REINVENTING SHAKESPEARE

ALSO BY GARY TAYLOR

Modernizing Shakespeare's Spelling, with Three Studies in the Text of "Henry V" (with Stanley Wells)

William Shakespeare, *Henry V* (editor)

The Division of the Kingdoms: Shakespeare's Two Versions of "King Lear" (editor, with Michael Warren)

To Analyze Delight: A Hedonist Criticism of Shakespeare

William Shakespeare, *The Complete Works* (general editor, with Stanley Wells)

William Shakespeare, *The Complete Works: Original Spelling Edition* (general editor, with Stanley Wells)

William Shakespeare: A Textual Companion (with Stanley Wells)

GARY TAYLOR

REINVENTING SHAKESPEARE

A CULTURAL HISTORY,
FROM THE RESTORATION
TO THE PRESENT

WEIDENFELD & NICOLSON

NEW YORK

Published by Weidenfeld & Nicolson, New York
A Division of Wheatland Corporation
841 Broadway
New York, New York 10003-4793

Published in Canada by General Publishing Company, Ltd.

Due to limitations of space, permissions appear on page 463.

Library of Congress Cataloging-in-Publication Data

Taylor, Gary, 1953–
Reinventing Shakespeare: a cultural history, from the Restoration
to the present / Gary Taylor. — 1st ed.
p.   cm.
Includes index.
ISBN 1-55584-078-7 (alk. paper)
1. Shakespeare, William, 1564–1616—Criticism and interpretation—
History.   2. Shakespeare, William, 1564–1616—Stage history.
3. Shakespeare, William, 1564–1616—Appreciation.   4. Great Britain—
Civilization.   I. Title.
PR2965.T39   1989
822.3'3—dc20
89-5784
CIP

Manufactured in the United States of America

This book is printed on acid-free paper

Designed by Irving Perkins Associates

First Edition

1   3   5   7   9   10   8   6   4   2

This book is dedicated to Rebecca Germonprez:

for whom
but for whom

CONTENTS

REINVENTING SHAKESPEARE

INTRODUCTION

For a while Shakespeare reinvented himself almost every day. He had to; he was an actor. In the Elizabethan repertory system, he might be expected to perform in six different plays on six consecutive days. Many times he would rehearse one play in the morning and perform in another that afternoon. On most days he probably played more than one character; Elizabethan actors doubled, tripled, quadrupled roles, their versatility helping to hold down costs.

When he was not acting in plays he was writing them. Like actors, Elizabethan playwrights were encouraged to demonstrate their adaptability. In less than twenty-four months at the turn of the seventeenth century Shakespeare wrote *Much adoe about Nothing, The Life of Henry the Fift, The Tragedie of Julius Cæsar, As you Like it*, and *The Tragedie of Hamlet Prince of Denmarke*, probably in that order, probably one right after the other. Even before he finished one play he had begun thinking about or even writing the next; toward the end of *Henry the Fift* he borrowed images from the same pages of Plutarch that he would use as source material for *Julius Cæsar*. As an actor he needed to become only two or three characters per play; as a playwright he had to perform all the parts in his head, momentarily recreating himself in the image of each. He juggled selves.

He did not stop juggling them when he stepped out of the theatre. "All the world's a stage," he wrote;[1] he also wrote, "my nature is subdu'd / To what it workes in, like the Dyers hand."[2] He could not stop being an actor any more than the globe itself could stop being a theatre. Like his characters, he played his part in family burials and marriages; he loaned money, bought property, invested venture capital, sued people, testified in court. He delighted civil audiences in an open-air theatre in the suburbs; he deferred to rowdy crowds indoors at court. He doubled one set of commitments in metropolitan London with another set in provincial Stratford-upon-Avon, like two roles in one play, like plot and subplot, like art and nature. He embodied mutability.

But gradually the pace of metamorphosis began to slow. At some time between 1603 and 1610 he seems to have stopped acting. After 1606 he wrote fewer plays; increasingly often, he collaborated with other writers. After 1608 he spent less and less time in London. After 1613 he stopped writing and commuting; geographically and imaginatively, his world contracted. Finally, on April 23, 1616, he stopped reinventing himself altogether. He was buried two days later.

We have been reinventing him ever since.

The study of Shakespeare has been in turmoil since at least the mid-1970s. Scholars are redefining what he wrote, how he wrote it, what it meant in his own time, and what it means to ours. Lines are being redrawn, even now; old stories are being told with new twists; our collective image of Shakespeare as a person and a poet is disintegrating and reforming. This book is a product and a chronicle of that crisis, in which I have played some part. But I will not start describing this recent revolution, directly, until Chapter 6. If I told you the story of this latest crisis only, it would read like an adolescent's account of a rebellion against parental authority—a true story, certainly, and a dramatic one, punctuated by angry quarrels and culminating in an achieved independence. I rather like such stories; I have lived them, and told them, and believed them. Indeed, one of the more memorable episodes in the current crisis occurred at a seminar held in Cambridge, Massachusetts, in April 1980, when one of the elder statesmen of orthodoxy, unexpectedly embattled and outnumbered in a crowded conference room, warned that we should not let the quarrel be portrayed as "the young Turks versus the Old Guard." He knew all too well how that story always ends. He did not like the way history was being plotted.

In its context, this protest was a futile effort to disarm, with mockery, an intellectual challenge that could no longer be ignored or withstood. But in a larger historical perspective it simply reminds us that the new hypothesis, the new image of Shakespeare (or of history, or of the universe), was generated by an old one and consciously or involuntarily incorporates some of its features. Like any child, it resembles the past that it rejects and replaces. We can trace this lineage of images of Shakespeare back to the middle of the seventeenth century.

Observing the changes in Shakespeare's image from the mid-seventeenth to the late twentieth century alters your perspective on the progress, geography, and substance of criticism. The important questions, the questions that matter beyond the intellectual enclosure of Shakespeare specialists, do not concern the meaning of particular words or the motives of particular characters; they concern the blunt fact of his cultural dominance. When did people decide that Shakespeare was the greatest English dramatist? The greatest English poet? The greatest writer who ever lived? Who did the deciding? What prejudices and convictions might have influenced their decision? On what evidence, by what reasoning, did they justify their verdict? How did they persuade others? How did they discredit rival claimants? And once Shakespeare's hegemony was achieved, how was it maintained?

The issue of the value accorded to Shakespeare's works cannot be disentangled from the values that people have found within those works. Unsurprisingly, different periods have interpreted Shakespeare in different ways. But how did one prevailing interpretation give way to another? When and why did people stop answering one question and start asking another? Shakespeare provides the best specimen in English, one of the best specimens in any language, for investigating the mechanisms of cultural renown.

Questions like these cannot be answered by a history of biographies of Shakespeare, or of theatrical revivals of his plays, or of critical interpretations of his work. Each of those histories is necessary, but individually it tells only part of the story. The whole story includes all these activities and many others. Which works are considered Shakespeare's in any given period, how they are edited, what kinds of commentary they generate, whether they are translated, into what languages, how often they are quoted, how they (and their author's name) are spelled, how they (and their author) are visually represented—cumulatively, such decisions define what "Shakespeare" means in and to any given period. And the balance of power between these activities shifts. Sometimes the theatre dominates, and when people think of Shakespeare they involuntarily recall a great performance of a popular play; but at other times people disparage the theatre and value Shakespeare as a writer of poetry. So the history of Shakespeare's evolving reputation must incorporate the annals of criticism, the theatre, and many other disciplines. The subject is so big that it has no name. We need a name for it, and so I will christen it "Shakesperotics." It embraces everything that a society does in the name—variously spelled—of Shakespeare.

But in order to interpret what a society does in the name of Shakespeare, you have to know what else that society does. You can hardly recount the history of the theatre, of publishing, censorship, journalism, education, morality, sex, without becoming entangled in the complex entirety of their host society, its economics, politics, ideology, its total social and material structure. And so a history of Shakesperotics becomes, inevitably, a history of four centuries of our culture.

∾

CHAPTER 1

RESTORATION

EXIT THE KING

On the tenth of January 1642, King Charles I, sensing irreconcilable differences, divorced himself from Parliament, left London and began garnering political and military support in the Midlands and the north of England. On August 22 he finally raised his banner at the head of a Cavalier army on the castle hill at Nottingham; on October 23, at Edgehill in south Warwickshire, the first real battle was fought, and the English civil wars had officially begun. In the interim, on September 2, a parliamentary edict temporarily forbade the performance of plays, claiming that "publike Sports doe not well agree with publike Calamities" and condemning "publike Stage-playes" as no more than "Spectacles of pleasure, too commonly expressing lacivious Mirth and Levitie."[1] The Globe theatre, the site of performances of Shakespeare's plays since 1599, was closed down; nineteen months later it was "pulled downe to the ground. By Sʳ Mathew Brand. On Munday the 15. of April, 1644, to make tennements."[2]

But the demolition of an empty theatre or the fighting of an indeterminate battle did not decide the issue. The Royalists and the theatres lost a prolonged war of attrition. The longer the military

7

campaigns dragged on, the more the king and his Cavalier supporters suffered their exclusion from metropolitan London, the source
of concentrated credit, trade, naval power, and population; the
longer the theatres stayed shut, the more the actors and playwrights
suffered their exclusion from metropolitan London, the source of
concentrated audiences, theatrical real estate, and enough excess
wealth to support a leisure industry. By a parliamentary decree of
October 22, 1647, the ban on performances, allegedly temporary,
was made officially permanent. On January 30, 1649, by order of a
parliamentary judicial tribunal, King Charles I was publicly beheaded. Kings had often been murdered before; but never had one
been put on trial, sentenced, and executed by an elected assembly.
Charles' death was the climax of modern Europe's first republican
revolution.

It was also the most spectacular and memorable theatrical event
of his reign. Contemporaries, hostile or sympathetic, almost invariably described his execution in the jargon and imagery of "publike
Stage-Playes":

> . . . thence the *Royal Actor* born
> The *Tragick Scaffold* might adorn:
>   While round the armed Bands
>   Did clap their bloody hands.
> *He* nothing common did or mean
> Upon that memorable Scene . . .3

Andrew Marvell, writing these words in the summer of 1650, knew
that "scaffold" could refer either to an executioner's platform or to
the boards of a stage; he knew that plays, when allowed at all, had
normally been performed on outdoor stages, before crowded audiences, many of them standing, drawn from all ranks of society; he
knew, too, that Charles I had participated in court masques at the
Palace of Whitehall in the 1630s; he knew, finally, that to his contemporaries the spelling "born" would be ambiguous, and that his
words could be taken to imply that Charles I, borne to the scaffold,
was a born actor.

Fifty years before, in what may have been the first play performed
at the Globe, Shakespeare had apologized for his own "*unworthy
Scaffold,*" wishing instead that he could command "*A Kingdome for a
Stage, Princes to Act, / And Monarchs to behold the swelling Scene.*"4 In

1649 Shakespeare's wish came true in a way he could hardly have foreseen and would probably have abhorred. But Shakespeare was, by some at least, held partly responsible for the king's fate. A contemporary defense of the execution claimed it would never have been necessary "had [*Charls*] but studied Scripture half so much as [he studied] *Ben: Johnson* or *Shakespear*."5 The imprisoned Charles I was indeed perusing Shakespeare's and Jonson's plays in the weeks before his death.6 And no less a figure than John Milton, in an attack on the executed king's supposed piety, took an illustration from "one whom wee well know was the Closet Companion of [King Charles's] solitudes, *William Shakespeare*." Milton quoted *Richard the Third* to demonstrate how predictably "pious words" issue from "the mouth of . . . a Tyrant."7 Milton clearly enjoyed turning Shakespeare against Charles, and one can hardly avoid the intimation that Charles may have learned his consummate hypocrisy and "Other stuff of this sort" from Shakespeare. The English monarchy and the English theatre fell together.

And when they rose again, they rose together. Immediately after Charles I's execution, royalists issued a commemorative medal, stamped with the image of a phoenix, that mythical bird whose offspring rises from the ashes of its unique parent. The image promised that a new king would spring from the blood of the old one. On May 25, 1660, the dead king's son and heir, Charles II, landed at Dover, welcomed by histrionic fanfares and acclamations. On August 21, less than three months after his own restoration to the throne, Charles II officially sanctioned the restoration of English drama, granting warrants to two courtiers "to Erect two Companies of Players Consistinge respectiuely of such persons, As they shall chuse and appoint, And to purchase builde and Erect or hire at theire Charge, As they shall thinke fitt, Two Houses or Theaters . . . for the Representation of Tragydies Comedyes, Playes, Operas, & all other Entertainments of that nature In Convenient places."8 But even before this grant was issued, public performances of old plays had begun at an old theatre in Drury Lane, known as the Phoenix. Shakespeare was back—along with the monarchy, the House of Lords, and the Anglican church.

REENTER SHAKESPEARE

The Restoration was an act of collective, willed oblivion. Charles II's reign was retroactively declared to have begun at the moment of his father's death, eleven years before. Only acts of Parliament approved by Charles I were deemed legal; all others were nullified. Eighteen years of legislation vanished from the statute books. Part of the past was legally abolished, as though a slice of time had been surgically removed, leaving no trace of discontinuity. A key piece of preparatory legislation that preceded Charles II's return was, literally, "An Act of Indemnity and Oblivion."

This collective amnesia was, naturally, only a polite fiction; but, like other fictions, it served a psychological and social function. Embittered Cavaliers complained that the Restoration was "an Act of Indemnity for the King's enemies and Oblivion for his friends."9 But in order for the new king to prevent a repetition and continuation of old social and political divisions, he had to forgive his former enemies and forget his former friends. Recognizing the tenuousness of his own position, he could not reward loyalty too extravagantly or punish rebellion too systematically; if he did either, he would rearm the passions that had toppled his father. Oblivion was a political necessity for the king and a psychological necessity for his subjects. After all, the overwhelming majority of the population had collaborated, actively or passively, consistently or occasionally, with the Puritan revolution. Like the French after 1945, the English after 1660 wanted to pretend that they had all supported the Resistance (a small, malign minority excepted).

But although the political amnesia was feigned, the failure to remember much of Shakespeare was real enough. The collected edition of his plays had not been reprinted since 1632. During the eighteen years between the official closing and reopening of the theatres, scores of old plays had been published, including a large and expensive collection of the plays attributed to Francis Beaumont and John Fletcher; but only three of Shakespeare's had even been reprinted (*The Merchant of Venice* in 1652; *Othello* and *King Lear* in 1655). Also in 1655 his tragic narrative poem, *The Rape of Lucrece*, was printed in a composite volume with John Quarles' *The Banishment of Tarquin: Or, the Reward of Lust.*

Despite the legislated ban on acting, surreptitious or private performances had been given sporadically during the 1640s and 1650s. We know of successful or unsuccessful attempts to perform Beaumont and Fletcher's *The Scornful Lady, A King and No King, The Bloody Brother,* and *Wit Without Money;* Jonson's *Sejanus;* the old anonymous *Mucedorus;* and a handful of miscellaneous works by Thomas Killigrew, James Shirley, Lodowick Carlell, Sir William Berkeley, Sir William Davenant, and other writers equally unfamiliar to modern readers.[10] But amid all these scattered records we do not hear of a single projected or achieved performance of a complete play by Shakespeare, who survived only in the form of "drolls," simplified adaptations of extracts from old plays, acted by vagabond players in fairgrounds, halls, and taverns. Twenty-six such drolls were collected and published in 1662;[11] three of them (hardly an impressive proportion) were taken from scenes in plays of Shakespeare: "The Merry Conceits of Bottom the Weaver" (based on *A Midsummer Night's Dream*), "The Bouncing Knight" (based on *Henry the Fourth*), and "The Grave-Makers" (based on *Hamlet*)—all clowns.

About Shakespeare's life Restoration readers knew almost nothing. Only one authoritative image of his physical appearance was generally available, the copper engraving first printed on the title page of the 1623 collected edition and reprinted, in deteriorating form, in subsequent editions. From it were copied, badly, two miniature engravings printed in 1640 and 1655; neither seems to have been widely known. A remarkably inaccurate engraving of the Shakespeare monument at Stratford was printed in 1656, among *Antiquities of Warwickshire,* a book not likely to have been familiar to many readers of Shakespeare.[12] In his lifetime Shakespeare must have written or signed hundreds of manuscripts, but by 1660 they were all destroyed, or disintegrating, or lost in the uncatalogued and unexamined chaos of public and private records. Restoration readers had no way of knowing that his signatures were usually spelled "Shakspere."

The Restoration occurred forty-four years after Shakespeare's death; from what we know about life expectancy in the seventeenth century,[13] few people alive in 1660 could have known Shakespeare, as adults, even at the end of his life. The first collected edition of his plays, the folio volume of *Comedies, Histories, and Tragedies* published in 1623, includes "The Names of the Principall Actors" who had performed them. The list names twenty-six actors; not one was still alive in 1660. Of his two surviving children, Susanna died in 1649,

Judith in 1662, both cocooned in the provincial market town of Stratford-upon-Avon. His only grandchild (eight years old in 1616, at the time of Shakespeare's death) died in 1670, childless, the last of his direct descendants. No doubt there were people in Stratford who remembered him, but the number of such memories and their reliability declined with each passing year. What reports we do have of Stratford memory in the second half of the seventeenth century are often garbled, impossible, or self-contradictory. In any case, such information remained private, jotted down in notebooks and diaries, if at all. No biography had been published—or would be, for another half a century.

Even an educated reader or spectator in 1660 could be expected to know only three things at most about Shakespeare's life: that he was an actor, that he had been born in Stratford, and that he was poorly educated by the standards of Restoration high culture (he had "*small* Latine, *and lesse* Greeke"). Notably, all this information could be gleaned from the 1623 folio or its 1632 reprint, and all of it came from or was confirmed by Ben Jonson.

Moreover, in 1660 Shakespeare had not yet become the object of literary criticism, as we would understand the term. His works had occasionally been plagiarized or echoed or quoted; collected editions of his plays and poems were prefaced by versified blurbs; individual works, or his canon as a whole, were sometimes summarily judged in passing, in published or private poems and prose. But the first extended specimen of critical analytical prose devoted to Shakespeare was not published until 1664.

Almost no publication, almost no performance, almost no biography, almost no criticism: we might take 1659 as the nadir of Shakespeare's posthumous history. The whole subsequent history of Shakespearian criticism, scholarship, interpretation, and performance is a history of the retrieval, analysis, and synthesis of what seemed lost by 1659.

This retrieval was by no means inevitable. Not every person or work that subsides into the quicksands of obscurity is pulled out. Even if we accept the dubious optimistic axiom that "Greatness will out," it does not tell us when or how or why "greatness" will be recognized. To understand Shakespeare's cultural resilience we need to understand why he resurfaced when he did. The year 1660 hosted two revolutions—one political, one literary—that have shaped the culture of all who speak the English language.

Shakespeare's restoration had its origins in the social and psychological circumstances of that era. Shakespeare and Jonson, the preferred reading of Charles I, returned from exile with Charles II, like all of the monarchy's other retainers and favorites. Their relative neglect during the preceding years was treated as a literary interregnum, a discontinuity regarded by them, and by almost all subsequent critics, as no less deplorable and unnatural than its political counterpart. And every succeeding age has reenacted this process of corrective nostalgia. The first scholarly monograph devoted entirely to Shakespeare, published in 1726, was called *Shakespeare Restored*. Two and a half centuries later, one of our most distinguished and respected Shakespeare scholars defended his own edition of the complete works in an article entitled "*Shakespeare Restored*—Once Again!"[14] The work of restitution never ends.

The king is dead; long live the king.

ENTER KILLIGREW AT ONE DOOR, DAVENANT AT THE OTHER

Shakespeare's restoration began in the theatres and was dominated by the theatre for the next half century.

Charles II quickly recognized two new companies, each led by a courtier-playwright who had begun his career during the reign of Charles I. Thomas Killigrew, the son of Queen Henrietta's vice-chamberlain, married one of the Queen's maids of honor; while carrying out various court duties in the 1630s he occasionally wrote plays, usually performed by the Queen's company of actors. William Davenant, by contrast, was the son of an Oxford tavern keeper. But by 1638 he had succeeded Ben Jonson as poet laureate; he composed plays for both the public and private theatres and wrote the last royal masque presented at Whitehall before the outbreak of the Civil War. During the war both men remained loyal to Charles I, and both supervised occasional private performances of plays while public drama was banned. The royal warrant of August 1660 rewarded their perseverance by giving what quickly became a theatrical monopoly to two companies: the King's Men (under Killigrew) and the Duke's Men (under Davenant). The record of the two managers seemed to promise that the theatres of the 1660s would restore both the political and theatrical traditions of the 1630s.

The same nostalgic assurance was held out by other aspects of the new companies. They competed with each other in advertising their credentials as reincarnations of past dramatic glory. Killigrew's company, consisting largely of actors from several of the London troupes that had flourished before the closing of the theatres, even took over the name of its most famous predecessor, "The King's Men." Davenant's company, composed mostly of younger actors, compensated by stressing the authenticity of their performances. Davenant's actors had been brought together by "Mr. *Rhodes*," a former "Wardrobe-Keeper . . . to King *Charles* the First's, Company of Comedians in *Black-Friars*."[15] Davenant himself had "seen Mr. *Taylor* of the [old] *Black-Fryars* Company Act" the title-role in *Hamlet;* Taylor had been "Instructed by the Author Mr. *Shakespear*"; Davenant, having seen Taylor, "taught Mr. *Betterton* in every Particle of it." The royal line thus descended directly from Shakespeare to Betterton. When Betterton came to perform *King Henry the 8th* he was again "Instructed in it by Sir *William,* who had it from Old Mr. *Lowen,* that had his Instructions from Mr. *Shakespear* himself."[16]

The questionable accuracy of such accounts matters less than the evident importance of authenticity. And in both cases the medium of that authenticity was Davenant. Shakespeare, in his journeys between Stratford-upon-Avon and London, stayed at the Oxford tavern owned by Davenant's father; Robert Davenant, William's brother, remembered that when he was a boy Shakespeare "gave him a hundred kisses"; Shakespeare was William Davenant's god-father—and, according to a rumor that Sir William countenanced and perhaps encouraged, his biological father, to boot.[17] The King's company might have more old actors, but the Duke's had inherited, at least in respect to Shakespeare, a unique link to the author.

This competition for authenticity originated in the commercial rivalry between the two companies, which also fundamentally affected the development of the theatrical repertoire. Killigrew's company seem to have established their rights to most of the plays formerly performed by the pre-1642 King's Men; the old actors still owned the old plays. Davenant's company, by contrast, initially had almost no plays to its name. Davenant responded to this situation, in part, by successfully begging for a few old scripts. Most of the plays he got were Shakespeare's; and he got them, at least in part, because they were considered disposable. They were older and less popular than Beaumont and Fletcher's, and even within the Shakespeare canon they were not the most lucrative or desirable items. Davenant was given the second-string plays of the second-string playwright. In the long run this arrangement worked to Shakespeare's advantage, for Davenant was the more energetic and innovative manager. With younger actors and few old plays, he could attract audiences only by creating the theatrical future. In this process he would make even his old plays seem new.

First, he introduced movable scenery. Using painted "flats" or side wings, slid along grooves, combined with painted backdrops or shutters, he could create a new visual background for any segment of the action. Davenant used such scenes in June 1661 in a production of his own play *The Siege of Rhodes;* but the technique was immediately applied to older plays too, for on August 24 Samuel Pepys witnessed a performance of *Hamlet,* "done with scenes very well." The King's company could not copy Davenant's innovation for almost two years, until their move into a new theatre; as early as July 1661 Pepys reported that Killigrew's theatre, "that used to be so thronged," was suffering badly as a result of Davenant's success.[18] Even if they had wanted to, they could not long resist the market pressure to compete with the new visual attractions.

Until this time, Shakespeare's plays had been performed in ornate theatres by actors lavishly costumed, but upon stages that gave no pictorial representation of place or time. The action in every play happened on a flat, dusty promontory between "the heavens" above (an overhang painted with astronomical symbols) and "hell" below (an invisible hollow, reachable by trapdoors). Location was signaled, if at all, by three-dimensional functional props like thrones, not by two-dimensional inert painted scenery. This definition of space is cosmic and human: "where we are" is determined by theological architecture and portable accessories. The post-Restoration definition of space was, in contrast, Cartesian and Newtonian: there was no theological frame, only a succession of spatial categories—unindividuated "stock" scenes, generic woods or gardens, city squares or interiors—neoclassical generalities of locale that framed recurring situations in many different plays.

Davenant's changeable scenery fundamentally altered the history of Shakespearian performance, criticism, and editing. In the first place, he initiated the tradition of theatrical anachronism; henceforth, any innovation or improvement in performance practices would be retroactively applied to the plays of Shakespeare and other dead dramatists. Although this procedure seems only natural to us, it was not inevitable. Noh and Kabuki drama in Japan, or the Comédie Française for much of its history, demonstrate that a vivid theatrical tradition can be sustained by scrupulous reproduction of past performances. But Davenant insisted that old texts should be performed in new ways: old matter, in a new manner.

In Shakespeare's case, changeable scenery also kept reminding audiences and critics of how often Shakespeare changed the scene. His violation of the prescribed unity of place became a recurring theme of literary criticism for the next century; it lay behind innumerable allusions, apologetic or accusing, to his lack of "Art." Performance on an unillustrated stage tends to minimize an audience's awareness of shifts in locale; Davenant's "scenes," by contrast, served as an inescapable repeated irritant, waving in front of spectators' noses an aspect of Shakespeare they disliked.

The new scenery came hand in hand with a new kind of stage and auditorium. Both companies at first converted old tennis courts into theatres, although Davenant's design was a more radical departure from previous architectural norms. Both were indoor theatres, with a small seating capacity and, consequently, high ticket prices; in this they resembled the so-called "private" theatres of the prewar period, not the great open-air popular theatres like the Red Bull and the Globe. Both managers, in gauging their potential market, decided not to overestimate its size; furthermore, they assumed that it would consist primarily of the upper reaches of the social pyramid. Whether or not this commercial prophecy was self-fulfilling we cannot tell, for the two companies had a monopoly on dramatic performances and targeted the same market share. As a result, English drama became more aristocratic; Shakespeare, to survive at all, would have to survive as an upper-class dramatist.

The actors' clientele changed in part because of the design of the new auditoriums, in part because of the changed relationship between the theatres and the court. The new managers, unlike the old ones, were courtiers, and Charles II visited the theatres almost every day when the court was in London; he suggested scenarios to Restoration playwrights, he had affairs with Restoration actresses. Before 1642 plays went to the monarch; after 1660 the monarch went to plays. Queen Elizabeth, James I, and Charles I had all, to varying degrees, enjoyed theatrical entertainments but never went to public theatres; plays were specially performed for them at court.

When Charles II publicly attended the theatres, he inevitably brought with him an entourage more interested in seeing the king than the play. And the new managements, blessed with the patronage of both the king and his courtiers, did their best to produce performances that resembled those offered at court in the 1630s. Those earlier command performances, particularly in the shape of the court masque, had offered a lavish, elaborately symbolic, sycophantic mixture of poetry, painting, and music, unlike anything available in the old public theatres. The new theatres gradually disengaged from the arcane symbolic substance of the masques but strove to reproduce or outdo their visual and musical surface. The masques of the 1630s became the operas of the 1660s.

"Opera" did not mean to Restoration audiences what it does to us. Operas were usually not sung throughout; one eighteenth-century critic called them "Semioperas, for they consisted of half Musick, and half Drama,"[19] spoken dialogue and song, both overlaid with conspicuous visual display. Thus, in *The Fairy Queen*, a spectacular operatic adaptation of *A Midsummer Night's Dream*, Shakespeare's words were spoken, not sung; Henry Purcell's music was confined to interpolated new episodes. Such works resembled nineteenth-century Italian operas less than they resemble twentieth-century Broadway musicals. Some of Shakespeare's plays could easily be adapted to fit these conventions; *Macbeth* and *The Tempest* became two of the most popular musicals of the age. The opening stage direction of the operatic *Tempest* (1674) gives a taste of Shakespeare's new flavor:

> *The Front of the Stage is open'd, and the Band of 24 Violins, with the Harpsicals and Theorbo's which accompany the Voices, are plac'd between the Pit and the Stage. While the Overture is playing, the Curtain rises, and discovers a new Frontispiece, joyn'd to the great Pylasters, on each side of the Stage. This Frontispiece is a noble Arch, supported by large wreathed Columns of the* Corinthian *Order; the wreathings of the Columns are beautifi'd with Roses wound round them, and several Cupids flying about them. On the Cornice, just over the Capitals, sits on either side a Figure, with a Trumpet in one hand, and a Palm in the other, representing* Fame. *A little farther on the same Cornice, on each side of a Compass-pediment, lie a Lion and a Unicorn, the Supporters of the Royal Arms of* England. *In the middle of the Arch are several Angels, holding the Kings Arms, as if they were placing them in the midst of that Compass-pediment. Behind this is the Scene, which represents a thick Cloudy Sky, a*

very Rocky Coast, and a Tempestuous Sea in perpetual Agitation. This Tempest (suppos'd to be rais'd by Magick) has many dreadful Objects in it, as several Spirits in horrid shapes flying down amongst the Sailers, then rising and crossing in the Air. And when the Ship is sinking, the whole House is darken'd, and a shower of Fire falls upon 'em. This is accompanied with Lightning, and several Claps of Thunder, to the end of the Storm.

An orchestra, a false proscenium arch decorated with the pictorial adornments of classicism and English royalty, spectacular visuals, flying spirits, thunder, lightning, and poetry—irresistible, then as now. The claps of the audience no doubt competed with the claps of thunder.

If the influence of the court pulled Restoration drama in the direction of the masque, it also had a direct practical effect upon the composition of the acting companies. In the past all female roles had been played by boy actors; after the Restoration they began to be played by women.

This revolution in theatrical practice had as many causes as consequences. Women began to appear on the stage partly to palliate the old Puritan objections to transvestism ("men in the habit of women").[20] But the introduction of women also brought the English theatre into line with French practice; during their years of Continental exile Charles II and his followers had seen and appreciated actresses in action. Moreover, the new companies had practical reasons for using women: the long interruption of playing had cut off the supply of apprentices, so that in 1660 there was no ready pool of boy actors well trained in the performance of female roles.

Whatever the motives, the introduction of actresses affected Shakespeare's plays along with everybody else's. Many spectators applauded the innovation, but the grounds of their judgment may have been sexual, not critical. Of the histrionic talents of one actress, for instance, Samuel Pepys noted, typically, only "The very best legs that ever I saw; and I was very well plesed with it"—the final pronoun ambiguously referring either to the play or to the display of female flesh. When not satisfied by the display on stage, Pepys, like other gentlemen, could visit the actresses' "Tireing rooms." Seeing Nell Gwyn "dressing herself" and "all unready," he found her even "prettier than I thought."[21]

Women began to appear on English stages at the same time that pornography began to appear on English bookstalls.[22] The first English translation of Aretine's *Ragionamenti* was published in 1658; thereafter homegrown porn as well as translations became an integral part of the London book trade. Pepys, in the years when he was attending the theatre, was also buying a translation of *L'escholle des Filles,* reading it, masturbating, and then burning the book.[23] This market for verbal erotica coexisted naturally with a market for visual equivalents, and after 1660 both patent theatres fished for audiences with sexual bait. The number of Restoration actresses who became mistresses to Charles II and/or to members of the aristocracy testifies to the perception, shared by male spectators and female performers alike, that the theatre was a shopwindow for tarts. Nell Gwyn, the most famous actress of the period, owes her reputation less to her roles on stage than to her performances in Charles II's bed.

The use of actresses does not seem to have increased popular or critical appreciation of Shakespeare's female characters. In his reminiscences of the Restoration theatre John Downes records only one detail about the performance of an actress in a Shakespearian role: in an adaptation of *Romeo and Juliet,* "Mrs. *Holden*" had played the equivalent of Lady Montagu, and one night, during the "Fight and Scuffle" in the first scene, she "enter'd in a *Hurry*" in order to restrain her husband, "Crying, O my Dear *Count!* She Inadvertently left out, O, in the pronunciation of the Word *Count!* giving it a Vehement Accent, put the House into such a Laughter, that *London Bridge* at low Water was silence to it."[24]

Restoration audiences found Shakespeare's men much more effective and affecting than his women; roles written for boys could not compete with the female roles, written for actresses, in new plays. Shakespeare's fondness for having boys play women who disguise themselves as boys lost some of its ironic point once actresses took over the roles; instead, "breeches parts" acquired a simpler appeal, as an opportunity for women to appear in male dress, which displayed their legs to better advantage than contemporary female attire. It can hardly be an accident that *Twelfth Night,* in which Viola wears breeches for almost the entire play, was the first Shakespearian comedy Davenant revived and the only one of his romantic comedies that achieved any currency at all in the 1660s. *The Taming of the Shrew* did become popular, but not in its original form; it was substantially rewritten by the comic actor John Lacey, who exploited the availability of actresses by adding a "Bed-Chamber" scene in which a male servant (played by Lacey himself) is ordered by Petruchio to undress Kate—in front of the audience—and tries to do so.[25] Nothing in Shakespeare offered that kind of titillation. Likewise, nothing in Shakespeare equaled the intelligent sexual frankness in the female roles created by Wycherley, Etherege, and Behn. When Shakespeare's plays were adapted for Restoration audiences, new female roles were often added, and the original female roles fleshed out.

Such adaptations—Lacey's *Taming*, Davenant's *Macbeth,* the Davenant/Dryden *Tempest*, Nahum Tate's *King Lear,* to name only the most successful—were, for later critics, the most obvious and deplorable aspect of the Restoration's treatment of Shakespeare. The adaptations added and subtracted characters and episodes, recasting the dialogue to a greater or lesser degree. The number of such adaptations increased from a handful in the 1660s to an actual majority of Shakespeare revivals in the 1690s. But such textual reimaginings are only the most obvious sign of a more general development. Shakespeare's text, even when the words remained intact, was adapted to new theatres, to new scenic conventions, to a new gender, to a new audience, to a new society. The meanings of the words changed, inevitably, even if the words themselves stayed the same. The Restoration differed from subsequent periods only in the extent to which this process of adaptation was conscious, flagrant, unashamed. Later ages would also, in their own ways, reinvent Shakespeare; but—unlike the honestly hypocritical Restoration—they would simply deny that they were adapting him at all. The Restoration at least knew what it was doing.

ENTER THE REPERTOIRE

What happened in the theatres in 1660 isolates, and so makes unusually clear, a process that affects works of art and thought all the time. Every year new works multiply, but only a small number are preserved and cherished in the next year. This process of cultural selection mimics the behavior of human memory. Our senses register, at any given moment, an encyclopedia of particulars, but only a sliver of those impressions is recorded for later use; most of them immediately go down the chute to oblivion.

A repertoire is a theatrical memory, and as such it can serve as a useful model of what literary critics call the "canon" of great literature. The works in a repertoire get played again and again; audiences come to know them intimately, to expect them, to take pleasure from their repetition. They become the familiar standards by which unfamiliar works are measured. At the same time, those who perform such plays come to be judged against the collective memory of previous performers. Can they equal or even surpass former interpretations? Can they perceive, and so reveal, new features of the beloved work?

The communal defining of a new theatrical repertoire in 1660 was a critical moment in the history of Shakespeare's reputation. The managers and actors of the new companies had to decide how to share out the repertoire between old and new plays; what share of the old plays to allot to various dramatists, including Shakespeare; and which of a dramatist's plays to choose as his most memorable and important. The choices made in establishing a Restoration repertoire would prove enormously influential not only in the theatre but also outside it.

By the spring of 1660, several months before the royal license was issued, two groups of actors were already openly performing plays in the capital. One company, created from "The scattered Remnant" of several troupes active before 1642, acted at the Red Bull, a popular open-air theatre built about 1603. A list of twenty plays, "acted by the Red Bull actors" and probably referring to this first season, includes Shakespeare's *Henry the Fourthe, Merry Wives of Windsor,* and *Othello,* along with nine plays from the Beaumont and Fletcher canon, three by James Shirley, and single plays by George Chapman, Ben Jonson, Thomas Middleton, William Davenant, and Thomas Killigrew.[26] Another company, apparently composed of younger actors, acted at the Phoenix in Drury Lane, a smaller indoor theatre built in 1616. Its repertoire included, among "divers others," eight plays from the Beaumont and Fletcher canon, Shakespeare's *Pericles,* and single plays by Philip Massinger, Thomas Middleton and William Rowley, William Davenant, and John Suckling.[27]

Most of the plays chosen in 1660 endured in later seasons, but one died in infancy. *Pericles,* the only Shakespeare play known to have been performed by the Phoenix company, defied all the commandments of Cavalier and Restoration taste. Ben Jonson had condemned it as early as 1631 as a "mouldy tale";[28] John Dryden in

1672 would include it in an account of plays "made up of some ridiculous, incoherent story, which, in one Play many times took up the business of an Age."29 It would not be revived again on the London stage in anything like its original text until 1854. *Pericles* nevertheless found itself in a select group of the first four Shakespeare plays revived at the 1660 reopening of the theatres, in a production memorable enough to be recalled half a century later when John Downes wrote his "Historical Review of the Stage" (1708).

Two factors account for this apparent incongruity. One was Thomas Betterton, the greatest actor of the second half of the seventeenth century. As Downes recalled, "Mr. *Betterton*, being then but 22 Years Old, was highly Applauded for his Acting in all these Plays [of the Rhodes' repertoire], but especially, for [five plays, including] *Pericles*."30 Downes also lists Pericles among Betterton's sixteen greatest roles. *Pericles* found a place in the Restoration theatre because of the opportunities its central role offered to an actor great enough to exploit them. Indeed, Betterton's performance must have been a tour de force, in part for the very features that Dryden and others found so objectionable in the play. As Dryden complained in 1695, "He who enter'd in the first Act, a Young man like *Pericles* Prince of *Tyre,* must not be in danger in the fifth Act, of committing Incest with his Daughter."31 The twenty-two-year-old Betterton had to portray Pericles not only as "a Young man" but also, equally convincingly, as an old one, aged not only by time but also by extraordinary suffering.

Betterton's Pericles illustrates, at the outset of this period, the extent to which a single actor's performance can bring a play into the theatrical repertoire. This association between the success of a particular performer and the fortunes of a play in the repertoire was not confined to Betterton or the Restoration period. The same thing happened in the eighteenth century, when the twenty-four-year-old David Garrick catapulted both himself and *Richard the Third* into stardom, simultaneously. A role is the meeting place for an actor and a play; if the actor triumphs so does the play.

Although Betterton's performance can explain why *Pericles* gained a brief toehold in the Restoration repertoire, it cannot explain why the play was chosen for revival in the first place. But *Pericles* and its protagonist were particularly appropriate to the opening months of 1660. The play tells the story of a young and

admirable ruler, unjustly driven from his country, reduced at one
point to dressing in the clothes of poor fishermen, but ultimately
restored to happiness and power. As the epilogue declares,

> In *Pericles,* his Queene and daughter [you have] seene,
> Although assaylde with Fortune fierce and keene
> Vertue preferd from fell destructions blast,
> Led on by heaven, and crownd with joy at last.

No audience in 1660 could have missed the relevance of that conclusion, or of the fable as a whole, to Charles II. Even particular
episodes of the play could be paralleled in the story of the "painful
adventures" of the newly restored monarch. After his triumphal
progress from Dover to London, any London audience could easily
imagine

> What Pageantry, what pheates, what shewes,
> What Minstrelsie, what pretty din,
> The Regent made in *Metalin,*
> To greete the King.[32]

In the most famous and dangerous episode of his struggle back to
power, Charles II, after the defeat of his army at the battle of
Worcester, had abandoned his entourage and started for London on
foot. To disguise himself he cut his hair and wore a pair of gray
cloth breeches, a leather doublet and a green jerkin, and "a greasy
gray soft hat without ribbon or linen."[33] In history as in the play,
such episodes gratify us by simultaneously asserting and denying
the equality of king and commoner. Charles II defeated at Worcester, Pericles shipwrecked and washed ashore on the coast of Penta-
polis—both look like and mix with ordinary folk; but even though
the people they meet may be fooled, we know all along that they are
kings, and that kings are not commoners, and that they will regain
their proper wardrobe and power. Indeed, their very capacity to
rise from such depths will confirm their right to govern.

Restoration playwrights and audiences habitually interpreted
plays in terms of contemporary politics. Many new plays depended
upon implied parallels between onstage characters or events and
their contemporary offstage counterparts. The same rage for parallels shaped adaptations of Shakespeare's plays. When Sir William

Davenant and John Dryden sat down to adapt *The Tempest* (1667), they found that Shakespeare's play already contained a subplot in which three menial, gullible, drunken characters (Caliban, Stephano, and Trinculo) conspired to murder the monarch of the isle; it took little imagination to modify these characters into unmistakable parodies of the Parliamentarians who had overthrown Charles I. Thomas Shadwell's adaptation of *Timon of Athens* (1678) highlighted parallels between Alcibiades' attacks on the Athenian Senate and the reforming Duke of Buckingham's attacks on the English House of Commons. From 1679 to 1681—the years of the Exclusion Crisis, when Charles II was at odds with Parliament over who would succeed him—at least seven Shakespeare plays were revived in new adaptations that emphasized their relevance to the political situation. Edward Ravenscroft's version of *Titus Andronicus* exploited the hysteria generated by the Popish Plot. Nahum Tate's adaptation of *King Richard the Second,* with its portrait of a *"Dissolute, Unadviseable [King], devoted to Ease and Luxury,"* so obviously ran the risk of reminding audiences of their own Charles II that it was banned before it could be performed. John Crowne's reshapings of *Henry the Sixth* highlighted the horror and hypocrisy of rebellion.

Pericles, like other plays, found its way onto Restoration stages by happy accident: the accident of Thomas Betterton, the accident of its relevance to the Restoration. Such accidents are the constants of theatrical history, and Shakespeare's plays—with their strong roles for star actors and their political subject matter—have attracted accidents with unusual frequency and regularity.

But although the causes that brought *Pericles* to theatrical attention in 1660 are common enough, the play itself remains anomalous within the broader pattern of the Restoration repertoire. Other aspects of the theatrical season of 1659–60 more obviously anticipate the taste of things to come. First of all, and to us most strikingly, the known list of plays performed does not include a single new work. In the three years following the resumption of regular theatrical activity in 1660, the London companies apparently performed more than eighty old plays but only nine new ones.[34] (By contrast, in the three years before the closing of the theatres the companies performed at least fifty new plays—and probably many more.)[35] At the beginning of the Restoration period the theatrical past wholly dominated the theatrical present.

This domination arose for simple economic reasons. Old plays were plentiful, and their authors did not need to be paid for their work. New plays, by contrast, require living playwrights, who in turn need to make a living. For almost two decades there had been no demand for new plays, and hence no market for playwrights, and hence no playwrights. The first new plays to appear were translations or works by aristocrats who did not need to worry about supporting themselves on the profits of playmaking. No playwright made a living from the theatre for the first five years after the Restoration, and not until 1669 was the professional status of a living playwright recognized by contract.

The situation in 1660 differs remarkably from that at another turning point in the history of English drama, 1576. In that year the first outdoor public theatre built to serve as such was erected in London; a second followed in 1577. But there was no significant preexisting repertoire. The theatres, actors, and audiences all needed plays, and a class of professional playwrights arose to supply them. By the mid-1590s, a single London theatre was consuming an average of eighteen new plays a year, coexisting with revivals of plays from one to ten years "old," weighted heavily toward the more recent end of the spectrum. From 1576 to 1642 there were never less than two, and sometimes more than five, prosperous theatres competing for weekly audiences of 18,000 to 24,000.[36] In these economic circumstances new plays were valuable commodities. The constant need for new plays encouraged companies to pay advances, which in turn created deadlines; pressures of time encouraged collaboration between two or more playwrights; collaboration acted as a form of apprenticeship for new writers; old plays were often adapted by new playwrights on the occasion of their revival. A tradition of collaboration within a constantly renewing repertoire created a workplace for playwrights that emphasized their rivalry and cooperation in a living fraternity, a loosely defined unofficial guild.

When Shakespeare began writing plays, in the late 1580s, the repertoire was disposable and the playwright indispensable; when John Dryden began writing plays, in the mid-1660s, it was the playwright who had become disposable. In 1660 several theatres built before 1642 were still standing; enough actors had survived or arose to form small companies (which may have been operating—occasionally, illicitly—during the interregnum); audiences of old devotees or curious newcomers could be attracted from the host multitudes of London. But a whole new race of playwrights could not be summoned into instant maturity. The actors and managers and audiences could not wait for a crop of new plays; they began with the old ones. Indeed, it was the old ones that they wanted, for the presentation of so many former favorites contributed to the warm communal illusion that the past was being restored. Only after satisfying this initial hunger for the resurrected past did they begin to ask for new plays.

In a theatrical system based upon a high turnover of plays, most of the texts performed in any given year will not survive into the next. A young playwright surveying the artistic landscape will see a little to admire but much to disdain, and that disdain creates a comfortable space for new work. But when the theatres reopened in 1660, actors turned naturally to the most popular, successful, and acclaimed plays of the period before 1642. This predictable procedure created an entirely false impression of the general standard of work in the earlier era. In the 1660s, for the first time, new playwrights found themselves competing not with their contemporaries but with the past and, what is worse, with an artificially selected, enthusiastically welcomed, massed anthology of the best of the past.

The institutional dominance of early plays must have been frustrating and dispiriting for new playwrights, but it obviously benefited Shakespeare. The more old plays performed, the greater his chances of being included in the new repertoire. The newly established King's company performed the same three plays earlier offered at the Red Bull (*Henry the Fourthe, Merry Wives,* and *Othello*). Toward the end of 1660 Davenant petitioned for the rights of "reformeinge some of the most ancient Playes that were playd at Blackfriers and of makeinge them, fitt, for the Company of Actors appointed under his direction."[37] On December 12 the Lord Chamberlain granted Davenant's troupe a license to perform, as he had requested, nine plays by Shakespeare, John Webster's *The Duchess of Malfi,* John Denham's *The Sophy,* and any of Davenant's own plays. Davenant also was given a two-month lease on six plays that had belonged to Rhodes' company (including *Pericles*).

Shakespeare looms much larger in this list than he does in the early repertoire of Davenant's company. Indeed, in 1660 and for the next forty years the plays of the Beaumont and Fletcher canon clearly outscored Shakespeare's in theatrical popularity.[38] By Restoration accounting Shakespeare wrote nearly as many plays as Beaumont and Fletcher, but he received fewer performances, whether we measure individual seasons or the period as a whole.* As Dryden claimed in 1668, the plays of Beaumont and Fletcher "are now the most pleasant and frequent entertainments of the Stage; two of theirs being acted through the year for one of *Shakespeare's* or *Johnson's*."39

Beaumont and Fletcher in their own lives anticipated the profile of the Restoration gallant, a figure familiar enough from the characters of Restoration and eighteenth-century comedy—and from the characters of some of the authors who wrote those comedies. Moreover, unlike Shakespeare, they were unmistakably quintessentially gentlemen, and this quality became a primary ingredient of their later fame. Dryden, for instance, comparing their plays with Shakespeare's, particularly noted that "they understood and imitated the conversation of Gentlemen much better; whose wilde debaucheries, and quickness of wit in reparties, no Poet before them† could paint as they have done."40 Likewise, Edward Phillips in 1675 distinguished Fletcher for his "courtly Elegance, and gentile familiarity of style"; James Drake in 1699 admitted that "*Shakespear* . . . fell short of the Art of *Johnson*, and the Conversation of *Beaumont* and *Fletcher*."41 These witnesses knew the kind of character, the style of behavior, they were describing; it figured prominently in their own culture. They also knew that Fletcher, or more generally the Beaumont and Fletcher canon, better illuminated that range of human behavior than had Shakespeare.

In 1647, Sir John Denham in a commendatory poem prefixed to *The Comedies and Tragedies of Francis Beaumont and John Fletcher* described Fletcher, Shakespeare, and Jonson as "the Triumvirate of wit"; in Denham's account, as in its many echoes, Fletcher is first

---

* Twenty-five of Shakespeare's plays can be traced in London theatrical records during these four decades; this total is lower than that for Beaumont and Fletcher and includes a much higher proportion of plays heavily adapted by Restoration playwrights, in some cases almost beyond recognition. Beaumont and Fletcher received, because they were felt to need, less frequent and less drastic adaptation. Shakespeare's plays ventured out one by one, as it were, and most of them sank on sight.

† In 1668 Dryden had originally written "no Poet can ever"; in 1684, revising the statement to "no Poet before them," he made clearer their superiority to Shakespeare and their origination of a mode that Dryden and his generation were ambitious to develop.

among equals. During much of the seventeenth century Shakespeare's plays seemed to most critics inferior to those of John Fletcher—and to those of Ben Jonson too.

Jonson's plays were mentioned oftener, quoted oftener, and praised oftener than Shakespeare's. On the basis of contemporary allusions, six of Jonson's comedies and tragedies, his poems, and his masques were more highly esteemed by the literary intelligentsia than anything written by Shakespeare; by such criteria Shakespeare's most famous work was *The Tempest,* which owed its preeminence almost entirely to the Dryden/Davenant adaptation.⁴² But Ben Jonson in his century, like James Joyce in ours, was the darling of the cultural elites, not of the general public; both Fletcher and Shakespeare surpass Jonson in the number of productions and editions of their work, which measure popular enthusiasm in the same way that allusions measure critical esteem.⁴³ As Aphra Behn declared, *"We all well know that the immortal* Shakespears *Playes . . . have better pleased the World than* Johnsons *Works."*⁴⁴

The opening season of 1660 suggests which Shakespeare plays "pleased the World" most. If we ignore *Pericles* as an anomaly, the new repertoire singles out three plays: the first part of *Harry the 4th, The Merry Wives of Windsor,* and *The Moore of Venice.* All three would continue to be both acclaimed and popular. If we ignore adaptations, *Othello, the Moor of Venice* and the first part of *King Henry the Fourth* were quoted or mentioned more often in the seventeenth century than any other texts of Shakespeare. John Downes listed them, together with *Julius Cæsar,* among the "Principal Old Stock Plays" and included *The Merry Wives of Windsor* among old plays that "were very Satisfactory to the Town."⁴⁵ His addition of *Cæsar* is supported by other evidence: *Cæsar* and *Othello* were Shakespeare's most often reprinted plays and were singled out among "the choicest and most applauded *English Tragedies* of this last age"⁴⁶ by critics as diverse as Thomas Rymer, Aphra Behn, and Charles Gildon.

Of the four most popular plays, three were performed almost immediately after the reopening of the theatres: clearly, the King's company judged their audiences' preferences correctly. Only *Julius Cæsar* was overlooked, apparently not entering the repertoire until 1669; but that omission clearly owed more to politics than to theatrical taste. In 1660 actors and audiences would have been uncomfortable applauding a play that dramatized the murder of Caesar by his republican opponents.

The Duke's company, under Davenant, could not begin with Shakespeare's most predictable successes; instead, they had to make successes of the plays given to them at the end of 1660. Downes included *The Tragedy of Hamlet, Romeo and Juliet, Twelfth Night,* and *King Henry the 8th* among the "Principal, which we call'd Stock-Plays" of the company's first five years. The company later added to its repertoire of hits Davenant's adaptation of *The Tragedy of Macbeth,* which "Recompenc'd double the Expence" and in 1708 was "still a lasting Play," and Shadwell's operatic adaptation of Davenant and Dryden's adaptation of *The Tempest,* which was performed "so Admirably well, that not any succeeding Opera got more Money."[47]

Such evidence of Restoration preferences can be confirmed more subjectively by the testimony of a single practiced playgoer. In some 350 visits to the theatre between 1660 and 1669 Samuel Pepys witnessed only fifteen performances of plays by Shakespeare and another twenty-seven performances of plays more or less heavily adapted from Shakespeare; by contrast, he attended seventy-six performances of Beaumont and Fletcher plays, only a handful of them adapted. Among plays associated with Shakespeare his favorites were Davenant's adaptation of *Macbeth* (which he saw nine times) and Davenant and Dryden's adaptation of *The Tempest* (eight times). He saw *Hamlet,* less drastically modified by Davenant, five times, always enjoying it enormously; he also saw *Henry the Fourth* five times, though usually unenthusiastically, on two occasions not even staying for the whole play. The predominance here of Davenant's company and of adapted plays cannot be overlooked. Pepys, at least, did not like his Shakespeare straight.

So Shakespeare was most admired for *The Moor of Venice, Julius Cæsar,* the first part of *Henry the Fourth, Merry Wives, Hamlet, Romeo and Juliet, Twelfth Night* (briefly), *King Henry the 8th, Macbeth,* and *The Tempest.* This list of favorites agrees remarkably well with the common judgment of later periods. It includes all the most famous tragedies except *King Lear* and from the comedies singles out *Twelfth Night* (for a while) and *The Tempest* (heavily adapted). It recognizes the primacy of Falstaff, whom Dryden called "the best of comical characters"; in performance the role "never fail'd of universal applause."[48] It may seem eccentric only in its elevation of *Merry Wives* and *King Henry the 8th.* But the latter clearly owed much of its theatrical success, then as in later ages, to spectacle. Critically, the play was not much approved; like Shakespeare's other history plays it seemed rambling and episodic. (*Henry the Fourth* escaped such critical censure only because Falstaff was irresistible.) By contrast, *The Merry Wives of Windsor* then enjoyed a critical reputation as great as its theatrical popularity and greater than in any other period. It fit Restoration prescriptions for comedy exceptionally well: Dryden twice acclaimed it as Shakespeare's most "regular" and "exactly form'd" play, conforming as it did to the contemporary critical preference for a classical unity of time, place, and action.[49] In its proliferation of readily identifiable, eccentric characters it also came closer than anything else in the Shakespeare canon to the comedy of Jonson, which the Restoration so admired.

Restoration audiences did not much care for Shakespeare's rambling history plays or his sentimental romantic comedies, and as often as not, they preferred Shakespeare *à la* Davenant (or Dryden, or Tate, or someone else) to Shakespeare *au naturel*. As Dryden wrote in the prologue to the adaptation of *The Tempest*, "Shakespear's *pow'r is sacred as a King's*";[50] but in England even the king was not above the law. Like others, Dryden conspicuously proclaimed the king's supremacy, while confining it in practice within the limits set by the national rational consensus.

ENTER, READING

The first performances in 1660 established a pattern, confirmed by the rest of the century, in which renewed theatrical exposure predictably stimulated a market for new reading editions. Immediately after the resumption of performances nine pirated editions of Beaumont and Fletcher plays stole onto the market—a sure sign of the plays' commercial vitality.[51] In the four decades between the Restoration and the end of the century over thirty editions of individual Beaumont and Fletcher plays were published.

Shakespeare was apparently not popular enough to be pirated, but in 1663 another reprint of his collected plays appeared, after a thirty-one-year hiatus. A second issue of this edition, dated 1664, announced on its title page that "unto this Impression is added seven Playes, never before Printed in Folio." These seven plays, now added to the thirty-six originally gathered in 1623, were *Pericles, Locrine, The First Part of Sir John Oldcastle, Thomas Lord Cromwell, The*

London Prodigal, The Puritan, and *A Yorkshire Tragedy.* Of these, only *Pericles* will sound at all familiar to modern readers, for only it has survived into modern editions. But all seven plays had been attributed to Shakespeare earlier in the century on title pages or in booksellers' lists of published plays. And Restoration readers, for the most part, treated them no differently than the familiar thirty-six.

None of the additional plays gathered into the canon in this period can have done Shakespeare's reputation much good. Several of them, by the standards of any era, are incompetent; none was likely to appeal to Restoration taste. *The Two Noble Kinsmen* (published in 1634, as a collaboration between Shakespeare and Fletcher) is dramatically and stylistically more assured than any of the others; but in 1679 it was reprinted in the Beaumont and Fletcher collection, and for almost three centuries thereafter it was kept out of editions of Shakespeare. *Pericles,* which stayed with Shakespeare, survived only in a text of bewildering unevenness. Taken together, the added plays inevitably reinforced the impression that his lifework was a mess, a collection of "indigested" plays that mixed genius and ineptitude haphazardly.

Restoration readers could not distinguish *Henry the Fourth* from *Sir John Oldcastle*; they could not distinguish *The London Prodigal* from *All's Well that Ends Well.* They had no map to help them negotiate the geography of Shakespeare's imagination. Their collected editions did not distinguish genuine plays from spurious ones or indicate Shakespeare's personal share in collaborative plays, or even specify which plays had been written collaboratively. Seventeenth-century editions did not identify when each play had been written, thereby depriving readers of any sense of Shakespeare's development from apprenticeship to maturity. Dryden thought—wrongly, we now know—that both *Troilus and Cressida* and *Pericles* were among Shakespeare's earliest compositions.[52]

The expanded collection of 1664 was reprinted in 1685 in an elegant and readable volume comparable in appearance to the best products of Continental printing or of English eighteenth-century bookmaking. Of the pre-Restoration dramatists, only Shakespeare, Beaumont and Fletcher, and Jonson were honored by folio collections of their plays in the late seventeenth century. Such editions testify to the cultural prestige of those dramatists; but that cultural prestige itself resulted in part from the publication of collected editions of their work in the first half of the century. The plays of Marlowe, Middleton, Dekker, Heywood, Chapman, Webster, Massinger, and Ford had not been collected; consequently their achievements were scattered in individual editions, long out of print, often unattributed. Even people who did not read all Shakespeare's or Fletcher's or Jonson's plays could see, merely from the table of contents in seventeenth-century folios, something of the range and scale of their work; but they had no such inkling of Marlowe's capacities, no such incentive or opportunity to explore and compare different provinces of Middleton's artistic diversity.

But although the availability of collected editions crucially influenced the creation and survival of reputations, not everyone could afford an expensive folio edition of Shakespeare. In fact, not everyone could read. In England in 1660 only about 30 percent of men and 20 percent of women could sign their names. Those who could were very unevenly distributed: literacy was high among the clergy, professions, and gentry; low among husbandmen, servants, and laborers. Yeomen, tradesmen, and craftsmen fell in the middle, in terms of status and literacy; but by 1700 the commercial classes in London were almost entirely literate.[53] The potential readership of Shakespeare's works was constrained by literacy, which was in turn constrained by the economic and social geography of Restoration England. It was further constricted by ideology. The author of the most enduringly popular of all Restoration books, John Bunyan, never once named or quoted Shakespeare and almost certainly never read him. Most of the households that owned a much-thumbed copy of Bunyan's *Grace Abounding to the Chief of Sinners* or *The Pilgrim's Progress* would probably not have cared to acquire Shakespeare's *Comedies, Histories, and Tragedies*. Finally, even among that fraction of the population able to read and willing to spend money on secular fiction, only a very few would want all thirty-six (or forty-three) plays.

More indicative both of popular preference and of theatrical influence are the smaller, cheaper quarto editions of individual plays: *Othello* (1681, 1687, 1695, 1705), *Julius Cæsar* (six editions between 1684 and 1691), and *Henry the Fourth* (1700). These editions claimed to offer the text of each play "as it is Now Acted at" one contemporary theatre or the other, and historians usually refer to them as "players' quartos." They differ from other editions of the period only in that their texts have undergone relatively little adaptation. But to a contemporary potential customer standing at a bookstall, who would not be collating them against earlier seventeenth-century editions, the 1681 edition of *Othello* would have seemed no different in kind from the 1676 edition of (Davenant's adaptation of) *Hamlet,* though the latter was more heavily cut and revised, or from the 1674 edition of (Davenant's adaptation of) *Macbeth,* which was substantially recast. Davenant's name appears on neither adaptation.

Other adapters advertised their presence, but they did not usually discriminate Shakespeare's dialogue from their own additions or alterations. Unless readers owned a folio edition and knew the original texts exceptionally well, they would find it difficult or impossible to know what was Shakespeare and what wasn't. Many eighteenth-century writers quoted, as though they were Shakespeare's, lines written by Davenant or other adapters. When David Garrick advertised in 1744 that he would revive *Macbeth* "as originally written by Shakespeare," James Quin, an older rival accustomed to Davenant's adaptation, retorted, "What does he mean? don't I play *Macbeth* as written by Shakespeare?"54 In this respect quarto editions of the plays, like their folio counterparts, progressively blurred the distinction between "Shakespeare" and "pseudo-Shakespeare." But this characteristic of printed editions, like the very demand for them, originated in the theatres. In the restoration of Shakespeare's reputation, publishers followed; actors led.

ENTER THE CRITIC, DISCONTENTEDLY

After actors, publishers; after publishers, critics. English dramatic criticism is defined from the beginning by its own belatedness, its after-the-factness. The great works of French criticism were written before or alongside the great works of French classical drama; but no significant or extended English dramatic criticism was written until half a century after Shakespeare's death. English criticism not only lagged behind English drama; it lagged behind French criticism too. Thomas Rymer, the first professional English critic, began his career with a translation of René Rapin's *Réflexions sur la poétique* in 1674. In 1677, emboldened by the success of his translation,

Rymer published his own critique of *The Tragedies of the Last Age*, concentrating his fire upon three plays by Beaumont and Fletcher. Sixteen years later, in *A Short View of Tragedy*, he finally zeroed in on Shakespeare.

Rymer objected, in part, to Shakespeare's linguistic extravagance. Quoting Othello's

> *O heavy hour!*
> *Methinks it shou'd be now a huge Eclipse*
> *Of Sun and Moon, and that the affrighted globe*
> *Shou'd yawn at Alteration,*55

he observed, sarcastically, that "It wou'd be uncivil to ask *Flamstead*, if the Sun and Moon can both together be so hugely eclipsed, in any *heavy hour* whatsoever. Nor must the Spectators consult *Gresham* Colledge, whether a body is naturally *frighted* till he *Yawn* agen."* Likewise, when complaining about the "ranting" of Cassius in *Julius Caesar*, Rymer rhetorically asked, what would "Sir *Will. Petty*"† think of such "raptures?"56

Rymer's allusions to contemporary scientists, made amid practical criticism of specific passages in Shakespeare's plays, remind us that English critical prose postdates the scientific revolution of the mid-seventeenth century. The Royal Society, England's first formal scientific institution, held its inaugural meeting six months after Charles II's restoration; Rymer belongs to the age of Isaac Newton, Robert Boyle, and Robert Hooke. For their part, the scientific geniuses of the seventeenth century had no time for Shakespeare. He is not mentioned anywhere in the voluminous personal and professional papers of Newton or Boyle or in the thirteen volumes of Henry Oldenburg's correspondence as Secretary of the Royal Society; he almost pops up once in Hooke's diary—"Saw Tempest. Paid 3sh"—but the price of the theatre ticket crowds out any reference to the author of *The Tempest*, which Hooke saw, anyway, in an utterly transformed operatic adaptation.57 Shakespeare had not yet become part of the mental equipment of every educated Englishman.

---

* John Flamsteed was appointed the first Astronomer Royal in 1675; Gresham College was home to the Royal Society.

† William Petty, a founder of the Royal Society, was an experimental scientist, mathematician, and linguistic reformer, who attempted to compose "A Dictionary of Sensible Words."

But although Restoration scientists did not waste much time on Shakespeare, they were fascinated and frustrated by the nature of language. On December 7, 1664, the Royal Society established a committee "for improving the English tongue," which numbered among its members the poets Abraham Cowley, Edmund Waller, and John Dryden; in 1667 Thomas Sprat's *History of the Royal Society* applauded the society's "constant Resolution, to reject all the amplifications, digressions, and swellings of style," advocating instead a "Mathematical plainness."[58] The greatest English philosophers of the century, Thomas Hobbes and John Locke, never mention Shakespeare, but they do wrestle with the deceptiveness of language. Hobbes' *Leviathan*, published in 1651, reserves two chapters for criticisms of style, particularly "the use of Metaphors, Tropes, and other Rhetoricall figures, in stead of words proper,"[59] and one of the four books of John Locke's *Essay Concerning Human Understanding* (1689) agonizes at length over the slippery properties "Of Words."

Sprat tells his readers that the Royal Society prefers "the language of Artizans, Countrymen, and Merchants, before that, of Wits, or Scholars."[60] According to Sprat, in describing natural phenomena one should speak like a merchant; according to Rymer, "In a Play one should speak like a man of business." In *Othello* the soldier Cassio, at a port in Cyprus, is asked about the arrival of a ship, and answers

> *Tempests themselves, high Seas, and houling Winds,*
> *The guttered Rocks, and congregated Sands,*
> *Traytors ensteep'd, to clog the guiltless Keel,*
> *As having sense of Beauty, do omit*
> *Their common Natures, letting go safely by*
> *The divine* Desdemona.[61]

Rymer, quoting this, snidely inquires, "Is this the Language of the Exchange, or the Ensuring-Office?" Like Sprat and the new empiricism he speaks for, Rymer demands a practical vernacular, an entrepreneurial idiom: Business English, or at least businesslike English. He does not find it in Shakespeare.

What he does find is exactly the kind of style that Sprat and other reformers criticized. Complaints about "the luxury and redundance of *speech*," criticisms of "this vicious abundance of *Phrase*, this trick of *Metaphors*, this volubility of *Tongue*, which makes so great a noise in the World,"[62] could be quoted from either and from many others. In Shakespeare's lifetime authors were most admired for copiousness, the ability to rephrase the same statement in many different ways: multiply fast, amplify most. In *Venus and Adonis,* his first published work, Shakespeare took 1,194 lines to tell the same story Ovid had told in 75. This relentless abundance simply exasperates Rymer. When Othello addresses the Venetian Senate—"*Most potent, grave, and reverend Signiors*"—for nineteen lines, Rymer reminds us succinctly that "All this is but *Preamble,* to tell the Court that He wants words."[63] Brabantio's "words flow in abundance" too; "no Butter-Quean could be more lavish." On such occasions Shakespeare slips out of pragmatic, disciplined bourgeois English into the uncontrollable gabble of the lower classes. Desdemona talks like "any Countrey Chamber-maid," Brabantio is insulted with "a rabble of Skoundrel language"; the language of the play could be appropriate only to a "*Bartholomew* Droll" or a performance at "*Southwark* Fair," crude entertainments performed in crowded fairs for illiterates. It is a short step for Rymer from the bottom of humanity to a state of linguistic bestiality: "In the *Neighing* of an Horse, or in the *growling* of a Mastiff, there is a meaning, there is as lively expression, and, may I say, more humanity, than many times in the Tragical flights of *Shakespear.*"[64]

When the linguistic reformer William Petty writes, as Rymer does, of a "rabble of words,"[65] he explicitly associates stylistic disorder with a tumultuous mob. For Restoration critics, tumultuous mobs inevitably recall the Puritan revolution and the Commonwealth. Sprat blames "the *dissention* of Christian Princes, the *want of practice* in Religion, and the like" upon ambiguous, obscure, and extravagant abuses of language; and he objects to the "many fantastical terms, which were introduc'd by our *Religious Sects*" during "our late *Civil Wars.*"[66] Likewise, describing *Julius Cæsar,* Rymer compares the noisy excesses of the play's action to the actions of Puritan regiments:

> The Thunder and Lightning, the Shouting and Battel, and alarms every where in this play, may well keep the Audience awake; otherwise no Sermon wou'd be so strong an Opiate. But since the memorable action by the *Putney Pikes,* the *Hammersmith Brigade,* and the *Chelsey Cuirassiers:* one might think, in a modest Nation, no Battel wou'd ever presume to shew upon the Stage agen . . .[67]

The Puritans had closed the theatres and banned Shakespeare's plays for eighteen years, but from the perspective of the Restoration, Shakespeare and the Puritans had two things in common: they were both noisy and both unmannerly. Both thrust clowns into the company of kings.

The argument about style could not be disentangled from arguments about politics and religion. The influential Anglican apologist Joseph Glanvill, also a member of the Royal Society, complained that during the Interregnum sermons were judged by every "Rustick and Mechanick," and as a result

> the most *empty* and *fantastical* Preachers were generally the most *popular:* And those that dealt most in jingles, and *chiming* of words, in *Metaphors,* and vulgar *similitudes,* in *Fanatick Phrases,* and *Fanciful* schemes of speech, set off by *pleasing similes,* and *melting Tones,* by *loudness* and *vehemency;* These were sure to be the *taking, precious* men, though their discourses were never so trifling, and ridiculous.[68]

Glanvill, like so many of his important contemporaries, shows no sign of having read or thought about Shakespeare, but his criticism of the "enthusiasm" of Puritan preachers belongs to the widespread Restoration renunciation of a style that Shakespeare shared with them. Anyone who disliked puns, metaphors, vulgar similitudes, fanciful schemes of speech, or excessive emotion could not care much for Shakespeare.

Rymer's father was executed, and his elder brother imprisoned, for leading an abortive Puritan rebellion against Charles II; in 1692, at about the same time his critique of Shakespeare was published, Rymer himself became Historiographer Royal under William and Mary. The son of a Puritan rebel became a Whig historian. Rymer repeatedly emphasizes that Shakespeare's drama derived from medieval religious pageants, in which "the Company for Acting *Christs Passion,* or the *Old Testament,* were Carpenters, Coblers, and illiterate fellows, who found that the Drolls, and Fooleries interlarded by them, brought in the rabble . . . so they got money by the bargain." He expects his Protestant readers to be appalled by this idolatry, or by the image of the Virgin Mary played by some "strawhatted, blew-apron'd, big-bellied" "stradling wench," "with her Immaculate Conception up to her chin"; but at the same time, like any royal apologist, he insists upon the mercenary illiteracy of these sacrilegious bumpkins. And "Our *Shakespear,* doubtless, was a great Master in this craft. These Carpenters and Coblers were the guides he followed. And it is then no wonder that we find so much farce and *Apochryphal Matter* in his Tragedies."[69] Like many anti-theatre critics before and after the Interregnum, Rymer complains that an audience's judgment of a play was entirely determined by "the *Show,* the *Action,* and the *Pronunciation*"; the scene in which Iago first infects Othello with jealousy had become "the top scene, the Scene that raises *Othello* above all other Tragedies on our Theatres," solely by virtue of "the Mops and the Mows, the Grimace, the Grins and Gesticulation" of the actors.[70]

Rymer is and is not a Puritan; he does and does not subscribe to the new scientific ethic. While scientists are busy overthrowing the authority of Aristotle as an observer of the natural world, Rymer is defending his authority as an observer of the literary world. But Rymer takes his tone and much of his style from the new science. Like the Royal Society, he attacks superstition. He tears down false idols (Fletcher, Shakespeare); he asks his readers not to be swayed by their emotions, not to be fooled by deceptive appearances, not to be overwhelmed by volleys of loud but hollow verbiage; he rejects traditional verdicts, appealing instead to Nature and to Reason. He sets up the authority of his belated criticism by demolishing the authority of an admired past. Most important of all, Rymer does not simply repeat or formulate general laws of aesthetics; he analyzes the particulars of specific texts. Like the "experimental philosophers" of his time, he puts the text under a microscope, he observes it, he reports his detailed observations.

Rymer first discovered, by such scrutiny, the embarrassing incoherence of temporal sequence in *Othello.* Shakespeare cannot decide whether Act Three "contains the compass of one day, of seven days, or of seven years, or of all together."[71] If you attend carefully to indications of the passage of time within the dialogue, it becomes apparent that Othello and Desdemona consummate their marriage on their first night in Cyprus and that he murders her on the second night, believing that she has "a thousand times committed" adultery with Cassio. Modern criticism dignifies and neutralizes this impossibility by calling it a "double time-scheme," and such two-timing can be found in most of Shakespeare's plays. The aberration is most often excused by noting that audiences never notice it; it can be praised—I have praised it myself—as evidence of Shakespeare's technical resourcefulness, exploiting simultaneously the plausibility of extended duration and the urgency of compacted events. But Rymer was right in detecting a radical discontinuity in such incoherences, a doubleness that cannot be synthesized away. Unreality is woven into the text; all realistic interpretations lose themselves, eventually, in the maze of applied fiction.

Rymer also objected that Desdemona did not behave as a noble Venetian woman should, that Iago did not behave as a soldier should. We are apt to dismiss such criticisms by saying either that Rymer had an unnecessarily restricted notion of human behavior or that he wished to impose upon drama an ideological definition of the behavior of certain social classes. But Rymer's objection is based upon the premise that any audience will inevitably interpret a dramatic character as the representative of a social type; for why should we take any interest in a character's behavior unless it is in some way representative? The twentieth-century objections of feminist and Marxist critics to Shakespeare's plays, their objections to *Othello* in particular, Jewish objections to *The Merchant of Venice,* are based upon exactly the same reasoning Rymer deployed in the seventeenth century: that audiences will take Shylock as a typical Jew, Othello as a typical black, and Desdemona as a typical woman. Rymer fulminates against Othello:

> With us a Black-amoor might rise to be a Trumpeter; but *Shakespear* would not have him less than a Lieutenant-General. With us a *Moor* might marry some little drab, or Small-coal Wench; *Shakespear,* would provide him the Daughter and Heir of some great Lord, or Privy-Councellor: And all the Town should reckon it a very suitable match:[72]

From Rymer's perspective Shakespeare was not bigoted enough; from our perspective he was too bigoted. But both perspectives recognize that roles in a play will be taken as models, that representations are taken to be representative and can accordingly be criticized if they are socially misleading.

HAMLET IS DISCOVERED

If you want a single representative of the Restoration image of Shakespeare, take *Hamlet:* adapted by Davenant, acted by Betterton, celebrated by Pepys, criticized by Dryden. It was one of the plays granted to Davenant's company in December 1660; on August 24, 1661, Pepys went "To the Opera, and there saw *Hamlet Prince of Denmarke,* done . . . very well." Other spectators responded differently. On November 26 of that year John Evelyn, in a less famous diary, noted that he "saw *Hamlet* Pr: of Denmark played: but now the old playe began to disgust this refined age; since his Majestie being so long abroad."[73] At the beginning of the era Shakespeare already seemed to some old-fashioned; by the end he seemed to others morally objectionable. In 1698 Jeremy Collier, in his now-infamous, then-influential *Short View of the Immorality, and Profaneness of the English Stage,* mentioned *Hamlet* only in order to complain of Shakespeare's "Lewd" and "unreasonable" characterization of Ophelia: in her madness the "young Virgin *Ophelia*" sings bawdy songs that "sully her Reputation," and then afterward Shakespeare rudely "drown[s] the Lady like a Kitten."[74]

Midway between Evelyn and Collier, in 1679, John Dryden in his only explicit allusion to the play cites a passage from *Hamlet* as a characteristic demonstration of Shakespearean bombast. Dryden quotes two passages from the scene in which Hamlet welcomes a company of strolling players; the first consists of "*an exclamation against Fortune*":[75]

> Out, out, thou strumpet fortune; all you Gods,
> In general Synod, take away her Power,
> Break all the spokes and fallyes from her Wheel,
> And bowl the round Nave down the hill of Heav'n
> As low as to the Fiends.

The second describes Queen Hecuba of Troy just after her old and defenseless husband King "Priam *was kill'd before her eyes*":

> The mobbled Queen ran up and down,
> Threatning the flame with bisson rheum: a clout about that head
> Where late the Diadem stood; and for a Robe
> About her lank and all o're-teemed loyns,
> A blanket in th' alarm of fear caught up.
> Who this had seen, with tongue in venom steep'd
> 'Gainst Fortune's state would Treason have pronounc'd;
> But if the Gods themselves did see her then,
> When she saw *Pyrrhus* make malicious sport

In mincing with his sword her Husband's Limbs,
The instant burst of clamor that she made
(Unless things mortal meant them not at all)
Would have made milch the burning eyes of Heav'n,
And passion in the Gods.[76]

Dryden's discussion of this passage can be taken as typical of the period. He writes with analytical relish—and accuracy, and intelligence—about its deficiencies as a piece of poetry.

> What a pudder is here kept in raising the expression of trifling thoughts. Would not a man have thought that the Poet had been bound Prentice to a Wheel-wright, for his first Rant? and had follow'd a Ragman, for the clout and blanket, in the second?

Poets, particularly those who aspire to write tragedies, should have nothing to do with wheelwrights or ragmen. Dryden articulates, as unabashedly as Rymer, the class prejudices that underlie Restoration aesthetics.

> Fortune is painted on a wheel; and therefore the writer in a rage, will have Poetical Justice done upon every member of that Engin: after this execution, he bowls the Nave downhill, from Heaven, to the Fiends: (an unreasonable long mark a man would think;) 'tis well there are no solid Orbs to stop it in the way, or no Element of fire to consume it: but when it came to the earth, it must be monstrous heavy, to break ground as low as to the Center.

Poetry must be reasonable; this passage is "*unreasonable.*" The Royal Society, which Dryden had joined soon after its founding, recommended that experiments be conducted publicly so that their results could be witnessed by as many members as possible. For us, an experiment's validity is confirmed only when it can be duplicated; for them, validity could be established by multiplying observers of a single event. An experiment was conceived as a theatrical demonstration of the laws of nature, with the experimenter playing playwright and the Royal Society playing audience. Many of those spectators were, like Dryden himself, not scientists at all, for the Royal Society was not a professional organization. Instead, it resembled, as the hard-core experimentalists often complained, a fashionable London club, open to anyone with enough curiosity, enough money to pay the membership dues, and enough vanity to be attracted by its intellectual prestige and royal patronage. These interested bystanders were exactly the class of people that patronized the Restoration theatre, and many came to meetings "only as to a Play to amuse themselves for an hour or so."77 Evelyn and Pepys, for instance, who attended performances of *Hamlet* in 1661, both belonged to the Royal Society. The spectators at an experiment who became the spectators of *Hamlet* the following night might easily regard Shakespeare's play, by contrast, as a dubious or rigged or failed demonstration of the laws of nature.

Modern readers and audiences usually do not sense such difficulty in the passage Dryden quotes—but only because we do not take seriously the cosmology of Dryden's (or Shakespeare's) era. We no longer find the passage difficult simply because we have lost part of its cultural context, a context still available to Dryden. If the passage seems sensible to us, that is not because we understand it better but because we understand it less.

> *His making milch the burning eyes of Heaven, was a pretty tollerable flight too; and I think no man ever drew milk out of eyes before him: yet to make the wonder greater, these eyes were burning. Such a sight indeed were enough to have rais'd passion in the Gods, but to excuse the effects of it, he tells you perhaps they did not see it. Wise men would be glad to find a little sence couch'd under all those pompous words; for Bombast is commonly the delight of that Audience, which loves Poetry, but understands it not:*

In this attack on "*that Audience*" Dryden simultaneously hits two targets. On the one hand, he alludes to the common belief that many of the barbarities of Shakespeare's plays could be explained by the barbarity of his audiences; on the other hand, he makes an equally pointed—and equally commonplace—complaint, from the perspective of a working playwright, about the appetite for rodomontade sadly discernible in a certain portion of Restoration audiences. He thus contrives in one sentence both to flatter and reprove his contemporaries. (He was, after all, the greatest English satirist of the seventeenth century.)

But what Dryden says of "*that Audience*" at either the beginning or the end of his century could equally well be said of audiences in our own century: "*Bombast is commonly the delight of that Audience, which loves Poetry, but understands it not.*" As every actor today knows, parts of any play by Shakespeare will be unintelligible to a handsome fraction of any audience. Contemporary British actors in particular, who cut their histrionic teeth on Shakespeare while importing more spectators than any other actors in the world, are often bemused by the masses of apparently insensible American and Japanese tourists who file obediently into their theatres during the summer season, appreciatively uncomprehending. But the audiences keep coming; they pay the bills, they keep the theatres open. Such modern auditors love Shakespeare without always understanding him.

Most modern readers would not understand him either if left to their own devices. As Dryden complains, Shakespeare "*often obscures his meaning by his words, and sometimes makes it unintelligible.*" A modern reader would need—at least, modern editions assume that they need—a note on *nave* (the hub of a wheel), *mobbled* (muffled), *bisson* (blind or nearly blind), *rheum* (moist bodily discharge; here, tears), *o're-teemed* (worn out by childbearing), *milch* (milk-producing), and *passion* (overpowering grief). To understand the passage fully we would also need to be told or reminded that Fortune was an allegorical goddess often portrayed in the Renaissance as a prostitute and as holding or standing upon a wheel. The line about Hecuba's worn-out loins makes sense only if we know that Priam had fifty sons; Shakespeare may not have assumed that Hecuba bore all of them, but even if he or his audience pedantically inquired about the numbers of her offspring they would have credited her with little fewer than twenty. We understand Shakespeare, when we do, only by virtue of the labors of centuries of annotators.

Dryden and his contemporaries not only had to make what sense they could of Shakespeare's difficult and obsolete language, without benefit of notes; they also had to make sense of texts progressively corrupted by decades of careless reprintings. In the text Dryden quotes, *fellies* (wooden pieces that form the rim of a wheel) has been transformed into a nonsensical *fallyes,* and *move* altered to a confusing *meant* ("Unless things mortal meant them not at all").

Dryden's discussion of this passage is characteristically ambivalent. On the one hand he performs a cold-blooded critical autopsy, treating the speech as a dead piece of poetry whose corpse must be cut up in order to demonstrate how diseased it was. On the other hand, he pretends not to be condemning Shakespeare at all. Feeling "forc'd to give an example" of the faults he criticizes, he explains:

> *but that I may do it with respect to* Shakespear, *it shall not be taken from any thing of his:* 'tis an exclamation against Fortune, quoted in his Hamlet, *but written by some other Poet.*

Dryden quotes *Hamlet* but claims that he is not quoting "Shakespear." This procedure probably seems whimsical to a modern reader. But Hamlet asks the visiting actors to perform a speech from "an excellent play" he once saw; the passage that Dryden quotes advertises itself, in context, as a quotation from some other text. In his plays Shakespeare sometimes "quoted" songs written by others; he sometimes regurgitated extracts from his historical sources with little or no change; *Hamlet* was itself based upon a lost play of the same name, probably written by Thomas Kyd.[78] We simply cannot assume that Shakespeare was self-evidently deceiving us in claiming that he took this speech from some other play.

But although Dryden's skepticism about authorship can be commended, in other respects his choice of this passage is disingenuous. The earlier part of the paragraph, leading up to this quotation and analysis, had been wholly devoted to Shakespeare; Dryden finishes the analysis of *Hamlet* in midparagraph, breaking off with a concession—"*But* Shakespear *does not often [write Bombast] thus*"—and then continuing to a discussion of *Julius Caesar*. That "*But* Shakespear," cunningly ambiguous, can be taken either to contrast him with the anonymous writer of the condemned passage or to concede that he did not usually write so badly. Moreover, this discussion occurs in Dryden's preface to his own adaptation of *Troilus and Cressida*, which, of all Shakespeare's works, might be singled out for the tortuous artificiality of its "*blown puffy stile.*" When Dryden complained about Shakespeare's occasional weakness for overwrought verbiage, he had been working upon and thinking about (and expecting his readers to think about) *Troilus and Cressida*.

Dryden says "*Hamlet*" but means "*Troilus and Cressida*"; he criticizes Shakespeare but claims to be criticizing someone else. His actions damn his great predecessor, but his words profess "respect"; he praises Shakespeare but imitates Fletcher. Such defensiveness characterizes the entire period. Some readers have concluded that Dryden's criticisms were conventional but his praise sincere; others decide that his praise was hypocritical and his contempt genuine. I suspect instead that a real admiration cohabited with a real contempt, and that the two attitudes tortured each other for the length of Dryden's life. In 1668 Dryden could say "I love *Shakespeare*"[79] and mean it—in the same way that an adolescent can honestly abstractly say, "I love my parents" while in practice hating them much of the time. It was Davenant who liked to believe and let others believe that he was Shakespeare's bastard, but it was Dryden who acted like a son—or, rather, an orphan—a posthumous child of uncertain paternity, constantly measuring himself against the image of his dead father, testing his legitimacy by his success, finding himself wanting, professing "respect" while chafing for some form of independence, hating what he loved, and hating himself for hating it.

Immediately after the preface to *Troilus and Cressida* is printed Dryden's prologue to his own adaptation, spoken by the "awful ghost" of Shakespeare himself, who asked:

> Now, where are the Successors to my name?
> What bring they to fill out a Poet's fame?
> Weak, short-liv'd issues of a feeble Age;
> Scarce living to be Christen'd on the Stage!

Thomas Betterton, who spoke this prologue, was most famous for his portrayal of Hamlet; Hamlet was haunted by his father's ghost; Dryden's play is haunted, preceded, simultaneously recommended and condemned, by Shakespeare's.

This crippling and creative double bind was not an accident of Dryden's personality or a universal constant of the artist's psyche. It was caused by the abrupt restoration of theatrical activity in 1660, which necessarily established overnight a repertoire of the best plays of an earlier period, a canon that dominated the theatres in which Dryden and other new playwrights would seek a place and an identity. Dryden, the foremost poet and critic of his generation, simply realized and expressed the situation better than anyone else:

> But it is to raise envy to the living, to compare them with the dead. [*Ben. Jonson, Fletcher,* and *Shakespeare*] are honor'd and almost ador'd by us, as they deserve . . . Yet give me leave to say thus much, without injury to their Ashes, that not onely we shall never equal them, but they could never equal themselves, were they to rise and write again. We acknowledge them our Fathers in wit, but they have ruin'd their Estates themselves before they came to their childrens hands.[80]

As early as 1668 Dryden knew that he and his contemporaries were compelled "either not to write at all, or to attempt some other way." Eighteen years later in his prologue to *Aureng-Zebe* he confesses:

> But spite of all his pride a secret shame,
> Invades his breast at *Shakespear's* sacred name:
> Aw'd when he hears his God-like *Romans* rage,
> He, in a just despair, would quit the Stage.

Shakespeare the father has become, by an easy slippage, God the father. Shakespeare is adjectived, increasingly often, as "Immortal," "*Godlike*," and "Divine."[81]

The strain of Restoration thought that hosannaed Shakespeare as an artistic god could hardly be expected to denigrate *Hamlet* as unceremoniously as Evelyn or Collier, or to tie itself up in the emotional ambivalences of Dryden. In 1695 London's two acting companies, engaged in particularly bitter rivalry, competed by throwing *Hamlet* at each other. Lincoln's Inn Fields announced a performance on Tuesday, Drury Lane promptly announced one on Monday; Lincoln's Inn Fields rescheduled its performance for Monday, Drury Lane backed down.[82] Such competition presumes a large public appetite for the play. Robert Gould, describing his own responses, no doubt spoke for many of his contemporaries:

> When e'r I *Hamlet*, or *Othello* read,
> My *Hair* starts up, and my *Nerves* shrink with dread:
> *Pity* and *fear* raise my concern still higher,
> Till, betwixt both, I'm ready to expire![83]

The Earl of Shaftesbury called *Hamlet* "that piece of [our old dramatick Poet], which seems to have most affected *English* Hearts, and has perhaps been oftnest acted of any that have come upon our Stage."[84]

Hamlet's popularity can also be surmised by its record of publication. In addition to the collected editions of 1664 and 1685 it was separately published in five quarto editions (two in 1676, others in 1683, 1695, and 1703), which give the text "As it is now Acted at his Highness the Duke of *York's* Theatre." This text, acted by Davenant's company, had apparently been prepared by Davenant himself and probably represents the acting version in use from the beginning of Restoration performances in 1661.[85]

By the standards of more notorious adaptations of the period, Davenant's *Hamlet* hardly seems adapted at all; he adds no new characters or episodes, nor does he restructure the action. But he does make more than three hundred small-scale changes in wording, some of which affect our interpretation of the action or characters. When Shakespeare's Hamlet discovers Claudius alone in Act Three he says, "Now might I do it pat, now he is praying"; Davenant's Hamlet first secures the audience's moral bearings by saying, "Where is this murderer" and then (sarcastically, or taken aback) notes that "he kneels and prays."[86]

But most of the minor changes have no such overt critical purpose. Some eliminate oaths or profanities; the patent of 1660 had required the new companies to purge the plays of any material objectionable to the pious. (After all, the pious had in the recent past closed the theatres and executed Charles I; Charles II did not want to offend them gratuitously.) Many changes regularize the irregular grammar of Elizabethan English or normalize Shakespeare's often abnormal word order. Others curtail the physicality, particularity, unembarrassed vulgarity, and sheer cussed strangeness of the language, rendering Shakespeare immediately comprehensible, easily digestible:

Shakespeare	*Davenant*
Perpend	Consider
coated	met
bray out	proclaim
In hugger mugger	Obscurely
Affront	meet
buzzers	whispers

In Hamlet's most famous soliloquy, where in Shakespeare human resolution "Is sicklied ore with the pale cast of thought," in Davenant it merely "Shews sick and pale with thought."[87] All these expressions, which Davenant thought unintelligible to his audience, are considered unintelligible to readers by modern editors, and our editorial glosses sometimes unwittingly echo Davenant's revisions. What later editors and commentators will put into the footnotes—paraphrases that explain Shakespeare's meaning—

Davenant simply sticks into the dialogue itself. The gloss displaces the text.

Not surprisingly, Davenant also cut the text of Shakespeare's longest play, which was *too long to be conveniently Acted.*" Beginning with the text printed in previous quartos, he deleted most of the passages deleted in the folio. Many of his cuts became standard, surviving as part of theatrical tradition until the end of the nineteenth century. He severely truncated the material dealing with Norway, eliminating entirely the parts of Valtemand and Cornelius, as well as Fortinbras' scene in Act Four; he cut most of Laertes' brotherly advice to Ophelia, Polonius' fatherly advice to Laertes, Polonius' meandering advice to Reynaldo, and Hamlet's histrionic advice to the Players. In general, Davenant disposed of diversions, tightening and accelerating the play's action. The protagonist, too, became more straightforward, less bedeviled by detours and moral ambiguities. Abbreviating the soliloquy at the end of Act Two, scene two ("O what a rogue and pesant slave am I!"),[88] Davenant produced a more practical Hamlet, who curtly reprimands himself for delaying and then at once settles down to a plan of action.

This reshaping of *Hamlet* satisfies a neoclassical preference for unambiguous heroes and villains, for moral as well as structural clarity and contrast. But these aesthetic motives were reinforced by political ones. In 1661 Davenant's company offered Restoration audiences a play about a wicked usurper who had murdered the true king and whose hypocritical prayers were gutted by his crimes. This usurper also tries to murder the old king's son, driving him out of his kingdom; but in the end that son returns and punishes the villain. In a scenario that so inevitably elicits parallels with English politics from 1642 to 1660, the hero needed to be made as straightforward, godly, and admirable as possible.

By erasing certain features of the play Davenant gave greater structural emphasis to what he saved. He did not cut the gravediggers' scene in Act Five; preserved as a "droll" even during the Interregnum, that scene was too popular to sacrifice. He also preserved all of Osric, whose foppishness presumably appealed to Restoration taste. This fondness for comedy can also be seen in the treatment of Polonius, who was played by James Nokes, a comic actor noted for "the ridiculous Solemnity of his Features": "He scarce ever made his first Entrance in a Play, but he was received with . . . a General Laughter, which the very Sight of him provoked, and Nature cou'd not resist; yet the louder the Laugh, the graver was his Look upon it . . ."[89]

The *Hamlet* performed in Restoration theatres was different from the play we know now, changed—sometimes blatantly, sometimes subtly—by deliberate cutting and rewording. But it also differed in some respects from the *Hamlet* offered to readers in the editions of 1676, 1683, and 1695. Those editions, for instance, do not simply omit the passages "*left out upon the Stage*"; instead, they print them enclosed in quotation marks. In the theatre such passages disappear; the edition simultaneously gives and withholds them, offering readers a synoptic vision of Shakespeare's play, book and performance side by side, each commenting upon the other.

If in such respects the Restoration editions give us more than a performance of *Hamlet,* in other respects they give us less. Pepys tells us that the play was being performed as early as 1661 "with Scenes"; the printed texts give no indication of their presence or character. Fortunately, a contemporary print offers an inkling of what one scene of *Hamlet* may have looked like on the Restoration stage; we can guess that a generic castle and churchyard would have been used to illustrate other scenes. Likewise, the texts divide the play— for the first time in print—into five acts, a division perpetuated in all subsequent editions of Shakespeare's works; but they do not tell us, as a contemporary playbill does, that in performance the play was "adorned and embellished with very curious dances between the acts."[90]

Nor can the printed texts re-create Betterton's performance. His acting of the title role had earned *Pericles* a moment in the Restoration repertoire; his performance of the Prince of Denmark had a similar but more enduring effect upon the fortunes of *Hamlet.* Surprising as it may now seem, when seventeenth-century readers thought of Shakespeare neither Hamlet the character nor *Hamlet* the play leaped first to mind. Among the plays of Shakespeare and Jonson it ranked thirteenth in reputation, judging by the number of contemporary allusions; among their characters, Hamlet ranked third, after Falstaff and Brutus.[91] References to both the play and the character cluster in the later decades of the century and probably reflect the impact of Betterton's performances. Pepys, for instance, saw *Hamlet* five times and on three of those occasions remarked primarily on Betterton's acting. On August 24, 1661, he "saw *Hamlet Prince of Denmarke,* done with Scenes very well. But above all, Batterton did the Prince's part beyond imagination"; on May 28, 1663, "saw *Hamlett* done, giving us fresh reason never to think enough of Baterton"; on August 31, 1668, "saw *Hamlett,* which we have not seen this year before, or more, and mightily pleased with it; but above all with Batterton, the best part, I believe, that ever man acted." Pepys was not being idiosyncratic. John Downes, who served as book-keeper and prompter to the Betterton company from 1662 to 1706, records that Betterton's "exact Performance of [*Hamlet*], gain'd him Esteem and Reputation, Superlative to all other Plays . . . No succeeding Tragedy for several Years got more Reputation, or Money to the Company than this."92

For the Restoration, Betterton's Hamlet was *Hamlet;* the two could not be separated. Although we cannot recover his performance, we can at least begin to imagine, from descriptions by contemporaries, how it affected spectators. Colley Cibber, who belonged to the next generation of actors, tells us that when Betterton encountered the Ghost of Hamlet's father he "made the Ghost equally terrible to the Spectator, as to himself!"

> the Passion never rises beyond an almost breathless Astonishment, or an Impatience, limited by filial Reverence . . . [the Scene] open'd with a Pause of mute Amazement! then rising slowly, to a solemn, trembling Voice . . . and in the descriptive Part of the natural Emotions which the ghastly Vision gave him, the boldness of his Expostulation was still govern'd by Decency, manly, but not braving; his Voice never rising into that seeming Outrage or wild Defiance of what he naturally rever'd.93

Thirty years after Betterton's death, another witness still remembered the expression on the actor's face and the rhythm of his voice; he had seen

> [*Betterton's*] Countenance (which was naturally ruddy and sanguin) in this Scene of the fourth Act, where his Father's Ghost appears, thro' the violent and sudden Emotions of Amazement and Horror, turn instantly on the Sight of his Father's Spirit, as pale as his Neckcloath, when every Article of his Body seem'd to be affected with a Tremor inexpressible . . . And when *Hamlet* utters this Line, upon the Ghost's leaving the Stage . . . *See——where he goes——ev'n now——out at the Portal:* The whole Audience hath remain'd in a dead Silence for near a Minute, and then,——

as if recovering all at once from their Astonishment, have joined
as one Man, in a Thunder of universal Applause.94

Betterton, coached in the role by accounts of performances before
the closure of the theatres, acting a text adapted just after the
Restoration, combined in his interpretation of Hamlet the twin
imperatives of authenticity and novelty. That performance illustrates, too, the extent to which the image of Shakespeare during the
Restoration originated in and always returned to the theatre. As
Nicholas Rowe would say, at the end of Betterton's career, "I cannot
leave *Hamlet,* without taking notice of the Advantage with which we
have seen this Master-piece of *Shakespear* distinguish it self upon the
Stage, by Mr. *Betterton*'s fine Performance of that Part."95

Betterton's performance dominated contemporary perceptions
of *Hamlet* partly because it was indeed "fine" but partly, too, because
of its sheer longevity. He performed the role for almost five decades,
from 1661 to 1709. In 1709 a new age began, and Nicholas Rowe
was its first voice.

CHAPTER 2

꩜

1709

On April 12, 1709, Richard Steele published the first issue of *The Tatler*. On May 2 Alexander Pope's poetry made its debut in print. By June 2 Nicholas Rowe's edition of *The Works of Mr. William Shakespear* had appeared. That same month the old Dorset Garden theatre was pulled down, and the old Drury Lane temporarily closed down; on September 20 Thomas Betterton played Hamlet for the last time. An allied army commanded by the Duke of Marlborough defeated the French at Tournai (September 5), Malplaquet (September 11), and Mons (October 20). On December 12 Parliament began consideration of "An Act for the Encouragement of Learning," a historic redefinition of the law of copyright. Collectively, the events of 1709 would transform the public perception of Shakespeare in the eighteenth century.

One man, a bookseller named Jacob Tonson, had a finger in them all. Described that year as "Chief Merchant to the Muses,"[1] Tonson joined his name to those of fifteen other wealthy printers and booksellers in petitioning Parliament to enact a new copyright law.[2] Tonson had also founded the famous Kit-Cat Club, an influential conclave of political and literary figures, including both Steele and Rowe; in December 1709 Marlborough was made an "extraordinary" member of that club, which ordered Tonson to dedicate to him a forthcoming edition of Julius Caesar's *Commentaries*.[3] Tonson published Rowe's edition of Shakespeare, published the anthology that introduced Pope to the reading public, and would later take over publication of *The Tatler*. He had published plays adapted by Betterton; Betterton had subscribed to Tonson's edition of Virgil; Tonson, like most of the Kit-Cat Club, regularly and conspicuously patronized the theatres and had joined other members in procuring a box at Betterton's benefit performance of *The Humours of Sir John Falstaff*. Indeed, the prologue to that benefit—written by Matthew Prior, another famous member of the Club and another Tonson client—alluded to the portly publisher himself: Betterton, playing Jack Falstaff, described Tonson as "old plump *Jack* in Miniature."[4]

The one man who, more than any other, shaped Restoration images of Shakespeare had been Sir William Davenant: Cavalier, courtier, playwright, theatre manager, adapter of texts, Shakespeare's alleged bastard son, tutor to Betterton, collaborator with Dryden. Dryden, Davenant's most famous protégé, became Tonson's most famous client. Mr. Jacob Tonson—publisher of Dryden, Betterton, Shakespeare; not a producer but a consumer of theatre; not a writer but a reader; not a Cavalier but a Whig; not a courtier but an entrepreneur—became for the first half of the eighteenth century what Davenant had been for the second half of the seventeenth: both maker and epitome of a new Shakespeare.

A THEATRE

Thomas Betterton made his final public appearance on May 2, 1710, when he was buried in Westminster Abbey. With him died an epoch of theatrical history, and the new epoch lacked the power and prestige of its predecessor. The stage sank as the bookshop rose. The decline was not unexpected or cataclysmic; it had been coming for decades. The theatre was dragged out and down by a political and economic undertow it could not escape or control. But although this slow drowning was less dramatic than the sudden deathblow administered in 1642, its consequences for Shakespeare's reputation were equally momentous.

By 1674, fourteen years after the Restoration, both of London's theatrical companies were playing in spanking new, specially built, neoclassical theatres. But this innovative prosperity did not last long. Over the next decade all the old leaders of the King's company—the actors who had made their start before the Civil War, the last living embodiment of the continuity of theatrical tradition— either expired or retired. In 1682 the King's company collapsed, and a single United Company, led by Betterton, was formed at Drury Lane theatre, combining the Duke's company with remnants of the broken King's. From 1682 to 1694 London had only one theatre and one company of actors; the lack of competition depressed standards and diminished the opportunities for new actors.

These internal difficulties were compounded by external ones. Charles II, patron of a quarter century of theatrical revival, died in 1685, and the political consensus he had created fell apart completely. His successor, James II, clumsily tried to make England safe for Catholicism but succeeded only in making it unsafe for the Stuart dynasty. Three years of political upheaval culminated in the Glorious Revolution of 1688. The birth of James II's first son confronted his subjects with the prospect of an endless succession of Catholic kings; they responded with a coup d'état, deposing James II and installing in his place the Protestant couple William and Mary. For the second time in less than a lifetime the English people had overthrown an unpopular government. But the Protestant parliamentarians who deposed James II—more cautious and experienced than those who deposed Charles I, less bitter because they had suffered less—did not abolish either the monarchy or the theatre; instead, both became subject to a newly defined social contract. Neither could safely flout the national moral consensus. In the case of the monarchy that social contract was written into law in the new bill of rights; in the theatre it was imposed by slow osmosis. The new monarchs tolerated drama, but they did not share Charles II's ostentatious enthusiasm for it, and the resulting loss of royalist prestige sapped it of artistic talent and aristocratic support. The theatre entered a period of hesitant redefinition and drift.

The new monopoly and the new monarchy predictably reshaped the repertoire. Initially, Betterton and his colleagues relished the opportunity to take over popular old roles, including most of Shakespeare's, previously owned by their rivals; and in the first five years of their new monopoly the United Company averaged only three new plays a year. Then, having left dramatists to starve for half a decade, the company realized that it needed them and expected to find fruit still growing on the neglected tree. After the crisis of 1688 the actors turned increasingly often, increasingly desperate, to new plays, thrashing around in search of new formulas to attract new audiences.5 But of the finest dramatists of the period before 1682, William Wycherley, Sir George Etherege, and Thomas Otway had all deceased or ceased writing by 1685; Aphra Behn died early in 1689, having concentrated her energies upon narrative fiction in the last five years of her life. The new formulas would have to come from new writers, and they did not come quickly.

The new audiences, influenced by and reflected in the bland probity of William and Mary, had less and less taste for the sexual and social comedy (on and off stage) of the 1660s and 1670s. This antipathy grew steadily after 1688. Jeremy Collier's dissenting Protestant attack on the *Immorality, and Profaneness of the English Stage* went through three editions in 1698. The pamphlet war Collier had started continued for a decade, and it did not spare Shakespeare. In an article in his thrice-weekly journal *A Review of the State of the English Nation* Daniel Defoe took characteristic exception to a performance of *Henry the Fourth* at Oxford: "Is not that Play as full of prophane, immoral, and some blasphemous Parts, as most now extant? Is not Religion banter'd in it, the *Church* ridicul'd, and your Maker dishonour'd?"6

Even before the furor created by Collier's pamphlet, the authorities had issued new instructions that "Obsenityes & other Scandalous matters" be deleted from plays.7 In May 1698 indignant reformers tried to get an indictment against Congreve and another playwright for writing objectionable plays, against the actors who acted them, and against Jacob Tonson and another bookseller for printing them. There was even talk of again closing the theatres, as in 1642.8 The theatres must either make themselves palatable to middle-class Protestant taste or close, if not by legal proscription then by commercial starvation. And so plays went where the playgoers wanted to go, from sexually erect to morally upright.

This change in the character of the audience reinforced changes in theatrical property, financing, and management, precipitated by the vagaries of venture capitalism. In 1692 Betterton lost his considerable personal fortune as a result of a disastrous commercial investment. In 1693 Davenant's son went bankrupt, and the United Company's royal patent accordingly passed from his hands into those of Christopher Rich, a moneylender and financial manipulator who had little interest in aesthetic values and no respect for actors. In 1694 Rich tried to cut costs by squeezing out the company's star names, replacing them with younger performers who would play for less money; Betterton, newly indigent, could not afford to be thus relegated, and in December 1694 he led a walkout. London again had two companies, at a time when public interest would hardly support one.

This revived commercial competition in an unfavorable economic climate intensified the need to identify and secure the loyalties of that new potential audience. Rich enjoyed a virtual monopoly on spectacular opera for the following decade, importing foreign virtuoso singers and dancers; and he tried to run his competitors out of business by feeding and developing the public taste for musicals and magicals. From this period dates the beginning of the practice, fully institutionalized and flourishing by the 1720s, of expanding the variety of entertainment offered by a visit to the theatre. In 1600 Hamlet could say, speaking for the century to come, that "the play's the thing"; in the eighteenth century the play was no longer "the thing" but simply part of the "whole show" that attracted audiences. It had become a mere "mainpiece" preceded, interrupted, and followed by other performances—music, dancing, puppets, pantomimes, juggling, acrobatics, overtures and afterpieces.

Meanwhile, the architectural spaces in which actors could act Shakespeare's plays—or anyone else's—were being redefined under the pressure of this prolonged economic crisis. Betterton and the other rebels soon realized that Rich could manage quite well without them but that they could not survive indefinitely in the cramped and outdated theatre at Lincoln's Inn Fields. On June 15, 1703, Sir John Vanbrugh had written to Tonson describing his plans for a large new theatre;9 in April 1705, after many delays, Betterton's company moved temporarily into the uncompleted building. But the new stage did not solve the old problems. It seems at first to have been an acoustic disaster, with the actors' voices sounding "like the Gabbling of so many People, in the lofty Isles in a Cathedral."10

The acoustics of Drury Lane had already been spoiled in the

1690s by Rich. To increase seating capacity—and income—he curtailed the forestage and put stage boxes in place of the downstage proscenium doors. These alterations combined to push the performers ten feet upstage and fundamentally changed the nature of the spatial and psychological relationship between actor and audience that had prevailed throughout the seventeenth century. Colley Cibber, writing in 1740, could not have been conscious of the historical implications of this departure from the acting conditions of Shakespeare's time; he complained, instead, simply from the perspective of a working actor:

> when the Actors were in Possession of that forwarder Space to advance upon, the Voice was then more in the Centre of the House, so that the most distant Ear had scarce the least Doubt or Difficulty in hearing what fell from the weakest Utterance: All Objects were thus drawn nearer to the Sense; . . . every rich or fine-coloured Habit [costume] had a more lively Lustre; Nor was the minutest Motion of a Feature . . . ever lost, as they frequently must be in the Obscurity of too great a Distance.[11]

In the seventeenth century the actors had been, by the very design of their stages, thrust into the midst of their audiences, vulnerable and palpable; in the eighteenth century they retreated increasingly into the upstage scenery. The old theatres created intimacy; the new ones, perspective (both visual and emotional).

By the time the theatrical civil war came to an end, it had inflicted incalculable damage on the actors, the buildings, and the less tangible but more permanent fabric that unites the theatre as an activity to its host society. As a result of actors' complaints, the Lord Chamberlain finally closed Drury Lane on June 6, 1709, leaving Rich without a company or a license. After Betterton's death the following year a new triumvirate of actor-managers (including Colley Cibber) took over Drury Lane and ran it for the next two decades. The age of Betterton was over; the age of Cibber had begun.

Cibber himself was not a great Shakespearian actor. In this, as in other respects, he typified his generation. When he played Richard the Third he reminded one spectator of "the distorted *Heavings* of an *unjointed Caterpillar*":[12]

> When he makes love to *Lady Anne,* he looks like a pick-pocket, with his shrugs and grimaces, that has more a design on her

purse than her heart; and his utterance is in the same cast with his action. In Bosworth-field he appears no more like *King Richard,* than *King Richard* was like *Falstaff:* he foams, struts, and bellows with the voice and cadence of a watch-man, rather than a hero and a prince.[13]

Cibber was a better comic than a tragic actor, just as the eighteenth century produced better comedies than tragedies; but throughout his life he insisted on attempting tragic roles, for which he was desperately ill-suited, just as playwrights kept laboring to concoct tragedies. Against the comedies of Farquhar, Vanbrugh, and Gay this period can offer only, at its best, Rowe's pseudo-Shakespearian *Jane Shore* and Addison's pseudoclassical *Cato.* This decline of contemporary tragedy, in progress since Dryden's *All for Love* (1677) and Otway's *Venice Preserv'd* (1682), itself contributed to the growth of Shakespeare's reputation. Most critics agreed that "his principal Talent and his chief Delight was *Tragedy.*"[14] In the period 1700–1728 Shakespeare's seven most popular plays were, in descending order, *Hamlet,* the adapted operatic *Macbeth, Julius Cæsar,* the adapted operatic *The Tempest, or the Enchanted Island,* the adapted *History of King Lear,* the first part of *Henry the Fourth,* and *Othello the Moor of Venice.*[15] Noticeably, five of the seven are tragedies; of the two exceptions *The Tempest* survived as a musical spectacular, and *Henry the Fourth* owed its continued success to Falstaff. The first three, moreover, all dramatize the successful overthrow of usurpers or tyrants, a theme predictably popular after the Glorious Revolution.

Shakespeare's tragedies held their place in the repertoire because no new serious drama rose up to replace them. As one reviewer remarked, "the Tragedies of *Shakespear* . . . are the great Support of our Theatre."[16] Of the twenty most popular plays of 1700–28, only Rowe's *Tamerlane* (sixteenth) and Addison's *Cato* (twentieth) were contemporary tragedies; but the list includes comedies by Vanbrugh, Farquhar, Gay, Dryden, Congreve, Cibber, and others. Since 1660 the English theatre had continued to produce new comedies that the public and the critics preferred to those of Shakespeare; but few of its new tragedies secured a foothold. For a good English tragedy you pretty much had to turn to Shakespeare—even if a rather beefed up, tidied up Shakespeare. And the repertoire, especially as it developed at the turn of the century, needed tragedies.

The new divertissements that now filled out an evening's entertainment, the entr'actes and afterpieces, were overwhelmingly farcical, musical, spectacular, or all three; so in order to offer a well-balanced theatrical meal some serious filling was occasionally needed. Shakespeare was kept on the menu because he was the only serious dish they knew how to cook.

Although Cibber was better at comedy than tragedy, his comic gifts were not ideally suited to Shakespeare. Betterton made the greatest Falstaff of his time as well as the greatest Hamlet; Cibber's most memorable Shakespearian role was Shallow, the country justice of the peace in *Henry the Fourth*, Part Two:

> Cibber's transition from asking the price of bullocks, to trite, but grave, reflections on mortality, was so natural, and attended with such an unmeaning roll of his small pig's-eyes, accompanied with an important utterance of tick! tick! tick! not much louder than the balance of a watch's pendulum, that I question if any actor was ever superior in the conception or expression of such solemn insignificancy.[17]

But however brilliantly performed, Shallow remains a small part in a play seldom revived. Falstaff is man expansive; Shallow, a shrunken remnant, a mere asteroid to Falstaff's Jupiter. Falstaff is intellectually multiplicitous, unputdownable, noncircumscribable; Shallow is . . . well, shallow.

Other star actors of the period were equally limited. James Quin, for instance, specialized in histrionic tantrums. In the famous quarrel scene between Cassius and Brutus in the fourth act of *Julius Caesar*,

> in the character of the mild patriot Brutus, [Quin] loses all temper and decorum; nay, so ridiculous is the behavior of him and Cassius at their interview, that setting foot to foot, and grinning at each other, with the aspect of two cobblers enraged, they thrust their left sides together, with repeated shocks, that the hilts of their swords may clash for the entertainment of the audience . . .[18]

Hardly anyone regarded these decades as a great era of English acting.

In part, this decline reflects the greed that increasingly pervaded English society. Cibber himself was notoriously mercenary; when the critic suggested that his Richard the Third seems to have had "a design on [*Lady Anne's*] purse," he was satirizing the actor's morals as much as his performance. The breakup of the United Company in 1695 had been precipitated by profiteering, and there are signs of increasing selfishness onstage as well as off. In 1735 a critic complained that contemporary actors

> *relax* themselves, as soon as any Speech in their *own* Part is over, into an absent Unattentiveness to whatever is *replied*, by *Another:* looking round, and examining the Company of Spectators, with an Ear only watchful of the *Cue;* at which, like *Soldiers,* upon the *Word of Command,* They start, suddenly, back to their *Postures,* TONE over the unanimating *Sound* of their *Lesson;* and, then, (like a *Caterpillar,* that has *erected itself* at the Touch of a *Twig*) *shrink again, to their* CRAWL, *and their* QUIET; and enjoy their full *Ease,* till *next Rowsing.*[19]

This deterioration probably reflects the environment in which actors had to work. Pushed back from the audience behind the proscenium arch; no longer foregrounded but on the same plane as the scenery; competing increasingly with both spectacle and music for the audience's attention—an actor's performance could easily become just one more set piece, an isolated demonstration of elocution no more related to the rest of the play than was the juggling or rope dancing that surrounded it.

Such tendencies were exacerbated for both performers and audiences by the example and influence of oratorio and opera, more popular in the early eighteenth century than they have ever been in England since, so popular that for a while they seemed capable of running spoken theatre out of business. Contemporary operas were dominated by *da capo* arias, formally, musically, and theatrically isolated; they offered little opportunity for ensemble, and the singer usually just left the stage after his or her aria. If singers simply sang their own parts, why shouldn't actors simply speak their own speeches with as much "TONE," effortless *glissando*, and *éclat* as they could muster? Shakespeare's plays particularly encouraged such treatment because they were, by critical consent, so uneven, such a ragbag of sublimity and ineptitude. An actor like Barton Booth would naturally be tempted to do what he was applauded for, sliding "with a kind of elegant negligence, [over] the *improprieties*, in a part he acted, while on the contrary, he would dwell, with energy, upon the *beauties*, as if he exerted a latent spirit, which had been kept back for such an occasion."[20]

The example of arias and recitatives probably also encouraged an exaggerated attention to rhythm. One witness observed that Quin's "utterance is a continual sing song, like the chanting of vespers, and his action resembles that of heaving ballast into the hold of a ship." In 1716 a playgoer objected that "the manner of speaking in our theatres in tragedy is not natural . . . Persons would call it theatrical, meaning by that something stiff and affected."[21] This stiffness in performance corresponds to the verbal turgor of contemporary tragedies, the effect in both cases arising from an exaggerated and inhibiting sense of the dignity appropriate to such subjects.

Cibber had no dignity at all. He turned to playwriting in order to create plum parts for himself as an actor, and his adaptation of *Richard the Third* (1699–1700) notoriously subordinated everything else in the play to Richard—played by Cibber, of course. The great age of adaptation had lapsed, and though Shakespeare adaptations continued to be ventured, none succeeded and fewer and fewer candidates stepped into the ring. In this, as in other respects, the early eighteenth-century theatre seemed satisfied to echo yesterday's Shakespeare. The most popular adaptations were Davenant's *Hamlet* (1661?) and *Macbeth* (1664), Shadwell's operatized version of the Davenant/Dryden *Tempest* (1672), and Tate's *King Lear* (1681)— most of them as old in 1720 as the originals had been when they were adapted. The favorites were still the same handful of tragedies; the most successful comedies still *The Tempest* and *The Merry Wives of Windsor;* the only successful histories still *Henry the Fourth* (for Falstaff) and *Henry the Eighth* (for spectacle).

The theatre succeeded in saving its pocketbook but only at the price, for the moment, of its prestige. The loss of royal enthusiasm between the death of Charles II (1685) and the accession of George I (1714) forced the actors to find a new audience among the middle class; but their appeal to that more demotic clientele provoked the disdain and dismay of the cultural elites that had for a century fed the theatres with talent and acclamation. In the last four decades of the seventeenth century, England's most vigorous writers had gravitated naturally toward the theatre: Dryden, Etherege, Wycherley, Otway, Behn, Congreve, Vanbrugh. In 1700 Congreve prematurely retired; Vanbrugh soon turned his best energies to architecture. Of the major writers of the first four decades of the new century, Addison and Steele made their reputations as essayists, not playwrights; Swift and Pope in effect boycotted the theatre; Defoe actively campaigned for its suppression. In the dedication to his 1709 edition of Shakespeare, Rowe complained that "The Present age is indeed an unfortunate one for *Dramatick Poetry;* she has been persecuted by Fanaticism, forsaken by her Friends, and oppress'd even by Musick, her Sister and confederate Art, that was formerly employ'd in her Defence and Support."[22] A decade later Rowe, the century's only important tragic dramatist, was himself dead, and a contemporary critic lamented with justice that " 'tis a melancholy thing to consider, that there is not at present in *Great Britain* one promising Genius, or promising Actor, growing up for the Stage."[23] The center of English culture was shifting from performance to print—and Shakespeare went with it.

A COFFEEHOUSE

Shakespeare appears in the very first issue of *The Tatler* and in the last, and in between he pops up more often than any other literary figure.[24] Richard Steele's new, popular, and influential periodical touted itself on its "moderation," a virtue both political and stylistic, and its treatment of Shakespeare typified that strategy. Shakespeare enabled Steele to defend the English theatre without, on the one hand, endorsing the allegedly immoral and atheistic works of the Restoration rakes, and without on the other hand appearing wholly subservient to French or classical models. Shakespeare was English, modern, and (mostly) moral.

Within two weeks of the first issue Steele specifically contrasted Shakespeare's plays with "that Heap of Vice and Absurdity," Edward Ravenscroft's comedy *The London Cuckolds* (1682). He assured his readers that the "low Gratifications" of Restoration comedy could be banished from the stage only if "People of Condition" set about "encouraging the Presentation of the Noble Characters drawn by *Shakespear* and others, from whence it is impossible to return without strong Impressions of Honour and Humanity."[25] For the most part Restoration plays are named only to be damned. Betterton's Hamlet was an exemplary hero, as actor and character;

by contrast, the hero of Etherege's *The Man of Mode* (1676) "is a direct Knave in his Designs, and a Clown in his Language" and the play itself "a perfect Contradiction to good Manners, good Sense, and common Honesty."[26] Moreover, the age Shakespeare lived in, "as is evident by many Passages in his Plays," had a "much greater Sense of Virtue than the present."[27] Steele's readers, if they doubted such conclusions, had only to look around them to see "Ladder-dancers, Rope-dancers, Juglers, and Mountebanks . . . strut in the Place of *Shakespear's* Heroes."[28]

Shakespeare could be used to cudgel the past and to shame the present. By contrast Ben Jonson, whose comedies teem with eccentric immorality, and John Fletcher, predecessor and patron of the Restoration gallant, could hardly serve that reforming impulse; and neither *The Tatler* nor its successor, *The Spectator*, spared them much attention. What had been the "Triumvirate" of great English dramatists contracted, as triumvirates so often do, to a single dominant strongman: Shakespeare, who had created "Heroes," illustrations of human excellence whose behavior could be recognizably quoted in polite society.

Seventeenth-century critics had praised Shakespeare, dispraised him, alluded to him; but *The Tatler*, more than anything else, quoted him. *The Tatler's* whole moral method depended upon quoting of one sort or another. On the day of Betterton's last performance of *Hamlet* it singled out certain beauties in Hamlet's behavior (his celebrated soliloquy "To be or not to be," his expostulation with his mother, his noble ardor on seeing the ghost, his generous distress over Ophelia's death); on the day of Betterton's funeral it singled out the beauties in Betterton's performance of Othello ("The wonderful Agony . . . when he examined the Circumstance of the Handkerchief"; "The charming Passage . . . where he tells the Manner of winning the Affection of his Mistress").[29] In the same manner, repeatedly, *The Tatler* quoted the beauties of Shakespeare's poetry—suitably poetic and profound arias like Caesar's "*Cowards die many Times before their Deaths*,"[30] or Richard the Third's soliloquy "*Give me another Horse—Bind up my Wounds!*"[31] or Hamlet's first soliloquy, "*That it should come to this! But Two Months dead!*"[32] or Macbeth's final one, "*To Morrow, to Morrow, and to Morrow*,"[33] or Othello's "*Farewel the Tranquil Mind! Farewel Content, Farewel the plumed Troops, and the big Wars.*"[34] In each case—Hamlet's conduct, Betterton's acting, Shakespeare's poetry—the very best exempla could be isolated and recited for admiration, contemplation, and imitation.

The Tatler did not quote at random. It particularly admired moments of middle-class simplicity:

> We see in Tragical Representations, it is not the Pomp of Language, or Magnificence of Dress . . . that touches sensible Spirits, but something of a plain and simple Nature which breaks in upon our Souls, by that Sympathy which is given us for our mutual Good-will and Service.

To illustrate this proposition Steele quotes two exemplary moments from Shakespeare: from *Julius Caesar,* Brutus' stoic revelation that *"Porcia is dead,"* and from *Macbeth,* MacDuff's anguished cry, *"What, both my Children! Both, both my Children gone—."*[35] Both heroes, coincidentally, suffer these familial griefs because of their manly resistance to absolutist political tyranny. Contemporary playwrights by contrast "depend mightily upon the Retinue of [a] Hero to make him magnificent." They think it is enough to "make Guards, and Ushers, and Courtiers, and Commons, and Nobles, march before" him. But that is a false method, *The Tatler* tells us; "The Man is to be express'd by his Sentiments and Affections, and not by his Fortune or Equipage . . . *Shakespear* [should be] your Pattern. In the Tragedy of *Caesar,* he introduces his Hero in his Night-Gown . . . without endeavoring to prepossess his Audience with empty Show and Pomp."[36]

With such democratic critical sentiments we can all be expected even now to agree. Unfortunately, although Shakespeare does bring Julius Caesar onstage in his nightgown, that incident does not occur until Act Two. In Act One he parades onstage at the head of a suitably magnificent entourage, including Mark Antony, Calpurnia, Portia, Decius, Cicero, Brutus, Cassius, Casca, Murellus, Flavius, a throng of citizens, and a Soothsayer, their entrance apparently accompanied by fanfares and acclamations. Such attendant numerical grandeur also accompanies Caesar's final entrance, in Act Three. Shakespeare thus frames the domestic gown scene between two public toga scenes; he permits us a glimpse of Caesar in deshabille only after he has already "prepossess[ed] his Audience with empty Show and Pomp." As a description of Shakespeare's play *The Tatler*'s encomium will not serve. But as a rebuke to the showy noisy emptiness of the eighteenth-century stage, as an affirmation of the literary primacy of "plain and simple" bourgeois humanity, it did very nicely indeed.

The Tatler was not exclusively or even primarily a literary magazine; its incidental criticism of Shakespeare and other writers served a larger social and political project. Richard Steele, its editor and chief contributor, was an outspoken supporter of the Whig political party, a party as English, modern, and moral as Shakespeare. Like Joseph Addison, his collaborator on *The Tatler* and its successor *The Spectator,* like their publisher Jacob Tonson, he was a member of the Kit-Cat Club, which included many leaders of the Whigs between 1688 and 1714. Horace Walpole was thinking of their political, not their literary, achievement when he described the club's members as "in reality the patriots that saved Britain."[37] For the Whigs were the architects and guardians of the Glorious Revolution of 1688, which deposed England's Catholic King James II and drove him into exile in France. The revolution turned Catholic France from an ally into an enemy, and it would remain England's geopolitical rival until the beginning of the twentieth century. For most of the eighteenth century that enmity pitted French political and religious absolutism against English political and religious compromise.

The Whigs were the ideologues of compromise. They compromised between regicide and submission by simply driving out an unwanted king and pretending he had abdicated. They compromised between the royalists and the parliamentarians by uniting a limited monarchy with a limited Parliament. They compromised between radical Puritanism and High Anglicanism by preserving the institutional national church but irretrievably weakening it when they formally accepted religious dissent. In the defense of monarchy they disposed of a monarch; in the defense of nationalism they put foreigners on the English throne; in the defense of state Protestantism they legalized religious freedom. Compromise was the instrument of consensus, and consensus was the foundation of stable power.

The Whigs' pragmatic moderation can be seen clearly enough in *The Tatler's* attitude toward the theatre, which lay somewhere between the crabbed Puritanism of Jeremy Collier and the aristocratic libertinism of Charles II. The theatre should not be condemned wholesale or endorsed wholesale but reformed (retail, as it were) to conform with the standards of mercantile morality and taste: not too hot, not too cold, but just right. (In practice, this meant tepid—as Steele's and Addison's own plays demonstrate.) As for Shakespeare, well, on the one hand he has his beauties, on the other hand he has his faults. This formula recurs in Addison, in the preface to Rowe's edition of Shakespeare's plays, in the preface to Pope's edition, in almost every lesser critic; it survives into the second half of the eighteenth century to achieve its apotheosis in the critical and syntactical balances of Dr. Johnson. Though not all these people were Whigs, they were all influenced by the pervasive pursuit of consensus that the Glorious Revolution had set in motion. Such pro-ing and con-ing can be seen in some earlier critics, but the seesaw became standard in the decades after 1688.

Shakespeare could not be divorced from the problem of literary theory, and the problem of literary theory could not be divorced from the problem of France. France, now the enemy militarily and ideologically, was also the source of the most sophisticated cultural theorizing of the age and of the most potent alternatives to native dramatic practice. Steele compares critics who insist upon (French) "Mechanical Rules" to "the Subjects of an Arbitrary Prince"; at the opposite extreme are critics "who despise Art and Method," who represent "a State of barbarous Anarchy"; right in the middle, naturally, is the (Whig) "free Critick, like a free *Briton*," who "is governed by the Laws which he himself votes for; whose Liberty is checked by the Restraints of Truth, and the Monarchy of right Reason."[38]

The English struggle against French power was personified by "the Hero of the Age,"[39] John Churchill, Duke of Marlborough. *The Tatler* compared him to Shakespeare's "*Harry* the Fifth," as each embarked for war with France ("*Then should the Warlike* Harry, *like himself,* / *Assume the Port of* Mars"), and to Shakespeare's Julius Caesar ("*with a Monarch's Voice,* / *Cry* Havock; *and let slip the Dogs of War*").[40] Marlborough himself, as if to ratify the association, claimed that his entire knowledge of English history was acquired from Shakespeare's plays.[41] Against the absolutist art of Corneille and Racine the English could defend themselves artistically only with Shakespeare, at least until some better weapon could be found.

Typically, Augustan critics compromised. Addison may be taken, in this as in other respects, as exemplary (not least because at times he carried Whig compromise to the point of assimilating Tory values). Like the French critics, he condemns tragicomedy—but thinks that the English use of double plots might be allowed if "an Under-Plot" was skilfully chosen.⁴² He ridicules the English theatre's enthusiasm for Thunder, Lightning, Alarm Bells, and Ghosts "to fill the Minds of an Audience with Terrour"—but concedes that there may be "a proper Season for these several Terrours."⁴³ He praises Shakespeare for having "incomparably excelled all others" in his dramatization of "several Species of Spirits"—a gift that uniquely qualified him to exploit "this weak superstitious Part of his Reader's Imagination."⁴⁴ On the one hand . . . on the other hand: evenhanded.

The earliest description of Addison's critical method is still the best: he would characteristically "Damn with faint praise . . . Just hint a fault, and hesitate dislike; Alike reserv'd to blame, or to commend."⁴⁵ Addison, as Pope realized, was a politician of literature. *The Tatler* and *The Spectator* were party papers, never more partial than when they insisted upon their impartiality.

But the format of Steele's and Addison's criticism of Shakespeare and English drama was as influential as its substance. The frequency and ephemerality of its publication helped to create a sense of spontaneity; its style and the carefully constructed persona of its putative editor, "Mr. Bickerstaff," contributed to the illusion of a personal voice addressing a particular reader. The periodical claimed to derive most of its material from London's innumerable coffeehouses, which were in turn its most important subscribers and distributors; *The Tatler* quite literally became part of the conversation of London's literate classes. It created an "audience" for itself, like the audiences at the theatre, sustaining the illusion of a shared oral and communal culture even as it effected the transition to the fragmented culture of print.⁴⁶

The Tatler became known as "The *Censor* of *Great Britain*."⁴⁷ Steele's organ of conformity was both judge and model of polite behavior, and it treated literature as a subdivision of polite behavior. Eccentricity was to be avoided; specialization was a form of eccentricity; a gentleman was an amateur, capable of coffeehouse conversation on any topic but never pedantically fixated upon one. Master of all trades, servant of none. And the literary expression of such social ideals was the periodical essay: not defensive, like a Restoration prologue or preface, the author's own critical views standing guard at the entrance to his work; not ill-tempered and long-

winded, like the erudite monographs on dramatic theory by
Thomas Rymer and Jeremy Collier; but likable, tasteful, digestible.
The literary equivalent of a sandwich: a compromise between a full
meal and an empty stomach.

The Tatler was not the first English periodical, but it created a
particularly influential and profitable formula for mixed literary
journalism. It immediately spawned imitators and rivals; it was
reprinted in collected editions, by Tonson among others; it was
succeeded by comparable journals, *The Spectator* being only the
most famous and successful—and it too was published by Tonson,
among others.

The influence of these journals may be measured in part by the
story of Addison's tragedy *Cato* and Steele's comedy *The Conscious
Lovers,* the first beneficiaries of journalistic hype: both were so
successfully promoted in advance by the authors' own ("disinterested") periodicals that they were the talk of the town even before
they opened at Drury Lane. In the early seventeenth century a
play's success onstage determined whether it would ever reach print
and how often it would be reprinted; by the early eighteenth century a play's advance reputation in print could determine its success
onstage.

The fourth "edition" of Addison's *Cato,* published by Tonson, was
advertised only twenty-five days after the play's first performance;
Shakespeare's *Julius Cæsar,* by contrast, did not reach readers until
twenty-four years after it reached its first audiences. The difference
reflects a change in the relationship between theatres and publishers in the intervening century. During the glory days of the
English Renaissance theatre, the number of first editions of
plays rose unevenly from only fourteen in the 1580s to 145 in
the 1630s,[48] not because so many more plays were written but
because an increasing proportion of them were printed. After the
Restoration the average interval between performance and publication gradually shrank.[49] By the eighteenth century, booksellers had begun acquiring rights in plays even before they were
performed—the better to exploit the large but usually temporary
readerly interest that the theatre could generate.[50] Successful
plays could be as lucrative for publishers as for theatres. And, as
Addison and Steele demonstrated, success was in large part a matter of marketing.

A MARKETPLACE

Jacob Tonson published plays for most of his career. His imprint first appeared in 1678, when he was twenty-three, and in that year his ventures already included plays by popular dramatists. The next year he copublished Dryden's *Troilus and Cressida* and thereafter remained Dryden's publisher for the rest of the century; in 1701, the year after Dryden's death, Tonson joined two other publishers to bring out a two-volume folio edition of Dryden's collected *Comedies, Tragedies, and Operas*. Tonson made a specialty of such prestigious literary collections. Rowe's edition of Shakespeare, published twice in 1709 and again in 1714, is the most famous today but only because, from our perspective, Shakespeare has eclipsed most of the other authors Tonson published; from Tonson's perspective Shakespeare was neither financially nor artistically exceptional. As early as 1681 Tonson had bought a share of *The Works of Mr. Abraham Cowley,* later acquiring sole rights. In 1683 he acquired half the rights to *Paradise Lost;* the new edition did not appear until 1688, but the delay proved profitable, for in the year of the Glorious Revolution Milton's parliamentary sympathies had become fashionable again, and within three years Tonson and his partner brought out another edition. In 1695 Tonson published, on his own, *The Poetical Works of Mr. John Milton.* Further editions followed, and Tonson by his own account made more money off Milton than any other author.[51] In 1693 he published a collected edition of translations of Juvenal and Persius, edited by Dryden, succeeded in 1697 by Dryden's rendering of *The Works of Virgil,* deservedly the most famous translation of the entire seventeenth century. In 1709 he brought out collections by Mathew Prior, Sir John Denham, and Sir John Suckling, as well as Shakespeare. The following decade produced comparable collections of Congreve, Beaumont and Fletcher, Waller, Otway, Spenser, and Ovid, along with further editions of authors already in the Tonson repertoire.

Tonson's list and its success depended upon the laws of copyright prevailing in his (as in Shakespeare's) lifetime. Copyright was held not by authors but by members of the Stationers' Guild, a trade cartel of printers and booksellers, who held those rights in perpetuity and could buy or sell them like any piece of real estate. Thus, a young bookseller like Tonson could purchase a piece of the publication rights to Cowley's poems, or *Paradise Lost,* after the death of both authors; later, with more investment capital at hand, Tonson could buy out his partners, acquiring sole rights, and thereafter reap all the profits of further editions and reprints. Ninety-three years after Shakespeare's death Tonson had a monopoly on publication of his plays; the House of Tonson kept its stock in Shakespeare until 1772, when the grandson of Jacob Tonson's nephew died and the family copyrights were auctioned. The Tonsons were sole or part publishers of all the great Shakespeare editions of the first two-thirds of the eighteenth century: Rowe's (1709), Pope's (1725), Theobald's (1733), Warburton's (1747), Johnson's (1765), and Capell's (1768). The Tonsons decided who would edit Shakespeare, in the period that cast the mold of all future editions of his work.

The Tonsons did not base those decisions on a simple judgment about who was best qualified to edit Shakespeare; they wanted editors who were already famous. Tonson chose Nicholas Rowe to edit his first edition of Shakespeare because Rowe was the best tragic dramatist of his generation. Shakespeare was appreciated primarily for his tragedies; presumably for that reason Tonson chose Rowe instead of, say, the admired comic dramatist William Congreve, another of Tonson's clients, who edited for him *The Dramatick Works of John Dryden.* Jacob Tonson, Jr., later chose Alexander Pope to prepare an edition to replace Rowe's, because Pope had by then earned himself an enviable and envied reputation as a poet and translator. Jacob, Jr., then chose Lewis Theobald to replace Pope, primarily because Theobald had aroused great critical and popular interest by his attacks on Pope. Theobald in turn was replaced by the Reverend William Warburton, who had first come to widespread notice as Pope's champion and confidant. In 1745 a little-known journalist and poet named Samuel Johnson imprudently issued proposals for a new edition of Shakespeare, to be published by a rival bookseller—an initiative that the Tonsons quickly squelched. But ten years later Johnson's historic *Dictionary of the English Language* and his periodical *The Rambler* had made him famous, and his new proposal for a Shakespeare edition received the Tonson imprimatur.

These editors were chosen for the market value of their reputations, which made their names as important to the reading public as Shakespeare's. The value of name recognition can be seen in the consistent policy of suppressing altogether the names of various

collaborators. For the 1714 reprint of Rowe's edition Tonson paid
John Hughes twenty-eight pounds seven shillings; in order to justify
such a sum Hughes' editorial work must have been substantial, but
only Rowe's name appeared in the printed volumes. Several friends
and scholars, including John Gay, helped Pope with his edition and
were paid for their contribution, but the edition as advertised was
Pope's alone.[52] Such tactics can be seen even more clearly in Warburton's edition, which was publicized as though it had been jointly
edited "*By Mr.* POPE *and Mr.* WARBURTON." Samuel Johnson's
1765 edition was revised by George Steevens in 1773 and 1778,
under the pretense that the famous Johnson had fully collaborated
with him on the revisions. Throughout the eighteenth century
other men's reputations ushered Shakespeare before the reading
public.

By initiating the practice of associating a particular reprint with a
well-known contemporary writer, Tonson simply applied to Shakespeare a marketing strategy employed and proven in earlier publications. In the same way, he had milked Dryden's reputation as
contributor and editor to encourage the visibility and sales of his
Miscellanies of poetry and his editions of Plutarch, Juvenal and
Persius. But in Shakespeare's case, because of the longevity of the
Tonsons' influence this strategy produced a string of editions inextricably associated with the dramatis personae of eighteenth-
century English literature. Nothing comparable can be found in the
history of editions of other writers, English or foreign. The practice
of theatrical adaptation, initiated during the Restoration, coupled
with Tonson's technique for appropriating reputations, meant that
for over a century the finest practitioners of the English language,
from Dryden to Pope to Johnson, contributed to the public
remodeling and transmission of Shakespeare's plays; while he in
turn contributed inevitably to the stylistic development of each,
immersed as they were for years in working over the minutiae of his
texts, adapting or editing them. By the end of the eighteenth
century Shakespeare had been, by such means, insinuated into the
network of English literature; he could not be extracted without
uprooting a century and a half of the national canon.

Pope succeeded Rowe, Theobald succeeded Pope, editor after
editor—a progress from one perspective tidied and linear but, from
another angle, jerking angrily forward, acrid with the smoke of
burning reputations as one short-lived editorial dynasty toppled

another, each defining itself in contemptuous opposition to its immediate predecessor. The invisibility of seventeenth-century editors had made them invulnerable to personal attack; no name to claim (by the publisher) meant no name to blame (by a rival). By contrast, the very prominence of the eighteenth-century editors, so useful to a publisher, made them obvious targets for hostile criticism.

Such attacks began immediately. Rowe's 1709 edition of the plays was followed in 1710 by an edition of the poems, which passed itself off as volume seven of Rowe's edition; but Charles Gildon devoted much of his introduction to berating Rowe. Pope did not fault his predecessor by name, but his entire preface and editorial practice declared the inadequacy of all previous editions—including, of course, Rowe's, the one most familiar to Pope's own readers. But Pope's implicit criticism of his predecessor was gentlemanly compared to the behavior of every subsequent editor. Pope's text appeared in 1725; the next year Theobald savaged it at length in *Shakespeare Restored: or, a Specimen of the Many Errors, as Well Committed, as Unamended by Mr. Pope in His Late Edition of This Poet*, which laces its argument with slurs on Pope's Catholicism, sarcasms upon his probity, and doubts about his honesty. Warburton says that his two predecessors, those "stupid editors" Theobald and Hanmer,

> left their Author in ten times a worse Condition than they found him ... The One was recommended to me as a poor Man; the Other as a poor Critic ... As to Mr. *Theobald,* who wanted Money, I allowed him to print what I gave him for his own Advantage ... What he read he could transcribe; but, as what he thought, if ever he did think, he could but ill express ... [*Hanmer,*] the *Oxford Editor* ... was absolutely ignorant of the Art of Criticism, as well as the Poetry of that Time, and the Language of his Author.53

In 1748, the year after Warburton's own edition was published, it was comprehensively debunked in a volume that professed to *"being a Supplement to Mr Warburton's Edition of Shakespeare . . . And Proper to be bound up with it."*54 The process repeats itself with every new edition.

The editorial venom of the eighteenth century did not merely seep through the cracks in a few flawed personalities; it poured unstaunchably out of the situation in which editors found themselves. Mere reprintings, after all, needed no defense; they satisfied a continuing public demand. By 1685 the collected edition of 1664 was merely out of print, not out of date. But new editions, with conspicuously proclaimed new editors, could be justified only if the new editor had something to do, something which could and should have been done before. You do not need Rowe, or Pope, or Johnson, unless each of them has something novel to promise. Tonson's marketing strategy depended on offering customers Shakespeare-with-Rowe or Shakespeare-with-Pope, a ploy that in turn forced editors to demonstrate and justify their advertised share in the collaboration. They could do so only by faulting the previous collaborator, with as much delicacy or crudity as they could muster. The system profited the publisher—and Shakespeare—at the expense of a succession of disposable editors.

Tonson's marketing techniques exploited, intuitively, the public's new appetite for competition. The constitutional settlement of 1689 had required parliamentary elections every three years, and the next quarter century gave birth to the two-party political system, with Whigs pitted against Tories in elections as boisterous as they were frequent. In 1695 the Licensing Act was allowed to lapse, thus creating by default freedom of the press and a consequent boom in periodicals, often overtly political. The pamphlet war initiated by Jeremy Collier's 1698 attack on the stage can be seen in one sense as part of the running political debate of those years of frequent elections, with the morality of the theatres and of public life at issue. More generally, the controversy demonstrates the extent to which the rise of journalism transformed the character of literary criticism: it became adversarial—and so it remains. Thomas Rymer's *A Short View of Tragedy* (1693) provoked responses by Dennis, Dryden, and Gildon; Collier (1698) provoked responses by Dennis, Dryden, Drake, Congreve, Vanbrugh, and others; Steele's defenses of the theatre in *The Tatler* (1709–10) provoked Defoe; Addison's defense of a few conventions of native drama against the strictures of Continental neoclassicists (1711–12) provoked Dennis—and so on and on, critique spawning countercritique. Aesthetic parties fought for public support, just like political ones, and in both marketplaces few rules regulated the conduct of competition. The history of the theatres in this period clearly belongs to the same economic and social climate. When the old United Company under Betterton broke up in 1695, the internecine rivalry between the two resulting companies was personal, bitter, and nasty, in a way that the gentlemanly competition between Davenant's and Killigrew's companies in the 1660s had never been.

But although Tonson's tactics epitomize a new economic ecosystem, his success depended in part upon the anachronistic survival of restrictive practices. In the seventeenth century copyrights were essentially monopolies, controlled by a self-regulating trade cartel. These monopolies could be bought, sold, or inherited; the most lucrative copyrights gave enormous power to the publishers who owned them.[55] The copyright act passed by Parliament in 1709 sought to liberalize competition in the publishing trade by abolishing the "Mammon-Monopoly" of perpetual copyright. In that spirit the 1709 statute restricted new copyrights to fourteen years' duration, renewable for another fourteen if the author were still alive. But the publishing lobby, in which Tonson played a prominent part, fought for and got a fateful compromise: copyrights in hand were extended for another twenty-one years, thus securing all Tonson's preexisting monopolies until 1730. The 1709 legislation (which Addison, a member of Parliament, supported)[56] would lead to a victory for liberalization in the long run, but in the short run it was a setback, and in that short run the Tonsons reshaped the Shakespeare landscape.

SHAKESPEARS HEAD

Jacob Tonson's 1709 edition of Shakespeare was to previous editions what an operatic Restoration adaptation was to the original performances: a spectacular new rendition, seasoned to contemporary taste. It had an overture: Rowe's expansive preface, including the first substantial biography of Shakespeare ever published. It had pictorial "sets": a frontispiece engraving for every play, making it the earliest illustrated edition of Shakespeare's works. The first such frontispiece was an engraving of the first scene of *The Tempest*, clearly based upon the 1674 operatic version. Just as, in performance, that first set for *The Tempest* had been adorned with symbolic compliments to the Stuart dynasty, so Tonson's edition was adorned with a preliminary dedication to Charles Seymour, sixth Duke of Somerset, a prominent member of the Kit-Cat Club and the Whig party. And just as, in performance, musical intervals or entr'actes divided a play into five segments, so Tonson segmented the works, replacing the huge, heavy, cumbersome single-volume folios of the seventeenth century with a more manageable set of six octavo volumes. There was even, unintentionally, a kind of afterpiece, when Edmund Curll published *Volume the Seventh,* Shakespeare's poems, "with Critical Remarks on his Plays, [and] an Essay on the Art, Rise and Progress of the Stage in Greece, Rome and England." Advertised in *The Tatler* soon after Tonson's edition was published, the volume was purposely indistinguishable in format and binding from Tonson's six volumes.

Although new to Shakespeare, such embellishments were not new to Tonson. In both the quality of their engravings and the amplitude of their commentary, Tonson's earlier editions of Milton overwhelm his Shakespeare. Rowe offered almost no explanatory notes on the plays; the engravings were a hodgepodge in conception, rising occasionally to mediocrity. Judged purely as material objects, as products of the art of bookmaking, Tonson's Shakespeare volumes do not, in page design or binding or typography, achieve the rococo elegance of his editions of Milton, Virgil, Ovid, or Racine.

Rowe's preface, his most lasting contribution to Shakespeare scholarship, also had Tonson antecedents. A biography of Abraham Cowley was reprinted in all Tonson's editions of that poet's works, and for the 1683 translation of *Plutarchs Lives* Tonson commissioned Dryden's substantial "Life of Plutarch." Both prefaces, like Rowe's, mixed biography with criticism and catered to the Restoration's burgeoning new popular and intellectual interest in the history of private lives.

Tonson's sense of the market demanded that the 1709 edition include "Some Account of the Life, &c. of Mr. *William Shakespear*"; and earlier prefatory biographies of literary figures provided Rowe with models, which shaped both his sense of what such a biography should include and how it should be written. Though writing almost a century after the death of Shakespeare, Rowe collected for the first time much surviving oral and documentary evidence; he omitted some stories that he must have heard but did not want to perpetuate (like Shakespeare's alleged adultery with Davenant's mother), and shaped the remaining scattered scraps into a proper biography that would be reprinted in every subsequent edition of Shakespeare's works for a century.

Rowe replaced the old engraving of Shakespeare, which had prefaced every seventeenth-century edition of the collected plays, with two new engravings: a frontispiece based upon the so-called Chandos portrait, followed in the preface by an illustration of the burial monument at Stratford. The disproportioned porcine staidness of the 1623 engraving yielded in these images to two attractive alternatives. In the monumentality of the Stratford image, any impression of the poet's own countenance is subordinated to the architectural frame, both classical and iconic—the English poet on his pedestal, so to speak, his social status evident in the prominent coat of arms. Alternatively, the Chandos portrait was, and still is, the most attractive and accomplished likeness with any claim to authenticity. Moreover, the Puritan contrasts of its black doublet and white collar offered the middle-class eighteenth-century viewer that "something of a plain and simple Nature" which Steele so admired in passages of *Julius Cæsar* and *Macbeth;* the painting's dominant black suited a great tragic dramatist; the alert attentiveness of the face promised a proper moral seriousness. (And the understated gold earring insinuated just enough exoticism—even almost decadence—to keep the portrait from subsiding into predictability.) Not surprisingly, the Chandos portrait proved the more popular, being regularly copied and engraved throughout the century. One derivative of the Chandos portrait became in 1710 the Tonson trademark, probably used as the sign of "Shakespears Head," Tonson's new bookshop on the Strand. The frontispiece to Rowe's edition places the Chandos image in the center of an ornate allegory, appropriated directly from the 1660 Rouen edition of Corneille:[57] Shakespeare adorned with French credentials.

The two images first given mass circulation by Tonson dominated eighteenth-century visions of the poet's face, and just as surely Rowe's preface dominated formulations of his life. The tidbits of biography that he managed (and chose) to snatch from the jaws of oblivion satisfied very well the appetites of contemporary social and literary criticism. Indeed, Rowe's first paragraph justifies his effort to record the details of Shakespeare's life on critical grounds, claiming that "the knowledge of an Author may sometimes conduce to the better understanding his Book." His treatment of biography in the preface conforms to this declared aesthetic intention. Rowe's cursory account of Shakespeare's birth and parentage, for instance, serves only as a prelude to the announcement that "His Father . . .

had so large a Family . . . that tho' [*William*] was his eldest Son, he could give him no better Education than his own Employment,"[58] a circumstance that prevented Shakespeare from developing a "Proficiency" in Latin. This brief biographical explanation leads naturally—indeed, inevitably for an eighteenth-century writer—into an extended discussion of the consequences for Shakespeare's art of his poor education.

After that critical excursus, Rowe returns to biographical narrative, disposing of Shakespeare's marriage in two sentences, before proceeding to account for his transformation from Stratford tradesman to London playwright:

> He had, by a Misfortune common enough to young Fellows, fallen into ill Company; and amongst them, some that made a frequent practice of Deer-stealing, engag'd him with them more than once in robbing a Park that belong'd to Sir *Thomas Lucy* of *Cherlecot,* near *Stratford.* For this he was prosecuted by that Gentleman, as he thought, somewhat too severely; and in order to revenge that ill Usage, he made a Ballad upon him. And tho' this, probably the first Essay of his Poetry, be lost, yet it is said to have been so very bitter, that it redoubled the Prosecution against him to that degree, that he was oblig'd to leave his Business and Family in *Warwickshire,* for some time, and shelter himself in *London.*[59]

This story may not be true; some of its details are impossible, and modern scholars tend to doubt the whole thing. But whether essentially true or false, it admirably recommended Shakespeare to an eighteenth-century sensibility and was accordingly repeated and embroidered throughout the century. It gives Shakespeare a passable excuse for his very unmiddle-class conduct in abandoning his family. It also reveals him as a practitioner, like any self-respecting poet of the late seventeenth or early eighteenth century, of personal satire in verse—a role further substantiated in Rowe's account of Shakespeare's supposed mock epitaph on a Stratford neighbor, John Combe. It offers a moral message too: the dangers of "ill Company," to which the young seem so prone. Finally, it molds the entire episode into an instance of that most consoling of all narrative tropes, the fortunate fall; what seems the worst moment turns out, in retrospect, to have been the best. Shakespeare's change of location and vocation was caused by an incident that "tho' it seem'd at first to be a Blemish upon his good Manners, and a Misfortune to him, yet it afterwards happily prov'd the occasion of exerting one of the greatest *Genius*'s that ever was known in Dramatick Poetry."[60] Oh lucky sin, indeed!

Elsewhere, the contemporary pressures that shape Rowe's narrative are even more transparent. "Queen *Elizabeth* had several of [*Shakespear*'s] Plays Acted before her, and without doubt gave him many gracious Marks of her Favour." Rowe has no evidence for such marks of favor, as his assertive "without doubt" confesses; but he wishes to contrast Shakespeare, whose art was fostered by royal recognition, with dramatists of Rowe's own generation, suffocating under the neglect or outright hostility of the monarchy. Queen Elizabeth had even "commanded [*Shakespear*] to . . . shew [*Falstaff*] in Love," thus prompting composition of *The Merry Wives of Windsor,* Shakespeare's most popular comedy; Shakespeare's Queen Elizabeth, unlike Rowe's Queen Anne, had actually commissioned plays, as it were. The Elizabethan aristocracy, too, had seen and supported Shakespeare's genius: "He had the Honour to meet with many great and uncommon Marks of Favour and Friendship from the Earl of *Southampton*," who "at one time, gave him a thousand Pounds." The story can hardly be true, but Rowe mentions it to illustrate "A Bounty very great, and very rare at any time, and almost equal to that profuse Generosity the present Age has shewn to *French* Dancers and *Italian* Eunuchs." The contrast between theatrical conditions in Shakespeare's time and in Rowe's, implied throughout the paragraph, surfaces, at last explicit, in that closing phrase and rises in the next paragraph, where Rowe assures us that "every one who had a true Taste of Merit, and could distinguish Men, had generally a just Value and Esteem for" Shakespeare, even in his own lifetime.[61] (Those were the good old days! People knew a genius when they saw one! But now . . .)

As evidence he cites several stanzas of a poem by Edmund Spenser on the subject of "*Our pleasant* Willy." Rowe immediately confesses that objections have been raised to the claim that Shakespeare was the Willy in question; after all, Spenser does say "*Our pleasant* Willy, *ah! is dead of late*," and Spenser died in 1599, long before Shakespeare. But Rowe can explain the discrepancy:

> Mr. *Spencer* does not mean that [*Shakespear*] was then really Dead, but only that he had with-drawn himself from the Publick, or at least with-held his Hand from Writing, out of a disgust he had

taken at the then ill taste of the Town, and the mean Condition of
the Stage.[62]

This Shakespeare sounds surprisingly like Rowe's friend and Kit-
Cat colleague William Congreve, who had "with-drawn himself
from the Publick" in 1700 after *The Way of the World* failed to receive
as much acclaim as he felt it deserved.

For Rowe biography contributes to an argument between the past
and the present; but it can also help arbitrate between rival claimants from the past. Rowe never explicitly addresses the widespread
Restoration conviction that Beaumont and Fletcher excelled Shakespeare in their characterization of "gentlemen" and of polite "conversation"; instead, he emphasizes that Shakespeare's family were
"Gentlemen" and that Shakespeare himself was "a most agreeable
Companion" who "made himself acquainted with the best Conversations of those Times."[63] Jonson, by contrast, had to be rebutted
frontally; Beaumont and Fletcher might be or might recently have
been rival contenders for Shakespeare's laurels, but Jonson, in addition to his formidable reputation as a dramatist, was also the most
familiar source of information about Shakespeare and, accordingly,
could not be ignored.

> [*Shakespear's*] Acquaintance with *Ben Johnson* began with a
> Remarkable piece of Humanity and good Nature; Mr. *Johnson*,
> who was at that Time altogether unknown to the World, had
> offer'd one of his Plays to the Players, in order to have it Acted;
> and the Persons into whose Hands it was put, after having turn'd
> it carelessly and superciliously over, were just upon returning it to
> him with an ill-natur'd Answer, that it would be of no service to
> their Company, when *Shakespear* luckily cast his Eye upon it, and
> found something so well in it as to engage him first to read it
> through, and afterwards to recommend Mr. *Johnson* and his Writ-
> ings to the Publick. After this they were profess'd Friends; tho' I
> don't know whether the other ever made him an equal return of
> Gentleness and Sincerity. *Ben* was naturally Proud and Insolent,
> and . . . could not but look with an evil Eye upon any one that
> seem'd to stand in Competition with him.[64]

This anecdote may well be true in its essentials; but for Rowe it also
serves the very useful purpose of discrediting Jonson as a critic of
Shakespeare. For the argument between critical theorists over the

respective merits of Art as opposed to Nature, technique against intuition, had resolved itself during the Restoration period into a battle between Ben Jonson (in the corner of Art) and William Shakespeare (in the corner of Nature), and Rowe's defense of Shakespeare throughout the preface repeatedly entails a corresponding spoken or unspoken denigration of Jonson.

For much of his information about Shakespeare's life Rowe was indebted to Thomas Betterton, whose "Veneration for the Memory of *Shakespear* . . . engag'd him to make a Journey into *Warwickshire*, on purpose to gather up what Remains he could of a Name for which he had so great a Value."[65] Rowe also owed most of the editorial innovations in his text to the theatre. He divided all the plays into five acts, supplying divisions in plays that had previously lacked them, thereby bringing the texts into conformity with stage practice. Rowe's decisions about where to place such divisions sometimes were even influenced by Restoration adaptations. Their thorough rewriting of the texts often made structural correspondence impossible, but Rowe did, for instance, begin Act Four of *Timon of Athens* at exactly the point that Shadwell had chosen (by no means inevitably),[66] and the act divisions that he added to *Hamlet* all corresponded with Restoration theatrical practice. In addition, Rowe divided each act into scenes (something much more rarely done in earlier editions), and in some plays he provided scenes with a "location." Thus, *Measure for Measure* begins with the announcement "*SCENE a Palace*," and other segments of the action are located in "*The Street*," "*A Nunnery*," "*A Prison*," and "*The Fields without the Town*." These editorial innovations undoubtedly reflect the scenic conventions introduced by Davenant after the Restoration. Both the generic quality of Rowe's locations, and the complete absence of specific locales for some scenes, mimic stage practice. Rowe's headnotes, like the theatre's painted flats, provided an occasional visual cue to the whereabouts of the action.

Rowe's own practical experience in the theatre alerted him to the importance of stage directions, particularly for exits and entrances, which are often deficient or misleading in earlier editions. Likewise, he recognized the convenience, long appreciated by prompters, of scripts that regularly identify characters by a single label in place of the sometimes bewildering variety of nomenclature in seventeenth-century texts. As a natural corollary to such standardizing of names he adopted another practice usual in editions of contemporary plays, prefacing each text with a helpful list of dramatis personae. The engraved frontispieces often reflected contemporary stage practice, however crudely. In his emendations of the dialogue itself Rowe sometimes behaved more like the adapters of the past than the editors of the future, systematically improving Shakespeare's grammar and, on one occasion, editing away an embarrassing anachronism. In *Troilus and Cressida* Hector of Troy refers to Aristotle, who was not born until centuries after Hector died; Dryden's adaptation omitted the offending sentence, and Rowe's edition charitably replaced the ineptly specific "*Aristotle*" with the innocuous generality "graver Sages."[67]

A PRIVATE GROTTO

Rowe's Whig edition looked backward to the stage; Pope's Tory edition looked forward to the book. Like Rowe, Pope knew Betterton, who had in fact been a hero of Pope's adolescence.[68] Like Rowe's preface, Pope's actually drew on Betterton as a source of information:

> It was, and is, a general opinion that Ben Jonson and Shakespear lived in enmity against one another. Betterton has assured me often that there was nothing to it.[69]

Pope accordingly devoted a vigorous paragraph to challenging the traditional opposition between Jonson and Shakespeare, a critical habit that had exaggerated their personal and artistic differences. But unlike Rowe's preface, Pope's does not mention Betterton at all; the passage quoted above comes not from the edition of Shakespeare but from Pope's conversation. Rowe, the playwright, advertised his association with and admiration for the actor; Pope, the poet, repressed it.

Pope repressed other things too. Rowe's preface had twice referred disparagingly to the critic Thomas Rymer, author of the most influential of all attacks upon Shakespeare's artistry. Pope reprinted Rowe's preface in his own edition but silently excised the two passages, with the result that they disappeared from subsequent reprintings of Rowe's preface throughout the eighteenth century.

The same fate befell Rowe's disparaging comments about Jonson.[70] Pope also got rid of the frontispiece engravings to each play, with their clumsy, often stagey, visualizing of the text. He threw out, for the first time, the seven plays added to the complete works in 1664. From the remaining thirty-six he omitted altogether, or suppressed to the bottom of the page, some 1,560 lines that seemed to him unauthoritative; "low" passages were relegated "below" the text. In the dialogue that remained, Pope, more enthusiastically than Rowe, removed bad grammar, bad logic, bad meter, and bad manners whenever he could.

More generally, Pope repressed the theatricality of the plays in favor of their readerliness. As material objects, as private possessions, Pope's volumes were to the eye and hand more elegant than Rowe's and, by virtue of their typography, easier to read. A glossary, provided for the first time and compiled from the best available authorities, made the text easier to comprehend. Pope helped readers to find Shakespeare's finest poetry by advertising and visually isolating "the most shining passages," as he called them, each signposted by prominent double commas in the left margin; and when an entire scene deserved such acclamation he heralded its "beauty" with a star. Rowe had called or re-called attention to a scattering of such gems in his preface, as had Addison and Steele in the new literary periodicals, but Pope more systematically and logically made this critical highlighting part of the texture of the text itself, at once reflecting and informing contemporary taste. In addition, his collaborators prepared several analytical indexes, one to characters, another to "Manners, Passions, and their external Effects," another to "Thoughts, or Sentiments," and an accompanying "Table of the most considerable [Speeches] in *Shakespear*." Such ancillaries told readers where to find reflections upon such topics as "*Adversity, the Advantages of it*" and "*Womankind, their Nature*." Both procedures, indexing and spotlighting, emphasized descriptive, sententious, narrative, undramatic passages, oratorio set pieces.[71] They fragmented each play into an occasion for a few admired poems.

Whereas Rowe's edition had achieved its originality by creative application of theatrical conventions to the printed text, Pope owed his originality to books. Rowe had been content to base his text upon the 1685 collected edition, the most recent and, from a historical standpoint, the most corrupt. He made virtually no textual use of the quarto editions of individual plays; typically, when he did consult quartos—as in *Hamlet* and *Othello*—he silently incorporated material from late seventeenth-century editions, which apparently represented the text as performed in the Restoration theatre; in the case of *Hamlet* he printed in Shakespeare's text lines adapted by Davenant.[72] Pope by contrast collected twenty-four early quarto editions of the plays,[73] advertised for others, and with the help of his colleagues collated them, comparing their texts with Rowe's. As a result he was able to correct hundreds of errors accumulated during the seventeenth century and to insert words, phrases, and sometimes whole passages undoubtedly written by Shakespeare but unavailable to readers since the Restoration and, in some cases, out of print for over a century. Moreover, Pope, unlike Rowe, called attention to places where he was drawing on readings in the early texts.

Pope's use of these books also appeared to unlock, at least in part, the great conundrum that had bewildered critics for decades: Shakespeare's unevenness. Taking a hint from Betterton, Pope's preface challenged the tradition that contrasted Shakespeare and Jonson as the opposed epitomes of Nature and Art; he continued this liberating critical reassessment by attributing much of Shakespeare's undeserved reputation for "want of learning" to "the many blunders and illiteracies of the first Publishers of his works," whose "ignorance shines almost in every page." In a conclusion endorsed by almost all subsequent scholarship, he recognized that Shakespeare himself had not overseen the printing even of those plays published in his own lifetime; consequently, the early quarto editions suffer from such "excessive carelessness of the press . . . that it's plain there either was no Corrector to the press at all, or one totally illiterate." Pope's attitude to the men who printed Shakespeare's plays is in such passages clearly shaped by his experience of unscrupulous Augustan publishers, like the notorious Edmund Curll.

But even so, according to Pope, the main source of corruption lay not with the printers but with "one source, the ignorance of the Players, both as his actors, and as his editors." Pope's books convinced him that the stage was to blame for obscuring Shakespeare's genius, which he proposed to restore by removing "those almost innumerable Errors" introduced by the acting profession. Strip away the accretions of the actors, and a Shakespeare emerged who was more palatable to the taste of eighteenth-century readers.

Pope set out to rescue Shakespeare from the theatre. Knowing almost nothing about theatrical conditions in Shakespeare's lifetime, he based his judgment of the acting profession upon the example of his own contemporaries. He accordingly found it easy, perhaps inevitable, to blame the actors for "the additions of trifling and bombast passages . . . mean conceits and ribaldries," and the vast expansion of "low scenes of Mobs, Plebeians and Clowns." The same culprits often omitted "beautiful passages," their only motive being a "willingness to shorten some scenes"; like Procrustes, they set about "lopping or stretching an Author, to make him just fit for their Stage." Likewise, sometimes "Characters were confounded and mix'd, for want of a competent number of actors"; at other times "a governing Player, to have the mouthing of some favourite speech himself, would snatch it from the unworthy lips of an Underling." Act divisions had been inserted not on rational principles but wherever the actors "thought fit to make a breach in [the performance], for the sake of Musick, Masques, or Monsters." Such conjectures leave no doubt that Pope, like Rowe, was thinking of the Augustan stage when he wrote about its Elizabethan counterpart.

Pope affected to deny any such implication, and in respect to someone like Betterton the denial may have been sincere; but he slides easily, as had Rowe, into a satire upon the imbecility of contemporary patronage. In contrast to the actors of Shakespeare's time, contemporary "Gentlemen of the Stage" were "plac'd at the Lord's table, or Lady's toilette"—this from the author of *The Rape of the Lock*!—and consequently, unlike their predecessors, actors now enjoyed the advantages of acquaintance with "the familiar conversation of our Nobility, and an intimacy (not to say dearness) with people of the first condition." King George I's patronage of the theatre consisted of a particular fondness for music, masques, monsters, and clowns; the "intimacy (not to say dearness)" between players and aristocrats manifested itself particularly in scandalous liaisons between actresses and lords. The gentlemanly pretensions of the more successful members of the profession were themselves an irritant to social conservatives like Pope. As an indignant pamphleteer complained, "Is it your Pleasure that Players dress like Lords . . . have their town and country Houses, and give Law to every Tavern and Coffee-House where they come? This many of them do already."74 For Pope the actors' rise into respectability was just another symptom of the decay of cultural standards.

Pope, the first editor of Shakespeare so hostile to the theatre, was also the first to make extensive use of variant early editions, and he set the pattern by which they would be interpreted for two and a half centuries. Most of the major differences between them he attributed to theatrical debasement. He did not read the 1608 quarto edition of *The History of King Lear* as one work of art and the 1623 folio edition of *The Tragedy of King Lear* as another; instead, he glanced at pieces of the 1608 edition, occasionally using it to supplement or improve the text of his immediate predecessor (Rowe, whose text was based on the folio). Pope regarded both early texts of a play as mere raw materials from which to reconstruct his own version of an ideal lost original; he used each to undermine the authority and integrity of the other.

All texts contain errors, of course; some information is lost in every transmission; one text, one transmission, may help us to correct the errors in another. But Pope declared that all the early texts of Shakespeare reeked of corruption; they could be saved only by wholesale adaptation. Just as Davenant's *Law Against Lovers* had combined materials from *Measure for Measure* and *Much Ado about Nothing*, just as Cibber's adaptation of *Richard the Third* included passages from *Richard the Second, Henry the Fourth, Henry the Fifth,* and *Henry the Sixth,* so Pope's *King Lear* freely combined Shakespearian dialogue from two different sources. In a gesture wholly representative of his editorial method, the engraving of Shakespeare in Pope's edition conflated two early images, grafting the Chandos face onto the Stratford monument. He did the same thing with early texts, transplanting quarto scenes and speeches into folio structures.

Pope, like Rowe, like Davenant, wanted and claimed to offer both authenticity and novelty. In his use of Elizabethan and Jacobean books he created a mechanism for serving both purposes. Apparently, textual criticism could heal the critical dilemma created by the puzzlingly imperfect texts of an admired author.

What textual criticism did not achieve, translation could. Pope turned to his edition of Shakespeare fresh from the artistic and commercial triumph of his translation of Homer's *Iliad*—still the finest transformation of that poem into English, just as Dryden's is still our most assured rendering of Virgil's *Aeneid.* Pope often consciously departed from what he knew that Homer wrote because he also knew that his own readers would not understand or like what

Homer wrote. Like every previous edition of Shakespeare's collected plays (including the first), Pope's text modernized the spelling, punctuation, and grammar of its predecessors, translating Early Modern English into Modern English. The very spelling of the playwright's surname had been modernized: since it is a compound obviously formed from a common verb and a common noun, printers spelled it as they would spell the words it compounded. The 1685 folio edition of the *Comedies, Histories, and Tragedies* consistently changed the obsolete spelling of the second syllable ("speare") to the preferred contemporary form ("spear");* for the next forty years it was almost universally adopted. Rowe accepted it, and so did Pope; Jonathan Swift joked that "In Queen *Elizabeth's* Reign" the English people first "attempted to deal in Tragedy, and began to SHAKE SPEARS."75 Pope simply carried this traditional modernizing process one step further, freely emending not only the spelling, punctuation, and stage directions but also the dialogue itself, in order to make it acceptable to eighteenth-century sensibilities. Pope could not decide, in Shakespeare's case, whether he was an editor or a translator; he wanted, impossibly, to modernize and to restore at the same time.

Pope's method was immediately and predictably turned against him, and would have been even if Lewis Theobald had never been born. Pope had opened a door that couldn't be closed. He had looked at more old editions than anyone else before him; but he had not looked at them all or noticed or used all that was in them. Theobald, for instance, returned to the form "Shakespeare" on the authority of the earliest printed texts; thus Pope is challenged by the very spelling of the first word of the title of Theobald's book (*Shakespeare Restored*). Theobald had more editions than Pope and examined them more thoroughly; other editors would in turn examine even more editions even more thoroughly than Theobald. And why limit the search to old books with Shakespeare's name on them? His text or meaning could often be illuminated by books written by his contemporaries. An author's words make sense only as part of an entire system of language, the linguistic and social code of his time and place. The fullness of meaning in an individual utterance can be recognized only in the context of everything said

*This spelling change had been anticipated on the title page of the 1664 issue (thus beginning the vogue of "Shakespear"); however, that edition left "Shakespeare" intact everywhere else in the preliminaries.

or sayable in the language in which that utterance is framed. So the fullness of Shakespeare's meaning is always just out of reach, postponed until we can read yet another old book, which would make clear to us some new aspect of what Shakespeare said or—just as significantly—deliberately avoided saying. Shakespeare's full meaning, his true text, is, in the new era initiated by Pope, always deferred.

We discover Shakespeare's meaning by relating what he said here to what he said there, or what he said to what others said, or what this book says he said to what that book says he said. But such differences, difficult enough to negotiate in themselves, are further replicated and tangled in the differences between any two editors or interpreters. Theobald sometimes challenged Pope's text not because he had access to additional information but because, after examining the same evidence Pope had examined, he came to different conclusions.

Pope's edition was an inevitable victim of the logic of language, the trap of differing and deferring, that ravenous hole which has swallowed every subsequent edition. Theobald, the predator, seeing Pope the victim in the bottom of the pit, leaped in on top of him and, in the process, transformed himself into the next victim, trapped at the mercy of the next predator-editor who peered down over the edge and who, in turn, . . .

A LIBRARY

At the end of his text Pope listed the twenty-seven early editions of Shakespeare that he had "made use of and compared"; eight years later Theobald's list boasted forty-three items.[76] For the first time, individuals had begun to acquire, deliberately, large private collections of Shakespeariana.

Both collections were financed at least in part by the Tonson firm, which kept records of how much it spent on books for each editor. More generally, the growth of such private libraries reflected the increasing proportion of England's national wealth that was being consumed in the manufacture and purchase of printed matter. The Tonsons prospered because more people had more money and more leisure to spend on books. This demand for books stimulated a boom in libraries, both private and public. By 1718 a handful of circulating libraries had been established in and out of London, and every subsequent decade witnessed an increase in the number of such collections, their geographical distribution, the size of their holdings, and the population of their subscribers.

The continued popularity of half a dozen of Shakespeare's plays in the theatre combined with the Tonsons' marketing expertise to guarantee him a place in these new libraries, but they did not determine what place it would be. Eighteenth-century English libraries had their own pyramid of social classes. Down among the masses tumbled all the gardening manuals, cookbooks, primers, sentimental fiction, and ephemeral plays—how to, what to do, boohoo, who's who; up among the mighty towered the Greek, Latin, and Hebrew classics, Milton, and Newton. Shakespeare's status would depend on where he was shelved.

In 1715 the Cambridge University library acquired for the first time a copy of Shakespeare's collected *Comedies, Histories, and Tragedies*.[77] A decade later George Sewell in the preface to a new edition of Shakespeare's poems complained that "Men of Learning and Leisure have usually buried themselves in reprinting the Works of the celebrated antient Authors in the *Greek* and *Latin* Languages"; such scholarly labors would be better expended on "our own great Writers, both in Prose, and Poetry," because such writers "are in some degree our *Classics*."[78] A few months later Theobald, at the beginning of *Shakespeare Restored*, agreed: "SHAKESPEARE stands, or at least ought to stand, in the Nature of a Classic Writer."[79] In both cases the definition of Shakespeare as a classic was expected to affect the editing of his work. Theobald deduced that Shakespeare's text "resembled That of a corrupt *Classic;* and, consequently, the Method of Cure was likewise to bear a Resemblance."[80]

Theobald took pride in stressing the similarity between his own textual method and that of the great classical scholar Dr. Richard Bentley. Bentley himself encouraged the parallel between the editing of classical works and vernacular classics by preparing a new edition of Milton's *Paradise Lost*, published by Tonson and others in 1732. Claiming that the first edition had been *"polluted with such monstrous Faults, as are beyond Example in any other printed Book,"* it proposed *"many Hundreds"* of new emendations.[81] Both Bentley and Theobald contended that an English classic had been ubiquitously corrupted by "*a bad Printer and a worse Editor*,"[82] that "*spurious Verses*" had been interpolated by a "*Friend or Acquaintance*" of the author,[83] that texts had been "imperfectly copied by Ear,"[84] and that "*the Proof-sheets of the First Edition were never read*" by or to the author.[85] In each case "no authentic Manuscript was extant"; in each case the author's works had for a long time been "republish'd from the faulty Copies without the assistance of any intelligent Editor: which has been the Case likewise of many a *Classic* Writer."[86]

Shakespeare's editors from Pope to Johnson shared most of these assumptions. But the plays of the great Athenian dramatists had suffered twenty-two centuries of textual corruption; the earliest surviving texts had been copied a millenium or more after the authors' deaths. Shakespeare's plays, by contrast, were little more than a century old; editions printed in his lifetime or shortly thereafter could still be found. These differences in temporal scale were ignored because it was in the interest of Shakespeare's editors not to see them. Like the great Renaissance humanists who had rescued classical literature from the Dark Ages, Shakespeare's eighteenth-century editors would rescue an English classic from the dark ages of the seventeenth century.

If Shakespeare was a classic, he should be edited like a classic—and criticized like a classic. But the precepts of Aristotle and Horace could not easily be reconciled with his practice, and he could be critically classicified only if a suitable alternative to Aristotle and Horace could be found.

The alternative was provided by Longinus, a shadowy first-century Greek critic unknown in the Middle Ages and the Renaissance until the publication in 1554, in Basel, of his single surviving work, *Peri hupsous*. For another century he remained invisible in England; even the formidably learned Ben Jonson never mentioned him, and not until 1652 did an English translation appear—which no one seems to have read. But in 1674 the critic and poet Nicolas Boileau, international arbiter of neoclassicism, published a French translation (*Le Traité du Sublime ou du Merveilleux dans le Discours*); and Longinus immediately became part of the common currency of European criticism. Dryden, for instance, who had never mentioned Longinus before 1674, did so eight times thereafter. A new English version that appeared in 1680 was, like subsequent translations, "Translated from *Boileau*'s Translation."[87]

Longinus was not immediately drafted into Shakespeare's service. Dryden did not use Longinus to defend Shakespeare; neither did Rowe, or Pope, or *The Tatler;* neither did John Dennis, though he was mocked for his excessive interest in the Greek critic.[88] Addison enlisted Longinus in support of his claim that Milton was "the greatest Poet which our Nation or perhaps any other has produced"; but he included Shakespeare among practitioners of "a false Sublime," and when condemning Shakespeare's puns he called Longinus as a witness for the prosecution.[89]

But in the same year as Addison's essay, 1712, Leonard Welsted— an altogether lesser writer than Addison, a minor poet and critic ridiculed by both Dennis and Pope—published his translation of *A Treatise on the Sublime;* in an appended essay he illustrated Longinian precepts with examples from Shakespeare. This precedent was followed by William Smith, a classical scholar and clergyman; about 1730 he wrote, and in 1739 published, an entirely new and influential translation based directly upon the Greek text. Shakespeare features prominently in Smith's commentary. Together, these two translations cemented an association between Shakespeare and Longinus for innumerable eighteenth-century readers.

This association gave English partisans of Shakespeare a prestigious Mediterranean ally; Shakespeare's artistic behavior was retrospectively validated by an ancient critic he had never heard of. But, as had happened with editing, this classical association also guided vernacular criticism of Shakespeare into particular channels. If Longinus was the only classical critic of much use in defending Shakespeare, then Shakespeare had to be defended on the grounds Longinus had prepared.

Aristotle had been chiefly concerned with taxonomic description; he identified the characteristic structure of different genres of writing, just as he did with different genera of animals. Augustan strictures on dramatic structure almost always depended, at one or more removes, upon Aristotle; and since Aristotle's descriptions did not fit Shakespeare's creations, comments on the overall shape of his plays were usually hostile. But Longinus was concerned with genius, not genus: he took samples wherever he found them—in epic, drama, oratory, or the Bible. Shakespeare's promiscuous crossbreeding of genres ceases to be a problem, if any genre can contain specimens of sudden splendor. Smith picks sublimities from *Cymbeline* as well as *Julius Cæsar,* Welsted quotes *King John* alongside *Othello.* Longinus gave Shakespeare's champions a precedent for ignoring dramatic construction altogether. And because Longinus typically illustrated his argument by quoting brief passages, he encouraged the tendency to break the plays down into quotable tidbits. Thus the preface to William Dodd's anthology of *The Beauties of Shakespear,* which went through thirty-nine editions between 1752 and 1893, promised "many fine passages" that "blaze in the robes of sublimity" and would "obtain the commendations of a *Longinus.*"[90]

Longinus gave Shakespeare's critics a warrant to ignore structural weaknesses and concentrate upon fine passages; he also let them turn Shakespeare's glaring faults into a badge of greatness:

> I readily allow, that Writers of a lofty and tow'ring Genius are by no means pure and correct, since whatever is neat and accurate throughout must be exceedingly liable to Flatness. In the Sublime, as in great Affluence of Fortune, some minuter Articles will unavoidably escape Observation. . . . its very Height and Grandeur exposes the Sublime to sudden Falls.[91]

This passage was quoted more than once by defenders of Shakespeare.[92] Even before then, it had become a commonplace of Augustan criticism: Pope affirmed that "Great Wits sometimes may *gloriously offend.*"[93] In both the corruption of his texts and the faults of his style, the very deficiencies of Shakespeare's plays confirmed his status as a classic.

But although Shakespeare found a place in eighteenth-century libraries alongside Longinus, Sophocles, and *Paradise Lost,* he also often found himself on a different set of shelves, serving a different kind of reader. Criticism and editing, which emphasized his classical credentials, were conducted by men, who spent much of their time comparing him with other male writers; but many of Shakespeare's eighteenth-century readers were female, and their enthusiasm for his work was instrumental in creating and maintaining his status as a popular author.

Women had read Shakespeare from the beginning. As early as 1605 a jealous husband in Thomas Middleton's *A Mad World, My Masters* felt compelled to take "all her wanton Pamphlets"—including *Venus and Adonis*—away from his young lascivious wife.[94] In a manuscript dating from about 1635, we hear of "A young Gentle Ladie" who, "having read ye works of Shakespeare," asked questions about Falstaff.[95] In a letter to a friend written on January 21, 1639, Ann Merricke regretted her lack of access to other "gentile recreationes": "I must content my selfe here, with the studie of Shackspeare, and the historie of woemen."[96]

In the second half of the seventeenth century female literacy in England increased: between the decade of Shakespeare's death and the decade of Pope's edition, female illiteracy in London declined from 91 percent to 44 percent. Shakespeare had envisaged Ophelia "sewing" in her chamber; in Davenant's adaptation sixty years later the courtier's young daughter instead spent her leisure time "reading."[97] In 1713 a male essayist explained women's passion for reading by claiming that the female half of the population "have more spare Time upon their Hands, and lead a more Sedentary Life"; since they often did their work communally, one woman could "read, while the others are at work."[98] Eliza Haywood recommended that a lady "make her Woman read to her, while she is dressing."[99] Whatever the causes, women constituted an important and visible sector of the reading market.

We know less about what they read, because much of our evidence comes from male witnesses, whose prejudices are often obvious. Addison in *The Spectator* purported to describe "a *Lady's Library*," treating its very existence as "a great Curiosity"; he used the occasion to satirize the reading habits of women, with their neglect of moral tracts and practical handbooks in favor of romances, modern novels, and English "Plays of all Sorts."[100] Addison does not specifically mention any of Shakespeare's "Plays of all Sorts" in his partial catalogue of a fictive lady's books, but the libraries of some real ladies did include him. The Duchess of Marlborough owned two copies of Shakespeare's works.[101] The glorious and notorious Lady Mary Wortley Montagu, honored by the Kit-Cat Club when she was only seven, owned a seventeenth-century folio edition of the plays, and her copy of Theobald's edition was "manifestly much read"; when in the country, away from her London library, she borrowed "a volume of Shakespear's plays" from Pope.[102] In 1696 *An Essay in Defence of the Female Sex*, "Written by a Lady," asserted that a woman could learn everything she needed to know from English authors without recourse to the Greek and Latin classics, for "who has given us Nobler, or juster Pictures of Nature than Mr. *Shakespear?*"[103] In 1709 *The Female Tatler*, "Written by a Society of *Ladies*," paired Shakespeare with Ben Jonson,[104] alluded casually to his most famous characters and plays, and complained that even "Immortal *Shakespear*" did not always "write up" to the standard created by his best work ("to the no small disappointment" of his admirers).[105]

But although many women read Shakespeare, active public discussion of his work was left almost entirely to men. The first critical prose essay on Shakespeare was written in 1664 by a woman, Margaret Cavendish, Duchess of Newcastle, who named Julius Caesar, Ovid, and Shakespeare as the "three Dead men" she had loved since her childhood.[106] Aphra Behn, the first English woman to earn her living as a writer, mentioned Shakespeare more than once in prefaces to her plays. Lady Montagu preferred *Julius Cæsar* to Addison's *Cato* because of its unity of action ("Caesar's death was [Shakespeare's] design and we hear of no Episodes not relating to that").[107] But Montagu's essay remained unpublished; Cavendish was politely ignored; the uninhibited Mrs. Behn was an embarrassment. By comparison with *The Tatler*, *The Female Tatler* had little to say about Shakespeare; and what it did say was soon forgotten, since, unlike its spectacularly influential male rival, it was never reprinted.

Nevertheless, in the late 1730s a group of women readers publicly intervened in support of Shakespeare's status as an English classic. In the winter of 1736–37 a "Shakespeare Ladies Club" was formed in London; we do not know who its members were, but "several Ladies of Quality" organized a "Subscription . . . for the Revival of *Shakespear*'s Plays."[108] In that theatrical season they prompted the first revival of *Cymbeline* in seventeen years, the first revival of *King John* in the eighteenth century, and a new adaptation of *Much Ado About Nothing*. The next season saw productions of *Richard the Second*, *Henry the Fifth*, and the first part of *Henry the Sixth*, which had not been performed in their original versions for more than forty years, as well as a new adaptation of *Pericles*. More generally, in these two years the proportion of London performances devoted to Shakespeare rose from 14 to 22 percent.[109] As a contemporary declared, "Some Ladies indeed have shown a truly public Spirit in rescuing the admirable, yet almost forgotten *Shakespear*, from being totally sunk in Oblivion."[110] Shakespeare hardly needed rescuing, but a female pressure group did succeed in persuading theatrical managements to offer more Shakespeare, and a greater variety of Shakespeare, to the London public. Since these women were encouraging the performance of plays that had not been produced in decades, their knowledge of them could have come only from reading.

In the seventeenth century the popularity of Shakespeare's plays with audiences had stimulated the publication of reading editions. In the eighteenth century, their popularity with readers stimulated new productions. Actors now followed where publishers had led.

A YAWNING RUIN

If you want a single exemplar of attitudes to Shakespeare in the first half of the eighteenth century, take *The Dunciad:* written by Pope, edited in part by Warburton, satirizing Theobald, satirizing Cibber, satirizing the new literary and political journalism, its publishers and those they published. Into its texts and notes crowd almost all the major and minor contributors to the image of Shakespeare in the Age of Cibber—including, of course, Jacob Tonson, "genial Jacob" who stimulates hacks to write bad poetry for profit, "great Jacob" whose "pace" other publishers seek to emulate.[111] "Books and the Man"[112] Pope sings, books that are now articles of commerce, gilded furnishings on shelves, purchased for reasons that have nothing to do with their contents. And to this group portrait of books and bookmen the little literati swarmed: "On the Day the Book was first vended, a Crowd of Authors besieg'd the Shop . . . to hinder the coming out of the *Dunciad:* On the other Side, the Booksellers and Hawkers made as great Efforts to procure it."[113] The poem's own history exemplifies the cultural situation it describes.

Pope's edition of Shakespeare was published in 1725; Theobald's attack on it appeared in 1726; in 1727 Theobald's play *Double Falshood* was performed, purporting to be his adaptation of an unpublished tragicomedy by Shakespeare and Fletcher. In 1728 a second edition of Pope's Shakespeare appeared, grouping "a thing call'd the *Double Falshood*" among "those wretched plays" which had been falsely attributed to Shakespeare.[114] But Pope's real answer to Theobald came in the scandalously popular *Dunciad,* published that same year with "pidling *Tibald*"[115] as principal dunce. The first edition pretended to be pirated; it was followed in 1729 by an official "*DUNCIAD VARIORVM,*" with an extensive commentary—beginning with a facetious note on Theobald's meticulous "preservation of this very Letter *e,* in spelling the Name of his beloved

Author" [*Shakespeare*]. After prolonged negotiations Tonson and Theobald in 1731 finally signed a contract for a new Shakespeare edition, which appeared in 1733. In the preface Theobald not only denied Pope's honesty and ability as an editor; he also devoted an entire paragraph to the "Libels" of the *Dunciad,* saying that "there are Provocations, which a Man can never quite forget" and threatening that "I shall willingly devote a part of my Life to the honest Endeavour of quitting Scores."[116] Theobald's edition was in some sense a reply to the *Dunciad,* from the editor's and the publisher's and the public's point of view. But although Theobald was right in prophesying that "impartial Posterity" would side with him, his scholarship made little headway at the time against Pope's poetry.

Pope, having crushed Theobald, lost interest in him. Colley Cibber had offended Pope as early as 1717 with his attacks on Catholics; in 1730 Cibber ascended to the diminence of poet laureate, an appointment that owed more to political patronage than to talent. In the 1730s Cibber summed up English culture: playwright, poet, actor, manager for two decades of Drury Lane, sycophant of the corrupt Walpole administration. Then in 1740 Cibber directly attacked Pope in several passages of his *Autobiography;* two years later he compounded the offense with a pamphlet retailing a damning sexual anecdote about Pope. Pope responded by composing a new version of the *Dunciad,* in which he dethroned Theobald and installed Cibber as the antihero of the poem. This revised *Dunciad* was published in 1743, fourteen years after the original. The gap between the two versions was, in at least one sense, a function of the copyright act passed by Parliament in 1709; by waiting until the old copyright had lapsed, Pope could make a further profit on the poem by reselling it with a "new and improved" formula.

The Dunciad is a masterpiece (two masterpieces, really) by one major interpreter of Shakespeare, attacking two other major interpreters of Shakespeare. Pope's poem is not about poems or plays; it is about "Books," about the materiality of art, including his own. Pope, who paid particular attention to the visual reality of his own publications and who had examined more old copies of Shakespeare's texts than any previous editor, realized that editing transformed one kind of book into another; emendations of individual letters or words made less impression than the total transformation of the work's physical context. Something similar was happening in the theatre, where, even if the text was not adapted, it was now performed in a radically new environment.

Shakespeare himself makes a few formal appearances in *The Dunciad,* always as a contrast to the degeneracy of eighteenth-century culture. In the very first note to the 1743 version Pope mentions the new "Monument in Westminster Abby" erected as a memorial to Shakespeare. Pope was a member of the august committee that planned that memorial, which was finally installed in 1741. Like other political and cultural conservatives, he associated Shakespeare with the glories of a vanished past epitomized by the royal bones anthologized in that abbey. The marble monument incorporates, alongside the full-length statue of Shakespeare, busts of Queen Elizabeth I and two of the many kings he characterized (Henry V and Richard III). Shakespeare belonged to and illustrated the retrospectively uncomplicated native royalist tradition, held up in imaginative contrast to the corrupt longevity of Robert Walpole's Whig administration (1721–42). The conservative opposition to Walpole naturally tried to enlist Shakespeare as a cultural ally. An opposition journal praised *The Life of King Henry VIII* because "Such a Representation as this, given us by so great a Master, throws ones Eye back upon our Ancestors"; in particular, the writer focuses on Shakespeare's portrayal of the *"wicked Minister"* Wolsey:

> the Character of this ambitious, wealthy, bad *Minister* is described in the very Words of *Shakespeare;* reflecting People may observe from this Picture how like human Nature is in her Workings at all Times.[117]

This anonymous critique uses Shakespeare to whip Walpole; Pope uses him to whip the cultural illiteracy of Walpole's era.

Pope employs the same artistic strategy when he juxtaposes Shakespeare and Cibber:

> o'er his Books his eyes began to roll,
> In pleasing memory of all he stole,
> How here he sipp'd, how there he plunder'd snug
> And suck'd all oe'r, like an industrious Bug.
> Here lay poor Fletcher's half-eat scenes, and here
> The Frippery of crucify'd Moliere;
> There hapless Shakespear, yet of Tibbald sore,
> Wish'd he had blotted for himself before.[118]

Pope himself commented on this passage in an appended note:

It was a ridiculous praise which the Players gave to Shakespear, "that he never blotted a line". Ben Johnson honestly wished he had blotted a thousand; and Shakespear would certainly have wished the same, if he had lived to see those alterations in his works, which, not the Actors only (and especially the daring Hero of this poem) have made on the *Stage,* but the presumptuous Critics of our days in their *Editions.*

Pope's own edition had been one of the most presumptuous of all time, and what he says of others could be applied with equal justice to himself—an irony that he could not prevent readers from appreciating and that he may even have appreciated himself, now that his edition was some eighteen years cold. The note reiterates his contempt for "the Players" who had first collected and published Shakespeare's works, and it squarely identifies the actors of Shakespeare's time with those of Pope's own. Shakespeare should, upon reflection, have omitted ("blotted") many of the lines he had written; because he did not he had opened opportunities to adapter/actors like Cibber and adapter/editors like Theobald, who disfigured ("blotted") his text with their own alterations. Pope equates theatrical adaptation and editorial titivation, treating both as forms of larceny—or perhaps one should say cannibalism. Shakespeare now wishes he had "blotted for himself before"; Pope, having learned this lesson, edits himself before anyone else gets the chance. The power of the editor for good or harm had become a theme not only of Shakespeare criticism but of literature itself.

But under the obvious ridicule of Cibber and Theobald lies an oblique rebuke to Shakespeare: he *should* have blotted those lines himself long ago, and in a way he has only himself to blame for what has now happened. The same ambivalence can be heard in the original version of the poem, where Shakespeare again serves as an exemplar of excellence contrasted with his debased interpreters; but at the same time Shakespeare himself emerges as an example of debased excellence. Thus, Theobald addresses the Goddess of Dullness:

> Here studious I unlucky moderns save,
> Nor sleeps one error in its father's grave,
> Old puns restore, lost blunders nicely seek,
> And crucify poor Shakespear once a week.[119]

The couplet that mentions puns contains one: Shakespeare is cruci-
fied by his interpreters but also "cruxified," as they publish in the
literary periodicals notes on the textual cruxes (or cruces) in his
plays. But while mocking Theobald, this passage also mocks Shakespeare, with his notorious puns and embarrassing anachronistic
blunders. Theobald's fastidious restoration of such blemishes is no
more tasteless than Shakespeare's creation of them. And when the
Goddess of Dullness surveys the "new-born Nonsense" of contemporary poetasters, their productions sound suspiciously like Shakespeare's own—featuring hundreds of puns, "motley Images," "a
Mob of Metaphors," the "jumbled race" of tragicomedy, a contented
imbecile disregard of the unities of time and place.[120] As an example of absurdities in descriptive poetry ("On cold December fra-
grant chaplets blow") Pope unmistakably echoes *A Midsummer
Night's Dream* ("on old [winter's] chin and icy crown / An od'rous
chaplet of sweet summer buds").[121]

Pope announces in the first lines of the poem that "Still Dunce the
second reigns like Dunce the first," in an image that compresses
politics and culture: the crown of England being passed like a
saltshaker from dumb King George I to dumb King George II,
while in literature the torch of acclaimed mediocrity is handed
down from one contemporary nonentity to another. But in some
sense too, perhaps the more important sense, Pope names Lewis
Theobald the inheritor (as dramatist) and executor (as editor) of
Shakespeare's faults. Shakespeare was, after all—as Dryden and
many others since had acclaimed him—the true "king" of English
literature. And in the revised version of the poem Cibber—as dramatist, actor, and adapter of other men's plays—can also claim to be
Shakespeare's successor.

In Pope's lifetime English power began to be felt increasingly on
the European continent; and where England led, Shakespeare followed. Pope had been visited by Voltaire in 1726, between the
publication of Pope's *Shakespear* and his *Dunciad*, and these two
epitomes of French and English culture in the early eighteenth
century shared a profound ambivalence about the king of English
literature. In 1733 Voltaire wrote the first French translation of any
of Shakespeare's work, a version of "To be, or not to be"; he introduced him to Europe as an important poet, full of moments of
genius. In the same breath he condemned Shakespeare's tragedies
as "monstrous Farces."[122] For Voltaire as for Pope, Shakespeare was

best represented by isolated "shining passages"—and even they needed to be translated into a more refined idiom.

Cibber and Theobald, by contrast, did not refine Shakespeare but further coarsened him. For Pope they personified two contrasting but equally deadening mechanisms for trivializing the culture of the past. On the stage, plays can be decorated to death, as audiences flock to see "A past, vamp'd, future, old, reviv'd, new piece,"[123] and the "Contending Theatres" compete with one another in mounting spectacular gewgaws. A debased theatre, catering to a debased public, can only debase any drama it touches.

But scholars too can reduce drama to dust. *The Dunciad Variorum* boasts commendatory and prefatory matter, voluminous explanatory notes, disquisitions on orthography, errata lists and appendices and indices following the text like theatrical afterpieces—all bogus of course, but by implication no more bogus than the real thing. Indeed, Pope's artificial scholarly apparatus can claim to be less bogus than the reality it parodies, for his notes are as literary, ironic, playful, and entertaining as the poem they stand under and understand. Theobald, by contrast, whose very plays inspire sleep, cannot be expected to awaken us when he descends to mere commentary.

Pope edited a modern classic, translated a Greek classic, and wrote more than one classic of English poetry; but it was Theobald and Cibber who pointed to the future. Pope's own poems would be in part unintelligible today without the commentaries to them. By the early eighteenth century Shakespeare had been dead for a century, and an increasing proportion of his meanings could be recovered only by people willing to devote long hours to poring over the decayed trivia of a culture's remains. Modern editors and readers are still indebted to the arcane notes of Theobald and the self-indulgent theatrical memoirs of Cibber. They have forgotten Pope's indexes, his highlighted and demoted passages, his efforts to translate Shakespeare into an Augustan idiom. Whether or not Pope approved of their power, Shakespeare could not survive without the pedant and the player. And his survival would be inextricably entangled with the power of George II's successor, Dunce the Third.

CHAPTER 3

 ༒

1790

On July 14, 1789, rioters stormed and burned London's three most notorious penal institutions, the Fleet, Newgate, and King's Bench prisons, setting free thousands of poor prisoners. As *The Times* reported, the "unlicensed populace" captured the governor and commandant of the garrison, "beheaded them, stuck their heads on tent poles, and carried them in triumph . . . through the streets"—a punishment also visited later that day on the "Lord Mayor."[1] Years afterward Jane Austen could still visualize with vivacious horror "a mob of three thousand men assembling in St. George's Fields; the Bank attacked, the Tower threatened, the streets of London flowing with blood."[2] Charles James Fox, leader of the parliamentary opposition, applauded the mob's action; but Richard Sheridan warned fellow members of the House of Commons that if the revolutionaries' plots succeeded "the whole of our constitution was to be overturned, and the Royal Family were to be murdered."[3] Not long afterward, Edmund Burke described how, on October 6, "A band of cruel ruffians and assassins . . . rushed into the chamber of the queen, and pierced with an hundred strokes of bayonets and poniards the bed, from whence this persecuted woman had but just time to fly almost naked, and through ways unknown to the murderers had escaped to seek refuge at the feet of a king and husband, not secure of his own life for a moment"; the king and queen were then led in triumph back to London, on foot, their parodic royal progress heralded and attended by "horrid yells, and shrilling screams, and frantic dances, and infamous contumelies, and all the unutterable abominations of the furies of hell."4 The Revolution that had liberated the prisoners imprisoned the royal family. On January 21, 1793, the king, like Charles I before him, was publicly beheaded. On February 1 France declared war on England. Thomas Paine's *Rights of Man,* the most famous of many pamphlets defending the revolution, was printed in a cheap edition deliberately aimed at a mass market, and by 1793 it had sold as many as 200,000 copies. But these early successes were followed by a period of brutal repression, described by contemporaries as a "reign of terror." Paine himself was arrested, tried, and imprisoned; then came the Report of the Committee of Secrecy, the Suspension of the Habeas Corpus Act, a series of treason trials in 1794, and the Treasonable Practices Act of 1795. For the next two decades the nation poured its money, blood, and energy into the prosecution of a worldwide war against its enemies, culminating in the decisive victory of a reactionary royalist coalition at Waterloo in 1815.

BOOK I

It did not happen quite like that, but it could have. Like Shakespeare in his history plays, I have freely combined material from varied sources, describing incidents widely separated in time and place. The weeklong Gordon Riots of 1780, which included those populist attacks on London's prisons, did not precipitate a revolution. *The Times* reporter in 1789 was describing events in Paris, not London; Jane Austen was imaginatively conflating the (native) Gordon Riots with the (foreign) storming of the Bastille in order to parody an immature Englishwoman's breathless Gothic nightmaring. The royal family imprisoned and then executed was Bourbon, not Hanoverian. The Revolution of 1789 happened over there, not in England. The French acted the tragedy; the English watched, exercised (or exorcised) their pity and fear, moralized upon the spectacle, and then—to quote *Hamlet*—"Did nothing."

I am exaggerating. The English did do something. They quoted *Hamlet*.

By his own account "Hamlet was the play, or rather Hamlet himself was the Character, in the intuition and exposition of which" Coleridge in 1798 first demonstrated his gift for "Philosophical criticism."[5] Three decades later he confessed, "I have a smack of Hamlet myself, if I may say so."[6] The Hamlet of which Coleridge had a smack was a character typified by "aversion to action," who

> is all meditation, all resolution as far as words are concerned, but all hesitation & irresolution when called upon to act; so that resolving to do everything he in fact does nothing. He is full of purpose, but void of that quality of mind wch wod lead him at the proper time to carry his purpose into effect . . . the great purpose of life defeated by continually resolving to do, yet doing nothing but resolve.[7]

You would hardly gather from this description that Hamlet actively isolates himself from the court by conspicuously continuing to wear mourning, or that he faces the Ghost alone, murders Polonius, forges an order for the execution of Rosencrantz and Guildenstern, leaps from his own ship in order to fight the pirates hand to hand on their own, leaps into Ophelia's grave, outduels Laertes, and kills Claudius. Whether or not Coleridge had a smack of Hamlet, the Hamlet he described had more than a smack of Coleridge, Wordsworth, and Southey, literary intellectuals who flirted with revolution but who could not "at the proper time" commit themselves.

Coleridge's interpretation of Hamlet distanced and idealized the political irresolution of his own generation. Coleridge projected that collective indecision onto Hamlet and then made an artistic fetish of his own weakness; even as he criticized it, he made "doing nothing" seem Shakespearian, heroic, and tragic. And, as if to ensure that we do not overlook such meanings, Coleridge himself intruded contemporary political parallels into his discussion of the play. In some notes for a lecture on *Hamlet*, written in 1813, he praised Shakespeare for his "tenderness with regard to all innocent Superstitions"; Shakespeare spares us "Tom Paine declarations and pompous philosophy." Coleridge proposed to end the lecture by speaking "of the honest pride of our Englishmen—Milton, Shakespear, Bacon, Newton—& now Wellington."[8] Elsewhere, Coleridge applauded "the wonderfully philosophic impartiality of Shakespeare's politics"; the phrase has since been echoed by innumerable

Coleridgettes, who do not usually notice that in the next sentence he claims that Shakespeare was "devoted to patriotism."9 For Coleridge "impartiality in politics" meant rejecting Thomas Paine's egalitarian *Rights of Man* in favor of the Duke of Wellington's monarchist victories.

In the same notes, describing Hamlet's "aversion to real action," Coleridge quoted the first line of the most memorable speech in Wordsworth's verse tragedy *The Borderers:*

> Action is transitory, a step, a blow—
> The motion of a muscle—this way or that—
> 'Tis done—and in the after vacancy
> We wonder at ourselves like men betray'd.10

The hero of that play is a noble, young, procrastinating, disgusted idealist; the text repeatedly, consciously or involuntarily, echoes *Hamlet* (and Shakespeare's other tragedies). Wordsworth was working on *The Borderers* from 1796 to 1799, and by his own account the play grew out of his "long residence in France, while the Revolution was rapidly advancing to its extreme of wickedness";11 the famous speech is spoken by a character named after and based upon an English Jacobin who was in revolutionary Paris at the same time as Wordsworth.

Like his elders Coleridge and Wordsworth, John Keats quoted *Hamlet* more often than any other play. In quoting it he too interpreted it. First, the title character could be identified with Shakespeare himself:

> a miserable and mighty Poet of the human Heart. The middle age of Shakspeare was all c[l]ouded over; his days were not more happy than Hamlet's who is perhaps more like Shakspeare himself in his common every day Life than any other of his Characters—12

Second, the title character could be identified with Keats himself:

> Hamlet's heart was full of such Misery as mine is when he said to Ophelia "Go to a Nunnery, go, go!" Indeed I should like to give up the matter at once—I should like to die. I am sickened at the brute world which you are smiling with. I hate men and women more.13

Keats=Hamlet=Shakespeare; by eliminating the middle term, Keats=Shakespeare. But eliminating it obscures the character of the two poets' proposed identity. They are identical because they are miserable and in love. Hamlet's political mission and social status have, in Keats, simply disappeared; Shakespeare has become the poet of love and melancholy. Coleridge and his Hamlet agonized inconclusively over a decisive political act; Keats and his Hamlet abdicated into a deliberately depoliticized private world.

Charles Lamb retreats even further, into the security of an elected insignificance:

> You might pit me
>   For height
> Against Kean.
>
> But in a grand tragic scene
>   I'm nothing.
> It would create a kind of loathing
>   To see me act Hamlet.
>   There'd be many a damn let
>   Fly
> At my presumption
>   If I should try
> Being a fellow of no gumption—[14]

Lamb has, he insists, the diminutive stature, but none of the talent of the actor Edmund Kean; Lamb cannot act either in the theatre or in the political world; he cannot even act Hamlet, let alone be Hamlet; he lacks "the gumption" even to play the part of a character who, in the prevailing Romantic interpretation, spent his life averting action. The flippancy of his rhymes advertises Lamb's pose of triviality.

Lamb's Hamlet could be acted by Kean, or someone else perhaps, but not Lamb; William Hazlitt's Hamlet could not be acted at all:

> We do not like to see our author's plays acted, and least of all, HAMLET. There is no play that suffers so much in being transferred to the stage. Hamlet himself seems hardly capable of being acted . . . Mr. Kemble plays it like a man in armour, with a determined inveteracy of purpose, in one undeviating straight line, which is as remote from the natural grace and refined

susceptibility of the character, as the sharp angles and abrupt starts which Mr. Kean introduces into the part. Mr. Kean's Hamlet is as much too splenetic and rash as Mr. Kemble's is too deliberate and formal.

No representation can be adequate to Hazlitt's idea of the character; and if he cannot have a perfect performance, Hazlitt wants none. In this attitude the critic resembles his Hamlet, "the prince of philosophical speculators," who, "because he cannot have his revenge perfect, according to the most refined idea his wish can form, he declines it altogether." Hamlet cannot be acted because Hamlet, at heart, does not belong on stage at all but in the audience. "It is *we* who are Hamlet" (Hazlitt's sociable "we" in place of Coleridge's egotistical "I"); whoever "goes to a play as his best resource to shove off, to a second remove, the evils of life by a mock representation of them—this is the true Hamlet." Hamlet is anyone who watches a play (like *Hamlet*) instead of confronting and opposing "the evils of life," particularly the evils of corrupt and illegitimate political power. "It is *we*," Hazlitt tells readers in 1817, "It is *we*" who, when we are "most bound to act," remain "puzzled, undecided, and sceptical" and dally with our purposes "till the occasion is lost."[15] Hazlitt defines himself and his contemporaries as the spectators to a performance, always inadequate, of a play about a character who would rather watch than act, because acting is always inadequate, and because watching the play is an alternative to changing the world. In Shakespeare's text the inset "Mousetrap" play contributes to the plot; in Hazlitt's text the inset *Hamlet* play is an alternative to plotting.

"We love Hamlet even as we love ourselves"; in Byron's mouth the Romantic glorification of Hamlet is phrased in terms that satirize its self-satisfaction. Byron himself, by contrast, declares, "O I am sick of this most lame and impotent hero"—and then falls asleep.[16] Physically lame himself, he is sick of lameness; politically impotent, he is sick of inaction. He might as well have said, "I hate Hamlet even as I hate myself." He makes these remarks in Pisa early in 1822. By then he is deeply involved in revolutionary Italian politics; a year later he will leave Italy to contribute physically and financially (and fatally) to the battle for Greek independence.

These interpretations of Hamlet, however varied and even contradictory, all belong to the Romantic obsession with works unfinished, closure postponed: Wordsworth's epic by titular definition a mere *Prelude*, itself deferred by endless revisions; Byron's unfinished and unfinishable *Don Juan*, formally promiscuous, knowing that no episode or orgasm can be any more definitive than the one before; Coleridge's volumes of fragments, notes, talk, plans— including plans for an edition of Shakespeare; Keats' abandoned *Hyperion*, his *Fall of Hyperion* suspended in midsentence; Edmond Malone's biography of Shakespeare, the goal and focus of a lifelong scholarly enterprise, published posthumously, a ragged fragment. (This experience—even glorification—of artistic incompleteness leads naturally, in the next generation, to the suggestion that one of Shakespeare's own plays, *Timon of Athens*, was left unfinished.)[17] Completedness, the rondure of achievement, is an aesthetic and spiritual injunction—Wordsworth describes his muse in a phrase quoted from Shakespeare, who had used it of the ghost of Hamlet's father[18]—but artistic and social wholeness seems unattainable.

In its place they have only fragments. They create fragments, like Coleridge's *Kubla Khan*, and they transform Shakespeare into a treasure-house of stray puzzle-pieces. In 1814 Edmund Kean bursts upon the London theatre with successive impersonations of Shylock, Richard III, Hamlet, Othello, and Iago; everyone faults his style as "fitful, flashy" and "spasmodic,"[19] but that unevenness cannot be separated from new and irresistible bits of business that "had an electrical effect" upon audiences. When Kean reaches the end of one of Shylock's famous set pieces ("You call'd me dog; and for these courtesies / I'll lend you thus much moneys"), his "struggle of outward humility and inner rage ends at the last word, the word 'moneys,' with an eerily prolonged laugh which suddenly breaks off, while the face, convulsively distorted into submission, remains for some time mask-like, unmoving, while the evil eye stares out of it, threatening and deadly"—that eye which observers described as "a magic lightning-flash, a fiery flame."[20] Kean's Richard III stands at Bosworth Field oblivious of those around him, "for some moments fixed in reverie, drawing figures on the sand" with the point of his sword.[21] To see Kean act was "like reading Shakspeare by flashes of lightning."[22]

As an actor Kean could make one moment— a line, a gesture— leap out of its context to demand attention (and applause). Audiences appreciated these revelations because they already knew the plays, and knew too how they had been performed by others; when-

ever Kean did something new his audience recognized the novelty
and could grasp its relevance to the whole character. In the same
way, writers could expect readers to recognize quotations from
Shakespeare and relish the aptness of an allusion or the novelty of
an interpretation. Shakespeare was quotable precisely because he
was already familiar. William Blake could entitle an image "Jocund
Day" or "Fiery Pegasus" and expect the two-word quotation to recall
its context in *Romeo and Juliet* or *Henry IV*.[23] The Reverend Thomas
Ford could publish in *The Gentleman's Magazine* one hundred and
fifty parodies of speeches from Shakespeare, including twenty-two
from *Hamlet* alone, and expect his readers to note and appreciate
how he was transforming each original.[24] As John Poole explained
in the preface to *Hamlet Travestie*, a popular burlesque of 1810, "to
derive entertainment from the perusal of a travesty . . . a familiar
acquaintance with the original is indispensable."[25] No English
writer was more familiar than Shakespeare; no play more familiar
than *Hamlet*.

Quoting *Hamlet*, and all the other plays and poems, the Romantics paste bits and pieces of Shakespeare into their lives and letters
and essays and poems. The main character in John O'Keefe's *Wild
Oats*, a theatrical hit of 1791–93, is a "Strolling Gentleman" named
Rover, who can apply and mix quotations from Shakespeare on any
occasion. Hazlitt quotes Shakespeare more than 2,400 times (and
over a fifth of those quotations come from *Hamlet*).[26] Keats declares
that in reading Shakespeare and Milton he looks "upon fine Phrases
like a Lover,"[27] presumably contrasting "Lover" with an implied
"pedant"; unlike editors of Shakespeare from Theobald to Malone,
Keats does not break down the poetic text into specimens for philological inquiry. But although Keats sees the lover and the pedant as
antithetical, both disintegrate the text into minute verbal constitu-
ents. The editor sections off obscure phrases; Keats sections off fine
phrases, both highlighting fragments at the expense of continuity.
This process can be seen not only in the quotiness of Hazlitt's essays
and Keats' letters but also in Keats' underlining of words and
phrases in the editions of Shakespeare he read.

The Tatler, at the beginning of the eighteenth century, had quoted
whole speeches; the Romantics quote phrases. In his edition of
Shakespeare, Pope had visually emphasized "the most shining passages" and had appended an index to sententiae; but those passages
were later wholly extracted from the text of the plays and printed in

enormously popular and influential collections like William Dodd's
The Beauties of Shakespeare (first published in 1752), William
Enfield's *The Speaker; or, Miscellaneous Pieces, Selected from the Best
English Writers* (1774), Elizabeth Griffith's *The Morality of Shakespeare's Drama Illustrated* (1775), and Vicesimus Knox's *Elegant
Extracts: or, Useful & Entertaining Passages in Poetry* (1789). Lord
Kames' *Elements of Criticism* (1762) owed much of its popularity to
the "numerous illustrations and quotations from Shakespeare" with
which its arguments were substantiated, making it another handy
anthology of purple passages.[28] All these books went through
numerous reprintings.

Shakespeare's plays had been, throughout the seventeenth century, actions. They happened; they enacted a story temporally; they
were acted out by particular persons from beginning to end; they
acted upon an audience assembled in a certain place at a certain
time. In the eighteenth century they became things; they became,
primarily, books. Books are spatial, not temporal; any reader can
skip backward or forward, dip in, pull out, pause, repeat. Books can
be cut up and rearranged, as time cannot. The transformation of
Shakespeare's actions into books thus permitted and encouraged
their disintegration into assemblages of quotable fragments. Unlike
a moment of time, the physical space of a book can also be systematically enlarged; and as the eighteenth century progresses Shakespeare editions surround the text with an expanding border of
annotation, an undertext of commentary that repeatedly interrupts
a reading of the uppertext. The commentary beneath the text
whispers to us visually, like a conversation at the next table, audible
but not comprehensible until we stop to listen, turning our eyes
away from Shakespeare to focus upon someone else. The experience of reading *Hamlet* in a late eighteenth-century edition was an
experience of directed action repeatedly interrupted, postponed by
eddies of subsidiary meditation. Books abstract, impersonalize, ide-
alize; what had been an interaction between a cast and an audience
became instead a kind of message left by an unreachable author for
any and all possible readers. The text became a thing, a perfect
timeless thing, and any attempt to transform it back into an action
came to be regarded as a transgression; any actualization diminishes the ideal by confining it to a particular time and place and
person. "*Action, Action, Action,*" Garrick had demanded of drama.[29]
The Romantics replied, "Action is transitory"; "We do not like to see
our author's plays acted."

The French Revolution enacted the philosophy of the Enlightenment: it turned books back into actions, ideals back into tangible particulars. It performed thought, and the performance was, predictably, inadequate. Edmund Burke, politician and aesthetician, sitting in a Channel-side seat, had an excellent view of the action and was seized at first by "astonishment at the wonderful Spectacle . . . what Spectators, and what actors!"[30] But within a year he had condemned the whole "monstrous tragi-comic scene."[31] It was monstrous to Burke in part because it was "tragi-comic"; in an ironic reversal of perspectives the English critic berated the French actors for abandoning neoclassical decorum and mixing dramatic genres.

Burke too quoted *Hamlet,* although the play hardly recommends itself to a critic contemptuous of tragicomedy. In his correspondence, as in that of Keats, it is quoted more often than any other Shakespeare play. Writing in 1790 of events in France, he declares, in Hamlet's words, "It is not nor It can not come to good."[32] In what would become the most famous sequence in *Reflections on the Revolution in France,* Burke condemned the French revolutionaries for their lack of "chivalry" toward Marie Antoinette. Burke's longtime friend and political associate Philip Francis, who saw the book in proof, particularly objected that this defense of Marie Antoinette was "pure foppery." Burke responded,

> What, are not high Rank, great splendour of descent, great personal Elegance and outward accomplishments ingredients of moment in forming the interest we take in the Misfortunes of Men? The minds of those who do not feel thus are not even Dramatically right. 'What's Hecuba to him or he to Hecuba that he should weep for her?' Why because she was Hecuba, the Queen of Troy, the wife of Priam, and suffered in the close of Life a thousand calamities. I felt too for Hecuba when I read the fine Tragedy of Euripides upon her Story . . .[33]

The quoted lines from *Hamlet* in the middle of this diatribe were (and are) so familiar that Burke did not even need to attribute them. They belong to the soliloquy in which Hamlet upbraids himself for his own cold inaction, contrasting it with the "passion" that an actor wastes upon a fiction. The quotation rose into Burke's mind because he was, like so many of his contemporaries, obsessed with English inaction. Hamlet is trying to rouse himself to kill a king; Burke was trying to rouse the English people to defend a king.

But Burke's quotation itself illustrates the extent to which Shake-

speare's lines had already floated free of their context; for in context
Hamlet finds it "monstrous"—the word Burke would use of the
Revolution—that the actor's passion is "all for nothing! For Hecuba!
. . . What would he do, / Had he the motive and the cue for passion, /
That I have?"34 As Burke uses the quotation, the "he" in question
has been transformed into a spectator, a reader not an actor; those
who are not moved by Euripides' play or Burke's book are not
responding as an audience should. Hamlet's incredulity at an exaggerated overemoting response has become Burke's condemnation
of a response (Philip Francis' or the English people's), which is not
extravagant or emotional enough. Burke argues that we should
indeed weep for the distant Hecuba and that consequently we
should, even more, both weep for and defend Marie Antoinette,
regardless of her guilt or innocence.

Burke's allusion to *Hamlet* here jostles with one to Euripides; in
his work as a whole, Shakespeare belongs with Milton, Virgil, Cicero, and the Bible among the venerable relics of a culture threatened by the irrational energy of change. In 1790 Edmond Malone
gave his fellow Irishman Edmund Burke a complimentary copy of
his edition of the *Plays and Poems of William Shakspeare;* Burke in turn
gave Malone a copy of "a pamphlet which I have lately published,"
*Reflections on the Revolution in France.*35 In the preface to his edition
Malone described The Right Honourable Edmund Burke as "a
great orator, philosopher, and statesman" who would rival Dr. Johnson as "the brightest ornament of the eighteenth century."36 Some
readers of Burke's *Reflections* explicitly compared its author to the
author of *Hamlet* ("Shakespeare himself is come again!").37 In 1796
Burke, congratulating Malone on his scholarship, congratulated
him on his politics as well: "Your admiration of Shakespeare would
be ill sorted indeed, if your Taste (to talk of nothing else) did not
lead you to a perfect abhorrence of the French Revolution, and all its
Works."38 Shakespeare's *Works,* for Burke and Malone, are natural
enemies to the "Works" of the French revolutionaries.

The quoting of *Hamlet* by English critics and poets in the decades
after 1789 not only expresses their obsession with political inaction
and artistic failure; it also constitutes, in itself, a form of cultural
inertia. As Jane Austen observed, Shakespeare's "thoughts and
beauties are so spread abroad that one touches them every where,
one is intimate with him by instinct.— . . . His celebrated passages
are quoted by every body; they are in half the books we open, and
we all talk Shakespeare, use his similies, and describe with his

descriptions"; consequently, "Shakespeare one gets acquainted with
without knowing how. It is a part of an Englishman's constitution."[39] "Constitution" was, of course, a word electrified with political meaning. An Englishman's political constitution was not, like the
new American or French alternatives, an identifiable piece of paper,
a rational construct, any more than an Englishman's physical constitution could be located in a specific organ of the body. Instead, that
mystical entity existed somehow, one had to believe, organically, as
an effusion of the whole. "Organic" was the adjective Coleridge
used to define and defend both the English class system and Shakespeare's poetry. Shakespeare's plays were broken down into fragments and then disseminated through the bloodstream of English
society, droplets of poetry suspended in a stable cultural solution.
By the end of the eighteenth century, Shakespeare had become part
of the English constitution.

As all their quoting from *Hamlet* demonstrates, the English managed to avoid a revolution in their literary institutions just as surely
as they avoided one in their political institutions. In the forty years
after the storming of the Bastille, Blake, Wordsworth, Coleridge,
Byron, Keats, and Shelley wrote their Romantic masterpieces, one
by one, and died or decayed, romantically, one by one. But Shakespeare and Milton, the twin crowned monarchs of the literature of
Great Britain—English poetry's royal family—still reigned at the
end of those forty years—if anything, even more secure in their
preeminence, no longer simply enthroned but also fixed atop "the
two glory-smitten summits of the poetic mountain."[40] Postrevolu-
tionary Romanticism in France toppled, temporarily at least, Racine
and Corneille; in Germany, Russia, and eastern Europe, Romanticism tore down neoclassicism and erected a new vernacular pantheon; in Italy it canonized Dante, after long neglect. But in
England literary loyalties held. Shakespeare and Milton still commanded the apex of the cone, on top and central.

It ought to surprise us that the English literary classes remained
so loyal to Shakespeare's reputation. After all, Hazlitt, describing in
1818 the writers of his own generation, recognized that the new
English poetry

> had its origin in the French revolution, or rather in those senti-
> ments and opinions which produced that revolution. . . . The
> change in the belles lettres was as complete, and to many persons
> as startling, as the change in politics, with which it went hand in

hand. . . . all was to be natural and new. Nothing that was established was to be tolerated.

Shakespeare, of course, was one of those unnew "established" things, which should have been intolerable, and Hazlitt repeatedly quotes him in cataloguing all that the new poets rejected:

> It could not be said of these sweeping reformers and dictators in the republic of letters, that 'in their train walked crowns and crownets; that realms and islands, like plates, dropt from their pockets' [quoted from *Antony and Cleopatra*] . . . They scorned 'degrees, priority, and place, insisture, course, proportion, season, form, office, and custom in all line of order' [quoted from *Troilus and Cressida*] . . . Their poetry . . . has 'no figures nor no fantasies' [quoted from *Julius Caesar*] . . . 'no trivial fond records' [quoted from *Hamlet*] . . . 'the marshal's truncheon, nor the judge's robe' [quoted from *Measure for Measure*]; neither tradition, reverence, nor ceremony, 'that to great ones 'longs' [quoted from *Measure for Measure*] . . .

Condemning such newfangled "metre ballad-mongering" (quoted from *Henry IV, Part I*), Hazlitt concludes that the typical Romantic poet "hates prose; he hates all poetry but his own; he hates the dialogues in Shakespeare."[41]

Hazlitt moves from prose to poetry to Shakespeare's mixture of poetry and prose. Politically, as Burke suggests, the long, costly, bloody war against France was undertaken to restore decorum; yet Shakespeare, jumbling prose and poetry, kings and clowns, was the most notorious of all disrespecters of aesthetic decorum. Shakespeare was a playwright; the English Romantics achieved their greatness in epics and essays, lyrics and lectures and letters, not drama. Shakespeare did not die young, did not leave fragments, did not despair, did not devote his poetry to prophecy or spiritual autobiography; proportionally, few of his lines stooped or rose to descriptions of nature; he could hardly be celebrated as an exemplar of the egotistical or geographical sublime. The Romantics valued originality far more than their predecessors had; Shakespeare had stolen much of his material from others. He could not be considered an exponent of the stylistic simplicity advocated by Coleridge's and Wordsworth's Preface to *Lyrical Ballads;* he had been condemned by every generation of critics since his own for his

deviations from simplicity, for verbal obesity and farfetched mutations of phraseology. When Hazlitt says that in the new poetry
"kings and queens were dethroned from their rank and station in
legitimate tragedy or epic poetry, as they were decapitated elsewhere,"[42] he was almost certainly defining "legitimate tragedy" in
terms of Shakespeare.

As Hazlitt's reference makes clear, aesthetic and political objections to Shakespeare went hand in hand. John Philip Kemble's
sympathetic portrayal of Coriolanus was one of the most successful
theatrical performances of the period, and according to Hazlitt,
"The whole dramatic moral of CORIOLANUS is that those who have
little shall have less, and that those who have much shall take all that
others have left." He concluded that "Shakespear himself seems to
have had a leaning to the arbitrary side of the question, perhaps
from some feeling of contempt for his own origin."[43] Even more
fundamentally, Hazlitt argued that tragedy itself was an absolutist
genre and that poetry and the theatre almost inevitably idealized
and romanticized tyrants like Coriolanus and Henry V. Likewise,
Tom Paine, the champion of democratic common sense in America
and France, condemned Burke's *Reflections on the Revolution* as "a
dramatic performance" full of "theatrical exaggerations"; for Paine
the theatre was a realm of aristocratic falsehood, and "Mr. Burke
should recollect that he is writing History, and not *Plays*."[44] When
Paine alluded to Shakespeare at all, he associated him with the
ancien régime; Burke's pamphlet and the system of government it
defended would soon disappear into "the family vault of all the
Capulets"; in England's corrupt Parliament "the Comedy of Errors
concludes with the Pantomime of HUSH."[45] William Cobbett, the
most influential English agitator of the period, objected to Shakespeare's "bombast and puns and smut" and characterized his plays
as a concoction of "wild and improbable fiction, bad principles of
morality and politicks, obscurity in meaning, bombastical language"; he complained that "hundreds of thousands of pounds had
been expended upon embellishing his works; [and] numerous commentators and engravers and painters and booksellers had got fat
upon the trade." Cobbett's explanation for Shakespeare's reputation
is equally damning. He asks, "What can make an audience in London sit and hear, and even applaud, under the name of Shakespear,
what they would hoot off the stage in a moment, if it came forth
under any other name?"—and he answers, "It is *fashion*. These

books are in fashion. Every one is ashamed not to be in the fashion."
Hamlet and *King Lear* are like fad foods; it is "the *fashion* to extol the
virtues of potatoes, as it has been to admire the writings of Milton
and Shakespear."[46]

Shakespeare could have been dethroned, just as George III could
have been, but for some reason neither was. Why did Shakespeare's
cultural supremacy survive and, indeed, expand during a revolutionary period when idols were being replaced all over Europe? It is
as though Hamlet had failed to kill Claudius.

But before we can explain why the English Romantics failed to
topple Shakespeare, we first have to explain when and how Shakespeare had made it to the top. The "when" is easy to define. Everyone agrees that, after a slow but steady upward climb, Shakespeare's
coronation as the King of English Poets finally occurred in the
middle of the eighteenth century, at some time between the death of
Alexander Pope (1744) and the birth of William Wordsworth
(1770); or, to put it another way, between the second Jacobite rebellion (1745) and the first year of Lord North's ministry (1770), which
would precipitate and then lose the war in America. In 1751–56
William Hawkins, Professor of Poetry at Oxford, gave (in Latin) the
first academic lectures on "Shakesperio" in a British university;[47] on
the Sunday before Christmas, 1772, Mrs. Hester Thrale "heard for
the first Time Shakespear's Plays quoted in the Pulpit the Passage
was from Hamlet."[48] Between 1751 and 1772 Shakespeare had
conquered both academia and ecclesia.

If you insist on naming a particular year, 1760 will do as well as
any. In 1760 a professor of Greek at Cambridge University publicly
declared that the excellencies of Æschylus, Sophocles, and Euripides were "all united and surpass'd in the immortal and inimitable
Shakespear"; in 1760 *The British Magazine,* comparing "the two
great dramatic genius's of France and England," found Corneille
"greatly inferior to Shakespear"; in 1760 *The Critical Review*
remarked that "our immortal Shakespear" possessed "vast powers
as a tragic writer [which] remain unrivalled"; in 1760 the first major
exhibition of contemporary English art included five paintings of
scenes or characters from Shakespeare; in 1760 a peer of the realm,
in a little book so popular that it ran through three editions in that
year alone, declared that "If Human Nature were quite destroyed,
and no Monument left of it except [Shakespear's] Works, other
Beings might know *what Man was* from those Writings."[49] It would
not be entirely perverse to suggest that in 1760 William Shake-

speare and George III together simultaneously ascended the English throne.

BOOK II

By every measure of material prosperity—wealth, military power, political stability, population growth, upward mobility, industrial innovation—the eighteenth century was good to England. The theatres prospered. From 1747 to 1776 David Garrick ran Drury Lane, combining the functions of leading actor and what we would call artistic director, to the considerable profit both of himself and the theatre. During that time he made repeated improvements and alterations to the building; its capacity gradually swelled from about 1,200 at midcentury to almost 2,300 by the 1780s. During Garrick's tenure the rival theatre at Covent Garden could accommodate almost 2,200 spectators; in 1782 it was expanded again, to hold another 300. During the early years of the French Revolution the two theatres ballooned once more: Covent Garden by September 1792 could hold 3,013 customers; while Drury Lane, having leap-frogged it in size, could open its doors to over 3,600 by the spring of 1794. This expansion of theatrical auditoriums in London was accompanied by the erection of new theatres in the provinces. Bath built a new theatre in 1705, York was supporting its own regular repertory company by 1730, by the 1740s Norwich had one; Birmingham, Bristol, Liverpool, Portsmouth—every English town of any size or self-importance had its own theatre. Outside London, England was better equipped with theatres in the late eighteenth century than in the late twentieth. Both the demand that justified such expansions and the capital that financed them demonstrate the commercial vitality of the entertainment industry.

Artistic vitality was another matter altogether. The expanding theatrical market created an increased demand for plays: twice as many new plays were written between 1750 and 1800 as in the preceding fifty years.[50] But in the century after John Gay's *The Beggar's Opera* (1728), English theatres produced only three and a half new plays that have been canonized by later generations: Goldsmith's *She Stoops to Conquer* (1773), Sheridan's *The Rivals* (1775) and *The School for Scandal* (1777), and his short comic afterpiece *The Critic* (1779). Noticeably, all were comedies; even more than at the

beginning of the century Shakespeare dominated the serious repertoire by default. In the three decades of Garrick's tenure at Drury
Lane, for instance, six of Shakespeare's seven most popular plays
were tragedies; all six featured among the twenty most frequently
performed plays of the period.[51] In the last quarter of the eighteenth century all but four of the most popular dramatic entertainments were comedies, many of them musical comedies; the four
exceptional serious plays were all by Shakespeare.[52]

Many critics throughout this period remarked upon the garish
shoddiness of new plays. Burke, for instance, complained that the
stage had "sunk . . . into the lowest degree; I mean with regard to
the trash that is exhibited on it"; but he did not blame this decline
upon "the taste of the audience" because when Shakespeare was
performed "the boxes, pit, and gallery, are crowded."[53] An enthusiasm for Shakespeare was proof, by definition, of good taste, even if
in every other respect the taste of such audiences seemed execrable.

As contemporary drama sank, theatre managers clung to the
wreckage of past success; and Shakespeare was the safest dramatist
in the repertoire. They exercised their ingenuity by attempting to
make greater use of a brand name that had attracted customers in
the past, scouring the canon for revivable or adaptable plays that
had been relatively neglected in previous decades. Thus, Garrick
made his own reputation in (Cibber's adaptation of) *Richard III;* in
his performances, it became the third most popular play of the
period. Earlier that year (1741) Charles Macklin, playing Shylock,
had transformed *The Merchant of Venice* into a thrilling tragicomedy,
which he went on playing for almost half a century.

In the same production Portia was played by Kitty Clive and
Nerissa by Hannah Pritchard. Actresses, too, were searching for
new roles, and they found many of them in Shakespeare's comedies.
In 1740–41 *Twelfth Night, As You Like It, The Winter's Tale,* and *All's
Well That Ends Well* were all revived for the first time in the eighteenth century; the last three had apparently not been performed
since the closing of the theatres in 1642. All four feature strong
female leads, and their successful reappearance on London stages
reflects the talent, ambition, and professional power of a new wave
of actresses. Clive and Pritchard teamed up as Celia and Rosalind,
or Olivia and Viola, or Katherine and Bianca. Clive also played Celia
to the Rosalind of Peg Woffington, who was particularly famous for
her liberated vitality on and off stage; she specialized in transvestite

roles and eventually played most of Shakespeare's major comic heroines. When Mrs. Cibber starred as Isabella in *Measure for Measure*,
revived for the first time in 1738, "the elegance of her figure, the
musical plaintiveness of her voice, and the gentleness of her manners" affected audiences as strongly as it did Angelo.54 Although
Falstaff had always been admired, since the Restoration Shakespeare had been primarily celebrated, in practice, as a tragic dramatist; these actresses pulled his romantic comedies up into the
repertoire. Garrick, by contrast, had no roles in what became, in
the middle of the century, Shakespeare's most popular comedies
(*The Merchant of Venice, As You Like It,* and *The Merry Wives of Windsor*).55

Romeo and Juliet, a romantic tragedy seldom performed (even in
adapted form) before midcentury, was even more successful. It was
revived in 1744, and Eliza Haywood praised it as "the very best and
most agreeable of all the Tragedies" of Shakespeare.56 Like other
plays that dominated the repertoire in this period, it pitted a strong
female lead against a strong male, and audiences took an active
interest in which of two popular performers would dominate the
other. This shifting balance of power generated much of the excitement when Pritchard and Garrick joined battle as Beatrice and
Benedict, or Lady Macbeth and Macbeth. Competition between
male and female lead was matched by competition between companies. For twelve successive nights in September and October 1750
both Drury Lane and Covent Garden offered alternative productions of *Romeo and Juliet,* with Garrick and Anne Bellamy billed
against Spranger Barry and Susanna Cibber in the title fight; thereafter it remained a staple of the London season. The two theatres
also competed with rival adaptations of *Cymbeline*.

Given the unique value of Shakespeare's dramatic capital within
the stock repertoire, either theatre could gain a considerable commercial advantage over the other by successfully linking, in the
minds of the playgoing public, its own name to William Shakespeare's. Such direct rivalry in marketing Shakespeare did not
become important until the 1740s. For most of the seventeenth
century Shakespeare's plays had belonged to one company or the
other. When the United Company broke in two in 1695 both halves
claimed Shakespeare, but no sustained rivalry developed; and from
1707 through the 1730s Drury Lane had a virtual monopoly on
serious drama, while its competitors devoted themselves to opera or

popular pantomime. Covent Garden, opened in 1732, for several years emphasized musical theatre; but by the early 1740s the two theatres were in direct competition for the same actors and audiences.

For the first time, though two rival companies both wanted to satisfy the public's proven willingness to spend money on Shakespeare, neither had legal preeminence or any obvious edge in Shakespearian credentials. Of the two managements, Drury Lane's proved the more adroit in appropriating the national dramatist. Garrick became a partner in the Drury Lane management in 1747; the theatre opened that autumn, 250 seats larger, with *The Merchant of Venice,* starring Macklin as Shylock and Clive as Portia, with a prologue written by Samuel Johnson and spoken by Garrick.

> When Learning's Triumph o'er her barb'rous Foes,
> First rear'd the Stage, immortal *Shakespear* rose;
> Each Change of many-colour'd Life he drew,
> Exhausted Worlds, and then imagin'd new:[57]

Garrick's admirers would later proclaim that he had, almost single-handed, rescued Shakespeare from generations of neglect.

But Garrick never did anything single-handed. The opening of the 1747 season at Drury Lane depended, characteristically, upon the combined talents of Macklin, Clive, Johnson, and Garrick, among others. That season brought together for the first time Garrick, Clive, Pritchard, and Mrs. Cibber, and the trio of great actresses was vital to the success of Garrick's management. When Henry Fielding remarked that, *"after the nicest strokes of a Shakespear . . .* some Touches of Nature will escape the Reader, which the judicious Action of a *Garrick,* of a *Cibber,* or a *Clive,* can convey to him,"[58] he treated Cibber and Clive as Garrick's equals—and elsewhere he added "Mrs. *Woffington*" to the list.[59] For Fielding, Clive was to acting what Shakespeare was to poetry and Hogarth to painting; for *"true Humour"* she was *"the greatest Actress the World ever saw."*[60] Pritchard was Garrick's partner in 652 performances, and Hester Thrale "always thought Pritchard superior to Garrick; he felt her so in one Scene of Hamlet, one of Macbeth . . . when all the spontaneous Applause of the House ran to *her."*[61] Garrick stopped acting *Macbeth* when Pritchard retired.

But Garrick was a man and a manager as well as a performer; for a quarter of a century he shaped Drury Lane, which in turn shaped Shakespeare. During Garrick's tenure Shakespeare accounted for 27 percent of the tragedies at Drury Lane, and 16 percent of the comedies.[62] As an actor Garrick was celebrated, with increasing frequency, as Shakespeare's "best Commentator."[63] As a producer he repeatedly claimed that he was bringing back the original texts, for the first time performing a play "As written by Shakespeare" or "with restorations from Shakespeare"; and he did consistently restore much of the detail of Shakespeare's language. He consulted contemporary editors about individual readings, from Warburton and Johnson for *Macbeth* (1744) to Edward Capell for *Antony and Cleopatra* (1758). He also collected an admirable personal library of early texts of Shakespeare and his contemporaries, of great value to editors in his own time and since.

For Garrick, as an actor, what was seen mattered as much as what was spoken. In 1755 he erected a "Temple of Shakespeare" on the grounds of his estate at Hampton; in 1758 he placed within it a specially commissioned life-size marble statue of Shakespeare, by Louis François Roubiliac, the most important sculptor working in England in the eighteenth century. Garrick's statue was intended to surpass Westminster Abbey's, and by general consent it does. Garrick himself allegedly posed as Shakespeare.

Garrick became what Alexander Pope had been before him, England's most painted, drawn, and sculpted cultural figure; and many of those likenesses showed him in his Shakespearian roles. In 1769 Gainsborough painted Garrick leaning against a bust of Shakespeare—but also, in the same gesture, folding it proprietorially in the crook of his right arm. In the same year Garrick achieved his marketing masterpiece, a "Shakespeare Jubilee" at Stratford-upon-Avon. Reported in newspapers throughout Europe, the jubilee spawned Stratford's literary tourism industry and Garrick's commemorative musical afterpiece, *The Jubilee*, which played for 152 performances at Drury Lane—making it more popular, in the period as a whole, than all but three of Shakespeare's own plays.

No doubt Garrick's admiration for Shakespeare was as genuine as anyone else's, but in promoting Shakespeare he was always successfully promoting himself and his company, too. His most popular role was Benedick, in *Much Ado about Nothing*;[64] he played that character for the first time just after his own marriage, so that all of the irony of the man's initial insistence that he would never marry, all of the satire on "Benedick the married man," reminded audiences of David Garrick the actor beneath Benedick the character. Both became deliciously vivid.

Garrick belongs beside Josiah Wedgwood and William Hogarth among the most astute eighteenth-century entrepreneurs of culture. Like most marketing claims before and since, his were misleading, if not deliberately dishonest. Shakespeare did not need Garrick to rescue him from any looming oblivion. As for restoring Shakespeare's words to the stage, in the case of *Macbeth* that meant cutting one-eighth of the 1623 text, retaining some of Davenant's scenic and musical elaborations in the witches' scenes, and writing a new death speech for Macbeth (played by Garrick). Garrick's *Macbeth* was undoubtedly much closer to Shakespeare's than Davenant's adaptation had been; but it was still a considerable distance from the play "as written by Shakespeare." Likewise, Garrick proclaimed his "Plan/To lose no *Drop* of that immortal Man" in the prologue to an adaptation of *The Winter's Tale* that omitted three of its five acts. Amid all the odes and ovations at the Shakespeare jubilee, not a word of Shakespeare was spoken. Garrick did not adapt all of Shakespeare's plays—but then, no one ever had. Like his predecessors, he adapted some but not others, and adapted some more heavily than others.

In his advertised aspirations to authenticity Garrick simply reverted to the appeal of the original patent companies at the Restoration. Like Davenant, he combined this authenticity with novelty: the novelty of new adaptations, of reviving plays that had not been seen before, of reverting to the original texts in place of adaptations, and throughout it all the novelty of Garrick's own interpretation of his roles. The advertisements for *Macbeth* juxtaposed the claim "As written by Shakespeare" with the promise "The Characters new Dress'd."

Such novelties should not obscure the essential conservatism of Garrick's appeal. Although he made a number of changes to the body of the theatre—gradually removing spectators from the stage itself, improving stage lighting and the artistry of set design—they all merely reformed and refined the spirit of the early eighteenth century without radically redirecting it. Garrick gave—and his audience welcomed—not much new but, rather, more and better of the old. The rise of Shakespeare coincided with the growth of cultural conservatism.

It also coincided with upsurgent nationalism and expansive imperialism. While Garrick managed Drury Lane, Britain fought and decisively defeated France in the Seven Years War; the Tories, after decades in the wilderness, were readmitted to some measure of influence at court; Samuel Johnson, the nation's most visible literary Tory, was granted a pension; and a series of ministries tried to impose Britain's will on its American colonies. In 1753 an impassioned reply to Voltaire's criticisms of Shakespeare observed that in Britain, "SHAKESPEAR is a kind of establish'd Religion in Poetry."[65] In 1756 Joseph Warton berated the "nauseous cant" of French and Frenchified critics who found Shakespeare "INCORRECT."[66] In 1760 an anonymous "Ode to the Muses," celebrating Shakespeare, recalled that in *Henry the Fifth* he had shown

> . . . how great Henry's vengeful lance
> Humbled the crested pride of France,
> With arms triumphant shook the haughty state,
> And rear'd his banners in their vanquish'd land;[67]

During the 1760s writers fell over one another in proclaiming Shakespeare the world's greatest dramatist and poet. Such praises were almost always nationalistic in tone and often specifically anti-French. In 1768 Capell's edition described Shakespeare's works as "a part of the kingdom's riches" that were "talk'd of wherever the name of *Britain* is talk'd of, that is, (thanks to some late counsels) wherever there are men."[68] The next year at the jubilee—sitting smack in the middle between the end of the French war and the beginning of the American one—Garrick proclaimed that "*England* may justly boast the honour of producing the greatest dramatic poet in the world."[69] (This speech was probably written for Garrick by Burke.)

Like the critics, the theatres were openly chauvinistic. The French-supported, pro-Catholic Jacobite rebellion of 1745 prompted successful revivals of Cibber's anti-Catholic satire *The Non-juror* and Shakespeare's *Henry V,* "With the glorious Victory of the English against the French in the Battle of Agincourt"; when Covent Garden produced *Papal Tyranny in the Reign of King John* (Cibber's adaptation of *King John*), Drury Lane responded with a revival of Shakespeare's play. In the same year the theatres began the practice, which would continue for two centuries, of commencing every performance with a rendition of "God Save the King." *Henry V* was revived annually during the Seven Years War; in 1761, incorporating a theatrical replica of George III's coronation procession, it achieved a phenomenal run of twenty-four performances in six weeks. During the reign of George III the king and queen regularly attended the theatres. In the 1790s Sadler's Wells produced a string of successful musicals glorifying English victories against the French, culminating in 1804 with the construction of a large tank filled with water for miniature reenactments of naval battles; the patent theatres responded with a spectacular new production of *Henry V; or, The Conquest of France* and with periodic revivals of *King John*. Henry V was one of John Philip Kemble's most acclaimed roles; his sister Mrs. Siddons was even more celebrated for her portrayal of Constance in *King John,* driven to madness and death by French perfidy.

England's victory in the Seven Years War was a decisive event in the growing international resistance to French political and cultural hegemony, and Shakespeare was the chief artistic beneficiary of that resistance. First in Germany, then successively in other parts of southern and eastern Europe, emergent literary nationalism and romanticism defined themselves, almost inevitably, in opposition to the dominant classical models. Politically, the only visible alternative to French absolutism was English liberty, as guaranteed by the English mixed constitution; aesthetically, the only visible alternative to the rules of the French Academy was the practice of English genius, a freedom from arbitrary critical decrees exemplified by the mixture of tones, genres, and social classes found in the plays of "Sachespir."[70] The English acclaimed Shakespeare as their greatest and most characteristic genius, as the paradigm of artistic freedom, in the very decade when England seemed to itself and others the modern world's most assured and successful experiment in political and social liberty. In that same decade Lessing's *Hamburgische Dramaturgie* praised the ghost in *Hamlet* and mocked the ghost in Voltaire's *Semiramis,* adopting as standards the dramatization of love in *Romeo and Juliet* and of jealousy in *Othello,* rebuking Voltaire's treatment of similar material in his most famous play, *Zaire.*

Most of the political revolutions of the later eighteenth century were attempts by disenfranchised peoples—American colonists, native Irishmen, colonized Italians, Haitian slaves, the French third estate—to claim for themselves liberties like those which native

Englishmen already enjoyed. One of those enviable English liberties was a right, and a determination, to celebrate their native
literature, in defiance of the fact that it did not conform to the
prevailing international aesthetic system. Any European critic who
wanted to raise the banner of Dante or Cervantes or medieval
romance could take comfort from English cultural independence.
The opposition between Shakespeare's practice and French aesthetic theory, the focus of critical argument for a century, became
the foundation of Shakespeare's expanding international reputation. Shakespeare became the exemplar of literary liberty, the titular champion of anyone who wanted to overthrow an exhausted
critical system.

This interpenetration of aesthetic and political values can be seen
clearly enough in Pierre Le Tourneur's preface to the first complete
French translation of Shakespeare's plays. The translation was
undoubtedly stimulated in part by Garrick's visits to Paris in 1763–
65 and by the international publicity generated by the jubilee in
1769; the first volume was published, coincidentally, in 1776. Le
Tourneur professedly does no more in his preface than string
together extracts from the prefaces to existing English editions
from Rowe to Johnson. But when he comes to Pope's statement that
"To judge . . . of *Shakespear* by *Aristotle*'s rules, is like trying a man by
the Laws of one Country, who acted under those of another," he
transforms it into "condamner Shakespeare d'après ces règles, c'est
juger un Républicain sur les loix d'une Monarchie étrangère."[71]
Pope's neutral opposition between one country and another has
been translated into Le Tourneur's image of an English republican
condemned by the laws of a (French) monarchy—a monarchy
defined, by the ambiguity of *étrangère,* not only as "foreign"
(from Shakespeare's perspective) but also as "strange, unnatural"
(from any perspective).

England's prosperity in the eighteenth century was built in part
on its success as a trading nation, and Shakespeare was one of its
most successful cultural exports. The English economy is still bank-
ing a handsome profit from the international market for Shakespeare opened up by eighteenth-century entrepreneurs. And once
that market had become truly international, foreign demand could
act as a periodic stimulus to domestic production. The *Hamlet* of
English Romantic criticism was, for instance, deeply in debt to
Goethe's novel *Wilhelm Meisters Lehrjahre* (1795–96) and August

Wilhelm von Schlegel's *Vorlesungen über dramatische Kunst und Litteratur* (1809–11); it was Goethe who, more memorably than any English writer, described the play as a story of "the effects of a great action laid upon a soul unfit for the performance of it," a story in which "There is an oak tree planted in a costly jar, which should have borne only pleasant flowers in its bosom; the roots expand, the jar is shivered."[72] Coleridge's appropriations from Schlegel and other German critics could be justified as nationalistic expropriations of foreign technologies, like the American theft of the design for the spinning jenny, expropriations designed to secure domestic markets for domestic producers. To the German "unser Shakespeare" Coleridge replied with "our Shakespear"; he appropriated and then further developed German critical innovations in order to ensure that England retained its threatened supremacy in the Shakespeare market.

England in the late eighteenth century exported Shakespeare; it also exported prints. English engravings, particularly caricatures, were the most popular art form of the 1790s and early 1800s. England's most successful exporter of prints was Alderman John Boydell. Like Garrick, Boydell set out to alloy Shakespeare, patriotism, and the profit motive. This must have seemed a natural combination, because Shakespeare was already the most popular source of allusions and captions in the work of English engravers.[73] In the late 1780s Boydell organized an exhibition of specially commissioned paintings of scenes from Shakespeare's plays, which were made the basis of a folio edition of large engravings. This ambitious project—and Boydell himself—was ruined commercially by England's war with France, which cut Boydell off from his vital Continental markets. Though in most respects the increasing association of Shakespeare with English nationalism fostered his European reputation, in France it created understandable hostility, lasting well into the next century: as late as 1822 a French audience, recognizing in Shakespeare "*un lieutenant de Wellington*," prevented *Othello* from being performed.[74]

But the commercial failure of Boydell's "Shakespeare Gallery" does not detract from its cultural importance. It was designed, among other things, to provide commercial encouragement for the development of "an *English School of Historical Painting*";[75] Shakespeare was chosen as the "one great National subject concerning which there could be no second opinion."[76] Boydell's new Pall Mall

Gallery opened on May 4, 1789, displaying what one reviewer acclaimed as "a treasure of graphic excellence in the highest degree creditable to British genius."[77]

Shakespeare had, along with Milton, already been instrumental in the development of a consciously English art during the eighteenth century. Hogarth, the first native visual artist to acquire an international reputation, in a self-portrait emblematically rests his palette on the works of Shakespeare, Milton, and Swift. Shakespeare provided matter, and a manner, that was perceived as quintessentially English; his artistic identity was defined for Georgian England in opposition to Continental traditions. Shakespeare, moreover, was the repository of a specifically English mythology, which artists could expect any educated viewer to recognize; in George III's England the satirical prints of Samuel Rowlandson and James Gilray quoted Shakespeare as automatically, and as confidently, as did Thomas Sheridan's parliamentary speeches and Horace Walpole's letters.

Shakespeare was also a dominant figure in two cultural forms that provided models for the native school of painting: books and theatres. Engravings could be used to illustrate books or could be sold separately as prints; often the same engraving served both purposes, and both incarnations could be bought in the same shop. At the same time, the theatre provided a new model, specifically native and contemporary, for the organization of visual space. Hogarth defined his own art in explicitly theatrical terms: "my Picture was my Stage and men and women my actors who were by Mean of certain Actions and express[ions] to Exhibit a dumb shew."[78] Popular actors and scenes from popular plays were among the most popular subjects for popular prints. And in an age when English art drew so much of its inspiration from the theatre, the theatre itself drew much of its inspiration from Shakespeare.

English artists were felt, and felt themselves, to be particularly adept at portraiture; since the Restoration, Shakespeare too had been especially praised for his portrayal of individuals, and his characters accordingly became natural subjects for Georgian artists. Portrait painting, and its ugly younger brother political caricature, expressed a more general Georgian fascination with individuality, a fascination bound up with the triumphal energies of expanding entrepreneurial capitalism, with the increasing upward pressure for political liberation of many kinds, with the rise of the

Methodist movement and lesser spiritualist sects. Garrick gave his last Shakespearian performance in the year which defined every individual's right to "life, liberty, and property" (the draft text) or "life, liberty, and the pursuit of happiness" (the revised text). This period also gave birth to the English eccentric, and Shakespeare's apotheosis took place during the eight years of serial publication of the greatest literary glorification of eccentricity, that unpredictable celebrity of the century, *Tristram Shandy*. (One of the eccentrics celebrated in that novel, Parson Yorick, is descended,—in fact,— fictitiously,—from "*Hamlet's Yorick*, in our *Shakespear*.")79

As the birth of political caricature demonstrates, this fascination with individuality does not entail untroubled endorsement of it. *Richard III,* that exorcism of grasping egocentric villainy, became after a century of neglect one of Shakespeare's most popular trage- dies, its title role played by the vulnerable little parvenu Da- vid Garrick; *The Merchant of Venice,* that exorcism of ruthless finan- cial villainy, became for the first time one of Shakespeare's most pop- ular comedies, its leading role played with sullen intensity by Macklin. But whether Shakespeare's enactments of egotism left Georgian spectators appalled or applauding—or, often, both— those enactments satisfied a newly intensified curiosity about the nature of individuality. The ambition of portrait painters who visualized Shakespeare's plays drew upon and contributed to an increasingly exclusive interest in defining characters. Commentators on and illustrators of Shakespeare's plays might be weak on over- all composition and structure, but they were keen on individual faces.

Such preoccupations shaped the very texts that eighteenth- century readers read. Rowe's 1709 edition had not only, for the first time, provided lists of dramatis personae and a consistent designa- tion of each character in speech prefixes; it had also sometimes substituted personal names for the generic labels found in the original texts. Rowe's successors carried this nominative process further, gradually mopping up any pockets of generic identification he had missed. "Bastard" in *King Lear* became Edmund, "Bastard" in *King John* became Falconbridge, "Bastard" in *Much Ado about Nothing* became Don John; "Clowne" in *As You Like It* became Touch- stone, in *Measure for Measure* Pompey, in *Love's Labour's Lost* Cos- tard; "King" throughout the English history plays and in half a dozen comedies and tragedies was broken down into individuated subsets. So long as a character was named at least once in the text, editors could impose that name throughout. Theatrical managers could go further, and invent individualities for characters Shakespeare had neglected ever to denominate. In *Henry IV, Part 1,* John Philip Kemble baptized with the good Scots nickname "Raby" a succession of speeches given to Hotspur's servant in scene 7 (2.4), to a messenger who reports to Hotspur in scene 12 (4.1), and to a messenger who reports to Hotspur in scene 17 (5.2), thereby creating an entirely plausible minor identity. In *All's Well That Ends Well* Kemble sorted the confusion of minor French lords into Lewis, Biron, Jaquez, and Tourville. *Et cetera.*

Speech prefixes were systematically relabeled in order to emphasize the individuality of all Shakespeare's characters; particular prefixes were also singled out for emendation in order to make the text more appropriate to received notions of character. One example out of many: in all editions of Shakespeare's plays from 1623 to 1732 Miranda had addressed Caliban as an "Abhorred Slave" and then violently rebuked him for another eleven lines;[80] in 1733 Theobald's edition, following the Dryden/Davenant adaptation, transferred the speech to Prospero, who kept it for two centuries. The coarse energy of the lines did not accord with editorial notions of feminine decorum.

The editorial rage for individuation was not limited to speech prefixes. Pope alphabetically indexed Shakespeare's characters (historical and fictional) by name, subdividing some of them into elaborated analytical outlines of their more important attitudes and actions. Johnson's commentary differed most obviously and memorably from that of his predecessors in its attention to critical assessment of character. In *Henry the Fifth,* for instance, the offstage death of Falstaff provokes a four-paragraph note on his character, the offstage execution of Bardolph another note, the final exit of Pistol yet another; an analysis of King Henry's character is appended to one of his speeches wooing Catherine; Johnson's endnote on the play devotes two of its five sentences to summary critiques of the characters of King Henry and Pistol.

The fascination with character was not limited to editors of Shakespeare. In 1774 William Richardson, Professor of Humanity at Glasgow University, published *A Philosophical Analysis and Illustration of some of Shakespeare's remarkable Characters,* which was soon followed by other influential works like *An Essay on the Dramatic*

Character of Sir John Falstaff by the civil servant Maurice Morgann (1777) and *Remarks on Some of the Characters of Shakespeare* by Member of Parliament Thomas Whateley (written 1768–69; published 1785). Excerpts from these and similar works soon found their way into editorial commentaries. To Johnson's edition Edmund Burke contributed a note on *Timon of Athens,* admiring Shakespeare's careful differentiation of Apemantus' misanthropy from Timon's;[81] to the later editions of Edmond Malone and George Steevens, Sir Joshua Reynolds contributed observations on the portrayal of Macbeth, Lear, and others.[82] Although we usually label those editions with the names of Johnson or Steevens or Malone or Boswell, their commentaries were in fact compilations that mixed the editor's own observations, those of previous editors, and those contributed by a widening circle of educated readers. In Steevens' case they also included notes written by the editor but facetiously or maliciously attributed to others. Those commentaries and texts were certainly shaped to a degree by the personalities of their titular editors, but they were also shaped by the social character of an entire period.

One spinoff of Boydell's Shakspeare Gallery was a new edition of Shakespeare, illustrated by small prints and edited by that ubiquitous Shakespearian, George Steevens. That edition, though of no importance to the history of editing, contributed to the incoming tide of Shakespeare texts, rising throughout the eighteenth century. Publishing of all kinds—of books, magazines, newspapers, prints—was one of the most successful industries of the period; in the bookshops as in the theatres, Shakespeare was a safe investment. Just as the audience capacity of theatres grew, so the number of editions of Shakespeare's complete works grew.[83] In the hundred years up to 1708 there had been four; in the hundred years after 1708 there were sixty-five, with each successive twenty-year period producing more such editions than its predecessor.

Theatres searched for new Shakespeare plays to perform and new ways to perform them; publishers searched for new ways to package the same old product. In 1709 Tonson shifted from single-volume folio to multivolume octavo. In 1711–12 Thomas Johnson began issuing *A Collection of the Best English Plays,* copying Shakespeare's texts from Tonson's 1709 edition but printing them "in small Volumes fit for the pocket"; they could be purchased separately but could also be bound together as a set of "10 handsom

Volumes."* Pocket books and serial publication became two of the
most profitable innovations in the eighteenth-century book trade.
Tonson responded with a pocket Shakespeare of his own; the 1714
reprint of Rowe's edition was published in a small duodecimo format. In 1725 Tonson published the six volumes of Pope's edition in
large elegant quartos, followed three years later by a second edition
in a more manageable duodecimo. In 1744 Sir Thomas Hanmer
published at Oxford an edition in quarto volumes even more sumptuous than Pope's. In 1773 readers could buy *Bell's Edition of Shakespeare's Plays, As they are now performed at the Theatres Royal in London;
Regulated from the Prompt Books of each House, by Permission;* in 1784
they could purchase the first new single-volume edition published
in a century. In 1795–96 American readers could buy an edition
printed on their side of the Atlantic.

But this proliferation of editions should not obscure the continuity and conservatism of the reading tradition. The editorial succession passed from Rowe to Pope to Theobald to Hanmer to
Warburton to Johnson to Steevens to Reed and Malone. Other
editions contributed to the marketing of Shakespeare throughout
and beyond the English-speaking world; but only that continuous
central tradition determined the text that others would dissemi-
nate. Moreover, that tradition was more homogenous in the second
half of the century than it had been in the first. Unlike his predecessors, Johnson chose his own successor, Steevens, who in turn
adopted Reed and Malone; Steevens and Malone eventually quar-
reled, but both continued to pay homage to Johnson, correcting
him politely or silently. Johnson was thus granted a retrospective
centrality that the quality of his editorial work hardly merited.
Steevens, Reed, and Malone—unlike their predecessors—each
worked on more than one major edition, so that between them they
wholly dominated Shakespeare editing from 1773 to 1821. And
each of the editions in that legitimate succession was based, literally,
upon its immediate predecessor; each editor created his own new
edition by marking up a copy of the previous edition, deleting some
of his predecessors' observations, adding his own, adding or sub-
tracting emendations, and then dispatching this palimpsest to the
printer. Johnson institutionalized the practice, already initiated to a

---

*Johnson, though an English bookseller catering to the English market, oper-
ated out of the Netherlands in order to evade the 1709 copyright act; his piracies of
Tonson's text were therefore legal.

lesser degree by Theobald and Warburton, of incorporating the remarks of previous editors even when he disagreed with them, and thereafter the main editions were relentlessly assimilative; as a result they grew in size from the eight volumes of Johnson in 1765 to the twenty-one volumes of Boswell in 1821.

Editions of Shakespeare grew organically, like the English constitution, like English law, by corporate incorporation, a prolonged and collaborative process of accumulation and inclusion. Moreover, old editions continued to be reprinted alongside the editions that superseded them. Thomas Hanmer's 1744 text, for instance, rose again in 1745, 1747, 1748, 1751, 1760, 1761, and 1771; that first American edition, of 1795–96, was simply a reincarnation of Johnson's edition, first published three decades earlier; the title pages of reprints continued to parade the names of Steevens and Malone until 1864. Like vestigial organs, outdated editions became part of the constitution of Shakespeare.

The form in which these editions reproduced themselves was conservative; the burden of material carried over from the past increasingly tended to dwarf the commentary original to each new edition. Editors wished to conserve as much as possible of the past. The material and intellectual relics of Elizabethan England had, for them, an intrinsic interest, beyond any question of their utility to the present. This privileging of the past soon liberated itself from any immediate pertinence to the text. Malone's prolix investigations of Shakespeare's biography and the history of the English stage did not limit themselves to questions that might affect the determination or explication of the text. Malone belonged to a society increasingly conscious of the difference between its habits and those of earlier epochs, increasingly curious about the texture of past cultures. After all, Edward Gibbon's *History of the Decline and Fall of the Roman Empire* was published in installments between 1776 and 1788; its author was a member of Dr. Johnson's literary club, to which Malone also belonged, as did the finest practitioner and theorist of the English school of historical painting, Sir Joshua Reynolds.

In this intellectual climate it is not surprising that Shakespeare's history plays became more popular than ever, both in and out of England. In 1768 Lessing wrote that Shakespeare's histories "stand to the tragedies of French taste much as a large fresco stands to a miniature painting intended to adorn a ring." Friedrich Schiller, whose achievement in dramatizing German history was inspired and guided by Shakespeare's example, earned his living as a professor of history from 1789 to 1791. A. W. von Schlegel described Shakespeare's cycle of English chronicle plays as "a historical heroic poem in the dramatic form";[84] of the seventeen plays he translated between 1797 and 1810, nine were English histories. And the nineteenth-century Briton most often compared to Shakespeare was not Keats or any of the Romantic poets but Sir Walter Scott, who redirected the energies of the English novel by creating an immensely popular model of historical romance.

As Scott's novels demonstrate, the eighteenth century's new historicism produced a new aesthetic appreciation of antiques. The works of antiquity had, of course, long been admired; but previous critics had extolled them for a universality that transcended the passage of time. Now, by contrast, evidence of the passage of time itself became part of their charm. *A Discourse on Ancient and Modern Learning* recognized that modern readers lose much of the meaning of an ancient work but suggested that in compensation such works "appear to us in the Splendor and Formality of Strangers," embellished with "several Graces that arise merely from the Antiquity of an Author."[85] Oldness became a relished attribute. The age that produced the run of great Shakespeare editions from Johnson to Malone was also the age that celebrated and even constructed ruins; that purchased innumerable curios carved from the wood of a mulberry tree Shakespeare had planted in Stratford; that avidly read *The Castle of Otranto,* the first Gothic novel, said to be printed from an ancient manuscript; that thrilled to the wrinkles of the ancient Gaelic bard Ossian; that discovered and acclaimed the poetry of the fifteenth-century Bristol monk Thomas Rowley.

This age of antiques was also, inevitably, an age of fakes. Rowley's poems, Ossian's epic, and *The Castle of Otranto* were all written by eighteenth-century writers, consciously creating the appropriately discolored documents of an imagined past, satisfying the appetite for antiques better than the antiques themselves. This impulse to create a literary past, to invent the manuscripts that should have been written, spread throughout Europe, from Britain to Bohemia, Russia to Rumania. To this period also belong the most famous of all Shakespeare impostures, a series of documents, poems, and plays forged by William Henry Ireland, admired at the time by many readers until they were discredited by Malone.

It is no coincidence that the rise of historicism coincided with a boom in literary frauds. In the historicist dispensation the value of an object no longer depended upon a judgment of its aesthetic merit but upon a determination of its origin. By putting a price tag on antiquity, this system of evaluation created a market for faked obsolescence and therefore needed to develop the critical machinery for distinguishing genuine from spurious. Malone began his career as a Shakespeare editor with an edition of the seven apocryphal plays added to the canon in 1664 and peremptorily ejected by Pope in 1725. Malone concluded, essentially, that Pope had been right about six of the seven (all but *Pericles*); but his method radically differed from Pope's. Pope had justified the expulsion of all seven plays on the basis of his own judgment of "all the distinguishing marks of [*Shakespear's*] style, and his manner of thinking and writing";[86] Malone documented those stylistic impressions and at the same time investigated the reliability of the documents that had assigned the plays to Shakespeare.

This pursuit of documentary authenticity contributed to the increasing critical dissatisfaction with performances of Shakespeare's plays. Even when eighteenth-century admirers praised Garrick as "the best commentator" on Shakespeare, they were unconsciously proclaiming the primacy of the book; actors were judged as commentators, marginal servants of the printed text. What reviewers called the "new readings" of performers were evaluated just as critically as the new emendations of editors. And for the most part, when the theatre was judged "by the book," it was found wanting. On the one hand the theatre continued to make use of adapted texts, performing passages that were "spurious" (because written by someone other than Shakespeare) and omitting passages that were "genuine" (because written by Shakespeare). On the other hand performances were not historically accurate in their treatment of costume and setting. Accordingly, Boydell's "first instruction" to the artists contributing to his Shakspeare Gallery was to "forget, if possible, they had ever seen the plays of Shakespeare, as they are absurdly decorated in modern theatres." Why? Among other reasons, because "In a playhouse, anachronisms are so little guarded against, that discordant devices, and modern arms, are frequently associated with ancient ensigns and weapons peculiar to distinct nations, and ages remote from each other."[87] The theatre was not authentic; the authentic Shakespeare could be found only in books or in paintings, in fixed historical idealizations.

We still rely upon documents first discovered by Malone and Steevens and their contemporaries; their conclusions about many matters of historical interpretation have been vindicated by subsequent scholarship. But the cast of mind that produced those discoveries also produced the political philosophy of Edmund Burke. Burke judged events in France against the native canonical standard established by the Glorious Revolution of 1688, a paradigm characterized by a limited program based on gentlemanly consensus and the unwritten common law. The French Revolution did not follow that pattern; instead, as always, the chaotic variety of the present contrasted painfully with the apparently perfect order and closure of the past. Burke and Malone judged the French Revolution as though it were a new work of literature or a new emendation, seeking admittance to the canon. They rejected it because, like French drama, it insisted that cultural practice should be governed by a logical, rigorous, unforgiving, formally articulated set of intellectual ideals. As the Glorious Revolution was to politics, Shakespeare was to literature: an ad hoc native model, scornful of a priori principles, adopting and adapting accepted national practice, endorsed by subsequent generations. In Malone's treatment of Shakespeare, as in Burke's treatment of the French Revolution, what is altogether new is by definition spurious; the past validates; past authority authenticates present actions. The most influential editors and interpreters of Shakespeare shared with Burke that compound allegiance to the past which Tom Paine questioned in *Rights of Man:*

> The circumstances of the world are continually changing, and the opinions of men change also; and as government is for the living, and not for the dead, it is the living only that has any right to it. That which may be thought right and found convenient in one age, may be thought wrong and found inconvenient in another. In such cases, Who is to decide, the living, or the dead?[88]

Malone and Burke would have answered in unison, "the dead." Shakespeare was part of that past which they wanted to protect from a radical future, part of the past with which they protected England from a revolution.

BOOK III

Neither Shakespeare nor George III was overthrown in 1789. That climactic nonevent was the culmination of a series of failed cultural revolutions that affected the perception and reception of Shakespeare throughout the eighteenth and into the nineteenth century.

The first would-be rebel against Shakespeare's aesthetic sovereignty had been Thomas Rymer, who haunted Shakespeare criticism from Dryden to Coleridge. In *The Tragedies of the Last Age* (1677) Rymer's devastating and thorough critiques of *A King and No King, Rollo Duke of Normandy,* and *The Maid's Tragedy* struck a blow at the reputations of Beaumont and Fletcher from which those dramatists have never recovered. He had originally intended to include a similar analysis of *Othello, Julius Cæsar,* and *Catiline* in the same volume, but in the event postponed consideration of those plays for another time. The promised second volume did not appear for sixteen years, so that the critique of Beaumont and Fletcher was irreparably separated from the critique of Shakespeare, making it possible to accept the first and reject the second, although both employed the same critical and rhetorical strategy. By contrast with his first book, *A Short View of Tragedy* (1693) was badly written and badly organized; it devoted most of its attention to *Othello,* seeming to belabor that play at inordinate length. By saying little about *Julius Cæsar,* by including a critique of Jonson's *Catiline,* by not discussing the increasingly popular *Hamlet,* Rymer lost the intensity of focus and breadth of attack that had made his reevaluation of Beaumont and Fletcher so persuasive. Shakespeare's admirers could parry Rymer's criticism simply by treating *Othello* as an uncharacteristically faulty work: although it continued to be performed, it lost the primacy among Shakespeare's tragedies that it had enjoyed for most of the seventeenth century. Shortly before *A Short View* was published Rymer had been appointed Historiographer Royal, a responsibility that occupied him for the rest of his life; he had neither the time nor the inclination to pursue his critique of Shakespeare. Finally, Rymer's arguments were taken up five years later in Jeremy Collier's wholesale condemnation of the English theatre, which anyone committed to the drama was bound to resist, tooth and quill. A critique of particular dramatic practices was swallowed up in an attack on the practice of drama itself.

Moreover, between *The Tragedies of the Last Age* and *A Short View,* Rymer had published his own single mediocre play *Edgar;* he had not been able to secure a performance, and the ineptitude of his own creative efforts made him an easy target for personal satire (particularly by successful playwrights). Dryden conceded that "Almost all the Faults which he has discover'd are truly there;

yet who will read Mr. *Rym*—or not read *Shakespear?*"[89] Addison facetiously announced that "the Plays of many unsuccessful Poets" were to be "artificially cut and shreaded" in order to provide theatrical snow showers: "Mr. *Rimer's Edgar* is to fall in Snow at the next acting of King *Lear*, in order to heighten, or rather to alleviate, the Distress of that unfortunate Prince; and to serve by way of Decoration to a Piece which that great Critick has written against."[90]

In these circumstances it is hardly surprising that Rymer did not succeed in undermining Shakespeare's reputation; he was an ingrown outsider, whose arguments were weakened by faults of style, organization, and presentation. His challenge was nevertheless so forceful that he became at once, and has remained, the bogeyman of Shakespeare idolatry. Dryden nationalistically accused Rymer of aiming "at the destruction of our Poetical Church and State."[91] Rowe wrote that, since he did not intend to "enter into a Large and Compleat Criticism upon Mr. *Shakespear's* Works," no one could expect him to "take notice of the severe Remarks that have been formerly made upon him by Mr. *Rhymer*." Having refused to deal in detail with Rymer's arguments, he nevertheless devoted a paragraph to speculating on Rymer's motives for attacking Shakespeare—was it "Vanity" or "Pique"? Rowe of course mentioned Rymer's own unsuccessful "Sample of Tragedy"; he objected to "the Tyranny of Pedants"; he opined that "the Beauties of *Shakespear*" should be mentioned alongside any discussion of his faults. In another paragraph Rowe again protested that he "won't pretend to enquire into the Justness of Mr. *Rhymer's* Remarks on *Othello*" but wished that he had "observ'd some of the Beauties too."[92] Theobald in 1733, Warburton in 1747, Johnson in 1765 all found it necessary to abuse Rymer.

Eighteenth-century critics, who for the most part accepted Rymer's social prejudices, could not reject his attack by rejecting his critical categories; they rejected it instead by claiming that Shakespeare had seen beyond categories. Johnson's critique of Rymer was decisive. His famous preface did not contribute any original arguments to the debate over neoclassicism, but it magisterially summed up and endorsed the scattered insights of lesser critics; what Johnson said mattered less than the fact that he was saying it—with all the verbal and cultural authority of the most respected conservative critic of the English Enlightenment. If even Johnson was abandoning neoclassical precepts, then clearly they were no longer defensible. Thus, in a passage often quoted, Johnson replied to "Rhymer

. . . and Voltaire" by stressing Shakespeare's indifference to "the casual distinction of country and condition":

> His story requires Romans or kings, but he thinks only on men
> . . . He was inclined to shew an usurper and a murderer not only
> odious but despicable; he therefore added drunkenness to his
> other qualities, knowing that kings love wine like other men, and
> that wine exerts its natural power upon kings. These are the petty
> cavils of petty minds.[93]

In fact, this passage does not prove that Shakespeare was indifferent to categories; it proves only that, in *Hamlet,* the character Claudius belongs to the category "murderous usurper," not to the category "king." Shakespeare never showed a legitimate hereditary king— like James I—as a drunkard. But Johnson's defense and others like it, however illogical, carried the day, thereby creating the myth that Shakespeare looked at experience directly, unrestricted by aesthetic models or epistemological categories. Rymer's critical uprising against Shakespeare was thus eventually suppressed.

Eighteenth-century England also put down two attempted revolutions in the theatre, which had long-term consequences for Shakespeare's cultural supremacy. The first had begun during the 1720s, when the practice of licensing plays before their performance gradually lapsed. During the same period the legal monopoly held by the two patent companies was flouted more and more regularly, so that by the mid-1730s as many as five companies were performing plays in London simultaneously. These changes effectively transformed the institutional shape imposed upon the English theatre by the Restoration. This new, unregulated, competitive situation produced a good deal of dramatic experimentation, much of it satirically directed against the Walpole administration. In June 1737 Walpole's Parliament retaliated by passing a new licensing act. This frankly punitive legislation reversed the theatrical revolution in progress for a decade. It restored the old two-theatre monopoly, confirming the exclusive royal patents held by Drury Lane and Covent Garden; it also required that all new plays and additions to old plays be approved in advance by an official licenser. Both provisions were enforced. If the act had been passed a decade earlier, *The Beggar's Opera* would almost certainly never have been licensed. The new legislation drove Henry Fielding out of business as a theatrical manager, transformed by act of Parliament from a dramatist into a novelist. What visibly and particularly happened to Fielding happened less visibly but more generally to literary talent everywhere. The press was a thronging competitive marketplace eager to exploit literary workmen; the theatre was an artificial duopoly offering a very limited outlet for new products.

The licensing act was not aimed at Shakespeare, but it affected his reputation in several ways. By discouraging literary talent from a career in the theatre it reduced the prospects that Shakespeare's work would be superseded by contemporary artists of comparable genius; by discouraging experimentation it tended to confine new work to the tired or hysterical reiteration of formulas handled with more freshness and assurance in the past; by weakening the quality of new work it made old work seem stronger in comparison. The act thus strengthened Shakespeare's domination of the English theatre for a century. As Eliza Haywood observed, "if the Town cannot have new Plays they will come to old ones"; old plays were preferred by theatre managers (who did not have to share their profits with living playwrights) and by actors (who were saved "the Trouble of studying new Parts").[94]

The act also intensified and accelerated the shift, already unstoppable, from the stage to the page. And the rise of the novel, though it depleted the imaginative resources and cultural authority of the theatre, actually enhanced Shakespeare's reputation. Novels did not need to worry about the unity of time or place, or the decorums of predetermined genres; they could, and often did, encompass an expansive sprawl of characters from every level of society. It did not take critics long to realize that "The plays of our SHAKESPEARE are many of them formed on the plan of novels, and of novels more evidently romantic";[95] Goethe's novel *Meister Wilhelm's Lehrjahre* claimed that all Shakespeare's plays—and *Hamlet* in particular—belonged to a literary genre halfway between drama and novel. One might summarize earlier neoclassical objections to Shakespeare by saying that his plays were too much like novels. Seventeenth-century critics had not phrased the issue in that way because novels had not been invented yet or, if invented, had not been recognized as a distinct and legitimate literary genre. But the burgeoning popularity of the novel in the eighteenth century acclimatized the reading public to conventions that had seemed unnatural and objectionable to earlier critics.

One attempted revolution in the theatre was ended in June 1737; another failed exactly fifty years later, in June 1787, when John Palmer opened his new 2,500-seat Royalty Theatre in east London. Palmer had hoped that he could simply ignore the patent monopolies, as other managers had done in the 1720s and 1730s; but the "legitimate" theatres were determined to enforce their royal prerogative, and Palmer's license from the governor of the Tower of London could not defend him against the licensing act. The Royalty Theatre opened only to close. Palmer's failure in one sense simply reinforced and prolonged the consequences of the parliamentary suppression of 1737, by confirming that a frontal assault upon the licensing act was suicidal. But in fact the monopoly could no longer be effectively enforced; Drury Lane, Covent Garden, and the Haymarket opera, all located in a small area of the West End of London, simply could not supply the public demand for entertainment in a city that had long since become the largest metropolis in Europe. As Palmer had argued, the more than 200,000 people residing in east London needed "a well formed and established Theatre" of their own.[96] The licensing act meant in effect that such markets could not be supplied with spoken drama or opera, so the demand for entertainment was supplied instead by various combinations of music and spectacle: puppet shows, equestrian circuses, ballets, pantomimes, the nonoperatic anything-goes music-drama called burletta. Begotten by ingenuity upon necessity, burletta evolved as an evasion of the licensing act and, in turn, gave birth to melodrama, the most popular dramatic form of the nineteenth century. The first English play calling itself a "Melo-Drame," Thomas Holcroft's *A Tale of Mystery*, opened on November 13, 1802. The age of literary Romanticism, and of Romantic criticism of Shakespeare, was the age of melodrama.

Holcroft's play was performed at Covent Garden. Against the challenge of burletta the patent theatres defended themselves with melodrama. Against the challenge of theatres outside the West End, catering to a large unsatisfied market, the patent theatres defended themselves by expanding their capacity. In the late eighteenth century, patents were held not by dramatic companies (who could build or buy new theatres) but by theatre buildings; as a result the patent owners could respond to increased demand only by enlarging their auditoriums. Soon after Palmer's challenge both patent theatres expanded yet again.

The new melodrama and the new auditoriums both affected perceptions of the theatre and, consequently, perceptions of Shakespeare. The huge auditoriums dwarfed actors. In an architectural volume where human beings seemed insignificant, dramatists and scene painters increasingly placed their characters, particularly at climactic moments, against vistas of immensity: a landscape, seascape, cloudscape impossible to escape. This tendency affected Wordsworth's *Borderers,* Byron's *Manfred,* and Shelley's *Prometheus Unbound* as surely as it did Holcroft's Gothic tragicomedies to music; in productions of *King Lear* petty humanity was measured against a vast storm and heath, in *Coriolanus* against the imposing (anachronistic) architecture of imperial Rome. John Philip Kemble's statuesque, heroic style suited such an acting space.

Eighteenth-century England twice failed to overthrow theatrical licensing; it also failed for sixty-five years to overthrow book licensing. Between 1695 and 1709 the book trade was unregulated, a free-for-all terminated by the copyright act of Queen Anne. That legislation extended existing copyrights for twenty-one years—a breathing space that enabled the most prosperous booksellers to entrench their position financially and institutionally. Thereafter, by a ruthless combination of restrictive practices and lawsuits, they succeeded in frustrating the intent of the legislation until 1774, when they lost a decisive court ruling in the House of Lords. By then the Tonsons had sold their Shakespeare holdings to a consortium of booksellers. Even after the 1774 ruling, those booksellers retained their copyright to the recent *commentaries* in Tonson's Shakespeare editions, a copyright extended and exploited by the variorum format of subsequent editions.

The success of this rearguard action not only postponed for two generations the consequences of deregulation; equally important, the booksellers defended their privileges in terms that fundamentally affected the definition of authorship in the eighteenth century and later. In lobbying for the reimposition of restrictive legislation, they did not defend copyright as a bastion of proprietary privilege in the book trade (which it was); that would have seemed too obviously self-serving. Instead, they claimed that copyright was needed to protect authors. Since copyright had until then been vested only in booksellers, this argument was, to say the least, an ingenious reinterpretation of the historical record; but it was tactically astute, for it transformed the booksellers' defense of their own interests into an altruistic campaign on behalf of authors. An author's text, they claimed, was the fruit of his labor; works were the product of work; they therefore constituted an author's property, and property needed to be defended by law. The corollary of this argument—the part that concerned the booksellers—was that literary works, like any other form of property, could be sold; once sold, they belonged, according to English common law, to the buyer and his heirs in perpetuity. The booksellers reiterated this argument in their legal and practical resistance to the abolition of perpetual copyright; Hogarth appropriated it in his own successful campaign for the Engravers' Copyright Act of 1735.

Although the 1774 House of Lords ruling (*Donaldson* v. *Beckett*) deprived booksellers of perpetual copyright in the works of deceased authors, it did not challenge the concept of authorship that the booksellers had so assiduously promulgated. It left intact the judgment, rendered in an earlier case, that "I do not know, nor can I comprehend any property more emphatically a man's own, nay, more incapable of being mistaken, than his literary works."97 By this definition, which came to be widely accepted in the eighteenth century, ideas are marketable commodities; thought is personal property. And if literary works are property, then they can be stolen. In *The Dunciad,* Pope in effect equated the piracy of unscrupulous publishers (like Edmund Curll, who infringed other booksellers' copyrights) with the piracy of unscrupulous authors (like Theobald and Cibber, who pinched material from other writers). In 1747 Milton was accused of wholesale plagiarism, an allegation lent credibility by the already extensive record of his literary borrowings; later in the century similar accusations were leveled against Laurence Sterne. In both cases the charges caused a prolonged scandal that did no good to either author's reputation. During this same period, by contrast, Shakespeare was being celebrated as an exemplary genius, "A Star of the first magnitude," in works like Edward Young's *Conjectures on Original Composition* (1759). Young's own originality lay in his articulation of what was, by the time he wrote, already an unconscious consensus.

Shakespeare, of course, was as guilty of theft, so defined, as any author. He belonged to an age in which—to quote the opinion of another judge, the author of a dissenting opinion in one of the century's key copyright trials—"the author has a property in his sentiments till he publishes them ... But from the moment of

publication, they are thrown into a state of universal commu-
nion."[98] Shakespeare stole with a clear conscience. He copied plots,
characters, speeches, images, and aphorisms from classical authors
and from his own contemporaries, without acknowledgment. But
Shakespeare stole for the most part from authors whom eighteenth-
century readers did not read—from the lower classes of literature,
as it were. Most readers automatically contrasted Shakespeare with
figures like Pope and Dryden, who made careers from the frank
imitation, translation, and adaptation of great men's work. They
contrasted Shakespeare with the derivative playwrights of their own
time. They still habitually contrasted Shakespeare with Ben Jonson,
who had so scrupulously recorded his borrowings in the margins of
Sejanus. Jonson stole conspicuously; Shakespeare stole surrep-
titiously. Edward Young, and the society for which he spoke,
deduced—unjustly, unsurprisingly—that Jonson "is as much an
Imitator, as *Shakespeare* is an Original."[99] The proprietorial concept
of authorial copyright, the criminalization of literary expropriation,
the entrepreneurial cult of originality—all were harnessed, like so
much else, to the bandwagon of Shakespeare's reputation.

The Copyright Act of 1710 was chiefly responsible, through the
Tonson family, for establishing a grand and orderly succession of
Shakespeare editors from Rowe to Steevens; after 1774 the sense
of succession was maintained by the variorum procedures of
Steevens, Reed, and Malone. The fifth failed revolution of the eighteenth century was Edward Capell's attempt to break into, and
break, that editorial tradition.

Capell, in a move entirely characteristic of the Enlightenment,
proposed that the editing of Shakespeare should start over again
from scratch. All the progressive sophistications and corruptions
introduced by intervening ages should be overthrown; reason and
purity could be restored only by a radical return to the primitive
state of nature. The state of nature, in editorial terms, was to be
found in the original texts, those published in Shakespeare's lifetime. Even the folio collection of 1623 was suspect, because it had
been published posthumously; no text published after 1623 had
any authority at all. By his own account, "a ray of light broke forth
upon him" at the moment when he realized that an editor should
"stick invariably to the old editions (that is, the best of them)."[100]
Capell did not, like everyone else, generate his own edition by
marking up the edition published by his immediate predecessor;

instead, he meticulously, calligraphically, and repeatedly transcribed the "best" sixteenth- or seventeenth-century text, which was usually the first. By this simple innovation he cleared away in one stroke at least hundreds, and probably thousands, of unauthoritative readings. He also cleared away the encrustations of editorial parasites; his edition of Shakespeare's plays was published without commentary, which appeared instead in three separate volumes.

Capell's demotion and separation of editorial matter was part of a larger ambition to redesign, from its foundations, the visual presentation of the text. Although Capell was not a printer, he controlled the design of each page of his text as absolutely and radically and eccentrically as William Blake. This control produced a spare and elegant edition, immediately distinguishable from any other. Capell's ambition also entailed a systematic scheme to extend and rationalize the written representation of speech. He introduced a new "note of punctuation to distinguish irony" (·); another, to denote "a change of the address . . . to whom the words are spoken" (_); a third, to call attention to "a thing shown or pointed at" (†); a fourth, to alert readers to "a thing deliver'd" (‡); a fifth, prefixed to words that are "spoke apart or aside" ("). He also used accents to indicate obsolete Elizabethan stresses (as in "triúmph").[101] In addition to "these new-invented marks" he deployed traditional punctuation in untraditional ways, using it for instance to define the metrical (rather than grammatical or logical) structure of a sentence. He also invented new words, including that inelegant, indispensable adjectival noun "Shakespearian."

Capell, as some of his semiotic codifications imply, paid far more attention than any other editor to details of staging; his innovations in the description of inferred stage business have survived into modern editions more often than his verbal emendations. His astute attention to the theatricality of Shakespeare's texts was probably a by-product of the fact that from 1737 to his death in 1781 a good deal of his income came from his appointment as deputy licenser of plays, a position created by the Licensing Act of 1737. The power over the fortunes of the London theatres that this appointment gave him probably accounts for his support from David Garrick. By an appropriate irony, the failure of one attempted revolution financed another: Capell's revolutionary text of Shakespeare's plays was made possible by an act of Parliament that repressed innovations in the theatre. Capell's edition, like his licensing, attempted to tame plays. An experienced censor soon discovers that words that look innocent on the page can be made politically embarrassing by "irony" of enunciation, or by "a thing shown or pointed to," or by lending statements the advertised surreptitiousness of an aside spoken directly to the audience, or by complementing dialogue with stage business of many kinds. Capell's text tries to prescribe the way readers will read and the way actors will act Shakespeare's plays. Capell's control of the text had to be total, for only a dictatorship could enforce revolutionary change.

Capell's revolution failed; his edition was never reprinted, and its importance did not begin to be appreciated for another century. It failed for many reasons. Capell succeeded in having his edition published under the Tonson imprint; but the Tonsons published it unenthusiastically, paying him less for his labors than they had any editor since Pope.[102] Capell himself was an outsider, an arrogant loner who did not belong to that privileged inner circle of literary London, the circle of Johnson, Boswell, Garrick, Burke, Reynolds, Steevens, Reed, Malone, and so many others. His attack on this clubbish editorial tradition was hopelessly fragmented and dispersed; his rare *Prolusions* (explaining his system of signs and signals) was published in 1760, his ten-volume edition of the plays in 1768, his first volume of notes in 1774 (quickly withdrawn), his revised full three volumes of notes in 1783 (after his death); his edition of the poems was never published at all. He further divided his commentary into separate lists of textual notes and variant readings; the third volume is entirely devoted to selections from Elizabethan and Jacobean works illustrating various matters in Shakespeare's text, a method of explication that gives priority to the original context at the expense of convenience. Even modern scholars sympathetic to Capell's ambitions find his consortium of publications damnably frustrating to use. Capell also lacked Johnson's gifts as a prose stylist and Steevens' gifts as a polemicist; even when he communicates his meaning, he does not do so forcefully or elegantly or memorably. Capell's enemies, like the enemies of the Jacobins in the 1790s, focused much of their satire upon deficiencies of style; arguments improperly expressed could not be worth answering.

From the perspective of modern scholarship Capell's editorial practice left much to be desired; but it was undoubtedly a great and radical advance upon prevailing methods. Subsequent editors slowly ransacked his work for its more obvious gems, all the while denigrating what they pillaged. There was no break with the past; accretion triumphed. Malone, the most characteristic editor of the second half of the eighteenth century, was a lawyer; and the edifice of Shakespeare editing, like the edifice of English jurisprudence, rose by progressive deposits of precedent sediment. Sir William Blackstone, the most influential figure in the history of English law, contributed notes to Malone's commentary on Shakespeare.[103]

Malone merely collaborated in the collective suppression of Capell; but he was personally instrumental in putting down another editorial revolutionary. In 1783 Joseph Ritson published a bookful of scholarly *Remarks, Critical and Illustrative, on the Text and Notes of the last Edition of Shakspeare;* like Theobald's critique of Pope, Ritson's critique of Steevens demonstrated his competence and declared his intention to prepare his own edition of "THE GENUINE TEXT OF SHAKSPEARE."[104] Malone moved quickly to squash Ritson's chances.[105] Shortly after the publication of Ritson's book, he decided "to produce a useful *family* Shakspeare"—a "portable edition" with minimal notes in the same format Ritson had announced; he admitted that "M[r] Ritson has in some measure been the cause of my undertaking this work."[106] Malone used his reputation and his circle of contacts to preempt Ritson, effectively locking him out of the London publishing world. Ritson was reduced to the role of a vociferous impotent pamphleteer. In *The Quip Modest* (1788) he pilloried the 1785 revision of Steevens' edition; in 1792 he published *Cursory Criticisms on the Edition of Shakspeare Published by Edmond Malone.* His targets treated Ritson the way they did Capell: they silently absorbed his corrections, "sometimes word for word,"[107] without crediting his contribution, and mentioned him only when they found occasion to rebuke him. Ritson fulminated against this old-boy network—"mischevious gangs of nocturnal banditti," slanderers who "escape the resentment of the injured, and the vengeance of the law," their gentlemanly malice invulnerable, while "offenders of comparative insignificance are almost every day exposed on pillories, or perishing in dungeons"[108]—but he fulminated in vain. Ritson was relegated to the sidelines of Shakespeare editing even more effectively than Capell, who at least succeeded in publishing an edition.

Ritson never published an edition of Shakespeare because, unlike Capell, he could not draw upon a large guaranteed income or an aristocratic patron. The son of a menial servant, Ritson earned his living as a legal conveyancer. Just as his social background differed from that of his editorial rivals, so did his politics. He had always been hostile to religion and the clergy; in the autumn of 1791 he visited revolutionary Paris; in 1793 he adopted the new Republican calendar; in 1794 his radical friends Horne Tooke and Thomas Holcroft were arrested. Ritson supported the opposition leader Charles Fox, proclaiming "Damn the king and all his adherents!"[109] (George Steevens, by contrast, subscribed a thousand pounds to Prime Minister Pitt's "Loyalty Loan," helping to finance the government's war effort against France.)

Had Ritson been able to publish an edition of Shakespeare, it would no doubt have been wrong as often as Malone's—but in different ways. It might well have created a radical alternative to the conservative tradition epitomized by Malone. For one thing, the social and political assumptions of Ritson's commentary would have differed from Malone's, as we can deduce from scattered remarks in his letters and pamphlets. Unlike Malone, Ritson praised Shakespeare's freedom from "the reigning superstition of the time"; Shakespeare was "addicted to no system of bigotry" and refused to subscribe to "the temporary religion" of one time or place.[110] Wholly indifferent to "Papish or Protestant, Paganism or Christianity," Ritson insisted that "the character of *Falstaff* was originally represented under the name of Oldcastle"; Shakespeare's comic hypocrite had been modeled on the historical figure of Sir John Oldcastle, revered by Protestants as a martyr. Though the original identity of Shakespeare's character was confirmed by a clutch of reliable witnesses, Malone rejected them all because they linked Shakespeare to Roman Catholic historiographers.[111] Unlike Malone, Ritson regrets that Shakespeare dramatized "the absurd and lying stories" about Joan of Arc, an "amiable, brave, wise, and patriotic female" who helped rescue her countrymen from English "usurpation and slavery";[112] Malone wishes that the whole of France could be "blotted from the map of the world."[113] Malone, in his own commentary, had denied Richard III's right to the throne; Ritson replies,

> King Richard, it is well known, had as good a title to the crown as the late king William or queen Anne, or the reigning house of Hanover. The issue of King Edward had been *bastardized,* the

duke of Clarence *attainted,* and himself *declared the undoubted heir of Richard duke of York,* BY ACT OF PARLIAMENT: and what better title has the present king?[114]

The difference between Malone and Ritson here would affect the interpretation of issues of political legitimacy throughout the history plays and several of the tragedies. For instance, Ritson enthusiastically defends the king-killer Hamlet against conservative complaints about "the immoral tendency of his character."[115] Ritson's critical hostility to kings is matched by a sympathy for "the common people," who "read a great deal" if given the chance. Unable to edit Shakespeare, he instead produced the first collection and critical edition of the folk tales built around the heroic popular figure of Robin Hood. In relation to a passage in *King John,*

> I saw a smith stand with his hammer, thus,
> The whilst his iron did on the anvil cool,
> With open mouth swallowing a tailor's news;
> Who, with his shears and measure in his hand,
> Standing on slippers, (which his nimble haste
> Had falsely thrust upon contrary feet,)
> Told of a many thousand warlike French,
> That were embatteled and rank'd in Kent:[116]

Ritson comments, "I have seen a fishwoman reading the journal of the [French] National assembly to her neighbour who appeared to listen with all the avidity of Shakspeares blacksmith."[117]

Ritson also differed from Malone in his attitude toward textual authority. Malone tolerated emendation less than his predecessors. In part his conservativism reflected a salutary historical awareness that many emendations were based upon ignorance of Elizabethan usage; but in part it resulted from Malone's own temperamental hostility to what he characterized as *"capricious innovation"*[118] in the text or the state. In preferring "the *true original reading* of the *only ancient authentic copy,*"[119] Malone equated antiquity with truth. Ritson objected, logically enough, that the oldest reading is not inevitably the best; the new is sometimes true. Thus, in the earliest surviving printed text of *As You Like It,* Malone found the following verse line

The body of Countrie, Citie, Court,[120]

which is metrically irregular. Every subsequent edition, from 1632 on, had produced a metrically regular line by inserting the word "the" before "country." This emendation presupposes a simple and common omission in the first edition. But Malone, in his deference to textual antiquity, retains the original reading, asserting that "*Country* is here used as a trisyllable."[121] As Ritson points out, Malone's conjecture would require us to pronounce Shakespeare's iambic pentameter line in an "utterly impossible" fashion:

The body of *coun-té-ry,* city, court.[122]

Ritson collects dozens of comparable examples, where Malone's reverence for textual authority leads him to reject obvious and probable improvements. Ritson was less afraid of change, more willing to see and attack "corruption" in the most venerable texts or institutions.

It is easy to glorify failed revolutions; we have never had to suffer the consequences of their success. But such foreclosed opportunities demonstrate that there was nothing inevitable or natural or rational about the rise and shape of Shakespeare's reputation in the later eighteenth century. They remind us that the triumph of one tendency depends upon the suppression of others; they expose the mechanisms of that suppression. And they begin to explain why the Romantic revolution did not depose Shakespeare.

BOOK IV

"Why did a revolution not happen in England?" The question is as important and as obvious as, "Why did one happen in France?" But most literary critics do not ask themselves why Shakespeare stayed on top during the Romantic period, because they assume that he belongs on top, and they assume too that continuity is normal. Inertial motion is, indeed, a large part of the explanation for his continued predominance; his reputation had developed so much momentum that it could have been stopped only by an obstacle or countermovement of enormous force. No such obstacle presented itself; instead, Shakespeare's momentum was accelerated.

In 1850 an aging Leigh Hunt recalled that at the end of the eighteenth century "people of all times of life were much greater play-goers than they are now." That addiction to theatre was actually intensified by events of the 1790s, for "the French Revolution only tended at first to endear the nation to its own habits."[123] As the history of the preceding decades so clearly demonstrates, Shakespeare, like playgoing, was one of those habits. An initially enthusiastic, or at least cautious, welcome for the French Revolution turned within a few years into a panicking chauvinistic rejection of it. Shakespeare's reputation had been fed by nationalism, and the intensified nationalism dominant during the twenty years of Napoleonic wars only fattened it further.

For England the balance did not tilt in 1789, the year of the fall of the Bastille, but in 1790, the year of Burke's *Reflections on the Revolution in France*. In 1790 Malone published his edition of *The Plays and Poems of William Shakspeare,* and Boydell became Lord Mayor. In the same year Isaac Reed, whose first edition of Shakespeare had been published in 1785, recorded in his diary that on April 23 "(Shakespeare's Birthday)," he had dined at Boydell's house, where the company included Sir Joshua Reynolds, Benjamin West, and Paul Sandby, who all contributed paintings to Boydell's Shakspeare Gallery. The next night Reed went to see *Twelfth Night;* on June 9 to *Hamlet;* on June 22 to *The Merchant of Venice;* on July 18, he "Dined at Mr Malone's with Boswell & Johnson. Afterw^ds Sr Joshua Reynolds came"; on October 21 he saw *Richard III* in the company of Dr. Richard Farmer, the Cambridge classicist who had written an influential *Essay on the Learning of Shakespeare.*[124] While France gave bloody birth to the future, the guardians of Shakespeare's England dined and theatred.

In the contest between French neoclassicism and English drama Shakespeare had been and would continue to be praised for his freedom from the rules, and that freedom had always had a political significance. But that political significance was altered and intensified by the French Revolution. There could no longer be a contrast between French absolutism and English liberty; the French had gotten rid of their king, the English still had one. Instead, the French (and American) belief that a society could be rationally planned, that a blueprint could be intellectually conceived and then imposed upon recalcitrant human materials, was contrasted with the English belief that a society naturally evolved, organically, by gradations and consolidations, like a tree, like Burke's British royal oak in particular. This political contrast has, obviously, its aesthetic corollary: French plays were constructed by rule, English drama grew organically.

The connection between these two ideas is expressed most directly in Coleridge's *Biographia Literaria*. Shakespearian critics tend to read the parts devoted to Shakespeare as brilliant exercises in critical theory or practice, because—along with published and unpublished passages from many other sources—they have been conveniently collected, organized, and decontextualized in various editions of *Coleridge's Shakespearean Criticism*. But as originally published they belong to a sustained argument for political and social reaction, written in the turbulent aftermath of Napoleon's defeat, when national self-defense could no longer be used as an excuse for repressing or postponing reform.

Shakespeare was not deposed *because* George III was not deposed; or, George III was not deposed *because* Shakespeare was not deposed. From 1790 on, the defense of political and social privilege was justified as a defense of the culture of the English people, and any such defense would inevitably entail the preservation of Shakespeare, already widely regarded as England's greatest artist. Indeed, Shakespeare was certain to be further glorified by such a movement. Milton, after all, had been an accomplice to the execution of an English king—a rather uncomfortable precedent in the years between 1790 and 1820. Shakespeare caused no such embarrassment. His mixing of genres, his representation of all ranks of society, clowns rubbing shoulders with kings, social diversity aesthetically united—the very aspects of his art that neoclassicism had found objectionable—became admirable, because culturally useful. The openness of Shakespeare's art embodied—indeed, proved—the openness of English society.

Like the Romantics themselves, in some moods, romantic readers believe in abrupt change, enjoy the excitement of cataclysms (avalanches in the Alps, and all that). Romanticism, on its own account, provides just such a cataclysm. The threat and promise of the revolution next door exhilarated English poets; the disparate elements of an evolving late-Enlightenment taste suddenly crystallized into a strong new aesthetic compound. Acolytes of Romanticism are interested in Milton or in Shakespeare only secondarily, because of their professed importance to the Romantics themselves; and they tend to believe the story the Romantics tell them. The Romantics tell them that the Romantics discovered Shakespeare—just as, in the middle of the eighteenth century, Garrick's admirers said that Garrick had discovered Shakespeare.

The historical record makes it perfectly clear that the playwright's works were in no danger of impending oblivion, in either case. But this is probably clearer to us than it was to them. Among authors quoted in literary anthologies from 1771 to 1801, Shakespeare ranks fourth (after Pope, Thomson, and Cowper).[125] Much of the most innovative criticism of Shakespeare in the second half of the eighteenth century was scattered in ephemeral periodicals and in books on other topics; it was not collected into a single widely accessible compendium until the 1970s. For the Romantics, what was accessible, what was inescapable, was the eighteenth-century editorial tradition, which brought Shakespeare's text into the nineteenth century encumbered with all the outmoded baggage of prefaces and critical notes from Rowe to Steevens. The Romantics took arms against the big books, against the anthologies, against the variorum editions, against the strictures in popular collected editions of *The Tatler* and *The Spectator*, against David Hume's *History of England*, its midcentury disparagements of Shakespeare monumentalized by reprintings, translations, and Hume's own prestige. In doing so they fought a battle won long before on the bloody fields of polemical journalism. Having mistaken him for David, the Romantics rushed to defend Goliath—and prided themselves on their part in his victory.

The Romantic attack on Shakespeare's eighteenth-century editors and critics belonged, socially, to a much more general attack on the intelligentsia. It was wrongly but widely believed that the French Revolution had been the work of a cabal of Enlightenment intellectuals and that a similar cabal of radicals, epitomized by Tom Paine and Mary Wollstonecraft, was at work in England. A conspiracy of pedants had overturned the French state and was busy planting its little lever under the foundations of the English one. The Romantic poets and critics were themselves, of course, intellectuals; they could not simply join the popular clamor against the class to which they belonged. But some of them did respond to the same emotions and, at the same time, usefully distanced themselves from such criticism, by attacking Shakespeare's eighteenth-century editors and critics, thus deflecting the outrage onto another set of intellectuals.

The English Romantics displaced their revolutionary fervor away from politics onto literature. Such displacements are also characteristic of their attitude toward Shakespeare. They did not challenge, but appropriated, Shakespeare or Milton; the energies of their rebellion against the literature of the past were channeled into attacks on lesser poets in the vernacular pantheon. Rather than confront Shakespeare, they directed their hostility onto his editors, critics, and adapters. Dryden, Pope, and Johnson conveniently belonged to both categories of target. Anyone familiar with political history will recognize such tactics: in the face of growing popular protest, the president/prime minister/general secretary/emperor sacrifices members of his staff. By toppling underlings a society presumes and ensures the inviolability of the high center of power. The Romantic manifesto did not call for the overthrow of the reigning literary dynasty; it called, instead, only for a change of ministry. Schlegel contended that English critics had never properly appreciated their greatest poet; they had abdicated, and Germany could therefore claim Shakespeare for herself. Coleridge and his contemporaries could endorse Schlegel's condemnation of eighteenth-century critical practice, but they wanted to retain English control of this strategic literary territory. The greatness of the "sovereign" Shakespeare would be better served and sustained by Prime Minister Coleridge than it had been by the corrupt pensioners of the old regime.

Shakespeare, simultaneously supreme and central, commanded the apex of the cone of English literature. Although given the opportunity and the injunction to overthrow the literary past, to make everything natural and new, the Romantics could not often, or for long, take arms against a sea of Shakespeare. Although he intended otherwise, the man whom Hamlet stabbed behind the arras was Polonius, not Claudius: the minister, not the king.

BOOK V

By their failure to confront Shakespeare directly the English Romantics marginalized themselves; their own work became a set of scribblings on the periphery of past literary history. The beginnings of this process can be seen even in Johnson: "I have confined my imagination to the margin,"[126] his preface declares, defining a policy of recording his own editorial conjectures in the commentary rather than adopting them as emendations of the text. But Johnson's commentary, however marginal, was published, monumentally, and was thereafter preserved in the edifice of subsequent eighteenth-century editions. By contrast, many of Coleridge's most astute critical observations on the plays are quite literally manuscript marginalia, not published until long after his death. But the best-known and most characteristic of such Romantic marginalia must be a poem by Keats:

> On sitting down to read King Lear once again.
>
> O Golden-tongued Romance, with serene Lute!
>   Fair plumed Syren, Queen of far-away!
>   Leave melodizing on this wintry day
> Shut up thine olden Pages, and be mute.
> Adieu! for, once again, the fierce dispute,
>   Betwixt Damnation and impassion'd clay
>   Must I burn through, once more humbly assay
> The bitter-sweet of this Shaksperean fruit.
> Chief Poet! and ye Clouds of Albion,
>   Begetter of our deep eternal theme!
> When through the old oak forest I am gone,
>   Let me not wander in a barren dream:
> But, when I am consumed in the fire,
> Give me new Phoenix Wings to fly at my desire.
>
>   Jan^{u}.22.1818.

The poem was written in Keats' copy of the 1808 facsimile of the Shakespeare First Folio, on the last page of *Hamlet,* which faces the first page of *King Lear.* The very existence of such a facsimile of the 1623 edition, and Keats' use of it, express a characteristic Romantic desire to do away with fussy intermediaries, to overthrow the editors and commentators of the eighteenth century, to read Homer in Chapman's translation instead of Pope's, to return to the imagined purity of a Renaissance font, typographical and metaphorical, that could bring them into direct spiritual contact with the poet himself.

The poem's title is as revealing as its location. *King Lear* has become a text to be read, not a play to be watched. From October 1810 until April 1820 it was not acted on any stage in London; since George III, like Lear, was old and mad and the king of England, any performance of the play would inevitably have suggested uncomfortable parallels with the living royal family. For Keats, *King Lear* existed only on paper. Whether or not political circumstances permitted a performance, Shakespeare's *King Lear,* like all his tragedies, was, as Lamb had said, "essentially impossible to be represented on a stage." Whereas "the reading of a tragedy is a fine abstraction," any performance reduced it to an imitation of mundane particulars: "The contemptible machinery by which they mimic the storm which he goes out in, is not more inadequate to represent the horrors of the real elements, than any actor can be to represent Lear: they might more easily propose to personate the Satan of Milton upon a stage, or one of Michael Angelo's terrible figures."[127]

"Michael Angelo's terrible figures" had been the inspiration for the efforts of William Blake and Henry Fuseli to create visual equivalents for Shakespeare's poetry. Blake invents spatial representations of verbal images: jocund day, fiery Pegasus, triple Hecate, pity like a naked new-born babe. Fuseli's compositions, which include the most original and memorable contributions to Boydell's Shakspeare Gallery, reconstruct the tragedies in terms that could never be realized in performance: frozen explosions of conflict, dominated by superhuman characters tensed and straining, muscled and flayed, invested with a sense of titanic energy only momentarily restrained within the frame. In contemporary theatres space dwarfed the characters; in Fuseli's painting, in the imagination of readers, characters overwhelmed space.

Keats sits down to read *King Lear* "again." Shakespeare's plays have become the objects of repeated readings. Keats not only knows before he begins how the story will end; he knows that he and his culture have defined the text as a masterpiece. The importance of this distinction can be made obvious by contrast with the title of another Keats sonnet, recording another literary encounter: "On first looking into Chapman's Homer." That sonnet records an experience of unexpected illumination, and it ends naturally with that surprised image of the discovery of the Pacific Ocean, a wild expanse seen from a mountaintop. "On sitting down to read King

Lear once again" records the experience not of an explorer but of a pilgrim-tourist, returning to a favorite shrine.

Keats' "again" inevitably recalls another famous encounter with *King Lear*.* Dr. Johnson had related, in his endnote on the play, that "I was many years ago so shocked by Cordelia's death, that I know not whether I ever endured to read again the last scenes of the play till I undertook to revise them as an editor."[128] Johnson found *King Lear* shockingly painful; he responded to Cordelia's death as he might respond to the actual death of a young woman he admired, even loved; he returned to the scene of the accident only when forced by circumstances to do so. Keats finds *King Lear* "bitter-sweet"; he does not mention Cordelia or any other character; their lives are allegorized into the intensity of a "fierce dispute, / Betwixt Damnation and impassion'd clay"; he responds to an old poem he admires, even loves; and although he claims that he "must" return to it, that imperative is self-imposed, not a practical duty but an imaginative commitment. In the half-century between Johnson's comment and Keats' sonnet, it had become a poet's duty to revisit *King Lear*. Because he is willing to "burn through" *King Lear* again, Keats may gain "new Phoenix Wings to fly at [his] desire"; Johnson, by implication, failed as a poet because he was critical of Shakespeare and reluctant to reread this play. Keats, like the other Romantics, defined his own poetry and his attitude toward Shakespeare in opposition to the eighteenth-century tradition.

The poem Keats wrote, as we can see almost without reading it, is a sonnet. His use of a sonnet to commemorate a rereading of *King Lear* is itself a formal act of homage to Milton, Spenser, and Shakespeare, while at the same time it places him among the poets of his own epoch. The sonnet had virtually disappeared from the repertoire of English poetic forms between the death of Milton and the death of Pope; its revival in midcentury was due almost entirely to the growing interest in Milton's minor poems and in Spenser. In the 1750s Benjamin Heath, one of its earliest eighteenth-century practitioners, appended more than fifty sonnets to editions of his *Canons of Criticism*, a volume wittily devoted to satirizing Warburton's

---

*Johnson's comment is reprinted at the end of *King Lear* in Keats' copy of an 1814 edition of *The Dramatic Works of William Shakespeare;* Keats often rebuked Johnson's comments on the plays in that edition. Keats could also have come across Johnson's remark in a number of other places: Leigh Hunt, for instance, quotes and criticizes it in *The Examiner* (May 28, 1808), 331–33.

edition of Shakespeare; Thomas Warton, another important critic of Shakespeare, more than any other writer reseeded the sonnet in the English literary imagination; but neither man was primarily influenced by Shakespeare. In the seventeenth century there had been fewer allusions to Shakespeare's sonnets than to any of his plays or narrative poems; first published in 1609, they were reprinted only once, in a textually eccentric edition of *Shakespeare's Poems* (1640). Neither Rowe's nor Pope's edition included the sonnets, though in each case a supplementary volume containing the poems was published to accompany their edition; subsequent editors also excluded them. Although Shakespeare's sonnets were available in a number of reprintings of the poems, those texts stood outside the editorial mainstream, and they followed the format of the 1640 text. That unauthoritative text regularly combined single sonnets to create formally spurious longer poems; in such conditions Shakespeare's poems were not likely to have much influence upon any revival of the sonnet form.

Shakespeare's sonnets contributed almost nothing to the form's renewed popularity in the second half of the eighteenth century, but Shakespeare's editors responded to it. In 1780 Malone published the first critical edition of the sonnets, returning to the format and sequence of the original 1609 edition, draping the poems in the full dignity of an introduction and commentary; in 1790 he incorporated them into his prestigious full-scale edition of the *Plays and Poems*, so that for the first time they became an integral element of the canon.

The rise of Shakespeare's sonnets in the late eighteenth century was a by-product of the rise of Milton and Spenser, a consequence of the popularity of contemporary sonneteers whom no one reads anymore. It also owes something to the steady expansion, in both popular interest and cultural respectability, of biography and autobiography and of literary biography in particular. This expansion, in progress throughout the century, culminated in Johnson's *Lives of the English Poets* (1779–81), itself topped in 1791 by the publication of Boswell's *Life of Johnson*. Malone's two editions of the sonnets belong to the same period and intellectual circle, and in his commentary he repeatedly stresses the biographical significance of the poems. This emphasis naturally and quickly led to George Chalmers' conjectural identification of the person to whom Shakespeare addressed the sonnets (1797); to A. W. von Schlegel's conviction that "These sonnets paint most unequivocally the actual situation and sentiments of the poet" (1797, 1808); to Wordsworth's declaration that in such poems "Shakspeare expresses his own feelings in his own person" (1815) and that "with this Key, Shakspeare unlocked his heart" (1827).[129]

Malone's editorial recovery of the sonnets was instrumental in transforming Shakespeare from the public dramatic poet of the Restoration and eighteenth century into a private lyric poet who could be embraced, celebrated, and appropriated by the Romantics. We can see the same process at work with Shakespeare's narrative poems, which before Malone had also been relegated to the editorial hinterland inhabited by the sonnets. Coleridge's scintillating analysis of *Venus and Adonis* in chapter fifteen of *Biographia Literaria* (1817), Keats' independent enthusiasm for the same poem in a letter written in November of that year,[130] signal a revolution in Shakespeare's reputation as a nondramatic poet. The admiration of these Romantic poets for Shakespeare's narrative poems follows Malone's historicist recognition that they were among Shakespeare's most popular and respected compositions during his own lifetime (1780) and his later historicist defense of them as the most accomplished "smaller pieces" of the Elizabethan or Jacobean age (1790).[131] Shakespeare remained, of course, primarily a dramatist; but the sonnets and narrative poems—freshly restored to the canon, as yet wholly neglected by critics—gave the Romantics an opportunity to enjoy the novelty of their own critical perspective, while claiming Shakespeare as a precursor in their own favored genres.

This new perspective was unabashedly biographical; it was intrigued by Shakespeare the individual, by the life of the Poet. Even Hazlitt, who resisted "the fashion of late to cry up our author's poems, as equal to his plays," interpreted them in the prevailing biographical terms. He found the sonnets "interesting as they relate to the state of the personal feelings of the author," and he blamed the poems' failings on Shakespeare's "modesty, and a painful sense of personal propriety" that inhibited him from writing comfortably in his own persona.[132] Hazlitt, so opposed to Wordsworth's "egotistical sublime," imagined a Shakespeare who exposed his personality chiefly through an aversion to exposing his personality. An interest in *The Characters of Shakespear's Plays* easily coincided with an interest in the character of Shakespeare.

Keats' poem on *King Lear* adopted not only the form but also the alleged biographical particularity of the sonnets. "On sitting down to read King Lear once again" is a private text: Keats did not publish the poem or most of his other sonnets. The privacy of a manuscript lyric contrasts with the public printed plays it sits between. Keats dated the poem, thereby defining it as both historical and autobiographical, part of the progress of his own life. The date appends to the poem a personal extratextual reality in which "this wintry day" not only anticipates the symbolic climate of *King Lear* but also recalls the actual weather in London on January 22, 1818.

This conjunction of the temporal and the personal, this interest in the development of a poet's mind and art, characterizes the Shakespeare scholarship of the late eighteenth century as well as the poetry of the Romantics. In 1709 Rowe had said that he would have been "pleas'd, to have learn'd from some certain Authority, which was the first Play he wrote; it would be without doubt a pleasure to any Man, curious in Things of this Kind, to see and know what was the first Essay of a Fancy like *Shakespear*'s"[133]—but he made no effort to satisfy this confessedly idle curiosity. Neither Rowe nor his successors attempted to establish a reliable chronology, though a certain amount of relevant information had already been accumulated in the late seventeenth century. The first such conjectural chronology of Shakespeare's works was published in 1778, by Malone; Capell's chronology was written earlier but not published until 1783; Malone further substantially revised his own account in 1790.[134]

Critics thereafter begin to talk of Shakespeare's works not only in terms of his artistic development but of his spiritual evolution as well. Coleridge supposes that *Love's Labor's Lost* was Shakespeare's earliest play, because it reflects the "scholastic pursuits" and provincial experience of his youth, before he had learned to observe human nature directly.[135] Keats sees *Hamlet* as a reflection of Shakespeare's melancholy middle age.[136] Leigh Hunt, assuring his readers that "*Twelfth Night* was the last work of SHAKSPEARE," marveled at "what a good natured play" it was; Shakespeare's "last thoughts" of the world were "kind and social," dwelling upon "the humours of good fellowship and the young trustingness of love."[137] According to modern scholarship Coleridge and Hunt are wrong— *Love's Labor's Lost* belongs to the end of Shakespeare's early period,

Twelfth Night preceded his retirement by a decade or more—and whether Keats was right depends upon your definition of "middle-aged" (Shakespeare was probably thirty-six when he wrote *Hamlet*). But the accuracy of such speculations matters less than their demonstration of the contemporary pressure to allegorize Shakespeare's biography, to find in it a tutelary philosophical progress, a model for poets and readers.

Keats, sitting down to read *King Lear,* is constructing such an artistic biography for himself; in this sonnet he creates and memorializes a turning point, a moment of revelation that rejects the "Syren . . . of far-away" and turns instead toward the "Chief Poet . . . of Albion," anticipating a movement through "fire" toward resurrection and ascension. Keats is trying to write a very tiny *Prelude*. And his poetic self-definition, like Wordsworth's, is in part nationalistic. Keats addresses both Shakespeare, England's poet, and "Albion," England's poeticized name for itself, which translates the reality of 1818 England into a timeless mythological ideal. In a letter written seven weeks after this sonnet Keats declares, "I like, I love England, I like its strong Men— . . . Shakspeare is fine, Hamlet is fine, Lear is fine, but dwindled englishmen are not fine"; elsewhere he hopes to be "among the English Poets" after his death.[138] Keats and Shakespeare and England have become tenaciously intertwined.

But Keats would never have earned his place "among the English Poets" if his reputation depended on this sonnet. It is not, to tell the truth, a very good poem; the context is more interesting than the text. In this it resembles most of Shakespeare's own sonnets: as isolated individuals only a handful of the 154 have ever attracted or rewarded as much enthusiasm as the story told outside and between them, a story that has excited the obsessive rearrangements, the speculative identifications of Mr. W. H. and the young man and the rival poet and the dark lady, the search for a narrative, the unraveling of thematic labyrinths, the etymological biographies of the cast of words and images, the conjectural sexual relations of persons and puns. In Keats' case, the poem's physical posture, its place and shape, its time and teller, the title above and the date below, are more memorable than the trail of words from "O" to "desire."

Keats' sonnet is more symptomatic than dramatic. The Shakes-pope of *The Dunciad* is only distantly related to the Keatspeare of "On Sitting Down." Keats' seeming opposition between the "Romance" of the octet and the "Chief Poet" of the sestet, the artistic choice that the sonnet constructs, dissolves upon even a cursory inspection. The "Queen of far-away" simply gives way to the long ago of *King Lear,* the "olden Pages" of Romance are replaced by the olden pages of the 1623 edition of Shakespeare's plays, the "Fair plumed Syren" metamorphoses into equally mythical "Phoenix Wings." In turning from Spenser to Shakespeare, Keats turns Shakespeare into Spenser. His Shakespeare inhabits and creates a world of clouds, dreams, wanderings, and old forests full of Edmund Burke's royal British oaks; he is epitomized by a Gothic fairy tale called *King Lear.*

Keats' poem on *King Lear,* written on the last page of *Hamlet,* sits with its back to *Hamlet* looking across the divided opening into *King Lear.* Keats quoted *King Lear* more than any other play except *Hamlet;* it was *King Lear* he chose to illustrate his famous axiom that "the excellence of every Art is its intensity, capable of making all disagreeables evaporate" (1817).[139] Hazlitt, who influenced Keats more than anyone, called *King Lear* "the best of all Shakespear's plays, for it is the one in which he was the most in earnest" (1817);[140] Shelley described it as "the most perfect specimen of the dramatic art existing in the world" (1821);[141] Coleridge regarded it as "the most tremendous effort of Shakspeare as a poet" (1822).[142] Although the Romantics quoted and criticized *Hamlet* obsessively, they seem to have admired *King Lear* more. Certainly, they admired it more than any previous generation. Even in Shakespeare's time, few allusions to the play have been found; it does not seem to have been especially popular with audiences or critics. The Romantics inherited a long-standing English admiration for *Hamlet;* they helped create the critical consensus that *King Lear* is an equal, perhaps a finer, achievement. What did they find so fascinating about *King Lear?* Why did Keats read it again?

King Lear is a parable of filial duty. Cordelia and Goneril and Regan and Edmund all rebel against their fathers and all die as a result. King Lear, moreover, unites the authorities of father and legitimate king; he embodies the traditional metaphorical argument that the king is a father, that his subjects are his children, that the preservation of society depends upon the child's obedience to the father and the subject's obedience to the king. In Shakespeare's play the children revolt against an old tyrannical father-king, one who bears an uncomfortable resemblance to George III. Such a rebellion might seem justifiable, even tempting. But no, the play tells us; no matter how old or mad or bad the father-king may be, revolt cannot be justified. Romantic critics identify not with the play's revolting young but with its toppled composite of power. In *The Prelude*, "As Lear reproached the winds," so Wordsworth reproached Robespierre, a vengeful "cruel son" who had made his birthplace groan. Old Edmund Burke, embittered and isolated, seeing himself as Lear, surrounded by currish ingratitude, quoted "The little dogs and all, / Tray, Blanch, and Sweetheart—see, they bark at me."[143] When we read the play "we are Lear—" Lamb declares, "we are in his mind, we are sustained by a grandeur which baffles the malice of daughters and storms."[144] Hazlitt said, in almost the same words, "It is we who are Hamlet"; but in *King Lear* the character parallel to Hamlet is, as Coleridge recognized, Edmund, "the main *agent* and prime mover." A Hamlet who acts becomes an Edmund, one of those "bold villains" Shakespeare uses "as vehicles for expressing opinions and conjectures of a nature too hazardous for a wise man to put forth directly as his own." And just as Burke had used all his art to make readers sympathize with poor Marie Antoinette, so in Shakespeare's text "All Lear's faults increase our pity," and the foolish intransigent monarch becomes merely "a fond father [who] has been duped."[145] *King Lear* excites the Romantics by acting out a total rebellion against the authority of the past, and in proclaiming its supremacy Hazlitt characteristically speaks of it in terms of "power," "force," and "strength."[146] But that sense of awesome and admirable power is located, paradoxically, in a feeble old man. That is why the Romantics' *King Lear* could not be acted: performance reminded them, jarringly, of the character's physical frailty. Keats, rereading *King Lear*, concluded that the "intensity" of great Art, left to itself, was "capable of making all disagreeables evaporate";[147] engrossed by "Beauty & Truth" we forget the temper tantrums and the slobber. For an imaginative reader, George III or King Lear might be transformed into a titanic tragic hero—but this illusion would be punctured by any encounter with material reality. In the mouths of the portly monarchs of contemporary Europe, Lear's heroic "every inch a king" could too easily become—as it did in Heinrich Heine's parody—"Jedes pfund ein König" (every pound a King).

King Lear gives revolution—and takes it away. As Hazlitt recognized in relation to *Henry V* and *Coriolanus*, "Poetry is right-royal" and "The language of poetry naturally falls in with the language of power."[148] The same principle animates *King Lear,* less obviously but all the more effectively. Lear gradually loses familial and political power, but he keeps his poetic authority, retaining in our readerly imaginations "The name and all th'addition to a king,"[149] a grandeur never granted to those who displace him. The power of an ancient power is intrinsic; you can temporarily peel away the trappings, but the organic core will always remain. Revolution is thus not only monstrous, ungrateful, and immoral; it is, in the end, impossible. And for the English Romantics, one of the revolutions that *King Lear* imagines and forecloses is a revolution against *King Lear* itself. Shakespeare had become one of the venerable authorities, one of the colossal father-kings, that his play defends.

CHAPTER 4

❧

VICTORIAN VALUES

Victorian . . . A. *adj.* Of or belonging to, designating, or typical of the reign of Queen Victoria (1837–1901).

Value (*sb.*) . . .
2. The material or monetary worth of a thing; the amount at which it may be estimated in terms of some medium of exchange or other standard of a similar nature . . .
6. The relative status of a thing, or the estimate in which it is held, according to its real or supposed worth, usefulness, or importance . . .
7. a. *Math.* The precise number or amount represented by a figure, quantity, etc.

A New English Dictionary on Historical Principles (1884–1928)

Victorian, *a.*[2] . . .
2. *fig.* Resembling or typified by the attitudes supposedly characteristic of the Victorian era; prudish, strict; old-fashioned, out-dated.

A Supplement to the Oxford English Dictionary (1972–86)

IN WHICH OUR HERO IS NOT INTRODUCED

Baron Georges Cuvier, one of the early mammoths of paleontology, concluded from his studies of the Paris basin that the history of life on earth had been regularly disrupted by catastrophes, abrupt crises that shaped the development of the biosphere:

> These repeated irruptions and retreats of the sea have neither been slow nor gradual; most of the catastrophes which have occasioned them have been sudden . . . Life, therefore, has been often disturbed on this earth by terrible events—calamities which, at their commencement, have perhaps moved and over-turned to a great depth the entire outer crust of the globe . . . [1]

These conclusions were articulated by a French aristocrat in 1812, in a work describing "les révolutions du globe." "Révolutions" was not a word used lightly by Frenchmen in 1812.

The chief antagonist of such theories was Charles Lyell, barrister and son of a wealthy landowner; in *Principles of Geology*, a textbook that immediately became famous, Lyell upbraided the "French spirit of speculation" and its desire "to cut, rather than patiently to untie, the Gordian knot."[2] He argued that we should stop "framing imaginary theories of catastrophes and mighty revolutions"[3] and recognize instead the powerful efficacy of "gradual mutations";[4] "sudden and violent revolutions of the globe"[5] were not needed if we put in their place "slow and tranquil causes,"[6] based upon "min-ute, but incessant alterations."[7] These words were written by an upper-middle-class liberal Englishman in 1832, the year that Par-liament passed the Great Reform Bill.[8] The French scientist in the early nineteenth century had experienced and believed in cata-clysm; the British scientist had experienced and believed in gradual change.

The theory of gradualism gradually prevailed, first in geology and then in biology. Lyell's victory over Cuvier was predictable; mere French science could hardly conquer English, not after Water-loo, in a century when the sun never set on the Pax Britannica. Lyell's friend Charles Darwin's victory over God was perhaps more surprising and certainly harder fought; but to wave the wand of individual creation over each species, or to wipe the earth clean with a flood—such theories sounded suspiciously similar to the discredited French ideology of cataclysm. Surely God, like any reasonable nineteenth-century Englishman, did not need to resort to extravagant catastrophes in order to re-form the plant and animal kingdoms. God, as an empirical practitioner of Liberalism and free trade, would surely depend upon the competitive laws of the biological marketplace. Revolutions were no more desirable or necessary in the natural than in the political world. In science, theology, politics, the writing of history, and the interpretation of literature, British bit-by-bitism slowly smothered the revolutionary theory of the one big bite.

No scientist dismisses Lyell's *Principles of Geology* or Darwin's *Origin of Species* simply because the authors of those books constructed an image of the planet's history that reflects the dominant features of British social experience in the nineteenth century. In the appropriate cultural conditions certain ideas are more likely to be thought, and having been thought are more likely to be communicated to others, and having been promulgated are more likely to win and sustain adherence. In retrospect, scientists may now realize that the hypothesis of gradualism, like the British Empire, overextended itself. By the late twentieth century geologists had come to accept the evidence for occasional cataclysms; among physicists the "big bang" is the most popular of all current cosmological theories. We can accept that these more recent models of the history of our cosmos improve upon the formulations of Victorian scientists, while acknowledging that this limited revival of catastrophism itself reflects the preoccupations of a thermonuclear age. A human culture, unlike a bacteriological one, cannot be preserved in sterilized isolation from its untidily teeming and changing environment. History and science contaminate one another. So do history and literature.

IN WHICH OUR HERO GRADUALLY
REVEALS HIMSELF

At 8 P.M. on Friday, March 13, 1874, Frederick James Furnivall called to order the first meeting of the New Shakspere Society. Furnivall himself had studied chemistry and mathematics, and in the prospectus announcing his foundation of a new society he had urged that "in this Victorian time, when our geniuses of Science are so wresting her secrets from Nature as to make our days memorable for ever," similar achievements could be expected from investigators of Shakespeare.[9] German Shakespeare scholars had already demonstrated how much could be done. Unfortunately, England was falling behind:

> Although the average Englishman may have read a play or so, he has no notion of the characteristics, the periods, or succession of Shakspere's works, and can tell next to nothing about the poet himself. He does not know whether *Love's Labour's Lost* comes after the *Tempest* or before it; whether Shakspere began with Comedy, History, or Tragedy; whether his mind and purpose grew greater and more earnest with advancing years . . .

This lamentable ignorance Furnivall was determined to overcome. "The purpose of our Society," he declared,

> is, by a very close study of the metrical and phraseological peculiarities of Shakspere, to get his plays as nearly as possible into the order in which he wrote them . . . and then to use that revised order for the purpose of studying the progress and meaning of Shakspere's mind . . .[10]

To know order was to perceive progress, and in progress would be found meaning.

The techniques that would be used to retrace Shakespeare's evolution were expounded in more detail in the first scholarly paper read to the new society. Its author was "the industrious flea," as he was nicknamed, the Reverend Frederick G. Fleay, who has been ably described by one of his contemporaries:

> A man of realities. A man of fact and calculation. A man who proceeds upon the principle that two and two are four, and nothing over, and who is not to be talked into allowing for anything over . . . With a rule and a pair of scales, and the multiplication table always in his pocket, sir, ready to weigh and measure any parcel of human nature . . .

Fleay, "a kind of cannon loaded to the muzzle with facts," fired off all the original papers printed in the first volume of the New Shakspere Society's *Transactions:* on metrical tests as applied to the plays

of Shakespeare, Fletcher, Beaumont and Massinger; on the authorship of *The Taming of the Shrew, Timon of Athens,* and *Pericles.* He
described his method in the paper read at that memorable first
meeting:

> Now, what I want is, Facts ... Facts alone are wanted in life ...
> Stick to Facts, sir! ... In this life, we want nothing but Facts, sir;
> nothing but Facts![11]

Actually, these are the words of Thomas Gradgrind, quoted from
the first chapter of Charles Dickens' novel *Hard Times,* not the words
of Frederick Fleay, quoted from the first chapter of the *New Shakspere Society Transactions,* twenty years later. Fleay's actual words
were:

> our analysis, which has hitherto been qualitative, must become
> quantitative; we must cease to be empirical, and become scien-
> tific; in criticism as in other matters, the test that decides between
> science and empiricism is this: "Can you say, not only of what
> kind, but how much? If you cannot weigh, measure, number your
> results, however you may be convinced yourself, you must not
> hope to convince others, or claim the position of an investigator;
> you are merely a guesser ..."[12]

The method of the New Shakspere Society would be scientific,
but the conclusions would be satisfyingly moral. "To understand
Shakspeare aright," Matthew Arnold advised, "the clue to seize is
the morality of Shakspeare."[13] Although the details had yet to be
worked out, it was already clear to Furnivall that the chronology of
Shakespeare's plays would show their author passing

> from the fun and word-play, the lightness, the passion, of the
> Comedies of Youth, through the patriotism (still with comedy of
> more meaning) of the Histories of Middle Age, to the great
> Tragedies dealing with the deepest questions of man in Later
> Life; and then at last to the poet's peaceful and quiet home-life
> again in Stratford, where he ends with his Prospero and Miranda,
> his Leontes finding again his wife and daughter in Hermione and
> Perdita; in whom we may fancy that the Stratford both of his
> early and late days lives again, and that the daughters he saw
> there, the sweet English maidens, the pleasant country scenes
> around him, passt as it were again into his plays.[14]

The New Shakspere Society offered Victorians a Shakespeare whose evolution could be measured with scientific precision, an evolution that confirmed the Victorian belief in progress, a progress that culminated in an affirmation of paternal pastoral "home-life."

This Victorian image of an evolving Shakespeare was itself a predictable phase in the evolution of Shakespeare's reputation. From the Restoration to the Romantics, the movement of Shakesperotics had been essentially vertical; assessments of the value of his work rose and rose. In the late eighteenth century his supremacy was consolidated; potential challenges were defeated or defused. But after the hyperbolic praise of Coleridge & Co., the limits of vertical evolution had been reached. In 1825 Thomas Lovell Beddoes could write without embarrassment of "the honey-minutes of the year / Which make man god, and make a god—Shakespeare"; in 1840 Thomas Carlyle described Shakespeare as "a *Prophet*" and "a Priest of Mankind," "a blessed heaven-sent Bringer of Light" who composed "a kind of universal Psalm," the "still more melodious Priest of a *true* Catholicism, the 'Universal Church' of the Future and of all times." Literary reputations can hardly rise higher. As Arnold testified, "The Bible and Shakspeare" were, by the Victorian period, naturally mentioned in the same breath and "imposed upon an Englishman as objects of his admiration."15 And as Arnold realized, the scientific assault on received religion perhaps made literature the more secure idol for a modern civilization.

This English estimate of Shakespeare's importance was simply confirmed by the growth of his reputation throughout Europe. Carlyle could say without hyperbole that "the best judgement not of this country only, but of Europe at large, is slowly pointing to the conclusion, That Shakspeare is the chief of all Poets hitherto; the greatest intellect who, in our recorded world, has left record of himself in the way of Literature." Shakespeare had already, before the end of the eighteenth century, conquered Germany; in the era which proclaimed that "Deutschland ist Hamlet," it is no surprise to find Brahms and Schubert composing music for songs from the plays, or Hegel writing of "the infinite breadth of his world-stage," or Heine affirming that "even though God claims for Himself the first place in creation, Shakespeare is next in line." But Shakespeare was also praised and imitated by the greatest Russian poet of the nineteenth century (Pushkin); he was adapted and translated by the greatest Russian playwright of the nineteenth century (Ostrovsky); he inspired symphonic fantasies, overtures, and incidental music by the greatest Russian composer of the nineteenth century (Tchaikovsky). Turgenev in a famous lecture of 1860 singled out Hamlet and Don Quixote as exemplary embodiments of "The Two Eternal Human Types," sceptics and idealists; ordinary Russians in Dostoievsky's novels quote and discuss Shakespeare, and the novelist himself affirmed "The universality, the all-comprehensive, the unexplored depth of the world types of man belonging to the Aryan race conceived by Shakespeare."[16] Similar proofs of Shakespeare's fame can be cited from every country in Europe. In 1858 the Hungarian composer Liszt composed a symphonic poem on Hamlet; between 1847 and 1893 the Italian composer Verdi composed operas based on *Macbeth, Othello,* and *The Merry Wives of Windsor;* in 1875–77 the complete works were translated into Polish; in 1895–96 the Danish critic Georg Brandes published an influential three-volume biography of Shakespeare.

Even the French had finally succumbed. Stendhal's *Racine et Shakespeare* was published in 1823, then again in an expanded edition in 1825. It not only praised individual plays ("Shakespeare's *Macbeth* is one of the masterpieces of the human spirit"),[17] it insisted that Shakespeare was a more relevant model for contemporary French dramatists than Racine. Stendhal's controversial pamphlet was followed in 1827 by the manifesto of French *romanticisme,* Hugo's epoch-making preface to *Cromwell* (1827), which equated "Shakespeare" with "drama." In 1839 Alexandre Dumas described Shakespeare as "the artist who has created most, after God." In the same year Paris heard a choral symphony by Berlioz based upon *Roméo et Juliette.* In 1862 Berlioz composed the last of his many works inspired by Shakespeare, a comic opera about *Béatrice et Bénédict;* in 1868 Ambroise Thomas composed a tragic opera about *Hamlet.* Shakespeare was the subject of adulatory volumes by Hugo in 1864 and by Lamartine in 1865; Hamlet was painted by Degas and poemed by Laforgue.

In this cultural environment Shakespeare's artistic supremacy had ceased to be debated; it was simply assumed. Consequently, the main movement of Shakesperotics now became lateral: his influence broadened, geographically and socially. What had been the river of his reputation was now "the ocean of Shakespeare,"[18] an ocean that surrounded and defined Great Britain. He became relevant to more areas of the cultural domain and the object of more kinds of cultural activity. Shakespeare's reputation, like Britain itself, entered a period of expansion and diversification.

The Victorians themselves were interested in the evolution of Shakesperotics; in 1847 Charles Knight published the first *History of Opinions on the Writings of Shakspere*. But they were more interested in the evolution of Shakespeare himself. If Shakespeare was—as everyone now affirmed—a genius, then he must have understood life; and therefore by understanding Shakespeare anyone else could understand life. But you could understand the fullness of Shakespeare's gospel only if you put his words, sentences, thoughts, in the right order. The chronology of his work provided the syntax of his message.

The interpretation of that syntax offered by Furnivall had been evolving since the eighteenth century, and its evolution characterizes the scholarship of the nineteenth century. Isolated contributions, widely separated, are gradually absorbed into a corporate progress that picks up mass as it gains momentum. As early as 1756 Richard Roderick had completed the first quantitative analysis of Shakespeare's verse, noting that *Henry VIII* contains an exceptional number of verse lines that end with a superfluous unstressed syllable and an exceptional number that place the caesura after the seventh syllable—conclusions later confirmed by the New Shakspere Society and by all subsequent investigators.[19] But Roderick could not relate his conclusions to the chronology of Shakespeare's work, because no such chronology was available in 1756. When Malone published the first such chronology, in 1778, he based his conclusions in part upon numerical assessments of style. Like Fleay a century later, Malone counted rhymes:

> their *frequency*, . . . is here urged, as a circumstance which seems to characterize and distinguish our poet's earliest performances . . . whenever, of two early pieces it is doubtful which preceded the other, I am disposed to believe, (other proofs being wanting) that play in which the greater number of rhymes is found, to have been first composed.

Largely on the basis of the "frequent rhymes with which it abounds," Malone concluded wrongly that *Love's Labour's Lost* was Shakespeare's first play.[20]

Little more was done with numerical measurements of style until the Victorian period. But between 1778 and 1874 Malone's prototype of the chronology was gradually improved. Capell's chronology was published in 1783, Malone revised his own in 1790, George

Chalmers revised Malone's in 1801, Malone's final version was published posthumously in 1821. New information, affecting the dating of individual plays, continued to float sporadically to the surface. In 1831 John Payne Collier discovered an early manuscript recording a 1602 performance of *Twelfth Night;* in 1832 the Reverend W. H. Black discovered an account of performances of *Macbeth, The Winter's Tale,* and *Cymbeline* in 1611; in 1842 Peter Cunningham published manuscript accounts of court performances of Shakespeare's plays in 1604–05 and 1611–12; in 1865 James Halliwell discovered a clear reference, printed in 1601, to *Julius Caesar.*[21] The particular names and dates here do not matter; what does matter is the number of names and the steady succession of dates. These revelations and others like them improved previous chronological scenarios; the tick-tick-tick of discoveries proved that the secrets of Shakespeare, like those of nature, were yielding to the inexorable energy and ingenuity of nineteenth-century Englishmen.

Moreover, these incremental improvements to the chronology, made haphazardly by many hands over the course of many decades, gradually distributed the plays into a sequence that, for the first time, seemed to possess some narrative coherence. For a century after 1623 Shakespeare's plays had been divided into three generic groups: the *Comedies, Histories, and Tragedies* defined by the First Folio collection. The "Histories" followed the order of the reigns they dramatised, from *King John* to *Henry VIII;* the "Comedies" and "Tragedies" were distributed—so it seemed—at random. In 1725 Pope had rearranged the plays into four categories, related but not identical to the original three: Comedies, Historical Plays (including *King Lear*), Tragedies from History (the four Roman plays, *Timon,* and *Macbeth*), and Tragedies from Fable (*Troilus, Cymbeline, Romeo and Juliet, Hamlet,* and *Othello*). The Historical Plays and Tragedies from History were arranged in historical sequence; for the Comedies he followed the haphazard arrangement of the folio, except that he moved *A Midsummer Night's Dream* so that it followed another "magical" play, *The Tempest* (which was placed first). Pope's arrangement survived in most editions for the rest of the eighteenth century, but it was hardly more satisfying than the original schema.

The first attempts at a chronological sequence were not enormously satisfying either. In the first place, the chronological tables were tucked away in introductions; until 1821 they did not affect the physical order of the plays in editions. In the second place, the rudimentary early chronologies afford little sense of development. Keats might be convinced that "Shakspeare led a life of Allegory; his works are the comments on it—"²² but the plot of that "continual allegory" was difficult to discern in chronologies that placed *The Winter's Tale* among Shakespeare's early works and *The Taming of the Shrew* among the late. Critics like Keats and Hunt might read a personal meaning in individual plays, like *Hamlet* or *Twelfth Night;* but such isolated explications did not give any meaningful shape to the sequence as a whole.

Coleridge did try to find an artistic and biographical pattern in the chronology of Shakespeare's plays, but in doing so he simply dismissed the scholarly evidence, arranging the plays in whatever sequence suited him at the moment. He justified this procedure by expressing contempt for "the fallacious and unsatisfactory Nature" of "external documents."²³ This disdain for Facts was not an attitude likely to persuade anyone else; indeed, from Coleridge's own changes of mind it never seems to have persuaded him for long. Coleridge idly busily constructed theories before enough reliable data had been collected; later theorists were not cleverer than Coleridge, but they had better data bases and respected them more. For example, Malone's discovery in 1808 of the nautical sources of *The Tempest* established that the play must have been written very late in Shakespeare's career, and in 1821 he placed it last. *Twelfth Night* had been a rival contender for that final position, but Collier discovered an Elizabethan manuscript account firmly relegating that play to the middle of the chronology. Malone's and Collier's independent documentary discoveries laid the foundations for the conjecture, first proposed in 1838, that,

> Shakspeare, as if conscious that ["The Tempest"] would be his last [work], and as if inspired to typify himself, has made its hero a natural, a dignified, and benevolent magician, who could conjure up spirits from the vasty deep, and command supernatural agency by the most seemingly natural and simple means.— ... Shakspeare himself is Prospero, or rather the superior genius who commands both Prospero and Ariel. But the time was approaching when the potent sorcerer was to break his staff, and to bury it fathoms in the ocean—
> Deeper than did ever plummet sound.²⁴

Thomas Campbell, the first proponent of this tempting hypothesis, could not equal Coleridge as a poet or a critic; but he could profit from the later, greater, new and improved Victorian understanding of The Facts.

Just as *The Tempest* gradually positioned itself as the valedictory culmination of Shakespeare's lifework, so other parts of the canon settled slowly into little subplots of their own. Almost all the English history plays, for instance, seemed to belong to the 1590s. The single serious anomaly was *Henry VIII*, which—as Capell knew and as Malone at last grudgingly realized—must belong to the seventeenth century. But this anomaly was removed, fortuitously, by James Spedding, who in 1850 asked the world, "Who Wrote Shakspere's Henry VIII?" and answered, "John Fletcher" (with a little help from Shakespeare).[25] Spedding's conclusion was based upon the most numerate and systematic analysis of Shakespeare's style that had ever been attempted, it explained many of the metrical peculiarities noticed by Roderick a century before, it established a model for the later investigations of the New Shakspere Society, and it has been confirmed by much subsequent scholarship. But it also had the effect of removing *Henry VIII* from the roll call of history plays wholly planned and completed by Shakespeare himself. The plays that satisfied those criteria all belonged, as far as the Victorians could see, to a few years before 1600. The concentration was even more remarkable if you disregarded, as most nineteenth-century critics did, the three early plays about Henry VI; according to Malone, Shakespeare had only touched up and tidied up those plays, which had initially been written by others. The data had gravitated into a pattern that Furnivall could characterize, reasonably enough, as "the patriotism . . . of the Histories of Middle Age."

The tragedies underwent a similar evolution. Both Capell and Malone had initially presumed a run of five or six tragedies beginning in 1607, partly from a feeling that all the plays based upon Plutarch's *Lives of the Noble Grecians and Romans* should have been written at about the same time. Some such concatenation of tragedies survived in all chronologies, and it led naturally to Henry Hallam's conjecture, first published in 1839, that

> . . . there seems to have been a period of Shakspeare's life when his heart was ill at ease, and ill content with the world or his own conscience; the memory of hours misspent, the pang of affection

mis-placed or unrequited, the experience of man's worser nature, which intercourse with ill-chosen associates, by choice or circumstance, peculiarly teaches;—these, as they sank down into the depths of his great mind, seem not only to have inspired into it the conception of Lear and Timon, but that of one primary character, the censurer of mankind. . . . These plays all belong to nearly the same period.[26]

But although this sequence of tragedies invited biographical speculation, it could not easily be related at first to the rest of Shakespeare's career. The late tragedies were widely separated from the end of the histories sequence and even further removed from Shakespeare's most famous tragedy, *Hamlet* (initially dated by Malone and Chalmers in 1596–97). But by 1821 Malone had gradually come round to the view, almost universally accepted since, that Shakespeare's *Hamlet* belongs to the beginning of the seventeenth century and that earlier references to Hamlet allude to a lost play on the same subject. Discoveries by Cunningham (1842) and Halliwell (1865) pushed *Othello* back to 1604 and *Caesar* back before 1601. The tragic series was thus preserved, but simply shifted backward along the time line of Shakespeare's artistic development.

With this shift in the position of the tragedies, Shakespeare's plays had at last separated out into four bands on a chronological spectrum. An early period dominated by experimental comedies led to an era of histories and mature comedies, then to a concatenation of tragedies, which gave way at the end to something else, as yet unnamed but typified by *The Tempest*.

IN WHICH OUR HERO'S PROGRESS IS DESCRIBED

The something else was named by Edward Dowden, a lecturer at Trinity College, Dublin, and an absentee member of the New Shakspere Society from its beginnings. Dowden called Shakespeare's final plays "Romances," and since then they have been called Romances by almost everyone else. Furnivall, adapting a scheme proposed by the German commentator Georg Gervinus, had divided Shakespeare's output into four periods; Dowden, in his popular "primer" *Shakspere* (1877), labeled and described those

four periods. If we measure success by influence, Dowden characterized Shakespeare's artistic and personal evolution more successfully than anyone before or since.

Dowden's division can be compared with another division, available at the time, which he did not use. In one of his most famous
speeches, memorialized in many later paintings and engravings,
Shakespeare had written of the "seven ages" of man;[27] in some of
his most famous paragraphs Dowden wrote of the four ages of
Shakespeare. The difference between these accountings results in
part from what Dowden subtracted. Dowden skipped over Shakespeare "the infant, / Mewling and puking in the nurse's arms" and
Shakespeare "the whining school-boy, with his satchel"; he omitted,
at the end, Shakespeare's "second childishness and mere oblivion, /
Sans teeth, sans eyes, sans taste, sans everything." Dowden thus
confined his "strange eventful history" to Shakespeare's four middle
periods—but characterized them rather differently than Shakespeare had:

> *In the workshop.* Shakspere was learning his trade as a dramatic
> craftsman ... The works of Shakspere's youth—experiments in
> various directions—are all marked by the presence of vivacity,
> cleverness, delight in beauty, and a quick enjoyment of exis-
> tence.[28]

Eighteenth-century painters and poets had imagined baby Shakespeare, like baby Jesus, already instinct with godhead, being presented with the gifts of the Magi or suckled by buxom Muses; but to
Dowden and his contemporaries it seemed obvious that Shakespeare "grew in wisdom and in knowledge" and in "self-control"
from year to year.[29] He must therefore have begun his career with a
period of "learning." Since the self-taught genius could hardly be
imagined acquiring that learning "In the Classroom," he must have
gotten it on the job. The workshop was, of course, an institution
familiar to Dowden's Victorian readers, who would find natural and
attractive the notion that Shakespeare, like many a bright and ambitious lad, worked his way up from the shop floor.

But Shakespeare himself, in cataloging the seven ages of man,
did not epitomize early manhood in an apprentice, a "craftsman"
learning a "trade"; it was personified for him by "the lover, sighing
like furnace, with a woeful ballad made to his mistress' eyebrow."
This description suits well enough the period that produced such

adolescent erotica as *Romeo and Juliet, A Midsummer Night's Dream, Venus and Adonis,* and other sexual comedies and poems, the period in which Shakespeare introduced love scenes into every play, including all three of the plays on Henry VI, *Richard III* and *Titus Andronicus.* It accounts for the "vivacity, cleverness, delight in beauty," the "quick enjoyment of existence" that Dowden describes—and for the awkwardness and the showing off, which he does not describe but which are equally characteristic both of those plays and of that period of early maturity. And in that age of "experiments in various directions," both sexual and intellectual, the delight in beauty walks hand in hand with an equally amoral delight in potency, the delight that created Richard III and Petruchio, the delight that celebrates virtuosity for its own sake.

Dowden's vision of the second period also differs from Shakespeare's own:

> *In the world.* But now Shakspere's imagination began to lay hold of real life; he came to understand the world and the men in it; his plays begin to deal in an original and powerful way with the matter of history . . . During this period Shakspere's work grows strong and robust.[30]

The workshop, the classroom, the bedchamber, the sonnet—these are real places, but they are also enclosures, and at some point mature manhood has to escape from them and venture out into the "world." Dowden here has adapted an old story. But for Victorian readers the size and pressure of that "world," the opportunity and the obligation to confront it, had become urgent and tangible as never before; the railroad and telegraph and steamship conspired to make it all, from war with China to the bombardment of Zanzibar, impend and impinge upon consciousness. English workshops sent products to, and took raw materials from, the whole globe; in an era dominated politically and economically by the classical liberal doctrine of free trade, English ingenuity had to be able to hold its own "in the world." As space imploded, so did time; the Victorians were fascinated by history, both geological and human. The Crystal Palace Exhibition of 1851, with its displays of paraphernalia from many places and periods, expressed and intensified the general preoccupation with time and space. It set Britain in the world, by bringing the world to London, and then bringing

an unprecedented hundreds of thousands of Britons into London
to see it.

Shakespeare, too, had come to London to see the world; but
that had apparently happened even before he began writing plays.
For Shakespeare the second phase of human maturity was personified by

> a soldier,
> Full of strange oaths and bearded like the pard,
> Jealous in honour, sudden and quick in quarrel,
> Seeking the bubble reputation
> Even in the cannon's mouth.

Soldiers must venture into the world, and Shakespeare's image can
to some degree incorporate Dowden's. But for Shakespeare that
period is combative, territorial, and ambitious. That time in a man's
life might generate the calculated aggrandizement of Bolingbroke
and Prince Hal, might deliberately humiliate Shylock and cold-
bloodedly reject Falstaff, might celebrate the imperialism of Henry
V (and the Earl of Essex in Ireland). During the period when such
plays were being written Shakespeare's ambitious theatrical company conquered the town; Shakespeare himself, "seeking the bub-
ble reputation," wrote what turned out to be the riskiest play of his
career, *Henry IV, Part 1* (turning the revered Sir John Oldcastle into a
hypocritical buffoon), and with the rest of his company he gave
what turned out to be the riskiest performance of his career, reviving *Richard II* on the eve of the Earl of Essex's abortive rebellion
against Queen Elizabeth. Shakespeare in that period did not stop
writing comedies, any more than a soldier stops having (or at least
desiring) sex; but the nature of the comedy changes. Characteristically, in *Much Ado* (as in *Henry V*) the male lovers are soldiers
fresh from a successful campaign, while in *Merry Wives* and *Henry IV,
Part 1* the passion is relegated to peripheral characters.

But Shakespeare did not stop here. And neither did Dowden, for
whom the third phase was epitomized by the phrase *"Out of the
depths"*:

> Before [the second period] closed Shakspere had known sorrow
> . . . the poet now ceased to care for tales of mirth and love, for the
> stir and movement of history, for the pomp of war; he needed to
> sound, with his imagination, the depths of the human heart; to

inquire into the darkest and saddest parts of human life; to study
the great mystery of evil ... Shakspere's genius left the bright
surface of the world, and was at work in the very heart and center
of things.

Shakespeare's experience had been broad; now it would become
deep. In the years between Charles Baudelaire's *Les Fleurs du Mal*
(1857) and Joseph Conrad's injunction "In the destructive element
immerse" (1900), between the death of Edgar Allan Poe (1849) and
the publication of *Dr. Jekyll and Mr. Hyde* (1886), Dowden envisaged
a Shakespeare submerged for a time in darkness. (Who knew what
lurked under the floorboards or in the sewers?) But, like the great
majority of his readers, Dowden did not want a Shakespeare who,
like Poe or Baudelaire or Dr. Jekyll or Lord Jim, willingly and
willfully explored corruption and degradation; and if Shakespeare
did not jump into the cesspit, he must have been pushed. As Carlyle
had asked, "How could a man delineate a Hamlet, a Coriolanus, a
Macbeth, so many suffering heroic hearts, if his own heroic heart
had never suffered?"[31] Dowden was accordingly forced to postulate
some "sorrow" that precipitated Shakespeare's descent into unhealthy morbidity. This emotional deus ex machina has often been
condemned by later critics and has become the most notorious of
Dowden's contributions to criticism; Dowden has been characterized for later critics by his most uncharacteristic maneuver. He
postulated no such catastrophe at the onset of the other periods,
which instead ease imperceptibly into one another; he did not need
any such explanation here, but he *wanted* to need one, so that he
could excuse Shakespeare's indulgence in experiences that were
morally repugnant but nevertheless necessary to the wholeness of
his achievement. Dowden's excuse made Shakespeare's third period
more palatable for Victorian readers; for modern readers this
period actually becomes more credible without Dowden's excuse for
it. A Shakespeare made sad by circumstance seems to us fortuitously sentimental; a Shakespeare who consciously dips his hand in
the vomit and then licks his forefinger would be, by contrast,
repulsively interesting.

For Shakespeare himself the third adult period was indeed personified by a connoisseur of crime; but Shakespeare's figure does
not look up from the depths. He surveys them from above. Rather
than focusing on the criminal or the victim, on the prosecution or
the defense, he singles out

the justice,
In fair round belly with good capon lined,
With eyes severe and beard of formal cut,
Full of wise saws and modern instances.

Middle-aged, potbellied, formal, observant, severe, his mind a repository of ancient principles and contemporary parallels, Shakespeare's justice presides over an unending daily ritual of tragedies and problem comedies; he ensures that the rules of the ritual are observed; he instructs the jury. Such a man might have written Shakespeare's mature tragedies or *Measure for Measure* or *Troilus and Cressida*. He need feel no personal sorrow, he need not dabble in degradation; he is, in fact, as Shakespeare seems to have been by the beginning of the seventeenth century, respectable, professional, and secure. He is purchasing property, enforcing the payment of debts, acquiring a visibly well-fed countenance, securing a family coat of arms, becoming a groom of the king's chamber.

But one phase still awaits him. Dowden pictures Shakespeare, at the end,

> *On the heights.* Whatever his trials and sorrows and errors may have been, he had come forth from them wise, large-hearted, calm-souled. He seems to have learned the secret of life, and while taking his share in it, to be yet disengaged from it; he looks down upon life, its joys, its griefs, its errors, with a grave tenderness, which is almost pity. The spirit of these last plays is that of serenity which results from fortitude, and the recognition of human frailty. . . . In these "Romances" . . . a supernatural element is present . . . Shakspere's faith seems to have been that there is something without and around our human lives, of which we know little, yet which we know to be beneficent and divine.[32]

Beginning from a center defined by the workshop, this Shakespeare moves out, then down, and finally up. This three-dimensional plot lets him master the whole of spiritual space, ending with a positive vertical movement (into "a pure and serene elevation"). Dowden's Shakespeare at last achieves a visionary acceptance, not doctrinal or theological but nevertheless unmistakably religious—and religious in so vague a sense that science could never imperil it.

Shakespeare's own vision of this period had been less optimistic, more relentlessly material:

> the sixth age shifts
> Into the lean and slipper'd pantaloon,
> With spectacles on nose and pouch on side,
> His youthful hose, well saved, a world too wide
> For his shrunk shank; and his big manly voice,
> Turning again toward childish treble, pipes
> And whistles in his sound.

The vision and the voice have deteriorated; the body has shrunk, the world has become too wide. Shakespeare in this period apparently gave up acting, wrote fewer plays, and finally gave up writing plays altogether; but he was, with his slippers and his moneybags, financially comfortable and, accordingly, surrounded with material comforts. The plays he wrote were comforting. Just as the voice slips back toward childhood, so the mind dwells increasingly upon the past. Shakespeare deliberately resurrects old-fashioned theatrical forms and plots, he recycles his own characters and themes, he tells the story of old men (Pericles, Leontes, Prospero) almost overwhelmed by the past.

Shakespeare's division of a man's life into seven ages was not original, and since he wrote the passage in his mid-thirties he could not have intended it as a comprehensive retrospective on his own life. Moreover, the speech is spoken by a willfully satirical observer, who emphasizes the folly and weakness of each phase. The familiarity of the sevenfold division would have made Jaques' bias evident to most of Shakespeare's audience; he could have expected us to accept each personification as a representative figure, while discounting some of Jaques' cynicism. Shakespeare did not want to imply—nor do I—that Jaques describes human life in general, or Shakespeare's in particular, wholly accurately or wholly. But Shakespeare's narrative does emphasize, by contrast, the very different ideological perspective of Dowden's.

In Dowden's account each period surpasses its predecessor in spiritual value; Shakespeare progresses from simple virtuosity to secular wisdom, from worldliness to profound moral examination, from philosophy to faith. In Shakespeare's account "All the world's a stage . . . And one man in his time plays many parts"; the periods are simply roles. Shakespeare was an actor and described the life of man in terms of an actor's life. At one end of his career an actor may naturally play juvenile lovers; at the other end he will more naturally play senescent pantaloons; the actor may, at the appropriate time, be equally adept at both roles, and both may be equally useful to his theatrical company. Early in his own career Shakespeare wrote *Richard III, A Midsummer Night's Dream, Romeo and Juliet,* young plays that in a way he never surpassed; late in his career he wrote *Cymbeline* and *The Tempest,* old plays, also unsurpassed but more sophisticated, less spontaneous, more difficult, almost private.

When Shakespeare divided human life into seven ages he was drawing upon the cosmology of his time; the seven ages were related to what astronomy then knew as the "seven planets" (the moon, Mercury, Venus, Mars, the sun, Jupiter, and Saturn). Dowden's division of Shakespeare's career draws, in the same way, upon Victorian science. For Dowden, modern science had demonstrated that "the whole universe was ever in process of *becoming.*"[33] Consequently, knowledge consisted of an understanding of the laws of process. In an introductory lecture on "The Teaching of Literature" he told students that in order to appreciate a literary masterpiece they needed to "know not only *what it is* but *how it came to be what it is.*"[34] The study of an author's oeuvre must be based upon "the scientific doctrine of self-development."[35]

Just as Dowden divided Shakespeare's career into periods, so he divided literature into "epochs," which he characteristically described in terms of the "vaster geological periods"[36] of the earth's history. Discussing the literary consequences of the French Revolution, for instance, he adopted Cuvier's catastrophic imagery, observing that "such epochs of flood and fire seldom pass without displacing old strata and creating a new stratum, from which flowers and fruits hitherto unknown will in due time arise."[37] In a periodical essay on "The Scientific Movement and Literature" he concluded that one chief consequence of scientific progress was a recognition that "all human knowledge is relative," which for a student of literary history meant that "Now, more than at any former time, we are impressed with a sense that the thought, the feeling, and the action of each period of history becomes intelligible only through a special reference to that period."[38] We must, accordingly, approach the past as "scientific observers." Coleridge had declared Shakespeare's works "organic"; Dowden, in the aftermath of Darwin, recognized that "In order that an organism—plant or animal—should exist at all, there must be a certain correspondence between the organism and its environment." Each epoch will favor different kinds of organism. If we examine Shakespeare's writings closely, we will find that "the laws of [their] growth" are determined by "the nature of the man, and the nature of his environment."39 The nature of each work depends upon the proper recognition of two factors: the period of literary history to which its author belongs, and the period of the author's history to which the work belongs.

Dowden not only accepted the implications for literature of the new understanding of evolution and environment; he also accepted the value of Facts. Literature deserves our attention because it reveals certain Facts. "A great poet is great ... because he has perceived vividly some of the chief facts of the world. . . ."40 A great poet, so defined, differs little from a great scientist; Arnold can couple "Shakespeare and Newton" without any sense of incongruity.41 Dowden's Shakespeare "accepted the logic of facts" and possessed "*a rich feeling for positive, concrete fact*"; "of concrete moral facts he had the clearest perception"; "The mere fact was enough without any theory about the fact."

But Shakespeare's "resolute fidelity to the fact"42 could not be understood in isolation from its environment. "Scientific observers," surveying the period in which Shakespeare lived, will perceive that "a rich feeling for concrete fact, was the dominant characteristic of the Elizabethan age."43 Elizabethan dramatists were distinguished by their "Capacity for perceiving, for enjoying, and for reproducing facts, and facts of as great variety as possible ... The facts were those of human passion, and human activity." The long reign of Elizabeth I, like the long reign of Victoria, was an Epoch of Fact, and "In that special environment Shakspere throve; he put forth his blossoms and bore fruit."44

Dowden's evolutionary vision of literature corresponds to Darwin's vision of life, and both belong to the dominant Victorian vision of society. Condemning Shelley and the French Revolution, Dowden contrasts their "revolutionary" idea of progress with the "scientific" one:

> No true reformation was ever sudden; let us innovate like nature and like time. . . . It is "from precedent to precedent" that freedom "slowly broadens down," not by extravagant outbursts of "the red fool-fury of the Seine." The growth of individual character, the growth of national well-being, the development of the

entire human race from animality and primitive barbarism—
each of these, if it be sound, cannot but be slow and gradual . . .
Let science grow from more to more; let political organizations
be carefully amended and improved; let man advance in self-
reverence, self-knowledge, self-control, and so from decade to
decade, from century to century, will draw nearer that "One far-
off divine event to which the whole creation moves."[45]

Noticeably, in describing this scientific idea of slow and gradual
progress Dowden finds himself quoting his fellow Victorians Alfred
Tennyson and George Eliot, exemplars of what he applauds as "anti-
revolutionary" art. No quotations from Shakespeare come to mind.
Shakespeare never used the words "develop," "development,"
"emerge," "emergence," "evolve," "evolution," "gradual," "improvement," "self-improvement," "self-reverence," "self-knowledge," "self-
control," or "scientific." For Shakespeare, an "invention" was a
literary composition; "innovation" meant a disturbance or commo-
tion, "progress" meant, neutrally, onward motion in general or, specifically, a state journey by a monarch—and "fact" meant "a crime."
(Just the facts, ma'am.)

IN WHICH OUR HERO ATTENDS THE UNIVERSITY

By his own criteria, we can fully appreciate Dowden's vision of
Shakespeare only by understanding the environment that produced it. When Dowden, in his hymn to scientific progress, urges
that "political organizations be carefully amended and improved,"
we hear an Anglo-Irish Protestant in the 1870s, a lecturer in Dublin's Protestant college, the son of a merchant-landowner, the
brother of an Anglican bishop, seeking to avert and defuse the
revolutionary violence of the Catholic Irish independence movement. Dowden's comment belongs to the decade that disestablished
the Anglican Church in Ireland (1869), passed the Irish Land Act
(1870), and almost reformed Irish education (1873).

But preoccupations specific to Dowden, though they may help
explain the genesis of his thought, do not explain its influence.
Dowden's audience was not limited to embattled liberal Anglo-Irish
intellectuals. *Shakspere: A Critical Study of His Mind and Art* went

through twelve British editions between 1875 and 1901 and is still in print. Dowden appealed to the Victorian public because his literary criticism reflected a communal social experience that had affected his readers too. Dowden and his contemporaries saw, wherever they chose to look, gradual change, beneficent evolution, progress.

The social processes that shaped Victorian thought are illustrated in the manufacture and sale of printed matter, an industry instrumental in shaping the public perception of Shakespeare. By 1803 a prototype of the first papermaking machine had been developed, and by 1807 it was being manufactured. The first steam-powered printing machines were operating by 1814. A machine for setting type was patented in 1822 and in commercial use by 1844. A typecasting machine was invented in 1838. In 1852 price-fixing by publishers and booksellers was outlawed. The invention of steam-driven machinery for folding (1856), sewing (1856), rounding and backing (1876), casemaking (1891), and gathering (1900) transformed the binding industry beyond recognition. In 1860–61 a chemical process was developed for making paper from cheap and plentiful esparto grass; this breakthrough was followed in 1866 by a chemical process for producing wood pulp. A hot-metal composing machine was being mass-produced by 1890. In every case the invention was followed by a period of progressive improvement and diversification. Cumulatively these innovations revolutionized productivity, efficiency, prices, and working conditions. In 1800 all paper was made by hand from rags; by 1900 one hundred times as much paper was being produced, by machine, usually from wood pulp, at prices averaging about one-tenth of those prevailing a century before. The machine presses developed for book production could work eight times faster than the manually operated presses they replaced, and average composition speeds increased by about 600 percent. Similar narratives of improvement and expansion could be told about other aspects of British life in the nineteenth century. Progress was a Fact.

Moreover, these technological changes were accompanied by equally momentous changes in the distribution of printed matter. Book prices fell, while literacy and real incomes rose. Literacy gave more people the desire—and the rise in middle- and working-class incomes gave them the wherewithal—to purchase reading matter. Taxes on newspapers and on paper were abolished. Between 1828 and 1853 average book prices declined 40 percent, with the decline led by reprints—including, of course, reprints of Shakespeare. The final destruction of the booksellers' copyright monopolies permitted an explosion of popular texts of English classics. Between 1709 and 1810 sixty-five editions of Shakespeare's works were published; a mere ten years from 1851 to 1860 witnessed the production of at least 162.[46] By 1887 over eighty school editions of individual plays had been published, making Shakespeare the subject of twice as many textbooks as any other English author. The abundance of cheap reprints of Shakespeare created a corresponding abundance of even cheaper secondhand copies.

The techniques of serial publication, so familiar to readers of Dickens, were also applied to Shakespeare. Between 1838 and 1843 Charles Knight's edition was published in fifty-five monthly parts, then collected into eight volumes; Julian Verplanck's New York edition burped out in monthly installments from 1844 to 1847 before being issued in a three-volume set. Publication in installments made it possible for families with limited incomes to collect an edition of Shakespeare piece by piece; in 1851 a Manchester bookseller testifying before a parliamentary committee estimated that 150 "penny numbers" of Shakespeare were sold every week.[47] Again like Dickens, both Knight's *Pictorial Edition* and Verplanck's *Illustrated Shakespeare* exploited new and cheaper techniques of lithography in order to embellish their texts with visualizations of the action. Staunton's edition (1857–60) boasted 824 illustrations. Likewise, the invention of photography led to photolitho facsimiles of the first and second edition of *Hamlet* (1858, 1859); a photographic reproduction of the entire First Folio appeared in 1866, another in 1876, another in 1895; meanwhile Furnivall and the New Shakspere Society produced a series of Shakespeare quarto facsimiles (1880–91).

Such facsimiles were aimed at a few hundred well-to-do readers. So were the nine volumes of a new edition of *The Works of William Shakespeare* published at one pound per volume between 1863 and 1866.[48] But in 1864 that text was separately printed, without notes, in a single affordable volume called "The Globe Edition." In their preface the editors explained their choice of title: "It seems indeed safe to predict that any volume which presents, in a convenient form, with clear type and at a moderate cost, the complete works of the foremost man in all literature, the greatest master of the language most widely spoken among men, will make its way to the remotest corners of the habitable globe."[49] This optimistic prediction proved accurate. The Globe edition immediately established itself and remained the standard text for almost a century. No other edition has ever achieved a comparable permanence.*

The unique cultural importance of this edition depended in large part upon the credentials of those who produced it. The editors of Shakespeare's works in the eighteenth century and the first half of the nineteenth had represented a variety of livelihoods. Rowe was a playwright, Pope a poet, Warburton a clergyman. Johnson was omnicompetent. Theobald wrote plays; Capell licensed them. Sir Thomas Hanmer edited Shakespeare after retiring as Speaker of the House of Commons. Charles Jennens was an eccentric millionaire. Both George Steevens and the Reverend Alexander Dyce were comfortably sustained by the wealth their parents had accumulated from the East India Company. Edmond Malone was subsidized by income from the family estates in Ireland. James Boswell the younger succeeded to his father's title as Lord Auchinleck. Charles Knight was an independent publisher and journalist. John Payne Collier began his literary career, like Dickens, as a parliamentary reporter, and his income from scribbling was later supplemented by a pension from the Duke of Devonshire and then another from the Civil List. S. W. Singer was bequeathed "a competency" sufficient to finance him for life by his friend the antiquarian Francis Douce. Howard Staunton was an international chess champion. James Halliwell supported himself with his pen, supplemented by profitable dealings in antiquarian books, until he was at last rescued from the need to earn a living by the death of his wealthy father-in-law. Beyond the fact that they were men, British, and born into the middle or upper class, these editors had only one thing in common: we would call them all amateurs. Some were educated at universities, but none were employed by universities.

By contrast the edition of 1863–66 was, as the title page declares, produced by three Fellows of Trinity College, Cambridge: William George Clark, John Glover, and William Aldis Wright. The text had been "Printed at the University Press" and was dedicated to "The Duke of Devonshire, K. G., Chancellor of the University of Cambridge." Understandably, this edition—from which the Globe edition derived its text and its authority—immediately became and

---

*As late as 1978 *The Annotated Shakespeare*—widely puffed in the popular media, hailed as "the definitive edition" by the *Wall Street Journal,* and still prominent in chains of American bookstores a decade later—simply reprinted the Globe text.

remains known as "the so-called 'Cambridge Shakespeare,'"[50] though that honorific appellation appears nowhere in the edition itself. The university's name mattered more than those of the individual editors, because what distinguished the edition from its predecessors was the involvement of professional academics from one of England's two ancient universities.

The Cambridge edition represented the first serious intrusion of academics into the history of Shakespeare's reputation. In the early eighteenth century Styan Thirlby, a Fellow at Jesus College in Cambridge, had made a number of useful suggestions to other editors, but his own plans for an edition succumbed to lassitude and alcohol. Although Hanmer's edition of Shakespeare was published by the Clarendon Press at Oxford, Hanmer himself was a landed gentleman, not a university don, and his edition epitomized amateurism in all the worst senses. Consequently, when Clark, Wright, and Glover edited their Cambridge Shakespeare, they knew, and readers knew, that they were setting a precedent. In the introduction to their first volume they asserted that "Cambridge afforded facilities for the execution of the task [of editing Shakespeare's works] such as few other places could boast of."[51] The trinity from Trinity declared that Shakespeare was a fit subject for academic research and that academics were the subjects best fitted to undertake such research.

What the academics undertook, they soon took over. The Cambridge Shakespeare was followed almost immediately by the Clarendon Shakespeare, a series of editions of individual plays published by Oxford University Press between 1868 and 1906, edited by Clark and Wright of Cambridge. In 1891 the Oxford Shakespeare offered the complete works in a single volume edited by W. J. Craig—a move that coincided with a second edition of the Cambridge Shakespeare, revised by Wright, in 1891–93. Commercial publishers continued to offer editions of Shakespeare; but increasingly those editions, if they had any pretensions to intellectual authority, were prepared by academics. Dowden, for instance, edited *Hamlet, Cymbeline,* and *Romeo* in the Arden Shakespeare series for Methuen and edited or wrote introductions for another ten editions by various publishers. The most influential of all Victorian Shakespeare critics, Dowden was also the first major Shakespearian who earned his living by college teaching. *Shakspere: A Critical Study of his Mind and Art* originated as a course of lectures at

Trinity College, Dublin. No less than the Cambridge Shakespeare, Dowden epitomizes the new academic age.

The professorial appropriation of Shakespeare accounts in part for the contrast between the unparalleled success of the Cambridge editors and the utter failure of Edward Capell a century before. Like Capell, the Cambridge triumvirate returned to the original editions and then critically and systematically reexamined the practice of subsequent editors; like Capell, they revolutionized the editing of Shakespeare. The similarity of the two projects is not fortuitous; Capell had donated his Shakespeare collection to Trinity College, Cambridge, and that collection formed the nucleus of materials upon which the Cambridge editors based their work. But Capell had been an isolated individual, trying to compete with the power of an eighteenth-century cultural oligarchy; the Cambridge editors were the shock troops of an expansive institution. Their immediate predecessors and rivals formed no club; they were scattered amateurs. Moreover, public confidence in those amateurs had been devastated by the allegations that John Payne Collier, the most able and respected of them all, had been forging documents for decades. Newspapers and popular periodicals printed charge and countercharge from 1853 to 1860, and the scandal tainted almost everyone involved. The Cambridge editors had not become involved: "We have," they announced, "no intention of entering into the controversy respecting the antiquity and authority" of the Collier documents, "nor is it necessary to enumerate the writings on a subject which is still so fresh in the memory of all."[52] After years of editorial civil war, a foreign power marched in, promising to suppress discredited factions and restore order; a relieved public welcomed the invader.

Intellectually, the Cambridge Shakespeare differed from all previous editions in its emphasis upon the factual history of the evolution of the text. The editors refrained from critical introductions or explanatory commentary, which would have compelled them to express subjective value judgments and to engage in unseemly bickering with rival editors. Instead, they printed only a text and an apparatus. In this strategic reticence about the editorial process they applied to Shakespeare norms already established in nineteenth-century editions of classical and Biblical texts, particularly by the influential German textual critic Karl Lachmann. Another German, Tycho Mommsen—younger brother of the great classical scholar Theodor Mommsen—had published in 1859 a historical collation of textual variants in every edition of *Romeo and Juliet* from 1597 to 1709; Mommsen provided his English contemporaries with a model of what could and should be done.

Printed at the bottom of each page, the Cambridge apparatus recorded with unprecedented thoroughness and accuracy the readings of previous texts, from the earliest quartos in the sixteenth century to the most recent Victorian editions. If the textual history of a passage was particularly complicated, the details were laid out in full in one of the few "Notes" appended to each play; but these appendages, like the main body of the apparatus, were confined to an objective transcript of the Facts. The apparatus did not catalog how many editors had adopted a particular reading; it was not designed as a democratic measurement of editorial taste. Instead, it identified the point at which each new reading had entered the historical record. It documented a textual continuum, which demonstrated that certain fossils appeared only in certain strata; readings originated in a certain edition and died out in another. In this way the Cambridge editors correctly established, in all but a handful of problematic cases, the genetic relationship between earlier editions.

The editors' collection and interpretation of this mass of data would have done credit to any Victorian scientist. It amassed in one place most of what an editor or critic needed to know about the textual tradition; anyone could create a new edition by modifying the Cambridge text to incorporate readings recorded in the Cambridge apparatus. By isolating and gathering together all that was original in previous editions, it collected all the power of the past into itself, rendering its predecessors superfluous and impotent. By its power to spawn derivatives it dominated the editorial future.

The Cambridge edition made no claims to originality in offering new solutions to textual problems. But the modesty of its own contribution only enhanced its authority as an arbiter of past contributions. Any conspicuous creativity would have called attention to its own presence; the text seemed instead to be transmitting the past directly into the future, overleaping the present entirely. The editors did not explain their choices—why, for instance, they spelled their author's name "Shakespeare." By justifying such decisions the editors would have advertised their own presence, their own personal standards of judgment. When the Tonson publishing family chose Nicholas Rowe, or Alexander Pope, or Samuel Johnson to edit Shakespeare, they expected those editors to exercise their personal judgment, and they expected readers to respect it. The Cambridge editors, by contrast, were not practitioners of imaginative literature; they were just experts. Their academic credentials and unequaled command of the Facts qualified them to establish the truth, impersonally. The impression of impersonality was abetted by collaboration. Eighteenth-century editors had cannibalized the work of their predecessors and had incorporated suggestions from many sources, but in the Cambridge edition the text of Shakespeare was decided for the first time by a committee. The individualities of the editors were submerged in their corporate cognomen. They are present everywhere but visible nowhere; their expertise guarantees and suffuses the entire text but never directly exposes the particulars of its operation. Invisible, inscrutable, impersonal.

The success of the Cambridge edition belonged and contributed to the rise of the "expert" (a noun first recorded in English usage in 1825) and the "specialist" (a noun first recorded in 1856). Nicholas Rowe had been an acclaimed playwright, author of the finest English translation of Lucan, an influential editor and critic and biographer of Shakespeare; Glover and Clark and Wright were editors, period. Clark and Wright were the most important, productive, and influential Shakespeare editors of the nineteenth century; but they would not even make a cameo appearance in any chronicle of Shakespeare biography, or theatrical history, or literary criticism. Likewise, James Halliwell, who contributed more to our knowledge of Shakespeare's life than any other nineteenth-century scholar, contributed nothing to the history of criticism and precious little to the history of editing. Dowden, like Halliwell, edited plays, but his achievements as a textual critic can be counted on the thumbs of one hand. And these were the giants of the age. Even Shakespearians were now experts in only a part of Shakespeare.

This division of intellectual labor is obviously related to parallel developments in science and industry. It resulted from, and in turn continually reignited, the explosion of knowledge that had begun in the nineteenth century. The sheer expanding bulk of acquired data forced a division of labor; the division of labor increased intellectual productivity; the increased productivity forced a further division of labor. Improving technology accelerated the dissemination of information throughout the system, while legislative reforms removed artificial impediments to the free flow of data. But even as information was being disseminated more widely than ever, it was being concentrated in a diminishing number of central data banks. In Shakespeare's case the process of collection had begun in the late eighteenth century, with a handful of individual antiquarians who amassed important private collections; but access to the information in them remained limited as long as the collections remained private. Capell gave his collection to Trinity College, Cambridge; Malone gave his to the Bodleian Library, Oxford; Garrick's went to what became the British Museum. By contrast, the Birmingham Shakespeare Library, which opened in 1868, was created communally, by the civic pride of a prosperous Victorian manufacturing town. Its supporters were fired by an ambition "to see founded in Birmingham a Shakespeare Library which should contain (as far as practicable) every edition and every translation of Shakespeare; all the commentators, good, bad and indifferent; in short, every book connected with the life and works of our great poet"—not to mention "portraits of Shakespeare, and all the pictures, etc., illustrative of his works."53 The creation of these national data banks democratized scholarship, making the raw materials of intellectual production available to a larger public; but it also gave enormous power to the new lords of access, the bureaucrats who controlled these concentrations of information. Members of the British Museum staff were instrumental in destroying Collier; the Cambridge editors Glover and Wright monopolized the post of librarian at Trinity College from 1858 to 1872. Cambridge, Oxford, Birmingham, and the British Library still dominate Shakespearian research in Great Britain.

A successful division of labor presupposes some agreed standard of reference, and the flood tide of Shakespeare editions made a common standard essential. In Germany it was provided by the Schlegel/Tieck translation, begun by A. W. von Schlegel in 1797 and completed by Ludwig Tieck and others in 1833; this version quickly became "Shakespeare für das Volk" and a recognized classic of German Romanticism. Rather than attempt to replace it, later German scholars simply corrected it (by emending away lexical errors) or restored it (by using Schlegel's manuscripts to remove corruptions from the printed text). In 1891 it was published in a cheap one-volume edition that sold 25,000 copies in two and a half years.54

This German best seller was clearly inspired by the success of the Globe edition. The Cambridge/Globe text immediately became the standard of reference for anyone who read Shakespeare in English (and "Shakespeare" he eventually became, under the relentless pressure of their use of that spelling). In its academic incarnation, with full scholarly apparatus, it was intellectually respectable; in its popular incarnation, without apparatus but with a larger readership than any other edition, it was universally recognizable. Moreover, the Cambridge editors for the first time enumerated Shakespeare's works. Other editors had subdivided each play into numbered acts and further subdivided each act into numbered scenes; but the Cambridge editors also decided "To number the lines in each scene separately, so as to facilitate reference."55 The Globe edition did the same. In this way the Shakespeare canon was subdivided into 114,792 line-units of approximately equal size.56 Every word of his work could thereafter be identified by citing its numeric coordinates in their edition; you could say that a certain expression occurred in the nth line of the nth scene of the nth act of play x, and any other reader would quickly be able to locate that area of the text and thus duplicate your observation. For instance, the longest word in Shakespeare, "honorificabilitudinitatibus," occurs in the Globe edition at line 44 of scene one of Act Five of *Love's Labour's Lost*, a reference that could be abbreviated for convenience to *L.L.L.* V.i.44 without losing its accuracy or intelligibility. This system of reference has become so familiar to literary scholars that we can hardly appreciate its revolutionary significance in facilitating data retrieval.

The availability of a universal standard of reference made possible the production of a series of standard reference works. In 1869 E. A. Abbott published *A Shakespearian Grammar: An Attempt to Illustrate Some of the Differences Between Elizabethan and Modern English;* a second and third edition followed within the year, and Abbott still remains the most widely cited authority on the grammar of Shakespeare and his contemporaries. In 1874–75 Alexander Schmidt published in Berlin a two-volume *Shakespeare-Lexicon,* which continues to be widely used, as it remains the only "Complete Dictionary of all the English Words, Phrases and Constructions in the Works of the Poet." Abbott divided his *Grammar* into 529 numbered paragraphs, for easy reference; for the same reason Schmidt divided his *Lexicon* entries for a word into parts of speech, with further subdivisions for distinct senses (identified by successive letters of the alphabet). All previous indexes and concordances were superseded in 1894 by John Bartlett's *New and Complete Concordance of the Dramatic Works and Poems of Shakespeare,* which is still in print. All these works are keyed to the line numbering of the Globe edition.

The most ambitious and important of these reference works was *A New English Dictionary on Historical Principles,* published by Oxford University Press and more familiar to modern readers by its later name, the *Oxford English Dictionary,* abbreviated for convenience to *OED.* The collection of materials for this edition was inaugurated in 1857, under the auspices of the Philological Society. The Philological Society, like the New Shakspere Society, was founded by Furnivall, that indispensable busybody (and model for the character of Toad in *The Wind in the Willows*). Furnivall took an intense personal interest in the dictionary project for decades and must be credited with its survival for the first twenty years, until James Murray was conned into becoming its editor. The first installment was finally published in 1878; the last volume appeared half a century later, by which time its over 16,000 triple-column folio pages had cost Oxford University Press some 300,000 pounds to produce. Hundreds of readers around the world collected quotations, which eventually filled 5–6 million individual slips of paper, which provided material for 1,827,306 illustrative quotations of the meanings of 414,825 words.

Charles Darwin, in a letter to Charles Lyell, recorded "how he wished some one would treat language as you had Geology, and study the existing causes of change, and apply the deduction to old languages."[57] The *New English Dictionary* attempted to trace the evolution of each word in the English language, determining "the etymology of each word strictly on the basis of historical fact, and in accordance with the methods and results of modern philological science."[58] The dictionary surpassed all others in English or any other language in both the scale of its attention to the development of the language and its documentation of that process. As Murray affirmed toward the end of his life, "Every fact faithfully recorded, and every inference correctly drawn from the facts, becomes a permanent accession to human knowledge."[59] The dictionary became an unparalleled repository of linguistic Facts, a museum of the history of the English language, an enormous philological data bank.

The dictionary cited Shakespeare more often than any other author; indeed, its compilers consistently favored him to the detriment of other writers, thereby exaggerating his contribution to the development of the language.[60] But the dictionary also, for the first time, made it possible to set Shakespeare's writing in the context of something approaching a comprehensive view of the English of his era. For a century and a half scholars and enthusiasts had been haphazardly accumulating Elizabethan parallels for Shakespeare's usage; the seventy years of organized collective enterprise that produced the *New English Dictionary* utterly transformed this primitive process. Any reader, simply by consulting the dictionary, could now understand more of the meanings of a passage of Shakespeare than Capell or Malone had been able to perceive after a lifetime of antiquarian research. The effect was compounded by the compilation during the same period of Joseph Wright's *English Dialect Dictionary* (1896–1905) and J. S. Farmer and W. E. Henley's *Slang and Its Analogues Past and Present* (1890–1904). For the first time, Shakespeare could be seen as a single moving figure in a total linguistic field. The full implications of this transformation have still not been fully absorbed.

Nineteenth-century Britain realized, more clearly than any previous society, that goods can be manufactured, and information can be processed, more efficiently when broken down into components. Shakespeare's writings were accordingly broken down into so many systematically arranged components of word usage, grammatical usage, metrical usage. Sometimes the books themselves were literally broken down into fragments; some of the early material collected for the *New English Dictionary* consisted of passages torn out of rare sixteenth-century books and pasted onto slips. Halliwell, too, regularly mutilated books in this way—including one of only two surviving copies of the first edition of *Hamlet*—cutting out pages or parts of pages and pasting them "for ease of reference" into notebooks organized by subject matter. In such cases information processing literally destroyed the whole in its eagerness to analyze and organize its parts.

By deconstructing Shakespeare, the Victorians could subject him to more vigorous examination and, at the same time, subject students to more rigorous examinations about him. In 1853 Parliament passed the India Act, which decreed that positions in the Indian civil service should be awarded by competitive examination, and in 1855 a commissioned report on the civil service of the East India Company recommended that English language and literature be included among the subjects tested in those exams. English was not only included; it could earn a candidate a thousand points—as much as mathematics and more than any other subject. That "glorious and inexhaustible subject, the LITERATURE of our country"[61] had already begun to infiltrate the college curriculum: University College, London, had a chair in English literature and history by 1828 (first held by the Reverend Thomas Dale, an Evangelical clergyman). But the civil service examinations formally legitimized the subject and increased pressure on the universities to supply the public demand for appropriate instruction. Dowden became the first Professor of English at Trinity College, Dublin, in 1867. At Cambridge, English formed a subdepartment in the Board of Mediaeval and Modern Languages, founded in 1878. At Oxford the Merton Professorship of English Language and Literature was established in 1884 (and a Germanic philologist appointed to the post); university examinations on the subject were instituted in 1893.

English elbowed its way into the curriculum during a period when the universities were being forcibly transformed by parliamentary decree. At the same time, beginning in 1870, Parliament created the state school system. Millions of schoolchildren sat waiting, "ready to have imperial gallons of facts poured into them until they were full."[62] The many new state schools required teachers, employed by the state; by taking responsibility for the educational system, Victorian government created a whole new class of civil servants, who in turn needed to be educated and examined. For thirty-five years Matthew Arnold, perhaps the most generally influential of all Victorian literary critics, earned his living as an inspector of schools.

Shakespeare became, in the late nineteenth century, the dominant component of the new subject of English Literature, itself an expanding part of an expanding educational system. This entire system depended—and in Britain still depends—upon examinations. The nineteenth century believed that intelligence could be quantified; it invented IQ tests and developed phrenology, measuring the cranium as an index to mental faculties. (Some enthusiasts wanted to dig up Shakespeare's skull and display it "in the phrenological shop-windows.")[63] A student's knowledge of Shakespeare had to be testable, because it had to be measurable. An examiner for the Indian civil service and the Council of Military Education, testifying before a parliamentary commission, defined "teaching English Literature" as "the reading and remembering as much as you can of as many authors as you can"; he recommended that examinations include "40 or 50 passages, selected from what I call fair authors—Shakspeare, Milton, Pope ... Sir Walter Scott and Tennyson."[64] Dowden defended the examination system on the grounds that cramming taught students to "acquire rapidly and accurately the knowledge of a mass of facts."[65] How useful such skills would be if a student ever became, for instance, Chief Secretary for Ireland or some other government minister, forced by a parliamentary question to acquire a sudden seeming expertise in the details of a policy or a subject of which he had been until then wholly ignorant! Dowden knew the value of cramming, because the Chief Secretary for Ireland had personally explained it to him.

Books written about Shakespeare in this period naturally began to take account of the Fact that Shakespeare was no longer simply read for pleasure but was actively studied with an eye to examinations. The Clarendon Press Series of Shakespeare's Select Plays, begun in 1868 by Clark and Wright, was *Designed to meet the wants of Students in English Literature.* Shakespeare became for the first time a textbook, and many publishers competed in the market for student editions. Fleay of the New Shakspere Society was a headmaster; Murray of the *New English Dictionary* was a schoolteacher. Abbott was headmaster of the City of London School, and in the preface to the third edition of his *Shakespearian Grammar* he expressed his "hope that this little book may do something to forward the development of English instruction in English schools." He also predicted in 1870 that "the time seems not far off when every English boy who continues his studies to the age of fifteen will study English for the sake of English; and where English is studied Shakespeare is not likely to be forgotten." His book therefore included 104 "Notes and Questions" on *Macbeth,* designed to test a student's comprehension of the rules of grammar and prosody.

Shakespeare was taken in hand by schools, universities, examinations, civil servants. In the opening chapters of *Hard Times* Thomas Gradgrind is accompanied by "a government officer," who "had it in charge from high authority to bring about the great public-office Millennium, when Commissioners should reign upon earth." This "gentleman" informs the Coketown students that they "are to be in all things regulated and governed by fact. We hope to have, before long, a board of fact, composed of commissioners of fact, who will force the people to be a people of fact, and of nothing but fact."[66] The Facts of English literature, mediated by the civil service, might Anglicize the Indian subcontinent; mediated by state schools, mechanics' institutes, workingmen's colleges, and extension lecturing, the Facts of English literature might Anglicize the working classes of England itself, convincing them that they belonged to a single, coherent, harmonious, long-established, triumphant national culture—or at least supplying them with materials from which they might construct an alternative (but still recognizably English) culture of their own.

Where English went, Shakespeare followed. And before it went anywhere else, English had gone to America.

IN WHICH OUR HERO CROSSES THE OCEAN

Americans began by being Englishmen abroad. The Puritans of New England and the Quakers of Pennsylvania, like their counterparts on the other side of the Atlantic, distrusted the theatre; other colonists were too busy or too dispersed to support an entertainment industry. But by the middle of the eighteenth century the new country could boast a few enclaves wealthy, leisured, and populous enough to afford some of the luxuries of "home." Colley Cibber's adaptation of *Richard III* opened New York City's theatrical season in 1750 and in 1751 opened the first theatrical season in Williamsburg, Virginia. The next year Lewis Hallam brought his "London Company of Comedians" to Virginia, where they began by performing *The Merchant of Venice*. Other plays and venues and companies followed. In five months of 1773–74 the aristocratic rice growers, plantation dwellers, and merchants of Charles-Town, South Carolina, were treated to twenty performances of thirteen different Shakespeare plays.[67] The Revolutionary War, like the Civil War of the 1640s, temporarily closed down the theatres, but they soon bounced back, and Shakespeare dominated the repertoire as before. What Walt Whitman called "the regular routine of Shakespearean plays"[68] accounted for one-fifth to one-quarter of performances. *Richard III, Macbeth, Hamlet, Othello,* and *The Merchant of Venice* were all performed at least once a year in New York between 1832 and 1862; in 1849 *Macbeth* was playing in three different theatres; the 1857–58 season accommodated ten productions of *Hamlet.* Nor was Shakespeare tied to the eastern seaboard. He made regular visits to theatres up and down the Ohio and Mississippi; he rode rafts with Huck Finn and steamboats with Mark Twain; he could be heard in Italian in Cincinnati, St. Louis, and New Orleans, passionately declaimed by touring European stars like Adelaide Ristori, Tommasso Salvini, and Ernesto Rossi. On the shores of the Great Lakes, in California, in small towns and mining camps, on custom-built stages or makeshift scaffolds, Shakespeare went wherever there was a demand for theatre. And in America, no less than England, theatre was the dominant medium of nineteenth-century popular entertainment.

America, too, experienced the boom in cheap publishing. In 1831 the French visitor Alexis de Tocqueville noted that "There is hardly a pioneer's hut which does not contain a few odd volumes of Shakespeare"; he had "read the feudal drama of Henry V. for the first time in a log-house."[69] People did not simply read these texts; they recited them. Since the middle of the eighteenth century, education in England and America had been organized around the study of elocution; in the great age of political eloquence—from Pitt and Burke to Webster and Lincoln—Shakespeare's big speeches supplied many of the practice texts for budding orators. Riding on New York omnibuses, Whitman often "spouted" "some stormy passage" from *Julius Caesar* or *Richard III* the whole length of Broadway.[70]

In these and other respects, for much of the nineteenth century Uncle Sam's treatment of Shakespeare simply duplicated John Bull's on a smaller scale. Tocqueville noted that "England supplies [American] readers with most of the books which they require."[71] The United States did not accept international copyright law until 1891; British editions and British criticism of Shakespeare could accordingly be reprinted cheaply, without paying royalties.

These publishing arrangements discouraged native scholarship. So did the absence of major libraries. British scholars could exploit public repositories in Oxford and Cambridge, or the British Museum and the Public Record Office in London; a few, like Collier, gained access to the large private libraries of ancient aristocratic families; others, like Halliwell, cultivated local records in Stratford. By contrast, American scholars had to rely almost entirely upon whatever books they could acquire with their own resources. Some of these collections were impressive: by 1884 Joseph Crosby, a grocer in Zanesville, Ohio, had collected 175 editions of Shakespeare's works, dating from 1709 to 1881, with another 300 editions of individual plays, and most of the important Shakespeare scholarship and criticism of the eighteenth and nineteenth century.[72] The only American with a better Shakespeare library was Horace Howard Furness of Philadelphia, who in 1871 published the first of a series of variorum editions of individual plays. Furness sought to collect in one volume everything important that had been said about a particular play. Like so many Victorian achievements, this vast project both simplified data retrieval and provided a record of chronological development; it was particularly useful for American readers, who usually lacked access to many important works of British and German scholarship.

Their private libraries enabled Crosby and Furness to sift with wit and sense through what others had written about Shakespeare; but neither man could acquire a working collection of Elizabethan and Jacobean editions. In the eighteenth century antiquarian books had been abundant and relatively cheap; by the late nineteenth century they had become rare and expensive—especially for Americans, who could purchase them only from Britain. The great British collectors of Shakespeariana had been literary scholars of private means; the great American collectors would be tycoons, like Henry Folger, president of Standard Oil, or Henry Huntington, California transportation magnate. Scholars usually gained access to such collections only after the death of the collector. Thus, the first major private collection in America did not become public until 1873, when the Boston Public Library bought Thomas Pennant Barton's two thousand volumes of Shakespeariana, including all four seventeenth-century folios and a copy of half of the quartos published before 1709.[73] In 1880 James Lenox's thirteen folios were acquired by the New York Public Library; at the turn of the century J. Pierpont Morgan began amassing books instead of money, acquiring eleven Shakespeare quartos and twelve folios, eventually housed in the Morgan Library in New York. In 1911 Yale University was given a private horde of twenty-six quartos and four folios. As an English scholar complained in 1898, Shakespeare's homeland was "being rapidly drained of its First Folios by the United States of America."[74] By the end of Queen Victoria's reign America had imported the raw materials it needed to support a productive native Shakespeare industry.

The first American Shakespearian of any consequence, Richard Grant White, had to make do without such resources. Nevertheless, he published a book-length contribution to the Collier controversy (1854), followed by an edition of the complete works (1857–66), a biography (1865), and a collection of *Studies in Shakespeare* (1886). White, who never let anyone forget his direct descent from one of the early English settlers of Massachusetts, also wrote two influential books campaigning for "correctness and fitness of verbal expression" and "the right use" of the English language. Contending that "The mental tone of a community may be vitiated by a yielding to the use of loose, coarse, low, and frivolous phraseology," he championed the "usage of the most cultivated society."[75] The English language had to be defended against most of the people who spoke it. White also published a six-hundred-page celebration of *England Without and Within,* which consciously ignores "mills and mines and everything connected with them."[76]

Most of the Americans who proselytized for Shakespeare in the nineteenth century were, like White, Anglophiles, Anglophiliacs, or Anglophonies. James Henry Hackett, for instance, occupied much the same position in the world of the theatre that White occupied in the world of books. Hackett created the first successful American Falstaff; he naturalized Shakespeare's fat braggart. But he also corresponded about matters Shakespearian with John Quincy Adams, at a time when the former president had become the reactionary opponent of every aspect of Jacksonian democracy. He first made a name for himself by mimicry of other actors, especially the Englishman Edmund Kean. And he was the first important native performer to export his talent to London, where he had himself billed as a "leading American comic actor."

Both White and Hackett, in their different ways, pioneered the transatlantic Shakespeare trade, which had advantages for both parties. England was America's most important trading partner; by 1846 they had negotiated away their major territorial disputes over hegemony in North America, and the intimacy of their economic and cultural relationship was facilitated by the development of clipper ships and then steamers. Like Henry James, American actors sought legitimacy and prestige in the United Kingdom; like Charles Dickens, British actors found adulation and profit in the United States. Most of the stars of the English stage—Edmund Kean, William Charles Macready, Charles Kean, Ellen Tree, Henry Irving and Ellen Terry—toured American cities between 1820 and 1883.

Along with British stars and British plays, American theatres also imported British production techniques. Since the 1820s major London revivals of Shakespeare's plays had begun taking pains to achieve historical accuracy in costuming and scenery, and this fashion reached New York in 1846, when Charles Kean mounted spectacular productions of *Richard III* and *King John*. With "antiquarian diligence" the productions reconstructed "the actual places where the events took place" and the authentic "costumes of all the characters."77 Fiction must respect the Facts of historical development, and Victorian actors were surrounded by onstage Facts, by factual helmets and factual facades, by actual factual crowds in convincing numbers. Such performances created onstage "illustrations" of history, like those in popular editions. A cheap subscription volume of *Antony and Cleopatra,* for instance, supplied portraits of Antony, Cleopatra, and Caesar (from coins in the British Museum) and views of Cleopatra's Needle, Pompey's Pillar, the Pyramid and Sphinx, the Atrium of Caesar's House (based upon excavations at Pompeii), and the prow of a Roman Galley ("From a Basso Relievo . . . found at Palestrina").78

The demand for historical authenticity also led British managements to begin ousting the adaptations that had held the stage for so long, replacing them with Shakespeare's own texts, heavily cut but otherwise little altered. This fashion, too, eventually emigrated to America. In 1838 Macready gave London audiences, for the first time in a century and a half, Shakespeare's *Tempest* (instead of the Davenant/Dryden version) and Shakespeare's *King Lear* (instead of the Tate version); by 1854 the restored *Tempest* reached New York (using a copy of Macready's own promptbook), and by the 1870s a restored *King Lear* began appearing on American stages.

Nahum Tate's tragicomic version of *King Lear* was not ejected from the theatre because popular audiences suddenly got tired of happy endings. After all, in the same period when tragedy was being restored to *King Lear* Dickens was being persuaded to abandon his original intentions and provide a happier ending for *Great Expectations*. The overtly melodramatic Cibber adaptation of *Rich-*

ard III and the version of *King Lear* with a love story and a happy
ending were part of "all the popularizing noise and show of broad
farce and blood-besmeared tragedy" which, as Melville complained, gave "the all-popular Shakspeare" most of his "mere mob
renown."[79] But this kind of rough theatre—attracting an audience
with its sleeves rolled up, smelling "of onions and whiskey," spitting
incessantly, shouting and thumping its feet when pleased,[80] using
"the egg as a vehicle of dramatic criticism" when displeased[81]—
grew more and more distasteful to the cultivated members of the
paying public. The theatre became increasingly respectable; by the
closing decades of the nineteenth century, melodrama and adapted
texts and burlesques based upon Shakespeare's plays ceased to be
respectable. Henry Irving was the first actor to abandon Cibber's
adaptation of *Richard III* (1877)—and the first actor to be knighted
(1895).

The educated insistence on an authentic text, like the insistence
on pictorial accuracy, belonged to the period's intensifying sensitivity to historical development. But that insistence created an awkward obstacle to American efforts to import Shakespeare, whose
plays belonged to an old epoch, an Old World, an old aristocratic
ideology that the New World had consciously rejected. "Democracy," Tocqueville declared, "gives men a sort of instinctive distaste
for the ancient" and "shuts the past against the poet."[82] In an 1852
article entitled "Imagination and Fact" an American critic concluded that "Shakspeare was a man of his era—"; "incapable of
sympathizing with the cause and feelings of the mass of the lower
classes," he "dreamed as little of the later evangils of democracy as
he did of the Daguerreotype and the electric telegraph."[83] Edwin
Forrest, the first important tragic actor born in the United States,
regularly performed a handful of standard roles from Shakespeare's plays, because only by doing so could he establish and
maintain his credentials as a great actor; but he also commissioned
new plays on American and democratic themes. Robert Taylor Conrad's *Jack Cade* was one of his (and the public's) favorites; at its
opening in 1841 it became the first play ever to run for a week at the
Park Theatre in New York. Since Shakespeare had also dramatized
the life of Jack Cade, American playgoers and journalists could
compare Conrad's Cade with Shakespeare's. The comparison did
not flatter Shakespeare. Forrest, in Conrad's play, presented Cade as
a tragic hero, a glorious martyr to democracy. Shakespeare, by

contrast, had portrayed Cade as a "wretched fanatic,"[84] obscuring "the *facts* in relation to [Cade's] extraordinary career," putting in their place a mere "mass of prejudice, bigotry and servility."[85] It did not take much imagination for Americans to realize that "The derision and contumely which have been heaped [by Shakespeare] on Cade, would have been heaped on those who achieved the liberty of this country, had they been equally unsuccessful in their struggle."[86]

Like Dowden, the best American critics in the late nineteenth century insisted that Shakespeare belonged to a particular literary epoch; but their portrait of that epoch could be less flattering than Dowden's. Whitman articulated the new American attitude more forcefully than anyone else. Literature, like man, evolves; a poet must be "a growth of the soil, the water, the climate, the age, the Government, the religion, the leading characteristics" of a people.[87] Shakespeare accordingly

> put such things into his plays as would please the family pride of Kings and Queens, and of his patrons among the nobility. He did this for Queen Elizabeth and for James I. His renderings of man, phases of character, the rabble, Jack Cade, the French Joan, the greasy and stupid canaille that Coriolanus cannot stomach, all these fed the aristocratic vanity of the young noblemen and gentlemen and feed them in England yet. Common blood is but wash—the hero is always of high lineage.[88]

The very name of Shakespeare's theatrical company declared its aristocratic loyalties: first the "Lord Chamberlain's Men," briefly "Lord Hunsdon's Men," eventually "the King's Men." In 1864 Halliwell announced the discovery of a document in which Shakespeare was allotted four and a half yards of "skarlet red cloth" in order to dress himself appropriately when he accompanied James I's procession through London in 1604.[89] Shakespeare belonged to a different time and a different place. For Whitman, "The great poems [of the past], Shakespeare included, are poisonous to the idea of the pride and dignity of the common people, the life-blood of Democracy."[90]

Foreign plays, glorifying a foreign feudal past, could become particularly objectionable when played by foreign actors. In 1825 Edmund Kean, by refusing to perform *Richard III* in front of an almost empty auditorium, was felt to have insulted the dignity of Boston, thereby provoking America's first theatre riot. In 1848 Macready returned to America for his third tour, billing himself, as by then he always did, as "The Eminent Tragedian"; his native rival Edwin Forrest, who had gradually come to hate Macready, followed the English actor everywhere, billing himself as "The National Tragedian." The conflict culminated on May 10, 1849, when Macready was performing *Macbeth* in New York; throughout the day handbills had urged "Workingmen! Freemen!" to "express their opinion this night at the English Aristocratic Opera House"; workingmen and freemen responded to the call. During the resulting riot one man exposed his chest and dared a soldier to shoot him: "Fire into this. Take the life out of a free-born American for a bloody British actor!"[91] Eventually the soldiers did fire on the crowd, killing thirty-one people.

Like other disturbances in the nineteenth-century theatre, the Astor Place Riot—pitting "Workingmen!" against an "Aristocratic Opera House"—had as much to do with class as nationalism. The division of labor and the growth of investment capital, which made possible the great Victorian intellectual and economic achievements, also deepened the alienations of the class system, which Karl Marx was busy analyzing in London. Indeed, in the same decade as the Astor Place Riot, Marx took as his text a passage from *Timon of Athens*, in which Timon discovers gold and condemns it as a "yellow slave":

> Shakespeare attributes to money two qualities:
> 1. It is the visible deity, the transformation of all human and natural qualities into their opposite, the universal confusion and inversion of things; it brings incompatibles into fraternity.
> 2. It is the universal whore, the universal pander between men and nations.

But if money could unite incompatibles, it could also divide fraternities. Under the pressure of class differences, the brotherhood of theatre audiences disintegrated. Increasingly, individual theatres began catering to particular markets: one theatre for the well-to-do ("culture"), another for the mob ("entertainment"). The choice of market affected the ticket pricing, repertoire, and acting style of each theatre.[92] Shakespeare was commandeered by "culture."

Shakespeare's American admirers, accordingly, soon began to discover that his culture was perhaps not so different from their own. James Russell Lowell contended that Shakespeare "arrived at the full development of his powers at the moment when" the language of his country had reached "its freshest perfection." Having "recruited itself, by fresh impressments from the Latin and Latinized languages, with new words to express the new ideas of an enlarging intelligence," it "admitted foreign words to the rights of citizenship"; "still hot from the hearts and brains of a people," it had not yet been "fetlocked by dictionary and grammar mongers." Like the language of nineteenth-century America, the language of sixteenth-century England had been new, fresh, firmly established but not too inhibited, receptive to immigrants. Shakespeare knew what the Americans needed to know: that "great poetry . . . can make any language classic."93 In Lowell's interpretation Shakespeare's epoch in the evolution of British literature corresponded to the epoch of Lowell and his contemporaries in the evolution of American literature. You could say—and Americans wanted to be able to say—that Whitman had more in common with Shakespeare than Tennyson did.

Whitman was an urban working-class journalist; Lowell was a Harvard professor from a patrician New England family. In America as in Britain the academics triumphed over the amateurs. In 1865 Harvard added a requirement in "reading English aloud" to its catalog. In 1873–74 it announced that "Each candidate will be required to write a short English composition . . . the subject to be taken from such works of standard authors as shall be announced from time to time"; in 1874 the list of six announced works was headed by "Shakespeare's *Tempest, Julius Caesar,* and *Merchant of Venice.*" Other colleges followed where Harvard led, and what the colleges demanded the high schools had to supply. Between 1886 and 1900 *The Merchant of Venice* and *Julius Caesar* (anti-Semitism and tyrannicide) were taught in more American high schools than any other works of literature; *Macbeth* ranked sixth, *Hamlet* eighth, *As You Like It* tenth.94 America's Anglophile cultural elite ensured that Shakespeare dominated the emergent curriculum of vernacular literature. Whoever wanted an American education would have to study English literature, and Shakespeare in particular.

But although everyone had to study English literature a little, some people studied it a lot. Most of those people were women.

IN WHICH OUR HERO MAKES THE ACQUAINTANCE OF A NUMBER OF YOUNG LADIES

The patrician (and promiscuous) American male Richard Grant White claimed that women generally don't like Shakespeare—"with the exception of a few who are not always the most lovable or the happiest of the sex."[95] Only unhappy unlovable women could enjoy the works of the man whom White, and almost everyone else, considered the greatest poet in the English (or any other) language.

Whether or not women liked Shakespeare, they certainly studied him in large numbers. Late in the nineteenth century women constituted two-thirds of the students in the new modern languages school at Cambridge and 79 percent of those who took the English examination in its first five years at Oxford.[96] As a parliamentary commission reported in 1868, "English literature occupies a more prominent position in the education of girls than of boys."[97] Indeed, since the middle of the eighteenth century, when the center of cultural life shifted from the coffeehouse to the salon, women had played an increasingly vocal part in Shakespeare criticism. The poet, novelist, and translator Charlotte Lennox wrote the first full-length book on Shakespeare by an American-born critic; her three-volume *Shakespear Illustrated* (1753–54), introduced by Dr. Johnson, was the first collection and analysis of Shakespeare's sources and was not superseded until 1831 (in German) and 1843 (in English). Elizabeth Montagu's *Essay on the Writings and Genius of Shakespeare*, defending "Our Shakespeare" against "the Misrepresentations of Mons. de Voltaire," was widely praised, went through seven editions between 1769 and 1810, and was translated into both French and Italian.

Lennox and Montagu were women, but their gender does not conspicuously govern their attitude toward Shakespeare. Lennox will occasionally rise to the defense of a female, like Queen Margaret in the *Henry VI* plays, whom she thinks Shakespeare has maligned; but she is just as likely to complain that he committed "an unpardonable Fault" in not punishing more severely "so vicious a Person" as Cressida.[98] Montagu can occasionally be priggish:

> Every scene in which Doll Tearsheet appears is indecent, and therefore not only indefensible but inexcusable. There are deli-

cacies of decorum in one age unknown to another age, but whatever is immoral is equally blamable in all ages, and every
approach to obscenity is an offence for which wit cannot atone,
nor the barbarity or the corruption of the times excuse.[99]

But comparable outbreaks of indignation occur in the works of
Johnson and her other male contemporaries.

But the last quarter of the eighteenth century saw the emergence
of a specifically "feminine" criticism. Mrs. Elizabeth Griffith, the
author of more than one guidebook to marriage, set out in 1775 to
illustrate *The Morality of Shakespeare's Drama;* she compiled from the
works of "our English *Confucius*" a 544-page compendium of observations upon "prudence, polity, decency, and decorum," concentrating especially on "those moral duties which are the truest source of
mortal bliss—domestic ties, offices, and obligations."[100] She quotes
Catherine's "admirable speech" at the end of *The Taming of the Shrew*
and Luciana's first speeches in *The Comedy of Errors* as illustrations of
"the duty and submission which ought to be shewn to a husband";
she praises Desdemona because "She speaks little; but whatever she
says is sensible, pure, and chaste." Indeed, Desdemona "seems to be
as perfect a model of a wife, as either this author, or any other
writer, could possibly have framed."[101]

Griffith was a preview of the nineteenth century. Two enduring
monuments to the new domesticity were erected in 1807: *The Family
Shakespeare* contained twenty plays edited by Henrietta Maria Bowdler; *Tales from Shakespear. Designed for the use of young persons* transformed twenty plays into prose stories, most of them written by
Mary Lamb. But the first edition of *The Family Shakespeare* did not
name any editor, and the second, in 1818, credited it to Henrietta's
brother Thomas Bowdler, M.D. (who was responsible only for
changes in the second edition). Likewise, the first editions of *Tales
from Shakespear* attribute them all to Mary's brother Charles Lamb,
who had written only six of the twenty. Mary Lamb's contribution
was not acknowledged until 1838; Henrietta Bowdler's was not
discovered until 1966. When nineteenth-century women tampered
with the text of Shakespeare, they did so anonymously or under the
covering fire of male authority—usually fraternal authority. In the
1860s Mary Cowden Clarke collaborated with her brother Charles
on an edition of Shakespeare's works. Like Dorothy Wordsworth,
who subordinated her life and talent to her brother William, these

women gave their siblings and their society a nineteenth-century exemplar of ideal womanhood: what Shelley invoked as "Spouse! Sister! Angel!" what Baudelaire addressed as "Mon enfant, ma sœur," a compound child-wife-sister.[102] In return, a brother gave these women what they needed (a male patron) but did not burden them with the complications or subordinations of sex and mother-hood. Mary Lamb had murdered her mother; she describes herself and Charles, writing the *Tales,* at "one table (but not on one cushion sitting) like Hermia & Helena in the Midsummer's Nights Dream"[103]—a Platonic pair, parentless, childless, sexless.

Tales from Shakespear and *The Family Shakespeare* were both aimed, for similar reasons, at a similar readership. During the second half of the eighteenth century children had become a major market: the new consumer culture mass-produced an increasing quantity and variety of toys, clothes, and books specially designed to be bought by parents for their children. In the Renaissance children had sometimes attended the theatre, and child actors had played female roles, but none of Shakespeare's texts had been written for children. Nevertheless, by the nineteenth century a familiarity with Shake-speare was expected of every educated person; the sooner aspirant middle-class children could acquire such knowledge, the better. Shakespeare was thus forcibly transformed into a children's author.

The Lambs wrote their prose condensations of Shakespeare pri-marily for "young ladies"; boys, who "are generally permitted the use of their fathers' libraries at a much earlier age than girls are," could skip the *Tales* and go straight to Shakespeare's own "manly book." Indeed, they encourage boys to initiate their sisters in a direct experience of Shakespeare, by reading to them passages from the plays (after "carefully selecting what is proper for a young sister's ear").[104] Henrietta Bowdler, likewise, selected "Twenty of the most unexceptionable of SHAKESPEARE'S plays" and then "endeavoured to remove every thing that could give just offence to the religious and virtuous mind," thereby producing a text fit "to be placed in the hands of young persons of both sexes."[105] Bowdler, like the Lambs, wanted to make Shakespeare safe for young women, by removing from his works anything to which a young woman should not be exposed. But this righteous ambition subjected her to an embarrassingly unrighteous paradox: she could protect other women only by exposing herself to material to which women should not be exposed. She could remove obscenities only if she understood things that no decent woman should understand. So to protect her reputation she published *The Family Shakespeare* anonymously—and later let her brother take responsibility for it.

Bowdler's anxious anonymity and anxious prudery are underscored by comparison with an earlier Englishwoman, Aphra Behn. One hundred and twenty years before the publication of *The Family Shakespeare,* Behn too had drawn attention to the amount of what Bowdler would call obscenity in plays like *Othello.* But Behn, writing under her own name, admitted to understanding such obscenities, defending them as artistically appropriate and objecting to the double standard that prevented her from dealing with such material.* Between the Restoration and the Regency, Behn's freethinking had become virtually unthinkable.

The sexual anxiety intensified as the nineteenth century wore on. Neither *Tales from Shakespear* nor *The Family Shakespeare* was an immediate best seller, but their popularity boomed during the reign of Queen Victoria. Bowdler's text was not reprinted for eleven years; but in the next seventy years it went through thirty editions. The fifteen editions of *Tales from Shakespear* printed between 1807 and 1873 were surpassed by the sixteen reprints of the 1880s alone.[106] Shakespeare was of course the greatest of all writers, but he was also to Victorian sensibilities potentially dangerous—in part because he was great. Mary Ann Evans (alias George Eliot) was described by a contemporary as "the greatest woman that has lived on the earth—the female Shakespeare, so to speak";[107] but "the female Shakespeare" had her doubts about the male one. In 1877 she declined an offer to write the volume on Shakespeare in a new and influential series on English Men of Letters being published by Macmillan. She did not explain her refusal, but elsewhere she wrote that a woman needed "as nice a power of distillation as the bee to suck nothing but honey from [Shakespeare's] pages."[108] She was not talking just about verbal obscenity; the ending of *Two Gentlemen of Verona,* in which Valentine nonchalantly hands over Silvia to his friend the would-be rapist Proteus, "disgusted" her.[109]

---

*"If I should repeat the Words exprest in these Scenes I mention, I might justly be charg'd with course ill Manners, and very little Modesty, and yet they so naturally fall into the places they are designed for, and so are proper for the Business, that there is not the least Fault to be found with them; though I say those things in any of [my Scenes] would damn the whole Peice, and alarm the Town": *The Luckey Chance* (1687), sig. A4.

In the nineteenth century, as never before, women and children shaped the prevailing image of Shakespeare. Most readers first encountered him in versions deliberately reshaped to make them fit for tender minds. They read Bowdlerized plays, either in *The Family Shakespeare* or in appropriately detoxified school editions. They read Lambsical stories, either in *Tales from Shakespear* or in its many rivals and imitators (almost all of them written by women). They read Mary Cowden Clarke's popular, stirring, illustrated accounts of *The Girlhood of Shakespeare's Heroines:* "The Magnifico's Child" (Desdemona), "The Physician's Orphan" (Helena), "Meg and Alice, The Merry Maids of Windsor." In France, Germany, and England, they read Heinrich Heine's expensive commentary on *Shakespeare's Maidens and Ladies,* commissioned to accompany a collection of handsome steel engravings by various English artists. Or they read passages from Shakespeare in the scores of popular anthologies that proliferated after 1800. In English anthologies Shakespeare was more popular than any other author—even Wordsworth, Cowper, and Longfellow.[110] And anthologies, which printed only choice selections from Shakespeare's work, never chose selections that would offend anyone's sense of decency. The anthologists and their public preferred passages like those which Matthew Arnold singled out as "touchstones," combining "*natural magic*" and "*moral profundity*"; they wanted poems (and women) to provide both ethical substance and "that rounded perfection and felicity of loveliness of which Shakespeare is the great master."[111]

As feminine virtues became more prominent in texts of Shakespeare, so too they became more visible in performances. Since the Restoration the ethereal Ariel had always been played by a woman, a tradition that continued even after Victorian managements abandoned the Dryden/Davenant adaptation. In 1838, when Macready produced *King Lear* "in the genuine text of the poet" for the first time in a century and a half, the wise Fool was played by a woman; in 1859 Mrs. Kean transformed the Chorus of *Henry V* into Clio, the Muse of History, who "formed the presiding charm, the keynote . . . of the entire production."[112] In 1899 Sarah Bernhardt played Hamlet himself. By casting women in the role of the poet's mouthpiece (Chorus) and his most famous character (Hamlet), such productions gave a physical shape to the new sense that Shakespeare's imagination was in some respects essentially unmanly. The weak moody femininity of Hamlet could also be seen in Romeo and

Richard II; critics like Dowden could not help but interpret such characters as aspects of the poet's own psyche. Having made such troubling observations about the plays, Victorians could hardly avoid connecting them to the Sonnets, with their even more troubling implicit homoeroticism, first publicly mentioned in 1824 and later elaborated in biographical fantasias by Oscar Wilde and Samuel Butler. If Shakespeare loved the Young Man of the Sonnets, he was either a homosexual—or a woman, as more than one crackpot concluded.

The nineteenth century sawed Shakespeare in two. The childlike Shakespeare of Lamb and Bowdler emphasized, by contrast, the dangerous sexual adult of the unexpurgated texts. The image of Victorian womanhood was also sawed in half, in the same way: pure head and heart above, dark whore below. When Victorian critics praised "all that magnificent array of womanhood"[113] in Shakespeare's plays, they were thinking not about Cleopatra and Cressida but about the spirited expurgated women of the comedies and romances or the pathetic expurgated women of the tragedies. Those women could be set on a pedestal—or an easel. Ellen Terry's performance as Hermione recalled the statue of Niobe in the Louvre; her Portia resembled "those stately Venetian dames who still gaze down from the pictures of Paolo Veronese"; her Ophelia looked like a pre-Raphaelite saint.[114] Harriet Smithson's "painfully intense" portrayal of the mad Ophelia inspired Hector Berlioz to compose the *Symphonie fantastique;* Elizabeth Siddal was the model for John Everett Millais' famous painting of the drowned Ophelia and for Dante Gabriel Rossetti's sketch of Desdemona. Drowned or strangled women made the best muses. Dead women, the pale fictions of a dead author, were more manageable, more easily idealized, than living ones.

IN WHICH OUR HERO IS MISTAKEN FOR
SOMEONE ELSE

The subject of Americans and the subject of women lead inevitably to Delia Bacon, who was both. In 1857 she published *The Philosophy of the Plays of Shakspere Unfolded,* a 675-page book proposing that the works so long attributed to William Shakespeare had actually been written by Francis Bacon. The proposition attracted innumerable adherents, including literary giants like Mark Twain, Walt Whitman, and Henry James. Delia Bacon has been, in a way, more influential than any other Shakespearian. The one thing everyone knows about Shakespeare is that, according to some people, Shakespeare didn't write Shakespeare's plays.

The arguments put forward in defense of this hypothesis have never been persuasive by any logical, legal, historical, or rhetorical criteria. They have never persuaded specialists. Bacon's own defense of her theory, being almost impossible to read, was seldom read, and the details had little influence on subsequent discussion. People who agreed that Shakespeare did not write the plays could not agree on who did write them; Francis Bacon was soon competing with a slate of rival candidates. The entire discussion is ultimately pointless. The theory that Shakespeare did not write Shakespeare's works belongs to the class of propositions that have no meaning, because they cannot under any circumstances be disproved. Any evidence against Delia Bacon's theory could be dismissed as a deliberate blind, designed to conceal the identity of the true author. And even if opponents produced decisive evidence against Bacon's claim, adherents could simply switch their allegiance to another candidate. Such theories are psychologically satisfying, because logically invulnerable; but only a vulnerable theory can ever be verified. A theory that could never be discredited cannot be credited. Nothing ventured, nothing said.

The success of the theory is therefore more interesting than the theory itself. It did not originate with the Victorians; late in the eighteenth century James Wilmot had concluded that Bacon wrote Shakespeare's plays but found his own hypothesis so disconcerting that he never published it. By contrast, in the Victorian period the idea occurred independently—by a kind of intellectual spontaneous combustion—to a number of writers, who did not hesitate to pass on the flame. In 1848 an American colonel, Joseph C. Hart, digressing from a panegyric on *The Romance of Yachting*, proposed that Shakespeare's only contribution had been to interpolate obscene passages into plays written by someone else; less than a decade later Delia Bacon and William Henry Smith, in mutual ignorance but within a year of one another, both nominated Francis Bacon as that someone else. Between 1856 and 1884 the controversy generated more than 250 books, pamphlets, and articles. It probably absorbed as much intellectual energy as any aspect of Shakespeare studies in the Victorian period. The question would continue to be argued in the twentieth century, but in the last half of the nineteenth it rapidly achieved a significance and urgency that it never had before or since. It was not peripheral or aberrant; it was central and typical.

"The authorship question," as it came to be known, had roots in the finest scholarship of the Victorian period. The first volume of *The New Shakspere Society's Transactions,* in 1874, was largely devoted to demonstrating that Shakespeare did not write large parts of *Titus Andronicus, The Taming of the Shrew, Timon of Athens, Pericles, Henry VIII,* and *The Two Noble Kinsmen.* Such doubts had been brewing for a long time. As early as 1687 his authorship of most of *Titus Andronicus* had been denied, and in 1709 Nicholas Rowe had observed that "there is good Reason to believe that the greatest part of [*Pericles*] was not written by [*Shakespear*]."[115] By 1725 Pope was conjecturing that Shakespeare had been responsible for "only some characters, single scenes, or perhaps a few particular passages" in *Love's Labour Lost, The Winter's Tale,* and *Titus Andronicus.*[116] In 1733 Theobald added the three Henry VI plays to the list of suspects. Such doubts were widely reproduced, and often endorsed and elaborated, by later editors. Victorian scholarship decisively extended skepticism into new areas of the canon: in 1840 Charles Knight published evidence that *Timon of Athens* was "not wholly a work of Shakspere";[117] in 1850 James Spedding, pursuing a suggestion made to him by Alfred Tennyson, denied Shakespeare most of *Henry VIII;* in 1869 Clark and Wright assigned much of *Macbeth* to Thomas Middleton.[118] Many of these doubts have weathered more than a century of subsequent investigation. Almost all scholars now accept that Shakespeare did not write certain passages in *Macbeth,* a clear majority believe that John Fletcher contributed to *Henry VIII,* and in the last two decades a range of linguistic evidence has confirmed the presence of a second author in *Timon of Athens.* These Victorian successes did not depend on guesswork or a pious desire to relieve Shakespeare of responsibility for material considered unworthy of his genius; they resulted in large part from the scholarly application of new analytical resources. The Victorians had accumulated more Facts and had developed new ways of accessing and organizing them.

But the new Facts, like those which Darwin brought back from the

Galápagos Islands, systematically undermined the authority of a sacred book. Modern literary science had established that Shakespeare could not have written large parts of a number of plays collected in the 1623 First Folio. That edition included material that Shakespeare had not written and omitted material that he had written: parts of *Pericles* and *The Two Noble Kinsmen* and also, as a member of the New Shakspere Society first realized in 1871, parts of an unpublished manuscript play, *Sir Thomas More*.

But Darwin at least offered a single unifying hypothesis, natural selection, to account for his Facts; in Shakespeare's case no such pattern could be discerned. No documentary or chronological principle defined the suspect plays, and several coauthors were involved. Only the Baconian hypothesis (or a variation) offered a single unified explanation: William Shakespeare was not the sole or prime author of any of the plays. In its daft simplicity, this hypothesis resembled Philip Gosse's claim that "God hid the fossils in the rocks in order to tempt geologists into infidelity."[119] Francis Bacon, likewise, might have deliberately and systematically concealed his responsibility for his creations. Gosse's book was published in 1857, the same year as Delia Bacon's. And in 1848, the year that Colonel Hart's *Romance of Yachting* first put "the authorship question" into print, another American had published a book devoted to *Historic Doubts Respecting Shakspeare; Illustrating Infidel Objections against the Bible.*[120] This book defended the historicity of Jesus Christ against the objections of atheists by facetiously demonstrating that the skeptics' objections could just as easily be leveled against the existence of Shakespeare. But this sword had two edges. If you doubted the authority of the Bible, why should you believe in the existence of God or Jesus? If you could not trust the Bible, why should you trust the First Folio? And if you doubted the authority of the First Folio, why should you believe in the existence of that incarnate deity of poetry, the "immortal" Shakespeare?

Lyell's and Darwin's Facts against the word of the Bible, Spedding's and Fleay's Facts against the word of the First Folio: fact against spirit. Increasingly, science and art seemed incompatible. Against the Facts of Gradgrind's bureaucratic-industrial school Dickens set the circus master, who would "enliven the varied performance at frequent intervals with his chaste Shaksperean quips and retorts."[121] Late in life, Darwin complained that his "mind seems to have become a kind of machine for grinding general laws out of large collections of facts," with the result that his youthful taste for poetry, music, and art had atrophied: "I have tried lately to read Shakespeare and found it so intolerably dull that it nauseated me."[122] The Baconian hypothesis healed this Victorian opposition between science and art by imagining a single figure who combined both: Francis Bacon, scientist, inhabiting the same body as "William Shakespeare," poet.

Although Dowden totally rejected the Baconian hypothesis, he did single out Bacon and Shakespeare—with the significant addition of the Anglican theologian Richard Hooker—as quintessential representatives of the Elizabethan epoch: "Bacon and Shakspere belonged to one great movement of humanity" epitomized by its desire "to attain the fact, and to ascend from particular facts to general."[123] By fusing these two figures into one, the Baconian hypothesis created a Bacspeare who could rival Goethe. Goethe, in Dowden's words, combined "a true synthetic genius in science, together with the artistic genius in its highest form."[124] What the nineteenth century admired in Goethe it yearned to see elsewhere. A satirist, astutely mimicking the Baconians, suggested that Dickens' novels had actually been written by Herbert Spencer;[125] during his lifetime Dickens was often compared to Shakespeare, and compounding him with the influential philosopher of contemporary science produced a synthetic superman no less appealing (and no more likely) than its Baconian prototype. But that prototype did not differ all that much in its appeal from Dowden's influential vision of Elizabethan England, a familiar compound ghost, conflating Bacon and Shakespeare and Hooker in a happy triumvirate of art and science and religion, dedicated to understanding the Facts of human experience.*

The Baconian hypothesis unified the disparate evidence against the canonical authority of the First Folio; it celebrated the marriage of science and sensibility. It also restored the congruence between art and life. As Dowden told his students, "The fruit-tree is more valuable than any of its fruits singly"; Shakespeare's works, like God's, deserved attention not only for themselves but also because they revealed "the living mind of the creator."[126] And since we are

---

*Dowden's lost paradise of synthesis does not differ all that much from T. S. Eliot's later, equally influential, vision of Elizabethan England, where naked thought and feeling unself-consciously cohabited before the flaming sword of a "dissociation of sensibility" forever sundered them.

1. The execution of Charles I. The scaffold juts out into the audience, like the stage in contemporary outdoor theatres; soldiers and spectators stand—like "groundlings" in the theatre—on three sides of the stage; the main characters can be easily identified by their emblematic costuming.

2. Sir John Falstaff and Mistress Quickly (the "Hostes") stand downstage in this 1662 collage of popular characters from the abridged "drolls" acted between 1642 and 1660. This is the first posthumous representation of any of Shakespeare's characters.

3. This engraving by Martin Droeshout was first published in the 1623 collection of Shakespeare's plays. The same copper plate was reused for the reprints of 1632 and 1663; the latter was reissued in 1664. The state shown here, from the 1664 frontispiece, would have been the image most familiar to Restoration readers; it is much coarser and darker than the 1623 original.

Iv. Grenhill pinx.   W. Faithorne Sculp.

S.ir William Davenant K.t

4. Sir William Davenant. This engraving served as frontispiece to the first edition of Davenant's *Works* (1673). In 1749 William Chetwood compared this image with Shakespeare's, trying to evaluate the rumor that Davenant was Shakespeare's bastard son. He concluded that Davenant's "Features seem to resemble the open Countenance of *Shakespear*, but the want of a Nose gives an odd Cast to the Face" (Davenant lost his nose to syphilis). The Davenant frontispiece also illustrates, by contrast, how unclassical, how old-fashioned, and how crude in its technique the Shakespeare image would have seemed to Restoration readers. All three characteristics matched prevailing views about the art of Shakespeare and his contemporaries, when compared to Davenant's own.

5. The earliest surviving playbill for a play by Shakespeare, advertising a 1697 performance of Dryden's adaptation of *Troilus and Cresida*. Typically, neither Dryden nor Shakespeare is mentioned.

6. *Hamlet* (1709). Like other aspects of Rowe's edition, this engraving probably reflects contemporary performances—as the curtain in the upper left-hand corner is meant to signal. Betterton plays Hamlet in contemporary attire (including a powdered wig); antic dishevelment is restricted to his right leg. The engraving confirms other testimony that Betterton responded to the appearance of his father's ghost by abruptly standing up, overturning his chair in the process; the portraits on the back wall may have been used as visual referents for Hamlet's demand that his mother "Look here upon this picture, and on this." The scenic flats, introduced by Davenant, explicitly define the setting as a domestic interior.

7. Shakespears Head. One of innumerable eighteenth-century copies of the "Chandos" portrait, this painting probably served as the shop sign of Jacob Tonson's bookstore in the Strand. Other copies served as personal icons: Dryden said of his (painted by Sir Godfrey Kneller), "With awe, I ask his Blessing e're I write;/ With Reverence look on his Majestick Face . . ."

8. William Hogarth, *Henry the Eighth and Anne Boleyn.* This engraving—one of the first visual images of a Shakespeare play, outside of printed editions of his work—illustrates the explicit topicality of Augustan interpretations of Shakespeare. Appearing at about the same time as the first version of *The Dunciad,* the engraving was inspired by Drury Lane's 1727 revival of *Henry VIII,* which had interpolated an elaborate procession celebrating the recent coronation of George II. Opponents of the government compared Cardinal Wolsey to Robert Walpole, on whom Hogarth's Wolsey, leaning on the throne, is explicitly modeled. The costumes and settings are all contemporary (as was usual in the theatres).

9. *Prospero on the Enchanted Island. The Enchanted Isle* was the subtitle of the Dryden/Davenant/ Shadwell adaptation of *The Tempest,* and this 1798 engraving portrays King George III as Prospero, wise and powerful lord of the magically invulnerable isle of "Albion." Like Prospero raising the seastorm that maroons his enemies on the island, George III is destroying the French fleet. Quoting Prospero's most famous speech, the King says (of the French Revolution), "Yea all which it inherit shall dissolve & like the baseless Fabric of a Vision leave not a Wreck behind."

10. Kitty Clive as Olivia, Peg Woffington as Viola. As the contrast in costuming demonstrates, a transvestite "breeches part" like Viola offered actresses like Woffington unique opportunities to display their normally concealed, consequently fetishized legs. But the comic dialogues between Viola and Olivia, Portia and Nerissa, Rosalind and Celia also gave eighteenth-century actresses strong scenes not dependent upon, or dominated by, men.

11. William Hogarth, *David Garrick as Richard III* (1745). One of the first, and most famous, English theatrical portraits, this painting epitomizes the period's emphasis on character and emotion. The sumptuous tent and costuming illustrate Shakespeare's ready adaptability to the broadly realist conventions of historical painting; but within them, the painting of Christ's crucifixion allegorically reminds the viewer of the moral reality that Richard turns his back on.

12. Henry Fuseli, *Titania and Bottom* (1786–89). The supernatural elements of *A Midsummer Night's Dream* fascinated Fuseli, as they did other Romantics. Unlike Hogarth, Fuseli visualizes the play in terms that the theatre could not reproduce: the emphatic glowing nudity of Titania; the wide range of physical proportions, from the gigantesque Bottom to the homunculus he holds in his hand; the control of light, illuminating several of the fairies but leaving the frame and bestial Bottom himself—particularly his genitals—in darkness.

13. William Blake, *Pity* (1795). Blake's interpretation of Shakespeare is even further removed from the theatre than Fuseli's. Here he pictorializes Shakespeare's verbal image of "Pitty like a naked new-born babe,/ Striding the blast, or heaven's cherubim,/ Hors'd upon the sightless couriers of the air" (*Macbeth* 1.7.21–23).

14. Facsimile of the signatures on Shakespeare's will (as reproduced by George Steevens in 1778). The first manuscript rediscovered in the eighteenth century that contained specimens of the author's handwriting, the will has no literary value but illustrates the period's fascination with documentary authenticity.

15. "Shakspeare's Cliff in 1836, seen from the North-east," from Charles Lyell's *Principles of Geology*. Among many examples of the effects of geological change within historical memory, Lyell observed that "Shakspeare's Cliff, composed entirely of chalk, has suffered greatly, and continually diminishes in height." Lyell deduced that "the view from the top of the precipice in the year 1600, when the tragedy of King Lear was written, was more 'fearful and dizzy' than it is now." The cliff was thought to be the site described by Edgar in Act Four of *King Lear*.

16. The Siege of Harfleur. This etching, made by George
Scharf, illustrates Macready's 1839 production of *Henry V*.
The Victorian theatre's desire for historical accuracy is
evident in the looming fortifications of the set, the authentic
shields and armor and crossbows and siege cannon, and the
army of supernumeraries.

17. J. M. W. Turner, *Juliet and Her Nurse* (1836). Turner's magnificent canvas illustrates, even
more clearly than Macready's *Henry V*, the dwarfing of text by context. Juliet and the Nurse
are tiny figures at the lower right, looking out across the dazzling splendor of sky and city
(the wrong city, Venice instead of Verona). In the eighteenth century Shakespeare illustration
had been dominated by engravings or by paintings in dark hues; the Victorian period is the
great age of Shakespeare paintings in vivid impressionist or pre-Raphaelite color.

18. John Hayter, *Miranda*. This etching of an idealized Victorian virgin is specifically keyed to Act I, scene two of *The Tempest*, Miranda's first scene, in which she spends most of her time listening attentively to Prospero. The upward tilt of the eyes, which in the context of that scene suggests the child looking up at her father, also recalls conventional images of heaven-gazing saints.

19. Eugène Delacroix, Ophelia (1843), one of several Victorian depictions of the drowning maiden. In Shakespeare's play this scene—like others favored by illustrators—is narrated but not dramatized. Ophelia, with her exposed breast and swooning abandon, about to be swept away by the current, invests the moment with an explicit eroticism, in addition to the voyeurism implicit in any viewing of her private bath/death.

20. The so-called "Janssen" portrait, which surfaced in 1770, was popularized as an authentic likeness by James Boaden in 1824. With a lace collar and silk-and-gold doublet, this is the most aristocratic image ever attached to Shakespeare's name. (Actually, it is probably a portrait of Sir Thomas Overbury.)

21. Max Beerbohm, *William Shakespeare, His Method of Work.* A suitably large, grumpy, and aristocratic Sir Francis Bacon stands behind a small, smiling, plainly dressed Shakespeare, who seems to be thinking hard and pacing the floor in the throes of creation. But the pacing can also be interpreted as slinking, and the thinking gesture as a conspiratorial finger aside the nose.

22. "Queen Katherine's Dream," in *Henry VIII* at the Princess' Theatre (1855). This scene from Charles Kean's production demonstrates one of many special effects resulting from improvements in lighting technology in the Victorian age, in a theatre made possible by Victorian legislative reform, which ended the old patent duopoly.

23. Wyndham Lewis, *Timon of Athens* (1912). These two harshly opposed, geometrical heads probably represent the slanging match between Timon and Apemantus in Act Four; but they also epitomize the period's preoccupation with a verbal/visual thematic image—what Ezra Pound called, in the same year, "an intellectual and emotional complex in an instant of time." The modernists generally favored Shakespeare's late plays—*Timon, Coriolanus, Macbeth, Antony, Pericles*—over earlier favorites like *Hamlet* and *Othello*.

TABLE I.—THE KITE IMAGE CLUSTER.

Context		Kite	Bed	Death	Spirits	Birds	Food
2 H. VI	3.1.249	kite^{249}		death^{245}	soul^{247}	chicken^{249} eagle^{248}	empty^{248}
	3.2.193		sheets^{174}	dead^{188}	ghost^{161}	partridge^{191}	feast^{184}
	196	kite^{193,196}	bed$_{212}$	dead^{192}			
	5.2.11	kites^{11}		deadly-handed^{9}	soul$_{18}$	crows^{11}	empty^{4} carrion^{11}
K. R. III	1.1.133	kite^{133}	bed$_{142}$	die$_{142}$	soul^{119}	eagle^{132} buzzards^{133}	diet$_{139}$
T. of S.	4.1.198	kite^{198}	bed$_{203}$ pillow, bolster$_{204}$ coverlet, sheets$_{205}$	kill$_{211}$	soul^{187}	falcon^{193} haggard^{196}	empty^{193} full-gorged^{194} eat no meat$_{200}$
J. C.	5.1.85	kites^{85}	canopy$_{88}$		ghost$_{89}$	ravens, crows^{85} eagles^{81}	gorging^{82} feeding^{82}
K. H. V	2.1.80	kite^{80}	Tearsheet$_{81}$ bed$_{87}$ sheets$_{88}$ warming pan$_{88}$	death^{65}	spirits^{72} devil$_{95}$	crow$_{91}$	couple a gorge^{75} pudding$_{91}$ food$_{97}$
Ham.	2.2.607	kites^{607}	(John-a-dreams$_{595}$)	murdered$_{612}$ blench$_{625}$	soul$_{630}$ devil$_{628}$	pigeon^{604}	offal$_{608}$
K. L.	1.4.284	kite^{284}	(sleep^{229})	marble-hearted^{281}	devils^{273}		epicurism^{265}
Mac.	3.4.73	kites^{73}		monuments$_{72}$ die$_{79}$ murders$_{81}$	devil$_{59}$ (ghost)		feed$_{58}$
A. & C.	3.13.89	kite^{89}	pillow$_{106}$	dying$_{95}$	devils^{89}		feeders$_{102}$
Cor.	4.5.45	kite^{45}	canopy^{42}			crows, daws^{45}	batten^{35}
W. T.	2.3.186	kite^{186}		death^{184}	soul^{181}	ravens^{186}	nurses$_{187}$
	4.3.23	kite^{23}	sheets^{23} linen^{23}	bleaching^{6} die$_{27}$	soul$_{67}$	lark, thrush, jay^{10}	dish for a king^{8}

The small figures refer to the number of the line in which the image occurs. They are placed above the image when it is on the same line as, or earlier than, the context image, and below the image when it occurs later than the context image.

24. The Kite Image Cluster. In this diagram, taken from Edward Armstrong's *Shakespeare's Imagination* (1946), Shakespeare has become a complex of tabulated and interrelated textual "images." Similar charts can be found in the work of L. C. Spurgeon, G. Wilson Knight, and E. M. W. Tillyard; they are characteristic modernist "portraits" of Shakespeare.

25. "Mr. Colin Keith-Johnston as Hamlet, in plus fours, in the graveyard scene" (in the words of the original 1925 caption). In the twentieth century photographs became the dominant visual medium for recording theatrical performances and for illustrating Shakespeare's texts; there was a corresponding sharp decline in the demand for, and production of, paintings, drawings, and engravings on Shakespearian themes.

26. *Twelfth Night* (1912). Orsino's court, in Granville-Barker's production, is dominated by a cubist curtain (designed by Norman Wilkinson). The costumes are deliberately eclectic and exotic; the actors are forced onto the narrow rim of the stage, often speaking

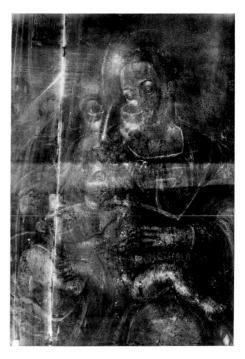

27. This X ray of the so-called "Flower" portrait of Shakespeare shows that it was painted over an earlier image of the Madonna and Child. The X ray enables us to detect later overpainting and touching-up of the portrait, but it also characteristically fragments the poet's image—demonstrating too how one text is created on top of another.

directly to the audience. By contrast with the huge theatres of the later eighteenth and nineteenth centuries, the Savoy stage and auditorium are relatively small, giving greater emphasis to the human figure but, at the same time, playing to a more restricted public.

28. *Richard II*. This 1984 sketch by C. Walter Hodges is designed to illustrate "A possible Elizabethan staging of Act I, Scene 3." The image is dominated by the ornate overarching architecture of the Elizabethan stage and is framed by the audience; Shakespeare's plays are seen as historically specific artifacts socially enacted, which visually enact historically specific social distinctions on stage. Their meaning depends not only on the words spoken but also on a network of semiotic codes: costuming, symbolic properties, music, the organization of space.

29. Valentina Shendrikova as Cordelia and Yuri Jarvet as Lear in Grigori Kozintsev's film (1969). Kozintsev's account of the making of *King Lear* is called *The Space of Tragedy;* here one of its most poignant moments—even more poignant when accompanied by Shostakovitch's score— is created by the space between two political prisoners as they are led away, together and apart, by a crowd of anonymous soldiers. Like Kurosawa, Kozintsev adapts Shakespeare to an epic cinematography of vast spaces and moving masses.

30. King Lear and the Fool in the storm, by Ian Pollock, from one of a series of full-color, full-text comic-book editions of Shakespeare's plays published in the 1980s. The postmodernist equivalent of the Lambs' *Tales from Shakespear*, the comic-book format translates the text into a succession of unrealistic, boxed, vivid, often garish and violent stills.

interested in Shakespeare's mind, we have to be interested in Shakespeare's body, for his character should have been expressed by his actions as well as his fictions. This expectation was confirmed by many examples of the demonstrable relationship between an artist's character and the character of his work, a relationship that becomes more obvious the more we know about his life. Dowden, like the Baconians, like most Victorians, assumed that the nature of Shakespeare's life must have strongly corresponded to the nature of his art.

But this assumption was disconcerted by the steadily accumulating testimony of the documents. Nineteenth-century scholarship unearthed much new information about the details of Shakespeare's existence, but the biography that emerged from those materials was a narrative of business transactions and actions at law. Shakespeare acquired property, Shakespeare dealt in commodities, Shakespeare made investments, Shakespeare sued people who owed him money. As Whitman summed it up, "He bought and sold, bargained, was thrifty, borrowed money, loaned money, had lawsuits."[127]

This emerging narrative satisfied some readers well enough. In the hands of Samuel Smiles, Shakespeare's life became another exemplary demonstration of the virtues of *Self-Help* (1859). An abiding best seller of the Victorian age, Smiles' book offered readers many inspiring *"illustrations of CHARACTER AND CON-DUCT"*; its Shakespeare was "a close student, and a hard worker," a man of "practical qualities" who consequently "prospered in his business, and realized sufficient to enable him to retire upon a competency."[128] Smiles' description of Shakespeare, although addressed to a popular audience, did not differ materially from what reputable authorities were writing in the same decade. In 1853 the British antiquarian James Halliwell assured readers that "the great dramatist most carefully attended to his worldly interests; and confirmations of this opinion may be produced from numerous early sources";[129] in 1865 the American editor Richard Grant White insisted that Shakespeare wrote his plays "solely that he might obtain the means of going back to Stratford to live the life of an independent gentleman."[130]

Shakespeare the self-made entrepreneur satisfied the mercantile mentality, but he was harder to relate convincingly to the sublimely imaginative poet who had been worshiped for more than a century.

Victorians coped with this disparity in various ways. Some quarantined the person from the poetry, so that their dissimilarity never obtruded itself. Since Rowe in 1709, every important edition of Shakespeare's works (and most unimportant ones) had housed an essay on his life; the Cambridge and Globe editions, by contrast, told readers nothing about him. This separation of powers, divorcing editors from biographers, suited the period's drive toward specialization and the division of labor.

For readers who nevertheless insisted on comprehensiveness, Dowden offered the most persuasive synthesis. Shakespeare the landowner sued a neighbor to recover money owed him for the delivery of malt; at about the same time he wrote Hamlet's speeches ridiculing courtiers "spacious in the possession of dirt" and lawyers with their "recoveries" and their buried skulls "full of fine dirt";[131] Dowden saw both actions as reflections of a single balanced personality. Shakespeare's intellectual achievement resulted, according to Dowden, from a triumph of "self-control." Shakespeare the practical man (a Bolingbroke, a Henry V, an Octavius Caesar) managed, barely, to contain Shakespeare the impulsive and emotional idealist (a Falstaff, a Romeo, a Hamlet).[132] Dr. Jekyll restrained but never wholly suppressed Mr. Hyde.

The Cambridge Shakespeare divided the works from the life; Dowden divided the lifework into two opposing impulses, precariously balanced; the Baconians divided the work into two contrasted lives, Bacon the hidden mind and Shakespeare the hired hand. All three responses, however different, presupposed an apparent incompatibility between the product and what was known of its producer. The Baconians simply concluded that the incompatibility resulted from fraud. And what better instrument of fraud than William Shakespeare the money-grub?

Since those who denied Shakespeare's authorship of the plays did not all agree on Bacon or any other candidate, they eventually came to be called "anti-Stratfordians"; whoever wrote the plays, it was not the man from Stratford. Stratford-upon-Avon epitomized the penny-wisdom they detested in Shakespeare himself. Its inhabitants had been cashing in on his name since the middle of the eighteenth century. As early as 1806 Stratford was attracting a thousand visitors a year.[133] In 1847 the American circus magnate P. T. Barnum tried to buy Shakespeare's birthplace; in response, the novelist Dickens and the actor Macready spearheaded a successful national campaign to purchase it by subscription for the nation. The arrival of the railway branch line in 1860 only intensified the town's commercial devotion to literary tourism. An estimated thirty thousand customers were lured to the tricentennial jubilee of 1864.[134] On April 23, 1879, the Shakespeare Memorial Theatre opened, and Stratford began hosting annual theatrical festivals. The jubilee and the festivals were subsidized by the Flower family, which dominated the town by virtue of the employment provided and the profits accumulated by their brewery. Small beer and Shakespeare—Shakesbeer fed and defined Stratford. The town personified the middle-class philistinism that Matthew Arnold descried and decried; it combined "provincialism" with the "commercial spirit." The town in which Shakespeare had been born and buried symbolized everything that was being rejected by the great Victorian critics of social consciousness.

The anti-Stratfordians are often accused by hostile critics of snobbery, but if so, it was an aesthete snobbery that they shared with John Ruskin, Walter Pater, and Matthew Arnold. Arnold, after all, assured us that "Shakspeare or Virgil,—souls in whom sweetness and light, and all that in human nature is most humane and eminent" would have found the Pilgrims "intolerable company."[135] Such snobbery encouraged many nineteenth-century authorities to believe that the aristocratic "Janssen portrait" was an authentic likeness of Shakespeare. Théophile Gautier's first novel included an idyllic account of a performance of *As You Like It* in the large orangery of a French country house, and Oscar Wilde celebrated an amateur production of the same play performed by Lady Archibald Campbell and the Pastoral Players in the garden of Coombe House: Orlando was played by Lady Archibald, the music was "quite exquisite," "the colour scheme was very perfect," and in conclusion "*As You Like It* has probably never been so well mounted."[136]

Such snobbery also informs some of the period's most characteristic music. By the nineteenth century Shakespeare was being served by major European composers of international reputation, at the tiptoe pinnacle of their powers, deploying entire orchestras. Mendelssohn, for instance, who had composed an orchestral overture to *A Midsummer Night's Dream* in 1826, wrote incidental music for a historic production of the play by the great German Romantic poet, playwright, and novelist Ludwig Tieck. This 1843 production included the "Wedding March," probably the most famous piece of music ever composed for a Shakespeare performance, played at the beginning of Act Five to accompany a long torchlit procession of the three bridal couples. The "Wedding March" adorned, in performance, a mere promenade, interpolated into the text; it gave symbolic sound to a dumb show. In Shakespeare's theatre such actions were accompanied by a simple flourish of trumpets, but in the nineteenth century such musical poverty no longer seemed adequate to the richness of the text. Shakespeare's plays deserved great music (just as they deserved to have been written by someone more significant than an actor from Stratford). And so Mendelssohn provided music of a complexity, variety, and formal assurance equal to Shakespeare's own poetry, music that inevitably accompanied subsequent nineteenth-century performances. The "Wedding March" itself—part of the incidental music commissioned by King Friedrich Wilhelm IV of Prussia—embodies, in sound, the theme of triumphant aristocratic marriage, focused and sustained during a procession five minutes long. Mendelssohn's collaborator on that production, Ludwig Tieck, had been the first critic to propose that the "germ" of Shakespeare's play had been "a felicitation" to celebrate the wedding of a particular Elizabethan nobleman.[137] There is no more hard evidence for Tieck's conjecture than for Delia Bacon's, but it became as popular with scholars as Mendelssohn's composition became with auditors; like Mendelssohn's music, like the Baconian hypothesis, Tieck's theory supplemented Shakespeare's text, grafting onto the original words a satisfyingly romantic and aristocratic paratext.

If Mendelssohn and Tieck and the Baconians can be accused of snobbery, so can the works attributed to William Shakespeare, which use variations of the word "lord" 3,296 times, of "king" 1,830 times, of "noble" 843 times, of "prince" 672 times, of "queen" 495 times, of "royal" 263 times, of "knight" 219 times. Speeches are regularly accompanied by deferential forms of address, recognizing social status: "sir" alone recurs 2,613 times, and the ubiquitous distinction between "thou" and "you" persistently signals nuances of rank. Moreover, the language of the plays and poems does not distinguish "gentle" as in "gentleman" from "gentle" as in "kind," or discriminate between "noble" as in "aristocrat" and as in "heroic" and as in "a gold coin"; "royal" could refer to a gold coin, a monarch, or the qualities of magnificence and munificence appropriate to monarchs; "sovereign" meant "royal" and "supreme" and "a gold coin." Etymology supports aristocracy: blue blood inherits virtue, and wealth properly belongs to those who have inherited titles. The plays are peopled with four emperors, thirty-two kings, seventeen queens, fourteen princes, two princesses, sixty dukes, five duchesses, and thirty-seven earls. Confronted with such Facts, the influential English journalist Walter Bagehot summed up Shakespeare as "the poet of personal nobility,"[138] and Walt Whitman, at about the same time, described him as the "artist and singer of Feudalism."[139] Confronted with such Facts, the Baconians decided that such plays can have been written only by an aristocrat.

The anti-Stratfordians believed that the plays were foundlings whose real parentage had long been obscured; but now the discovery of some vital clue, some neglected artifact, would at last demonstrate their aristocratic lineage. The plays had been fathered by Francis Bacon, Lord Verulam, not by the lowly country fellow Shakespeare. Likewise, in the plays themselves Philip Falconbridge turns out to be the bastard son of King Richard the Lion-Hearted; Viola is not a servant fit to attend Orsino but a lady fit to marry him, Marina is not a seamstress but the child of King Pericles, Perdita is not a shepherd's daughter but heir to the kingdom of Sicily, Guiderius and Arviragus are not rustics but princes, Imogen is not a page but a princess. Status (like murder) will out. Such stories appealed to Victorian readers as much as they had to Renaissance playgoers; Oliver Twist, after all, raised in a workhouse for paupers, is eventually reunited with his half sister and restored to his inheritance. The Baconians simply transferred this family romance from the plots of the plays into a plot that explains the authorship of those plays.

The Baconians saw plots everywhere. Their hypothesis required a conspiracy; nothing less could have concealed Bacon's authorship of the plays in his lifetime, by planting so much false evidence attributing them to Shakespeare. And from the Baconian point of view, only the existence of a hostile conspiracy could explain why their theories, once promulgated, were not immediately and universally accepted by the cultural establishment. No doubt some of the Baconians, like their archetype Delia Bacon herself, would now be diagnosed as neurotics, but the movement as a whole cannot be explained in terms of individual neurosis; too many people succumbed. The Baconian hypothesis required paranoia, and it could never have succeeded unless it had been supported by mass paranoia.

In the Gothic novels of the late eighteenth century isolated heroes

or heroines had found themselves at the mercy of a despotic aristocrat; in the great Gothic novels of the early twentieth century they
would find themselves at the mercy of a despotic bureaucracy. The
scene of middle-class European nightmares, the nightmares of the
common reader, shifted from Horace Walpole's *The Castle of Otranto*
(1765), written by the fourth earl of Orford, to Franz Kafka's *The
Trial* (begun in August 1914), written by a government insurance
clerk. This cultural shift in the focus of fictional paranoia corresponded to a real shift in social power, and the Baconian movement
emerged during the transition between aristocracy and bureaucracy. It arose at the moment when Shakespeare was institutionalized and expropriated by the new civil servants of literature.
The Baconians were all amateurs writing for amateurs against specialists; the Baconian myth represented and still represents the
revolt of the layman. An enthusiast, armed only with the truth,
struggles against the massed repressive powers of a corrupt establishment. The maverick upsets the mandarin.

Delia Bacon was a contemporary of Charles Dickens. In Dickens'
novels protagonists were victimized by named and characterized
sadistic villains who represented the coercive institutions of a mass
society: the school (*Nicholas Nickleby*), the workhouse (*Oliver Twist*),
the legal system (*Bleak House*). In most of those struggles Dickens,
unlike Kafka, still envisaged the triumph of the individual over the
organization. The early Baconians, likewise, confidently expected
an imminent victory against the Shakespeare establishment.

The theory that Shakespeare did not write Shakespeare's plays
continues to appeal to amateurs, precisely because it has been
utterly rejected by professionals. If it were ever accepted by the
academic establishment, it would immediately lose its hold on the
popular imagination. The theory shifts in order to satisfy the paranoia of the moment. While science was widely perceived as an
advocate of new truth, courageously challenging the establishment,
Francis Bacon was the favored candidate; but now he is out of favor
because science has itself become one of our most powerful and
distrusted bureaucracies. In recent science fiction romances, like
E.T. or *Flight of the Navigator,* scientific bureaucrats have unmistakably assumed the role of villains, frustrating the natural and applaus-
ible impulses of ordinary folk. The myth that the pyramids were
built by extraterrestrial astronauts satisfies the same popular hunger as the myth that Shakespeare's plays were written by extratex-

tual aristocrats. In both myths credit for a great achievement has been misplaced, and the accredited experts are discredited. The structure of both myths encodes a rebellion against the authorities of culture. Shakespeare and the professional Shakespearians are ousted by Bacon and the amateur Baconians; Shakespeare is ousted in order to oust the Shakespearians.

Conspiracies are an essential feature of the Baconian plot, and coded messages are a natural accessory to conspiracies. In 1882 two Americans, Catherine Windle and Ignatius Donnelly, independently concluded that Bacon had left proof of his authorship by embedding appropriate crytographic messages in the text of "the So-Called Shakespeare Plays." Thereafter the discovery of ciphers and cryptograms multiplied. The methods and the results of those many amateur essays in cryptanalysis have been blown away by professional cryptologists; but the resort to codes and ciphers in the first place deserves some attention, because it represents an original, characteristic, and enduring Victorian contribution to literary criticism.

Codes and ciphers were not invented by the Victorians, but they first became objects of general public fascination in the second half of the nineteenth century. The invention of the telegraph in 1844 made Morse code a fact of daily life; many commercial codes enabled customers to disguise the messages they transmitted through telegraph clerks; military cryptology was utterly transformed. The popular press, dedicated to revealing secrets, and private codes, dedicated to concealing them, both profited from new technology. Not surprisingly, they soon came into conflict: in 1878—only four years before the first discovery of a Bacon "cipher"—an American newspaper ruined the political career of a presidential candidate by deciphering and publishing his coded attempts to buy votes in the electoral college. The most famous of many Victorian detectives, Sherlock Holmes, decipherer of secret codes and detector of hidden clues, made his public debut in 1887. This interest in contemporary codes coexisted naturally with an interest in the codes of the past. Samuel Pepys' diary, quoted above in discussing the Restoration theatre, had been written in a shorthand cipher and was not decoded or published until 1825. The Rosetta stone had been deciphered, and Egyptian civilization made legible, in 1822; Babylonian cuneiform finally succumbed in 1857.

The past speaks in code; in order to understand it you must decipher its language. The fossils in the rocks, the hieroglyphics in Egyptian monuments, the manuscripts Pepys had bequeathed to Magdalene College, Cambridge—the messages had been there all along, but no one knew their meaning until the code was cracked. Egyptian hieroglyphics, Babylonian cuneiform, were languages; but to outsiders they concealed their meanings as effectively as the most complicated modern military cipher. Not only could any language be encoded; any language was by definition a code. The study of past languages and literatures therefore required critical techniques that resembled cryptanalysis.

The Baconians treated Shakespeare's texts as a coded message requiring decipherment, but so did many other Victorian scholars. The need for cryptanalysis itself reinforces the power of "experts." The critical history of the sonnets throughout the nineteenth century consisted of attempts to decipher the private narrative they implied and to determine the real identities of the patron, the dark lady, and the rival poet; these attempts, as contradictory and prolific as theories about the real author of Shakespeare's plays, depended upon the discovery and interpretation of cryptic "clues" embedded in the texts, which sometimes had to be rearranged in order to make the narrative clear. The search for private messages, so obsessive in the poems, naturally invaded the plays too. Fleay proposed that four characters in *Love's Labour's Lost* (Armado, Moth, Nathaniel, and Dull) satirized four of Shakespeare's fellow writers (John Lyly, Thomas Nashe, Robert Greene, and Anthony Munday).[140] In 1874 the New Shakspere Society heard a paper on "The Politics of Shakspere's Historical Plays" that discovered numerous "indirect references and allusions to contemporary politics"; for instance, Shakespeare had repeatedly departed from his historical sources in order to draw parallels between King John and Queen Elizabeth.[141] Government censorship of the drama forced him to speak of certain subjects in riddles, circumlocutions, and allegories. Such interpretations presuppose that the plays were written in part in a private language, only properly understood—then and now—by an elect elite. Like the Baconians, they again split Shakespeare in two, this time separating the public meaning from the private one.

The Victorians were not wrong in treating Shakespeare's language as a code, not wrong in attempting to decipher it, not wrong in believing that it was saturated at times with a half-private meaning. Such impulses may have generated the Baconian myth, but they also generated much of the best criticism and scholarship of their century and our own. The search for a message from beyond the grave produced Ignatius Donnelly's silly Baconian book, *The Great Cryptogram;* but it also produced the philosophical scholarship of A. C. Bradley's *Shakespearean Tragedy.*

IN WHICH OUR HERO MEETS AN EXTRAORDINARY FIGURE, WHO RESOLVES SOME PUZZLES, AND AT LAST EXPLAINS THE PURPOSE OF HIS LIFE, AND THE MEANING OF HIS MANY ADVENTURES

Dowden, in his introductory lecture, promised that a student of English eventually "passes from the biographical and the historical to the philosophical study of literature."[142] Like literature itself, the study of literature evolves; as biological evolution culminated in man, so critical evolution culminated in philosophy. A terrier, dissatisfied with the tasteless dogfood pellets in his bowl, leaps onto the table to enjoy the steak abandoned by a higher species; the Victorians, dissatisfied with the bitty gristle of Shakespearian biography, leaped onto the high table of Shakespearian philosophy.

A. C. Bradley, born in 1851, was the son of an evangelical clergyman; he numbered among his older brothers a master of University College, Oxford, and the Oxford philosopher Francis Herbert Bradley. At Oxford, Bradley studied and, for a while, taught philosophy. In the nineteenth century philosophy had not yet divorced itself from literature. Arnold was not alone in seeing a "high seriousness" in Shakespeare's work,[143] a "criticism of life," "a source of illumination and joy to the whole human race for ever."[144] Hegel, Nietzsche, and Schopenhauer all wrote on Shakespeare, Delia Bacon's magnum opus unfolded *The Philosophy of the Plays of Shakspere*, Anna Jameson based her categorical description of *Characteristics of Women* upon an analysis of *Shakespeare's Heroines* (as her book was later retitled).

Bradley's own career as an Oxford philosopher was terminated by a dispute with the master of Balliol College, the formidable Benjamin Jowett, who disapproved of the Liberal politics and Idealist philosophy of Bradley's circle. Bradley left Oxford, not exactly voluntarily, and found employment as the first King Alfred Professor of Modern Literature at the University of Liverpool (1882), then as Professor of English Literature at Glasgow University (1889). In 1900 he was elected Professor of Poetry at Oxford, and during the five years of his tenure he delivered the lectures eventually incorporated in *Shakespearean Tragedy* (1904) and *Oxford Lectures on Poetry* (1909). Of the eleven pieces collected in the latter, four are wholly devoted to Shakespeare. Both books were published after the death of Queen Victoria, but they represent the public formulation of a critical method developed and articulated during the last two decades of the nineteenth century. Bradley's lectures on Shakespeare were the most highly developed and influential specimens of the Victorian epoch of literary scholarship.

Typically, Bradley's criticism, like Dowden's, takes the form of academic lectures designed for undergraduates, subsequently collected and published by the lecturer. To these circumstances his work owes much of its accessibility. The lectures were designed to serve, and can still serve, as a ritual of initiation; the experienced master carefully guides an innocent neophyte into the intricacies and intimacies of a restricted discipline. Bradley therefore does not dazzle; he does not deal in startled images that jump up out of their context; he is no purveyor of phrases that attach themselves like lint to our memories. Kean, Keats, and Coleridge illuminated Shakespeare with the fitful lightning of isolated brilliant moments of imaginative contact; Bradley uses the lower, steadier voltages of an electric bulb. What dazzles may cause momentary confusion; too memorable a phrase may distract us with its own elegance, luring us into speculations of our own when we should be attending to the lecturer's next paragraph. Bradley inducts us into routine. He proses methodically:

> The question we are to consider in this lecture may be stated in a variety of ways. We may put it thus: What is the substance of a Shakespearean tragedy, taken in abstraction both from its form and from the differences in point of substance between one tragedy and another? Or thus: What is the nature of the tragic aspect of life as represented by Shakespeare? What is the general fact shown now in this tragedy and now in that? And we are putting the same question when we ask: What is Shakespeare's tragic conception, or conception of tragedy?[145]

The first paragraph of the first lecture of *Shakespearean Tragedy* illustrates Bradley's intellectual method throughout. He imposes a relentless clarity on his material; he defines by a steady aggregation of phrases, of examples, of arguments. Meaning piles up.

Bradley has had so many followers because his meaning is so easy to follow. He parcels his analysis into digestible, bite-size portions. *Shakespearean Tragedy* begins with two general introductory lectures ("The Substance of Shakespearean Tragedy" and "Construction in Shakespeare's Tragedies"), then devotes two lectures apiece to *Hamlet, Othello, King Lear,* and *Macbeth;* the book concludes with thirty-two short "Notes" on such questions as "Hamlet's age" and "When was the murder of Duncan first plotted?" cumulatively occupying a quarter of the book's pages. All these separate elements are self-contained; in his preface Bradley explains that readers who "prefer to enter at once on the discussion of the several plays" may skip the first two lectures entirely.[146] Within the individual lectures the material is organized into a series of subsections. The lecture on construction, for instance, has four numbered sections; the second section identifies three numbered "methods by which Shakespeare represents the rise and development of the conflict"; the third section lists eight methods—lettered "(*a*)" to "(*h*)"—that Shakespeare employed in order to overcome the natural sagging of interest in Act Four of his plays; the fourth section enumerates seven "real defects"—lettered "(*a*)" to "(*g*)"—in dramatic technique occasionally evident in Shakespeare's tragedies.[147] Large portions of the lectures on each tragedy readily disconnect into separate descriptions and analyses of the individual characters.

This pattern should by now be familiar. Dowden divided Shakespeare's work into four periods; Bradley divided Shakespeare's tragedies into two groups—the big four (*Hamlet, Othello, King Lear, Macbeth*) and the rest. Professionals were divided from amateurs; the new university departments divided literary history into epochs, assigning each period to a different specialist; biography was divided from editing, and both from criticism; the elite "legitimate" theatre was divided from popular entertainment; Shakespeare's texts were divided into separately printed installments, into elite (Cambridge) and popular (Globe) texts, into British and American, male and female, adult and child versions; Shakespeare's share was divided from that of his collaborators; Shakespeare's works were, by the Baconians, divided from Shakespeare. The price of expansion was diversification. Everything was efficiently broken down into manageable fragments, which only a heroic act of synthesis could reunite. Bradley's verbal and organizational style mirrors the structure of Victorian culture.

Once the lectures were published, with Bradley's own helpful analytical index at the end, they naturally fissured in students' hands into so many crammable digests of Bradley's answers to examination questions.

> I dreamt last night that Shakespeare's ghost
> Sat for a Civil Service post;
> The English paper for the year
> Had several questions on *King Lear*
> Which Shakespeare answered very badly
> Because he hadn't read his Bradley.[148]

University instruction, examinations, the civil service, and the philosopher Bradley had, by the end of the Victorian period, wholly institutionalized Shakespeare. This poem, written in the 1920s, satirizes but also recognizes how completely the status of literature had changed. Shakespeare was a mere amateur; if he did not now conform to the routines of the institution, the institution could deprive him of professional credentials.

Bradley asked "several questions on *King Lear*" that Shakespeare might have answered badly. For instance, Bradley commented upon the sudden upsurge of sexual loathing in some of Lear's mad speeches. When the blinded Gloucester, recognizing the king's voice, kneels to his sovereign, Lear takes him as a prisoner kneeling for clemency.

> I pardon that man's life. What was thy cause?
> Adultery?
> Thou shalt not die: die for adultery! No:
> The wren goes to't, and the small gilded fly
> Does lecher in my sight.
> Let copulation thrive; for Gloucester's bastard son
> Was kinder to his father than my daughters
> Got 'tween the lawful sheets.
> To't, luxury, pell-mell! for I lack soldiers.
> Behold yond simpering dame,

Whose face between her forks presages snow;
That minces virtue, and does shake the head
To hear of pleasure's name;
The fitchew, nor the soiled horse goes to't
With a more riotous appetite.
Down from the waist they are Centaurs,
Though women all above:
But to the girdle do the gods inherit,
Beneath is all the fiends';
There's hell, there's darkness, there's the sulphurous pit,
Burning, scalding, stench, consumption: fie, fie, fie! pah, pah![149]

According to Bradley, "while it is natural in Timon to inveigh against female lechery when he speaks to Alcibiades and his harlots, there is no apparent reason why Lear in his exalted madness should choose this subject for similar invectives." Bradley interprets Lear's diatribe as evidence of the "undercurrent of disgust" toward "sexual corruption" that "becomes audible" in Shakespeare's work in the years 1602–06; this disgust expresses Shakespeare's own "discouragement and exasperation" during this "unhappy period."[150] We hear in these lines Shakespeare's personal preoccupations.

Or are they Bradley's personal preoccupations? For Bradley, the irruption of extraneous material, like Lear's sexual loathing, could be explained only by assuming that Shakespeare had momentarily lost artistic control, allowing the pressure of personal turmoil to push alien subterranean matter violently to the surface. This explanation may be correct. But it depends upon a decision that certain material is extraneous. What seemed extraneous to the Victorian critic may not have seemed so to a Jacobean audience.

Certainly, these passages can be interpreted and defended as an integral part of the play. For one thing, Lear's speeches here pick up earlier strands of the plot. Long before the play began, Gloucester had indeed committed adultery; his bastard son Edmund, the fruit of that adultery, commits adultery with Lear's daughter Goneril; the unfilial behavior of Goneril and Regan had driven Lear himself at one point almost to suspect his own sainted dead wife of adultery. And this repeated narrative emphasis upon unauthorized sex is deeply implicated in the themes of the play. *King Lear* dramatizes a breakdown of authority, parental and political. In Shakespeare's lifetime political authority depended upon parental authority, because the structures of political power were familial in origin; in particular, political legitimacy depended upon legitimacy of birth; a child's right to rule, to assume a title, or to own certain property depended upon the inheritance of royal or noble blood, which in turn depended upon the sexual conduct of the child's mother. As the wives of Henry VIII learned the hard way, in a royal family adultery is treason. Given such ideological and biological assumptions, a seventeenth-century play about the breakdown of political authority is naturally—perhaps inevitably—also a play about adultery and lust. In *Hamlet* the political usurper is also a sexual usurper: Claudius has unlawfully inserted himself into his brother's rightful place, in both the throne room and the bedroom. Richard III, too, fraudulently commandeers England's crown and Lady Anne's genitals.

Bradley does not discuss the Renaissance connection between illicit sex and political illegitimacy, nor does he discuss the Renaissance connection between mental and political instability. Both William Shakespeare and Charles I wrote of the "Soveraignty of Reason" over the soul.[151] Both imagined the structure of the mind in political terms: royal reason must govern the lower orders. When someone like Brutus contemplates rebellion, "the state of man, / Like to a little kingdom, suffers then / The nature of an insurrection."[152] As the legitimate monarch is deposed, reason is deposed in the minds of men; in *Titus Andronicus, Hamlet, King Lear, Macbeth,* political illegitimacy gives birth to madness. Hamlet, appalled by his mother's "blind" concupiscence, describes it as a condition in which "Rebellious hell" mutinies, and "reason pardons will";[153] lust is a rebel, and reason, which should be sovereign, pardons vulgar appetite—just as the sovereign Lear (mad) pardons his adulterous subject Gloucester (blind). When Shakespeare revised Hamlet's speech, he intensified the condemnation by changing the verb, so that reason no longer simply pardons but actively "panders" to sexual appetite. The revision combined two images he had used before: "reason is the bawd to lust's abuse" (describing a ruler's rape of one of his subjects) and "made his majesty the bawd" (describing Machiavellian political maneuvering in sexual terms).[154]

Shakespeare equated monarchy and monogamy, the superego and the state. Bradley did not, nor do we. Few English-speaking readers of Shakespeare today would characterize the revolutions of 1642, 1688, and 1776 in terms of madness, unbounded sexual appetite, or filial ingratitude. Shakespeare's monarchic interpretation of the psyche has been replaced by a constitutional one; mental health depends—in Dowden's interpretation of Shakespeare no less than in current folk psychology—upon a system of checks and balances, upon perpetual negotiation and compromise of competing interests, upon a daily rapprochement between repression and liberation.

Bradley did not explain Lear's speeches in terms of sexual or psychological politics because Bradley did not think like Shakespeare; Bradley thought like Dowden. In 1909 he affirmed, "In everything that I have written on Shakespeare I am indebted to Professor Dowden."[155] Like Dowden he saw Shakespeare through and beyond his texts, "as through a glass darkly." According to Bradley we study poetry "in order to reproduce in ourselves more faintly that which went on in the poet's mind when he wrote."[156] We aspire toward direct contact; like Stanley in pursuit of Livingstone, we trek through the textual jungles until we can at last face our hero and say, "William Shakespeare, I presume." Shakespeare, like Livingstone, will be rescued, whether he wants to be or not.

John Stuart Mill had argued that "To the many Shakespeare is great as a story-teller, to the few as a poet." And what was a poet? Since, according to Mill, "all poetry is of the nature of soliloquy," a poet is someone whose soliloquies we overhear. For Mill poetry had no utility; indeed, he turned to it as a reaction against utilitarian values. But most readers wanted to know what the poet we were overhearing was like and what he had to tell us. If "poetry is *over*heard,"[157] was it worth listening to? Bradley, like Dowden and almost every other major Victorian critic, therefore set out to deduce from Shakespeare's work Shakespeare's philosophical conclusions about the nature of human life. To Bradley his tragedies were dissertations upon "the tragic fact" (a formula he repeats ten times in the very first lecture of *Shakespearean Tragedy*). And the central "fact"—"the inexplicable fact" to which all other "facts" were subordinated—was the fact of "waste" and of "the worth of that which is wasted." Something of value has been wasted; something useful has been unused or misused. The moral calculus of the universe is inefficient. "And this fact . . . is tragedy."

But what does that have to do with Lear's mad speeches about adultery? Nothing. Bradley does not discuss those speeches in *Shakespearean Tragedy* at all, nor do they form part of the substance of *King Lear,* as he defines it there. He discusses those speeches, instead, in relation to "Shakespeare the Man," one of the *Oxford Lectures* published separately five years later. Lear's mad speeches belong to the psychobiography of William Shakespeare, not to the tragedy of *King Lear.* In determining the author's meaning we must in some sense subtract the author; we must ignore his lapses from perfect artistic command of his material. Just as, in determining the truth about characters and events in a play, we must disregard evidence that comes from unreliable characters, so too, in isolating the universal truths that a text conveys, we must disregard evidence tainted by the merely personal circumstances of the author. At the beginning of his first lecture Bradley goes out of his way to insist that the view of life extractable from Shakespeare's tragedies need not have "corresponded with [Shakespeare's] opinions or creed outside his poetry." Bradley, like so many other Victorians, in practice divided the man from the work.

Among the author's merely personal and therefore extraneous circumstances must be counted the fact that he wrote for the theatre. Bradley addresses himself to readers of Shakespeare and repeatedly analyzes the effect of passages and events when read. *King Lear,* in particular, he considered a great work of art but a poor play. Bradley attended performances of plays by Shakespeare and others; he wrote an interesting historical lecture on "Shakespeare's Theatre and Audience"; he could at times pinpoint precisely the differences between the text as read and the text as performed. But such activities remain peripheral to his achievement; theatre mattered less to the dominant consciousness of Shakespeare in Bradley's time than it had in the two preceding centuries.

Bradley has been often accused of treating Shakespeare's plays as though they were Victorian novels. He did not. But the accusation persists because *Shakespearean Tragedy* itself reads like a Victorian novel. It is big, serious, moral, eloquent in a stiff sort of way, verbally polite. It was originally presented to the public in installments. It goes on a bit too long. It loses itself from time to time in curious alleyways. Dryden the dramatist had cast his criticism of Shakespeare in the form of a dialogue *Of Dramatick Poesie;* the journalists Steele and Addison had inscribed Shakespeare in shapely prose essays; Keats and Coleridge had been the greatest practitioners of a mode of criticism typified by lyrical fragments. In Bradley's hands Shakespearian criticism became a philosophical novel.

❦

CHAPTER 5

GOOD-BYE
TO ALL THAT

I

"On or about December, 1910, human character changed."[1] It doesn't matter whether the statement is true; Virginia Woolf, characteristically, mocks her modernist affirmation even as she makes it. Why 1910? Why December? She never says. She might have expected her audience to remember that King Edward VII, Victoria's son, had died in 1910—but that was in May. The Liberal government had been returned to office in that December's general election—the second election that year, called to confirm that government's authority against the House of Lords. The Lords had vetoed a proposed "super-tax" on high incomes and a tax on land; the second Liberal victory in 1910 took a bite out of the power of the aristocracy and the bank accounts of the upper classes. It also left the Liberal government dependent, for the first time, on support from the Labour Party, which in turn depended upon the trade unions. Throughout 1910 those unions squeezed the economy with more strikes, more effective strikes, than ever before. The triumph of the mere masses loomed.

But Virginia Woolf does not mention any of these public events. Arnold Bennett or H. G. Wells or John Galsworthy might have mentioned them; but their novels, she later assures us, with their conscientious expositions, confident explanations, solid stolid characters, belong to the world that 1910 had left behind. Woolf notices that the behavior of servants has changed—one's cook now has opinions about everything—but she does not say why. Did the cook attend the first Post-Impressionist Exhibition, which opened in London on November 8, 1910? Did the cook have opinions about the founding in 1910 of the International Psycho-Analytical Association? E. M. Forster published *Howard's End* in 1910; in 1910, at a railway station, with the international press scavenging outside, cameras in wait to film his funeral, Tolstoy coughed and died—but Virginia Woolf does not mention any of this. Nor does she mention—did she even know?—that in 1910 a midwestern philosophy student at Harvard began writing "The Love Song of J. Alfred Prufrock."[2] T. S. Eliot's character defines himself in opposition to Shakespeare's most famous character ("No! I am not Prince Hamlet, nor was meant to be"), just as Eliot himself will later define his own poetic practice in opposition to Shakespeare's practice in *Hamlet*.

And how do we know that human character has changed? Because the characters we meet in books have changed. Like Eliot, Woolf defines the character of her new art in opposition to the characters of someone else's old art. She does not provide an analytical exposition of the differences in human character before and after 1910; instead, she recounts her encounter with a woman in a railway carriage. This "Mrs. Brown," visibly old, probably poor, the well-meaning worthy novels of Wells and Galsworthy would have characterized in their own old-fashioned way; but E. M. Forster and D. H. Lawrence and James Joyce (and Woolf herself), the novelists who represent the new world that began in 1910, would characterize Mrs. Brown rather differently, more allusively, elusively, illusorily, elliptically, cryptically. Against the philosophical novels of the Victorians, Woolf sets the poetic novels of the modernists. Woolf did not speculate on what William Shakespeare would have done with the character of Mrs. Brown; but Shakespeare, after all, did write his plays before 1910, before human character changed.

Woolf, tactfully, does not mention any of this. But not everyone was so discreet. While she was saying good-bye to character—or, at least, good-bye to character as previous novelists had defined it—in another part of the critical forest E. E. Stoll and Levin Schücking were saying good-bye to character as Shakespeare had defined it—or, at least, as previous critics had defined how Shakespeare defined it.

Shakespeare, for instance, would almost certainly have given Mrs. Brown a soliloquy, in which she could directly and unambiguously inform us of the thoughts which she did not express to any of her fellow passengers in the railway carriage. But how should we interpret what Mrs. Brown confides to us? When Hamlet catches Claudius praying, he decides not to stab him in the back where he kneels; Hamlet says that he doesn't want to kill the villain at a moment when he might go to heaven; he wants Claudius damned as well as dead. Do we believe this explanation, or do we think—as was first suggested in the second half of the eighteenth century—that Hamlet is grandstanding an excuse in order to postpone yet again a decision he lacks the moral strength to make? According to the American Professor Stoll and the German Professor Schücking, we have to believe Hamlet's explanation, because soliloquies do not lie. Of course, in real life, people lie to themselves as often as they lie to other people—maybe more often. But soliloquies are not real life. In real life there is no appended auditorum to which we can at any moment confidentially reveal our motives. Soliloquies are a convention; conventions are a code; if we don't accept the rules of the code we will mistranslate the message. Real life doesn't enter into it. If Shakespeare's Mrs. Brown said, solilogistically, that the Virginia Woolf who had just obtruded herself into the railway carriage was a nosy snob, we would have to believe her; against a Shakespeare soliloquy there is no appeal.

Other codes shape other characters. Henry V belongs to the conventions of heroism, Richard III to those of villainy, Shylock to those of anti-Semitism. Macbeth, "like most Elizabethan and Shakespearean characters, . . . comments on his feelings instead of uttering them." Rather than be himself, he describes himself. Moreover, in describing himself, Macbeth, like Shakespeare's other villains, unrealistically adopts the author's moral perspective. As Stoll observes, modern criminologists have repeatedly demonstrated that "in criminals signs of repentance, remorse, or despair are seldom to be detected. Among four hundred murderers Bruce Thompson found signs of remorse in but three, and of seven hundred criminals Ferri found only 3.4 per cent who showed signs of repentance or who appeared at all moved in recounting their misdeeds"; "Far from evincing Shakespearean remorse," real murderers are inclined, like "Dostoieffsky's Raskolnikoff," to "hate their victim after the crime more than before it."[3] Shakespeare has artificially implanted the conscience of the audience into the thorax of a criminal; he has also planted a poet's tongue in a soldier's mouth. Most of Shakespeare's characters speak verse; people speak prose. Characters speak in the images that seem most poetically or rhetorically effective to Shakespeare—not those which would come most naturally to a person of a certain background in a given situation.

Schücking and Stoll both insist upon interpreting Shakespeare's characters in terms of the theatrical conventions of his own time. That literary code could be read so easily in the second decade of the twentieth century because its last inherited remnants had by then been displaced by a new code: the conventions of Ibsenism. After the long artistic drought of the nineteenth century, the English theatre had begun to leaf again. The best plays of John Galsworthy and Harley Granville-Barker were all written in the first ten years of the century; George Bernard Shaw's career had begun in the 1890s, but he did not achieve any real popularity until 1904–07, when Granville-Barker ran ten of his plays in repertory at the Royal Court Theatre. The influential critic William Archer had been championing Ibsen since the 1880s; by the 1890s Ibsen had achieved an international reputation, and Archer's English translation of his collected works was published in 1906–08. Archer lauded Shaw and Galsworthy, and in 1904 he and Granville-Barker issued a *Scheme and Estimates for a National Theatre.*

Collectively, Galsworthy, Granville-Barker, Shaw, and Archer had by 1910 created a new English drama, and its newness helped to define by contrast the oldness of the drama that it dislodged. Virginia Woolf opposed new characters to old characters; Eliot opposed Prufrock to Hamlet. Maurice Baring, minor playwright and prolific jack-of-all-genres, published in that epochal year 1910 a collection of *Dead Letters,* its title wittily compounding undelivered correspondence and obsolete literature. Baring parodically transformed Shakespeare's characters by making them speak like people in Edwardian plays and novels, as when Goneril the suburban hostess writes to her sister, complaining about "Papa's Fool":

You know, darling, that I have always hated that kind of humour. He comes in just as one is sitting down to dinner, and beats one on the head with a hard, empty bladder, and sings utterly idiotic songs, which make me feel inclined to cry. The other day, when we had a lot of people here, just as we were sitting down in the banqueting-hall, Papa's Fool pulled my chair from behind me so that I fell sharply down on the floor. Papa shook with laughter ... of course Albany refused to interfere. Like all men and all husbands, he is an arrant coward.4

On this point, Shaw differed from Baring only in being a better writer. Like Baring he opposed his *Caesar and Cleopatra* (1906) and *Saint Joan* (1923) to Shakespeare's portrayal of the same historical figures, opposed his *Cymbeline Refinished* (1937) to Act Five of Shakespeare's play.

With the exception of Galsworthy, the key figures in defining the new English drama were also instrumental in redefining Shakespeare for the twentieth century. Granville-Barker became the most influential producer of Shakespeare revivals, and one of the most influential Shakespearian critics, of his generation. In 1908 the Archer/Barker/Shaw campaign for a British National Theatre formed an unlikely alliance with the campaign for a Shakespeare memorial, creating the Shakespeare Memorial National Theatre Committee; in 1919 this committee, at Archer's urging, helped to fund the establishment of the first permanent repertory company at the Memorial Theatre in Stratford-upon-Avon, which would evolve into the Royal Shakespeare Company. In 1923 Archer changed his mind, shifting his support to the Old Vic, which would eventually evolve into the National Theatre. Between them the Old Vic/ National Theatre in London and the Memorial/Royal Shakespeare Theatre in Stratford would dominate the history of British Shakespeare revivals from the 1920s on. In 1923, the year that the Shakespeare Memorial National Theatre Committee gave a thousand pounds to both the Old Vic and the Memorial Theatre, Archer published *The Old Drama and the New*. What T. S. Eliot called a "brilliant and stimulating book" celebrated the new drama as a big blessed advance over the primitive conventions of the Elizabethans, which Archer disemboweled with the gusto of a hyena. Tactfully, like Woolf, he did not mention Shakespeare personally—or rather, as Eliot said, he "facilitated his own task of destruction, and avoided offending popular opinion, by making an exception of Shakespeare." But, as Eliot and everyone else recognized, the same mud-dled conventions could be found everywhere in Shakespeare's plays, producing "faults of inconsistency, faults of incoherency, faults of taste . . . faults of carelessness."5

What Archer implied but did not have the courage to say George Bernard Shaw had been saying loudly for thirty years. Orlando, Adam, Jaques, the banished Duke, Touchstone, Rosalind and the rest are simply "impostures." "This is not human nature or dra-matic character; it is juvenile lead, first old man, heavy lead, heavy father, principal comedian, and leading lady." Tybalt is "an unmer-cifully bad part"; Enobarbus exemplifies Shakespeare's "bogus characterization."6

Granville-Barker, Shaw, and Eliot were (or became) playwrights of considerable originality; even Archer wrote one lucky play. Of course, none of them could compare with Ibsen, Strindberg, or Chekhov. But for the first time since Dryden and Rowe, criticism of Shakespeare was again being shaped, after a two-hundred-year interregnum, by important dramatists. Like Dryden and Rowe before them, Granville-Barker and Shaw and Eliot, living and cre-ating a new set of conventions, were exceptionally sensitive to the differences between their practice and Shakespeare's. Like Dryden, they were all—as Eliot insisted that most great critics are—practi-tioners of the art they criticized.7 Eliot himself, almost single-handed, pulled Dryden out of the ditch of oblivion, brushed off a century of disheveled neglect, and set him back up in the ranks of major English poets and critics. Ben Jonson, too, poet and play-wright and critic, was resurrected: in 1919 Eliot essayed to rescue his reputation from "the most deadly . . . conspiracy" of an-tiquarians, and in 1921 *Volpone* and *Bartholomew Fair* were again revived on the English stage, after an absence of (respectively) 136 and 190 years. Jonson was, for Eliot—just as he had been for Dry-den—an alternative to Shakespeare. But Eliot, unlike Dryden, had no use for Beaumont and Fletcher; instead, he built his alternative theatrical tradition from the plays of John Webster, Thomas Mid-dleton, Cyril Tourneur, John Ford, Thomas Kyd, and Christopher Marlowe, who had all been almost wholly neglected in the English theatre ever since the Restoration. Webster and Middleton jostle with Shakespeare for quoted pride of place in *The Waste Land*.

For the first time in almost two centuries, Shakespeare had com-pany on the Everest of English drama. Dowden had defined the Elizabethan epoch by aligning Shakespeare with Hooker and

Bacon—thinkers, not playwrights; not poets but expositors in prose. Stoll and Schücking and Archer and Eliot, by contrast, all put Shakespeare back in his theatrical context. But each did so for different reasons. The likes of Stoll emphasized the conventions that Shakespeare shared with his contemporaries and did not share with modern drama; Eliot, by contrast, sought in Shakespeare's contemporaries what he could not find in Shakespeare. Stoll saw one tradition, in which Shakespeare participated; Eliot saw a split tradition, with Shakespeare dominating one side of the divide. Jonson and Webster and Middleton could not offer Eliot, or anyone else, an alternative to Shakespeare's conventions. They offered, instead, an alternative to Shakespeare's music.

Crude conventions, magnificent music. Imagining a performance of *Othello* in Shakespeare's lifetime, Virginia Woolf pictured "A black man . . . waving his arms and vociferating . . . the actors running up and down a pair of steps and sometimes tripping, and the crowd stamping their feet and whistling, or when they were bored, tossing a piece of orange peel on to the ice which a dog would scramble for." But "Rough though the staging was," nevertheless "the astonishing, sinuous melody of the words" stirred her, "like music."[8] Shakespeare's characters might be, by modern standards, cardboard, but even curmudgeonly George Bernard Shaw had to admit that the cardboard was "transfigured by magical word-music."[9] Shaw has been called "the best music critic who ever lived";[10] he did not use the metaphor "word-music" casually. He declared that "it is the score and not the libretto that keeps [Shakespear's] work alive and fresh";[11] consequently, only a musician "has the right to criticize works like Shakespear's earlier histories and tragedies", which

> depend wholly on the beauty of their music. There is no deep significance, no great subtlety and variety in their numbers; but for splendor of sound, magic of romantic illusion, majesty of emphasis, ardor, elation, reverberation of haunting echoes, and every poetic quality that can waken the heart-stir and the imaginative fire of early manhood, they stand above all recorded music . . . It is not enough to see Richard III; you should be able to *whistle* it.[12]

Only Shakespeare's music can explain the fact that people have for so long been hypnotized into affirming the reality of Shakespeare's embarrassingly unreal characters. "Tested by the brain, [Othello's part] is ridiculous; tested by the ear, it is sublime."[13]

In addition to *The Quintessence of Ibsenism,* Shaw wrote a book on *The Perfect Wagnerite,* and the new British dramatists redefined Shakespeare between the opposing models of Ibsen and Wagner, between argumentative prose realism and musical myth. Ibsen exemplified what Shakespeare did not do and what Shaw and company wanted to do; Wagner, although equally revolutionary in reshaping European drama, could be more easily adjusted to Shakespearian apologia. As early as 1876 and periodically thereafter, promoters of the newborn theatrical festival at Stratford-upon-Avon had invoked comparisons with Bayreuth, and the auditorium of Stratford's Memorial Theatre (rebuilt in 1932 after a disastrous fire) consciously echoed Wagner's design. Wagner himself wrote only one awkward early opera directly indebted to Shakespeare (*Das Liebesverbot,* in 1836, based on *Measure for Measure*); but while Wagner concentrated on German mythology, his contemporaries were setting Shakespeare's myths to music. Giuseppe Verdi and Arrigo Boito, composer and librettist, triumphantly demonstrated—in 1887 with *Otello* and six years later with *Falstaff*—what could be achieved by the Wagnerian fusion of a modern orchestra with a Shakespearian text. Eliot rejected Ibsen's recipe for the rejuvenation of modern drama; but he was—like Shaw, Forster, and Lawrence—a perfect Wagnerite. *The Waste Land* arguably owes more to Wagner than to any other model, and in his criticism of drama Eliot demands, as did Wagner, a fusion of musicality and myth held together by wholly artificial theatrical conventions. Like Shaw, Eliot defined dramatic poetry in metaphors of music, and the analogy informed his perception of verbal organization from the rhythm of an individual phrase to the composition of an entire work. Drama by definition depends upon "rhythm," the rhythm of "words, sounds, and movements of the body," a rhythm that informs the tricks of jugglers or the films of Charlie Chaplin; it originates in ritual, it is a kind of dance, properly accompanied by "The Beating of a Drum."[14] The "philosophy of Shakespeare" cannot be verbalized—as Bradley had tried to verbalize it—in a set of propositions; "it really has more in common with, let us say, the philosophy of Beethoven"; we feel a meaning but "cannot confine it in words."[15] In his essays on Elizabethan dramatists Eliot was particularly anxious to define their verse technique; Marlowe, for instance, deserves our attention because he "introduced several new tones into blank verse."[16] In his own poetry Eliot appropriated and transformed the "tones" of Shakespeare's Jacobean contemporaries more successfully than any other poet.

In 1930 Eliot wrote an introduction to G. Wilson Knight's influential book *The Wheel of Fire,* praising it particularly for its "search for the pattern below the level of 'plot' and 'character,' " a pattern of "subterrene or submarine music" that organizes the whole work.[17] Knight's book brought Shaw's and Eliot's Wagnerian interest in Shakespearian music into the mainstream of criticism. Shakespeare's plays become "dramatic symphonies"; critics begin to "think of them in terms of orchestration, counterpoint, *leitmotiv* and the rest, because the language appropriate to musical composition seems . . . less misleading than any other."[18] Knight writes a chapter on "The *Othello* Music"; he writes a book on *The Imperial Theme.* In Knight's handling "theme" becomes an insistent leitmotiv in the vocabulary of Shakespearian interpretation, fusing the word's musical definition ("a melodic subject, developed with variations") with its rhetorical one ("the subject on which one writes"). The object of Shakespeare criticism, as defined by Knight, is to identify the theme of each play. Thematic tones and images recur in the speeches and actions of diverse characters; character and plot serve only to illustrate theme.

G. Wilson Knight in 1930 subordinated character to music; L. C. Knights in 1933 rejected character altogether. Facetiously asking "How Many Children Had Lady Macbeth?", Knights attacked Bradley for his excessive finicky attention to the fictive biographies of dramatis personae in Shakespeare's texts. It was high time we said good-bye to "character criticism," good-bye to the whole misguided tradition of Shakespeare criticism since the Restoration:

> the only profitable approach to Shakespeare is a consideration of his plays as dramatic poems . . . the total response to a Shakespeare play can only be obtained by an exact and sensitive study of the quality of the verse, of the rhythm and imagery, of the controlled associations of the words and their emotional and intellectual force . . . We start with so many lines of verse on a printed page which we read as we should read any other poem.

When Macbeth confronts Banquo's ghost the words of different characters "repeat a theme" that "is taken up in the final orchestration"; when Lady Macduff and her young son are murdered, the scene "echoes in different keys the theme of the false appearance." Shakespeare's characters could no longer be defended as plausible representations of human personality; the scholarship of men like Stoll and Schücking, the dramatic practice of men like Ibsen and Shaw, had demonstrated that. "*Macbeth* has greater affinity with *The Waste Land* than with *The Doll's House*." In Shakespeare's play, unlike Ibsen's, the characters are simply the instruments of a complex verbal music, a music not dependent upon the conventions of a primitive theatre, not dependent upon a theatre at all. When Knights wants a parallel for Shakespeare's attitude toward the musical instruments called "characters," he finds it not in other plays but in the novels of Joseph Conrad, James Joyce, D. H. Lawrence—and Virginia Woolf.[19]

II

But when you say good-bye to character, you say good-bye to biography too. In 1934, the year after L. C. Knights disposed of Shakespeare's characters, C. J. Sisson disposed of Shakespeare's character. Knights attacked Bradley; Sisson attacked Dowden. Victorian readers had extrapolated a personality, an emotive history, from the words of texts; the word was made flesh. But the words would not support such inferences. Text was just text, a fleshless complex of intellectual messages. For Sisson, as for Knights, Shakespeare was simply "a great and disinterested poet and thinker," "the master-mind, the supreme craftsman and artist."[20] He did not let the ephemera of his own emotions or the detritus of contemporary events obtrude into the circle of his art.

When, in 1930, E. K. Chambers published his study of Shakespeare's life—the most admired and influential work of its kind in the first half of the twentieth century—he did not call it "A Biography" but *A Study of Facts and Problems*. Its two volumes, still invaluable, devote only two chapters to a narrative of Shakespeare's life: one on his "Origins" and another on his theatrical "Company," totaling a mere 61 pages out of 1,056. Where did he come from, with whom did he play? The rest of the book describes theatrical conditions and printing practices in Shakespeare's lifetime; surveys problems of authenticity and chronology; catalogs records, dates, pedigrees; transcribes documents. It records and classifies, for instance, the eighty-three documented spellings of the playwright's surname. Shakespeare becomes a collage of appendices. "These fragments I have shored against my ruins";[21] Chambers' *William Shakespeare* meticulously collects and records the broken pottery, but it does not even speculate on how the pieces might be put back together to form the ancient vase of a life. "Do I dare?" Prufrock asks. "And how should I begin? And how should I presume?" No, Chambers answers, at the end of his first chapter: "It is no use guessing."[22]

James Joyce, by contrast, did presume. Rather than catalog orthographic variants of William's surname, he invents new ones of his own, ranging from the archetypal "Great Shapesphere" to the domesticated "*Shakefork.*"[23] Stephen Daedalus and his cohorts carry on, off and on, about Shakespeare for seventy pages of *Ulysses* (first published by a small Paris firm named Shakespeare and Company). *Hamlet* is, in a *franglais* pun, a "*Pièce de Shakespeare*" and a piece of Shakespeare; Anne Hathaway, the older woman, seduced Shakespeare in a rye field outside Stratford; she committed adultery with Shakespeare's younger brothers Richard and Edmund;

> his mother's name lives in the forest of Arden. Her death brought from him the scene with Volumnia in *Coriolanus*. His boyson's death is the deathscene of young Arthur in *King John*. Hamlet, the black prince, is Hamnet Shakespeare. Who the girls in *The Tempest*, in *Pericles*, in *Winter's Tale* are we know. Who Cleopatra, fleshpot of Egypt, and Cressid and Venus are we may guess.[24]

If you have not read *Ulysses*, if you are wholly dependent on my summary and quotations, you might mistake this for biography, imaginative biography, the re-creation of a character. But Joyce, like Chambers, never snuggles down to narrative. The conversation bobs and meanders, chopped by arrivals and departures, sidetracked by asides. "What the hell are you driving at?" the text asks, attributing the question to no one in particular and never answering it. "Shakespeare? he said. I seem to know the name." But other names intrude. Goethe, Coleridge, Whitman pop in, familiarly, and "Mr Justice Madden in his *Diary of Master William Silence* has found the hunting terms," and then too there is "Good Bacon: gone musty." Joyce creates not only a conversation between several fictional characters on June 16, 1904, in the National Library at Dublin, but also a conversation among Shakespeare's biographers, who become in Joyce's hands equally fictional. He plays with pieces from the Danish biographer Georg Brandes, pieces from the Jewish biographer "Mr Sidney Lee, or Mr Simon Lazarus," pieces from the "Catamite" biographer Oscar Wilde, pieces from the Irish biographer Edward Dowden ("William Shakespeare and company, limited. The people's William. For terms apply: E. Dowden, Highfield house . . ."). "And we ought to mention another Irish commentator, Mr George Bernard Shaw. Nor should we forget Mr Frank Harris." In case you have forgotten, Mr Frank Harris published in 1909, that last year of the old dispensation, *The Man Shakespeare and His Tragic Life-story*, a sensational Irish rendering of the bard's full-blooded genital-groping life and rimes. As for Hamlet, "Has no-one made him out to be an Irishman?"

And while they (and we) are on the subject of Irishmen, we may as well mention that Joyce is the last of his line. Malone and Dowden in their different ways each shaped the international perception of Shakespeare for a generation or more, while Harris and Shaw and Yeats and Joyce collectively helped shape his modernist image. Since then Shakespeare has lost his Irish accent. *Ulysses* was finished, its last line tells us, in 1921, the year that Ireland (most of it) gained its independence from Great Britain. They still teach Shakespeare in Eire, of course, they talk and write about him, but in 1921 he became a foreigner again. "As an Englishman," one of Joyce's voices glosses, Shakespeare "loved a lord." As an Englishman, loving lords, mocking the stage Irishman MacMorris and the bogs of MacMorris' homeland, Shakespeare aroused mixed feelings in the new Eire. In 1924 George William Russell concluded that Shakespeare, "the first supreme artist in literature who seems to be absorbed in character for its own sake," had led "literature into a blind alley"; in the same year George Moore claimed that W. S. Landor was greater than Shakespeare. Neutrality became national policy.

Joyce, self-consciously Irish, mocks the Irish pride in Irish Shakespeare criticism, but his mockery is catholic: he mocks them, scholars, one and all. The whole episode dramatizes, as Ezra Pound immediately recognized, *"une vanité universitaire"*.[25] The critics bobble out of their footnotes into Joyce's scholastic comedy; they "fingerpond nightly each his variorum edition of *The Taming of the*

Shrew," perpetually contradicting each other, their passionate theories incongruously jumbled in a tumbling conversation, entrusted to untrustable spokesmen, whole books compressed into sentences, misapplied, garbled, offhand, the whole machinery of pedantry dramatized as an amusing round of intellectual gossip:

> Do you believe your own theory?
> —No, Stephen said promptly.

Like Chambers, Joyce does not believe any of the biographies; they are all fiction, no less and no more so than *Ulysses* or *King Lear.* "In the reading of *King Lear* what facts verifiable by science, or accepted and believed in as we accept and believe in ascertained facts, are relevant?" a contemporary critic asks, and answers "None whatever."[26] Good-bye to all those Victorian Facts. The Victorians saw Fact even in literature; the modernists see fiction even in the facts of life.

Like Chambers, Joyce gives us, instead of a life, a montage of fragments, scrupulously collected from many sources. Shakespeare has become a ghost, the ghost behind and within *Hamlet,* Hamlet's ghost.

> —What is a ghost? Stephen said with tingling energy. One who has faded into impalpability through death, through absence, through change of manners.

And the "divine," the "immortal" Shakespeare celebrated since the seventeenth century, has become in the twentieth as impalpable as every other Holy Ghost. "The playwright who wrote the folio of this world and wrote it badly"—is Joyce writing about God or Shakespeare? "(He gave us light first and the sun two days later)"; Joyce is, in the parenthesis at least, writing about God, reminding us that the time scheme of Genesis is as impossibly confused as the time scheme of *Othello.*

Ulysses can be fairly confusing too. Joyce's fiction, like Chambers' scholarship, addresses itself to a select readership. For the uninitiated both are intimidating, difficult, unhelpful. Victorian Shakespeare had been commandeered by specialist professionals, but that elite still sought and got the attention of a mass audience. *The Globe Shakespeare,* like *The Origin of Species,* made the complex-fresh achievements of specialists accessible to literate laymen. Charles Knights' *William Shakspere: A Biography* (1842–43) was written by a populist publisher, Sidney Lee's *Life of William Shakespeare* (1898) began life as an entry in the *Dictionary of National Biography;* from the beginning of Victoria's reign to the end, scholarly biography addressed itself to the same public that read the novels of Charles Dickens and George Eliot. By contrast, E. K. Chambers—a career bureaucrat who rose to be Second Secretary in the Education Department of the British government—wrote a white paper for his fellow civil servants of literature. He methodically surveyed and evaluated all the evidence, he broke the material down into a series of discrete problems, in each instance he considered the policy options available, in some cases he suggested that the balance of probabilities favors one interpretation rather than another, in other cases he did not venture an opinion. You do not read Chambers' *William Shakespeare;* you use it.

You use it, particularly, when you are puzzled by a problem. Chambers redefines Shakespearian biography as *A Study of Facts and Problems;* Schücking pondered *Character Problems in Shakespeare's Plays;* W. W. Greg devoted a lifetime to elucidating *The Editorial Problem in Shakespeare.* For Sisson "the artistic problems Shakespeare set himself" matter more than "the problems life set Shakespeare."[27] For Eliot, " 'Hamlet' the play is the primary problem"; Hamlet the character is a merely "secondary" problem.[28] Granville-Barker considers "The Producer's Problem" in *Love's Labour's Lost,* "The Problem of Double-Time" in *The Merchant of Venice,* "The True Problem" of that play's construction. He tells us that "*Othello* is dominated by the problem" of why Othello falls victim to Iago, and he analyzes how Shakespeare solved the "problem" of keeping Cleopatra prominent during the almost two-fifths of the play when the plot has no need of her. The great dramatist creates and solves harder problems than other dramatists. In 1896 an academic borrowed "a convenient phrase from the theatre of to-day" and classified *All's Well that Ends Well, Measure for Measure, Troilus and Cressida,* and *Hamlet* as "Shakspere's problem-plays."[29] The new category proved as popular among critics as had Dowden's description of the late plays as "romances." *Hamlet* had always been popular, but the other "problem-plays" had, until now, attracted little attention and less enthusiasm. But Shaw puffed them as tirelessly as he puffed Ibsen, and for the same reasons. In *All's Well,* for instance, Shaw saw

Shakespeare conducting an "experiment, repeated nearly three hundred years later in *A Doll's House*."[30] In 1907, for the first time since Shakespeare's lifetime, *Troilus and Cressida* was revived on an English stage, and in 1923 it was given its first professional production in London for over three hundred years. Shakespeare had become a collection of problems, a creator of problems, a something to be solved. And who would solve it? The critic, of course, the scholar, the literary professional.

By redefining Shakespeare as a complex of problems, critics and scholars redefined themselves as problem solvers. Like science, criticism was a set of techniques for eliciting solutions from the controlled examination of artificial objects. Expectant authors, at the same time, saw themselves as problem setters. Their works aspired to furnish material for questions in the university examinations of the future. James Joyce anticipated that *Finnegans Wake* would keep scholars busy for hundreds of years; readers setting out across *The Waste Land* were escorted by a party of poker-faced endnotes and some suggestions for further reading. Such texts demand and reward professional readers.

And so good-bye to all those amateur enthusiasts who had enjoyed Tennyson and Dickens, good-bye to all that mass literacy which the Victorians had so industriously cultivated. Real Literature, important literature, belonged to, and could only be preserved by, a cultural elite. Poetry is "a superior amusement."[31] Bloomsbury, walled within its own high brows, fully booked its social calendar; Eliot pronounced himself an Anglo-Catholic royalist; Pound promoted fascists; W. H. Auden, Louis MacNeice, Stephen Spender, and C. Day Lewis wrote their poems for each other and their Oxford chums.

Such attitudes permeated the best modernist criticism as surely as they did the best modernist literature. At Cambridge the young I. A. Richards, one of the first academics to hail *The Waste Land* as a masterpiece, wrote a textbook on *Practical Criticism*, an instruction manual on how to create an adequate reader, a reader fit for literature, who could join with other adequate readers to form a cultural vanguard, trained to resist "the more sinister potentialities of the cinema and the loudspeaker," the radio, the best seller, the advertisement.[32] Richards' readers were taught to despise "*Stock Responses*."[33] Down with stereotypes! Up with archetypes! Stereotypes were mass-produced, generating crude Pavlovian responses in an undifferentiated mass of readers, jerking the strings of emotion. Archetypes were the heraldic emblems of a cultural aristocracy, passed down through the generations, permanent, to be savored by a subtle circle of readers who could appreciate their resonance, their intellectual bouquet. At Cambridge the young Q. D. and F. R. Leavis—champions of Lawrence, Eliot, and Pound—rallied "an armed and conscious minority"[34] of literary critics to resist the "herd" mentality of mass culture. "The teaching profession is peculiarly in a position to do revolutionary things"[35] and must help to create "a kind of freemasonry and syndicalism of the intellect"[36]—a Bolshevik party of Bohemians—able to withstand the bland dishings of pop pap. At Cambridge the young William Empson, writing poems of imploded paradox, also wrote *Seven Types of Ambiguity*. His influential taxonomy of literary doubletalk found multiples of meaning packed into what had seemed simple sonnets. Only a professional reader could unravel the intestinal contortions of Empson's own poems or those he praised.

Dryden, many years before, had objected to the difficulty and obscurity of much of Shakespeare's poetry. But that difficulty, once a source of critical embarrassment, now became a literary virtue. As early as 1892 a paper delivered at a conference of the Modern Language Association of America had observed that American professors "can now make English as hard as Greek."[37] By making the study of English literature difficult, they made it respectable; English displaced Greek and Latin in the educational curriculum by demonstrating that it, too, could furnish the raw materials for complex pedagogical exercises. But those exercises were initially philological. Elizabethan English was treated as a dead foreign language, like Latin, which the student must learn to parse. For nineteenth-century teachers and their students Shakespeare's works were not born difficult; they had become difficult, as the passage of time defamiliarized their grammar and vocabulary. For Richards and Leavis and Empson and their kind, Shakespeare's writing, like all the best modern writing, was intrinsically difficult; it had always been difficult; in difficulty lay its claim to our intellectual attention. Shakespeare furnished Empson more knots of ambiguity than any other writer.

But the decades that rediscovered Shakespeare's difficulty also rediscovered his adherence to the simplistic conventions of a primitive theatre. Stoll and Empson both published books in 1930. How to reconcile these incompatibles? Divide Shakespeare's audience in two. In 1907 Robert Bridges (former Etonian, future poet laureate) had argued that Shakespeare "deliberately played false to his own artistic ideals for the sake of gratifying his audience"—an audience enamored of "mere foolish verbal trifling," "bad jokes and obscenities," "extravagant grossness," "disgusting details," and "an extra-brutality of conduct." Consciously "taking advantage of their stupidity," Shakespeare created his most striking dramatic effects by exploiting logical "inconsistencies and impossible situations" that his customers would be too dumb to notice or too lax to condemn.[38] Bridges divided Shakespeare from his audience; the contemptuous sophisticate looked down upon a herd of primitives. Surely, though, Shakespeare was not alone on his side of the division. "Most of the audience," Q. D. Leavis explained, "could not possibly understand" *Hamlet*.[39] But if "most" did not, then implicitly "a few" did. *Hamlet* must have been aimed at the more cultured members of Shakespeare's audience. And so Shakespeare's plays could be interpreted on two levels of intellectual sophistication corresponding to the social division between educated upper classes and uneducated masses.

How could a play satisfy two such different sensibilities at once? Ambiguity. In 1919 Gerald Gould, promulgating "A New Reading of *Henry V*," announced that *"The play is ironic."* Shakespeare's portrayal of Henry V's victories in France was not intended to glorify war, as actors, audiences, and readers had hitherto naively assumed. The hideous "Prussianisms" of the title character were part of Shakespeare's satire "on imperialism, on the baser kinds of 'patriotism', and on war." Seen from one perspective the play derides what, from another perspective, it seems to praise. "No doubt the irony of *Henry V.* was meant to 'take in' the groundlings," but Shakespeare expected the more perceptive members of his audience to detect the sarcasm.[40]

The reasoning that Gould here applied to Shakespeare had already been applied by the controversial classical scholar A. W. Verrall, not long before, to Euripides. (And Verrall came down from Cambridge, saying, behold, Euripides did mock the superstitions of a foolish people, and yet so cleverly did he mock them, that they understood it not, for he spake only to the wise among them, filling his works with contradiction and with parody, that the wise might smile, seeing his irony, but the multitude, in their ignorance, did not.) The life of Euripides—professed intellectual, outspoken opponent of convention, author of unpopular plays—at least condones Verrall's interpretation; the life of Shakespeare—poorly educated, outwardly conventional, always popular—does not provide such promising material. Nevertheless, Gould initiates an era of "new readings" not only of *Henry V* but of every other work in the Shakespeare canon. Such readings always presume or create a disjunction between the apparent meaning of the text, perceived by the mass of readers and spectators, and the real meaning, perceptible only to a smirking connoisseur. Irony embraces snobbery.

Shakespeare, accordingly, moved in the best society. "Great Art is NEVER popular to start with," Ezra Pound declared; "and the Elizabethan drama . . . was a court affair."[41] D. H. Lawrence was sure that "if *Hamlet* and *Œdipus* were published now, they wouldn't sell more than 100 copies."[42] Defiantly defensive about their own unpopularity, modernists made rejection a badge of greatness and awarded it posthumously to Shakespeare. Virginia Woolf, describing a Bloomsbury day ("the gramophone playing Mozart"), exclaims "How Shakespeare would have loved us!"[43] She imagines Lytton Strachey "Reading Shakespeare . . . and occasionally making a note very neatly in a very beautiful book";[44] at Vanessa Bell's party "we were all awfully nice: I kept thinking of Shakespeare. We were so mellowly and good fellowly";[45] "tea—Shakespeare, Joyce—and so on" in concert produce "a very exciting life."[46] Shakespeare also makes several guest appearances in the diary of Mary, Lady Monkswell:

> I had the great interest & pleasure of going with Mr. Justice Wills & Lucy Wills to see *"Twelfth Night"* acted in the splendid old Hall of the Middle Temple. I had marked down the notice of it some weeks before, but as seats for it were things money could not buy I had given up hope of going. Then to my great joy Mr. Justice Wills wrote last Sunday to ask me to go with them. The Shakespeare Society, all amateurs, who acted it try to give it exactly as it was given the first time it was acted (in the same Hall), before Queen Elizabeth in 1601. The same music, the same Elizabethan costumes; 3 ladies instead of 3 boys for Olivia, Viola & Maria, & the Prince of Wales instead of Queen Elizabeth. The Hall was crammed, it was quite a brilliant scene. In the front row sat the Prince of Wales & Princess Louise & the Duke of Teck, Lord Esher (Master of the Rolls), the Lord Chancellor, the Lord Chief

Justice—Lord Russell,—the new Bishop of London, who has written a great deal on the Elizabethan period, & [his wife] Mrs. Creighton whom I beheld for the first time, a square-looking woman with an unpleasant suggestion of German-governess about her. I saw a multitude of Judges, Chitty, Macnaughten, Sir Richard Webster, Davy, little Mr. Justice Wright, little Dean Bradley of Westminster, F.M. Sir Evelyn Wood—all with their orders & ribands on—a most gay scene. The acting was delicious, they all spoke such good English.[47]

We have, as it happens, no evidence that Queen Elizabeth attended the first (or any other) performance of *Twelfth Night;* the play was indeed acted at the Middle Temple in 1602 (1601 by the old calendar); but that performance was probably not the first, and its audience was certainly bestudded with fewer celebrities than Lady Monkswell saw.

Virginia Woolf would no doubt have regarded Lady Monkswell as a moron; Q. D. Leavis and Robert Bridges would have been as contemptuous of one another as they both were of the bulk of Shakespeare's audience. Two different cultural elites were colliding. Monkswell represented a relatively closed old elite defined by social status and based largely on inherited wealth; the Leavises represented a more open-ended elitism, a new cultural meritocracy accessible to anyone with intelligence who could secure the right kind of education. Each elite excluded, by definition, most members of the other. But the hostility between them should not obscure the fact that in the early twentieth century both groups cooperated in reshaping Shakespeare. For their different reasons, they both insisted that Shakespeare the old popular playwright did not belong to the populace.

Scholars soon began to produce interpretations of Shakespeare that corresponded to the theories of Ezra Pound and the experiences of Lady Monkswell. In 1916 E. K. Chambers himself, skepticism in tweed, conjectured that *A Midsummer Night's Dream* had perhaps been written to celebrate the aristocratic wedding of Elizabeth Carey and Thomas Berkeley.[48] In 1929 Peter Alexander conjectured that *Troilus and Cressida* had been specifically written for the educated elite that attended dramatic performances at the Elizabethan Inns of Court.[49] In 1930 John Dover Wilson conjectured that *Twelfth Night* was "written for a polite audience" and designed for a special presentation on the Feast of the Epiphany.[50]

In 1931 Leslie Hotson conjectured that *The Merry Wives of Windsor* had been specifically written for the Garter ceremonies held by the court at Whitehall Palace in 1597.[51] In 1934 Frances Yates conjectured from *A Study of Love's Labour's Lost* that it had been specifically written to support one court faction (the Earl of Essex's) against another (Sir Walter Ralegh's). In 1950 J. W. Draper conjectured that the first night of *Twelfth Night* had been a court performance in 1601, for which the play had been specifically written.[52] The absence of historical evidence for these conjectures did not discourage their proliferation in respectable circles. These imaginative revisions of theatrical history, which soon influenced conclusions about chronology and textual transmission, all provided Shakespeare with a cultured minority audience of the kind in which Lady Monkswell sat, a Bloomsbury audience. The Blackfriars theatre took on a new importance for the same reason. After 1608 Shakespeare's company performed plays in both the large outdoor Globe theatre and the smaller indoor Blackfriars. Far fewer spectators could fit into the Blackfriars, and they had to pay more for the privilege; in 1948 G. E. Bentley conjectured that Shakespeare's final plays were specifically written to satisfy this more discriminating minority audience.[53]

The growing conviction that Shakespeare addressed his best work to a cultural elite also found expression in less orthodox venues. In 1920 J. Thomas Looney identified Shakespeare, in *"Shakespeare" Identified*, as Edward de Vere, seventeenth earl of Oxford. Oxford rapidly replaced Bacon as the favored candidate of those who doubted Shakespeare's title to the works published in his name. The aristocratic credentials of Oxford, son-in-law of Lord Burghley, surpassed those of Bacon; Oxford, unlike Bacon, traveled extensively in Europe and wrote plays admired by his contemporaries. Looney did not convince literary scholars. But the amateur's identification of Shakespeare with Oxford satisfied many of the same yearnings as the professionals' identification of so many plays with coterie occasions. Both conjectures assigned the plays to a humanist intellectual writing for an educated and powerful cultural elite.

The search for an elite audience worthy of Shakespeare's complexity naturally enlisted the poems too. Since Rowe everyone had known that *Venus and Adonis* and *Lucrece* were dedicated to an aristocrat; since Malone biographers had argued over the identity of the young man to whom Shakespeare addressed so many of his sonnets. Such episodes had been seen as biographical curiosities, detours on the high road to the theatre; now they expressed, more explicitly than the plays, the true intellectual loyalties of a man attentive to the arbiters of culture in his time. In 1922 Charlotte Stopes published an expansive *Life of Henry, Third Earl of Southampton, Shakespeare's Patron*, sensing the presence of Southampton in much of Shakespeare's work, lyric and dramatic. At the same time the poems were being upgraded in critical esteem. Throughout the nineteenth century the sonnets had been admired as romantic lyrics and studied as biographical documents; in the twentieth century they rose toward the summit of Shakespeare's artistic achievement. I. A. Richards defended *The Waste Land* by reference "to Shakespeare's greatest sonnets or to *Hamlet*," taking it for granted that the short sonnets belong alongside the longest and most famous of the plays.[54] "Bare ruined choirs, where late the sweet birds sang" in Sonnet 73 was the first exemplary line of poetry quoted and analyzed in *Seven Types of Ambiguity*. In 1934—the year after he had asked his sarcastic question about Lady Macbeth's children—L. C. Knights wrote an equally influential essay on the poetic techniques and themes of "Shakespeare's Sonnets."[55] "The Phoenix and Turtle," that most cryptically difficult of all Shakespeare's poems, had been published in a volume celebrating an aristocratic couple; by 1922 its "obscure, mystical, and strictly unintelligible" verses were being praised, for the first time, as "the most perfect short poem in any language."[56]

The man who wrote poems for such elite readers, plays for such elite audiences, must have been educated. Ye shall know the tree by its fruit, and complexity does not grow on louts. Since the middle of the eighteenth century it had been generally assumed that Shakespeare possessed little if any firsthand knowledge of classical literature. But in 1944 an American professor, T. W. Baldwin, devoted 1,525 pages to *William Shakspere's Small Latine & Lesse Greeke*, demonstrating from the evidence of quotations, echoes, and allusions in the plays and poems that he must have been given a secondary education of the kind provided by English grammar schools—like the one at Stratford—in the late sixteenth century. And since Elizabethan universities placed little emphasis on literature, "If William Shakspere had the grammar school training of his day—or its equivalent—he had as good a formal literary training as had any of his contemporaries."[57]

Baldwin, single-handed, with one Titanic effort, identified what Shakespeare would have read if he had attended grammar school; an army of academics, less conspicuously, more slowly, identified what Shakespeare would have needed to read when he came to write individual plays. A meticulous and sustained scrutiny of details revealed that in writing each of his Roman and English history plays Shakespeare had drawn upon several historical and literary sources. If this was true of some plays, where historical details could be isolated and traced to separate accounts, it might well be true of others, entirely fictional. The routines of academic scholarship accommodated and rewarded the search for sources; decades of collective trawling found dozens of new antecedents and influences beneath the surface of Shakespeare's texts. This steady expansion of Shakespeare's library in turn altered the perception of received facts. For instance, when writing *Othello* he could have read Giraldi Cinthio's *Hecatommithi* in the original Italian; scholars no longer needed to suppose that Cinthio's influence was filtered through a lost translation or a lost play on the same subject. Once scholars stopped inventing lost entities to explain extant facts, it seemed apparent that Shakespeare had read French, Italian, much Latin, some Greek—not to mention prodigious quantities of English.

By midcentury Shakespeare looked as polyglot as Joyce and Eliot and Pound, his poetry, like theirs, the product of a cosmopolitan intellect. He read foreign languages and acquired foreign friends. In 1910 Charles and Hulda Wallace, an American academic couple living in London, proved that in the early seventeenth century Shakespeare had boarded for some time with a French Huguenot family living in London. Through their shared patron Southampton, Shakespeare could easily have met the Italian tutor John Florio; he seems to have read Florio's translation of Montaigne two to three years before it was published. John Dover Wilson even speculated that Southampton and Shakespeare might have toured Italy together.[58]

How does Wilson's speculation about Shakespeare in Italy differ from Joyce's speculation about Shakespeare seduced by Anne Hathaway in a rye field outside Stratford? Little enough. Both want to imagine a credible character; neither entirely believes his own imagination. Wilson subtitles his book *A Biographical Adventure*. A ride on the roller coaster: uneven fun, but it deposits you back where you started.

In the early twentieth century if you wanted to obtain a human likeness you could take a photograph, and prose realism aspired to a comparable social accuracy in the theatre, and the no-nonsense criticism of Schücking and Stoll and Archer and Shaw measured Shakespeare's characters against a photographic norm, and the "exact" scholarship of Chambers defined Shakespeare by a scrupulous transcription and examination of authenticated documents. *A Study of Facts and Problems* includes thirty illustrations, most of them photographs, mostly of documents. Shakespeare himself was dead; ghosts could not be photographed. Shakespeare now existed only as a collection of texts: biographical records (of the kind examined by Chambers), source books (of the kind examined by Baldwin), dramatic documents (of the kind examined by W. W. Greg). Texts he appeared in, texts he read, texts he wrote. And if Shakespeare was a collection of texts, then Shakespeare properly belonged to editors, bibliographers, paleographers, the scientists of text. Chambers himself devoted half of *Facts and Problems* to editorial questions. His friend Greg, the greatest textual critic of the twentieth century, made editing the most innovative and confident department of the literary civil service.

Both the epistemology of science and the technology of mechanical reproduction encouraged an emphasis upon precise, impersonal, verifiable observation. Texts, being material objects, could be observed and described as scrupulously as scientists observed and described other material objects. Before you could have a plausible hypothesis, you had to have reliable readings, and editors controlled the instrumentation that recorded readings. "Accuracy is always desirable," Greg affirmed, "even when one is working on Shakespeare."[59] By "working on Shakespeare" Greg meant "working on matters of inconsequential detail"; a rhetorical substitution made the accurate transcription of minutiae seem as important as Shakespeare himself, while implying that "Shakespeare" was nothing more than a compendium of incidentals. Before there could be anything else—any biography, any criticism, any history—there must be simple accuracy in reproducing texts. But simple accuracy could not be easily achieved. More than once Greg lamented the innate fallibility of "the imperfect human machine."[60] Where possible, human instruments should be supplemented or replaced by mechanical ones. In 1931, the year after Chambers' *Facts and Problems,* Greg published two epoch-making volumes of *Dramatic Documents from the Elizabethan Playhouses;* the second volume, measuring

fifteen by twenty inches, consisted entirely of photographs juxtaposed with transcriptions. The next year Greg completed an
equally important collection and description of *English Literary
Autographs 1500–1650,* again interleaving photographs and transcriptions. His summary achievement as an investigator of dramatic
texts, *The Shakespeare First Folio: Its Bibliographical and Textual History,*
was originally intended to introduce a new photographic reproduction of the 1623 collected edition. That facsimile never mate-
rialized, but Greg did supervise a new, more reliable series of quarto
facsimiles.

Like the search for sources, the insistence upon accuracy lent
itself to the new academic culture; creativity could not be routinely
measured, but correctness could. Chambers demolished the reputation of Fleay and other Victorian scholars by showing that their
observations on metrical practice could not be duplicated, that their
criteria were not systematically applied, that their figures varied
from one publication to the next, that their columns did not add up.
Amateur scholars could not be trusted, because they were careless.
"Arm-chair editors" could not be trusted, because they neglected
their fieldwork, relying on other people's transcriptions, other people's proofreading, other people's eyes.[61]

Amateur readers could not be trusted either, because they relied
upon unreliable modern editions. For three centuries each new
edition of Shakespeare had updated the spelling and punctuation
of his texts, to make them more intelligible for contemporary readers. But a responsible editor should reproduce the text
accurately; he should not modify it for the convenience of a mass
readership. Consequently, Greg insists that "modern opinion is
unanimously in favour of preserving the spelling and punctuation
of the original authority." The resulting "critical" edition, the
proper object of a scholar's labor, will be used by "critics"; it should
not be confused with a mere "popular or reading edition." Greg
admits that the second category exists, but it does not interest him;
indeed, it positively disgusts him. "To print *banquet* for *banket, fathom*
for *fadom, lantern* for *lanthorn, murder* for *murther, mushroom* for *mush-
rump, orphan* for *orphant, perfect* for *parfit, portcullis* for *perculace,
tattered* for *tottered, vile* for *vild, wreck* for *wrack,* and so on, and so on,
is sheer perversion."[62] It does not matter that such "perversion"
removes thousands of obstacles to ordinary understanding; it does
not matter that old-spelling editions, however accurate, render

Shakespeare inaccessible to *"the great Variety of Readers"* who had been addressed in the preface to the 1623 collected edition of his plays. Greg's scholarship, financed by a private family income, addressed only "the most able" of readers. The great Victorian editor W. A. Wright—still a fellow of Trinity College, Cambridge, when Greg was a student there, and instrumental in Greg's appointment as Trinity College librarian—had lent his energies to the populist Globe Shakespeare and to the Clarendon series of Shakespeare editions for use in schools. Greg, though he devoted his long productive life to editing, never produced a popular edition; indeed, he never produced any edition of Shakespeare at all. He wrote specialist monographs; he edited many old-spelling editions of works by minor writers, most of them unemended transcripts, most of them for limited circulation by the Malone Society. His only sustained contribution to literary criticism, an early and influential book on *Pastoral Poetry and Pastoral Drama* (1906), celebrates the period's nostalgic yearning for a preindustrial, preurban community. Nor were his politics only the politics of literary criticism. Greg later proudly recorded that in 1926 he had scabbed for Scotland Yard, doing his bit—alongside many Oxford and Cambridge undergraduates—to help break the General Strike.[63]

The insistence that William Shakespeare should be pictured in old spelling, that he should not be anachronistically re-dressed in contemporary orthography, not only closed the doors to popular comprehension, ordinary appreciation, and mass meaning; it also increased the need for accuracy. It was no longer enough to get the words right; the scholar now needed to reproduce exactly every letter, every point of punctuation, every eccentricity of typography, in an archaic linguistic system unfamiliar to modern copy editors, compositors, and proofreaders, all the fallible intermediaries between the scholar and his readers. Greg and Chambers not only fought for Accuracy; they expanded the territory Accuracy claimed.

This change in standards reflected and reinforced the change of readership. Major works of scholarship were aimed at a more circumscribed audience. (Fewer readers; more critics.) The growth of graduate schools, the redefinition of universities as research institutions, the new legitimacy of English studies, greatly expanded the total scholarly base. In the early twentieth century the number of people employed to study, teach, and write about Shakespeare increased exponentially. More and more names clamor for scholarly attention, like the crowd of ghosts Dante had seen milling on the threshold of hell or the crowd of commuters Eliot saw flowing over London Bridge: "so many, / I had not thought text had undone so many."[64] A representative history of Shakespearian criticism devotes 163 pages to the seventeenth, eighteenth, and nineteenth centuries combined and 230 to the first sixty years of the twentieth.[65] This community of specialists exercised most of its energies in checking and contesting each other's work, a process most economically conducted in scholarly reviews. The publication of academic periodicals boomed. Greg helped found the *Modern Language Review;* Greg's fellow bibliographer A. W. Pollard founded *The Library;* Greg's lifelong friend and fellow editor R. B. McKerrow founded the *Review of English Studies;* Eliot founded *The Criterion;* the Leavises founded *Scrutiny.* Greg himself was a fierce, destructively demanding reviewer, especially at the beginning of his career, while establishing the authority of his new discipline. The reputation of academics, and accordingly their professional standing, depended upon how well they stood up to this process of rapid, routine, rigorous peer review. Academics expected their books to be read and judged primarily by other academics.

Other academics demanded accurate transcription of documents; they also demanded accurate documentation. Conclusions could be tested quickly, results could be duplicated easily, only if readers were informed of the precise whereabouts of a scholar's sources. Moreover, a scholar's individual contribution to the collective thought-hoard could be instantly evaluated only if the scholar discriminated precisely between new ideas and old ones, between primary original thoughts and secondary thoughts borrowed from others. This process of discrimination necessarily involves scholars in a routine of hyperbolic self-differentiation; you define your own originality by contesting and modifying the theories of others. At the same time, the texts you contest, the hypotheses you reject, the influences you acknowledge, must all be materially embedded in your own text; you define yourself by citation, by references to other texts. Hence, as in Joyce's *Ulysses,* Shakespearian scholarship became a dialogue of texts talking to one another in the National Library, calling each other by name, engrossed in a private conversation. And Shakespeare himself became such a text, echoing and modifying other texts. As scholars systematically identified their own sources, acknowledging their own intellectual debts, so they systematically identified Shakespeare's sources, the intellectual influences that shaped his "contribution," the theatrical precedents that preformed his dramatic structures. And the need for proper citations affects scholarly attitudes toward biographical evidence. Chambers distinguishes, in descending order of reliability, between "Records," "Contemporary Allusions," and "The Shakespeare-Mythos." Put your faith in the documents, Chambers advises; do not trust posthumous accounts that fail to cite their sources.

Photography produces a certain sort of human likeness more accurately than any earlier technology of visual representation, and Chambers produces a certain sort of human likeness more accurately than any earlier Shakespearian scholar. But by the early twentieth century most artists—certainly the most interesting artists—had decisively rejected the kind of likeness photography could supply. Postimpressionism, expressionism, cubism, futurism, constructivism—every available artistic ism abandoned the attempt to compete with mechanical devices in accurately reproducing the recognizable visual surfaces perceived by human optical equipment. Instead, they focused upon essence. Photography could reproduce only surfaces; art could re-create a superior reality beneath or beyond or within or behind the visible. The artist could see what the camera could not. Wilhelm Roentgen discovered X rays in 1895; in 1896 Antoine Becquerel discovered radioactivity; Ernest Rutherford discovered alpha and beta rays in 1898; in 1900 Paul Villard discovered gamma rays; by 1903 radiation, a whole domain of energies beyond the visible spectrum, had already begun to mesmerize the international imagination, featuring in newspaper articles, public lectures, and popular books. In 1900 Sigmund Freud published *The Interpretation of Dreams,* soon to be followed by *The Psychopathology of Everyday Life* (1904) and *Jokes and Their Relation to the Unconscious* (1905); the first book on psychoanalysis in English appeared in 1912, and the next year the London Psycho-Analytical Society was founded by Freud's disciple Ernest Jones. In the years between Roentgen's discovery of X rays and Freud's dissection of the unconscious, Konstantin Stanislavsky, producing plays by Chekhov and Tolstoy and Gogol and Shakespeare at the Moscow Art Theatre, developed a system of acting that emphasized an exploration of the "subtext" of a role, demanding a disciplined tapping of the subconscious. The energies that structured the physical world, the human mind, the actor's performance—all lay below the visible surface, beyond the camera's range, inside the outside. The text of reality, the surface of language, was simply a frail material manifestation of invisible energies in motion.

Dover Wilson set out on what his subtitle calls *A Biographical Adventure* in order to find what his title calls *The Essential Shakespeare*. Where Chambers seeks facts, Wilson wants essence. "Here, in a nutshell, is the kind of man I believe Shakespeare to have been."[66] Like Virginia Woolf contemplating the mysterious Mrs. Brown, Wilson aches to know how Mr. Shakespeare's thoughts felt, how the world tasted in his mouth, why he was what he was, the "thousands of ideas" and "thousands of emotions" that coursed through his brain, "met, collided, and disappeared in astonishing disorder" every day.[67] Photographable documents, the brittle shell of material verity, will not satisfy such hungers. Wilson wants to ride the stream of Shakespeare's consciousness, to smell that burning essence. But he does not know how.

Caroline Spurgeon knew how. In a monograph on *Leading Motives in the Imagery of Shakespeare's Tragedies* (1930), in a British Academy lecture on "Shakespeare's Iterative Imagery" (1931), in an acclaimed book on *Shakespeare's Imagery and What It Tells Us* (1935), she showed how. Her method was less vulnerable than Wilson's. Wilson, trying to illustrate the essence of Shakespeare's mind, narrated instead the history of his body, an account dependent on events, relationships, chronologies, the thicknesses of a material world. But in order to substantiate such a narrative, Wilson needed more documents. He did not have them; so he conjectured. No one believed his conjectures. Spurgeon instead constructed an image of Shakespeare's essence out of Shakespeare's own images. The material world did not matter. Spurgeon could dismiss "the dry records of legal documents and law-suits."[68] The only documents she needed were Shakespeare's own texts. T. E. Hulme, articulating the aesthetics of modernism, had found in poetic imagery "the very essence of an intuitive language";[69] Spurgeon found in Shakespeare's imagery the very essence of Shakespeare:

> it is chiefly through his images that [a poet], to some extent unconsciously, 'gives himself away'. He may be, and in Shakespeare's case is, almost entirely objective in his dramatic characters and their views and opinions, yet, like the man who under

stress of emotion will show no sign of it in eye or face, but will
reveal it in some muscular tension, the poet unwittingly lays bare
his own innermost likes and dislikes, observations and interests,
associations of thought, attitudes of mind and beliefs, in and
through the images . . .[70]

Accordingly, in Spurgeon's book "*all* his images are assembled,
sorted, and examined on a systematic basis," then compared with
images in works by Bacon, Marlowe, Jonson, Chapman, Dekker, and
Massinger. From these images Spurgeon concludes that Shakespeare "was healthy in body as in mind, clean and fastidious in his
habits, very sensitive to dirt and evil smells," "a countryman
through and through," who "does not like noise," "a competent
rider" who "loved horses, as indeed he did most animals, except
spaniels and house dogs," "an expert archer," generally "deft and
nimble with his hands." As for the inner man, "five words sum up
the essence of his quality and character as seen in his images—
sensitiveness, balance, courage, humour and wholesomeness."[71]

"Miss Spurgeon was a Lady," a later critic remarked, rejecting the
exaggerated gentility of this portrait of Shakespeare; "naturally,
certain areas of experience were closed to her."[72] But at least Shakespearian scholarship was not closed to her. Spurgeon led a generation of her gender into positions of some power within the academic
world. Already Professor of English Literature at University College, London, after World War I she was appointed to the select
Newbolt committee on the teaching of English, which greatly
expanded the importance of literature in the postwar curriculum.
The only victors in World War I were women. When the army
sucked hundreds of thousands of British men into the mud of
France, women took their places in shops and factories, opening up
professions previously closed to them; 750,000 of those men never
came back, another two and a half million returned wounded or
disabled, prolonging for a generation the shortage of men and the
corresponding surplus of unmarried women. In 1918 the franchise
was extended to women over thirty; after 1928 electoral law made
no distinction between the sexes. In 1929 I. A. Richards reported
that his women students were, in general, better read and more
discerning than their male colleagues.[73]

During the postwar years women became an increasingly visible
contingent of Shakespeare scholarship. Madeleine Doran chal-

lenged orthodox opinion on the texts of *Henry VI* (1928) and *King Lear* (1931) before turning her attention to Shakespeare's imagery.[74] In 1932 Muriel St. Clare Byrne published a celebrated critique of the kinds of evidence used in determining the authorship of disputed or collaborative plays.[75] Una Ellis-Fermor's influential interpretation of *The Jacobean Drama* appeared in 1936; by the late 1940s she had become Hildred Carlile Professor of English at Bedford College and the first general editor of the new Arden Shakespeare series. Muriel Bradbrook's prizewinning Cambridge essay on *Elizabethan Stage Conventions,* published in 1932, launched a Shakespearian career more than half a century long. Another Cambridge graduate, Alice Walker, during the 1930s acted as R. B. McKerrow's junior collaborator on a projected old-spelling edition of Shakespeare's complete works; after McKerrow's death she succeeded him, establishing herself as one of the most influential textual critics of midcentury and the first woman to make any appreciable contribution to the history of Shakespeare editing.

All of these women helped shape the image of Shakespeare prevalent in the middle of the twentieth century. In contrast to their Victorian predecessors, none of them called attention to her own gender. A recent bibliography of "Women and Men in Shakespeare" does not mention Spurgeon, Byrne, Ellis-Fermor, Bradbrook, or Walker at all.[76] Their contemporary Virginia Woolf had asked, in the name of women, for *A Room of One's Own,* a place of their own in which women could create a literature of their own, the kind that might have been written by a woman who "had Shakespeare's genius" and was given the chance to use it. "Shakespeare's sister," as Woolf calls this fictive woman, would not have characterized Cleopatra and Octavia so conventionally; Shakespeare's sister would have recognized that women "have other interests" besides love and domesticity.[77] Spurgeon quoted a passage from Woolf as an epigraph to *Shakespeare's Imagery,* but she did not apply Woolf's feminist program to criticism. The first wave of women Shakespearians did not claim to interpret the world or Shakespeare's work from a woman's point of view; they claimed implicitly that gender made no difference to their perspective. Behind their unisex initials "C. F. E." Spurgeon, "M. C." Bradbrook, and "U. M." Ellis-Fermor could not be distinguished from "L. C." Knights, "I. A." Richards, and "E. E." Stoll.

But the fact remained, "Miss Spurgeon was a Lady." Unlike

Tiresias in *The Waste Land*, she had never crossed the border between male and female. The word "sex" does not even appear in the expansive analytical index to *Shakespeare's Imagery*, and though Spurgeon must have seen the intertwined, multiplying images of fornication in Shakespeare's work she did not stop to count, distinguish, or discuss them.

Men could be less inhibited (though some of them paid dearly for their frankness). Like other characters in *Ulysses*, Joyce's Shakespeare had visible genitals and used them. Living in "an age of exhausted whoredom," seduced in a rye field where Anne Hathaway bent over him "as prologue to the swelling act," fathering his children in "An instant of blind rut," Shakespeare was for Joyce both "bawd and cuckold," in the sonnets performing "the holy office an ostler does for the stallion," in *Hamlet* and most of the other plays obsessively enacting his wife's adulteries. Sex haunted Shakespeare's art, but Shakespeare himself could never "play victoriously the game of laugh and lie down."[78] Lawrence, likewise, saw in Shakespeare and his contemporaries "a horror of sexual life," particularly visible in Hamlet's "horrible revulsion from his physical connexion with his mother," which in turn produced a "similar revulsion from Ophelia"; Lawrence attributed "*some* of Shakespeare's horror and despair, in his tragedies" to "the shock of his consciousness of syphilis," whether or not he ever personally contracted the disease.[79] According to Eliot, Hamlet was "dominated by an emotion" connected to his mother's sexual guilt but nevertheless "in *excess* of the facts as they appear"; and Hamlet's creator, "under compulsion of" some unknown but traumatic "experience," felt the same inexpressible horror, a proper subject of study for "pathologists."[80] The pathologist Ernest Jones, elaborating on a hint from Freud, had already subjected the "problem of Hamlet" to psychoanalytic study. In an essay first published in 1910, gradually expanded over the decades until in 1949 it achieved book-length embodiment in *Hamlet and Oedipus*, Jones read *Hamlet* as a classic account of the Oedipal complex—and Hamlet's "conflict is an echo of a similar one in Shakspere himself."[81] Claudius did what Hamlet unconsciously wanted to do: kill Hamlet's father and marry his mother. The scene in which Hamlet confronts his mother, hitherto neutrally known as "the closet scene," located in an unspecified private room—that scene became in Dover Wilson's 1935 account of *What Happens in "Hamlet"* explicitly "the bedroom scene," Hamlet in mama's boudoir trying to kill her husband. In 1927, in a Prague production, the scene had, apparently for the first time, featured a prominent bed and Gertrude nightgowned; by the 1940s the bed had become almost obligatory in revivals. Laurence Olivier's 1948 film consciously visualized Hamlet's Oedipal unconscious.

The resurrection of sex was not limited to *Hamlet*. In 1938 Olivier had enacted an equally Freudian Iago, whose hatred of Othello was energized by suppressed homoerotic desire. As early as 1909 sexual obsession had motivated Shakespeare's own *Tragic Life-story*, as told by Frank Harris: "the dark lady of the sonnets" haunted Shakespeare's consciousness, reappearing in almost all his plays and poems, disguised now as Rosalind, now as Cleopatra, imaginative "lust in action" transforming her into innumerable dream images. The fascinated sexual disgust of the "problem plays"—*Troilus and Cressida, Measure for Measure, All's Well That Ends Well*—ceased to be a problem and became in fact an asset. In 1921 *Pericles* was given its first unexpurgated revival since the seventeenth century, brothel scenes and all; like the problem plays it earned itself a small but secure place in the theatrical repertoire and a larger place in the critical canon. Eliot defended unexpurgated performances generally, claiming that "the sense of relief, in hearing the indecencies of Elizabethan and Restoration drama, leaves one a better and a stronger man";[82] Wyndham Lewis condemned the "congealed moralism" and "sex-obsession" that had in the previous century bowdlerized Shakespeare's texts.[83] "I admit," Virginia Woolf admitted, with a characteristic abbreviation, "that I adore—Sh[re] at his bawdiest."[84] Such attitudes led to an increasing recognition in editorial commentary of Shakespeare's ubiquitous double entendres. In 1947 Eric Partridge published the first dictionary of *Shakespeare's Bawdy*.

These changes in the interpretation of Shakespeare correspond to wider social changes in the interpretation of sex. In *The Descent of Man* (1871) Darwin had made "selection in relation to sex" central to the evolution of the human race; three decades later Freud made sex central to the development of the human mind. Henry Havelock Ellis produced six volumes of *Studies in the Psychology of Sex* between 1897 and 1910 and a seventh in 1928; in 1918 Dr. Marie Stopes wrote the first best seller about contraception, launching a public campaign for sex education. In the 1920s inhibitions fell as skirts rose.

But sex did not simply become more visible, more audible; it became a mechanism for generating secret meaning. The hidden motor that had powered human evolution, sex also caused neuroses, textual errors, psychoses, slips of the tongue, systems of ethics, jokes, the structure of the family. Freud himself was, above all, a literary critic. He constructed his entire system by interpreting verbal narratives: a play by Sophocles, a patient's account of a dream, the Book of Genesis, a joke in a magazine—all stories, all axiomatically cryptic, their real meaning teeming beneath the crust of an ostensible narrative. In Freud human beings became texts; and literature, like every other human utterance, became a symptom. And the symptom could be properly diagnosed only by a specialist. Like Verrall with Euripides and Gould with *Henry V*, Freud created two layers of meaning, one visible to the masses, another and more important discernible only by the specialist. Freud founded the clerisy of psychoanalysis at the very moment when universities were founding the clerisy of academic criticism. As the critic to the text, so the psychoanalyst to the patient: privileged interpreter. Not surprisingly, the champion of secret meaning became a champion of secret identity too: Freud endorsed Looney's belief that Shakespeare's plays were written by the Earl of Oxford.

According to Eliot, in order to interpret *Hamlet* "We should have to understand things" about Shakespeare "which Shakespeare did not understand himself."[85] Psychoanalysis, of course, performs such miracles routinely, and Spurgeon justified her own study of Shakespeare's imagery with images from psychoanalysis:

> the repeated evidence of clusters of certain associated ideas in the poet's mind . . . throws a curious light on what I suppose the psychoanalyst would call 'complexes'; that is, certain groups of things and ideas—apparently entirely unrelated—which are linked together in Shakespeare's subconscious mind, and some of which are undoubtedly the outcome of an experience, a sight or emotion which has profoundly affected him.[86]

Shakespeare, for instance, inevitably associated dogs or spaniels with images of fawning, licking, candy, sugar, sweets, thawing, melting; almost any one of these images will quickly summon up the others.

> Be not fond,
> To think that Caesar bears such rebel blood
> That will be *thaw'd* from the true quality
> With that which *melteth* fools, I mean, *sweet* words,
> *Low-crook'd court'sies* and *base spaniel-fawning,*
> Thy brother by decree is banished:
> If thou dost bend and pray and *fawn* for him,
> I spurn thee like a *cur* out of my way.[87]

It is not Caesar's imagination that ricochets from *thaw'd* to *cur;* it is Shakespeare's, because the same pattern imposes itself on Hamlet, Hotspur, Antony, Timon, and Cassius.

Spurgeon's brief account of such complexes was convincingly extended in 1946 by Edward A. Armstrong, whose study of *Shakespeare's Imagination* demonstrated the existence of several additional clusters: goose/disease/bitterness/seasoning/restraint, for instance, or kite/bed/death/spirits/birds/food. But Armstrong also supplied a much more sophisticated model of that "active and subtle organising principle" which operated "below the level of consciousness," allowing Shakespeare "to leave the ordering of the images to his subliminal mind" while he concentrated upon problems of plot and dramatic purpose.[88] Armstrong rejected Freud's particular patented blueprint of the psyche, but he did agree that the "processes involved in the imagination" worked "subliminally" and that those processes could be retraced through the wiring of associated imagery. By such means Shakespeare's unconscious spoke to ours, his images "awakening chains of not fully conscious associations which co-operate in the reader's mind to give emotional tone" so that "his subconscious thought" could arouse corresponding "harmonics in our minds," as "levels of consciousness lower than that of conscious attention respond to the undertones of the poet's song."[89]

Armstrong returns us, on the train of psychology, to the image house of music. Spurgeon, too, explicitly compares Shakespeare's "recurrent images" to the recurrent themes or motifs of Wagner's operas.[90] Like Shaw and Eliot and Knight, Armstrong and Spurgeon describe the power of Shakespeare's poetry by musical analogies, in images of tone, theme, harmony, song. "From the echo of one word is born another word, for which reason, perhaps, the play seems as we read it to tremble perpetually on the brink of music": Virginia Woolf writes more musically than either scholar, her prose trembles, but she says much the same thing. She believes, like them, that such lingual music plays in the echo chambers of the writer's subconscious: "Shakespeare is writing, it seems, not with the whole of his mind mobilized and under control but with feelers left flying that sport and play with words so that the trail of a chance word is caught and followed recklessly."[91] She believes, like them, that the writer's subconscious speaks to the reader's, if only writer and reader can just relax on the couch, momentarily still the conscious clamor, and let the subliminal music be heard. In an essay "On Being Ill," published in Eliot's *Criterion*, she praises illness, because it weakens our conscious control. "In health meaning has encroached upon sound. Our intelligence domineers our senses."[92] But in illness, "with the police off duty,"

> words seem to possess a mystic quality. We grasp what is beyond their surface meaning, gather instinctively this, that, and the other—a sound, a colour, here a stress, there a pause—which the poet, knowing words to be meagre in comparison with ideas, has strewn about his page to evoke, when collected, a state of mind which neither words can express nor the reason explain.

In this state of heightened weakness, the mind opens Rimbaud, and Rimbaud intimates Mallarmé, and Mallarmé melts into Donne, and Donne, at last, summons Shakespeare. "Rashness is one of the properties of illness"—and praised be illness for it—"and it is rashness that we need in reading Shakespeare." Illness "in its kingly sublimity" sweeps aside "all the views of all the critics"; illness silences that "buzz of criticism" which Joyce had sardonically dramatized; illness leaves us alone, "nothing but Shakespeare and oneself" in the room, patient and visitor. "It is not that we should dose in reading him, but that, fully conscious and aware, his fame intimidates and bores." Illness debilitates our inhibitions; "the barriers go down, the knots run smooth, the brain rings and resounds with *Lear* or *Macbeth*"—rings and resounds, like music.

And music, which leaps the barriers of consciousness, also crosses the borders between languages. "The Chinese," Woolf thinks in 1926, "must know the sound of *Antony and Cleopatra* better than we do" because for them the tongue retains its strangeness. Granville-Barker discovers in 1921 that "French actors can speak Shakespeare better than English actors" because they unaffectedly appreciate "the fine sound and poise" of "beautiful speech," its "swiftness, intensity, precision, variety, clarity, and above all, passion."[93] Eliot and Joyce in 1922 slip casually in and out of English, tantalizing readers of *The Waste Land* and *Ulysses* with that musical strangeness of a foreign language. *The Waste Land* and *Ulysses* quote Shakespeare too. Three hundred years after publication of the First Folio, Shakespeare's English had acquired some of the aural glamour of French and Chinese, Hindi, Latin, Greek, elusively foreign, almost, trembling at times on the brink of sheer sound. Eliot lilts,[94]

> O O O O that Shakespeherian Rag—
> It's so elegant
> So intelligent

and his words echo and transmute the chorus of a hit song of 1912:

> That Shakespearian rag,—
> Most intelligent, very elegant,
> That old classical drag,
> Has the proper stuff, the line "Lay on Macduff"[95]

Out of *Macbeth* the lyricists picked up "proper stuff" and "Lay on Macduff" (spoken by different characters, 1,020 lines apart)[96] and, juxtaposing the phrases, turned them into music, a music at once peculiar and familiar. Eliot, of course, like Joyce, like Knight, like Spurgeon and Armstrong, programmatically did the same thing.

But where O where has the author gone? He has disappeared again, fallen between the interstices of his own images. For Armstrong, Shakespeare's images do not reveal anything about the poet's own physical or temporal life; they display only the impersonal operations of a poet's imagination, which "achieved a high degree of autonomy" and can be used as a model of imaginative process in all minds. Shakespeare has simply become the medium by which one unconscious speaks to all others. For Eliot poetry occurs "when a bit of finely filiated platinum is introduced into a chamber containing oxygen and sulphur dioxide"; with the platinum present, the two gases combine to form "sulphurous acid":

> This combination takes place only if the platinum is present; nevertheless the newly formed acid contains no trace of platinum,

and the platinum itself is apparently unaffected; has remained inert, passive, and unchanged. The mind of the poet is the shred of platinum.[97]

Shakespeare, the passive catalyst, compounds images. How can you write the biography of a shred of platinum?

III

But if you say good-bye to character and biography, you must also say good-bye to actors—good-bye at least to actors who want to portray biographical character. "We do not know Shakespeare," Eliot complains; "we only know Sir J. Forbes-Robertson's Hamlet, and Irving's Shylock, and so on." As "strained through the nineteenth century," Shakespeare "has been dwarfed to the dimension of a part for this or that actor."[98] Shakespeare had to be saved from the actors.

He was saved by William Poel, Edwin Gordon Craig, and Harley Granville-Barker. Poel always used amateur actors. Craig subordinated actors to the set designer. Granville-Barker subordinated actors to the director.

Beginning in 1881 with a performance based upon the 1603 edition of *Hamlet,* William Poel devoted five decades to iconoclastic productions of Shakespeare's plays that were as sui generis as they were avant-garde. That performance of *Twelfth Night* which Lady Monkswell attended was organized by Poel, for instance, and although he did not normally draw such a society audience, in other respects the production was typical enough. The play was performed "exactly as it was given the first time it was acted," in Elizabethan costume, without sets, on a bare stage, furnished only with a table and chair. "The absence of the changing & shifting of the scene was very restful," Lady Monkswell thought; not needing to interrupt the performance with the long scene-changes typical of Victorian productions, the actors "went straight thro' . . . without a pause, even at the end of the acts."[99] The music, too, was authentic, being played on "an Italian virginal of about 1550, a treble and a bass viol, and a Venice-made lute of about the same period," using original settings where possible and—where the originals were lost—music specially composed by Arnold Dolmetsch in the Elizabethan manner.[100] For the first time since the Restoration, Shakespeare was being performed in conditions approaching, as closely as possible, those for which the plays were originally designed.

In part such work developed naturally out of the historicism of Victorian scholarship; Shakespeare's plays belong to a different epoch, and in order to understand them we must attend to the environment in which they flourished. Poel, like Macready or Irving or Booth, pedantically insisted upon historical accuracy. But Macready and Irving and Booth had tried to reconstruct the historical reality that the plays themselves envisaged; *Richard II* set in the material circumstances of fourteenth-century England, *Hamlet* in tenth-century Denmark. Instead, Poel—like Stoll and Schücking—denied that the plays reflected any historical reality. In order to understand Shakespeare you did not need to know anything about the real world or real people; you simply needed to understand the conventions of Elizabethan art.

Shaw claimed that Shakespeare's plays could not be defended as representations of human behavior; they could be appreciated only as musical scores for several voices. Poel operated on the same assumption. Like Shaw, he objected to the way Victorian performances cut and rearranged Shakespeare's texts; such alterations destroyed the "design" of the composition, just as they would destroy a Mozart symphony. In his own productions Poel's

> first step was to cast the play orchestrally. He decided which character represented the double-bass, the cello, the wood-wind, so to speak, and chose his actors by the timbre, pitch and flexibility of their voices ... Before starting rehearsals, he had worked out the melody, stress, rhythm and phrasing of every sentence ... at the end of, say, two weeks [the play] had become as fixed in musical pattern as if written in an orchestral score.[101]

In determining the score of each Shakespeare play, Poel paid particular attention, for the first time, to the scene divisions, stage directions, and punctuation of the earliest editions; he wanted actors to work from cheap facsimiles of the original quarto and folio texts.[102] Like Greg, Poel rejected anachronistic modernized editions. Like Poel, Greg wanted to rediscover the material conditions and theatrical conventions that governed performances of Shakespeare's plays.

Old-spelling editions and old-staging productions originated in the same insistence upon material authenticity.

In both cases the desired authenticity could not be achieved. For Shakespeare's original audiences Elizabethan dress and Elizabethan conventions had been ordinary and hence invisible; for Poel's audiences Elizabethan dress and Elizabethan conventions were exotic, foreign, obtrusive. For Shakespeare's original readers Elizabethan spelling and punctuation had been natural; for Greg's readers it was artificial. What was once modern had become antique. You could restore that antique with faultless accuracy, but you could not make it modern again.

Paradoxically, Poel's method quickly led to its natural antithesis. If Shakespeare's actors had originally performed in contemporary costumes, then it would be more "authentic" for modern actors in a modern revival to perform in equally contemporary costumes. In 1923 Barry Jackson's Birmingham Repertory Theatre produced *Cymbeline* in modern dress, and in 1925 they brought their modern-dress *Hamlet* to London. The courtiers sported monocles, drank cocktails, smoked cigarettes; Hamlet wore plus fours; Laertes showed up in Oxford "bags"; Ophelia bobbed her hair and wore a skirt of "inescapable shortness";[103] the characters played jazz and bridge.

"Hamlet in Modern Dress," as the production advertised itself, exploited the same "mythical method" epitomized by *Ulysses* and *The Waste Land*, "manipulating a continuous parallel between contemporaneity and antiquity."[104] In the same years David Jones, trying to put the experience of World War I into verse, equated "Mr. X adjusting his box-respirator" with Shakespeare's description of "young Harry with his beaver on"; "Trench work brought [Shakespeare's *Henry V*] pretty constantly to the mind"; the sight of "infantry in tin-hats, with ground-sheets over their shoulders, with sharpened pine-stakes in their hands" inevitably recalled "the very casques / That did affright the air" at Shakespeare's Agincourt.[105]

In Jones' poem modern British Tommies became Renaissance characters; in Jackson's production a seventeenth-century prince became "a modern youngster," "naturally currish and then driven to despair by self-torturing philosophy," whose "gabbling cynical world-hatred" and "fiery mood of relentless raillery" achieved "a perfect expression of a shell-shocked world."[106] Laertes, a seventeenth-century aristocrat who leads a rebellion against his king, was translated into "an ordinary decent undergraduate, warped by a rancorous hatred in his heart for the young man who he thinks has seduced his sister."[107] Jackson's production rejuvenated *Hamlet*, throwing onto the scrap heap the moldy leftovers of an exhausted theatrical tradition, "the incredible clothes and the wigs and the beards" and "the whole accumulation of conventional characterization."[108] But Jackson's production also threw away the very pastness of the past, its estranged particularity. An "ordinary decent undergraduate" may be our closest equivalent to Laertes, but something has been lost in the translation. If Poel's methods recall Greg, Jackson's recall I. A. Richards—who, in the same decade, set examinations in practical criticism that systematically removed all evidence of a poem's date and circumstances, every historical referent that might send a student out of the poem into that poem's world.

Poel's productions and Jackson's, apparently so different, both depended upon a cultural translation and therefore concentrated power in the translator himself. Each actor could manage his own role; but in order to achieve systematic antiquarianism or modernity, someone—be he Poel or be he Jackson—had to take responsibility for the entire production. In the past a company's leading actor had also been its director, just as an orchestra's lead keyboard player or violinist had once been its conductor. But the conductor and the director eventually emerged as separate specialities. The rise of the orchestral conductor in the nineteenth century had resulted in part from the increasing popularity of older music, which compelled orchestras to handle unfamiliar styles and notations, correspondingly increasing their collective dependence upon a single expert who could master the historical background. Poel's authority likewise depended upon his knowledge of unfamiliar conventions. But nineteenth-century orchestras also needed conductors because new music was becoming more complicated, and the new breed of conductors were all, at first, composers: Weber, Mendelssohn, Berlioz, Wagner. Shaw, likewise, directed the first productions of most of his own plays; Granville-Barker directed his own plays and other people's. And just as the increasing complexity of nineteenth-century music led to more precise and prescriptive notation, so the increasingly detailed realism of drama led to more precise and prescriptive stage directions. In the printed texts of Shaw's and Granville-Barker's plays authorial directions overwhelm dialogue. And the same control that Granville-Barker exerted over his own plays authorially he exerted over his revivals of Shake-speare's plays directorially. His *Prefaces to Shakespeare* describe and prescribe every facet of the play, from the interpretation of each role to the speaking of the verse, sets, costumes, intermissions, music, the structure of the play, its text, its themes. In print or in rehearsal the entire performance was subordinated to one man's compelling vision.

On November 11, 1937, *Julius Caesar* opened at the Mercury Theatre in New York City in a production directed by Orson Welles, who also starred as Brutus. Like the original production in 1599, Welles' *Julius Caesar* was performed, *à la* Poel, on a bare stage; but in 1937 Caesar's supporters wore brown-shirted military uniforms. Welles explicitly compared Caesar to Mussolini. But after all, Mussolini also explicitly compared himself to Caesar (and wrote plays). Theatre was political, and politics theatrical, and although Welles was condemning Mussolini he was also exploiting the same trope. Like Mussolini's propaganda, like Barry Jackson's *Hamlet*, Welles' *Julius Caesar* depended upon the audience's appre-ciation of a metaphor, its sustained attention to the similarity and disparity of vehicle and tenor. In the theatre and outside it, the terms of the metaphor became whole cultures, distant societies yoked forcefully together. In *The Golden Bough* James Frazer treated Christ as simply another variation on the myth of the Hanged God. In *Ulysses* Joyce conflated Homeric Greece and con-temporary Dublin. In urban Europe, Eliot quoted the Hindu *Upanishads* at the end of *The Waste Land* ("Shantih, shantih, shan-tih"); in a New Mexico desert, witnessing the explosion of the first atomic bomb, J. Robert Oppenheimer recalled the *Bhagavad-Gita* ("I am become death, the shatterer of worlds").

As an actor Orson Welles played Brutus, the enemy of political dictatorship; but as director of the production he played the part of artistic dictator. Total theatre, not for the first time, bore an uncom-fortable resemblance to its contemporary, totalitarianism. Hitler the would-be scene designer appropriated not only Wagner's myths but also his music, his subordination of all arts to a single emotive purpose; the architecture of light in Albert Speer's Nuremberg rallies realized the ambitions of Adolphe Appia and Edward Gor-don Craig for a theatre composed of abstract planes of mass and light, wholly dwarfing the individual human performers. Craig wanted the individual actor to become a kind of *Übermarionette*, subordinating himself to "the art of the theatre," which meant in practice subordinating himself to a director/designer. In his designs for the 1912 Moscow production of *Hamlet* the entire court sheltered under King Claudius' enormous gold cloak, which visually and physically dominated the court as completely as Craig's designs dominated the cast. After Craig's gold cloak came Granville-Barker's equally famous gold fairies, in his 1914 revival of *A Midsummer Night's Dream:* hair like gold wood, gilded skin, beards like coiled golden rope, metallic moustaches, gold-flaked costumes, standing utterly motionless like posts or stones, their movements "jerky" and "puppet-like," like carved figures on a clock, or "gilded steam radiators" that "had become mechanically animate."[109] That depersonalizing directorial gold returned in the most memorable sequence of Olivier's 1944 film of *Henry V,* the charge of the French cavalry at Agincourt. Shakespeare's text does not include the charge at all and characterizes the French army in a handful of clearly delineated individuals; Olivier's film shows multitudes in motion, an army under the artistic command of director Olivier, horses and gorgeous armor moving to the music of William Walton's heroic score.

In a world of mass production, mass transportation, mass war, mass unemployment, mass politics, mass media, human beings looked like moving multitudes of puppets. Individual "character" seemed an irrelevance. The most exciting and influential theatrical event of the London season of 1911 was not a play at all but the first of many appearances in Britain of Serge Diaghilev's Ballets Russes. Eliot, eight years later, wanted poetic drama to create "an effect as immediate and direct as that of the best ballet," an effect obtained by "the design of a scene, of costume, of movement, and the excitement of something very fine taking place before a number of people."[110] Characters do not figure in this prescription. "Anyone who has observed one of the great dancers of the Russian school" will have realized that

> In the Ballet only that is left to the actor which is properly the actor's part. The general movements are set for him. There are only limited movements that he can express. He is not called upon for his personality. . . . a true acting play is surely a play which does not depend upon the actor for anything but acting, in the sense in which a ballet depends upon the dancer for dancing . . .

Drama and dance fail whenever "the human being intrudes."[111]
This definition of theatre fits Prokofiev's ballet of *Romeo and Juliet*
better than Shakespeare's play.

The ballet was art for an elite; the cinema was entertainment for
everyman. The coming of film affected Shakespeare more directly
and permanently than the Ballets Russes. The world's first building
specially designed as a cinema opened in 1907; even before then, in
1899, Herbert Beerbohm Tree and a huge cast appeared on film in
a scene from Tree's production of *King John*. Thereafter Shakespeare's plays were adapted, usually radically, to provide scenarios
for hundreds of silent films; in 1908 American studios alone produced ten Shakespeare films, more than in any subsequent year of
the century. With the coming of sound, films could even incorporate
Shakespeare's dialogue when it suited them. In 1929 Douglas Fair-
banks played Petruchio, taming a shrewish Mary Pickford in the
first Shakespeare talkie. The most successful of these early films,
before the coming of Olivier and Welles in the 1940s, was Warner
Brothers' 1935 rendition of *A Midsummer Night's Dream*, a British
play produced by an American film studio and codirected by the
Austrian impresario Max Reinhardt. Reinhardt had directed his
first production of the play in Berlin in 1905 and returned to it a
dozen times over the next three decades; more consistently and
influentially than any British contemporary, in the first decades of
the twentieth century Reinhardt epitomized the new status of the
director, integrating music and movement, setting and speaking
into a unified theatrical score. Reinhardt's Hollywood cast included—to name only those familiar to any filmgoer—Olivia de
Havilland (coed Hermia), Mickey Rooney (Puck's irrepressible
naughty Huck Finn grin), Joe E. Brown (the almost mute, pained
face of Flute), and James Cagney (a Bottom compounded of "union
weaver, Chicago hood, and Ugly Duckling").[112] These performers,
like all the others, lost most of the language Shakespeare had given
them, because the text was heavily abridged; but they nevertheless
left on celluloid indelible images of their characters. Those images
moved among other images, equally memorable, of giant trees and
palace pillars, shiny pools and shiny floors, frogs and fairies, moon-
light and Mendelssohn—"imaginary gardens with real toads in
them."[113]

Individual Shakespeare films, however eccentrically unforgetta-
ble, affected the interpretation of Shakespeare only sporadically;

but the advent of film radically redefined the nature of drama for both practitioners and patrons. Audiences went out of the playhouse and into the movie house. Live theatre became, conspicuously, a minority taste; directors like Poel and Granville-Barker worked in smaller theatres than the great nineteenth-century showmen. Literary critics like Richards and Leavis condemned films as crude mass entertainment, pandering to the lowest commonplace denominator of the human psyche. But while champions of the theatre were condemning film they were also, like Welles with fascism, appropriating its techniques. The camera ruthlessly controlled point of view; film forced every spectator to watch what the camera watched, from the cameraman's perspective. Theatre labored to achieve the same singleness of purpose, the director's megaphone magnifying one voice above the others, funneling every aspect of a performance through a single perspective. For thirty years silent film produced images of human beings, deprived of the particulared complexities of speech, their emotions simplified by mime and music, moving on-screen as jerkily as Craig's *Über-marionetten* or Granville-Barker's golden fairies.

And film was fast. It could cut instantly from one scene to the next—unlike the Victorian theatre, which wasted long empty minutes changing sets. The Ballets Russes and the Keystone Kops delighted the eye not with scenic stills but with moving figures. So did Granville-Barker's revivals of Shakespeare at the Savoy. Poel and Granville-Barker abandoned the cumbersome scene changes of the mainstream Victorian and Edwardian theatre, reduced the number of intermissions, pared away elaborate comic business, insisted that the actors speak their speeches rapidly, without the measured pomp of traditional declamation. The old entr'actes and afterpieces had already disappeared. These changes all restored Elizabethan theatrical practices; moreover, by speeding up the delivery of the text, they enabled a performance of tolerable length to deliver the text whole, for the first time in hundreds of years. But these reforms also achieved, in the theatre, "scenic changes almost as rapid as the kinematograph,"[114] revivals that rivaled the pace of modern life, as Europe accelerated into a century of motorcars, airplanes, and radios. Authenticity satisfied the impatience of modern spectators.

Authenticity also spared the theatre from a competition it could not win. The Elizabethan stage had no sets, no artificial lighting, no period costumes, no actresses; it had only a wooden peninsular platform atop which actors directly addressed in rhetorical verse a shoe-shifting and sibilant audience that visibly half-surrounded them throughout the performance. By restoring authentic Elizabethan conditions, Poel and his followers necessarily abandoned visual realism; but this loss came to be seen as a gain. Shaw praised Poel's productions because they substituted "a few well-understood conventions" for any attempt at "an impossible scenic verisimilitude."[115] Scenic verisimilitude was not, in fact, impossible—it was perfectly possible in the cinema—it was just impossible in the theatre. The stage could not compete, as Edward Gordon Craig realized, with "the strenuous photographer."[116] Scene painters, like other painters, had to find an art beyond the reach of photochemistry.

Craig found it on screens. The cinema could project any number of images onto a blank screen; the theatre could construct any number of geometrical moods by shifting and lighting blank screens, and by doing so as quickly as film cut from one take to another. Developed for the Moscow *Hamlet,* Craig's screens were almost immediately adopted by W. B. Yeats at the Abbey Theatre in Dublin. Yeats from the beginning had hailed Craig's work, "the first beautiful scenery our stage has seen," because it epitomized an art of the theatre that was no longer "naturalistic."[117] The Ballets Russes, Craig's designs, Granville-Barker's productions of Shakespeare were "all examples of the new decorative method."[118] That new decorative method appealed to Yeats because it satisfied his own prescriptions for poetic drama. You could not speak poetic dialogue in an Ibsenite drawing room, any more than you could "stage Galsworthy and Shakespeare in the same way."[119] Unnaturalistic but imaginative sets complemented unnaturalistic but imaginative speech in a marriage of verbal and visual imagery.

Yeats wanted to revive verse drama; so did Eliot, then W. H. Auden and Christopher Isherwood, Maxwell Anderson, Christopher Fry, and Archibald MacLeish, among many others. Poetic drama offered the theatre the one thing that cinema could not supply: spectacular speech. Films at first could not talk at all; when speech came in the late 1920s it was prose. In its own defense the theatre emphasized its advantages over the cinema. This new celebration of conscious artifice naturally affected productions of Shakespeare, from the stylized set of a 1913 *Taming of the Shrew* to the futuristic curtains of a 1923 *Cymbeline,* from the cubism of the black-and-red-triangled curtain in Granville-Barker's 1912 *Twelfth Night* to the extravagantly multicolored costumes of Nigel Playfair's 1919 *As You Like It*. But the interest in poetic drama also affected, even more fundamentally perhaps, critical attitudes. What distinguished the drama of Shakespeare and the other Elizabethans from naturalistic plays and films was precisely their artificiality. The art is in the artifice; artifice and poetry, conventions of language and action, became the focal objects of scholarly and critical attention.

In abandoning naturalism Poel, Craig, and Granville-Barker set in motion "something of a revolution in the English Theatre,"[120] a revolution that defended itself as a literal and genuine revolve, a circling movement that returned to the authentic artifice of an earlier period. But this artifice was riven by the same contradictions that beset editions in original spelling and productions in original costuming. Modern poetic drama, modern revivals of old poetic dramas, consciously defined themselves in opposition to naturalistic plays and films; they turned away from realism. For its own audiences, though, in its own time, the artificial Renaissance theatre had been more naturalistic, more realistic, than any known alternative. Marlowe's blank verse, however rigid its rhythms seem to modern ears, sounded—and still sounds—more natural than the dialogue of any of his Tudor predecessors, and Shakespeare's later sounded more natural than Marlowe's, and Middleton's later sounded more natural than Shakespeare's. Renaissance actors dressed in spectacular costumes because they copied and sometimes borrowed the real accoutrements of real kings, real aristocrats, real ecclesiasts, real foreigners. Renaissance plays were interspersed with dance and music because music and dance punctuated the lives of the society they dramatized. Renaissance audiences thrilled to *The True Tragedie of Richard Duke of Yorke* and to a play on the reign of Henry VIII that promised *All is True*.

It soon became apparent, even to the moderns, that although Shakespeare could not be defended or staged using naturalistic criteria, neither was he artificial enough to serve as the model for a new poetic drama. Eliot complained that "the Elizabethans themselves admit the same criteria of realism" that governed modern drama: "A play of Shakespeare's and a play of Henry Arthur Jones are essentially of the same type," and if you wanted to see drama of a different type you had to go all the way back to the medieval morality play *Everyman*.[121] In 1890 Pollard had published a collection of *English Miracle Plays, Moralities and Interludes* that went through eight editions in the next forty years; in 1901, for the first time since the sixteenth century, Poel had triumphantly revived *Everyman*, prompting a series of productions of English morality plays. Elizabethan drama could now be evaluated—unfavorably— by comparison with the drama it had supplanted. Eliot in practice combined medieval and Greek models; Yeats' best plays owed more to Japanese Noh than Shakespeare. Shakespeare stood, uncomfortably, halfway between the artificial drama of an archaic culture and the realism of modern film.

G. Wilson Knight, reviewing Warner Brothers' cinematic rendering of *A Midsummer Night's Dream*, "was impressed by the way in which the producer brought out, *what is in the poetry*, the nightmarish fearsomeness of the woods and its wild beasts" onto the screen; he also "liked Oberon on his black horse."[122] However insistently the champions of poetic drama differentiated it from photography and the cinema, photography and the cinema transformed their critical perspective. The movement Ezra Pound dubbed Imagism in 1912 declared by its title the primacy of visual impressions, and in 1914 Vorticism set those images in violent motion, briefly compounding the plastic and the visual and the verbal arts. What distinguishes Shakespeare for Virginia Woolf is precisely "the power to make images" and the speed of those images, pouring out in "the volley & volume & tumble of his words":

> I never yet knew how amazing his stretch & speed & word coining power is, until I felt it utterly outpace & outrace my own, seeming to start equal & then I see him draw ahead & do things I could not in my wildest tumult & utmost press of mind imagine. Even the less known & worser plays are written at a speed that is quicker than anybody else's quickest; & the words drop so fast one can't pick them up.[123]

Caroline Spurgeon and Edward Armstrong, analyzing Shakespeare's word clusters, described the behavior of visual images in motion, one generating another; Wolfgang Clemen traced *The Development of Shakespeare's Imagery*, both within individual speeches and progressively through the canon. Wilson Knight himself, the most influential of these critics, visualized "the Lear-theme rushing, whistling in air, a sudden visionary brilliance, and many colors across the heavens";[124] indeed, Knight pictured the whole Shakespeare canon as a progression of charged images, a sequence of symbols, from tempest to music.

Knight also insisted—like the camera, like the director, like the dictator—upon unity of effect, singleness of vision. Invariably, a "play's thought and action derive their significance" from a "central idea." "Death is truly the theme" of *Hamlet,* for instance, "for Hamlet's disease is mental and spiritual death."[125] Spurgeon, likewise, identified "dominating pictures" in each play: "certain groups of images ... stand out in each particular play" because "the theme [Shakespeare] is handling raises in his imagination as he writes some picture or symbol which recurs again and again in the form of simile and metaphor throughout the play," creating "an undertone of running symbolic imagery."[126] In *Henry V* images of "swift and soaring movement" are "dominating"; in *A Midsummer Night's Dream* "the woodland beauty of a dreaming summer night" impresses itself upon us "overpoweringly"; "The dominant image in the *Tempest* ... is the sense of *sound*"; in *Romeo and Juliet* "The dominating image is *light*"; disease dominates *Hamlet,* food *Troilus and Cressida;* the imaginative world of *Othello* is dominated by "animals in action."[127]

This oneness of vision presupposes the presence of only a single executive imagination, controlling every feature of the work. Throughout the eighteenth and nineteenth centuries scholarship and criticism had agreed that some, perhaps many, of Shakespeare's plays were written in collaboration with other authors, sometimes nameable, sometimes not. But in 1924 E. K. Chambers, delivering a decisive lecture to the British Academy, rejected and rebuked this "Disintegration of Shakespeare." Chambers did concede the presence of a collaborator in a few plays, but the reaction he initiated soon overwhelmed even the most entrenched doubts. In 1929 Peter Alexander reclaimed the whole of the Henry VI trilogy for Shakespeare; in 1933 L. C. Knights insisted upon "the indivisible unity" of *Macbeth,* simply ridiculing those who discerned a "ubiquitous Interpolator" in certain passages; A. M. Sampley in 1936, and Hereward T. Price in 1943, influentially defended the integrity of *Titus Andronicus;* in 1942 Una Ellis-Fermor gave Shakespeare all of *Timon of Athens.*[128] Spurgeon's study of the imagery in *Henry VIII* convinced her that Shakespeare wrote more of the play than had been generally assumed; Wilson Knight concluded that *Pericles* was "as authentic as any of Shakespeare's works."[129]

A monocular theory of textual transmission anticipated and assisted this monocular theory of authorship. Until the twentieth century it had been widely accepted that the surviving early editions of Shakespeare's texts were printed from corrupt manuscripts several times removed from the author. In 1756 Samuel Johnson, in a passage often quoted thereafter, had declared that Shakespeare's manuscripts, once he sold them to the theatre,

> were immediately copied for the actors, and multiplied by transcript after transcript, vitiated by the blunders of the penman, or changed by the affectation of the player; perhaps enlarged to introduce a jest, or mutilated to shorten the representation; and printed at last without the concurrence of the authour, without the consent of the proprietor, from compilations made by chance or by stealth out of the separate parts written for the theatre . . .[130]

As late as 1902 Sidney Lee, in less memorable but equally pessimistic language, affirmed that "The greater number of the quarto editions of Shakespeare's plays which were published in his lifetime seem to have been printed from more or less imperfect and unauthorized playhouse transcripts which were obtained by the publishers more or less dishonestly."[131] This editorial orthodoxy was overturned in 1909 by A. W. Pollard, a librarian employed in the British Museum's Department of Printed Books. The preface to the 1623 First Folio had warned readers not to trust "diuerse stolne, and surreptitious copies"[132] of Shakespeare's plays, previously published; this phrase had been taken by editors as a condemnation of all the early quartos. Pollard instead argued that the ambiguous phrase, and particularly the ambiguous word "diuerse," indicted only a distinguishable few of the early editions, which he characterized as "bad" quartos; the remaining quartos were by contrast "good." ("Do you know the difference between the Quarto's and the folios?" Virginia Woolf asked a correspondent; "I never did, till last night."[133])

Pollard's interpretation was widely applauded as a revolutionary breakthrough, and specialist textual studies of individual plays soon began to confirm that "the early editions . . . are a good deal closer to the original manuscripts from [Shakespeare's] pen" than previous "text-builders" had allowed.[134] In 1934 Dover Wilson, in the most characteristic and influential example of such studies, devoted two volumes to a demonstration that a quarto published in

1604 had been printed directly from *The Manuscript of Shakespeare's 'Hamlet'*—leaving only one thin intermediary between us and that singular authorial text. And in one play we could get even closer. In 1916 the British Museum paleographer E. Maunde Thompson offered expert evidence that three pages in a British Museum manuscript had been written out by Shakespeare himself. In 1923 Thompson joined forces with Greg, Pollard, and Dover Wilson to press the case for *Shakespeare's Hand in The Play of 'Sir Thomas More.'* By "*Hand*" they meant "handwriting"; but the noun's ambiguity conveyed some of their excited sense of the author's corporeal presence.

The technical and paleographical evidence for Shakespeare's authorship of the three pages was bolstered by another contributor to the *Sir Thomas More* colloquium, R. W. Chambers, who examined "those subtle links of thought" by which ideas and images "are associated in one mind."[135] Chambers' essay directly applied the analysis of imagery to problems of authorship. The new studies of Shakespeare's text depended on the same method as the new studies of his imagery: in both cases minutiae scattered throughout the text were systematically examined in pursuit of a single originating agent. Dover Wilson tabulated orthography, the formulas used in stage directions, the frequency and distribution of certain kinds of punctuation, variations in speech prefixes—features of the text neglected by previous editors—and from such atomistic evidence propounded a unifying hypothesis about the nature of a text. By such means Dover Wilson identified Shakespeare's hand in the manuscript behind the 1604 edition of *Hamlet;* by such means F. P. Wilson identified the hand of Ralph Crane, a professional theatrical scribe, in a number of texts and suggested that "one or more" manuscripts "in his handwriting" may have been used by the printers of the 1623 First Folio.[136] By similar means Spurgeon and Knight, tabulating images, identified a unifying principle that explained innumerable details of the text, organizing the chaos of disparate trivia into a satisfying ordered whole. As the preface to the First Folio had declared, Shakespeare's "mind and hand went together"; in the early twentieth century the techniques for studying mind and hand went together, too. R. W. Chambers' essay in *Shakespeare's Hand* reappeared sixteen years later, expanded as a chapter in *Man's Unconquerable Mind.*

If Shakespeare's mind and hand went together, then a play by

Shakespeare was unified not only by a single executive imagination but also by a single moment of creation. The paleographers concurred that the three pages of *Sir Thomas More* had been written at great speed; behind the 1604 edition of *Hamlet* or the 1600 edition of *Henry IV, Part 2* we could apparently see Shakespeare's own "foul papers," a complete manuscript of the play, the material text achieved in a single sustained act of composition, showing—like *Sir Thomas More*—evident symptoms of haste. Shakespeare uttered his thoughts so masterfully so quickly, that he need never return to the scene of his creation; he finished off a play in one fell swoop. On the third day Shakespeare created *Much Ado About Nothing*, and he saw that it was good, and so he left it alone and busied himself with other matters. The unity of the text was not disturbed by more than one author, or more than one period of composition.

This new interpretation of Shakespeare's methods of creation had to overcome certain inherited obstacles. It had been widely assumed, since the eighteenth century, that some of Shakespeare's plays, first printed in the 1623 First Folio, were mere reworkings of earlier texts written either by Shakespeare himself or by other authors. Thus, the text of *Henry VI, Part 2* printed in 1623 reworked the text of *The First Part of the Contention*, printed in 1594; *Henry VI, Part 3* reworked *The True Tragedy of Richard Duke of York* (1595); *The Taming of the Shrew* reworked *The Taming of a Shrew* (1594); *King John* reworked *The Troublesome Reign of King John* (1591); *Romeo and Juliet*, *Henry V*, and *Hamlet* all reworked inferior texts with the same titles, published in earlier editions. These inferior texts, banished from the authorized congregation of Shakespeare's works, had always been treated as a special suspect category; but, like every supplement, they helped define the work to which they were appended and from which they were excluded. Whether written by Shakespeare or someone else, the apocryphal texts defined the canonical texts as reworkings, rehandlings of work by an other or an earlier hand. Eliot's 1919 verdict on *Hamlet*—"most certainly an artistic failure"—was prompted by just such considerations; Eliot summarized and endorsed J. M. Robertson's analysis of the play's gradual textual evolution. Thus "the whole action of the play" was not, as ideally it should have been, solely "due to Shakespeare's design"; Shakespeare's design had been, instead, unsuccessfully "superposed upon much cruder material."[137] Robertson attributed the cruder antecedents to Thomas Kyd and George Chapman; but even if the cruder material had been Shakespeare's own early work, Eliot's objection would remain equally valid.

But Robertson's textual scholarship was already old-fashioned by the time Eliot endorsed it. In 1909 Pollard had redefined most of the suspect texts as "bad quartos," the results not of an earlier process of crude composition but of a later process of corrupt textual transmission. The 1600 text of *Henry V*, for instance, did not represent an antecedent of the play, by Shakespeare or anyone else; it constituted only an unauthorized, mangled derivative of Shakespeare's own text. Other scholars had anticipated Pollard's interpretation of some of these suspect texts, but he formulated the hypothesis much more cogently, offering a coherent intellectual mechanism for systematically resolving a range of textual problems. Other scholars soon expanded and developed Pollard's hypothesis. In 1929 a monograph by Peter Alexander—with a preface by Pollard—relegated *The First Part of the Contention* and *Richard Duke of York* to the roster of derivative texts; in 1928 John S. Smart (Alexander's teacher) had added *The Taming of A Shrew* to the same category; in 1950 E. A. J. Honigmann (Alexander's pupil) added *The Troublesome Reign*.[138] Other scholars substantiated similar claims about the first editions of *Hamlet* (1941) and *Romeo and Juliet* (1948).[139] Dowden's Victorian map of Shakespeare's progress had placed his first period "In the Workshop," an apprentice reworking other people's plays; by the middle of the twentieth century Shakespeare's texts had been relieved of any such dependence on earlier hands.

The new theories of authorship and of textual transmission were united, characteristically, in E. K. Chambers' pivotal diatribe against "The Disintegration of Shakespeare." In attacking proponents of multiple authorship, Chambers also attacked, more generally, proponents of what he called "continuous copy," the notion that a dramatic text would be extensively reworked by its author or by another dramatist at a later date. Chambers targeted both collaboration and revision, because both processes threatened the wholeness of Shakespeare's texts; and since Shakespeare had become in twentieth-century biography merely a set of texts, anyone who disintegrated them was disintegrating Shakespeare.

Chambers successfully demolished a good deal of nonsense, but neither he nor Pollard could save Shakespeare from the temporal world. Shakespeare's new integrity was riddled with fault lines.

Whether or not the 1603 edition of *Hamlet* represents earlier re-
daction or, as seems more likely, corrupt transmission, the fact
remains that Hamlet had been the subject of a popular play at least
a decade before Shakespeare wrote the text that would be included
in editions of his work. Shakespeare's text developed out of other
texts. Moreover, the very text that brought us closest to "Shakespeare's Hand," *Sir Thomas More*, was a collaborative play; attention
focused upon Shakespeare's three pages, which were repeatedly
reproduced in isolation from their dramatic context, but our only
glimpse of "Shakespeare's Hand" discovered it in the company of
other hands, presumably reworking a passage originally written by
one of those other hands. Ellis-Fermor, in reclaiming *Timon of
Athens* for Shakespeare, had to label it an "unfinished play"; *Timon*
showed us what a Shakespeare text looked like before it had
received its final authorial revision, before Shakespeare turned his
original couplets into blank verse—rather like Eliot (or Pound)
turning the original couplets of *The Waste Land* into free verse.
Ellis-Fermor could preserve authorial integrity only by sacrificing
temporal integrity: if the play was written by only one author, then
it must have undergone more than one period of composition. But
the sacrifice of temporal integrity could easily be overlooked,
because after all the second stage of the text—like the earlier play
about Hamlet—had fortunately not survived. And so Shakespearians could continue to act, like Coriolanus, "as if a text were
author of itself, and knew no other kin."[140]

Good-bye to all that collaboration, good-bye to continuous copy.
The text did not reflect a temporal continuum; the text was timeless; the text was both conceived and born in a single moment, of a
single parent; the text was a single, large, complex image. And, as
Wilson Knight realized, images belonged in space:

> One must be prepared to see the whole play in space as well as
> time.... there are throughout the play a set of correspondences
> which relate to each other independently of the time-sequence
> which is the story; such are the intuition-intelligence opposition
> active within and across *Troilus and Cressida*, the death-theme in
> *Hamlet*, the nightmare evil of *Macbeth* ... Now if we are prepared
> to see the whole play laid out, so to speak, as an area, being
> simultaneously aware of these thickly-scattered correspondences
> in a single view of the whole, we possess the unique quality of the
> play ...[141]

And so, good-bye to narrative. Narrative, the "story," hardly matters to the best modernist criticism of Shakespeare, any more than it matters to Eliot's *Waste Land* or Pound's *Cantos* or Joyce's *Finnegans Wake*. After all, without characters, how can you tell stories? The Victorians had written poems by extracting Shakespeare's characters from his plays, letting them loose to tell their own story: "Mariana" in Tennyson's moated grange, "Caliban upon Setebos" in Browning's Island. Eliot's "Marina," his "Coriolan," instead reiterate images, rehearse themes, arealy, aerially, like someone looking down from an airplane, with one glance taking in a landscape it would have taken Shakespeare a day to walk across.

> Now come the virgins bearing urns, urns containing
> Dust
> Dust
> Dust of dust, and now

Eliot's "Coriolan"[142] asks to be seen, as Knight asks for Shakespeare's *Coriolanus* to be seen, spatially, as an area of text.

And just as we must see the individual play as a whole and single entity, so we must see the canon of an author's work, and the canon of literature, as wholes. Against Victorian diversity and fragmentation the modernists insist upon an ascetic unity. The individual play, like a single dream, can be properly analyzed only by the critic or psychoanalyst in the context of the playwright/patient's other plays, other dreams. Eliot's doctoral dissertation on the philosophy of F. H. Bradley insists that "without the implication of a system in which it belongs the fact is not a fact at all" (1916); his seminal essay on "Tradition and the Individual Talent" (1919) insists, likewise, that

> The existing order is complete before the new work arrives; for order to persist after the supervention of novelty, the *whole* existing order must be, if ever so slightly, altered; and so the relations, proportions, values of each work of art toward the whole are readjusted.[143]

Thus, as a result of the new work of Eliot and his fellow modernists Shakespeare's most popular tragedies and comedies lost a little of their old centrality, displaced in the ranks of critical esteem by seldom acted, verbally complex works like *Coriolanus, Timon of*

Athens, and *Pericles.* But even those new favorites could not be understood in isolation:

> the full meaning of any one of his plays is not in itself alone but in that play in the order in which it was written, in its relation to all of Shakespeare's other plays, earlier and later: we must know all of Shakespeare's work in order to know any of it.[144]

Literary tradition—like social reality in the two decades that witnessed the Bolshevik Revolution, the Irish war of national liberation, the British General Strike, the Great Depression, the Spanish Civil War, the rise of Hitler and Mussolini—poses "a problem of order." Traditions create "systems in relation to which, and only in relation to which, individual works of literary art, and the works of individual artists, have their significance;"[145] in the new era of mass civilization, individuals, too, have their significance only in relation to the larger social systems that they help collectively to constitute. Even more fundamentally, words themselves attain significance only by virtue of the total linguistic system to which they belong; so declared Ferdinand de Saussure in a series of lectures delivered at the University of Geneva between 1906 and 1911, posthumously published as *Cours de linguistique générale* (1915). An individual word made sense only in relation to a system of language; an individual action, in relation to a system of conventions; an individual image, in relation to a system of images; an individual character, in relation to a system of characters; an individual work of art, in relation to a system of works of art. Tiny atomic particles had no significance in themselves; they were given significance by the colossal energies that bound them together into systems.

What, then, was Shakespeare? A potent vacuum. An engrossing (w)hole.

IV

I have not yet mentioned Cleanth Brooks. I have been saving him—as an ape does an apple, Hamlet would say, in the corner of my jaw, fully intending to squeeze him dry, but not until dessert. One of the most influential American critics of the twentieth century, maker of textbooks, propounder of critical and pedagogical method, Brooks in the summer of 1945 published a famous essay on *Macbeth* that was later included in his 1947 book *The Well Wrought Urn: Studies in the Structure of Poetry*.[146] Like Pope's *Dunciad,* Keats' "On Sitting Down to Read King Lear Once Again," and Bradley's *Shakespearean Tragedy,* Brooks' essay comes toward the end of a period of Shakesperotics that, in many ways, it epitomizes.

Unlike those previous epitomes, Brooks did not live or work in the little country that Shakespeare had been born in. The story of English literature in the twentieth century is not, at its best, an English story. Joyce and Yeats and Shaw were Irish; Eliot and Pound—and Robert Frost and Wallace Stevens and William Carlos Williams—were American. For a few decades England, and more particularly Cambridge, still dominated literary studies. Greg and McKerrow, as undergraduates at Trinity College in the 1890s, plotted the revolution in textual studies that became the New Bibliography. Cambridge University Press published the most interesting and innovative edition of the early twentieth century, Dover Wilson's New Shakespeare; and Cambridge in the 1920s and early 1930s housed Richards, Knights, Bradbrook, Empson, and the Leavises. But the sheer number of universities that the American population could fill and the American economy could fund soon began to make itself felt. World War II—so damaging to the United Kingdom, so beneficial to the United States—accelerated a process that was in any case demographically inevitable. American academics appropriated English literature, just as American soldiers appropriated England itself; "This royal throne of kings, this sceptred isle"[147] was leased out as an unsinkable launching platform for the joint Anglo-American invasion of Normandy. In the summer 1945 issue of *The Yale Review* Brooks' essay was surrounded by titles such as "The Rehabilitation of Europe" and "The War Converges on Japan."

Brooks' essay was entitled "Shakespeare as a Symbolist Poet." This title openly defined Shakespeare as a poet, not a dramatist, and associated him with a particular strand of modernist poetry pioneered by the French symbolists (Mallarmé, Verlaine, Rimbaud, Laforgue), championed in England by Arthur Symons' influential book on *The Symbolist Movement in Literature,* and epitomized in English by Eliot and Pound and Stevens. Its title situates Brooks' essay in the field of modernist poetry, and the essay itself echoes the reiterative thematic imagery of modernist criticism. He discerns "an elaborate pattern in the imagery" of *Macbeth;* certain symbols "dominate the play." To understand "the play as a whole" we must attend to its "inner symbolism," a symbolism that Shakespeare's "unconscious" may have generated. Like a good scholar, Brooks substantiates his argument with numerous citations from appropriate authorities—T. S. Eliot, I. A. Richards, Coleridge, *The Shakespeare Glossary,* "Miss Spurgeon," Robert Penn Warren, Yeats—assuming in each instance that his readers will immediately recognize and respect them. Except for Coleridge, they all belong to the first decades of the twentieth century, and Coleridge had been made an honorary ex officio member of the same visionary company, owing the revival of his reputation as a critic to the enthusiasm of Richards and Eliot. T. M. Raysor's standard edition of *Coleridge's Shakespearean Criticism,* for instance, was published in 1930.

Brooks invokes his contemporaries so habitually because he believes, like Eliot and Knights, that the "essential qualification" of the "true Shakespeare critic" is "a lively interest in the present and the immediate future of poetry."[148] We can understand the individual play or poem only as part of the larger literary system to which it belongs, a system that the poetry and criticism of the present are themselves helping to shape. Consequently, in *The Well Wrought Urn* Brooks' essay on *Macbeth* takes its place among essays on poems by Donne, Milton, Herrick, Pope, Gray, Wordsworth, Keats, Tennyson, and Yeats. Brooks asks us to understand *Macbeth* as a component of a larger literary system, which he defines. Noticeably, this system includes, *Macbeth* excepted, only poems; and the intrusion of *Macbeth* implies, what Knights had not long before explicitly declared, that "*Macbeth* is a poem."[149]

Another oddity: although the other chapters of the book follow the chronology of English literature from Milton to Yeats, *Macbeth* enters out of sequence. The book begins with Donne, then back-pedals to Shakespeare before resuming its forward motion.* Indeed, in the original version of the essay Brooks introduces Shakespeare as "Donne's great contemporary," suggesting that "our

*The exact date of Donne's "The Canonization" was and is not clear; Brooks would probably have consulted *The Poems of John Donne,* ed. Herbert J. C. Grierson, 2 vols. (1912), II, 8–10. However, the poem's reference to "the King" indicates that it belongs to the reign of James I; *Macbeth* by general consent belongs to the early years of that reign. Brooks did not know whether the play or the poem was written first; he nevertheless began with the younger of the two writers (Donne was born eight years after Shakespeare).

practice in reading Donne" may "enable us to read Shakespeare more richly"; both formulations make Shakespeare secondary to Donne.[150] In *The Well Wrought Urn* Brooks eliminates these telltale phrases and goes out of his way more than once to affirm that Shakespeare is a different and a greater poet than Donne; nevertheless, in the second paragraph of the essay on *Macbeth* he concedes that the "new criticism" has "tended to center around the rehabilitation of Donne and the Donne tradition." The book's organization makes it clear enough that Brooks places Shakespeare in a tradition epitomized by Donne—by "telescoped conceits," by poems of "metaphysical" intellectual complexity circulated privately among an educated elite.

Brooks enters *Macbeth*, characteristically, by way of a problem—or rather two problems. Macbeth compares pity to

> a naked new-born babe,
> Striding the blast, or heaven's cherubim, hors'd
> Upon the sightless couriers of the air . . .

"The comparison is odd, to say the least," Brooks comments. "Is the babe natural or supernatural—an ordinary, helpless baby, who, as newborn, could not, of course, even toddle, much less stride the blast? Or is it some infant Hercules, quite capable of striding the blast, but, since it is powerful and not helpless, hardly the typical pitiable object?" Likewise, in "An even more interesting" passage, Macbeth describes his discovery of the murder:

> Here lay Duncan,
> His silver skin lac'd with his golden blood;
> And his gash'd stabs, look'd like a breach in nature,
> For ruin's wasteful entrance: there, the murderers,
> Steep'd in the colours of their trade, their daggers
> Unmannerly breech'd with gore . . .[151]

Brooks notes that eighteenth-century editors were so repulsed by the image "breech'd" in the final line that they tried to emend it away; he quotes an unnamed "nineteenth-century critic" who objected that "There is little, and that far-fetched, similarity between *gold lace* and *blood,* or between *bloody daggers* and *breech'd legs.* The slightness of the similarity, recalling the greatness of the dissimilarity, disgusts us with the attempted comparison." (The critic in question had in fact continued, "Language so forced is only appropriate in the mouth of a conscious murderer"[152]—thus explaining the imagery in terms of character. Brooks has no interest in character and does not quote that final sentence.)*

These passages confront a modern critic with a simple problem: Shakespeare, a great poet, in one of his greatest plays, written in his "mature style," has employed two images that "must still shock the average reader" by their apparent ineptitude. But "in neither case is there any warrant for thinking that Shakespeare was not trying to write as well as he could." In the twentieth century we assume that Shakespeare, trying to write as well as he could, would have written as well as anyone ever could; so that our distaste for these particulars contradicts our general estimate of his artistic intelligence. The problem, if given as a modern examination question, might have been phrased in this way:

> 1. Demonstrate that these two passages can be reconciled with the consensus that Shakespeare was a great poet; if possible, organize your demonstration so that it also affirms Shakespeare's adherence to "the tradition of Donne."

John Dryden and Alexander Pope and Samuel Johnson, confronted with this kind of question, would obviously have failed the examination. Analyzing *Hamlet,* Dryden also quoted (as Brooks does) a passage full of dizzy metaphors; but for Dryden such a passage simply demonstrated that a great poet could make mistakes. Moreover, for Dryden, or any other major critic from the Restoration to the twentieth century, Donne did not set a standard by which English literature should be judged; the Restoration compared Shakespeare to Fletcher, the Romantics to Milton. Brooks defines and then "solves" a problem that did not exist in those terms for earlier critics. And, in posing the problem, he also defines the terms of an acceptable solution. When Brooks asks, "Is the passage vague or precise? Loosely or tightly organized?" there can be little doubt,

---

*Brooks does not supply exact references in either version of the essay, but for his knowledge of editorial commentary on this crux he was almost certainly dependent on the New Variorum edition of *Macbeth,* ed. Horace Howard Furness (1873), rev. ed. H. H. Furness, Jr., (1903). The 1873 edition quotes the passage in full (p. 122); the 1903 edition, from which Brooks presumably quoted, omits the final sentence (p. 160).

within the terms of the critical system that he assumes and articulates, that "vague" and "loose" mean "sloppy," while "precise" and "tight" mean "exact." Brooks defines good poetry with the criteria of good scholarship: accuracy, organization, novelty, intellectual grasp. Since Shakespeare is by definition a "good" poet, we can be sure that the two passages will emerge, in Brooks' solution, as examples of "precise" and "tightly organized" imagery.

Brooks constructs his solution by relating each passage to "the play as a whole." He connects the image of daggers "breech'd with gore" to Spurgeon's "discovery" of a pattern of "old clothes" imagery in *Macbeth*. But "Miss Spurgeon has hardly explored the full implications of her discovery"; and Brooks proceeds to demonstrate that the play contains more clothing imagery—and a more coherent system of clothing imagery—than Spurgeon had realized. Thus, "the series of garment metaphors which run through the play is paralleled by a series of masking or cloaking images" including, in particular, Macbeth's line, "Let's briefly put on manly readiness," where the verb "put on" metamorphoses the abstract noun "manly readiness" into a kind of clothing. Likewise, although Spurgeon did not notice it, the play includes "a great many references to babes," which can be supplemented by references to human children in general or to offspring of any kind. From this larger perspective "the babe signifies the future"; but it also "symbolizes all those enlarging purposes which make life meaningful" and all those "emotional and . . . irrational ties which make man more than a machine." Moreover, these two patterns of reiterative images, clothing and children, interact, complementing and opposing one another:

> The clothed daggers and the naked babe—mechanism and life—instrument and end—death and birth—that which should be left bare and clean and that which should be clothed and warmed—these are facets of the two great symbols which run throughout the play. . . . the image of the garment and the image of the babe are so used as to encompass an astonishingly large area of the total situation.

The two disturbing passages thus contain "telescoped conceits," tied by tentacles of metaphor to complexes of symbolic significance throughout the play. Problem solved. Q.E.D.

In *The Well Wrought Urn* Brooks' essay is retitled "The Naked Babe and the Cloak of Manliness." This new title epitomizes his method, juxtaposing images from widely separated parts of the play. The passage on the "naked babe" is cited, as he notes, from "Act I scene vii." He does not locate the second passage, describing the daggers as "breech'd with gore," which belongs to Act II, scene iii—313 lines later. Throughout the essay Brooks provides few scene references and no line numbers for the passages he quotes, thereby eliding any sense of the great tracks of text he flits across. Moreover, his title alters both quotations. He omits "new-born" from the first phrase, thereby compressing it into symbolic adjective "naked" and symbolic noun "babe." The second phrase he simply invents: "cloak of manliness" does not appear anywhere in *Macbeth,* or anywhere in Shakespeare, who never uses "manliness" at all. In the compressed image "cloak of manliness" Brooks summarizes his analysis of a series of actions and metaphors throughout the play, and does so in a two-term compound that neatly contrasts "naked" with "cloak" and "babe" with "manliness." Brooks creates in his title a complex metaphorical polarity, a single poetic image of the play as a whole. He makes no attempt to explain how an audience could garner such significances from a performance. Brooks admits that "the most obvious symbols" in the play, darkness and blood, "appear more often" than the images he analyzes; "darkness and blood," whether or not we notice their reiteration, cumulatively create "atmosphere." But Brooks' images do not create atmosphere, do not work cumulatively; in order to understand their significance we must remember, analyze, and interrelate a mass of dispersed verbal detail—something an audience cannot do within the performance conditions of Shakespeare's time (or anyone else's). The bewilderment of earlier critics, which Brooks cites at the beginning of his essay, indeed demonstrates empirically that even readers, not bound by theatrical restraints, had missed the alleged connections between these two passages and the rest of the play. Brooks is not embarrassed by the fact that no one else seems to have noticed the relationships he describes; indeed, he rejoices in it. Like Donne's poems, Brooks' essays advertise the novelty of their own conceit.

Brooks treats all parts of the play as though they were simultaneously present and visible to the viewer, collapsing time into a single dimension; and he does the same thing to literary history. All the poems analyzed in *The Well Wrought Urn,* from Shakespeare to

Yeats, are subjected to the same critical method, which deliberately ignores history. As the preface declares, the book sets out to answer a "question": "whether a poem represents anything more universal than the expression of the particular values of its time." Of course Brooks answers yes; and he achieves this universality, as Eliot and Joyce and Pound did, by a "mythic method," brazenly juxtaposing material from widely separated historical periods. He avoids any discussion of the social and political, cultural and ideological, assumptions of Shakespeare's era. At the simplest level, the dead king's blood is golden, his skin is silver, the spatter of blood on skin is lace, because gold and silver and lace befit a king; the blood on the grooms is like ink or dye on a tradesman's hands, their daggers are "breech'd", because work stains and britches befit domestic servants. Likewise, in a society based upon hereditary monarchy "a naked new-born babe" can be both pitiable and potent; a king's heir—and Macbeth is talking, after all, about the death of a king—inextricably combines pitiable human frailty with terrifying social potency. The king's two bodies, mortal and divine, frail and infallible, coexist in the one figure. This paradox would have been especially vivid for Shakespeare when writing *Macbeth,* to be performed by the King's Men, not long after the accession of a new king. For the first time in Shakespeare's lifetime England had a royal family, including royal children. Such social details inform the imagery of both passages, helping to make them "precise" and "tightly organized" in ways that an audience can understand at once; but Brooks ignores them all. He also ignores the evidence that *Macbeth* was adapted after Shakespeare's death. He suppresses history, including the history of texts. He wants a significance that transcends temporal particulars.

His insistence that a poem convey something "more universal than the expression of the particular values of its time" itself expresses the particular values of his time. As the preface announces, Brooks seeks in poetry something that will combat "The temper of our times," which is "strongly relativistic." This relativism, moreover, "bears very definitely on the much advertised demise of the Humanities." Brooks wants a definition of poetry that will cure the ills of his own godless culture and, at the same time, increase the prestige of his own profession. For the rise of academic literary scholarship, in the half century from 1875 to 1925, had not resulted in any corresponding rise in the public's appreciation of poetry; paradoxically, the expansion of the discipline had diminished its subject. Historical scholarship, demonstrating so convincingly that Shakespeare's plays depended upon particular theatrical conditions and antiquated dramatic conventions, in one sense brought critics closer to Shakespeare but, at the same time, made him seem farther away than ever. Critics were caught in the same dilemma as editors and directors: the more authentically they restored Shakespeare's texts or performances or meanings, the more artificial he became. Brooks solved this problem by saying good-bye to historical scholarship, and hence good-bye to theatrical scholarship, and hence good-bye to the theatre. If a performance in Elizabethan costume was unsatisfactory, and a performance in modern costume was unsatisfactory, then the critic might as well forget about performances altogether.

Brooks' methodological solution influenced so many people because it fit so perfectly the circumstances of American academics. England is a small country, with a few centrally located repositories of early books and documents and a thriving network of theatres heavily dependent on revivals of "classic" plays; the country lends itself to historical scholarship and practical theatrical criticism. America was a vast country with, at the time, few research libraries comparable to those in London and Oxford and Cambridge; its theatrical industry, concentrated in New York City, paid less attention to Shakespeare and, in any case, was less confident about its own revivals. When he published "Shakespeare as a Symbolist Poet" Brooks was teaching at Louisiana State University, and *The Well Wrought Urn* was dedicated "To the members of English 300-K (Summer Session of 1942, University of Michigan) who discussed the problems with me and helped me work out some of the analyses." How much access did such students at Michigan or Louisiana State—or even their teachers—have to the materials that made possible original historical research or original dramatic criticism? Although the Huntington Library in Los Angeles published its first *Bulletin* in 1931, and the Folger Shakespeare Library opened in Washington in 1932, there was no National Endowment for the Humanities to fund research trips to these institutions on either coast; air travel was expensive and uncommon; university teachers were badly paid. By 1983 America could boast thirty-one Shakespeare "festivals" in theatres scattered around the continent; though their quality varies wildly, they at least make Shakespeare performances available to a wide variety of students. But the oldest of these Shakespearefests, the Oregon Shakespeare Festival in the isolated town of Ashland, was not founded until 1935. "New Criticism," as practiced by Brooks and innumerable other American academics, required only a (modernized) text and *The Shakespeare Glossary*.

If Brooks' method appealed to American academics in midcentury, so did his message. In American classrooms at the end of World War II, Brooks defined Macbeth as a murderous usurping dictator who "made war on children." (Hitler sent schoolchildren into the Battle of the Bulge, and Hirohito put them into kamikaze planes.) More generally, Macbeth founds his career on an "overbrittle rationalism," rejecting "the emotional ties which make man more than a machine." Indeed, Brooks quotes Robert Penn Warren to the effect that "all of Shakespeare's villains are rationalists." Brooks and Warren had collaborated on two influential anthologies, *Understanding Poetry* (1938) and *Understanding Fiction* (1943); like their contemporaries John Crowe Ransom and Allen Tate, both were Southerners, defining their cultural stance in active opposition to the soulless "abstraction" of Northern/urban/mass/industrial life.

For Brooks, as for many others, the search for universal values leads only to a confirmation of current values. "Eternity" is a euphemism for the isolationist present, which retrospectively commandeers the past.

V

It was an age of good-byes. Eliot and Pound and Hemingway and Stein left America; Pound later left England, and so did Auden and Isherwood; Joyce left Ireland, Diaghilev and Nabokov left Russia, Reinhardt and Brecht left Germany. Millions left the countryside to live in cities; millions left their homes to die in battles or in concentration camps. Husbands left their wives, and wives their husbands, as divorce was normalized. Laymen left the church. People became more mobile than ever, both geographically and socially. In this new *Aufwiedersehenskultur*, humanity became addicted to impermanence.

Some people were even inclined, at first, to say good-bye to Shakespeare. In 1913 Ford Madox Ford warned a young writer to "forget about Shakespeare" and all the other obsolete poets; a few years earlier T. E. Hulme had advocated "the complete destruction of all verse more than twenty years old."[153] Pound recommended a moratorium on "study of Shakespeare" for thirty years; to twentieth-century readers Shakespeare's "embroidery of language" was "rank affectation."[154] Eliot branded *Hamlet* "an artistic failure," and Shaw repeatedly poked fun at its author. But none of these threatened good-byes was very serious; they smelled of posturing and paradox.

The paradox was epitomized by Robert Graves in his best-selling 1929 memoir *Good-bye to All That*. Graves was born in 1895, and his earliest recollection was of "looking up with a sort of despondent terror at a cupboard . . . filled to the ceiling with octavo volumes of Shakespeare." His father had organized a Shakespeare reading circle, and Graves later recalled "the lemonade glasses, the cucumber sandwiches, the *petits fours,* the drawing-room knick-knacks, the chrysanthemums in bowls, and the semi-circle of easy chairs around the fire," as his parents and their friends read aloud *The Taming of the Shrew.* The nostalgic contempt with which Graves fondled the details of this domesticated Edwardian gentility characterized the entire autobiography and the generation it spoke for and to. Graves swept up all these remnants of his past—including Shakespeare—in order to clear them out of his mental attic once and for all; he dispatched them to oblivion. But to free himself definitively of the past, he needed to remember everything he wanted to forget. He saluted all that, in the very act of dismissing it. An age of good-byes overlapped with an age of nostalgias. And Shakespeare belonged to that idyllic, preindustrial, premodern, prewar past. In a world where everything was changing, he could be called permanent. So when Graves voluntarily returned to the horrors of the Western Front he took with him "Shakespeare and a Bible, both printed on india-paper."[155] *Good-bye to All That* was dedicated to Laura Riding, with whom Graves wrote "A Study in Original Punctuation and Spelling" in Shakespeare's sonnets—arguing, characteristically, that we could understand Shakespeare anew by making him old again.[156]

So there was no good-bye to Shakespeare; but people still needed to find something new to do with him. Greg's demonstration (1908) that several early Shakespeare quartos had false dates on their title pages and Pollard's division of all the early quartos into "good" and "bad" (1909) initiated a revolution in textual scholarship that soon came to be called the New Bibliography. Granville-Barker, directing *Twelfth Night* in 1912, proclaimed that "A new formula, a new convention, has to be found" for staging Shakespeare; "To invent a new hieroglyphic language of scenery, that, in a phrase, is the problem."[157] In 1919 Gerald Gould published "A New Reading of *Henry V.*," the first of innumerable new readings. In 1931 Caroline Spurgeon announced "a new method of approach to Shakespeare."[158] In 1941 John Crowe Ransom published *The New Criticism*, retrospectively christening a movement begun in the 1920s with Richards, Empson, Leavis, and Knights. "MAKE IT NEW" Pound demanded, and Eliot, the archbishop of New Criticism, celebrated "the new (the really new)."[159]

"The scientist," Pound explained, "does not expect to be acclaimed as a great scientist until he has *discovered* something."[160] Modern science institutionalized and valorized the routine production of novelty (and, therefore, obsolescence). Scientists discovered their novelties partly by conducting experiments. I. A. Richards conducted an experiment on Cambridge undergraduates by asking them to evaluate poems without knowing who wrote them or when they were written; he documented and analyzed the results of that experiment in *Practical Criticism*. Granville-Barker urged actors and directors to begin "experimenting on the living body of the play" in order to "prove" that Shakespeare was a master of stagecraft;[161] the theatre could serve as "something like a laboratory in which theories and deductions could be put to practical test."[162] *The Times* praised "Sir Barry Jackson's experiment in putting *Hamlet* on the stage in the dress of to-day."[163]

If modern interpreters of Shakespeare experimented, then you could be sure that Shakespeare himself had experimented too. Eliot, at least, was sure: "Shakespeare was one of the slowest, if one of the most persistent, of experimenters."[164] According to the scholarship of the eighteenth and nineteenth centuries, Shakespeare had been a play botcher, rehashing other people's plots and dialogue; but from the new theories of text and authorship he emerged as a true "upstart," launching his career with a tetralogy of plays based on the English chronicles, virtually creating the genre of the vernacular history play.

"On or about December, 1910," Virginia Woolf was just saying, "human character changed." Why did it change? Why so many good-byes? *Anna Karenina*, Woolf explains, started it all.

> *That* is the origin of all our discontent. After that of course we had
> to break away. It wasn't Wells, or Galsworthy or any of our medi-

ocre wishy washy realists: it was Tolstoy. How could we go on with sex and realism after that? How could they go on with poetic plays after Shakespeare? It is one brain, after all, literature; and it wants change and relief. . . . Literature is all one brain.[165]

Or, literature is all one body, which periodically changes its mind.

CHAPTER 6

⤬

PRESENT TENSE

EAST BERLIN

April 2, 1986. We take the S-bahn to Friedrichstrasse station. There, under the alert indifference of cameras and armed guards we descend several flights of steps to a scruffy tiled hall, stand in line for forty-five minutes, nervously discussing nothing. Finally, I enter a narrow stall. The door behind me locks as it closes. An officer sits boothed behind glass; as I deliver my passport, I have to decide whether to smile (suspiciously ingratiating?), look him in the eye (provocative?), or avoid his gaze (guilty?). However I organize my face, its signifiers might be misinterpreted. The quiet man in uniform reads my passport and reads me. He collates the face in my photograph with the face I am wearing, his eyes moving from one image to the other, three times, like an editor searching for variants. He gives me back my passport, takes my five deutschmark visa fee, and presses a button that, with an electrocuted squeal, automatically unlocks the exit from this stall. Beyond that door I must buy, at a farcically inflated exchange rate, twenty-five East German marks, which I must spend before returning to West Berlin. I then pass two more sets of guards, who could—but today do not—check my belongings and passport. Finally, as I emerge from *Passkontrolle* into the drizzle of a gray spring, I see, just across the dark river, the lighted marquee of the Berliner Ensemble.

We have come to see Shakespeare's *Troilus und Cressida,* directed by Manfred Wekwerth. The Prologue is spoken by Thersites. Ekkehard Schall's Thersites—a short, round, bald, irreverent veteran, one eye permanently asquint—stands at ease downstage, occasionally lifting one foot and shaking it stiffly, as though he had stepped in something unpleasant or were easing the release of an impeded fart. He pretends to half-forget the play's most famous names, satirizing simultaneously the hoary familiarity of the Troy story and the deteriorating memory of an aging great actor.

This scabrous vaudeville sergeant coexists with an effortlessly moving portrayal of the two young lovers, nowhere more so than in Cressida's alternately stunned and violent shock when Troilus betrays her, the morning after, by acquiescing in her exchange for Antenor. In Corinna Harfouch's performance, Cressida is physically beautiful but emotionally brittle, never predictable, always believable, her body by turns defensively rigid or voluptuously fluid, every movement as naturally disciplined as a dancer's. Her struggle to escape Troilus' grip develops imperceptibly into a brief pas de deux. She removes her ballet shoes (or are they slippers?) when she leaves Troy, led away barefooted and fur-coated, opulent vulnerability personified; by her final corrupting interview with Diomed she is wearing trashy red high heels.

The Berliner Ensemble, as its name testifies, aspires to the theatrical socialism of ensemble acting. Schall and Harfouch share the stage with a vivid red-haired fox of a Ulysses (Hermann Beyer) in animal furs and brown hat; an angular, black-suited, deliberate Pandarus (Arno Wyzniewski); a wiry little Latin Ajax (Alejandro Quintana). During the vicious communal kissing of Cressida by the Greek generals, Ajax sporadically appears at the back of the stage, jogging ridiculously past, warming up for his coming bout with Hector.

These performances and others bloom in a set (designed by Manfred Grund) of great imaginative fertility and flexibility, achieved by the simplest of means. A vast white nylon cloth is by turns lifted, lowered, pulled, twisted—sometimes by the actors, sometimes by black-hooded stage hands—to suggest in turn the sail of a Greek ship, high walls, tents, and private apartments. Helen and Paris are discovered when part of the canvas falls forward, framing them in a room with white back wall and floor, the floor covered with flowers; at the end of that scene the canvas is raised, spilling the flowers onto the stage, which thus becomes Cressida's garden, with a pattern of mottled light now projected onto the canvas, suggesting the moon and clouds. Stagehands twist the lower third of the canvas into a rough pillar, transforming it into a tree, the same pattern of mottled light now metamorphosed into foliage. Later, in Cressida's final interview with Diomed, the canvas suggests both a tent and a stage; Cressida acts out her betrayal of Troilus in front of Troilus, Ulysses, Thersites, and us.

Shakespeare's texts of the play require Troilus to give Cressida a memento, which she later surrenders to Diomed, who wears it into battle to taunt Troilus. Here the memento is a red ribbon; when Cressida and Troilus part she ties back her hair with it. At the end of her scene with Diomed, she ties the ribbon as a garter high on her thigh. That movement is itself shocking; until then she has been scrupulously discreet physically. Diomed takes the garter from her thigh, then abruptly transforms it into a choker, forcing her tethered neck backward into a brutal kiss. In the Epilogue, Pandarus tosses the ribbon, and the long evening glove that Cressida had given Troilus, onto the white canvas of the set, like flowers onto a grave.

This may be one of the finest performances *Troilus and Cressida* has ever been given, but it is also a performance wholly characteristic of the late twentieth century. A story that has always been understood as a misogynist parable of female infidelity is now seen as a misandrist parable of male betrayal and brutality. As if to demonstrate the pervasive influence of feminist thought, only a few blocks away men are being portrayed in an equally unflattering manner in the Deutsches Theater's production of *Sommernachtstraum* (*A Midsummer Night's Dream*). In the first scene Theseus shamelessly handles Hippolyta's taut body, like a man obsessively stroking a recalcitrant cat that has had its claws and teeth pulled and its legs tied. Egeus enters carrying a screaming Hermia over his shoulder, drops her on the floor like a sack of coal, and puts a knife to her throat. Demetrius almost rapes Hermia in the forest; Thisbe, in rehearsal, is a balloon-breasted drag caricature who promptly falls on her back spread-eagle under Pyramus; Bottom, transformed into an ass, is bestially phallic; Theseus' hunting party pursues not a fox or rabbit or deer but Hippolyta herself. Every relationship is brutally sexual, and the women are always victims. The Berliner Ensemble *Troilus* works more subtly, but no less insistently, to portray men as oppressors and women as victims.

This shared emphasis on the exploitation of women belongs to a larger concern with the social and political implications of drama in general and Shakespeare's plays in particular. The most influential work of German Shakespeare scholarship from the first half of the century had been W. H. Clemen's *Shakespeare's Bilder. ihre Entwicklung und ihre Funktionen im dramatischen Werk* (1936), translated and revised as *The Development of Shakespeare's Imagery* (1951); by contrast, the most influential such work from the second half of the century is Robert Weimann's *Shakespeare und die Tradition des Volkstheaters: Soziologie, Dramaturgie, Gestaltung* (1967), translated and revised as *Shakespeare and the Popular Tradition in the Theater: Studies in the Social Dimension of Dramatic Form and Function* (1975). Weimann rejects the "purely formal ... image-symbol-myth" approaches to Shakespeare criticism, epitomized by Clemen, just as he rejects "Romantic character analysis," epitomized by Goethe and Schlegel; instead he insists upon "the function of theater in society" and "the unity and vitality of Shakespeare's work as a social and cultural force."[1] Clemen savored aspects of dramatic form; Weimann savors drama as a form of social behavior. Clemen taught in Munich; Weimann teaches in East Berlin.

Weimann's book is dedicated in part to Manfred Wekwerth, a "friend in the theatre" whom Weimann praises for having "come closest to a modern Shakespeare in the popular tradition." Wekwerth's production of *Troilus* embodies Weimann's criticism. Weimann the Berliner sees the Elizabethan theatre as a place at once united and divided; Shakespeare's stage combines "literature" and "play," realism and convention, convincing illusion and nonrepresentational performance, emotional engagement and intellectual distance. The people on stage move back and forth across an invisible border between *locus,* the imagined locale in which characters enact their fictional individualities, and *platea,* a platform, a place, anyplace, the spot where an entertainment is at this instant being performed by a group of actors before and for a group of spectators. At one moment Thersites/Schall stands on the very lip of the forestage, talking to us moderns; at the next he retreats into the cavernous mouth of the fictional past, talking to the other ancients who populate the Trojan War. But however engrossed he and we become in the story, he can at any moment step "Back to the Future," into our presence.

Behind Weimann and Wekwerth stands Bertolt Brecht, the greatest German playwright and dramatic critic of the twentieth century, who helped found the Berliner Ensemble in 1949. Wekwerth himself, after Brecht's death, directed the first production of Brecht's unfinished adaptation of *Coriolanus;* and Schall, who acts Thersites, is Brecht's son-in-law. Weimann and Wekwerth and Schall are not Brecht clones, and in some two hundred references to Shakespeare Brecht changed his mind and contradicted himself as often as any other great critic. But Brecht insists—and Weimann and Wekwerth agree—upon three simple principles. First, a play results from the interaction of characters and the collaboration of actors; it should not be subordinated to the self-importance of a star performer or a dramatic "hero," any more than society should be subordinated to one individual's will. Second, the audience must remain alert and critical, ready and able to disengage, aware that it is watching a parable; it should not surrender itself completely to illusion, any more than the spectators of a political rally or a television commercial should. The dramatic interest should be divided among several characters; the audience's consciousness should be divided between engagement and distance. Third, enacting a play is—cannot help but be—a social and political act.

The very decision to perform *Troilus und Cressida* at all is a social act. It is only the third Shakespeare play that the Berliner Ensemble has produced in four decades. Why, out of the brimming Shakespeare kettle, bob for this slippery apple? It has never been popular in the theatre or among the general reading public; it seems not to have elicited a single production anywhere between its first performances, in London in the first decade of the seventeenth century, and 1898–99, when a much abbreviated adaptation was revived in Munich and then in Berlin. It did not receive a fully professional production in England for three full centuries after the 1623 publication of Shakespeare's collected plays, and no English production achieved a critical or popular success until the Royal Shakespeare Company's revival of 1960. The first professional English production took place in the disillusioned aftermath of World War I; the first successful English production—on a set covered with sand—took place after the humiliating and tainting English involvement in the Suez crisis and after fifteen years of the cold war. Since the 1960s the play has been regularly performed around the world and is now a favorite among critics.

The Berliner Ensemble's decision to perform *Troilus und Cressida* reflects the play's recent intellectual prestige among an international cultural elite, its reputation as a disillusioned dissection of the causes and conduct of war. These motives might account for a performance anywhere in the world. But Berliners in particular perhaps also relish, for private reasons communally shared, the sardonic tragedy of a historied city under interminable siege; of a wearying, indecisive struggle between two juxtaposed armied camps; of divided families held hostage to emotional blackmail. The play's irreverent pressure-cooker sex also probably appeals to them; returning to my hotel in West Berlin, ignoring the prostitutes, I pass a shopwindow displaying T-shirts imprinted with a composite image of Princess Diana's face smiling atop an amply bare-breasted torso.

But if the decision to perform *Troilus und Cressida* is a social act, so too, just as inevitably, is my decision to begin this chapter with a description of that production. By doing so I set postmodernist Shakesperotics in the context of the political, economic, military, and ideological contest that has shaped the postwar world; I give one problematic, intellectual, unpopular play pride of place; I give theatre pride of place; for the first time in this book, I begin a chapter outside of England. Of course I could introduce this chapter in other ways, but all the alternatives would be equally political. For in organizing this account I must, like any other social being, make uncomfortable choices about the distribution of finite resources; I must decide which points of view will be represented and how their representatives will be chosen. Such decisions must be made in every chapter: each word of this book is an action, and each action forecloses others.

And so I begin by being unforgivably arbitrary. In schematizing previous, less crowded periods I could rely on a preformed consensus about which works of criticism and scholarship turned out to be important and influential; the brutal hierarchy of priorities had already been constructed for me, and I merely inherit it. But in coping with the overpopulated present, the teeming recent past, I have to decide which works to canonize and which to ignore. I need somehow to focus the hurricane of material generated by the last forty years of Shakesperotics. I am doing so by taking a two-dimensional slice out of the hurricane. I am picking, out of the chronological hat, the year 1986.

Kurt Vonnegut in *Galapagos* also picks 1986, which is in his science fantasy the last year of the old human race and the first year of the new. After 1986 Shakespeare survives only as a few quotations in the electronic memory of a laptop computer. A few years later the computer is thrown in the sea, and Shakespeare sinks with it. For Vonnegut 1986, the year of an imagined global catastrophe, marks a stark boundary between one period and another. But for me 1986 is just another year, not especially important, only average. It is, by virtue of its very ordinariness, typical. For postmodernist historians, one year will do as well as any other. And so *Troilus und Cressida* earns its pride of place here, in part, simply because I saw it in 1986. The chapter might just as easily have begun with the Beijing-Shanghai Shakespeare festival of April 1986, which featured twenty-eight different productions;[2] but in April 1986 I was in Germany, not China.

As this example illustrates, I cannot prevent this part of my narrative from becoming autobiographical. These are my times; I am no longer an observer but a participant. There can be, now, no pretense of objectivity or aesthetic distance.

LONDON

May 1, 1986. Howard Davies' production of *Troilus and Cressida* is opening at the Royal Shakespeare Company's Barbican Theatre. Since the completion of its Barbican complex in 1982, the RSC has been headquartered in London, but it does not have a monopoly on the city's Shakespeare market. The National Theatre is also based in London, on a three-theatre site opened in 1976; it, too, regularly performs Shakespeare and in December 1986 mounts a new production of *King Lear*. The British Broadcasting Company, meanwhile, another powerful cultural bureaucracy operating out of London, is still making money off foreign sales of the first televised cycle of all thirty-seven plays in the canon, the fruits of a six-year project begun in 1979. Shakespeare is also being performed in London's commercial West End theatre district; for eight weeks in the summer of 1986 you can see Vanessa Redgrave and Timothy Dalton in *The Taming of the Shrew* or *Antony and Cleopatra* at the Theatre Royal, Haymarket. And there are down-market, open-air

performances in Regents Park. In November 1986 a new international touring group, the English Shakespeare Company, baptizes
itself with *Henry IV* and *Henry V.**

Nevertheless, the RSC dominates Shakespeare production in
London; by its standard other London companies are judged. And
by the theatrical standards of London other cities, in and out of
Britain, are judged. The RSC, unlike its rivals in the capital, oper-
ates nationally and internationally. Though new to London, this
production of *Troilus and Cressida* has already completed an
extended run in Stratford-upon-Avon. The RSC runs two theatres
in London and three in Stratford; it performs for five weeks a year
in Newcastle upon Tyne too; during the 1986–87 fiscal year transferred or touring RSC productions are also showing—to overwhelmingly middle-class, educated audiences—in two West End
theatres, in Manchester, in New York and Los Angeles and Washington, D.C., in Adelaide and Melbourne and Brisbane.[3] In the second
half of the twentieth century the RSC is the most influential and
successful theatrical organization in the Western world.

The current name and structure go back to 1960, with the
appointment of Peter Hall as artistic director. Hall transformed
what had been a summer festival by Londonizing the company. He
leased a West End theatre, thereby enabling the company to trans-
fer productions from provincial Stratford to Europe's largest city;
with two venues the company could now perform Shakespeare year-
round, and in London it could supplement Shakespeare with new
plays and with old plays by other authors. This access to a mixed
repertoire and to a metropolitan audience helped Hall attract and
retain acting talent, and he initiated three-year contracts; at the
same time the expenses of the London operation helped him to
attract and retain government grants. In this way he created a
subsidized, unusually stable theatrical company, explicitly modeled
on the Berliner Ensemble, which had visited London in 1956. Like
Brecht's company, Hall's became a showcase of cultural nationalism.[†] The Berliner Ensemble takes its *Troilus und Cressida* on tour to

---

* The availability of Shakespeare in London has further increased since 1986
with the creation of the Renaissance Theatre Co. and the beginning of Jonathan
Miller's regime at the Old Vic.

† In 1973, Hall became director of the National Theatre, another cultural monument; in 1988, he left it to form his own West End production company. His career
thus epitomizes the shift from youthful socialism in the 1960s to the establishment
privatization of the 1980s.

Edinburgh in 1987, just as the RSC takes *Richard III* to Australia or *Coriolanus* to Paris and Vienna and Berlin. But Britain, unlike East Germany, encourages foreign visitors. Britain and the RSC exploit the new age of mass tourism far more successfully than their rivals in eastern Europe.

This success depends in part upon rapid turnover. In 1986 the RSC performs new productions of six of Shakespeare's plays; between 1960 and 1985 it mounts some 170 major productions. *Troilus and Cressida,* for instance, is revived in 1960, 1968, 1976, 1981, and 1985. Popular plays like *Romeo and Juliet* and *Twelfth Night* recur even more frequently. Historically, the sheer quantity of new productions matters more than individual interpretations of any given play. By contrast, Harley Granville-Barker directed only five Shakespeare productions; David Garrick originated only fourteen. The second half of the twentieth century witnesses a steady acceleration in the rate of Shakespeare production.

This acceleration is not confined to the RSC. In 1953 Tyrone Guthrie founded Canada's equivalent of the RSC, Ontario's Stratford Festival, an internationally recognized company producing a clutch of new Shakespeare productions annually. In 1954 Joseph Papp started the New York Shakespeare Festival; lesser Shakespeare festivals proliferate, particularly in the United States. Moreover, with the rise of rapid international travel and instant international communications a major new production in London, Berlin, New York, or Ontario at once becomes the intellectual property of theatrical professionals and Shakespeare scholars worldwide. Accelerated productivity and magnified exposure build instant obsolescence into every new production. Consumed today, replaced tomorrow.

This boom in transient interpretation affects the academic world as much as it does the theatre. The World Shakespeare Bibliography for 1986 contains 4,069 items, compiled by informants in twenty-nine countries.[4] To arouse any interest in its authors or readers, all of this writing must appear to be doing something new. But the new thing which it does cannot be definitive, or it would preclude the production of more new things next year. The interpretive work published in 1987 can adopt one of only two possible attitudes toward the colossal output of 1986: ignore it or criticize and revise it. Either strategy ensures the transience of previous interpretations.

In this cycle of shared ephemerality academics feed the theatre, and the theatre in turn feeds academics. The 1960 RSC production of *Troilus and Cressida* was codirected by Peter Hall and John Barton, a recent graduate of the Cambridge English Department and a former Fellow of King's College, Cambridge. Barton—having since married the Shakespeare scholar Anne Righter, a Fellow of Trinity College, Cambridge—is still directing for the RSC a quarter of a century later. Some of the RSC's most acclaimed productions—the 1962 *King Lear*, the 1963 *Wars of the Roses*, the 1965 *Hamlet*, the 1970 *Midsummer Night's Dream*—are explicitly indebted to the theories of Jan Kott, formerly Professor of Drama at Warsaw University. John Russell Brown, Shakespearian critic and editor, becomes dramaturge at the National Theatre. On the same line, traveling in the opposite direction, two RSC directors address the 1986 World Shakespeare Congress, which also hears from a German director on "Recent Shakespeare Production in the GDR" and hosts an entire session on changing theatrical interpretations of Shakespeare's characters; a panel of four RSC actors and actresses is featured at the 1986 International Shakespeare Conference. *Shakespeare Quarterly*, the major American journal wholly devoted to matters Shakespearian, apportions about one-fifth of its space to reviews of recent productions; *Shakespeare Survey*, its British counterpart, includes an annual review article on the theatre alongside similar articles assessing current criticism, scholarship, and editing. The academic debutantes of 1986 include a book on *Harley Granville Barker: A Preface to Modern Shakespeare*, a history of *Macbeth in the Swedish Theatre 1838–1986*, one on *"Amletto" in Italia nel Novecento*, a 972-page global guide to "notable postwar revivals" from Adelaide to Zurich, and a new volume—the latest installment of a series—on *Measure for Measure: Text and Performance*.[5] Much scholarly labor is now consigned to recording and interpreting theatrical interpretations. The theatre and the academy multiply and interbreed.

But this explosion in the interpretation population threatens to deplete the raw materials that sustain it. In physics, too, in economics, in the hard and soft sciences generally, knowledge expands at an accelerating velocity; but the physical and social universe still dwarfs the scratchings of the insects exploring its surface. In Shakespeare's case, by contrast, the rising inverted pyramid of interpretation balances precariously upon a single point: a collection of works, written over the course of only twenty-five years, easily contained within the boundaries of one book. Can so small a datum really support so many interpretations, critical and theatrical? For forty years in the second half of the eighteenth century a Stratford entrepreneur sold curios allegedly carved from the wood of a single mulberry tree planted by Shakespeare; the very abundance of the relics eventually cast doubt upon their authenticity. In the second half of the twentieth century interpretations of Shakespeare, all claiming to be genuine, multiply even more rapidly than the fruit of that mythical mulberry, and the sheer productivity of the interpretation industries ought to undermine consumer confidence in their product.

It does not. Instead, the interpretation industries undermine consumer demand for authenticity. The RSC and the parallel institutions of criticism gradually persuade themselves and their customers that an author's original intention is irrelevant. If a production succeeds as theatre, does it matter whether Shakespeare would approve? If a scholarly essay succeeds as criticism, does it matter whether Shakespeare would approve? In 1986 Terence Hawkes, a white British Shakespearian scholar, describes literary criticism in terms of "jazz music, that black American challenge to the Eurocentric idea of the author's, or the composer's, authority":

> For the jazz musician, the 'text' of a melody is a means, not an end. Interpretation in that context is not parasitic but symbiotic in its relationship with its object. Its role is not limited to the service, or the revelation, or the celebration of the author's/composer's art. Quite the reverse: interpretation *constitutes* the art of the jazz musician. The same unservile principle seems to me to be appropriate to the critic's activity. Criticism is the major, in its largest sense it is the *only* native American art . . . criticism makes Americans of us all.[6]

Jazz here derives much of its cultural prestige from its origins in an oppressed class; the metaphor elevates critics to the romantic status of a subject people, at last successfully rebelling against their servitude. Of course, by the time those words are written, interpretation is the master and literature its slave. The metaphor reverses the true distribution of power, so that interpretation can exercise its tyranny with a good conscience, in the name of perpetual insurrection. For jazz is simultaneously the music of the oppressed and the anthem of a superpower; the predominance of jazz—and of criticism—is confirmed by America's economic, military, and therefore cultural dominance. Criticism has a right to its independence, because it has been unjustly oppressed; but criticism also has a right to its independence, because it is irresistibly powerful. The metaphor excuses while it threatens. Moreover, jazz itself has by now been safely marmorealized, neutered and legitimated. A music that prided itself on spontaneity is frozen onto recordings; particular improvisations become "classics"; a canon of collectors' items is defined. In an age of rock music, criticism calls itself jazz and celebrates the routines of institutionalized spontaneity.

Though interpretation may now reject "the Eurocentric idea of the author's ... authority," the Royal Shakespeare Company nevertheless depends upon the cultural authority of its eponymous hero. Both the Berliner Ensemble and the RSC owe their identity and the core of their repertoire to the plays of a single author, but their attitude toward him differs. Brecht was alive when the Berliner Ensemble was founded; after his death in 1956 his wife, the actress Helene Weigel, took control of the company; Wekwerth became artistic director in 1977, having worked with both his predecessors. Shakespeare, by contrast, is safely dead centuries before the RSC moves to London; Peter Hall is a director, an artistic administrator, not a playwright. The Berliner Ensemble is haunted by loyalty to an author, by a widowed yearning for fidelity to the dead; some of its productions of Brecht's own plays become, consequently, museum pieces, like an empty room carefully preserved after the death of its beloved occupant.

The RSC has no such inconvenient loyalties to the past; it feels no guilt about ignoring the author's will. George Bernard Shaw asked that most of his estate be dedicated to the reform of English spelling, and George Orwell asked that no biography of him should ever be written; soon enough, both behests are disregarded. Shakespeare has been dead far longer, and his intentions are in any case less explicit; why should the RSC make a fetish of one dead man's plans? Indeed, why make a fetish of any author's intentions, alive or dead? More than once, the RSC bans living playwrights from its property during rehearsals of their own plays; director Peter Brook searches for a form of theatre that can dispense with authors and texts altogether. Against the authority of authors the RSC sets up the authority of interpreters; against the authorial past it sets up the directorial present.

This distaste for the past can be clearly seen in the RSC's attitude toward efforts to build a working replica of the Globe theatre in London. On June 25, 1986, Southwark County Council agrees to abide by its earlier commitment to lease a large site on the south bank of the Thames to the Globe Trust. By the end of the twentieth century it may again be possible, for the first time since the Restoration, to witness professional performances of Shakespeare's plays on the site and in the kind of building for which they were first written. The impetus to reconstruct such buildings reflects the same conviction that leads the Academy of Ancient Music to perform Mozart on eighteenth-century instruments or reconstructions of them. The art of an age depends upon the artistic technology of that age and is distorted by the application of alien future technologies. A theatre is the instrument on which a play is played, and Shakespeare composed his plays for a certain kind of instrument.

But within months of the Southwark settlement RSC director Adrian Noble rejects such experiments, even before they have been tried: "The answer is not to go back to Globe playhouses. I think that's a nonsense . . . because the world has moved on."7 RSC actors, more than once, express the same patronizing skepticism. The world has indeed moved on. But Shakespeare's plays are as old-fashioned as the instruments he fashioned them for. If, as the RSC insists, we have outgrown the instruments, why haven't we outgrown the plays? If we no longer want the Globe, why should we want *Hamlet*?

Hamlet, we are assured, is still relevant. From 1961, the book *Shakespeare Our Contemporary* influences theatrical interpretation more profoundly than any other critical work of the period. In the 1960s Peter Hall formulates "one simple rule" that governs the practice of the RSC: "that whenever the Company did a play by Shakespeare, they should do it because the play was relevant, because the play made some demand upon our current attention."8 Thus, in 1965 David Warner's Hamlet is a disaffected 1960s teenager, rejecting the corrupt world of his elders, teetering between radical political commitment and total dropout withdrawal. The RSC affirms the pertinent contemporaneity of *Hamlet,* just as the Polish academic Jan Kott affirms that the play "like a sponge . . . immediately absorbs all the problems of our time,"9 just as the East German academic Robert Weimann affirms the "vitality of Shakespeare's work as a social and cultural force in the present world."10 The plays are now celebrated for their social value, for the perspective they offer on contemporary communal problems.

The RSC's annually new repertoire and endless updated revivals define the world as a place that changes with routine rapidity, and defines Shakespeare's plays as a set of texts that can accommodate any such change. The RSC, like other postwar institutions of interpretation, admires Shakespeare precisely because "he can be interpreted in so many different ways." To confine the plays of such an author to a single permanent genuine meaning is not only unnecessary; it is now positively wrong; it is in fact not genuine. Shakespeare is defined as someone who resists definition. He does not communicate any particular meaning; he promises instead an inexhaustible plurality of meaning. He is artistically infallible, because infinitely malleable. Every new interpretation of his work appears to confirm the boundless intellectual hospitality of his genius.

Shakespeare, so defined, gives his interpreters authority, without constraint. The figurehead artistic monarch of the Royal Shakespeare Company legitimates but does not restrict the behavior of his ministers. His text is a blank check.

OXFORD

October 28, 1986. Dr. Stanley Wells performs before an audience in the Sheldonian Theatre, celebrating the publication by Oxford University Press of a new text of Shakespeare's works. The Sheldonian Theatre, an edifice serving both dramatic and academic functions, is an appropriate setting for this performance, for Wells is a theatre historian as well as an editor, both a governor of the Royal Shakespeare Theatre and a Fellow of Balliol College. Like Rowe, but in contrast to the subsequent editorial tradition initiated by Pope, Wells edits Shakespeare in the light of theatrical practice. From 1725 to 1985 editors had labored to peel away what they saw as the debasing influence of the stage, seeking to recover Shakespeare's own literary, pretheatrical text. By contrast Wells declares that "The theatre of Shakespeare's time was his most valuable collaborator"; and his edition "chooses, when possible, to print the more theatrical version of each play."[11]

In its emphasis upon theatrical practicality the new Oxford edition reflects not only Wells' personal interests but also the new interpenetration of theatre and scholarship characteristic of his generation. Not surprisingly, one feature of the edition that Wells emphasizes in this inaugural lecture is "our treatment of stage directions":

> Editorial theorists, preoccupied by the words to be spoken, have almost totally ignored the subject of stage directions, even though

they are central to a presentation of Shakespeare's, or any dramatist's, art . . . What happens on stage during a play is not merely a
kind of optional descant to the dialogue; it is an absolutely integral part of the author's vision.[12]

This intensified scrutiny of stage directions affects every play.
Oxford's Shakespeare calls for French prisoners to be killed onstage
in *Henry V*, clarifies the spectacular staging of Prospero's masque in
The Tempest, attends to the removal of Emilia's corpse in *Othello*,
scrupulously details the arrangements for the morris dance in *The
Two Noble Kinsmen*.

This fresh focus on details of implied stage action extends beyond
the Oxford edition and beyond editing. Alan Dessen identifies the
set of implied stage directions coded into Shakespeare's text whenever it calls for characters to enter "*from dinner*" (napkined, brushing
real or imaginary crumbs from their clothes) or for women to signal
that they are either "*mad*" or have been "*ravished*" (disheveled clothes
and loose hair).[13] Ann Pasternak Slater explains how *Shakespeare the
Director* prescribes the movement of his actors: shaking hands, kissing, embracing, kneeling, weeping.[14] G. K. Hunter analyzes Shakespeare's use of "diagrammatic movement" and stresses that
costuming ubiquitously defines social status.[15] John Doebler shows
that the staging of the wrestling match in *As You Like It* icon-
ographically associates Orlando with Hercules, and Huston Diehl
publishes "an alphabetical compilation of every icon in every
English emblem book" printed in the Renaissance.[16] David Bevington, declaring that *Action Is Eloquence*, describes *Shakespeare's
Language of Gesture*. In the late seventeenth century Rymer had
been appalled by the way any actor playing Othello "rolls his eyes
and gnaws his nether lip as he prepares to kill Desdemona"; for
Bevington these gestures are merely "the kind of stage action that
an Elizabethan audience would recognize as a conventional sign of
furious distress."[17]

A book like Bevington's reflects the new deference toward the
theatre among Shakespearian scholars; but it also belongs to a
larger intellectual climate manifest in events like the Toronto inter-
disciplinary conference on "The Language of Gesture in the
Renaissance."[18] We have become conscious of the way people communicate without words. "Body language" enters the popular lexicon in 1970, riding the title of an international best-seller;[19] it now

authenticates the babble of every talk show host and advice colum-
nist in North America. According to political mythology, Richard
Nixon lost the 1960 presidential election because he looked
unshaven and haggard during a television debate; Margaret
Thatcher, likewise, wins the 1979 general election after the advertising firm of Saatchi and Saatchi gives her voice lessons and a new
hairdo.

Indeed, television itself, the dominant communications medium
of the postwar world, continually subordinates verbal to visual signals. Even within print media, photography becomes increasingly
prominent, first in magazines, then newspapers. The study of film
inexorably infiltrates the curriculum of university literature departments. The 1986 volume of *Shakespeare Survey* devotes itself to
"Shakespeare on Film and Television."[20] And the finest Shakespeare films of our time—Russian director Grigori Kozintsev's
Hamlet and *King Lear,* Japanese director Akira Kurosawa's *Throne of
Blood* (based on *Macbeth*) and *Ran* (based on *King Lear*)—do not
even have English sound tracks.

In such a society, semiotics, the science of signs, naturally triumphs over literary criticism. Criticism analyzes language; but language is—as we now cannot help but realize—just one set of signs.
Semiotics does not confine itself to language but studies any and all
signs—aural, visual, physical. Drama makes use of more semiotic
systems than, say, fiction; Renaissance drama is the site of a particularly complex and influential conjunction of literary and theatrical
codes. Critics now devote whole books to Shakespeare's textual
silences, the points where he made performers convey pivotal
choices without words or by the gestures and inflections that may
accompany ambiguous words.

In its intensified attention to stage directions the new Oxford
Shakespeare is a semiotician's edition, the product of a self-
consciously semiotic culture. The edition does not confine its minis-
trations to the words Shakespeare wrote; it attends, systematically,
characteristically, to all the signals conveyed by spelling, punctuation, stage directions, lineation, typography, act and scene division,
line numbering. In all of these areas it alters received practice. A
new sign, a crippled bracket (⌐), alerts readers to speculative stage
directions; another new sign, a geometrical rose (⬡), stands for an
interval between acts. Even if the Oxford edition had not changed a
single word of dialogue, its changes to so many other signifying

systems would still produce what one reviewer calls "perpetual slight surprise."[21] (That is, of course, exactly the effect achieved by a typical RSC production.)

In its emphasis upon the theatre the 1986 edition reflects the world view of its editors and their peer group. But the editors are only one part of the work force that produces this latest repackaging of Shakespeare's texts. The shape and influence of the first eighteenth-century edition was determined as much by the publisher (Jacob Tonson) as by the editor (Nicholas Rowe); what was true in 1709 remains true in 1986. In fact, by 1986 an individual editor's role has, if anything, diminished. In the eighteenth century editions were identified with the name of a prominent man of letters (Rowe, Pope, Johnson); by the late twentieth, editors' names matter less than a corporate trademark. Most people now buy the Penguin or Bantam or Signet or Swan Shakespeare without knowing anything about their apparently interchangeable editors. Most purchasers of the 1986 edition could not name its general editors; they are simply buying a text published and accredited by Oxford University Press.

OUP, like the RSC, is a large nonprofit corporation based in Britain but operating internationally, with branch offices in seventeen countries. Thanks to its charitable status it pays neither taxes nor dividends; as a department of the University of Oxford it is not vulnerable to hostile corporate takeover. Its favored institutional status makes it, like the RSC, an unusually stable medium of cultural production.

Like the RSC and the Berliner Ensemble, OUP owes much of its success to its authority as the most reputable purveyor of a core product. Until the twentieth century it was sustained by its half of the legal monopoly on printings of the Authorized Version of the English Bible. But religion declines, while literacy rises; sales of the Bible decrease, sales of dictionaries increase, and the *Oxford English Dictionary* becomes the unbeatable flagship of a fleet of profitable dictionaries of every description. This gunboat authority over English usage, when combined with the company's network of international bases, decisively strengthens OUP's share in another major global market, the trade in textbooks for teaching English as a second language. These profitable core products supply the capital that finances an unrivaled variety and quality of academic monographs. In this way OUP becomes, in the second half of the twentieth century, the world's most important academic publisher.

Shakespeare, like God and the English language, is a valuable commercial property on the international culture market. OUP's new Shakespeare is marketed in every available format, in order to reach every conceivable user. Victorian readers could buy the same text either in the expensive Cambridge edition (for specialists) or the cheap Globe edition (for laymen); but in our time the fission of the reading public demands a much greater variety of packaging. Oxford publishes its edition in two versions, one in old spelling, the other in modern spelling. The latter will be followed, within a year, by a boxed three-volume set of comedies, histories, and tragedies, intended primarily for book clubs; then will come a cheap compact text for those with small book shelves and pocketbooks, as well as other editions in a variety of formats and price ranges—including one on computer-readable floppy disk.

The financial stability of OUP and the predictable profitability of its new multibodied Shakespeare edition make possible its investment in research and development. By 1986 the Oxford Shakespeare project is employing four full-time scholars, two full-time production assistants, and half a dozen part-time proofreaders, keyboarders, and copy editors. The project consumes uncounted machine hours on the company's own mainframe computer, and draws on two other mainframes in Oxford and Munich. By comparison with the overheads of contemporary scientific or industrial research, this commitment may seem paltry; but within the insect world of literary scholarship it is colossal. Like the pharmaceutical industry, or IBM, OUP depends upon the security of its international markets to finance development of a new product.

What has long been true of scientists is becoming true of scholars and critics: we are not romantic individualists, harvesting the vineyards of solitude; we depend on hierarchic, subsidized, bureaucratized, corporate, global institutions (publishers, universities, research institutes, grant-giving agencies and foundations). We submit to the power of such institutions because their resources enable kinds of research that would otherwise be impossible.

Thus, as a consequence of OUP's investment, the text of Shakespeare that emerges from Oxford in 1986 is—as even its detractors concede—the most thoroughly researched edition of Shakespeare ever published. As such it naturally invites comparison with the Cambridge edition of 1863–66. But the old Cambridge edition had been an epic achievement of consensus and consolidation; the new

Oxford edition is instead, as Stanley Wells insists, "a work of deconstruction, an attempt to see Shakespeare afresh, to cut through the accretions of the centuries." The edition is, like an RSC production, self-consciously new; it is also, like an RSC production, self-consciously transient. Wells already anticipates the day when his own edition will be "relegated to library basements," having laid down "one thin layer in the coral reef"[22] of editorial history. (The individual dies; the corporation is eternal.)

Alongside this recognition of the transience of scholarship lies a consciousness of the mutability of language itself. "One of the first tasks" Wells sets himself as general editor is "a study of the principles of modernization." He recognizes that the subject may seem trivial, even to an audience of academics. However difficult and important it might be to determine which words Shakespeare wrote, deciding how to spell them is "merely"—as another scholar has offhandedly and dismissively remarked—"a secretarial task."[23] And indeed, although editions of Shakespeare have been modernizing his spelling for almost four centuries, the task has until now largely been left to an underclass of compositors, copy editors, secretaries, the functionaries of standardized discourse. An almost universal practice "has been attended by surprisingly little discussion" of how it should be done.

Suddenly, however, spelling has become the subject of surprisingly much discussion. In 1974 the Riverside Shakespeare, the most widely respected American edition, conspicuously departs from past practice by preserving "a selection of Elizabethan spelling forms that reflect, or may reflect, a distinctive contemporary pronunciation";[24] this policy leads to the retention of such forms as "Dolphin" (Dauphin), "fadom" (fathom), "vild" (vile), and hundreds of comparable orthographic antiques. In 1978, at a Canadian conference on editing, Randall McLeod precipitates an intellectual crisis by objecting to the way old-spelling editions standardize or modernize typographical details of the original documents; in Renaissance English, he argues, typography often determines orthography.[25] In 1984 A. L. Rowse, a Fellow of All Souls College, Oxford, issues the first volumes of "The Contemporary Shakespeare," a series that promises to "translate" not only archaic spellings but also all obsolete and archaic words and aberrant grammatical forms.

Oxford's 1986 edition does not accept any of these models. In the first place, Oxford publishes a critical old-spelling text of the complete works alongside its modern-spelling rendition of the same "text," a juxtaposition that reveals how thoroughly modernization transforms the text. This is not simply a matter of the metamorphosis of individual meanings; it shapes the entire experience of reading. Moving from seventeenth to twentieth century spellings of Shakespeare's sonnets, Thomas M. Greene senses the degree to which modernizing systematically conceals "the different status of the word itself in a prelexicographical culture," shielding readers from "the problematic contingencies of the original," stripping away "the seclusion and the particularity of its unique inflection."[26]

Oxford's old-spelling edition radically historicizes, in a typically postmodernist way, Shakespeare's texts; but by also publishing a modern-spelling version Oxford emphasizes, in an equally postmodernist way, the irreducible arbitrariness of text. And to many readers Oxford's modern-spelling version looks, in many of its details, as unfamiliar as its old-spelling fraternal twin. Wells, like his contemporaries, makes modernizing an urgent editorial issue. He also, like his contemporaries, abandons past practice, and his new principles transform the spelling of hundreds of words: "Ancient" Pistol becomes "Ensign" Pistol, the Forest of "Arden" becomes the Forest of "Ardenne."

Rowse professes to "translate" Shakespeare's English into contemporary equivalents, and the problems of modernizing resemble those of translation. Translating, like modernizing, is now increasingly subjected to scholarly attention. In 1974 Toshikazu Oyama founds a new journal wholly devoted to Shakespeare Translation worldwide.[27] There are, for instance, some twenty different Polish verse translations of Hamlet, representing most periods and styles of two centuries of Polish literature; Szekspirze does not, for Polish readers or playgoers, belong to any fixed sedimentary layer of the language. When East Berlin's Deutsches Theater retrieves a clumsy 1775 translation of A Midsummer Night's Dream, it does so in order to alienate audiences and strip the play of its traditional lyricism. None of six East German productions of Twelfth Night in 1985–86 use the classic Schlegel-Tieck translation of the play, dating from the early nineteenth century; all prefer contemporary versions.[28] A new version is no less or more authoritative than the old; both, after all, are just translations. Consequently, for foreigners Shakespeare can always speak in the present tense.

Native speakers of English are not so lucky. For them Shakespeare, even in a modern-spelling edition, remains half-fixed in a
language four hundred years old, like a fly wriggling to free itself
from a drop of drying paint. The fact that " 'tis" has now become
archaic in English, while "it's" has become commonplace, does not
affect Boris Pasternak, trying to render Shakespeare into modern
Russian; but it inevitably affects every modern English reader. The
commentary to any English-language edition of Shakespeare
awards a disproportionate share of its attention to obsolete words,
not because they were especially significant or conspicuous to the
original author or audience, but simply because a modern reader
needs to be told what they mean. Elizabethan English is retrospectively divided into two classes: those words which readers still
understand correctly, and those which they understand not at all or
in the wrong sense. The Elizabethans themselves would not have
recognized this distinction. We cannot avoid it.

A modern editor, therefore, must constantly engage in one form
of translation or another. Either the word is left incomprehensibly
intact in the text and translated in the commentary; or the text itself
is translated, either by modernizing its spelling or by substituting
some other word. The Riverside policy reminds readers of the
strangeness of Shakespeare's English by throwing nuggets of exotic
orthography in their way; the Oxford policy assures readers of the
familiarity of Shakespeare's English by removing the anachronistic
obstacles of an alien orthography whenever possible. The difference between these policies reproduces, in miniature, the difference
between old-spelling and modern-spelling editions, which has tor-
mented Shakespeare's editors since the beginning of the twentieth
century. Both strategies attempt, impossibly, to recover for a modern reader the experience of readers four centuries ago.

About a block from the Sheldonian Theatre lies the Oxford
college where Terry Eagleton teaches. Wells is a Fellow of Balliol and
general editor of a series published by Oxford University Press;
Eagleton is a Fellow of Wadham and general editor of a series
published by another Oxford publisher, Basil Blackwell. As a general editor each controls one of the key networks of academic
patronage in our time, and each uses his power in conspicuously
subversive ways.

Like Wells, Eagleton publishes, in 1986, a widely read and
reviewed interpretation of Shakespeare. Like the Oxford edition,

Eagleton's *William Shakespeare* is "an attempt to see Shakespeare afresh, to cut through the accretions of the centuries." This violent rebellion against tradition can be seen clearly enough in Eagleton's response to *Macbeth:*

> To any unprejudiced reader—which would seem to exclude Shakespeare himself, his contemporary audiences and almost all literary critics—it is surely clear that positive value in *Macbeth* lies with the three witches. The witches are the heroines of the piece, however little the play itself recognizes the fact, and however much the critics may have set out to defame them.[29]

Eagleton dismisses the *Macbeth* seen by Shakespeare's critics, Shakespeare's contemporaries, Shakespeare himself. He sets in its place *Macbeth* as it would be understood by a certain brand of modern intellectual encountering it for the first time. Imagine you are an alien archaeologist, and you have just dug up *Macbeth*. What do you make of it?

Eagleton knows that this attitude will seem perverse to many readers. He anticipates, savors, and mocks our outrage. He taunts us with one aggressively facetious paradox after another. "Though conclusive evidence is hard to come by, it is difficult to read Shakespeare without feeling that he was almost certainly familiar with the writings of Hegel, Marx, Nietzsche, Freud, Wittgenstein and Derrida."[30] That cautious modifying clause—"conclusive" evidence for an impossible proposition is indeed "hard to come by"—caricatures the language and the practice of traditional scholarship. Bullfighter Terry toys with the lumbering stupidity of the Shakespeare establishment; in the stands we are supposed to laugh and gasp at every adroit flick of his nonchalant wrist.

Eagleton belongs to the lower-middle-class generation that, thanks to the socialist victory in the 1945 election, stormed the barricades of British higher education and tiptoed into Oxford and Cambridge *en masse*. The defensive insecurity this situation produced in those students can be seen in Eagleton's first book, *Shakespeare and Society* (1967), 208 careful pages on seven plays, written by "Terence Eagleton." Now, two decades later, on top, himself the most name-dropped of Oxford critics, Eagleton can dispense with all that hateful decorous deference. Reverting to the colloquial "Terry," he takes on all of *William Shakespeare* in a mere 108 small pages and twenty-three footnotes. His subject is still, like Weimann's, "Shakespeare and Society"; his interpretations have not changed all that much; he is still, despite his fame, defensively insecure; but he now writes in a cocky, anarchic, ironic tone. His book has the moral fierceness and the parodic joy of all good satire.

Like all good satire, it hits more than one target. Aimed partly at academic scholarship, partly at contemporary capitalist society, Eagleton's *William Shakespeare* also, like Dryden's *MacFlecknoe,* guys its titular hero. In Eagleton's mock epic, as in Dryden's, the very brevity of the work falls indecorously short of the narrative magnitude that the genre demands and the subject deserves; Eagleton compares his book to a game "in which contestants are given twenty seconds to summarize the plot" of Proust's *A la recherche du temps perdu.* We expect Shakespeare to be the hero of *William Shakespeare;* instead, three witches are the heroines. Eagleton praises what Shakespeare dispraised; in celebrating the witches of *Macbeth* he criticizes the author of *Macbeth.* And why does Eagleton find the witches so admirable? "Exiles" from "a society based on routine oppression and incessant warfare," they "live in community, not as individual entrepreneurs of the self"; "poets, prophetesses and devotees of female cult, radical separatists who scorn male power," the witches "figure as the 'unconscious' of the drama, that which must be exiled and repressed as dangerous." They "strike at the stable social, sexual and linguistic forms which the society of the play needs in order to survive."[31] Eagleton's witches are the champions of feminism, socialism, the unconscious, the ambiguous, the repressed. We *ought* to like them. Eagleton wants us to feel guilty for not cheering them on.

Stanley Wells does not personally delight in paradoxical effrontery, and no one could mistake him for a Marxist. But the differences between Wells and Eagleton as individuals matter less than the institutional and historical situation they share. Oxford's *William Shakespeare: The Complete Works,* no less than Eagleton's *William Shakespeare,* repeatedly shocks its readers, and knows that it will. Like the naked red breasts of Gertrude in Peter Zadek's 1977 Bochum production of *Hamlet,* OUP's 1986 edition confronts the Shakespeare-loving public with a full-frontal challenge to its sense of propriety. It declares that Thomas Middleton wrote a third of *Timon of Athens* and that *Measure for Measure* was posthumously adapted; it changes the title of *Henry VIII* back to *All Is True,* the name of Falstaff back to Oldcastle, Imogen back to Innogen; it includes poems never before printed in any edition of Shakespeare's works; it offers not one but two versions of *King Lear*, each different from the text readers and critics and audiences have appreciated since the eighteenth century. You don't have to know or accept the scholarly reasons for such decisions, but you can't help noticing the consistency and scale of Oxford's affront to textual orthodoxy.

Like Eagleton, the Oxford editors belong to an age that permits—even encourages—shockingly deviant behavior. Eagleton can get away with saying outrageous things because his outrages are legitimated by Oxford University. So too with the Oxford Shakespeare. Like IBM and the Berliner Ensemble and the RSC, OUP can afford to experiment, because its risky innovations are subsidized by its safe market leaders. The Oxford editors, too, can afford to experiment, because they know that the global power and prestige of OUP will be mobilized in support of their experiments. Their shocking edition is empowered by and, in turn, empowers the multinational business interests of Oxford University Press, just as Eagleton's Marxist monograph is underwritten by and underwrites the capitalist family firm of Basil Blackwell Ltd.

CHICAGO

May 1986. At the University of Chicago, Professor Allan Bloom is finishing *The Closing of the American Mind,* a conservative lament that will become an unexpected national best-seller. In its closing pages he explains that "much of the philosophic instinct in America . . . is now veering off toward certain branches of literature and literary criticism." This might seem a promising development. Unfortunately, as philosophy has been hijacked by literary criticism, so literary criticism itself is now held hostage by a gang of foreign thugs:

> Comparative literature has now fallen largely into the hands of a group of professors who are influenced by the post-Sartrean generation of Parisian Heideggerians, in particular Derrida, Foucault and Barthes. The school is called Deconstructionism, and it is the last, predictable, stage in the suppression of reason

and the denial of the possibility of truth in the name of philosophy. The interpreter's creative activity is more important than the text; there is no text, only interpretation.

Bloom condemns and resists the "endless debates about methods—among Freudian criticism, Marxist criticism, New Criticism, Structuralism and Deconstructionism, and many others," all of which read literature as mere raw material for "some contemporary theory—cultural, historical, economic or psychological."[32]
But of course Bloom, the scourge of academic interpreters, is (like me) an academic interpreter, treating literature as raw material for his own contemporary theory. He has written a book on *Shakespeare's Politics* ("Shakespeare is no democrat").[33] Weimann writes *Studies in the Social Dimension* of Shakespeare's theatre; Eagleton studies *Shakespeare and Society;* Bloom is Professor in the Committee on Social Thought. Though he may not approve of Eagleton's or Weimann's Marxism, he too believes that "Shakespeare was an eminently political author."[34]
Critical contras like Bloom are not hallucinating the revolution they deplore; it has occurred. Contemporary critics and students are indeed asking, in Bloom's words, "After all, what do Shakespeare and Milton have to do with solving our problems? Particularly when one looks into them and finds that they are the repositories of the elitist, sexist, nationalist prejudice we are trying to overcome."* Accordingly, teachers no longer say, "You must learn to see the world as Homer or Shakespeare did." Critics disparage the "effort to read books as their writers intended them to be read."[35] Instead, a large body of contemporary literary theory and critical practice contends that the responses of readers matter more than the intentions of authors. And those responses are determined in part by the mechanics of human sensory perception. Even Bloom would concede that we must see marks on paper in order to interpret them properly. But scientists and psychologists also discover that we must interpret the marks on the paper in order to see them properly. The aesthetic implications of these laboratory studies of

---

* Such attitudes have become so common that they now appear in avowedly popular works, like Arthur C. Clarke's 1986 best-seller, *The Songs of Distant Earth.* Clarke's novel—an orthodox example of the most important new genre of the second half of the twentieth century, science fiction—simply assumes that future generations will find Shakespeare's works a repository of intolerable prejudice and superstition.

visual perception naturally impinge upon art historians like E. H.
Gombrich and Rudolf Arnheim before they disturb literary critics.
But the disturbance inevitably spreads. In an influential essay on
Henry V, for instance, Norman Rabkin draws his key concept—that
the play is constructed so that readers can and must interpret it
alternately as either "a rabbit" or "a duck," either a condemnation
or a celebration of war—directly from Gombrich.[36] A reader confronting a poem on paper does not differ materially from a spectator confronting a drawing on paper. In either case, perception
depends upon interpretation.

Reader-response criticism accordingly tries to define exactly
what happens when a reader encounters a text. Every act of reading
is an act of imaginative collaboration. On this side you have a set of
signifiers; on that side you have an individual reader; literature
results from their interaction. But every reader will interact differently with any particular set of signifiers; and since literature cannot occur without the reader, since the reader is an essential
ingredient, the work itself has no fixed meaning. There are as many
meanings as there are readers. Stephen Orgel describes Shakespeare's plays as "collaborative fantasies."[37]

This kind of criticism depends upon certain demonstrable constants of human perception, but it also depends upon certain
assumptions about the production and consumption of literature.
In particular, it presumes a set of social practices that have become
dominant in our culture only since the invention of the printing
press. Reader-response criticism presupposes that literature is characterized by anonymity, absence, isolation, and silence. Anonymity,
because authors have no control over the process by which their
work is distributed; once a book is printed it can be sold by anyone
to anyone, and the author does not know who bought it, and the
reader does not really know who wrote it. Absence, because the
author is not physically present when the product is "consumed" by
the person who has acquired it. Isolation, because the printed book
is a portable product that individuals buy and then carry away with
them to consume in private. Silence, because the absence of the
author, the isolation of the reader, makes speech superfluous; a
reader does not need to vocalize the text in order to consume it.

It is hardly surprising that a critical method based upon such
premises has become so fashionable. It reflects and indeed applauds
the dominant anonymity, absence, and isolation of contemporary

experience. We can shop without leaving home, watching a television shopping channel and then, using our credit cards, phoning in an order delivered by mail. Politics and religion no longer depend upon long speeches at mass gatherings but on television, which brings prepackaged fragments of absent politicians and evangelists, popes and presidents, into isolated and anonymous homes. Portable radios and cassette players with earphones cocoon any pedestrian within an individual musical shell. Almost half the American homes with television sets also have videocassette recorders, which enable each isolated viewer to interact personally with a film, pausing or fast-forwarding or rewinding. William Montgomery, one of the editors of Oxford's new Shakespeare edition, also collaborates on an interactive computer game keyed to the text of *Macbeth*. According to reader-response criticism, *Macbeth* is a computer game with so many variables that it can satisfy the operators of an infinite number of individual terminals indefinitely.

Of course, our society differs in certain obvious material respects from Shakespeare's. Though the printing press was invented a century before Shakespeare's birth, most of his work was not designed for printed distribution. The theatre—and particularly Shakespeare's theatre—does not accept the assumptions of reader-response criticism. It instead presupposes presence, recognition, community, and sound.

In the theatre, authors are present—always potentially present, usually actively and practically present—when their plays are first performed; the author is there, and so is the audience, in one place at one time. Shakespeare was there, at the first performances of *As You Like It;* the actors, too, were physically present. Even today, audiences are drawn to the theatre by the promised presence in the flesh of famous performers. Shakespeare's original audiences were equally susceptible to the corporeal actuality of actors like Burbage and Alleyn, Tarleton and Armin and Field. If the author also acts, he may present himself in both capacities: Shakespeare playing Hamlet's ghost, Molière playing Tartuffe.

In the theatre authors can recognize how other people respond to their work and can modify it accordingly. Moreover, individual spectators recognize that their own responses are shared by other spectators. Precisely for that reason, the political authorities of Shakespeare's England, like other authoritarian regimes, feared drama and tried to control it. The potential political power of the theatre depends upon its capacity to "bring people together" both literally and imaginatively; it depends upon the compounding of presence with recognition. The official censor demanded changes in *1 Henry IV* and *King Lear*, not because he expected each individual to interpret the text differently but because he feared that three thousand spectators would respond collectively to Shakespeare's dangerous irreverence and would thereby recognize their own subversive cohesion. The Essex conspirators paid for a revival of *Richard II* because they expected it to remind its audience of the possibility—even desirability—of collective rebellion. The theatre can enable isolated dispersed individuals to recognize that they form part of a cohesive, and therefore powerful, present group consensus. Groups are less inhibited than individuals. The consciousness of belonging to a crowd tempts and enables an individual to do things that, left alone, s/he would resist—something any censor understands.

This awareness of community occurs to some extent even in modern auditoriums; an experienced Shakespearian actor informs me that "a good house," a sensitive and responsive audience, actually "breathes together."[38] But a typical contemporary auditorium, like the RSC's new Barbican, is artificially darkened, its stage artificially lighted; our attention is focused on "them," the actors, not on "us," the spectators. This enforced distinction itself decreases our sense of a shared physical and mental space. The individual seats in which we sit, the darkness, the silence, the restriction of physical movement, the armchair partitions that carefully separate us in tiny cubes of purchased private space—all these conventions of modern theatregoing do not destroy but do diminish our sense of belonging to a group. They mimic, insofar as possible, the experience of sitting at home alone watching television. New studio theatres like The Other Place and The Pit, in which many of the most acclaimed recent productions have been mounted, push Shakespeare even closer to electronic conventions, giving actors and audiences who have been raised on television whole plays in close-up. Moreover, the audience at an RSC performance of *Troilus and Cressida* or any other Shakespeare play has no predetermined social cohesion. It consists of people from all over Great Britain, combined with a significant proportion of foreign tourists from North America, the European Community, and Japan. Shakespeare is the only thing they have in common, and Shakespeare is not enough to unite them.

By contrast, in a Renaissance theatre you could not escape the sense of communal response, of a common sensing. The physical crowding of three thousand people into a small arena—many of them standing on the undemarcated floor of the pit, the rest huddled together in galleries stacked precipitously one on top of another—ensured that they all remained conscious of one another. Shakespeare and Jonson complained about the smell. The audience was as visible and present to itself as the actors onstage; indeed, there were spectators on the stage itself. The audience may have included a few tourists and provincials, but Londoners wholly dominated it. Shakespeare's theatre was not an international or even a national institution; it belonged to one city, in some senses to one neighborhood. It exploited jingoistic and parochial sentiment. Jacobean city comedy was played in London for Londoners by Londoners about Londoners. Likewise, the Jacobean court masque depended upon the visible presence of the monarch and on the participants' recognition that they formed an elite community.

Drama is conveyed aurally by music and speech, and audiences respond to it aurally by applause or hissing, by the static of restless boredom or the rapt silence of engrossed attention. For a modern audience silence is the polite norm, broken only by polite applause. For a modern reader, even more strongly, silent reading is the norm; the experience of literature is ocular. But for an actor or Renaissance audience, a text is oracular, and silence is just one extreme of a meaningful continuum of sound. Sound—heard similarly and simultaneously by everyone present—helps to bind us into a group. The temporary community of Shakespeare's audience, in Shakespeare's presence, hears the sound of Shakespeare's words and interprets them collectively. Their perception, like all perception, still depends upon interpretation; but that interpretation is not only recognizably corporate but also holistically corporeal; each of us is a body among bodies, reacting viscerally.

Allan Bloom does not say any of this. He fumes at the results of reader-response criticism but does not criticize its premises, because he shares them. Like his adversaries, Bloom defines interpretation in terms of reading, individual meditation, isolated intellectual activity; and like his adversaries, he addresses and admires an educated elite. The academic appropriation of Shakespeare begun by the Victorians is now virtually complete. Consequently, any account of postmodernist Shakesperotics must take account of the economics, politics, and social rituals of academic life.

Bloom cares little about the interpretive community of Shakespeare's theatre; but, characteristically of our time, he cares passionately about the interpretive community of university professors. The University of Chicago interests him more than Shakespeare. He wants to show, in the words of his subtitle, *How Higher Education Has Failed Democracy and Impoverished the Souls of Today's Students.* He attributes that failure to the current demand that a university education have some "relevance" to contemporary life. He offers as an alternative Plato and, through Plato, Socrates; he yearns for an Athenian Academy, for an oral community of philosophers that can close itself off from the democratic chaos of the society around it, just as the safe and wealthy University of Chicago enclaves itself from the surrounding slums, just as the safe and wealthy colleges of Oxford literally wall themselves off from what has become a depressed manufacturing town.

Like Eagleton's *William Shakespeare,* Bloom's *Closing of the American Mind* sucks much of its energy from satire of the author's own profession. Both books belong to the era of the academic novel. The heroine of Malcolm Bradbury's *Eating People is Wrong,* a postgraduate student in the Department of English at a provincial British university, is "writing a thesis on fish imagery in Shakespeare's tragedies."[39] Just as Pope mocks the characters of the *Dunciad* with the incongruous grandeur of allusions to the *Aeneid,* so Malcolm Bradbury and David Lodge mock their graduate students and professors of English, satirically juxtaposing the incompetent gossippy clutter of academic life with the resplendent literature it purports to serve. For Lodge's characters, Jane Austen or Shakespeare or Hazlitt is simply "a ticket to ride":

> All over the world, in hotels, university residences and conference centres, in chateaux and villas and country houses, in capital cities and resort towns, beside lakes, among mountains, on the shores of seas cold and warm, people of every colour and nation are gathered together to discuss the novels of Thomas Hardy, or the problem plays of Shakespeare . . .[40]

There are too many of these people, the satirist implies, and they are having too much fun. The narrator here seems to yearn, like Bloom, for "The old teachers who loved Shakespeare or Austen or Donne, and whose only reward for teaching was the perpetuation of their taste"; but those selfless innocents of yore "have all but disappeared."[41] Instead, criticism has been cosmopolitanized, with disastrous consequences. Bloom interprets *Othello* as the tragedy of "Cosmopolitan Man," a dangerous fool who believes that he can be "liberated from the influence of and need for the laws and ways of a particular nation." Mixed marriages are a mistake, and "Shakespeare appears to tell us that it is not good to introduce influences that are too foreign."[42] But Shakespeare's modern critics have ignored this warning.

Lodge's novel reaches its comic climax at the "mega-conference" of the Modern Language Association of America. A few months before Bloom finishes his *Closing of the American Mind* some ten thousand literary academics from all over the world gather in Chicago for their annual migratory winter festival. Among the 661 separate sessions, they discuss "Gender and Sexuality in Shakespeare" and "The Elizabethan Theater-State" and "The Canonization of Shakespeare" and "Iconography and Iconoclasm in Shakespearean Drama"—and more. But the topics change every year; the conference abides. The convention embodies the dominant, shaping institutional context of postmodernist Shakesperotics.

This enormous conference, like all its lesser siblings in the family of literary criticism—like all its distant, more powerful, wealthier, scientific cousins—gives the contemporary intellectual what the Elizabethan theatre gave its audiences: presence, recognition, community, and sound. On a platform at the front of the room speakers perform their rehearsed speeches; spectators, in the same even light, sit, stand, walk in, walk out, talk among themselves, make faces, applaud, ask questions. Scholars normally communicate through print; here they make contact orally and aurally. Much of the excitement is generated by sheer presence—so many academic "stars" present in this one place, presenting new papers, defining the present of literary criticism. Out of this turbulent confluence of presences comes the personal recognition of new ideas and old friends, the communal recognition of achievement.

But if a community can give you a sense of belonging, it can also make you feel like an outcast. The greater the mass of an object, the greater its inertial momentum; the greater its inertia, the more opposing force will be needed to alter its velocity or direction. More people teach and study literature than ever; more people teach and study Shakespeare than any other author; more people read English than any other language; for centuries, more criticism has been written about Shakespeare than about any other writer of English. As a result, Shakespeare has now accumulated more inertial mass than any other object in our literary universe. Accordingly, responses to Shakespeare in this period are inevitably affected by the sheer mass of his reputation. The laws of inertia account both for the entrenched conservatism represented by Bloom and for the opposing shock tactics represented by Eagleton. Bloom senses that the whole vast mass has, since the 1960s, begun moving in a direction he doesn't like; Eagleton senses that the whole vast mass has been moving for centuries in a direction he doesn't like. Bloom wants to get it back on track; Eagleton wants to derail it. Both sides feel like outcasts in the only community they know.

The arbiter of victory in such circumstances is not Shakespeare or Shakespeare's text but the academic community. The text is the site of a struggle; the community is audience, judge, and umpire.

STRATFORD-UPON-AVON

August 21, 1986. Stephen Booth of the University of California at Berkeley is addressing an audience of scholars at the Twenty-second International Shakespeare Conference. The conference is hosted by the Shakespeare Institute, founded in 1951 by Allardyce Nicoll. Thanks to Nicoll, who also founded the conference, Stratford becomes, for the first time, a seedbed of Shakespeare scholarship during the very years that the Royal Shakespeare Company is rising to international prominence.

Booth is explaining that he likes *Julius Caesar;* he would like himself more if he liked *Julius Caesar* less. It is not a friendly play: "There is no significant character in *Julius Caesar* on whom we are not invited to exercise our contempt." And while we are feeling contempt for the characters, the author is feeling contempt for us, the audience. Booth demonstrates that "we—an audience contemptuous of the forgetfulness and inconsistency in the characters put before us by the play—are as indifferent to intellectual constancy as the contemptible, audience-like mob." The success of Shakespeare's play depends upon the forgetful malleability of an audience; Shakespeare knows that he can manipulate us as easily as Antony manipulates the plebeians. "*Julius Caesar* seems to me to be its author's cynical experiment with the limits of his power to make puppets of theater audiences." Booth strongly suspects that "Shakespeare felt malicious pleasure in making us victims of a practical joke so mean that it denies its victims the ultimate dignity of knowing they have been victimized and thus knowing that their attacker considers them *worth* dignifying." Shakespeare constructs a play "that would make its audiences make fools of themselves and compound their folly by blindness to it."[43] Booth's *Julius Caesar* is not a nice play; Booth's Shakespeare is not a nice guy.

"William Shakespeare, Businessman" is not a nice guy either. He is described by E. A. J. Honigmann of the University of Newcastle upon Tyne, formerly a Fellow of the Institute, who now sits in the audience listening to Stephen Booth. A century earlier Honigmann's German grandfather published an article in *Shakespeare Jahrbuch;* and Honigmann's emphasis on Shakespeare's financial acumen looks at first glance like a reversion to Victorian values. Honigmann's Shakespeare becomes, like his Victorian counterpart, "a very rich man";[44] but Honigmann expects that his audience will now find Shakespeare's wealth "shameful," embarrassing, suspect. This Shakespeare, moreover, is no self-made man; as eldest son in a social system founded on primogeniture, he inherits and develops a diversified family business. Honigmann refuses to assert that "Shakespeare is Shylock" but makes the suggestion even as he retracts it; for this Shakespeare is a moneylender. William, like his father, like Shylock, charges interest on his loans. This Shakespeare may be called "gentle" only because he is a certified member of the gentry; as a businessman he drives a hard bargain even when dealing with his neighbors; as a theatrical professional he "spoke scathingly to his fellow-actors when he felt he had to." This Shakespeare is not necessarily made a shareholder of the Globe in recognition of his artistic talent; he may have bought his way in, like any other venture capitalist with sufficient liquidity. This Shakespeare does not intentionally retire to Stratford because he wishes to end his life in Victorian serenity. As head of the family business he simply has to spend more time in Stratford after 1608, when his mother dies. With both parents dead, he can no longer rely on others to manage his "very extensive business interests in Stratford" routinely and efficiently. This Shakespeare's final statement, the summa of his life, is not *The Tempest,* written in 1611, but his will, written five years later, shortly before his death, full of complicated and cunning financial provisions.

Honigmann, like Eagleton, enjoys shocking his audience. So does the dramatist Edward Bond, who achieves early fame for a play that features the stoning to death of a baby in its pram. Bond's play *Bingo*, performed by the RSC in 1976 here at Stratford, offers a portrait of Shakespeare no more flattering than Booth's or Honigmann's. Bond's Shakespeare is "closer to Goneril than Lear," a "reactionary blimp" or, more charitably, "senile."[45] Subtitled "Scenes of Money and Death," Bond's play begins after all Shakespeare's plays have already been written. Shakespeare has stopped writing, not because he has achieved personal serenity but because he realizes that his art has done nothing to change the world. In Stratford he makes a deal with the unscrupulous local businessman William Combe; he lends his support to the enclosure movement, which dispossesses poor tenants and aggrandizes wealthy landowners. At the end he asks himself, despairingly, "Was anything done?" and commits suicide. His daughter, finding him dead, starts looking for his will.

Bond's British play takes place entirely in Stratford after Shakespeare's theatrical career has ended; Leon Rooke's Canadian novel takes place entirely in Stratford before Shakespeare's theatrical career has begun. The novel watches the most famous of poets from the perspective of *Shakespeare's Dog*. Rooke makes the dog the more admirable character. More humane than his master, he saves a poor old woman accused of witchcraft from being murdered by a mob; he saves dispossessed and despised vagrants from starvation; he saves Shakespeare himself from drowning in the Avon. Young Snakespit, meanwhile, shuttered in his upstairs room, "scratching dandruff from his empty head," scribbles inanities: "Love this and Flower that and other such juvenile twaddle." The dog wants "hot revolution"; young Shakespizzle is "strict in his conformity" and hates equality. The "cocky versifier" "could see men hanged for stealing a biscuit and smile at this prettily"; for "Better a thousand vagabonds perish for bread than one strand of our Queen's hair be ruffled." "Word-blower!" his wife yells, utterly exasperated: "Thou shitted stool!"[46]

Shakespeare irritates Rooke and Bond. They focus that irritation by concentrating on the underside of his career, his half-life in Stratford. The fiery disk of literary glory in London blinds any observer who looks at it directly; the shadow world of Stratford can be visualized more easily. Honigmann also emphasizes Stratford for similar reasons. His Shakespeare has one set of businesses running in London, another rather different network headquartered in his hometown. In this he resembles the Royal Shakespeare Company. But, for the RSC, Stratford and London simply represent two branch stores that sell pretty much the same product. In Shakespeare's lifetime, by contrast, Stratford and London constitute different worlds, three days apart by horseback. Shakespeare somehow contrives to belong to both communities, metropolis and market town, international port and provincial home, center and periphery. The most respected biography of Shakespeare in the second half of the twentieth century, S. Schoenbaum's *Documentary Life,* begins by declaring that "The story of William Shakespeare's life is a tale of two towns," Stratford and London.[47] He begins and ends his life in Stratford; his family stays behind there during the twenty or more years he makes a name for himself in London; he returns home at least once a year, probably during the summer. Honigmann insists that "William Shakespeare, Businessman," most visible in the Stratford community, coexists with "William Shakespeare, Poet," most visible in the London community. The two personalities belong to one person.

A related dichotomy empowers one of the most popular and potent concepts of postwar criticism. Honigmann's paper is delivered the same year that *Northrop Frye on Shakespeare* is published. The book's title, in which the dead British playwright and the living Canadian critic share equal billing, says something about Frye's own eminence and more about the contemporary balance of power between author and interpreter. Frye rocketed to prominence in 1957 on *The Anatomy of Criticism,* a systematic description of the literary universe in terms of recurring mythical cycles and phases. Even in that book, which purports to map the whole of literary history, Frye cited Shakespeare more often than any other author, and thereafter Shakespeare became one of the primary objects of his criticism.

Frye describes Shakespeare's plays in terms of a recurring symbolic journey from city to country and back. *A Midsummer Night's Dream,* for instance, contrasts "the two worlds of the action"; the characters leave the sophisticated court world of Athens and venture into an older, superstitious "wood-world" inhabited by "creatures of legend and folk tale and mythology and abandoned belief." At the end, they return to the court, but by then they have been transformed by their journey into and through a less urban, more natural, "green world." This pattern cannot be attributed to Shakespeare's sources, since he constructed the plot out of his own imagination. The same transforming transport in and out of the natural world organizes the action of plays as diverse as *As You Like It* and *King Lear, The Two Gentlemen of Verona* and *Cymbeline.*

Frye frowns on biographical speculation; he does not relate Athens to London or the "wood-world" to Stratford. But his narrative scheme does have explicit psychological concomitants. He contrasts "the waking world of Theseus' court," the world of law and artifice, with a natural dreamworld of "sexual license" that "has affinities with what we call the unconscious or subconscious part of the mind." This Freudian topography creates, for the resolution of the play's plot, the same problem that Shakespeare's dual residence creates for the resolution of his biography: how, at the end, to dissolve the dichotomy by incorporating both places in a single transcendent whole? Honigmann and Frye, in their different ways, both define Shakespeare as the function of a contrast and contest between two sites.

Frye describes the "green world" as a place of "dissolving identities,"[48] and one of the identities it helps dissolve is Shakespeare's own. This process of fragmentation can be seen even more clearly in another book published in 1986, C. L. Barber's posthumous *The Whole Journey: Shakespeare's Power of Development.* Barber, like Frye, is most famous for an original and influential piece of anthropological criticism published in the late 1950s; Barber compared *Shakespeare's Festive Comedy* (1959) to Elizabethan holiday entertainments. The plays mold their audience into a community partly by mimicking contemporary communal celebrations like May Day, Twelfth Night, and Midsummer Night. Such festivals are strictly confined in time and space; at holiday's end characters and auditors alike must return to the workaday world. London-Stratford, Athens-wood, workday-holiday: Shakespeare emerges from the tension between copresent polarities.

The Whole Journey takes this postulate the whole distance. In *The Comedy of Errors,* for instance,

> the young dramatist has split himself into a stay-at-home twin, married, and carrying on in a commercial world (as Shakespeare might have, had he followed his father in "uprightness of dealing" as a successful merchant in Stratford), and into a wandering,

searching twin for whom the world of Ephesus, including the situation of marriage, is strange.49

Antipholus of Ephesus-Syracuse, Shakespeare of Stratford-London: the one fertile egg divides into two personalities, each defined geographically. But the London-Stratford fault line is only one of many. Shakespeare's success as a playwright depends upon his capacity for exploiting the divisions within his own riven psyche. Thus, in *Hamlet* Shakespeare "splits" his father-figure into a wholly lovable dead Ghost and a wholly hateable live Claudius. Barber quotes approvingly a contemporary critic who observes that such splitting is "a basic Shakespearean strategy" for managing psychic conflict.50 He quotes approvingly another contemporary critic who notices that Shakespeare's very profession rested on an unstable polarity: "a professional playwright in a mainly commercial theatre, writing for, and even in a sense creating, a national public, but depending first and last on aristocratic favour".51 Does Shakespeare speak to, identify with, the aristocracy or the bourgeoisie?

Such tensions create the explosive imaginative energy so admired by Shakespearians; but they also produce, sometimes, disquieting side effects. Like Booth, Barber recognizes that irony, the technique fundamental to so much of Shakespeare's art, is psychologically "a form of aggression." Richard III is "Shakespeare's first great exploitation of theatrical aggression."52 Shakespeare, like his audience, condemns and applauds Richard; like his audience, he hates what he loves. Shakespeare is and is not Richard.

At the same time, Richard is and is not Richard. The critical disarticulation of Shakespeare's own psyche runs in tandem with a drive to disarticulate his characters. In an essay dedicated to Barber, Randall McLeod urges editors to "dehomogenize and denormalize" the standardization of the names of Shakespeare's characters, traditional since the eighteenth century. The stage directions and speech prefixes of the earliest texts of *Richard II,* for instance, sometimes label the protagonist "Richard," sometimes "King"; these "episodic discontinuities" reflect the "mythillogical word of Elizabethan English" and provide shifting perspectives on the character, the play, and its author.53

Modernist critics had said good-bye to character analysis and biographical narrative; postmodernist critics say hello again to both—an aggressive, knowing hello. Although narrative has returned, it now brings with it the recognition that "character" (authorial and fictional) is itself shaped by the conventions of narrative, by the logic of a logos. Every personality is a narrative performance, shaped in part by its audience and the structure of its theatrical frame. Character has returned, but now it is multiple, contradictory, overlapping, ad hoc, an inevitably rickety construct built by a quarreling committee for questionable motives from unstable materials.

Barber's own book enacts the dissolution of identity that it describes and prescribes. As the mosaic of citations from other critics suggests, Barber often speaks through the voices of others. Within the profession he is widely and affectionately remembered for his stimulating encouragement of younger scholars; late in life he remarks half-jokingly that his "young friends" are writing his books for him.[54] Barber dies before finishing the book on which he labored for two decades; he entrusts its completion to Richard P. Wheeler, a former student, now an accomplished critic in his own right, who soon discovers that Barber's papers can be "brought to fruition" only if Wheeler himself becomes, effectively, as Barber had wished, coauthor. Throughout the text the authorial pronoun wavers uncertainly between "I" and "we." The author of *The Whole Journey*, like its subject, has no center, no single secure self. An author, like an atom, has no identity beyond the interaction of particles and energies.

Shakespeare's plays, like *The Whole Journey*, result from a process of imaginative collaboration. Sometimes Shakespeare collaborates with himselves, sometimes with other people. The difference between these two situations begins to seem less material than it once did. Traditional literary scholars (American Cyrus Hoy, Australian David Lake, New Zealander MacDonald P. Jackson, Englishman R. V. Holdsworth) and a new breed of literary mathematicians (Toronto statistician B. Brainerd, Belfast computer scientist M. W. A. Smith) demonstrate that the man from Stratford did collaborate with other playwrights on at least half a dozen plays.[55] All these studies depend upon semiotic surveys of a whole community of practicing playwrights. For instance, the investigator breaks the second person pronoun into two signs, "you" and "ye." (By the early seventeenth century they had come to share the same meaning but not the same shape.) The investigator then traces the recurrence of "ye" and "you" throughout a large body of texts, written by many different authors during the first decades of the seventeenth century. It becomes apparent that some texts prefer one body, and some the other. By accumulating data on the distribution of a sufficient number of these arbitrary binary pairs, the investigator gradually builds up a statistical profile of several separate identities within the community of texts. These statistical profiles strongly correspond to a range of historical evidence linking certain biological entities (now dead) with certain texts (still present). The age of quantum mechanics undermines the old classical causalities of authorship. An author is just a statistical probability.

These calculations of minutiae slowly overcome the inertia of the Shakespeare establishment. The RSC's new Stratford theatre, the Swan, opens in April 1986 with the company's first revival of *The Two Noble Kinsmen,* by Shakespeare and Fletcher. In the same year, that play appears for the first time in a single-volume British edition of the complete works. In twenty years the play has inched itself firmly into the accepted canon. The three pages of *Sir Thomas More* are there too, Shakespearian piecework. The new Oxford edition goes further than any of its predecessors in publicly acknowledging the presence of other authors in "Shakespeare's" plays: Fletcher, Middleton, Wilkins, Nashe, perhaps others as yet unnamed.

Even when no second playwright intrudes, Shakespeare's texts are shaped by other collaborators. Shakespeare is a company man. For most of his creative life he works with and for a single theatrical organization, the Chamberlain's Men, later called the King's Men. His plays are produced not by one man but by a group, acting together, interacting. The text is not fixed when the ink dries on the final page; it evolves under the pressure of comments from readers, rehearsal by actors, performance before audiences. Drama, as an art form, cannot be produced by a single individual; like the building of a medieval cathedral, it requires a community. This community produces a "socialized text"[56] compounded of contributions from many sources. The playwright's contribution may dominate, but it can no longer be disentangled from all the others.

Something similar happens to Shakespeare's poems. Shakespeare, after all, did not print them himself. In the Renaissance, printers almost always took responsibility for the spelling, punctuation, and layout of texts. In the second half of the twentieth century a generation of textual scholars—epitomized and often taught by

Fredson Bowers, editor for forty years of *Studies in Bibliography*—demonstrates the pervasive contribution of Elizabethan and Jacobean printers to the particulars of the books they made. Shakespeare's two narrative poems, *Venus and Adonis* and *Lucrece*, are printed by Richard Field; like Shakespeare, Field is a Stratford native come to London; the printed poems result from a material collaboration between two displaced Stratfordites. Shakespeare's plays, too, can be published only by passing through the minds and hands of workmen in a printing house. Charlton Hinman discovers that the compositor responsible for setting most of the First Folio may have been named "John Shakespeare."[57] Like William, John came from Warwickshire and worked in London. In the First Folio William's handiwork often cannot be disentangled from John's. Shakespeare's text is a communal construct.

WEST BERLIN

April 1–6, 1986. The International Shakespeare Congress meets every five years. Many of this year's participants fly to Berlin directly from the fourteenth annual Shakespeare Association of America conference, held this year in Montreal in March. Many of them meet again, in August, at Stratford.

The program of the 1986 congress announces that its 640 registered participants will concern themselves with "Images of Shakespeare." This declared theme, a typical bureaucratic compromise, has been designed to include any and everything. "Images" here has so many meanings that it has no meaning; or, rather, its meaning resides wholly in the permissive plurality of its final letter. No one image of Shakespeare takes precedence.

These Shakespeares and Shakespearians come from all over Europe and North America. India, Japan, China, New Zealand, Australia, Africa, and the Middle East, though not so heavily represented, have also sent accredited emissaries. And the diversity is temporal as well as geographical. Literary criticism has been institutionalized; it has been given tenure; its average life expectancy has increased. A bright young critic, publishing her first articles in her twenties, may still be writing about the same subject half a century later. The same year that witnesses the publication of Eagleton's

William Shakespeare also brings forth a posthumous new collection of *Essays on Shakespeare* by William Empson and a new essay on Shakespeare's comedies by M. C. Bradbrook.⁵⁸ The characters of Chapter 5 threaten to impinge on Chapter 6.

For Shakespearians at the Berlin conference, the past is present, the absent is present. Old interpreters, interpreters from faraway places, old interpretations, interpretations from faraway places— "Images of Shakespeare" can accommodate anything. Participants hear about "Undercurrents in Victorian Illustrations of Shakespeare" and about "*King Lear* in Czechoslovak Folklore"; they are shown "Changing Images of Romeo and Juliet, Renaissance to Modern"; they ponder how "Shakespeare's Plays," approached with "an Indian Sensibility," may yield "A Possible Sense of Community." All of space and time is sucked into the black hole of the here and now.

But not every Shakespeare critic on the planet can be fitted onto the program of a four-day conference. Many call, but few are chosen. A very few are invited to deliver hour-long plenary papers; some are allowed to speak to a smaller audience for twenty minutes; more participate in seminars, where their papers are not publicly presented at all but simply circulate in advance to some dozen people, who then meet in a classroom to discuss the issues raised. Even among the elect, speech is rationed, hierarchically.

Feminists begin to be heard in the 1970s. In 1975 Juliet Dusinberre publishes *Shakespeare and the Nature of Women;* in 1976 Carolyn Ruth Swift Lenz organizes the first special session on feminist criticism of Shakespeare at the MLA convention. This leads to the publication in 1980 of *The Woman's Part,* an influential collection of eighteen essays edited by Lenz, Gayle Greene, and Carol Thomas Neely. The collaborative nature of that collection, and of the special session, prefigures the unusually communal tone of this critical coalition. ("Feminism is a corporate venture; mutual support is essential to its survival.")⁵⁹ No single voice, no single point of view, dominates. In 1983 Lisa Jardine publishes *Still Harping on Daughters: Women and Drama in the Age of Shakespeare;* in 1985 Neely publishes *Broken Nuptials in Shakespeare's Plays;* in 1986 Jardine and Neely, British and American, cochair a seminar on "Images of Gender and Power in Shakespeare and Renaissance Culture." Between 1976 and 1986, between the MLA special session and the Berlin seminar, feminists are among the most productive and visible exponents of a new wave of Shakespearian criticism.

Their cultural legitimacy is recognized, within months of the Berlin conference, by Oxford University Press. Its new "concise introduction" to *Shakespeare,* in the popular paperback "Past Masters" series, is written by Germaine Greer, best known for her polemical manifestos *The Female Eunuch* (1970) and *Sex and Destiny* (1984). Before those best-sellers liberated her from academic drudgery, Greer had been a lecturer in English literature at Warwick University; she wrote her Ph.D. dissertation at Cambridge University on Shakespeare's early comedies.[60] Now, with the blessing of Oxford University Press, she assures her readers that Shakespeare "rejected the stereotype of the passive, sexless, unresponsive female and its inevitable concomitant, the misogynist conviction that all women were whores at heart."[61]

As Greer's curriculum vitae illustrates, the feminist demand for a voice within the academic community cannot be disentangled from their demand for a voice within society at large. The feminist Shakespearians gathered at Berlin live in an epoch that has seen mass distribution of effective contraceptives; the legalization of abortion; a steady rise in the number of working women; the passage of legislation banning sexual discrimination and sexual harassment; increased sensitivity to sexual violence, pornography, and discriminatory language; and a marked shift in the balance of power within heterosexual relationships, in and out of marriage. These social changes affect Shakespearian critics whether or not they consider themselves feminists.

Allan Bloom condemns feminism as "the latest enemy of the vitality of classic texts"; he assumes that "*all* literature up to today is sexist" and therefore unpalatable to liberated tastes.[62] He also assumes that if you've seen one feminist, you've seen them all. But not all feminists dismiss all "classic texts"; indeed, many of them applaud Shakespeare (not always for the same reasons). Greer finds in his plays an ideal of "egalitarian marriage," an appreciation of female "steadfastness," a recognition of mutual physical sexuality. Dusinberre admires Shakespeare's effort "to dissolve artificial distinctions between the sexes."[63] *The Woman's Part* sets out "to see and celebrate his works afresh." Coppélia Kahn argues that Shakespeare "was critically aware of the masculine fantasies and fears that shaped his world, and of how they falsified both men and women"; he questioned the "cultural definitions of sexual identity" that modern feminists like herself also question.[64] This attitude toward

Shakespeare goes back to the earliest feminists of all. In 1792, in *A Vindication of the Rights of Women*, Mary Wollstonecraft expresses a good many "Animadversions" on the portrayal of women by contemporary writers; but she does not, there or elsewhere, criticize Shakespeare, although she alludes to him frequently. Those allusions demonstrate, in passing, the width of her learning and hence contribute to her argument that women are the intellectual equals of men. Two centuries later some feminists are still trying to appropriate Shakespeare's cultural authority. So interpreted, Shakespeare endorses contemporary feminism, and contemporary feminism endorses Shakespeare.

By admiring Shakespeare, feminists redefine him, as admiration always redefines its object. In particular, they construct a new hierarchy of critical value. They champion characters—Gertrude and Goneril, Cressida and Cleopatra—that other readers have tended to rebuke. They insist on the structural and thematic importance of characters, like the three mothers in *Richard III,* that other readers have tended to minimize. They disparage as spurious, destructive, macho, fragile, the values of characters—from Mercutio to Prospero, Hamlet to Troilus, Othello to Coriolanus—that other readers have tended to admire. They celebrate *Romeo and Juliet* and *Antony and Cleopatra,* plays with dual protagonists, which the critical tradition personified by A. C. Bradley has tended to exclude from the private club of real greatness.

More radically, they challenge the class system of genre. Most critics from Aristotle on put tragedy on top; as the tragic hero towers over other mortals, so tragedy itself towers over other genres. Many feminists reverse this traditional position and put comedy on top. They find in Shakespeare an equation of gender and genre, formulated in the title of Linda Bamber's book *Comic Women, Tragic Men.* Plays in which women watch over the action—women like Portia and Rosalind—achieve comedy and community, laughter and life; plays dominated by men—men like Hamlet and Claudius, Iago and Othello—disintegrate into tragedy, death, desolation. Such feminists tell us that Shakespeare tells us that, if men would just let them, strong women will organize a happy ending. Moreover, in Shakespeare's own development comedy takes precedence chronologically and structurally. In *The Comic Matrix of Shakespeare's Tragedies* Susan Snyder reminds readers that Shakespeare created most of his great comedies and comic characters before the run of great tragedies initiated by *Julius Caesar;* she then demonstrates that the tragedies depend upon structural formulas taken over from comedy. Comedy is the matrix, the nurturing mother of tragedy.

Moreover, tragedy itself is defined by its attitude to gender. For Madelon Sprengnether "Shakespeare's tragedies demonstrate, with terrible consistency, the ways in which love kills." Sprengnether, like many other feminists, unites psychoanalysis and literary criticism. She sees Shakespeare's tragic heroes torn between heterosexual and homoerotic impulses:

> The heroes of *Romeo and Juliet, Othello,* and *Antony and Cleopatra* retreat from their initial gestures towards heterosexual union to a world of masculine loyalties embodied in a companion who disdains or avoids the love of women and who bases his identity on his definition of himself as a fighter.

Coriolanus, the last of the tragedies, focuses this conflict about gender and identity into "a deep fantasy of maternal destructiveness."[65]

And after the tragedies Shakespeare returns again to the mother, to comedy, to Stratford, to the late romances. In David Lodge's mythical MLA convention, the novel's central, elusive female critic contends that tragedies "move inexorably to what we call, and by no accident, a 'climax'—and it is, in terms of the sexual metaphor, an essentially *male* climax—a single explosive discharge of accumulated tension." Against this exhausted male genre she sets Romance, the art of "multiple orgasm," of the inexhaustible "vagina" that "comes and comes and comes again."[66] But the vagina, "The Woman's Part," is an organ of birth as well as sex, and Shakespeare's romances celebrate birth and rebirth. *The Woman's Part* is dedicated to C. L. Barber "for his nurturing, demanding support of us, of other women, and of feminist criticism," and for Barber *The Whole Journey* of Shakespeare's development culminates in "a recovery of deep relation to the maternal presence,"[67] a recovery dramatized in the family romance of the late romances.

In their exaltation of the romances Barber and some other feminists may seem to echo Victorian critics like Dowden. But there is nothing Victorian about contemporary feminism. The old-fashioned protagonist of Lodge's novel is embarrassed by "the stream of filth" that laces the critical vocabulary of his beloved feminist. He would be more embarrassed by Erica Jong's *Serenissima.*[68] In

Jong's first-person fantasy, a glamorous American professional woman, finding herself in an exotic European city, travels back in time and becomes one of those admired females of Shakespearian comedy (Jessica, from *The Merchant of Venice*). Like *Shakespeare's Dog*, she saves Shakespeare's life. Like the dog, she describes Shakespeare having sex with other characters, male and female. Unlike the dog, she has sex with Shakespeare herself. The novel could be subtitled "Erica Jong fucks William Shakespeare." Jong and her generation refuse to be ashamed of explicit female sexuality.

With a slight change in the angle of vision, that explicitness easily becomes pornography. The rise of feminism in the late twentieth century takes place in a society saturated with pornographic magazines, books, advertisements, films, videos, and live performances. For some feminists Shakespeare's women are, as surely as those in *Playboy* and *Deep Throat*, the objects of male masturbation. Iago, for instance, asks Othello what it would take to convince Othello of his wife's infidelity.

> Would you, the supervisor, grossly gape on?
> Behold her topp'd?

Kathleen E. McLuskie in a paper for the Berlin seminar observes that "Iago's imagery of sexual transgression . . . has all the appeal of the 'dreams' of pornographic fantasy." This fantasy is not limited to Iago. In the final scene of the play, Othello strangles Desdemona in bed:

> As an emblem on stage, glossed by Othello's language, Desdemona provides a focus for the combination of violence and reverence that informs pornography. Nineteenth-century theatrical tradition, recognizing the sexual import of this scene, hid the strangling behind the bed curtains. More recent productions from Maggie Smith in the 1960s to the 1985 production at the [Royal Shakespeare Theatre] openly offer up the figure of Desdemona to the audience's view, placing her center stage on the structure that is part bed, part altar. The place of Othello's fantasy is shared with the audience.[69]

McLuskie's Shakespeare, like Booth's, like Honigmann's, like Bond's, is not a nice guy.

For McLuskie, Shakespeare remains "The patriarchal bard."[70] He can be understood only as a product and producer of a social

system dominated by men: a phallocentric cockocracy, a phallogo-
centric cocktalkocracy. Feminists like McLuskie insist on the importance and recurrence of what Peter Erickson calls *Patriarchal
Structures in Shakespeare's Drama.* Sometimes the patriarchy is tyrannical, sometimes benevolent; but, according to Erickson, it is always
there. Even in *As You Like It,* where Rosalind speaks more than
any other character, Shakespeare "participates in male wish-
fulfillment."[71] Likewise, Linda Woodbridge concludes that "Shakespeare's transvestite heroines reveal his essential conservatism about
sex roles."[72]

Patriarchy is literally a social system ruled by fathers. The new
feminist attention to the sociological and psychological structures of
patriarchy calls attention to the relationship between fathers and
daughters in Shakespeare's plays, a love-and-death struggle in
which daughters regularly must choose between "domination and
defiance."[73] At the same time, critics become increasingly sensitive
to the problems posed for patriarchal theory by the reign of Elizabeth I; to the articulation of patriarchalism as "a viable political
theory" by Shakespeare's contemporaries (including King James);
to the Jacobean "anxiety about the sexuality of the young" evident
in plays like *All's Well that Ends Well* and *Measure for Measure,* "in
which the father-ruler seeks to control the sexuality of his subject-
children."[74]

A patriarchal bard can be understood only if we understand
patriarchy; studies of Shakespeare's works take on the methods and
vocabulary of anthropology. Literary and social criticism interpenetrate. Indeed, any feminist reading of Shakespeare, positive or
negative, repeatedly moves back and forth between text and society—our society, or Shakespeare's, or both. That oscillating juxtaposition of fiction and fact, that superposition of the image of one
culture on the image of another, throws into relief the differences
between them. Feminism privileges difference. The feminist novelist Marilyn French constructs a Berlin Wall of values, separating
positive "feminine" "Gender Principles" from negative "masculine"
ones, calling it *Shakespeare's Division of Experience* (1981). French's
book is a forced march; other feminists lead exploratory expedi-
tions. But they all converge on the same terrain. They all focus upon
differences between the representation of men and the representation of women.

The scholarly identity of these feminists depends upon difference; the analysis of sexual difference differentiates them from

other Shakespearians; it gives them something new and significant to say and a right to be heard. Just as they must reorganize the hierarchy of social relationships and the hierarchy of the literary canon, so they must reorganize the hierarchy of academic value. The analysis of gender must be accepted as a critical activity as important as any other scholarly subdiscipline—perhaps more important. The power of feminists within the community of Shakespearian scholars depends upon the power of gender as an analytical tool. The study of gender cannot be disentangled from the study, and the exercise, of power.

WASHINGTON, D.C.

October 10, 1986. Not everyone plays the international conference circuit. Peter W. M. Blayney, for instance, sits in the Old Reading Room of the Folger Shakespeare Library, examining books. The outstanding Shakespearian bibliographer of his generation, Blayney would be welcomed at as many conferences as he wanted to attend; but he does not attend. Indeed, he even publishes rarely.

This principled isolation does not, however, preserve him from the internationalism of contemporary Shakesperotics. Blayney himself is an Englishman who did his graduate work at Trinity College, Cambridge, before moving to an academic appointment at the University of Chicago and then to the Folger, where he is subsidised by the National Endowment for the Humanities. His current reputation is founded upon *The Texts of "King Lear" and their Origins*, which required his personal examination of texts in thirty-one libraries in England and Scotland, and another thirteen in the United States.[75]

Blayney visits so many libraries searching for difference, for variants between different copies of the same book. Proofs of a modern book are read and corrected before printing begins; every copy of this book should be identical; an error or revision in one should be repeated in all. But Renaissance printers continued to proofread a text while the individual sheets were being machined; if they found errors, they stopped the press, made corrections, and then resumed printing. They might stop and start in this way more than once. As a result, some copies of each page were corrected, and some were not;

the proportion varies, depending on when the correction was made. When it came time to sew the sheets together into a book, the printer did not throw away the uncorrected copies or even put all the corrected pages together in one set of copies and all the uncorrected pages together in another set; instead, he left their distribution to chance. Each copy of the book may contain a different combination, and you can be sure that you have caught every variant only if you examine every copy of the book. (Since most copies are now lost, complete confidence can never be achieved.)

Since the late eighteenth century individual editors of Shakespeare have occasionally noticed variants between two copies of the same edition, but until the middle of this century no one attempted to catalog all the variants in all the surviving copies of one edition. Such a project could not be attempted until the publication of library catalogs, the improving technology of photography, and the increasing ease of international travel made it possible. In 1940 W. W. Greg published a monograph listing and discussing all such variants in the first edition of *King Lear*. Thereafter many bibliographers contribute to an international collective effort to identify and record the variants in widely scattered copies of the early editions of Shakespeare and other Renaissance dramatists. In order to study *The Printing and Proof-Reading of the First Folio of Shakespeare* Charlton Hinman examines "some fifty-odd copies of the Folio throughout" (and parts of another twenty-five), mostly in the Folger;[76] on the basis of this study he prepares *The Norton Facsimile*, which brings together photographs of pages in many different copies. Michael Warren's more comprehensive facsimile edition of *The Complete King Lear* reproduces pages from individual exemplars at Yale, Harvard, Oxford, London, the New York Public Library, the Folger Library, and the Huntington Library.

This collective scholarly achievement fundamentally alters our definition of the text of a work. In the Renaissance no individual copy contains the whole of a book. The whole is, instead, distributed communally among a group of physical objects that were once related but are now widely scattered. The text, like the author, is plural. Composite facsimiles like Hinman's and Warren's construct the textual equivalent of a conference.

Moreover, Hinman's study of the First Folio demonstrates that the thirty-six plays in that volume were not printed separately, one after the other. Instead, compositors were often simultaneously setting pages from different plays; work on one play was interrupted while one or more others were being finished; *Troilus and Cressida*, two-thirds of the way through the book, was set into type last. In these circumstances it no longer makes sense to edit any of the plays in the First Folio individually. Solutions to the problems in one play depend upon evidence scattered throughout the volume. In the second half of the twentieth century the identification of individual compositors working on the Folio absorbs more bibliographical effort than any other single problem in Shakespearian editing. By 1986 the Oxford editors postulate eight different workmen. In the same year Canadian Paul Werstine publishes a comprehensive study of verse and prose lineation in the Folio; he demonstrates that different kinds of mislineation are strongly associated with different compositors and that decisions about the lineation of a single speech must take into account patterns visible only across hundreds of pages of text.[77]

Nevertheless, though the Folio contains many texts, it is still only one book, a book of obvious enough importance to any editor of Shakespeare. By contrast, the daily operations of Cambridge University Press in the late seventeenth century involve many books, none with any obvious relevance to Shakespeare. But those operations happen to be more extensively documented in surviving records than any other early English printer's. New Zealander D. F. McKenzie, studying those records, discovers that books are not printed one at a time, one after the other; instead, early printers often work concurrently on several titles.[78] Separate publications of one printer, like separate plays within the Folio, are not separate at all. McKenzie defines bibliography as "the study of the sociology of texts."[79]

Blayney epitomizes the new era of contextual bibliography, initiated by Hinman and McKenzie. He does not visit all those libraries simply in order to look at copies of the first edition of *King Lear*. He also looks at copies of every other surviving book produced by the same printer in the years before and after. He examines the proofreading, the type, the paper, of as many of these books as possible. The printing of *King Lear* cannot be understood as an isolated event; it belongs to a continuum of operations in a particular business, the Jacobean printshop of Nicholas Okes. In Okes' production schedule for December 1607 and January 1608 William Shakespeare's play *The History of King Lear* is flanked by *The Cobler of*

Canterburie (an anonymous jestbook) and John Pelling's *A Sermon of the Providence of God*. Bibliographically, these books belong to a single community. And Okes' books belong to an even larger society of texts. Blayney is now investigating "The London Print Trade, 1590–1610," meticulously examining every known surviving copy of every book printed in London during the two decades that spanned most of Shakespeare's London career.

While Blayney peruses typefaces upstairs, downstairs Stephen Greenblatt is inaugurating the Folger's new Center for Shakespeare Studies. A block from the U.S. Capitol, catty-cornered from the Supreme Court, the Folger is visited by about one thousand scholars a year, for periods ranging from days to months; in the 1985–86 fiscal year 12 percent are foreigners, from fifteen different countries. In the same year the Folger hosts thirteen seminars and workshops, twelve public lectures, and a large number of colloquia. Most of these are organized by the Folger Institute, cosponsored by the library and twenty-two universities.[80] Although the Folger serves scholars of all kinds, specialists on Shakespeare retain pride of place, accounting for a full quarter of the library's users. The Folger also edits and publishes *Shakespeare Quarterly,* founded in 1950; it publishes Folger Books, which in 1986 issues four new titles devoted to Shakespeare and his contemporaries; it houses a small mock-Elizabethan stage, which it leases to an independent repertory company, the Shakespeare Theatre at the Folger; and now, thanks to an initial grant of $232,000 from the Educational Division of the National Endowment for the Humanities, it has its own Center for Shakespeare Studies. The Folger has become a kind of permanent Shakespeare conference, the site of a continuous international interdisciplinary information-exchange.

Today's special is Stephen Greenblatt, Professor of English at the University of California at Berkeley, cofounder of the avant-garde journal *Representations,* general editor of a series of volumes devoted to "Cultural Poetics," founder and godfather of the critical movement called new historicism.[81] He recounts and analyzes a 1552 sermon by Hugh Latimer, Dudley Carleton's description of an abortive execution in 1603, William Strachey's narrative of a troubled colonial expedition to Virginia in 1610, and H. M. Stanley's recollections of a perilous encounter with Moa tribesmen in central Africa in May 1877. He also talks about *The Tempest.* In fact, only *The Tempest* brings together the diverse materials of his paper, as it brings together the diverse individuals in his audience. But *The Tempest* occupies only a fraction of his text.

Greenblatt's originality and success are rooted in his narrative technique. His title, his opening anecdote, create a mystery: how does all this relate to Shakespeare? As in any good mystery story, we are both curious and complacent; no solution is evident, but one will surely materialize—or, rather, many will materialize. Greenblatt does not aim at that single interpretive climax, epitomized by tragedy or scientific discovery; he does not offer us, at the end, a formula, any critical $E = mc^2$ that incorporates and subsumes and so devalues the foregoing narrative. His narrative is, like romance, full of incident, a kind of prolonged and inventive intellectual foreplay, simultaneously creating and releasing tension. And he sees the same techniques in the "theatrical technology" of Renaissance England. Shakespeare's plays arouse us in order to relieve us, stimulate anxiety in order to direct and dissipate it.

Part of the interest of Greenblatt's narrative arises from its novelty. Until now, no one has related Shakespeare's play to Latimer's sermon or Carleton's account or Stanley's memoirs. Since 1808 critics have realized that *The Tempest* is indebted to Strachey's description of the Virginia expedition; but Greenblatt avoids the passages of direct and obvious verbal indebtedness, so often discussed by others. He talks, instead, about the passages in between the passages that other critics quote—everything represented by the ". . ." that those critics place between the passages they reproduce. He analyzes Strachey's account as an interesting narrative in its own right, a narrative that interested Shakespeare. "I assume," he says, "that Shakespeare read the whole thing," and so he reads the whole thing. No one has ever related *those parts* of Strachey's narrative to Shakespeare's play before. Shakespeare is familiar, but all of the other characters in Greenblatt's narrative—Latimer, Carleton, Stanley, even Strachey—surprise us.

Greenblatt needs these novel characters because Shakespeare himself can no longer hold our attention. Laboratory studies of the psychology of perception demonstrate that we simply stop seeing an object if it remains in our visual field for a long time without changing or moving. Basically, we notice only difference; in a homogeneous and static universe we would be senseless. Criticism must therefore find a way of making us see Shakespeare's plays in a new way, from a different angle, if we are to see them, effectively, at all.

We have made love to *The Tempest* so many times that the act of textual intercourse itself has begun to bore us. Greenblatt offers us a new way of doing it. And his way of doing it resembles the narrative technique of the plays themselves. Shakespeare's double plots, his insistence on weaving together two or more stories, irritated neoclassical criticism; New Criticism found in that narrative multiplicity a thematic unity, a single intellectual thread tying together disparate materials. Greenblatt takes the multiple plot not only as a subject but also as a narrative model for his own criticism. Like Tom Stoppard (whose play *Travesties* brings together Lenin, James Joyce, and the dadaist Tristan Tzara in the Zurich of 1918), like Terry Johnson (whose play *Insignificance* brings together Einstein, Marilyn Monroe, Joe DiMaggio, and Senator Joseph McCarthy in the New York City of 1953), Greenblatt brings together Latimer, Carleton, Strachey, and Shakespeare in the London of 1611. Greenblatt thinks, he writes, by interweaving a plurality of seemingly unrelated anecdotes, whose enfolded diversity defines the unique signature of a time and place.

Shakespeare thus becomes just one facet of a fractal narrative. The incident Carleton describes, for instance, belongs to a series of spectacular executions at the beginning of James I's reign, executions designed to demonstrate the new king's power and authority. On this occasion, however, when the condemned conspirators are standing on the scaffold—"together on a stage, as use is at the end of a play" in Carleton's words—a messenger arrives at the last moment with a pardon from the king. The dramatic timing of this pardon has been stage-managed by the (absent) king; it elicits from the assembled crowd a spontaneous "plaudite," a burst of applause. The pardon dramatizes the king's mercy.

This incident leads Greenblatt into reflections upon the importance of royal pardon in the legal system of Renaissance England; it also relates to the subject of Latimer's sermon. In Latimer's Christianity, which becomes the official theology of England in Shakespeare's lifetime, every human being is born under sentence of death. We are guilty and have been justly condemned; but we can be pardoned, royally, by God if in his mercy He chooses to save us. The English church, like the English state, creates in the English people a "salutary anxiety"; it reminds them vividly and repeatedly of the horrific punishments to which they are subject, while assuring them of the benevolence of the power who watches over them. In the same way Prospero's chief magical device is to harrow other characters with anxiety, to create in them a state of "managed insecurity." Shakespeare himself creates a corresponding anxiety in the audience. Will the characters on the ship drown? Will Antonio murder Alonso? Will Caliban murder Prospero? In the end, of course, no one comes to any harm. Shakespeare's play, Latimer's sermon, Carleton's narrative, are all tragicomedies; deaths are threatened but do not materialize.

But Greenblatt does not want us to conclude that Shakespeare's theatre merely appropriates a social strategy; Anglican Christianity and Jacobean jurisprudence are not merely "sources" for Shakespeare's play. That way of thinking makes history a footnote to literature; it elevates one set of texts (Shakespeare's plays, literature generally) above others (sermons, letters, factual narratives, memoirs). Greenblatt's narrative and critical method treats all these materials equally, as comparable examples of "discourse," of "writing." The ceremonies of the church, of the state, of the theatre, all speak the same language. They all exemplify what another Shakespearian critic calls *Power on Display*.[82]

Politics and theology are themselves permeated with aesthetic techniques. Carleton explicitly compares the scene of an execution with a moment in the theatre. "This complex circulation between the social dimension of an aesthetic strategy, and the aesthetic dimension of a social strategy, is," Greenblatt assures us, "the half-hidden meaning of literary history." With this formula he proclaims the equality of discourses and warns critics that literature cannot be understood except as a form of history. At the same time, however, he claims history itself for literary criticism. While demoting literature itself to the status of just one discourse among many, he colonizes all other discourses in the name of an expansionist literary criticism. Sermons, diaries, memoirs, factual narratives, legal codes, theology—they are all discourses. Their "half-hidden meaning" is best elicited by people professionally trained in the interpretation, the sensitive decoding, of complex texts: professors (aggressors) of English literature.

The subject of all this discourse is, in this instance, anxiety. Anxiety permeates postmodernist criticism; Harold Bloom has built an entire critical method on the concept of "the anxiety of influence." For Bloom everyone *but* Shakespeare is anxious;[83] for Greenblatt, Shakespeare belongs to a culture awash with anxiety.

The contemporary scholar, like the contemporary scientist, must keep routinely producing new ideas at an accelerating rate, while keeping up with everybody else's new ideas. It is impossible to satisfy either expectation, and so everyone is anxious. The intellectual economy demands and subverts individual originality; in a situation where multitudes of people with similar talents and training, starting from similar positions, working with similar tools, influenced by similar experiences, are all driven by the imperative of novelty, it is inevitable that dozens of people will independently arrive at a new idea at approximately the same time. The knowledge that this is likely to happen only makes every investigator more anxious; somebody else may get to "your" idea before you can publish it.

Greenblatt analyzes anxiety so subtly because he and his audience swim in it. And his own discourse stimulates anxiety in his academic audience ("isn't literature being devalued? and how can I possibly become a historian in my spare time?")—but also allays it ("the discipline is expanding; and I can generate all sorts of new interpretations of my own, if I combine literature and history in this way"). Like semiotics, like deconstruction, like feminism, Greenblatt's historicism subjects a whole new continent of texts to the technologies of an imperialist literary criticism and critical theory. Greenblatt's lecture not only discusses but itself enacts the display of power.

The "mimetic economy of Jacobean England" depends upon what Greenblatt calls "an institutional circulation of culturally significant narratives." (So does the contemporary academic economy, of course.) William Shakespeare's *The Tempest* and William Strachey's *True Repertory of the Wracke* are both generated by shareholding companies, nominally under Crown patronage but in effect independent corporations founded with investment capital. The circumstances that produce such texts are "corporate and institutional." Like Blayney, Greenblatt sees any individual Shakespeare text as part of a larger, corporate operation; like Blayney, Greenblatt illuminates Shakespeare's text by juxtaposing it with a number of apparently unrelated nonliterary texts. Both study "the sociology of texts."

Blayney and Greenblatt both demonstrate the relevance of the irrelevant. Greenblatt speaks of "a network of resemblances" linking the different discourses of Renaissance England; the networking of his style essays to catch as many of those resemblances as possible. This is the age of the network: computer networks, mass media networks, the personal "networking" that conferences and institutions like the Folger facilitate. Networks convince us of the intricate interrelationship of seemingly unrelated details. The international news media bombard us with the distant repercussions of events all over the planet. The extinction of one species disrupts an entire ecology. In the ubiquitous fantasies of time travel, changes to a few trivial events in the past trigger a chain reaction of unpredictable consequences for the future-present. And the whole new science of "chaos" attempts, like Greenblatt, to describe the circulation, turbulence, and multidimensional self-similarity that organize complex nonperiodic systems.[84]

Everything is related to everything else. So everything is relevant to Shakespeare, and Shakespeare is relevant to everything. Shakespeare, the apex of the inverted pyramid of interpretation, is also the tip of a funnel through which the whole world can be poured. And that tip belongs to criticism.

HONDURAS

September 9, 1929/1986. The first entry of Edward Harrison's journal, describing his journey to Honduras, was composed in 1929; but it is first published in Malcolm Evans' *Signifying Nothing* in 1986. Evans reports that "the authenticity of Harrison's journal is in considerable doubt"; he ascribes to it "no more authority or truth than if it were, in fact, only a work of literary fiction."[85] Evans, citing and analyzing Harrison's journal, deliberately invites confusion about whether it is past fact or present fiction, whether written by Edward Harrison or Malcolm Evans.

Whether Evans wrote the journal or only found it, he has decided to use, as a point of critical departure, its account of the visit to British Honduras of a young graduate of Cambridge University; "enter Harrison bearing culture for the natives." But Harrison, far from celebrating the achievements of English literature, sets about "arming Caliban, 300 years later, against Prospero." Like Greenblatt, Harrison and Evans home in on the colonial narrative in and behind *The Tempest;* they see that colonial narrative repeated as successive waves of English imperialism radiate outward. In 1638 the "first British inhabitants settle" in Honduras "after shipwreck"; Harrison, recalling that shipwreck, cannot resist quoting *The Tempest*.[86] H. M. Stanley, marching across central Africa in 1877, takes Shakespeare with him. Greenblatt, in the Chesapeake basin, and Evans/Harrison, in Honduras, both see Shakespeare as an instrument of cultural imperialism and look back upon the history of his conquests from the perspective of a conquered people.

Geographically, Evans is no colonial; he teaches at the Polytechnic of North London. In resisting the traditional veneration of Shakespeare, scholars like Evans also resist the dominance of the English upper classes over the "colonized" masses of Britain and Ireland. After all, England exerted its military hegemony over the independent nations of Wales, Scotland, and Ireland before it established colonies in North America, Honduras, or Africa. Malcolm Evans is bilingual, and his book on Shakespeare begins with a dedicatory poem in Welsh.

In its overt solidarity with colonized and suppressed cultures, Evans' criticism echoes a long British debate about Scottish and Welsh devolution and the bloodier issue of independence in Northern Ireland. But these British preoccupations belong to a larger international movement that seeks to secure the independence and integrity of minority cultures; the Basque separatists in Spain, the Palestinians, the Quebecois in Canada, Biafrans in Nigeria, Maori in New Zealand. The argument emerges from the period of decolonization in the aftermath of World War II, when entire imperial superstructures were taken conspicuously down. The independence achieved by so many peoples in the Third World occurs alongside the civil rights movement in the United States and the struggle to dismantle white hegemony in Rhodesia and South Africa. Suppressed minorities, suppressed majorities, demand equal time.

Evans appropriates for British criticism the heroic mythology of national liberation. Like many contemporary radicals, he envisages the canon of English literature as an oppressive empire of culture, which needs to be dismantled. He treats that canon as a kind of apartheid, which artificially distinguishes between "literature" and other forms of discourse, and then systematically discriminates in favor of "literature." Even within the elite literary classes, the canon favors natives of England at the expense of Americans, Canadians,

Australians, New Zealanders, and all the other Anglophone peoples of the world; although India contains more speakers of the language than any other country, no Indians have yet secured entry into the canon. Shakespeare himself is the keystone atop this triumphal arch of "English" "literature," and by removing him from that position Evans hopes to bring the whole structure crashing down. At the end of a book on Shakespeare he proposes—as arch and outrageous as Eagleton, glorifying Macbeth's witches—that Shakespeare be suspended from the curriculum, to make room for authors like Abiezer Coppe and Gerrard Winstanley. Shakespeare, shareholder in a capitalist playhouse, is the patron saint of corrupt bourgeois values; Winstanley and Coppe, radical partisans of the English civil war, are the champions of activist egalitarianism. Evans celebrates the Puritan revolutionaries whose brethren closed down the theatres in 1642.

The Puritans regarded the theatre as the instrument of a hostile ideology; Evans sees the institutions of our own time in the same way. The fictional or factual diarist Edward Harrison teaches English literature; and his alter ego Evans, also "a hired purveyor of culture," naturally discusses Shakespeare's place in the British educational system. Likewise, half of *Political Shakespeare*—an influential collection of radical essays edited by Alan Sinfield and Jonathan Dollimore—analyzes the contemporary uses to which Shakespeare is put in the classroom and the theatre, on television and film. Shakespeare has been used to support conservative interests. Shakespeare serves the dominant culture, and so the dominant culture serves us Shakespeare.

British critics feel Shakespeare's cultural hegemony, and England's past responsibility for suppressing alternative cultures, much more keenly than their counterparts in North America or continental Europe. As a result, to those outside Britain the fervor of these neo-Marxist critics can easily seem hysterically parochial. The United States, after all, has no equivalent to the RSC or the BBC; its educational system has always been more diversified and decentralized; it sees itself as a melting pot of immigrants or a stew compounded of many ethnic ingredients; and Shakespeare has become a minority taste, always politically marginalized. Nevertheless, American scholars now dominate Shakespeare criticism, just as Washington, D.C.—not London—now dominates Honduras. Uncle Sam has power over Shakespeare; as in *Richard III* the royal orphaned nephew exerts little reciprocal influence over his dangerous uncle. Stephen Greenblatt can say that "the living Shake-speare," the art that perpetually renews itself in the present, does not interest him; his criticism dissects "the dead Shakespeare," the art that belongs to a coffined moment of the past.[87] But for Evans, Sinfield, Dollimore and other radical British critics, Shakespeare is neither living nor dead, but both.

A valid criticism of the past therefore must entail a criticism of the present. In his play *Lear*, Edward Bond utterly rewrites Shake-speare's story, transforming it into a parable of violent oppression and violent resistance; Lear begins the play trying to build, and ends the play trying to tear down, a fortified wall (like the one in Berlin). Evans begins *Signifying Nothing* by analyzing the text of Queen Elizabeth II's 1982 Christmas message to the Common-wealth, supporting the Conservative government's war against Argentina. The last essay in *Political Shakespeare* begins by analyzing the text of a 1983 newspaper interview with the Conservative chan-cellor of the exchequer, who quotes *Troilus and Cressida* and *Cori-olanus* as evidence that "Shakespeare was a Tory, without a doubt."[88] Alan Sinfield in a 1986 essay on *Macbeth* compares the two doctors in that play to contemporary "conservative and liberal" literary critics; he remarks upon the "almost uncanny resemblance" between the failed Gunpowder Plot of 1605, an acknowledged influence on Shakespeare's play, and the Irish Republican Army's failed attempt to blow up the entire Conservative cabinet at Brighton in 1984. Delivering a lecture at Harvard in the week of President Reagan's April 1986 attack on Libya, Sinfield suggests that Reagan, like Macbeth, sends armed emissaries to "attack the citadel of his opponent and kill one of his children."[89]

Sinfield and Dollimore are general editors of a new series devoted to "Cultural Politics."* Shakespeare's plays, like any other social product, cannot be disentangled from the power struggles of the past and present: "Culture is not simply a reflection of the economic and political system, but nor can it be independent of it."[90] If Shakespeare has almost always buttressed conservative positions, then either he must be abandoned entirely, or ways must be found of radicalizing responses to his texts.

The liberation of suppressed classes, cultures, and discourses necessitates the liberation of suppressed meanings. Evans demon-

---

* Sinfield and Dollimore resigned in 1988, after Manchester University Press refused to publish one volume in the series, Simon Shepherd's *Positively Gay*. They are now suffering from the cultural backlash represented by Allan Bloom.

strates that a seemingly pleonastic clause in *As You Like It*—"If truth holds true contents"—has a multitude of potential meanings. The word "truth," for instance, can also mean "troth"; "holds" can contain the neutral sense "contain" and the active sense "restrain"; "true" incorporates both "accurate" and "faithful"; "contents" can refer either to the "contents" of a container or, in Elizabethan English, to contentednesses. Adding grammatical and theatrical ambiguities to these lexical ones, Evans mathematically establishes that the five words can be arranged into 172 different dispositions, though not all of them yield combinatory senses. "There is repetition, back-tracking, tautology, nonsense and *reductio ad absurdum.*" But who decides how many permutations we will allow? "Where and by what authority do you draw the line beyond which the interpretation of these words itself ceases to hold true contents?"[91] No one can or should limit the free play of signifiers. No one has a right to impose his or her culture, his or her meanings, on anyone else.

Evans' analysis of the clause "If truth holds true contents" applies equally well to the institutional situation of contemporary Shakespeare criticism. What Evans does to one phrase in *As You Like It*, S. Schoenbaum does in the same period to the whole of Shakespearian biography. In *Shakespeare's Lives*—again that telltale plural—Schoenbaum writes a massive history of biographies of Shakespeare, from the seventeenth century to our own time. Schoenbaum sees every biographer constructing an idol more or less in his or her own image. And as Schoenbaum's convivial skepticism recounts the follies of past scholarship, he genially hollows out a vacuum at the center of Shakespeare studies, a biographical *aporia*, a chasm of infinite unmeaning, which generates and consumes all our meanings. For Schoenbaum and for Evans, in their very different ways, Shakespeare is a hollow god. But neither can resist the temptation to fill his abysm.

WILLIAMSTOWN

October 11, 1986. We have been assuming until now that, however many meanings it might have, there is still only one text. We have been making this assumption since the eighteenth century. Steven Urkowitz is busy unmaking it.

In his 1980 book *Shakespeare's Revision of 'King Lear'* Urkowitz argues that the two early editions of that play—one printed by Nicholas Okes in 1608, the other incorporated in the First Folio of 1623—represent distinct authorial versions. Since 1725 all editors have combined elements from both editions to produce a single catchall text, which supposedly restores Shakespeare's own single version of the play. Urkowitz argues that all the editors are wrong, that there never was a single version of the play, that Shakespeare wrote two versions, that either of his versions makes better sense than the hybrid produced by two and one-half centuries of scholarship. Similar explanations are soon floated for the disparities in other texts. In 1986 the new Oxford edition offers readers of Shakespeare's complete works two texts of *King Lear;* the edition displays varying degrees of revision in the sonnets, *Hamlet, Othello, Troilus and Cressida,* and a dozen other plays. At the Berlin conference Urkowitz, looking at "Five Women Eleven Ways," argues that revision affects even more texts.[92] And now, at a special session of the New England Renaissance Conference of the Renaissance Society of America, held at Williams College, he urges his audience to understand "Shakespeare as a Revising Artist."[93]

These revisionist theories of authorial revision inevitably disintegrate the Shakespeare of traditional scholarship and criticism. Characters in the conflated text have been celebrated by two centuries of critics as unified and coherent wholes, rich in interpretive possibilities; they are now dismissed as mules, sterile offspring of the bestial union of two different texts, their ill-fitting assortment of traits awkwardly stitched together. And just as the admired unity of individual characters disintegrates, so does the admired unity of whole plays. Innumerable critics have admired the aesthetic wholeness of texts that are being described, now, as inept collages of radically incompatible material, scissored and pasted together. And if the unity of the text goes, so does the unity of the author himself. Shakespeare could not make up his mind about how best to dramatize the Lear story—or, rather, he made up his mind more than once. Shakespeare had a plurality of incompatible intentions.

Urkowitz and his subversive colleagues do not convince everyone. On the same panel G. K. Hunter—once a colleague of Germaine Greer's at Warwick, now Professor of English at Yale—seeks to define "The Logical Limits of Disintegration."[94] His talk is "not a defence of the traditional text of *King Lear,*" because that text, for him, "needs no defence."[95]

This championship match between Urkowitz and Hunter reenacts an earlier confrontation at another conference at the other end of Massachusetts. In April 1980 the annual Shakespeare Association of America conference convenes at Cambridge, and the textual seminar considers *King Lear.* At all SAA conferences a dozen or so registered participants sit around a table, but any number of other scholars may enter the room and listen. The textual seminar that year draws a larger audience than ever before or since; it brings together, for the first time, four radical and as yet relatively unknown exponents of revision: Urkowitz, Randall McLeod, myself, and Michael Warren.* The stimulus for the seminar was created by Warren, who had urged a bifurcation of the traditional conflated text of *King Lear* four years before, at the World Shakespeare Congress in Washington, D.C.[96] The chairman of the seminar, G. B. Evans of Harvard—editor of the Riverside edition—asks three respected senior scholars to comment on the work of these upstart revisionists: Hunter from Yale, Wells from Oxford, and the respected bibliographer and editor George Walton Williams from Duke. Both Wells and Williams announce their conversions to the revisionist cause; so does another participant, Thomas Clayton of the University of Minnesota. Hunter, champion of an orthodoxy that has lasted for centuries, finds himself suddenly surrounded and embattled.

As in all the best plays, this peripeteia excites the audience; the revisionist position immediately acquires the intellectual glamour that David achieved by slaying Goliath. Its new academic credibility results from a classic moment of theatrical recognition. The unexpected conversions of Wells, Williams, and Clayton offer the participants and the audience a compelling model of anagnorisis; suddenly, the scales fall from my eyes, and I can see the light. At the same time, the revisionists themselves—like a theatre audience brought together in one place, responding in the same way to the same stimulus—recognize that they constitute a unified and hence potentially powerful community. The revisionists recognize their own strength; the spectators, too, recognize that strength; the revisionists recognize that the spectators recognize that strength.

---

* It is a measure of the intense hostility initially generated by the revisionists' work that, when Warren's seminal essay on *King Lear* was rejected by the Modern Language Association's journal in 1975, the reader's report concluded that "This paper ought not to be published anywhere."

Directly out of this seminar grows a collection of essays, *The Division of the Kingdoms: Shakespeare's Two Versions of "King Lear,"* edited by Warren and myself. This collection is immediately hailed and attacked as the manifesto of a new movement. Its impact results in part from the same sense of communal potency so important at the 1980 seminar. It brings together essays by eleven revisionists from Britain, North America, and New Zealand; it brings together an equally obvious variety of critical and scholarly approaches. Coincidences conspire to enhance this sense of a new community. Urkowitz' book on *King Lear,* another book on *King Lear* by Peter Stone, and my essay on "The War in *King Lear,*" all challenging the traditional conflated text, are all published in 1980, the year of the seminar.97 Cambridge University Press publishes Peter Blayney's big book on *The Texts of 'King Lear'* in 1982, followed in 1983 by Oxford University Press' big book on *The Division of the Kingdoms.*

In contending that Shakespeare revised his work, these scholars themselves revise the accepted paradigms of editorial and critical practice. Their collective challenge to 250 years of Shakespeare texts does more than alter or displace hundreds of lines and stage directions in a dozen plays. Revisionism insists that texts are made; they become—they do not flash instantaneously into perfect and unalterable being. Over a certain period an author makes a text; during a later period, in response to internal or external stimuli, that author remakes the same text; the revised version results from a kind of posthumous collaboration between a deceased younger self and a living older self. Later, the text is remade again, by eighteenth-century editors. Thereafter, the text is continually remade, in small ways, although the received structure remains intact. Now we see that text being remade again, fundamentally.

Whatever the cogency of Hunter's arguments, the very fact that he is here—in Williamstown, debating Urkowitz—strengthens Urkowitz' position. The audience can see for itself that there are now at least two texts of *King Lear:* Hunter's and Urkowitz'. Neither recognizes the legitimacy of the other. The debate itself demonstrates that Shakespeare's text is a contested site, that what we read must be decided by the likes of Hunter or the likes of Urkowitz. The text, which had been taken for granted, has now become a matter of debate, hence a matter of choice; therefore it has always been a matter of choice; therefore it will always remain a matter of choice.

Shakespeare himself cannot walk onto the platform at the end of the session and declare in favor of Urkowitz or Hunter. So it is we, the audience, who make the decision. The nature of the occasion demonstrates to everyone present that Shakespeare's text is a contemporary communal construct.

Hunter can offer his audience nothing new; in an intellectual economy based upon the constant production of novelty, he stands for an old text. But the revisionists, by doubling the number of texts of *King Lear* (or *Hamlet,* or *Othello*), more than double the potential for critical interpretation. At a stroke, all existing interpretations are rendered suspect; they must all be looked over again, in the light of this new theory. At the same time, critics are invited to examine two fresh new texts where before they had one stale old text. Moreover, the doubling of *King Lear* creates a third object of interest, an immaterial text potentially even more fascinating than the two material ones. Critics are not only invited to interpret the two rediscovered, restored, independent texts, each a work of art in its own right; they can, and do, also interpret the differences between them. They are offered a whole new technology for generating new readings of old plays: what Randall McLeod calls "differential reading," reading "between the texts."[98]

McLeod himself is married to a feminist photographer, and his contribution to *The Division of the Kingdoms* argues that the revised version of *King Lear* portrays Goneril more sympathetically than critics have recognized; Beth Goldring's essay in that collection contends that the ambiguous speech prefix "*Alb.Cor.*", hitherto all but universally interpreted by male critics as "Albany and Cornwall," instead unites "Albany and Cordelia"; Urkowitz finds that "some of the most striking instances" of textual variation "occur among female characterizations."[99] Like the feminists, the revisionists privilege difference.

Our new sensitivity to the cumulative effect of such seemingly minute differences develops naturally from our consciousness of the networking that links everything unpredictably to everything else; as the scientists of chaos declare, complex systems harbor a "sensitive dependence on initial conditions," so that inconsequential changes can spin out vast consequences. In 1973, the year after Peter Blayney begins work on *The Texts of 'King Lear',* the two leading actors in John Barton's acclaimed and influential RSC production of *Richard II* come forward every night before the performance and (pretend to) decide who will play Richard and who Bolingbroke. In 1980, the year of the Cambridge seminar on *King Lear,* audiences at the National Theatre can see Alan Ayckbourn's new play(s) *Sisterly Feelings* in four different versions; simple choices by the characters produce complex variations in the plot, and if we go to the theatre four times we can see the results of every alternative. Ian Richardson or Richard Pasco as Richard II, the two different endings of *King Lear,* the four permutations of Ayckbourn's comedy; the versions advertise their differences, while declaring their equality. "You pays your money and you takes your choice."

What happened when Shakespeare finished *King Lear?* According to the traditional story, he never revised his work, and so after he had written the last page of *King Lear* he closed the book—and that was that. But fewer and fewer critics believe in closure. Shakespeare may at some point have closed the book; but he could reopen it again whenever he wanted. There is no Last Judgment anymore. You can appeal your conviction; you can remarry your ex-wife. Even death is no longer final; we resuscitate the dead, we put them on life-support systems, we distinguish between heart death and brain death. Roman Polanski's film of *Macbeth* ends with an added scene in which Malcolm visits the witches, restarting the sequence that has just seemed to end. Peter Brook's film of *King Lear* ends with the thunder of an approaching, returning storm. The year 1986 begins for me with a screening of Kurosawa's film *Ran;* the Japanese adaptation of *King Lear* ends with an image of a blind man standing on the edge of a precipice.

Closure arbitrarily privileges one moment out of a continuum of equal intervals. Terence Hawkes asks "When *does* the play close?" Does *Hamlet* end when "the dialogue stops and when the soldiers carry the bodies off and the music and the explosion of the cannons is heard?" No, he answers; "there follows applause" and then "the curtain-call," which "the actors rehearse," just as they rehearse the author's script. By choosing one of these moments as "the end" we artificially unchoose others. And this suspicion of arbitrary closure affects beginnings as well as endings, for the commencement of one state necessarily ends another. Birth has become as problematic for us as death: at what arbitrary point does a fetus become a human being? Predictably, Hawkes also questions when *Hamlet* begins. "Is it when the first sentry walks out on to the stage? Or has the play already begun in our mind's eye as we enter the theatre?" No. "In our society," he concludes, *Hamlet* "has, for complex social and historical reasons, always already begun."[100]

The beginning of *Hamlet* is always a rebeginning. This axiom applies even to Shakespeare. His *Hamlet* is a rewriting of someone else's lost play, just as his *King Lear* is a rewriting of someone else's *King Leir;* later, First Folio *Hamlet* is a rewriting of Second Quarto *Hamlet,* First Folio *King Lear* a rewriting of Quarto *King Lear.* Every writing is a rewriting.

PARIS

January 8, 1986. Back in the United States, *Shakespeare's Perjured Eye,* which will eventually win the MLA's James Russell Lowell Prize for 1986, is being published today by the University of California Press. But its author, Joel Fineman, associate professor of English at Berkeley, is on sabbatical in Paris. Director Peter Brook is also there; in 1970, after his acclaimed RSC production of *A Midsummer Night's Dream,* Brook established in Paris Le Centre International de Recherche Théâtrale. Shakespeare familied in Stratford and acted in London; for more than a century after the Restoration, Paris was the capital of a critical domain that thoroughly repudiated Shakespeare. So what draws contemporary Shakespearians to Paris, that city of displaced desire?

In the early twentieth century Paris had played host to Ernest Hemingway, James Joyce, Ezra Pound, Gertrude Stein, Marcel Proust, Pablo Picasso, the Ballets Russes. In the second half of the century it is culturally associated with Roland Barthes, Jacques Derrida, Michel Foucault, Jacques Lacan, and Claude Lévi-Strauss, that gang of "Parisian Heideggerians" so detested by Allan Bloom. The names on the old list are artists; the names on the new list are interpreters. Within the critical community as a whole, these writers are more eagerly read, more controversial, the source of more excitement and debate, than any contemporary poet or novelist or dramatist.

But it has taken them a long time to impinge directly upon the interpretation of Shakespeare. Although these five figures achieve a kind of intellectual hegemony in France during the 1960s, their techniques do not penetrate Shakespeare criticism until the mid-1980s. Shakespearians do not rush to meet the new theories, and the new theories busy themselves elsewhere. Lévi-Strauss is an anthropologist, Derrida a philosopher, Foucault a philosophical historian, Lacan a psychoanalyst; only Barthes could be classified as a literary critic. Shakespeare has never been central to the culture to which these men belong, and he remains peripheral to their thought and work. Even Fineman, who makes more use of Lacan's general theories than any previous Shakespearian, admits that "Lacan's comments on Shakespeare are often disappointing."[101] Moreover, the first wave of literary theorists in America to form an intellectual alliance with the new French philosophers—Geoffrey Hartman, Paul de Man, J. Hillis Miller—all specialize in Romantic and modern literature. Only gradually does the new army of theory extend itself backward toward the Renaissance.

With Fineman, postmodernism faces Shakespeare. Later in 1986 Jonathan Goldberg publishes *Voice Terminal Echo,* a set of essays that attempts to correlate *Postmodernism and English Renaissance Texts;* the same ambition generates, in the same year, *Literary Theory/Renaissance Texts,* edited by Patricia Parker and David Quint. But, historically, the effect of this encounter may matter less than its belatedness. From Dryden to Eliot every previous revolution in English literary theory and practice has, from the beginning, confronted or appropriated Shakespeare. To today's revolution Shakespeare has been irrelevant. By the mid-1980s Barthes, Foucault, and Lacan are already dead, and Lévi-Strauss inert.

A comparable time lag afflicts most departments of postmodernist Shakesperotics. The critical technology and vocabulary of British radicals like Alan Sinfield and Jonathan Dollimore derives from an earlier generation of Marxist critics like Raymond Williams and Stuart Hall, who are not Renaissance specialists; as Sinfield observes, "Significantly, the prophets come from outside Shakespeare."[102] Likewise, in recognizing the fact of authorial revision and its implications for both editing and criticism, the textual revisionists of the 1980s are simply applying to Shakespeare, at last, ideas and procedures that have long dominated scholarship on most other writers. Even Bloom—who warns us in Shakespeare's name against foreign influences—notes that "The idea" for his essay on *Julius Caesar* "was originally given me by Leo Strauss,"[103] to whom *Shakespeare's Politics* is dedicated; Strauss was an émigré German Jew who came to the United States in 1938. Shakespeare no longer leads; he catches up. He is already losing his intellectual centrality.

Fineman's thesis depends upon his sense of Shakespeare's belatedness in his own time. Shakespeare writes his sonnets at the end of a long wave of European sonneteering that stretches back to Petrarch, and a more immediate English wave initiated by Sidney. Consequently,

> when Shakespeare writes his sonnets the literary vitality of such traditional epideixis . . . is to a considerable extent exhausted . . . This exhaustion is a decisive fact for literary history, for when Shakespeare comes to write his sonnets—long after what even Sidney, at the inaugural moment of the Elizabethan sonnet, calls "poor Petrarch's long-deceased woes"—the poetry of praise has lost so much of its original and traditional force that Shakespeare can no longer uncomplicatedly employ a poetic mode that he must nevertheless think of as orthodox. This is the general situation that leads Shakespeare to develop in his sonnets a new poetics . . .

This is also, of course, though Fineman does not say so, the general situation of a Shakespearian critic in the late twentieth century: how do you praise persuasively when so much praise has already been written?

The traditional poet (or critic) experiences and offers us a vision; the belated poet (or critic) experiences and offers us re-vision, rewriting.

> Shakespeare rewrites praise through the medium of epideictic paradox . . . It is important to emphasize here the "re-" of "rewrite," because it is part of the point I want to make that both the novelty and the effect of Shakespeare's sonnets derive in good measure from the way they noticeably duplicate, from the way they call attention to the fact that they repeat with a difference, the epideictic tradition they succeed.[104]

Fineman's critical thesis is reinforced, simultaneously, by postmodernist scholarship. John Kerrigan's 1986 edition prints and discusses variant texts of several sonnets. Kerrigan—an early advocate of the thesis that Shakespeare revised *King Lear*—concludes that, although most of the poems were written in the 1590s, Shakespeare revised and reorganized them into a collection after 1603. The private panegyrics of 1590, circulated in manuscript among friends, become public, printed "recapitulative Jacobean labors," consciously anachronistic—in which, conspicuously and ironically, readers are never even told the name of the object of Shakespeare's praise.[105]

Shakespeare, finding himself at the end of an exhausted tradition, rewrites the sonnet. Shakespearians, drowning in their own dismayed abundance, rewrite criticism. Stanley Wells writes *Re-Editing Shakespeare for the Modern Reader,* Terry Eagleton writes a book about Shakespeare in a series called *Rereading Literature,* E. A. J. Honigmann writes "Re-enter the Stage Direction" for *Shakespeare Survey.* (Gary Taylor writes *Reinventing Shakespeare.*) In the 1980s Shakespearians read and write essays in collections called *Representing Shakespeare, Shakespeare Reproduced,* and *Rewriting the Renaissance.*[106] Shakespeare, the untutored original of Romantic poetics, becomes the retooling retailing reteller of postmodernism.

All this rewriting must be repeatedly reread in order to be understood at all; but the rereadings are rewarding and rewarded. Kerrigan observes that "the sonnet as a form ... most aptly finds resolution in a critical apparatus." The 400-page "analytic commentary" of Stephen Booth's edition of *Shakespeare's Sonnets*—which in 1977 won the same prize that Fineman's book on the sonnets wins a decade later—unravels (and restitches) a bewildering compressed complexity of reference in poems that were once celebrated as a transparent window onto Shakespeare's heart. Booth's commentary makes the sonnets more difficult to read than ever before. Ten years later Jonathan Goldberg, deliberately abandoning "literary tact," makes his own criticism of those poems as difficult to read as Booth's sonnets:

> The interior/eternal text of sonnet 122 is a reiteration-with-a-difference of all that has been written already; the mind is a place prepared beforehand to receive the impression of the character of the beloved. Eternity is retraced and retracted in the second quatrain of sonnet 122 ("Or, at the very least . . ."); the status of memory and texts as what *remains* replaces the eternal monument—temporality, and with it the present/presence of the text/mind (of "nature," in short), as erosion, erasure, forgetfulness. "Rased oblivion" is the apparent end (Hegelian *telos*) of what remains.[107]

If you compare Goldberg's prose with Bradley's you will get some idea of how radically Shakesperotics has been transformed in the last eighty years. Goldberg does not write this way because he is foolish or incompetent. His style, like Fineman's, like Derrida's, Lacan's, Barthes', Foucault's, deliberately convolutes and obstructs. It does not trust language. Language is treacherous, and its treachery—the flight of the signifier—has become the obsessive focus of contemporary philosophy, from Wittgenstein to Austin to Derrida.

This fascinated distrust of language motivates the circling wariness of Fineman's style; but it also motivates, according to Fineman, the originality of Shakespeare's own style. Poet and critic are both wrestling Proteus, the teeming malleability of verbal signs:

> It is this visionary subject fully present to his object, to himself, and to the speech he speaks, that Shakespeare rewrites by revising the visual poetics of the poetry of praise. Very briefly, I argue that in his sonnets Shakespeare substitutes for this ideal and idealizing characterization of visionary language—"To hear with eyes belongs to love's fine wit" (Sonnet 23)—a different account that characterizes language as something corruptingly linguistic rather than something ideally specular, as something duplicitously verbal as opposed to something singly visual. The result is a poetics of a double tongue rather than a poetics of a unified and unifying eye, a language of suspicious word rather than a language of true vision.[108]

"The truth of language is that, compared to vision, it is false." This linguistic duplicity everywhere informs Shakespeare's awareness of "verbal density and texture"—what Kerrigan calls "the mendacity of metaphor," what Fineman calls "the 'languageness' of language."[109] ("Word thickens, and the crow makes wing to th' booky wood."[110])

Like Booth and Greenblatt, Fineman teaches at Berkeley, and he shares his sense of the viscous (vicious) materiality of language with a new generation of San Francisco Bay poets. The year of Fineman is also the year of Silliman. Ron Silliman's anthology of American "language poetry" *In the American Tree* celebrates a literary genre that abandons plot, syntax, and reference, attending instead to "the word as such," or breaking down the word as such into a collage of disarticulated graphemes; "language appears as a material applied to a surface; the analogy is to paint."[111] "I HATE SPEECH," Silliman's introduction begins; and the sentence would serve equally well as an introduction to Derrida's attack on the phonocentrism of Western philosophy or as an epigraph to Mark Medoff's 1986 Academy Award–winning film about deafness, *Children of a Lesser God.* It might also serve as a motto for the work of Randall McLeod, concrete poet turned textual critic, who sometimes signs himself Random Cloud.

McLoud does not hate speech any more than Derrida and Silliman do; but he, like them, typically, typographically, typologically, speaks about the unspeakable, the utterly unutterable. "Text is experienced as visual pattern, before it is sound, before it is logos." Mclodd insists that "SHAKE-SPEARES SONNETS" cannot be properly understood unless we read them in the original book with that title printed by George Eld in 1609. Kerrigan, too, emphasizes the physical integrity of the 1609 collection—which includes, like his own edition, not only the Sonnets but also *A Lover's Complaint;* Kerrigan shows that English Renaissance sonnet sequences often end with such a narrative coda. But McClod goes further: for him, all subsequent editions are "translations" or "translacings" into modern graphic conventions, anachronistic conventions that "deny and frustrate the very medium of Renaissance English literature." They disfigure (and literalize, "dis-figure") the original "textual icon" by changing "its body-language."[112]

Silliman's anthology includes a piece by Bruce Andrews called "MISREPRESENTATION," which is "(*A text for* The Tennis Court Oath *of John Ashbery*)." That text deliberately breaks down the boundaries between poetry and prose, citation and creation, reading and writing. Andrews disassembles, quotes and echoes Ashbery's text in the act of building up a new text of his own. Rereading becomes rewriting; the Berlin Wall between interpretation and creation, criticism and literature, is torn down. If literature is just one among many equal varieties of discourse, then criticism is too, and it need no longer accept its subservience to literature. Criticism may be produced for a small, specialized audience; but then, so is most modern art. In another contribution to Silliman's anthology, Steve Benson describes the situation of contemporary poetry in terms equally applicable to contemporary criticism:

> The truism that the only people who now read poetry are themselves poets is thus understood rather as potential than limita-

tion: the reader is presumed not as a consumer of the experience sustained by the poem but as a fellow writer who shares contentiously in the work and can willingly answer the uses of the medium which the writer feels impelled to undertake.[113]

Criticism feeds on previous texts; but literature also feeds on previous texts. According to a generation of critics like Northrop Frye, literature is a self-enclosed system in which texts breed texts, without contamination from the "real" world. In this conversation between texts, how can we distinguish the voice of criticism from the voice of literature?

The two voices are so often the same voice—Jonson, Dryden, Pope, Johnson, Coleridge, Eliot—and they are so often saying the same things. A whole critical subgenre describes Shakespeare's plays in terms of "metadrama": each play is a comment upon, a critique of, the nature of plays. James L. Calderwood, in another Californian book published in 1986, argues that when writing *Macbeth* Shakespeare "systematically opposed" that play to *Hamlet,* deliberately producing its "inverse," a "counter-*Hamlet*"; at the same time Shakespeare's "major preoccupation" in *Macbeth* is "the nature of tragic action," which becomes "not only a means of representation, a way of ordering the doings of the hero, but an object of representation."[114] *Macbeth* is thus a text about *Hamlet* (like Calderwood's previous book, *To Be and Not to Be*) and a text about "Tragic Action" (like Calderwood's current book). The poet Shakespeare interests Calderwood precisely to the degree that he behaves like a critic.

And at the same time dramatists rebegin rewriting Shakespeare, as they did in the Restoration and the eighteenth century. Charles Marowitz, the keynote speaker at the 1986 Stratford conference, creates his own adaptations of *A Macbeth* and *The Shrew* by rearranging fragments of Shakespeare's text in a new, deliberately subversive collage. John Barton, a plenary speaker at the 1986 Berlin conference, creates the RSC's epic dramatization of *The Wars of the Roses,* three plays formed by mixing selections from four plays by Shakespeare with about one thousand lines of Bartonian pastiche. Peter Brook commissions Ted Hughes to "translate" *King Lear* into modern English poetry. *Rosencrantz and Guildenstern Are Dead* juxtaposes archaic and contemporary idioms—"a bit of Shakespeare," Tom Stoppard explains, and then "a bit of me, a bit more of that, off with me, on with some Shakespeare."[115] Bond's *Lear* and Kurosawa's *Ran* likewise depend upon and rebel against *King Lear.* In Eugene

Ionesco's *Macbett* two ugly witches disguise themselves as Duncan's beautiful wife and her attendant gentlewoman; Macbett and Banco are at times interchangeable, mouthing the same political slogans used by Glamiss and Candor; at the end of the play Macol, having defeated Macbett, begins quoting Shakespeare's text, promising to "pour the sweet milk of concord into Hell."[116] Like Davenant's London *Macbeth*, Ionesco's Parisian *Macbett* inextricably mingles criticism and literature, the past and the present. Such adaptations differ from Shakespeare quite deliberately, and with that act of defiant deference they declare the *liberté, égalité, fraternité* of discourses.

SILVER SPRING

May 1987–January 1989. If you want a single symptomatic exemplar of Shakesperotics in the late twentieth century, the book you are reading now will do as well as any other. It would be arrogant to historicize others without at least attempting to historicize ourselves. And the very effort to make this book fold back upon itself is, in any case, altogether typical of the self-conscious reflexivity of postmodernist literature and criticism. Moreover, *Reinventing Shakespeare* (which was written in Silver Spring, a suburb of Washington, D.C.) has at least one advantage over other specimens of the contemporary Shakespeare industry: I can assume that you are familiar with its contents. This does not necessarily mean that you have (or will) read it from cover to cover. Even for hard-core Shakespearians, lifers, it is impossible to digest the hundreds of books and thousands of articles published on this subject in any year.

These circumstances, in which contemporary Shakespeare criticism is produced and distributed and consumed, affect the shape and content of the product. *Reinventing Shakespeare* is, typically, a modular book. A set of apparently self-contained historical packages, like sections of a Tootsie Roll, it permits readers to bite off whichever chapter happens to appeal to their own personal or professional appetites. But modular construction depends for its convenience upon tidy modules, and their very tidiness misrepresents the fluidity of history. When do Romantics become Victorians? When do Victorians become modernists? You could easily and legitimately subdivide the history of Shakesperotics differently than I have done, devoting a chapter to the Biedermeier Shakespeare of the mid-nineteenth century or the Eisenhower Shakespeare of the mid-twentieth, distinguishing each from the periods and paradigms that flank it. The categories in which I have divided this very chapter—feminist, Marxist, new historicist, and all the rest, lined up like so many booths at Bartholomew Fair—are equally arbitrary; most real persons belong to several of these overlapping and conflicting groups. Even the apparently fixed boundaries of the year 1986 prove, upon examination, as uncertain as the boundaries of any text. I have included work published in 1986, work completed in 1986 but published later, work given orally at conferences, work first paperbacked in 1986, work title-paged 1986 but actually issued at some other time, work issued in 1986 but given some other date on the title page. As in fractal geometry, every period can itself be divided into smaller periods, each equally detailed and divisible. Every boundary is infinitely long and infinitely complicated.

Nevertheless, modular books abound. Terence Hawkes' *That Shakespeherian Rag,* to pick one example arbitrarily, consists of an introduction, a conclusion, and four interloping chapters, each devoted to a different Shakespeare critic of the early twentieth century: A. C. Bradley, Walter Raleigh, T. S. Eliot, John Dover Wilson. Each chapter is intelligible in its own right, and indeed three of the four have already been published in separate journals or collections of essays—each more than once.[117] The four studies do gain something by being viewed together, like Van Goghs collected in one room; but each can be appreciated independently of its companions, and components could easily be added or subtracted without disturbing the structure.[118]

Self-deconstructing modular books—like Hawkes' Shakespeherian ragbag, or mine—readily accommodate the argument that every book is self-deconstructing, that the unity sought and praised by earlier writers is an illusion. Wholeness is impossible. The most celebrated essay in Hawkes' book is called "Telmah," which is *Hamlet* spelled backward. That essay seeks "to undermine our inherited notion of *Hamlet* as a structure that runs a satisfactorily linear, sequential course from a firmly established and well-defined beginning through a clearly placed and signalled middle to a causally related and logically determined end which, planted in the beginning, develops, or grows out of it."[119] The boundaries of a play or book of critical prose are arbitrary. What right has Shakespeare, Hawkes demands, to demand that we read the text in a certain arbitrary sequence?

Modular books can be constructed and consumed in a variety of shapes; they also make use of individual modules that can be, and often have been, used elsewhere as components of other structures. Most new books about Shakespeare, including this one, contain material already published elsewhere, in some other format. Such recycling permits writers a steady flow of productivity, a thin continuum of ephemera periodically coalescing into books.

Naturally enough, my professional colleagues and I begin to notice similarities between our working conditions and Shakespeare's. In Honigmann's vision of "William Shakespeare, Businessman," the playwright may have turned a double profit from each play and a triple profit from some: selling the script to a theatrical company (like any other playwright), pocketing a percentage of the earnings from performances of the play (like any other theatrical shareholder), and in some cases selling the manuscript to a publisher (like any other author). Stephen Orgel argues that the text of Shakespeare's plays might have been revised any time they were revived. Michael Hattaway contends that plays were deliberately designed for re-production in a variety of different theatrical spaces, from permanent London playhouses (indoor and outdoor), to disparate provincial touring sites, to court banqueting halls.[120] All these contemporary theories emphasize the recyclable adaptability of Shakespeare's product.

Contemporary criticism needs to be recyclable because power—in the academic world as in the theatre—depends upon visibility. If a play or essay appears in two places, twice as many people may see it. Invisibility is impotence, and visibility is getting harder to achieve. The sheer volume of transmissions being generated by the Shakesperotics industry makes the entire critical process dependent upon subsidiary systems of information management: bibliographies, reviews, surveys, innumerable instant evaluations of the current state of research. The chapter you are reading belongs, of course, to the same genre.

The book you are reading belongs to a related genre: the history of interpretation. Just as the annual survey article in *Studies in English Literature* gives us a map of the contemporary terrain, so the History of Shakespeare Studies gives us a map of past terrain. In both cases we need a map because the territory is so vast that we would get lost without one. So we rely on a tour guide. Guided histories of Shakespeare studies have become increasingly popular as the century wears on;* individual periods of Shakespeare criticism are now the subject of whole books in themselves. In 1986 Arthur Sherbo devotes a volume to *The Birth of Shakespeare Studies* in the eighteenth century, Jonathan Bate focuses on *Shakespeare and the English Romantic Imagination,* Richard Foulkes edits a collection of essays on *Shakespeare and the Victorian Stage,* and Terence Hawkes composes *That Shakespeherian Rag.* Shakespearian critics discover that they belong to a community that has a history, to a history that has in itself a meaning. Increasingly, we tell stories about ourselves.

The story *Reinventing Shakespeare* tells, and the way it tells that story, is inextricably bound up with the circumstances of the author, the publisher, and the society that produce it. In its emphasis upon the theatre, its efforts to pay more attention to the contributions of women, its attention to the complex social interaction between literature and culture, its criticism of New Criticism, its treatment of academic life as the stuff of satirical fiction, in many other ways that you will no doubt have noticed, this book is obviously generated by the attitudes and priorities I have been describing in this chapter. I can see—and warn you about—some of the ways in which it fits the paradigm that currently prevails. But, by definition, I cannot see all of them. You will see more of them than I do: by the time you read this book, its titular "present" will already be part of the past. But I, here in my present, could see all of the ways in which my thinking is typical of this period only if I could somehow get outside of our paradigm, if I could rise above it and look down upon it so that its edges became apparent. But if I could rise above our paradigm, I would no longer be in it. If I could show you all that was wrong with our paradigm, I would have destroyed that paradigm and constructed another one. Paradigms cannot be avoided; they can only be replaced.

* David Nichol Smith's account of *Shakespeare in the Eighteenth Century* (1928) was followed by Augustus Ralli's two-volume *A History of Shakespeare Criticism* (1932), Ivor Brown and George Fearson's *Amazing Monument: A Short History of the Shakespeare Industry* (1939), F. E. Halliday's *The Cult of Shakespeare* (1957), Louis Marder's *His Exits and His Entrances: The Story of Shakespeare's Reputation* (1963), Alfred Harbage's *Conceptions of Shakespeare* (1966), Arthur Eastman's *A Short History of Shakespearean Criticism* (1968), S. Schoenbaum's *Shakespeare's Lives* (1970), and Brian Vickers' six-volume anthology and commentary, *Shakespeare: The Critical Heritage* (1974–81), covering the years from 1623 to 1801.

CHAPTER 7

❧

SINGULARITY

Most histories of Shakespeare's reputation belong to the genre of academic romance, written from the perspective of an omniscient present tense. Scholarly writer and enthusiastic reader, knowing so much more than the critics of the past, hand in hand survey the follies and frolics, eccentricities and excesses, of their predecessors. The story originates with Shakespeare and terminates in our own orthodoxies about him. Shakespeare is the alpha, we are the omega; literary history is an interregnum, just a survey of middlemen.

One of the orthodoxies that every previous history of Shakespeare's reputation has perpetuated, usually without argument, is an assurance of Shakespeare's place among the world's greatest writers. Who would write or read a history of interpretations of Shakespeare, unless they believed that Shakespeare was worth writing and reading about? Many critics would claim (and have claimed) that Shakespeare is the greatest poet, the greatest playwright, of all time. From a closetful of such testimonials, all much alike, we can pick a representative sampler by Alfred Harbage, late Professor of English at Harvard University, author of a collection of astute essays on Shakespeare's reputation, and one of the most widely respected American Shakespeare scholars of this century. Harbage assures us,

"We can say that [Shakespeare] was the greatest dramatist of all times with our eyes open—the image is true."[1]

But even if it is true, how do we know it is? As I have tried to tell it, the history of Shakesperotics raises those questions insistently and makes any proposed answer uneasy. Charting the shifting sandbars of critical opinion, the social and cultural tides that have swept and shaped Shakespeare's reputation, it becomes increasingly difficult to discern what makes Shakespeare a "great" writer, let alone "the greatest." Let us assume, for the moment, that Shakespeare qualifies as a great writer. This assumption could be challenged, but most readers of this book will probably accept it, and I don't wish to attempt here any defense of a proposition so generally regarded as self-evident. But "great" does not mean "greatest." Anyone who claims that Shakespeare is the "greatest" poet or playwright must define Shakespeare's preeminence, his superlative uniqueness— what has been called in our own time "The Singularity of Shakespeare."[2] What, if anything, makes Shakespeare so different from—so much better than—everybody else? We can answer only by looking, however briefly, at the "everybody else" that it dismisses; we must compare the history of Shakespeare's reputation with the history of other great literary reputations.

I might as well warn you before we begin that none of the proposed defenses of Shakespeare's singularity is convincing. Shakespeare may indeed be a great writer; but we have no compelling reasons to consider him *uniquely* great. Moreover, the very fact that so many people have perpetuated and endorsed such unsatisfactory arguments raises another set of questions. What had been an issue of literary theory—"Why is Shakespeare singular?"—is transformed into an issue of literary history. Why do people think Shakespeare is singular, and how does thinking he is singular affect their attitude toward him and toward others?

*

It would be convenient if Shakespeare's primacy could be defined by objective criteria, and his biographers have accordingly tried to oblige. S. Schoenbaum speaks with a biographical authority unequaled in our time when he says that

Shakespeare's combined achievements as actor, sharer, and playwright made him ... "the most complete man of the theatre of
his time." Few in any age have served the stage so variously. Not
Racine or Ibsen or Shaw; only Molière, besides Shakespeare,
among playwrights of world stature.3

This is of course not true. The Roman comic dramatist Plautus
"served the stage" just as variously, having allegedly been a stage-
hand, actor, and director.4 Plautus, it might be said, is no longer
regarded as a dramatist of "world stature"; Schoenbaum's silent
exclusion of Plautus might therefore be defended.

But it would be hard to defend the neglect of Sophocles. His
stature as a great dramatist can hardly be denied, and we know he
was an actor, singer, and musician.5 Aeschylus seems to have acted,
too. We have no knowledge that Euripides or Aristophanes did so,
but they certainly, like Sophocles, directed their own plays—a job
that included choreographing the dances. All four Greek dramatists also usually composed the music for their own choral lyrics.
The songs in Shakespeare's plays, by contrast, are simpler, shorter,
and less important; Shakespeare did not write the music for them;
in several cases, he did not even write the words. As a writer of
singable poems Shakespeare was surpassed even in his own time by
the lyricist and composer Thomas Campion, who (like Cole Porter,
Stephen Sondheim, and the Greek dramatists) was equally adept at
both the literary and musical sides of songwriting.

Sophocles was a playwright, actor, singer, director, choreographer,
and composer; Aeschylus, Euripides, and Aristophanes performed
most of the same functions. More particularly, even as actors Sophocles and Molière share a distinction that Shakespeare cannot possibly claim. Sophocles made a name for himself as a performer;
Molière was the greatest actor of his era. The only two roles we can
associate with Shakespeare, on any early authority, are the old
servant Adam in *As You Like It* and Hamlet's father's ghost, both
small parts. Shakespeare was no doubt a competent professional;
but he could not compete with the likes of Richard Burbage and
Edward Alleyn.

None of these facts proves that Molière or Sophocles—or
Aeschylus, or Euripides, or Aristophanes—was a greater dramatist
than Shakespeare. But then, equally, Shakespeare's varied theatrical
experience does not prove that he was a greater dramatist than

Racine or Ibsen or Shaw. One might as well say that Shakespeare
was the Colley Cibber of the Elizabethan stage; both men did a little
of everything. Schoenbaum does not mention Cibber, or Noël Cow-
ard, because such examples would destroy the force of his implicit
logic, which says "Shakespeare's singular greatness is reflected in
the exceptional variety of his engagement in the theatre." By such
criteria we can deduce only that Shakespeare belongs to that subset
of dramatists which includes Cibber and Sophocles; even in that
constellation he is not the star of greatest magnitude.

Our greatest living authority on the Elizabethan and Jacobean
stage, G. E. Bentley, describes Shakespeare as "the most complete
man of the theatre of his time," by virtue of "the comprehensiveness
of his participation in all aspects of the theatrical enterprise, as
professional playwright, as actor, as 'sharer', and as theatre owner."[6]

But Bentley's statement is, if not literally false, at best debatable
and misleading. It is sophistry to describe Shakespeare's position as
a sharer as though it constituted in itself an "achievement." A sharer
was simply a shareholder in a theatrical company. To become a
shareholder required, it is true, some contribution to the collective
equity of a theatrical company. In Shakespeare's case that contribution could have been partly, indeed perhaps wholly, pecuniary: he
might have made a substantial capital investment in the new company, either through his personal ownership of play texts[7] or by
drawing on his family's financial resources (he was the eldest son);[8]
he might even have received, as Nicholas Rowe reported, a gift from
the Earl of Southampton, who was apparently his patron in the
months before the establishment of the new company.[9]

Nor was Shakespeare the only man of his period to combine the
roles of writing, acting, and shareholding; so did Thomas
Heywood. Like Shakespeare, Heywood wrote popular histories,
tragedies, and comedies; he also, unlike Shakespeare, wrote civic
pageants, court masques, a prose pamphlet on acting, and domestic
tragedy. Moreover, Heywood had "*either an entire hand, or at the least a
maine finger*" in the composition of some 220 plays[10]— more than
five times Shakespeare's output. Objectively considered, on the evidence of engagement in the greatest possible diversity of theatrical
experience, Heywood has a better claim than Shakespeare to be
hailed as "the most complete man of the theatre of his time."

Shakespeare's multifaceted commitment to the theatre probably
says more about Shakespeare the businessman than Shakespeare

the artist. Shakespeare achieved more financial security than any other playwright of his period, primarily because he was an actor and sharer in his company, not just a playwright. This arrangement put him in the same position as Molière, who was also the most financially successful playwright of his time.[11] In the seventeenth century a handsome living could not be secured simply by writing plays. After he had made his fortune, and before he was fifty, Shakespeare apparently retired to Stratford and lived off his investments, including his shareholding in the profits of the theatrical property and the theatrical company he had left behind. Having, as Rowe tells us, gathered "an Estate equal to his Occasion," he stopped writing.[12] Probably none of Sophocles' seven surviving plays was written before the age at which Shakespeare abandoned the theatre.

*

Nothing in the facts of Shakespeare's life can define or support his alleged supremacy among the world's writers. But where biography fails, history might succeed. Historical arguments, like biographical ones, have the benefit of seeming objectivity. Dr. Johnson was summing up an entire tradition of aesthetics when he declared that "length of duration and continuance of esteem" was the only measure of the merit of a work of art; "no other test can be applied."[13] Harry Levin made Dr. Johnson's test the cornerstone of his argument for what he called "The Primacy of Shakespeare."[14]

Levin's essay was provoked by a remark of Northrop Frye's. Frye had said that to call Shakespeare "one of the great poets of the world" was "not a statement of fact" but a mere "value-judgement," to which "not a shred of systematic criticism can ever be attached."[15] Levin, in order to refute this theoretical stricture, simply recited the "facts": the duration and extent of Shakespeare's fame, his early and sustained reputation as a supreme poet and dramatist, a reputation which has endured "all the vicissitudes save neglect," a reputation that in our time makes him more widely performed and studied than any other dramatist or poet.

Almost all of Shakespeare's modern apologists employ this defense, explicitly or implicitly. They seem curiously blind to the fact that none of Shakespeare's works is more than four hundred years old. This may be a long time in terms of Western culture; but if we want to compare Shakespeare's reputation now with those of, for instance, the great Greek dramatists (to whom he has been constantly compared since the seventeenth century), we must look at their reputations three to four hundred years after their deaths. In the century before the birth of Christ the plays of Aeschylus, Sophocles, Euripides, Aristophanes and Menander were studied and performed throughout what was then the entire "civilized" world. Shakespeare certainly does no better than the Greeks, on such a scale. And after all, despite our fondness for fools' prophecies, we cannot really know what kind of reputation Shakespeare will enjoy, in the theatre or the library, two thousand years from now.

In the first place, we cannot even be sure that any of his work will physically survive. Shakespeare's words are disappearing before our eyes; their sound is lost already, tentatively reimagined in specialized monographs written and disputed by phonologists and linguists, but spoken by no one, not even by critics who spend their lives reading Shakespeare, reading him silently or out loud in sounds he never heard; and the shape of his words, too, like their sound, is gone, or going; the code that communicated his meanings becoming unintelligibly obsolete, joined by grammatical constructions we no longer recognize or tolerate, their social register and resonance often inaudible to us, their spellings involuntarily renovated or, if left unmodernized, now encrusted with a strangeness that was no part of their first purpose; and the words themselves are going the way of their eccentric spellings and unhelpful punctuation, the substantives scheduled to suffer the fate already endured by the incidentals. Modernizing the spelling is no longer enough; Shakespeare will need to be translated—indeed, is already being translated—out of his English into ours, individual obsolete bricks in the facade being replaced—tactfully sometimes, crassly as often—by modern equivalents or the closest we can get to equivalents. Shakespeare, like Chaucer, like Sophocles, will have to be translated for his own countrymen.

Shakespeare's works are no more immortal than the scores of plays by the great Greek dramatists that have evaporated. Those plays succumbed to the fall of old power structures and the rise of new ideologies. Christianity had little use for pagan plays. The fall of the Roman Empire in the West, the rise of Islam (including the burning of the library of Alexandria in 641), the collapse of Byzantium (including the sack of Constantinople in 1453), all contributed to the slow but relentless erosion of Greek dramatic texts. Texts are material objects, like buildings; without maintenance they decay.

Shakespeare is just as vulnerable to accidents of war and shifts of ideology, just as helpless against the political power of a reigning orthodoxy. If the English revolution of the 1640s had sustained itself, if France had won its wars against England, if England like other countries had been culturally transformed by the upheavals of the late eighteenth century, then Shakespeare would almost certainly not have achieved or retained the dominance he now enjoys. In the future, from Christian and Islamic fundamentalism he could expect at best neglect, at worst persecution; some brands of Marxism might be no more friendly. From 1965 to 1977 the Cultural Revolution banned all translation, production, and criticism of Shakespeare in China.[16] And Nigerian playwright Wole Soyinka, winner of the 1986 Nobel Prize for Literature, has been rebuked by some African critics for his interest in and indebtedness to Shakespeare, who for them epitomizes European cultural imperialism.

But those who deplore such political intrusions upon cultural destiny must first acknowledge that what may in the future do Shakespeare harm has in the past done him good. The history of Shakesperotics repeatedly demonstrates that his reputation is a function of larger social and cultural movements. Native English competitors to his predominance in the theatre were severely discouraged by centuries in which the theatre was censored but the press free. The spread of his reputation in Europe depended largely upon his usefulness as a subversive alternative to French neoclassical hegemony. Some considerable proportion of Shakespeare's current international reputation is the fruit not of his genius but of the virility of British imperialism, which propagated the English language on every continent. They say that an Englishman is branded on his tongue; England branded the world's tongue. English is, in consequence, the lingua franca of our time, the dominant language of our international culture. Where English imperialism faltered—in most of Central and South America, for instance, where Spanish remains the prevalent colonial language—Shakespeare has made little headway. But the global currency of English has given him an insurmountable advantage, in the potential market for his words, over rival literary exports from France,

Spain, Italy, Germany, Russia, Japan—not to mention ancient Athens and Rome.

*

The uncertainty of physical survival cannot be underestimated in evaluating the most common of all critical arguments for Shakespeare's supremacy, the evident variety of his oeuvre.

> We may agree that, whatever our veneration for Greek tragedy, Shakespeare is no less powerful and far more varied; and again that where Racine is supreme in French tragedy, as Molière in comedy, Shakespeare combines the two ... the extraordinary width and range of his work [is] quite beyond Racine or Molière, Aeschylus or Euripides.[17]

A. L. Rowse's recent summation of the case for Shakespeare echoes a long line of critics, whose praises have been consciously quoted innumerable times and reiterated unconsciously innumerably oftener. As early as 1598 a shameless name-dropper named Francis Meres began the liturgical chant, claiming that "As *Plautus* and *Seneca* are accounted the best for Comedy and Tragedy among the Latines: so *Shakespeare* among yᵉ English is the most excellent in both kinds for the stage."[18] For much of the seventeenth and eighteenth centuries Shakespeare's comedies and histories were little admired, but even so Dryden credited him with "the largest and most comprehensive soul" of "all Modern, and perhaps Ancient Poets."[19]

Whether or not Shakespeare had the largest and most comprehensive soul, he certainly has one of the largest and most comprehensive bodies of extant work. When critics estimate Shakespeare's imaginative range, they take account of almost everything he ever wrote. For Sophocles, by contrast, we possess only seven plays, out of approximately 120 originals: 5 percent of his output. Five percent of Shakespeare would be only two plays. For neither Sophocles nor Aeschylus do we have a single surviving complete example of a genre that composed a full quarter of their output: the satyr play, a mythological burlesque that accompanied each set of three tragedies offered at the city festival.

Fate has been kinder to Euripides. Thanks to the chance survival of a single manuscript containing nine extra plays, we can read altogether about a quarter of his output, including one satyr play (*Cyclops*) and another dramatic hybrid (*Alcestis*) that was performed in the position usually reserved for satyr plays. The same manuscript preserves our only text of another play, *Heracles,* regarded by many modern critics as one of Euripides' greatest achievements. That single manuscript also contains all the surviving examples of his late tragicomedies: *Helen, Iphigeneia at Aulis, Iphigeneia at Taurus,* and *Ion.*

The lucky survival of those four plays supplies the most telling rebuttal to one of the commonplaces of Shakespeare hagiography. From 1598 to 1985, from Meres to Rowse, we have been told—have told ourselves—that Shakespeare was the first dramatist to succeed in both tragedy and comedy. But Euripides, though better known to us as a tragedian, was also "the inventor, for the stage, of what we know as comedy."[20] Euripides not only wrote tragedies and satyr plays and comedies; he also initiated a tradition of comedy that Shakespeare merely inherited. Euripides' primacy was recognized in antiquity: a papyrus fragment refers to the conflicts of husband and wife, father and son, master and servant, "and also the whole business of vicissitudes, raping of young women, substitutions of children, recognitions by means of rings and necklaces . . . these are of course the main elements of the New Comedy, and Euripides brought them to perfection." Euripides, not Menander, invented New Comedy.

Euripides also wrote tragedies, of course. But although Aristotle called him "the most tragic of poets,"[21] Euripidean tragedy embarrassed or annoyed most classical scholars of the eighteenth and nineteenth centuries. At a time when Euripides' comedy was misclassified and his tragedy misunderstood, he could hardly pose a serious challenge to Shakespeare's critical supremacy. And in the twentieth century, as Euripides' stock among classicists has risen, the number and prestige of classicists has fallen. Euripides' reputation has been ascending the stairs to the upper decks of an ocean liner that is sinking faster than he can climb.

The relationship between Shakespeare's reputation and Euripides' is not one of those unfortunate coincidences which result from the random interaction of independent agents; it is not just the cultural equivalent of my son coming in the front door while I go out the back door to look for him. The two reputations have been linked since the early seventeenth century: the reinventing of Shakespeare has always entailed a reinventing of Athenian drama. In the panegyric that prefaced the very first collected edition of Shakespeare's plays, Ben Jonson promised to "*call forth thund'ring Æschilus, / Euripides, and* Sophocles" in order to praise Shakespeare. Jonson did not give Shakespeare preference over the Greek triumvirate; but he did assert equivalence. The Greek tragedians were the obvious standards of achievement in serious drama; any new candidate had to be measured against them.

Jonson's proposed equivalence between Shakespeare and the Greeks was disputed for most of the seventeenth century. But, for the most part, these first controversies took the form of neoclassical attack and vernacular defense. When neoclassical critics pointed to features of Shakespeare's plays that violated the rules abstracted from certain interpretations of Aristotle and Horace, defenders of Shakespeare could then respond in two ways. Either they could point to similar deviations in classical plays, thus claiming that Shakespeare was no more irregular than the accepted models; or they could deny the universal applicability of classical practice, thus claiming that ancient and modern standards, though different, were of equal value. Both tactics were logically defensible, and both supported Jonson's claim to equivalence; but the first tended to draw attention away from Shakespeare, into the narrow detail of classical texts, while the second opened a wider front. It directly challenged the universality of prevailing theory: it entertained the possibility of two equally valid but incommensurable paradigms.

This shift of theoretical perspective was made possible by an ambiguity in the word "law": it could apply to the laws of nature or to the laws of nations. As Pope put it in 1725, "To Judge therefore of *Shakespear* by *Aristotle*'s rules, is like trying a man by the Laws of one Country, who acted under those of another."[22] Through this logical maneuver the defense of Shakespeare was justified by, and justified, a more general provincialism of the imagination. England could define crime and art in any way it wanted; there was no universal court of appeal that could arbitrate upon the justice of individual national verdicts, judicial or aesthetic. This new critical pluralism obviously belongs to the same intellectual climate that produced the political and religious pluralism of eighteenth-century England. But just as theoretical pluralism produced an actual hegemony of Whigs and Anglicans, so the seeming even-handedness of literary nationalism produced in practice an hegemony of native literature. Aeschylus, Sophocles, and Euripides sank to the status of foreign nationals. Greek tragedies were not performed; they could be read by only a minority of the literate population. How could they compete on equal terms with Shakespeare, whose plays dominated the theatres and flooded the bookshops?

The European intelligentsia did not stop reading Greek tragedies, or comparing them with Shakespeare's tragedies, or seeking universal aesthetic prescriptions for tragedy. On the contrary, from the middle of the eighteenth century writers and critics in many parts of Europe developed a sharpened new enthusiasm for Greek literature and the Greek spirit. But they appreciated that culture, now, for its very foreignness, its Greekness. The important thing about Greece was that Greece was not Georgian England. Within this new system of evaluation, Greek authors were inevitably judged by the degree to which they satisfied, not the old universalist aesthetics but the new conception of Greekness. Homer, Aeschylus, and Sophocles were properly Greek, precisely by virtue of their sustained difference and distance from modern European thought; but Euripides was too much like us, too modern, too un-Greek.

Euripides was not sufficiently *other;* hence, paradoxically, he was reviled for those very aspects of his art which were, at the same time and sometimes by the same people, being praised in Shakespeare: his mixing of tones, the colloquialism of his language, the inconsistencies and contradictions in his plots, his disregard for tradition and the rules, his shifts from the sublime to the risible, his refusal to invest kings and heroes with a decorously heroic and kingly dignity, his representation of men (in Sophocles' own description of Euripidean practice) "not as they should be, but as they are." Euripides, it was said, had resisted the natural genius of his nation (as defined by Victorian classicists); Shakespeare, by contrast, had conformed. The comparability of their artistic practice, which in the late seventeenth century had been used as evidence in Shakespeare's defense, by the nineteenth century became evidence against Euripides.

Greek tragedy was the culture of a foreign country; but it was also, in England, the culture of a country within a country. From the middle of the eighteenth century the classical languages were institutionalized, with increasing rigor, as mechanisms of class distinction. In 1748 we are told that "The word *illiterate,* in its common acceptation, means a man who is ignorant of [Latin and Greek]." In the 1790s political conservatives praised the classical languages for "making the language and thought of the higher orders distinguishable from that of their social inferiors."[23]

After 1805, as the result of a court decision, Greek and Latin became the only subjects that could be taught in free schools, thus accelerating and hardening the transformation of the old grammar schools into vehicles of elitism and class division. Greek tragedy became a weapon in the hands of the British upper classes. And in the schools themselves the methods of teaching—with their relentless emphasis upon philology, memorizing, construing, "gerund-grinding"—transformed the plays themselves into instruments of pedagogical oppression. This educational system predictably made Greek and Latin the focus of hostility for those excluded from it and for those subjected to it. Greek tragedy represented compulsion, the enforcement from above of a mind-grinding rule; Shakespeare, again, by contrast, seemingly embodied imaginative freedom. First against the French neoclassical dramatists, then against the Athenian classical dramatists, Shakespeare triumphed because he was associated (rationally) with English linguistic nationalism and (irrationally) with freedom.

In our society Shakespeare has become the subject, in most schools and universities, of "required courses"; for almost a century now, students have been compelled to study him, as they were once compelled to study Greek and Latin. The badge of cultural elitism and the instrument of pedagogical oppression, Shakespeare now finds himself needing to be constantly justified against the determined boredom, the soaking resentment, of conscripts. Captivated audiences have become captive classrooms. At the same time, modern scholarship has made us increasingly conscious of the perimeters that constrained Shakespeare's art: political and religious censorship, the inherited conventions of the Elizabethan theatre, the legal need for patronage, the hostility of London's civic government, the dimensions of the stage, the theatre's limited technical resources, the size and organization of acting companies, the limited number of boy actors available to play female parts, the need to double roles, the need for plots that facilitated doubling, the expectations of audiences. Such preconditions bound Shakespeare no less than the neoclassical rules bound Racine. The old no longer believe Shakespeare was free; the young no longer experience him freely.

Shakespeare's charisma has been thoroughly institutionalized, and we have yet to see whether, or in what shape, he will survive the resultant concretion of his talent. Only then will we be in any position to measure Shakespeare's achievement on the scales of "length of duration and continuance of esteem." But Dr. Johnson's scales should, in any case, be reexamined by the National Bureau of Standards. Why does Dr. Johnson repose such trust in "length of duration and continuance of esteem"? Because, as the most famous of England's Tory journalists assures us, "What mankind have long possessed they have often examined and compared, and if they persist to value the possession, it is because frequent comparisons have confirmed opinion in its favor."[24] Rival products have come and gone; consumers have tasted and tested them; if the consumers of culture continue to prefer Brand X, then it must be superior. But this argument presupposes an absolutely free and rational market; it presumes that consumers' choices have not been distorted by false advertising, or state intervention, or institutional monopolies, or inequalities of investment and distribution, or inertia. It ignores the influence of prevailing systems of belief—like Johnson's own unconscious equation, in eighteenth-century Europe's most advanced capitalist society, of literature with a "possession" periodically assessed by its owner, an owner defined as "mankind," though in Johnson's England "mankind" effectively consisted of a thin crust of about twelve thousand London intellectuals.[25] Sometimes what rises to the top is not cream but scum.

Dr. Johnson has another argument: "what has been longest known has been most considered, and what is most considered is best understood."[26] Prolonged familiarity breeds knowledge, knowledge of both weakness and strength; if a work survives such scrutiny, it must deserve the esteem awarded it. But such reasoning modulates all too easily into Edmund Burke's defense of tradition against change. What has been "most considered"—God, for instance—is not always, as a result, "best understood." The Bible, the *Aeneid,* Homer, Shakespeare, the U.S. Constitution, the Communist Manifesto—once a society enshrines a text, that text accumulates all the meanings of the clerisy of its interpreters. In that excess of meaning, meaning disappears altogether, just as too much light blinds. I doubt whether anyone who professes literature in the English-speaking nations really knows anymore whether Shakespeare is "as good as they say." Our judgment is bewildered past recall by the babble of acclamation and explication; our tongues make noises but can no longer taste.

*

> ... one man cannot be more than one man; there might have been six Shakespeares at once without conflicting frontiers; and to say that Shakespeare expressed nearly all human emotions, implying that he left very little for anyone else, is a radical misunderstanding of art and the artist—a misunderstanding which, even when explicitly rejected, may lead to—

May lead to what? May lead—has led, certainly—to the belittlement of subsequent English drama. May lead, has led, to the impossible insistence that new talent contort itself to fit the Shakespeare pattern. In the last twenty-five years, when the British theatre has midwifed more new good plays than at any time since the seventeenth century, Alan Ayckbourn is berated because he can write "only" comedy, Tom Stoppard is put in his place because he cannot create sufficiently rounded "characters," Edward Bond has to be dismissed because he does not have or want Shakespeare's "wonderful philosophical impartiality." May lead, has led, to our underestimating the drama of other nations. We assume that Shakespeare's thirty-odd plays contain more of humanity than the five hundred plays of Lope de Vega that we have not read. May lead, has led, to misdefinition of Shakespeare himself and of the other playwrights of the late sixteenth and early seventeenth centuries whose plays he watched and read and acted. May even lead, has led, I do not doubt, to our neglecting all those aspects of humanity which Shakespeare neglected, on the assumption that anything outside the circle of his art does not exist.

But that was not how T. S. Eliot ended the sentence. Eliot, characteristically, displaces the argument into a minor key; having, like an American gangster, pressed the point of his knife against someone's solar plexus, he then, rather embarrassed by his own extravagance, steps back and, elegantly, like an English valet—so elegantly indeed that you hardly notice the altered trajectory—pricks the pinkie of his left hand. Assuming that Shakespeare had exhausted the possibilities of language and of human nature may, as Eliot sternly warns us, lead to

> our neglecting the effort of attention necessary to discover the specific properties of the verse of Shakespeare's contemporaries.[27]

Eliot was, as these final phrases remind us, an epicure of metrics, the rightful heir of Alfred Tennyson and Robert Bridges, the recognizable contemporary of A. E. Housman.

But even if we restrict ourselves to technicalities of form, as Eliot here invites us to do, it can be hard to see Shakespeare's limitations unless we willfully temporarily estrange ourselves from the critical assumptions we have been raised on. It takes an effort of the imagination for a modern critic to comprehend how, in 1846, Walter Savage Landor could describe Shakespeare's sonnets as "hot and pothery: there is much condensation but little delicacy; like raspberry jam without cream, without crust, without bread, to break the viscidity."[28] The sonnets don't taste that way to us—perhaps because we have been eating them for as long as we can remember.

We don't take Landor's criticism seriously partly because we don't take Landor's poetry seriously anymore. If you compare Shakespeare's dramatic verse with that of post-Restoration English drama, with Dryden's *The Conquest of Granada* or Addison's *Cato,* you will almost certainly, like other readers for the past three hundred years, come away convinced of Shakespeare's superiority as a verbal artist. Looking around for explanations of that superiority, you could easily attribute it—most critics do—to the very characteristics of Shakespeare's verse that the Restoration deplored: its clinching puns, its hodgepodge of verbal strata, its metaphor-clotting. But Racine and Sophocles explode that hypothesis; both distill meaning from "imaginative bareness,"[29] a tightened vocabulary, an idiom stripped and squeezed and hard. They channel the power of their pleasures. Racine and Sophocles and the tradition they define contradict the easy assumption—easy at least for those raised on Shakespeare—that verbal authority is a function of the features Dryden disliked. If Shakespeare succeeds, he succeeds for more complicated reasons, which we will never recognize unless we respect, at the same time, an alternative poetry, equally powerful but different in kind. Anyone who admires the achievements of

English baroque in architecture and music, Christopher Wren and Henry Purcell, should be able to imagine a corresponding verbal elegance, palisaded but not pallid. The Restoration produced no comparable achievement in dramatic verse; but that failure does not justify an assumption that there is no worthwhile alternative to Shakespeare's style.

In the late seventeenth century Gerald Langbaine, presenting himself as "a Champion in the Dead Poets Cause, to vindicate their Fame" against the criticisms of Dryden, claimed that Dryden's "Improprieties" were as great as Shakespeare's.[30] This complaint echoes down through the centuries: in a book published in 1987 Harry Levin snidely complains that "with due cognizance of [Dryden's] own imperfections as a playwright," his criticisms of Shakespeare appear "two-faced."[31] Such ad hominem criticism of Dryden distracts attention from the real issue. "It does not follow," as George Bernard Shaw insisted, "that the right to criticize Shakespeare involves the power of writing better plays"; even Shaw did not "profess to write better plays."[32] In any case, could Gerald Langbaine, or Harry Levin, write as well as Dryden? If Dryden had no right to criticize Shakespeare, what right have they to criticize Dryden?

*

We can understand what Shakespeare did only if we understand what he didn't do and understand too that what he didn't do was worth doing. What he did is a matter of substance as well as style: not only how he talked but what he talked about. What Shakespeare left out is as important as what he put in. You don't have to buy psychoanalysis to recognize that the subjects people avoid are as significant as the ones they belabor.

To take just one example, *Measure for Measure* tells the story of a puritanical governor who sets out to eliminate sexual corruption in Vienna. Shakespeare tells the story in a way that repeatedly undercuts this ambition. Angelo, the governor, himself succumbs to lust; the most visible victims of his crusade are a likable young engaged couple, guilty of nothing more heinous than consummation before consecration (dessert before saying grace). By concentrating upon the hypocritical governor and the unlucky lovers, Shakespeare distracts attention from the real focus of sexual corruption, Viennese prostitution. The sex industry is represented in his play by a dimwitted john (Froth, described by the list of characters in the Folio itself as "a foolish Gentleman"), by a witty pimp (Pompey Bum, his surname punning on the British sense "buttocks," incongruously juxtaposed with the classical pomp of "Pompey"), and by an old bawd (Mistress Overdone, punning on the slang sense "fucked too much"; perhaps the modern equivalent would be "Mrs. Overlaid"). A crew of harmless comics: dumb customer, daffy pimp, dizzy madam. The names themselves assure us that we have entered the world of happy whoredom. But where, pray tell, are the prostitutes?

Shakespeare shows us the customers and the management, but the sexual work force itself, the women who ride up and down the shaft to the coal mines of prostitution, them we never see, never hear, hardly hear of. The worst punishment that can be devised for Lucio, at play's end, a punishment many modern critics consider neurotically severe (on the Duke's part or Shakespeare's), is "Marrying a punk"—being forced to husband a prostitute he had impregnated. Likewise, in *Pericles* we see the husband-and-wife duo of brothel owners comically complaining about the local whore shortage, and we see their eager underling Bolt (a name both phallic and functional, since he bolts the door); but nary a prostitute do we see. The management buys and then tries to sell Marina; but she, in a delectable little dramatic fantasy, moralizes the lust out of her customers, so that they pay her for sermons instead of sex. Indeed, one of them, who happens happily to be the most eligible bachelor in town, falls in love with her and, in due course, proposes marriage.

Prostitution, like theatre, had rapidly expanded during Shakespeare's lifetime, catering to a demand generated by the increasing density of population in London. Its supply of female raw material was fished up from the widening pool of displaced and destitute families caused by agricultural contraction, periodic commercial recessions, plague, conscription for war, disregard for disabled veterans, persistent inflation and a steady decline in real wages. The rise of capitalism made more families more vulnerable economically, at the very time when political and demographic change tended to isolate individuals from earlier mechanisms of social protection. The dissolution of the monasteries in the mid-sixteenth century destroyed the central institutions of organized charity, while the new thousands pouring into London, the country's social sewer, found themselves packed into poorly policed, unplanned slums, cut off from the old networks of neighborliness and parish charity. Then as now, prostitution fed, and fed upon, urban alienation, and like other forms of private enterprise it expanded as capitalism did. People who sell, sell people. In a favorite pun of Jacobean city comedy, bordellos and boardrooms unite in their devotion to "(w)holesale."

London's playhouses went up alongside its whorehouses, in areas just beyond the reach of civic authority, and from the building of the first theatres to their closing in 1642 critics and apologists alike recognized that "Strumpets, Pandors, Bawdes, Adulterers, Whoremasters, Drunkards, Prodigals,) doe flocke by troopes to Stageplayes, with greedinesse and delight."33 Prostitution and playing are both service industries; both cater gainfully to the market for real fantasy. According to the Puritan opposition, theatres did not just attract whores; they produced them. A theatre was "the school of Bauderie," where spectators saw and passively assented to romantic and erotic gestures, actions, situations: "in the representation of whoredome, al the people in mind plaie the whores."34 The audience enacted imaginatively what the play acted out. Players and prostitutes worked in the same buildings, lived off the same customers; both simulated passions they did not feel; both went through the motions without the emotions. Whorehouse and playhouse alike stood on the uncertain periphery of the city and the law: condemned but condoned, persecuted and permitted. The contradiction persisted until the outbreak of civil war: in 1642 the theatres were closed; in 1650 Parliament made unlawful fornication a crime, subject to three months' imprisonment, and adultery a felony, punishable by death.

Just as Shakespeare suppressed, consciously or not, the actual prostitutes in *Measure for Measure* and *Pericles*, so he suppressed the kinship between the world's oldest profession and his own. The actor-playing-Hamlet marvels at the actor-playing-an-actor who,

> ... in a fixion, in a dreame of passion
> Could force his soule so to his whole conceit
> That from her working all his visage wand,
> Teares in his eyes, distraction in's aspect,
> A broken voyce, an his whole function suting

With formes to his conceit; and all for nothing,
For *Hecuba*.
What's *Hecuba* to him, or he to *Hecuba*,
That he should weepe for her?

The actor-playing-Hamlet, prompted by this histrionic model, then launches into a rhetorical tirade of his own—only to cut himself off in disgust, exclaiming

... what an Asse am I ... That I ...
Must like a whore unpacke my hart with words,
And fall a cursing like a very drabbe;
A scullyon, fie uppont, foh.[35]

What was the behavior of an actor has become, thirty lines later, the behavior of a whore: from harlequin to harlot in one speech. But neither Hamlet nor Shakespeare makes the connection explicit, and audiences catch it subliminally if at all. Shakespeare's imagination made the equation but kept it on the periphery of the poetry, in the suburbs of consciousness. Thus, the pimp in *Measure for Measure* is consistently called, in stage directions and speech prefixes, "Clowne"; but the spoken text never addresses the relation between his sexual and theatrical function.

In Shakespeare's time actors were male, prostitutes were female. The difference of gender made it easier to deny the likenesses between the two professions; but it also tended to channel that denial into misogyny. The protagonist of *Hamlet* welcomes and praises a troupe of strolling players, commissioning a performance from them; the protagonist of *Timon of Athens* berates and drives off a pair of strolling prostitutes, having commissioned them to spread syphilis as widely as possible. Shakespeare wasted no sympathy on the women lured or conned or forced into prostitution. The working women who do appear in his plays are accused of murdering their customers outright (Doll Tearsheet, in *Henry IV, Part 2*) or of murdering them piecemeal, with disease (Phrynia and Timandra, in *Timon of Athens*), in both cases without compunction or compulsion. Shakespeare's contemporary Thomas Middleton could sympathize with the "Distressed needlewomen and trade-fallne wiues," the "poore spirits" and "poore shifting sisters," "hungry things" caught on the "hooke" baited by urban pimps;[36] but Shakespeare himself never considers, or asks his audience to consider, the circumstances or motives of such women.

Shakespeare sees prostitution from the outside, or rather from the male side, the side of the customer or the pimp; the women either do not exist at all (as in *Measure for Measure* and *Pericles*) or deserve contempt (as in *Henry IV, Part 2* and *Timon of Athens*). Curiously, unrealistically, they are never young, never beautiful, never genuinely alluring. To make them attractive would be to admit their power; but it might also force male actors to equate themselves with female prostitutes. An actor can play a comic pimp comfortably enough; to do so simply concedes that whores ply their trade in the actors' building, that actors by their performances bring together in one place male customers and willing women. The pander in *Pericles* contemplates retiring, once he has made enough money to set himself up in some more honorable profession. The first great Elizabethan actor, Edward Alleyn, had done just that, and at the time *Pericles* was written Shakespeare was doing the same thing. Shakespeare could tolerate, barely, the image of the actor as a jovial, harmless, male pimp; but he never pictured the actor as an oppressed, alluring, female whore.

With one hand Shakespeare denied the connection between common players and common prostitutes; with the other he assumed their identity. Because actors enjoy acting, whores must enjoy whoring; after all, if they didn't, then they could, like Marina, just refuse to do it, and marry a prince. In *Measure for Measure* the contemporary Puritan enemies of the theatre are personified in Angelo; but in the play Vienna, unlike London, has no theatres, and Angelo's reforming zeal is directed at sexual license, not theatrical licenses. Shakespeare, accordingly, can discredit Angelo's moral crusade by making him personally guilty of sadistic lust. By displacing the moral issue onto sexuality, by suppressing any hint of a parallel campaign against theatres, Shakespeare can undermine the opponents of playing, without ever arguing the merits of their case and without ever conceding, to himself or his audience, the connection between whorehouse and playhouse. It took Jean Genet—who ate infamy with as much relish as Shakespeare accumulated respectability—to insist, theatrically, upon that connection.

But the absence of prostitutes (and theatres) from *Measure for Measure* does not just testify to Shakespeare's suppression of an association, social and psychological, that he found disturbing. It also belongs to a more general discrepancy between the world of

Shakespeare's plays and the world outside them. *Measure for Measure* contains five women; seventeen men are specified, in addition to the many unnamed lords, officers, citizens, and servants, all male, who populate the periphery of the text. Isabella, the most visible and voluble of the five women, speaks less than half as many words as the Duke; all five combined speak only 18 percent of the text. Still, by comparison with other plays, women do rather well in *Measure for Measure: Hamlet* specifies two women to twenty-eight men, *Julius Caesar* two women to thirty-eight men. Men are overrepresented in Shakespeare, as they are in Congress and Parliament. That is part of the meaning of Shakespeare's plays and, indeed, of all the plays of the English Renaissance.

Before 1660 female roles were impersonated by boy actors, and boys could not be expected to play mature women as easily as very young ones. Most of Shakespeare's women are, accordingly, girls; they belong to that liminal age when boy meets girl, when boyness meets girlness, and the two states easily interpenetrate, before sexual distinctions have hardened into barriers. In *Measure for Measure* Isabella, Mariana, and Juliet are all, in an idiom significantly sexless, "young things." Mistress Overdone, by contrast, belongs to an alternative female class: hags. Old women can be caricatured by young males no more improbably than girls can be played by boys; consequently Shakespeare's females are generally either pretty young or ugly old. Exceptions can be cited; tendencies are never absolute; that does not diminish their significance. The very structure of theatrical companies before 1660 discouraged the presentation of women in the prime of life. In its paucity of females, and their age, the English Renaissance theatre fundamentally misrepresented English Renaissance demography.

And why do so many of Shakespeare's women—Kate and Bianca, Hero, Lear's three daughters, Desdemona, Miranda, Ophelia, the list goes on—have onstage fathers but seemingly no mothers? In prescientific gynecological myth women were thought to be relatively superfluous even in the process of human reproduction. The mother (Latin *mater*) simply provided the vessel, the test tube, the "matter" or "mater" (both spellings were current in Shakespeare's time) in which a male seed developed. In this biological hypothesis, children had only one essential parent, and that parent was male. Women's bodies were simply the medium through which male messages were transmitted from generation to generation.

Female roles were played not by adult males but by boys. In the ideology of Western patriarchal cultures, formally articulated by Aristotle, a woman is simply an immature, not fully developed, more primitive form of man. Shakespeare's young women, when for some reason or another they wish to disguise themselves as males, often pretend to be "pages"; not surprisingly, the wit of Shakespeare's comic women, of Rosalind or Julia, played by boy actors, resembles the wit of Shakespeare's comic pages, played by the same boy actors. Both kinds of character deal in the precious and the precocious; like the child stars of modern film and television, they amuse audiences by displaying an impertinent intelligence, a witty insubordination, even at times a talent for sexual innuendo, not expected from and deliciously incongruous in such mouths. Shakespeare's clever women are clever boys in drag; sometimes, his clever women are clever boys in trousers. And the role of page accurately defines the status of the boy actors who played such roles. Within the dramatic companies themselves, which were modeled on craft guilds, the actors who played female roles were apprentices, under the charge of a specific adult actor, their "master"; the drama of female subordination, played out onstage, reflected the reality of economic subordination backstage.

That economic subordination ran the risk of becoming, or of appearing to become, sexual subordination. The young apprentice was required to dress as a woman and then to act out romantic episodes with older males, sometimes perhaps the same male who was his master, the master in whose house he lived. If the aroma of forbidden sexuality attached itself to the Elizabethan theatre in general, suspicion focused particularly upon those transvestite boys. To cast such a boy in the role of an alluring whore, brought before the public by an older male actor impersonating a pimp, would come uncomfortably close to exposing the equation between prostitution and playing.

The absence of prostitutes from *Measure for Measure* is already overdetermined; it originates in the social and institutional conditions of Elizabethan theatre and in Shakespeare's own ambivalences about prostitution, about acting, about women. But it also belongs to a more general pattern of attitudes toward the working class. Of the twenty-one specified adult characters in *Measure for Measure*, only four belong to the vast majority of the population beneath the rank of gentleman: Mistress Overdone the bawd, Pompey the pimp, Elbow the constable, and Abhorson the executioner—criminals and clowns. These characters in combination speak less than 11 percent of the text. It would be absurd to demand some sort of quota system, by which the characters in each play are proportioned demographically along lines of gender and class; but what happens in *Measure for Measure* happens in the other plays too. Like women, the lower and middle classes are systematically underrepresented by Shakespeare. They are also, as the sample from *Measure for Measure* makes clear, misrepresented. They are all, like Shakespeare's prostitutes, seen from above.

What I am doing here to Shakespeare could be done to any of us. Drawing attention to the holes and displacements in Shakespeare's texts, the blind spots and distortions in his vision, reminds us that he was human, therefore limited, therefore specific to a time and place. Coleridge found *Measure for Measure* a "hateful" and "disgusting" work;[37] it is, no doubt, in part—not, as the conservative Coleridge would object, because it contains too much reality, but because it contains too little.

*

Shakespeare cannot claim any unique command of theatrical resources, longevity or reach of reputation, depth or range of style, universality or comprehensiveness. But critics continue to exalt him, and the logic of their superlatives can be illustrated by *The Comedy of Errors*, which serves this purpose particularly well, since Shakespeare based it, undoubtedly and unabashedly, upon a Latin original, *The Menaechmi* of Plautus.

Recent scholarship would place *The Comedy of Errors* somewhere toward the end of the first quarter of Shakespeare's career—not, by a long shot, his earliest play or even his earliest comedy.[38] But most of the critics I am about to quote consider it his first work, and yet they feel no compunctions about repeatedly asserting that, in every sort of way, it surpasses a mature work by one of the two acknowledged masters of Roman comedy. David Young, for instance, writing in an acclaimed reference book, simply assumes without discussion that *The Comedy of Errors* was "Shakespeare's earliest comedy," in which he "dutifully" followed the "rather dubious" classical models of Plautus and Terence; this single "exercise in Plautine comedy proved to Shakespeare that he could imitate the ancients closely and that he did not particularly care to observe such boundaries in future."39 Anthony Burgess, in a popular biography, considers *Errors* "the first work of any length that Shakespeare completed"; it began as a simple translation, but developed into an adaptation; it marks the transition between Shakespeare's career as a schoolmaster in the country and his career as a playmaster in the city.40 In both Burgess and Young, novelist and academic, Shakespeare starts where the classics left off, and immediately surpasses them; he "outPlautuses Plautus." He breaks out of the "dutiful . . . dubious . . . boundaries." The very placement of *The Comedy of Errors* on the starting line of the Shakespeare canon—despite the absence or hostility of the evidence—imposes a predetermined shape and scale and meaning on Shakespeare's career and his achievement.

Both Plautus and Shakespeare tell the story of male twins, identical in name and appearance, separated at birth, and of the arrival of one of these twins in the town inhabited by the other, where numerous comic confusions of identity occur. But Shakespeare adds two twin servants, both named Dromio, one attached to each of the twin brothers. Every modern critic remarks that Shakespeare, by doubling the twins, doubles the confusions of identity. In the words of one of them, he has "made *The Comedy of Errors* structurally as much a tour de force as one of the great Bach fugues."

A different perspective on such changes comes from editions of Plautus, which tell us that "Shakespeare, who wrote in an age of Mistaken Identity plays, spoils *The Menaechmi* by adding the two Dromios."41

The difference between the Shakespearian and the classicist here makes it obvious that neither has proven anything. Tweedledum blasts Tweedledee. To say that Shakespeare complicated his source does not prove that he improved it. In complicating the story he also made it more improbable, and the same critics who here praise implausible complication will elsewhere applaud Shakespeare's efforts to simplify and plausify the stories he stole from other sources. Shakespeare's play is, as almost everyone points out, twice the size of its Latin original. But expansiveness need not be, by definition, virtuous. The most obvious difference between Shakespeare and the classical dramatists—Corneille, Racine, and Molière included—is epitomized in this very distinction between *The Comedy of Errors* and *The Menaechmi:* complexity and expansion opposed to simplicity and concentration. Either strategy can work; neither has a monopoly on merit. The classical alternative gives us, in contrast to Shakespeare, what Eliot in another connection called "A condition of complete simplicity / (Costing not less than everything)."[42]

Another intriguing set of critical dicta huddles around Shakespeare's demotion of the character that Plautus names Erotium. In Plautus' plot she plays a larger, more important, more explicit part; in Shakespeare's play she has no name, and we only know that she is a "Courtezan" if we read the stage directions and speech prefixes of a printed text. The word never appears in the dialogue and so is never heard in the theatre, and her profession can accordingly be communicated, if at all, only by caricatures of costume or behavior.

What do we make of such changes? According to Paul Jorgensen, in the introduction to an edition widely used in college classrooms, "Plautus is Roman comedy at its most cynical. Elizabethans preferred a wife rather than a prostitute as the central female character . . . The English audience preferred in general some softening of the derisive, satirical spirit that constituted comedy for the Romans."[43] David Bevington, in an edition even more recent and even more popular, enunciates this position even more clearly:

> the softening touches of Shakespeare's maturity are unmistakably present as well . . . He adds characters to the Plautine original in order to enhance the love interest and to reconcile Plautus with English moral conventions . . . *The Comedy of Errors* is quite far removed from *The Menaechmi* in tone and spirit. Gone are the cynicism, the satirical hardness, and the amoral tone of the Roman original . . . The Courtezan's role is no longer prominent. Instead Shakespeare creates Luciana, the virtuous sister of Adriana . . .[44]

It is no doubt symptomatic of my own cynicism, amorality, and satirical hardness that this description of the superiority of Shakespeare's play makes me want to read Plautus. I am reminded of Joe Orton's wish that he should never write anything "as bad as" Shakespeare's first plays.[45] Are we to deduce from Bevington that courtesans are less legitimate as the subjects of great art than "virtuous sisters"? Must every comedy "enhance the love interest"? The phrase could have been excerpted from a movie magnate's memo to a hack scriptwriter. Is it the business of a great artist to reshape his material in order to "reconcile" it with the moral values of his time and place? Euripides would hardly agree, nor for that matter would Solzhenitsyn.

The very ease with which Shakespeare accommodated himself to the values of his age perhaps explains in part Wittgenstein's distrust of him. Unlike Tolstoy or Goethe or Dante or Kafka, Shakespeare does not seem to have struggled, to have been outraged or oppressed by the confines of his times; and without such struggle facility becomes facile, the poet contracting to a mere technician of language, a verbocrat in the literary meritocracy. What was a calling becomes a job. Emerson, despite his admiration for Shakespeare's art, did not consider him a true "poet-priest,"[46] and Santayana was disconcerted by the complete absence of "true religious feeling" in Shakespeare's work (in contrast to Homer, Lucretius, Dante, or Goethe).[47] Wittgenstein feels a similar unease:

> "Beethoven's great heart"—nobody could speak of "Shakespeare's great heart" . . . He is *not* true to life . . . And if Shakespeare is great, as he is said to be, then it must be possible to say of him: it's all wrong, things *aren't like that*—and yet at the same time it's quite right according to a law of its own . . . In other words he is completely unrealistic. (Like a dream.)[48]

Shakespeare discommoded reality. He dramatized the daydreams of his culture.

Tolstoy in the first paragraph of an infamous essay declared that his "own long-established opinion about the works of Shakespeare" directly opposed "that established in the whole European world" and supported by "all civilized men of the Christian world." Tolstoy, too, found Shakespeare's plays unreal:

> In Shakespeare everything is exaggerated . . . the exaggeration of events, the exaggeration of emotion, and the exaggeration of effects. One sees at once that he does not believe in what he says . . . In all of [Shakespeare's works] one sees intentional artifice; one sees that he is not *in earnest*, but that he is playing with words . . .

Not only unreal but immoral, because that intentional artifice is employed in the service of a degenerate philosophy; "moderation in everything," the conservation of established institutions, "Chauvinist English patriotism," a philosophy that "despises" the working classes and "repudiates" religious and humanitarian efforts toward "the betterment of the existing order." And Shakespeare's defenders refuse to recognize such weakness and corruption because they adopt "exactly the same attitude" toward Shakespeare "which is usually met, in the defenders of any dogmas accepted not through reason, but through faith."[49] Tolstoy here echoes an observation made by an Englishman in the 1760s, soon after Shakespeare's installation as the monarch of English literature: "A Veneration for Shakespear seems to be a Part of [an Englishman's] National Religion, and the only Part in which even your Men of Sense are Fanatics."[50] Shakespeare is the spokesman and the beneficiary of superstition.

In their criticisms of Shakespeare, Wittgenstein and Tolstoy enact the stance they admire: they struggle against the idolatries of their day, they set up the emotional honesty of their own responses against the cant and convention they hear all around them and in Shakespeare himself. They play the fool, the deflator of common (non)sense. And they have generally been treated as though, by criticizing Shakespeare, they had made fools of themselves. George Orwell explains Tolstoy's criticisms of *King Lear* as a function of Tolstoy's own uncomfortable similarity to Lear;[51] as usual, since the days of Dryden and Rymer, the critique is not rationally answered but taken as proof of personal weakness. Hume and Wittgenstein and Santayana were philosophers; philosophers can't be trusted. Voltaire and Emerson and Tolstoy and Wittgenstein were foreigners; foreigners can't be trusted. Hazlitt and Cobbett were radicals; radicals can't be trusted. Oliver Goldsmith condemned Shakespeare's "forced humour, far fetch'd conceit, and unnatural hyperbole";[52] Samuel Johnson said that "Shakespeare never has six lines together without a fault";[53] Matthew Arnold complained about Shakespeare's sloppy "workmanship" and his often "detestable" style;[54] A. E. Housman confessed that "it gave him no pleasure to read a play of Shakespeare's from beginning to end, for though some parts were magnificent, there were others so slovenly that the effect of the whole was disagreeable."[55] But Goldsmith and Johnson and Arnold and Housman—and Jonson and Milton and Dryden and Pope and Wordsworth and Byron and Landor and Whitman and Shaw and Eliot, who all expressed similar reservations—were rival

writers; rival writers can't be trusted. Rymer was a disappointed
poet; disappointed poets can't be trusted. George III—that corpu-
lent embodiment of English ordinariness, as endearingly commonplace as Elizabeth II's frowsy hats and scarves—confided to Fanny
Burney that he thought Shakespeare's plays contained a good deal
of "sad stuff":

> "Was there ever" (cried he) "such stuff as great part of Shake-
> speare? only one must not say so! But what think you?—What?—
> Is there not sad stuff? What?—what?"56

But George III was mad; madmen can't be trusted. Ezra Pound
admitted that "Hunks of Shxpr *bore* me; I just can't read 'em";57 but
Pound was a rival poet, a madman, a foreigner, and a fascist to boot;
mad fascist foreign poets can't be trusted. Or, rather, any of these
categories of human being can be trusted when they praise Shakespeare but not when they venture objections.

I am not as brave as Tolstoy or Wittgenstein and do not wish to
appear as mad as George III; rather than pressing their strategic
attack, I will retreat to the tactical battle over *The Comedy of Errors*. In
my quotations of contemporary admirers of the play I have deliberately chosen critics I respect and descriptive statements widely
endorsed. In each case I agree with the description of Shakespeare's
play, and of its difference from *The Menaechmi;* what I can't accept is
the conviction that Shakespeare's changes are improvements. The
key antithetical terms are "hardness" (Bevington's word) and
"wholesomeness" (my own). What I personally admire about
Plautus and other writers like him is what Shakespearians so regularly deprecate: hardness, toughness, exuberant and fantastic amorality. And what I dislike about Shakespeare's comedies—and
tragedies—is their softness, their central mushiness, their inevitable
"love interest," their wholesomeness.

In order to celebrate the gentle wholesomeness of Shakespeare,
critics devalue the hard-core exuberance of Plautus. This tactic is
articulated characteristically by one of the subtlest contemporary
apologists for Shakespearian comedy, Anne Barton:

> [*Menaechmi*] is tightly constructed, lively and inventive, full of the
> atmosphere of a bustling harbor town. It would be difficult,
> however, to claim that it has any object or concern other than to

turn the normal world upside down and to evoke laughter of a simple and unreflective kind.58

Plautus' play is tightly constructed, lively, inventive, bustling: artfully packed full of life. But it has no proper "object," no legitimate "concern."

If we want a different perspective we need only turn, again, from Shakespearians to classicists. Six years before Barton's introduction was published, Erich Segal, in what is probably the most respected modern interpretation of Plautus, had described the *Menaechmi* as a dramatization of "the conflict of *industria* and *voluptas,* holiday versus everyday," acted out in "a magnetic field between personifications of restraint and release." It tells the story of two brothers, one "a lowly stranger who arrives in town, is mistaken for someone of greater importance, and fulfills the comic dream: everything for nothing, or more specifically, food, sex, and money"; another who, by contrast, "suffers a double *damnum,* physical as well as fiscal, for the significant reason that he has gone to work on a holiday."59 Shakespeare's changes in the plot destroy this polarity; the local Antipholus does not suffer because he works when he shouldn't, and the overlaid antics of the second set of twins in any case confuse any clear opposition between insider and outsider, worker and tourist.

Barton's description, typically, underestimates the intelligence of Plautus. But the local inaccuracy of her description of the *Menaechmi* matters less than the critical principle she articulates, in preferring Shakespeare's play. She diminishes the value of Plautus because he does nothing more than evoke a rather "simple" laughter. Presumably, therefore, great comedy does something more than make us laugh. In other words, great comedy is great precisely and only for those elements in it which are not funny; in other words, comedy is great insofar as it is not comic. This may well be true; but it is not, on the face of it, a very encouraging line of approach. It presumes, as a fundamental but unspoken premise, what it claims to substantiate, the central assumption of all Shakespeare's work: the artistic validity, indeed the artistic necessity, of tragicomedy, of a mixing of modes. (Incidentally, it was Euripides who pioneered that mixing of modes; Shakespeare, like others, followed in his inkprints.)

Plautine comedy does no more than "turn the normal world upside down." There is something almost immoral, something psychologically unhealthy, about the whole idea of turning the world upside down. What is it, after all, but an indulgence in disruptive fantasy?

What I miss most in Shakespeare, the thing I find in Aristophanes or even a minor modern like Joe Orton, is fantasy, the exhilaration of fantasy. By "fantasy" I do not mean the invention of minor extranatural figures, like the fairies in *A Midsummer Night's Dream,* or Ariel or Caliban, or the witches in *Macbeth* (which probably owe as much to Middleton's imagination as to Shakespeare's, anyway). The Greeks played that kind of game all the time; they were positively addicted to it; and a gift for picturesque deity-making, despite the praise lavished upon it by Romantic critics, hardly constitutes the prince of imaginative faculties. Shakespeare once comes close to the kind of fantasy I am describing, when he sticks an actual ass's head on Bottom, in *A Midsummer Night's Dream.* But even that example has to be disqualified, since the transformation takes place in a magic forest night, neutralized and framed by urban daylight—and even the daylight is long ago, far away. Puck's trick on Bottom is just that, a trick; it's all a game. Other writers, by contrast, fantasticate the here and now: actual people, actual conduct, in the actual human world. A man breeds and feeds a giant dung beetle on which to fly to heaven in pursuit of peace; another man awakens to find himself transformed into a cockroach; a third awakens to discover that he has been asleep and over-parked for two hundred years; one woman is buried to her waist in sand, another woman hanging out laundry is translated bodily to heaven, an old man mistakes windmills for giants, a traveler finds himself a giant in one country and a minim in another. Such fantasy is not "unreflective." The upsidedown inevitably comments upon the rightsideup. In fact, turning the world upsidedown may be one of the only ways to make us see it at all. It defamiliarizes the familiar, it reveals the arbitrariness of what had seemed inevitable, the artificiality of what had seemed natural. A painter makes us conscious of the extraordinary shape and form of a chicken egg by painting one in the middle of a desert, where we don't expect it, where as a consequence we look at, and are startled by, an object we blindly manipulate every morning. Shakespeare did many things; turning the world upsidedown was not one of them.

Since the early essays of *The Tatler* and *The Spectator,* staggering depositions of critical prose have testified to the moral wholesomeness of Shakespeare's work. That wholesomeness was originally defined in explicit contrast to the sexual frankness and skeptical experimentation of Restoration drama; Shakespeare was used to sweep away the naughty likes of Etherege, Wycherley, and Behn and to give stage room to the sedated glories of Addison and Steele. David Garrick, likewise, found Shakespeare a convenient ally in his effort to make the undignified profession of acting socially respectable. In both cases the impulse behind the glorification of Shakespeare's morality was essentially conformist and proved culturally debilitating. Shakespeare became ethically respectable in the century when English drama died. That was also a century in which much of the sexual slang that lurks beneath his dialogue had become, by linguistic obsolescence, illegible to the overwhelming majority of readers, inaudible to auditors; and as later scholars gradually uncovered this verbal sludge, moralists either cut it out of the plays entirely or left it to harden in its own harmless, and purposely unalleviated, unintelligibility.

For us, "wholesome" may be practically defined as "suitable for schoolchildren and impressionable young adults to read." I and my professional colleagues are engaged in teaching Shakespeare to schoolchildren and impressionable young adults; we must therefore convince ourselves, and the society that employs us, that Shakespeare is fit for such people to read. No doubt, read the right way, he is. But do the underlying values of his plays actually mesh, as is often implied, with the values and beliefs of our own age? Do we really believe anymore, do students believe, do we want them to believe, in the overwhelming moral importance of premarital female virginity? Do we believe in the assumption, implicit in Shakespeare's very vocabulary and the material of his plots, that "nobility" is more characteristic of "nobles" than of the rest of the population? Or that "gentlemen" are "gentle"? Or that lower-class characters who display such virtues will turn out to have had upper-class parents? Do we believe that illegitimate children are, and behave like, "bastards"? It may be objected that these questions are not moral but sociological; but they reflect our view of the nature of society and the causes of human conduct, and that view will in turn determine which questions we consider "moral" and how we answer them. Do we believe that people with money, or people whose parents had money, should be dignified by speaking verse, while people without money are relegated to speaking prose? Do we believe Joan of Arc was a witch?

Do we even believe in witches? Do we satirize the ills of contemporary society by complaining that nowadays there are "No Heretiques burn'd"?[60] Do we think cuckolds are uproariously funny? Do we think wars are decided by single combat between the men who stand to gain or lose most by the outcome? Do we believe in the influence of the planets? Do we worry ourselves about the divine right of kings? Do we believe in Hamlet's ghost? Do we actively believe, all of us, in the fundamental premises of Christianity?

And these are all fairly straightforward questions, where Shakespeare's own beliefs can hardly be doubted. I could give many more, were it not for a modern critical tendency to reconcile our morality with Shakespeare's by presuming that Shakespeare almost always wrote with his tongue in his cheek. In this way you can turn any moral statement insideout, thereby proving that Shakespeare endorses all your own ethical prejudices—which of course only goes to show how very wholesome he is. Too much modern criticism appropriates Shakespeare ("Shakespeare thought just like me"); if criticism is going to have any value beyond confirming our own complacencies, it should instead distance, in order to define ("Shakespeare is another country").

Shakespeare's intellectual and moral preoccupations are not necessarily ours; he by no means exhausts the moral universe. That simple fact explains why so many people, to the bemusement and frustration of professors of literature, continue to prefer second-rate new literature to first-rate old literature. "Merrie England" knew unemployment and economic exploitation, inflation and dislocation, in even crueler forms than our own; but if we want to see such realities dramatized we will have to look elsewhere. Shakespeare decided not to write about that misery around him.

*

Finally, Shakespeare's characterization has been acclaimed more often than any other feature of his art. Claims that Shakespeare's portraiture surpassed every other dramatist's began in the Restoration and continue into our own day. As recently as 1981 Kenneth Muir reiterated that "Shakespeare is the most popular world dramatist because of his unrivalled powers of characterization."[61] "The

Singularity of Shakespeare," according to Muir, arises from the ambiguity of his characters, their complexity and multiplicity, their layered life.

But it is worth remembering that, until the mid-twentieth century, a vocal minority had always denied the plausibility and cohesion of Shakespeare's characters. That minority was effectively silenced by two hermeneutic techniques developed during the decade of World War I. The "ironic strategy," pioneered by Gerald Gould's "New Reading of *Henry V*" in 1919, took any apparent implausibility or inconsistency in a character's speeches and conduct as evidence that Shakespeare was conspicuously undermining that character's point of view. In such readings, all defects are ironic and deliberate; all defects of detail serve a larger thematic perfection. The "psychoanalytic strategy," pioneered by Sigmund Freud's 1913 essay on "The Theme of the Three Caskets," took any apparent implausibility or inconsistency in a character's speeches as evidence that Shakespeare was conspicuously calling attention to some feature of the character's unconscious.[62] In such interpretations, the circularity of much psychoanalytic reasoning contributes to the greater glory of Shakespeare. His characters are assumed to have a three-dimensional psyche; all defects are deliberate and symptomatic; all defects of detail serve a larger psychological perfection.

By such techniques, as innumerable critics soon discovered, any apparent blotch in Shakespeare's characterization can be transformed into a subtlety of genius. Moreover, these techniques were developed in a period when the critical community found them difficult to resist. In the early twentieth century literary criticism was taken over by academics. Within the esteem-culture of the academic tribe, it is hard to win friends by pointing out deficiencies in the local totem.

But let us, for the moment, accept Muir's claims about the integrity and complexity of Shakespeare's characters. Certainly Shakespeare characterizes his major figures with more detail than Sophocles, partly because Shakespeare's plays are longer and contain more variety of incident. But mere detail surely does not in itself make a character more "real"; if it did, novels would always surpass plays. The exaltation of Shakespeare's plays and characters coincided with the rise of the novel in the eighteenth century, and it can hardly be doubted that his reputation benefited from the application to drama of expectations and standards created by the emergent narrative form, which dominates our own literary culture. But although Shakespeare's plays may be more like novels than Racine's, they are still plays. Furthermore, if the guardians of Shakespeare's reputation apply novelistic standards in order to distinguish his plays from those of other great dramatists, they also insist that such standards are irrelevant to any discussion of the relative merits of his plays and, say, Dostoievsky's novels.

In their biographical variety and detail Shakespeare's characters resemble real people; but real people do not speak intensely charged verse, sometimes rhymed, full of rare words, neologisms, archaisms, rhetorical constructions, classical allusions, cultivated ambiguities, multiple meanings, dense aural and rhythmical patterning. Shakespeare's apologists will defend such peculiarities— properly in my opinion—by saying that such artistry enables Shakespeare to multiply and intensify the amount of felt life he can squeeze into a few hours of playing time. But such a defense amounts to saying that when Shakespeare's plays resemble life we praise them for being mimetic, and when they do not resemble life we praise them for being artistic. And if we can legitimately combine these two broths of analysis to the particular mix of reality and irreality in Shakespeare's plays, we can combine them just as easily and legitimately to the rather different mix found in French or Greek drama.

In measuring the nuanced circumplexity of Shakespeare's characters, you posit, consciously or not, aesthetic principles, ways of thinking, ways of seeing, that have been dominant in Europe and North America for two centuries. You also draw upon four centuries of almost continuous interpretation of Shakespeare's plays by actors and critics. That tradition has teased and tested, explored and expanded, the possibilities impacted within each role. And that tradition feeds our readings. Our interpretations accrete around those characters, relentlessly endowing each with further layers and strata of psychological truth. These constant critical and theatrical reinfleshments inevitably make Shakespeare's characters seem more real, for English-speaking peoples, than the characters created by Euripides, Lope de Vega, or Racine. But that seeming is, in the sweep of human culture, just a trick of perspective: a local illusion.

*

By overestimating Shakespeare's importance and uniqueness, Shakespearian critics insult the truth. They glorify one writer by denigrating many.

But they also harm Shakespeare himself. For instance, if we believe that Shakespeare's work was perfect and all-encompassing, we cannot edit it. If everything he did was done ideally, then anything in the extant texts that dips temporarily beneath our own waterline of perfection will be stigmatized as corrupt, textually corrupt, a blemish of transmission that should accordingly be emended out of existence, so that the text can float back up to the surface of our (and its) complacency. In such circumstances, editing becomes unending cosmetic surgery, the face perpetually reshaped to suit the latest fashion. Alternatively, if we believe that Shakespeare's mind was all-encompassing, singular by virtue of its unique plurality, not limited by the artificial boundaries of a physical mind or a local time, then the extant texts can hardly be emended at all. Even the most contorted phraseology, for which his own work and the work of his contemporaries offer no parallels, and which might easily arise from the simplest and commonest of printing errors, even such readings just might be another instance of Shakespeare's limitless and therefore wholly unpredictable genius—a genius so all-swallowing that those who have dared to fault him have been filleted by subsequent scholarship for the paucity of their own understanding. For such editors it is unsafe to emend anything, because Shakespeare is so much smarter than you that your cleverness today will inevitably look like stupidity tomorrow. It is safer to praise than to think.

In pondering whether or not to emend, editors have to decide what Shakespeare actually did or did not write. Such problems extend beyond the authority of individual words to the authenticity of whole works. The Victorian and Edwardian campaign that E. K. Chambers epitomized and stigmatized as "The Disintegration of Shakespeare" depended in part upon the belief that England's perfect poet could do no wrong; therefore, if something in his plays, or even whole plays, seemed bad, the offending bit must have been writ by some lesser wit. (Such attitudes have not disappeared; in the controversy over the authenticity of "Shall I die?" we were repeatedly assured that Shakespeare could not have written such a "bad" poem.) Hermeneutics accomplishes the same act of critical salvation with a similar formula: if Shakespeare wrote something that appears to be awful, then in fact it must be brilliant, if only you look at it carefully enough. Blemishes need not be emended, if all blemishes can be redefined as beauty marks.

Such editorial and critical maneuvers attempt to cope with apparent defect in a canon arbitrarily predefined as fault-free, Shakesperfect. Another strategy extends the physical boundaries of a canon already arbitrarily predefined as unboundable. Critics sometimes claim, for instance, that it doesn't really matter whether or not Shakespeare wrote all of *All Is True*. In one sense, this is true; the work should be judged independently of its origin. But this socialist theory (that works of art are not private property, that authorship doesn't matter) leads in practice to a monopolistic corporate takeover (as Shakespeare appropriates the entire work). Since Shakespeare's "comprehensive soul" could have written anything, one might as well assume that it did write everything. As Theobald expressed the prejudice in 1728, "my Partiality for *Shakespeare* makes me wish, that Every Thing which is good, or pleasing, in our Tongue, had been owing to his Pen."63

This attitude is still operating. In 1968 two critics independently related aspects of *Timon of Athens* to the comedies of Thomas Middleton. Brian Gibbons, in an influential book on *Jacobean City Comedy*, suggested that "Shakespeare in Act III of *Timon of Athens* may be indebted to Middleton's art of comedy."64 Philip Edwards observed that if *Timon* had not survived, "we should not have known . . . of Shakespeare's power to write satirical merchant comedy in a style which only Middleton could equal."65 Neither scholar records the fact that doubts about Shakespeare's authorship of the whole of *Timon of Athens* had been regularly expressed since 1840 and that Middleton had been independently nominated as his collaborator by two investigators in the early 1920s.66 Since 1968, studies by David Lake, MacDonald P. Jackson, R. V. Holdsworth and myself have shown that, on the evidence of every independent objective linguistic criterion, Middleton, not Shakespeare, wrote Act Three of *Timon of Athens*, the scenes that demonstrate such a remarkable gift for "satirical merchant comedy."67 The proposed proof of Shakespeare's unpredictable range emerges in retrospect as a demonstration of his predictable limitations; Shakespeare could not write urban satire of Middleton's caliber, Middleton's caustic comic intelligence. But Philip Edwards continues to attribute *Timon* wholly to Shakespeare,[68] ignoring recent scholarship as confidently as he ignored earlier scholarship. In the same way, critics and theatres continue to credit Shakespeare with the whole of *Macbeth* and *Pericles* and *All Is True,* despite the relentless accumulation of evidence that parts of each were written by others. The same aggrandizing impulse has led scholars at one time or other, for some reason or other, to attribute to him every competent play—and some incompetent ones—written in the 1580s or early 1590s. Thus in 1986, Eric Sams gave Shakespeare sole credit for every play included in the First Folio, as well as the anonymous plays *Edmund Ironside, Edward III, The Troublesome Reign of King John, The True Chronicle History of King Leir, The Famous Victories of Henry V,* and a lost early play on Hamlet, among others.*

Moreover, if Shakespeare was perfect, then he never needed to revise any of his work. This attitude was articulated by his first editor, Nicholas Rowe, discussing Shakespeare's habits of composition:

> Perhaps we are not to look for [*Shakespear's*] Beginnings, like those of other Authors, among their least perfect Writings; Art had so little, and Nature so large a Share in what he did, that, for ought I know, the Performances of his Youth, as they were the most vigorous, and had the most fire and strength of Imagination in 'em, were the best ... what he thought, was commonly so Great, so justly and rightly Conceiv'd in it self, that it wanted little or no Correction, and was immediately approv'd by an impartial Judgement at the first sight.[69]

This statement—which, with the rest of Rowe's "Account of the Life," was prefixed to every major edition for a century—sets the problem of revision within the prevailing critical dichotomy between Nature and Art. Since Shakespeare did not pay any attention to the "rules" of dramatic writing, as they were understood by the eighteenth century, then he could not owe the success of his plays to any "Art," any critical artifice, at all; he depended upon

---

* Sams, a retired civil servant and music critic, represents a contemporary version of the "revolt of the layman," epitomized by Victorian Baconians; he attributes any rejection of his theories to a conspiracy of blinkered academics.

"Nature," which naturally expressed itself in his first thoughts. Within the system of critical discourse available to Rowe, Shakespeare could be defended only as an exemplar of Nature; Nature did not revise; therefore, Shakespeare did not revise.

This attitude has long outlived the critical vocabulary that gave it birth, despite the steady accumulation of textual and historical witnesses against it. When confronted by two early versions, both purportedly by Shakespeare, editors since Rowe and Pope have simply asserted that one text or the other is corrupt. Indeed, by the end of the eighteenth century the antipathy to revision had actually hardened. Rowe and Pope were willing to admit that Shakespeare made mistakes; a century later, such fault-finding had come to seem disrespectful. Once Shakespeare was enthroned as an infallible genius, it became almost impossible to believe that he revised his work. God doesn't make mistakes, and God doesn't change his mind. Editing and criticism since the eighteenth century have defined "Shakespeare" in a way that makes it logically impossible for "Shakespeare" ever to have revised his own work; their definition, as Wittgenstein would say, "fills the whole of logical space, leaving no point of it for reality."[70]

*

A singularity (represented by the symbol *) is the center of a black hole; it is a mathematical point in space having no length, breadth or depth, a point at the center of a once vast, now collapsing star where matter is crushed by its own irresistible gravity into literally zero volume. Even light cannot escape from a black hole; time itself stops.

If Shakespeare has a singularity, it is because he has become a black hole. Light, insight, intelligence, matter—all pour ceaselessly into him, as critics are drawn into the densening vortex of his reputation; they add their own weight to his increasing mass. The light from other stars—other poets, other dramatists—is wrenched and bent as it passes by him on its way to us. He warps cultural space-time; he distorts our view of the universe around him. As Emerson said, "Now, literature, philosophy, and thought are Shakespearized. His mind is the horizon beyond which at present we do not see."[71]

But Shakespeare himself no longer transmits visible light; his stellar energies have been trapped within the gravity well of his own reputation. We find in Shakespeare only what we bring to him or what others have left behind; he gives us back our own values. And it is no use pretending that some uniquely clever, honest, and disciplined critic can find a technique, an angle, that will enable us to lead a mass escape from this trap. If Shakespeare is a literary black hole, then nothing that I, or anyone else, can say will make any difference. His accreting disk will go on spinning, sucking, growing.

Before he became a black hole, Shakespeare was a star—but never the only one in our galaxy. He was unusually but not uniquely talented. He was indeed singular, not because he surpassed all other writers, but simply because he was a unique and unrepeatable individual, living in a unique and unrepeatable time and place. He was no less and no more singular than anyone else. Shakespeare remains, like every other somebody, like us but not us. We are attracted and defeated, educated and mystified, by his strangeness, his otherness, his contradictory incompleteness, his whole, his holes, his permanent personal opacity, his multiplicity. He reinvented himself imaginatively and prolifically, but not infinitely. He, too, was limited, confined by space and time and the boundaries of his own perception. He is not us. But he is like us. The culture that turns him into a god produces a schizophrenic criticism, mixing abasement and appropriation.

Within our culture, Shakespeare is enormously powerful. Power corrupts and disfigures. The power of a politician easily corrupts his entourage, and the power of a poet easily corrupts his apologists. The courtier/critic's "candied tongue," in Hamlet's withering description, will all too readily "licke absurde pompe, / And crooke the pregnant hindges of the knee."[72] But criticism, at its best, struggles to be free; like the press at its best, its function is to doubt what we have been told; it is skeptical; it is suspicious of power. Sycophancy is no more admirable in literature than in politics.

ACKNOWLEDGMENTS
AND REFERENCES

In writing this book I set myself an impossible task. I have tried to encourage you throughout the foregoing narrative not to trust me; the documentation I append below is designed to enable you to retrace my steps, skeptically, in the pursuit of facts I have overlooked or suppressed.

I have systematically recorded the sources of direct quotations from primary sources, but I have had to restrict severely the citation of secondary sources. I have recorded any indebtedness to unpublished work to which I have been given access by living scholars; I have also, though no doubt less consistently, noted my sources for important statements of fact, particularly if they involve observations that are absolutely or relatively new or new in their application to this context. I have made no attempt to document my indebtedness to other people's ideas, their ways of thinking, though such debts are undoubtedly the most material of all.

However, I must record the unpublished kindnesses of several individuals. Rebecca Germonprez, Robert Hazen, Elizabeth Joyce (three non-Shakespearian friends), Stanley Wells, Gary Williams, and George Walton Williams (three Shakespearian friends) each read a draft of the entire text; they have collectively improved it more than I care to admit to myself. So have my editors at Weidenfeld and Nicolson, Mark Polizzotti and Dan Green; my editor at Chatto & Windus, Jenny Uglow; and my copy editor, Joel Honig. Michael Dobson, Margreta de Grazia, Robert Hume, John Jowett, Robert Mahoney, William Montgomery, Virgil Nemoianu, S. Schoenbaum, Francis Spufford, and Michael Warren all read more than one chapter; Hans Walter Gabler, Russell Jackson, Glen Johnson, Nancy Maguire, Joseph Sendry, and Michael Shaw all read individual chapters. Peter Blayney, John Kerrigan, Jon Mikalson, Jeanne Roberts, and Deniz Şengel answered questions; Richard Hardin xeroxed a distant source.

"Present Tense" is something of a special case. Because it deals with living authors, I sent a draft of that chapter to almost everyone whose work is discussed in it and to several other interested parties. Not everyone replied to my unsolicited queries, but I am grateful to Stephen Booth, Kent Cartwright, Jonathan Dollimore, Malcolm Evans, Howard Felperin, Margreta de Grazia, Werner Habicht, Terence Hawkes, E. A. J. Honigmann, G. K. Hunter, David Lodge, Philip Maguire, Randall McLeod, Barbara Mowat, Carol Neely, Virgil Nemoianu, Alan Sinfield, Steven Urkowitz, Kim Scott Walwyn, Michael Warren, Robert Weimann, and Paul Werstine.

Colleagues have also been generous in giving me access to unpublished work. Don Wayne and Walter Cohen sent me advance copies of their essays in *Shakespeare Reproduced;* Werner Habicht and Roger Pringle let me see the proofs of *Images of Shakespeare;* Stanley Wells provided proofs of *Shakespeare Survey 40* (and much else); Barbara Mowat arranged for me to listen to a tape of Stephen Greenblatt's 1986 talk at the Folger. Margreta de Grazia and Marion Trousdale showed me unpublished papers on the New Bibliography. I am indebted to all the members of Nancy Maguire's seminar on Restoration Shakespeare at the 1988 Shakespeare Association of America conference, both for their comments on my work and for the opportunity to read their forthcoming essays.

Libraries are harder to thank than individuals. For most of this book I could count on the Catholic University of America Mullen Library and the Folger Shakespeare Library; I have also drawn upon the books and the patience of the Library of Congress, the British Library, the Bodleian, the Kenneth Spencer Research

Library at the University of Kansas, and libraries at the University of Maryland (College Park) and the University of Virginia.

All quotations from Shakespeare are identified by references to the lineation of the new Oxford edition, *The Complete Works* (1986) and *The Complete Works: Original-Spelling Edition* (1986), gen. eds., Stanley Wells and Gary Taylor. Conclusions about authorship, date of composition, and textual status are based upon Stanley Wells, Gary Taylor, *et al.*, *William Shakespeare: A Textual Companion* (1987), which provides full documentation. References to Shakespeare texts are given in the form "modern-spelling act.scene.line number/original-spelling continuous line number." However, although the line numbering of this edition is used, quotations are taken from the text current in the period under discussion. Thus, in the first chapter I reproduce (p. 40) Dryden's quotation of *Hamlet* as it stood in his text and quote *Pericles* (p. 23) from the quarto of 1635, the most recent edition available in 1660; in both cases, however, my note identifies the passage by its line numbers in the Oxford edition. I hope that this procedure will enable readers to find in current editions the passages discussed and yet to experience them as they would have been known to readers and critics of the past. For the same reason I have in the text given the titles of plays and the names of characters in use during each period: thus, although it seems clear that Shakespeare and Fletcher's play was originally called *All is True*, it would be misleading to refer to it by that title in a discussion of Restoration productions or Victorian scholarship. Plays are listed in the index under the Oxford form.

The spelling of Shakespeare's name causes special difficulties. I had originally intended to spell the name as erratically in my own prose as in the historical record, changing the spelling whenever one of my quoted sources did so; this has the desirable effect of continually deconstructing a reader's confidence in the familiar "Shakespeare." However, it soon becomes—as my publisher pointed out—an irritating distraction. "Shakspere," which seems to have been his own preferred spelling, would be equally disconcerting for a modern reader, without the advantages of reflecting past practice. In the end I have had to concede that my work, like all those it discusses, is a product of its own time. In our time "Shakespeare" is normal, and I have therefore grudgingly perpetuated it.

NOTES

Introduction

1. *As You Like It*, 2.7.139/1063.
2. Sonnet 11.7–8.

Chapter 1: Restoration

1. G. E. Bentley, *The Jacobean and Caroline Stage*, 7 vols. (1941–68), II, 690.
2. "Continuation of Stowe's Survey of London" (ca. 1658), Folger MS. V.b.275.
3. "An Horatian Ode upon Cromwel's Return from Ireland," in *The Poems and Letters of Andrew Marvell*, ed. H. M. Margoliouth, rev. Pierre Legouis and E. E. Duncan-Jones, 2 vols. (1971), I, 92–93, 294–303.
4. *Henry V*, Prologue, 3–4/3–4 (quoted from the 1623 folio).
5. John Cook, *King Charls his Case: or, an Appeal to all Rational Men, Concerning His Tryal* (1649), 13.
6. *Perfect Occurences of Every Daies iournall in Parliament*, No. 104 (December 22–30, 1648), 778 (entry for "*Wednesday the 27. of December.*").
7. John Milton, *Eikonoklastes* (1649), 11.
8. British Library Add. MS 19256, fol. 47. The patent is reproduced in Percy Fitzgerald, *A New History of the English Stage*, 2 vols., (1882), I, 23.
9. Ronald Hutton, *The Restoration: A Political and Religious History of England and Wales 1658–1667* (1985), 135.
10. Gunnar Sorelius, *'The Giant Race Before the Flood': Pre-Restoration Drama on the Stage and in the Criticism of the Restoration* (1966), 34–35.
11. Henry Marsh, ed., *The Wits, or, Sport upon Sport* (1662). For the most recent discussion see R. A. Foakes, *Illustrations of the English Stage 1580–1642* (1985), 159–61.

12. For these seventeenth-century engravings, see S. Schoenbaum, *William Shake-speare: Records and Images* (1981), 162, 171–72.

13. Lawrence Stone, *The Family, Sex and Marriage in England 1500–1800* (1977), 51.

14. G. Blakemore Evans, "*Shakespeare Restored*—Once Again!" in *Editing Renaissance Dramatic Texts, English, Italian, and Spanish*, ed. Anne Lancashire (1976), 39–56.

15. John Downes, *Roscius Anglicanus* (1708), ed. Judith Milhous and Robert D. Hume (1987), 42 [17]. (Page numbers in brackets identify the pagination of the 1708 edition.)

16. Downes, *Roscius Anglicanus*, 51 [21], 55 [24].

17. Bodleian MS. Aubrey 6, fol. 46. John Aubrey's memorandum on Shakespeare and the Davenant family is transcribed in E. K. Chambers, *William Shakespeare: A Study of Facts and Problems*, 2 vols. (1930), II, 254. See also Mary Edmond, *Rare Sir William Davenant* (1987), 13–26.

18. *The Diary of Samuel Pepys*, ed. Robert Latham and William Matthews, 11 vols. (1970–83), July 4, 1661. References to Pepys will be quoted from this edition, by date of the entry.

19. *Roger North on Music*, ed. John Wilson (1959), 353.

20. Percy Fitzgerald, *A New History of the English Stage*, 2 vols. (1882), I, 80. I quote from the revised Killigrew patent, issued on April 25, 1662; Davenant's revised patent is similarly worded.

21. Pepys, October 5, 1667.

22. See David Foxon, *Libertine Literature in England 1660–1745* (1965) and Roger Thompson, *Unfit for Modest Ears: A Study of Pornographic, Obscene and Bawdy Works Written or Published in England in the Second Half of the Seventeenth Century* (1979).

23. Pepys, February 9, 1668.

24. Downes, *Roscius Anglicanus*, 52 [22].

25. John Lacey, *Sauny the Scott: Or, The Taming of the Shrew: A Comedy* (1698), 25. Although not printed until 1698, this adaptation was being performed by 1667.

26. "Names of the plays acted by the Red Bull actors," allegedly compiled by Sir Henry Herbert, probably around August 14, 1660; the original document is lost and is now known only through the printed account of it in Edmond Malone's "An Historical Account of the Rise and Progress of the English Stage"; see *The Plays and Poems of William Shakspeare*, ed. Malone, 10 vols. (1790), vol. I, pt. 2, p. 265.

27. Downes, *Roscius Anglicanus*, 43 [18].

28. Ben Jonson, "Ode," appended to *The New Inne* (1631), sig. H2.

29. John Dryden, "Defence of the Epilogue. Or, An Essay on the Dramatique Poetry of the last Age," in *The Conquest of Granada by the Spaniards: In Two Parts* (1672), 163.

30. Downes, *Roscius Anglicanus*, 43 [18].

31. C. A. Du Fresnoy, *De Arte Graphica. The Art of Painting . . . Translated into English, Together with an Original Preface containing A Parallel betwixt Painting and Poetry. By Mr. Dryden* (1695), xl.

32. *Pericles* 22.110–13/2376–79, 22.6–9/2272–75; quoted from the 1635 quarto edition, sig. I2, H4^v.

33. Antonia Fraser, *Royal Charles: Charles II and the Restoration* (1979), 112–28, 179.

34. William van Lennep, ed., *The London Stage, 1660–1700* (1965). This figure is based on known performances through December 1662; I do not include

revivals or adaptations of plays performed in any circumstances before 1660. See also Robert D. Hume, "Securing a Repertory: Plays on the London Stage 1660–5," in *Poetry and Drama 1570–1700: Essays in Honour of Harold F. Brooks,* ed. Antony Coleman and Antony Hammond (1981), 156–72.

35. Alfred Harbage, *The Annals of English Drama 975–1700,* rev. S. Schoenbaum (1964), 138–42. I have based these figures upon the seasons of 1639–41; 1642 was badly disrupted, even before the parliamentary closure.

36. Alfred Harbage, *Shakespeare and the Rival Traditions* (1952), 24–25, 47.

37. Public Record Office LC 5/137, p. 343.

38. *The London Stage, 1660–1700,* cxxviii–cxxix.

39. *Of Dramatick Poesie, an Essay* (1668), in *The Works of John Dryden,* vol. XVII, *Prose 1668–1691,* ed. S. H. Monk *et al.* (1971), 57.

40. Dryden, *Of Dramatick Poesie,* 56.

41. Edward Phillips, *Theatrum Poetarum* (1675), 108–9; James Drake, *The Antient and Modern Stages survey'd* (1699), 201.

42. G. E. Bentley, *Shakespeare and Jonson: Their Reputations in The Seventeenth Century Compared,* 2 vols. (1945), I, 107–9.

43. D. L. Frost, "Shakespeare in the Seventeenth Century," *Shakespeare Quarterly* 16 (1965), 81–89.

44. Aphra Behn, "An Epistle to the Reader," *The Dutch Lover* (1673), sig. a1.

45. Downes, *Roscius Anglicanus,* 17–27 [6–9].

46. Thomas Rymer, *The Tragedies of The Last Age consider'd and Examin'd by the Practice of the Ancients, and by the Common sense of all Ages* (1678), in *The Critical Works of Thomas Rymer,* ed. Curt A. Zimansky (1956), 17.

47. Downes, 56, 71–2 [24, 33].

48. Dryden, *Of Dramatick Poesie,* 59; Gerald Langbaine, *An Account of the English Dramatick Poets* (1691), 456.

49. Dryden, *Of Dramatick Poesie,* 54; "The PREFACE to the Play," *Troilus and Cressida, Or, Truth Found Too Late* (1679), sig. a3.

50. Sir William Davenant and John Dryden, *The Tempest, or the Enchanted Island. A Comedy* (1670), sig. A4.

51. Johan Gerritsen, "The Dramatic Piracies of 1661: A Comparative Analysis," *Studies in Bibliography* 11 (1958), 117–31.

52. Dryden, *Troilus,* sig. A4^v; Dryden, "An Epilogue" [to Charles Davenant's *Circe* (1677)], first printed in *Miscellany Poems* (1684), 292.

53. David Cressy, *Literacy and the Social Order: Reading and Writing in Tudor and Stuart England* (1980), 176–77, 119.

54. See for example *The Tatler,* No. 68 (September 14, 1709)–quoted in the next chapter—and Arthur Murphy, *The Life of David Garrick, Esq.,* 2 vols. (1801), I, 71.

55. *Othello,* 5.2.107–10/3004–7; quoted from Rymer, *A Short View of Tragedy, It's Original Excellency, and Corruption. With Some Reflections on Shakespeare, and other Practitioners for the Stage* (1693), in *Works,* 161.

56. Rymer, *Tragedies of the Last Age,* in *Works,* 59–60.

57. *The Diary of Robert Hooke, 1672–1680,* ed. Henry W. Robinson and Walter Adams (1935), June 20, 1674.

58. Thomas Sprat, *The History of the Royal Society of London* (1667), ed. Jackson I. Cope and Harold Whitmore Jones (1958), 113.

59. Thomas Hobbes, *Leviathan* (1651), 20 (part I, chap. v).

60. Sprat, 113.

61. *Othello,* 2.1.69–74/751–56; quoted from Rymer, *Short View,* 86.

62. Sprat, 111, 112.

63. *Othello*, 1.3.76–94/362–80; quoted in Rymer, *Short View*, 139.
64. Rymer, *Short View*, 134, 144, 138, 154, 155, 136.
65. William Petty, *The Advice of W. P. to Mr. Samuel Hartlib for The Advancement of some particular Parts of Learning* (1648), 12.
66. Sprat, 113, 42.
67. Rymer, *Short View*, 170.
68. Joseph Glanvill, "Anti-fanatical Religion and Free Philosophy," in *Essays on Several Important Subjects in Philosophy and Religion* (1676), 41–42.
69. Rymer, *Short View*, 145.
70. Ibid., 87, 149; referring to *Othello* 3.3.94–482/1542–1929.
71. Rymer, *Short View*, 154.
72. Ibid., 134.
73. *The Diary of John Evelyn*, ed. E. S. de Beer, 6 vols. (1955), III, 304 (November 26, 1661).
74. Jeremy Collier, *A Short View of the Immorality, and Profaneness of the English Stage* (1698), 10.
75. Dryden, *Troilus*, sig. b2ᵛ–3.
76. *Hamlet*, 2.2.495–99, 2.2.507–20/1425–29, 1437–50 (as quoted by Dryden).
77. "Proposals for the Advancement of the Royal Society," Royal Society Domestic Manuscripts, V, 12: see also Michael Hunter, "The Social Basis and Changing Fortunes of an Early Scientific Institution," *Notes and Records of the Royal Society* 31 (1976), 9–114.
78. On the lost *Hamlet* play, see *Textual Companion*, 137–38.
79. Dryden, *Of Dramatick Poesie*, 58.
80. Ibid., 72–3.
81. *The Shakspere Allusion-Book: A Collection of Allusions to Shakspere from 1591 to 1700*, ed. C. M. Ingleby *et al.*, 2 vols. (1909; 2nd. ed. 1932), II, 338, citing examples from 1678, 1680, 1690, 1696: see also II, 243 (1678); Aphra Behn (1673), sig. a1, and Gildon (1698?), 92.
82. Colley Cibber, *An Apology for the Life of Mr. Colley Cibber, Comedian, and Late Patentee of the Theatre-Royal* (1740), 117–18.
83. Robert Gould, *Poems Chiefly consisting of Satyrs and Satyrical Epistles* (1689), 177.
84. Anthony Ashley Cooper, *Soliloquy: or, Advice to an Author* (1710), 117.
85. Hazelton Spencer, *Shakespeare Improved: The Restoration Versions in Quarto and on the Stage* (1927), 174–91; but see also Mongi Raddadi, *Davenant's Adaptations of Shakespeare* (1979), 64–78.
86. William Shakespeare, *The Tragedy of Hamlet Prince of Denmark* (1676), sig. H2 (*Hamlet*, 3.3.73/2189).
87. *Hamlet* (1676), sig. F4: 3.1.87/1623.
88. Ibid., sig. F2: 2.2.551/1481.
89. Cibber, *Apology*, 120.
90. Lennep, *The London Stage 1660–1700*, 225.
91. Bentley, *Shakespeare and Jonson*, 109, 124.
92. Downes, *Roscius Anglicanus*, 52 [21].
93. Cibber, *Apology*, 60–1.
94. *The Laureat* (1740), 31–2.
95. Nicholas Rowe, "Some Account of the Life, &c. of Mr. *William Shakespear*," in *The Works of Mr. William Shakespear*, ed. Rowe, 6 vols. (1709), I, xxxiii–xxxiv.

Chapter 2: 1709

1. Edward Ward, *The Secret History of Clubs* (1709), 360.
2. *Journals of the House of Commons*, Vol. XVI: *1660–1745*, 240.

3. Historical Manuscripts Commission, *The Manuscripts of His Grace the Duke of Portland*, vol. II (1893), 209.

4. The prologue was printed in *Wit and Mirth: or, Pills to Purge Melancholy*, ed. Henry Playford, *The Second Part* (1700), 314. For the whole incident see Kathleen M. Lynch, *Jacob Tonson, Kit-Cat Publisher* (1971), 56–57.

5. Richard D. Hume, *The Development of English Drama in the Late Seventeenth Century* (1976), 380–81.

6. Daniel Defoe, *A Review of the State of the English Nation*, August 10, 1706.

7. Emmett L. Avery, ed., *The London Stage, 1700–1729*, 3 vols. (1960), I, xl.

8. Joseph Wood Krutch, *Comedy and Conscience After the Restoration* (1924; rev. 1949), 166–85.

9. *The Complete Works of Sir John Vanbrugh*, ed. Bonamy Dobrée and Geoffrey Webb, 4 vols. (1927–28), IV, 8.

10. Cibber, *Apology*, 183.

11. Ibid., 241.

12. Aaron Hill, in *The Prompter*, No. 3 (November 19, 1734).

13. *Grub Street Journal*, No. 253 (October 31, 1734), letter signed "Some-body."

14. John Dennis, *An Essay on the Genius and Writings of Shakespear* (1712), in *The Critical Works of John Dennis*, ed. Edward Niles Hooker, 2 vols. (1939–43), II, 13, 432–33.

15. George Winchester Stone, Jr., "The Making of the Repertory," in *The London Theatre World, 1660–1800*, ed. Robert D. Hume (1980), 197.

16. *The Guardian*, ed. John Calhoun Stephens (1982), No. 37 (April 23, 1713) (John Hughes).

17. Thomas Davies, *Dramatic Miscellanies*, 3 vols. (1784), I, 306–7.

18. Tobias Smollett, *The Adventures of Peregrine Pickle*, 4 vols. (1751), II, 139–40.

19. Hill, in *Prompter*, No. 62 (June 13, 1735).

20. *The Works of the Late Aaron Hill Esq.*, 4 vols. (1753), II, 115–16; Hill's letter describing Booth had previously been quoted by W. R. Chetwood, *A General History of The Stage* (1749), 94.

21. Smollet, I, 139; *The Diary of Dudley Ryder 1715–1716*, ed. William Matthews (1939), 360 (November 6, 1716).

22. Rowe, I, A2ᵛ.

23. John Dennis, dedicatory epistle to *The Invader of his Country* (1720), in *Critical Works*, II, 179.

24. Richmond P. Bond, *The Tatler: The Making of a Literary Journal* (1971), 98–100.

25. *The Tatler*, No. 8 (April 28, 1709). Quotations from *The Tatler* refer to the edition by Donald F. Bond, 3 vols. (1987).

26. *The Spectator*, No. 65 (May 15, 1711). *The Spectator* is quoted from Donald F. Bond's edition, 5 vols. (1965).

27. *The Tatler*, No. 111 (December 24, 1709).

28. Ibid., No. 12 (May 7, 1709).

29. Ibid., No. 167 (May 4, 1710).

30. *Julius Caesar* 2.2.32/927, as quoted in *The Tatler*, No. 53 (August 11, 1709).

31. *Richard III* 5.5.131/3222, as quoted in *The Tatler*, No. 90 (November 5, 1709).

32. *Hamlet* 1.2.137–8/293–94, as quoted in *The Tatler*, No. 106 (December 13, 1709).

33. *Macbeth* 5.5.18/1999, Davenant's adaptation, as quoted in *The Tatler*, No. 167 (May 4, 1710).

34. *Othello* 3.3.350/1797, as quoted in *The Tatler*, No. 188 (June 22, 1710).

35. *The Tatler*, No. 68 (September 15, 1709), quoting *Caesar* 4.2.201/1938 and *Macbeth* 4.3.219–20/1766–67 (in Davenant's adaptation).

36. *The Tatler,* No. 53 (August 11, 1709), alluding to *Caesar* 2.2/Sc. 5.

37. Horace Walpole, *Anecdotes of Painting in England,* 4 vols. (1760–70), III, 111.

38. Richard Steele, *The Englishman,* ed. Rae Blanchard (1955), 31 (No. 7: October 20, 1713).

39. *The Tatler,* No. 3 (April 16, 1709).

40. Ibid., No. 137 (February 23, 1710), quoting *Henry V* Pro. 1, 5–8/1, 5–8, and *Caesar* 3.1.273–76/1360–63.

41. Bryan Bevan, *Marlborough the Man* (1975), 15.

42. Joseph Addison, *The Spectator,* No. 40 (April 16, 1711).

43. *Ibid.,* No. 44 (April 20, 1711).

44. *Ibid.,* No. 419 (July 1, 1712).

45. Alexander Pope, *An Epistle to Dr. Arbuthnot* (1735), 201–5, in *The Twicken-ham Edition of the Poems of Alexander Pope,* gen. ed. John Butt: vol. IV, ed. Butt, 110.

46. Charles A. Knight, "The Literary Periodical in the Early Eighteenth Century," *The Library* VI, 8 (1986), 232–48.

47. *The Tatler,* No. 162 (April 22, 1710).

48. W. W. Greg, *A Bibliography of the English Printed Drama to the Restoration,* 4 vols. (1939–59).

49. Judith Milhous and Robert D. Hume, "Dating Play Premières from Publication Data, 1660–1700," *Harvard Library Bulletin* 22 (1974), 374–405.

50. Shirley Strum Kenny, "The Publication of Plays," in *London Theatre World,* 313–15.

51. Joseph Spence, *Observations, Anecdotes, and Characters of Books and Men,* ed. James M. Osborne, 2 vols. (1966), I, 333.

52. Folger MS S.a. 163 (a quarto sheet headed "Paid the Editors of Shakspear").

53. "Preface," *The Works of Shakespear,* ed. William Warburton, 8 vols. (1747), I, x–xii.

54. Thomas Edwards, *The Canons of Criticism* (1748). The book was repeatedly reprinted and expanded until 1765.

55. On the background see John Feather, "The Book Trade in Politics: The Making of the Copyright Act of 1710," *Publishing History* 8 (1980), 19–44.

56. Peter Smithers, *The Life of Joseph Addison,* rev. ed. (1968), 179.

57. David Piper, *The Image of the Poet* (1982), 52.

58. Rowe, I, ii.

59. Ibid., v.

60. Ibid.

61. Ibid., I, viii, ix, x.

62. Ibid., xi, xii.

63. Ibid., ii, viii.

64. Ibid., xii–xiii.

65. Ibid., xxxiv.

66. For an argument that the division belongs elsewhere see Rolf Soellner, *"Timon of Athens": Shakespeare's Pessimistic Tragedy* (1979), 40–42.

67. Dryden, *Troilus and Cressida,* 11; *Troilus and Cressida* 2.2.165/1114 (Rowe, IV, 1841).

68. Maynard Mack, *Alexander Pope: A Life* (1985), 89–94.

69. Spence, *Observations,* I, 23.

70. Rowe, I, xv–xvi, xxxiv–xxxv (Rymer), xiii, xiv–xv (Jonson); Pope, ed., *The Works of William Shakespear,* 6 vols. (1725), I, xxxii, xli (Rymer), xxx (Jonson).

71. John Butt, *Pope's Taste in Shakespeare* (1936).

72. Barbara Mowat, "The Form of *Hamlet*s Fortunes," *Renaissance Drama* 19

(1989); Thomas L. Berger, "The Second Quarto of *Othello* and the Question of Textual 'Authority' " (paper presented in the seminar on text at the International Shakespeare Conference, Stratford-upon-Avon, August 1988).

73. *The Prose Works of Alexander Pope*, Vol. II: *The Major Works, 1725–1744*, ed. Rosemary Cowler (1986), 35, n. 51.

74. [James Ralph], *The Case Of our Present Theatrical Disputes* (1743), 59.

75. Jonathan Swift, *A History of Poetry, In a Letter to a Friend* (1726).

76. Pope, VI, sig. Oooo1–2ᵛ; Theobald, VII, 495–503 (unnumbered pages following 494).

77. David McKitterick, *Cambridge University Library: A History: The Eighteenth and Nineteenth Centuries* (1986), 96 (a copy of the 1685 edition).

78. George Sewell, "The Preface," in *The Works of Mr. William Shakespear. The Seventh Volume*, ed. Sewell (1725), vii.

79. Theobald, *Shakespeare Restored*, v.

80. Theobald, "The Preface," I, xxxix.

81. "The Preface," *Milton's Paradise Lost. A New Edition*, ed. Richard Bentley (1732), sig. a2.

82. Ibid., sig. a3.

83. Ibid., sig. a2ᵛ, a1ᵛ ("*whoever he was, to whom* Milton *committed his Copy and the Overseeing of the Press*"); Theobald, "Preface," xxxvii (on "Mutilations or Additions made" by the actors).

84. Theobald, "Preface," xxxvii–xxxviii (on transcription of plays by auditors at a performance); Bentley, sig. a1 (corruption of Milton's text by "*The Amanuensis*").

85. Bentley, sig. a3; Theobald, who believes many of the early texts were published "without the Poet's Knowledge" ("Preface," xxxviii), nowhere challenges Pope's views on proofreading, and in practice implicitly accepts them.

86. Theobald, "Preface," xxxvii, xxxix; Bentley, sig. a2ᵛ, a2.

87. Swift, *On Poetry: A Rhapsody* (1733), line 265.

88. [Alexander Pope], *The Narrative of Dr. Robert Norris* (1713), 18.

89. *The Spectator*, No. 409 (June 20, 1712), No. 285 (January 26, 1712), No. 61 (May 10, 1711).

90. William Dodd, *The Beauties of Shakespear. Regularly Selected from each Play*, 2 vols. (1752), I, vi.

91. Dionysius Longinus, *On the Sublime*, trans. William Smith (1739), 78–79 (Section XXXIII).

92. See for instance the anonymous *An Examen of the New Comedy, Call'd The Suspicious Husband. With Some Observations Upon Our Dramatick Poetry and Authors* (1747), 23–24; Peter Whalley, *An Enquiry into the Learning of Shakespeare, with Remarks on Several Passages of his Plays* (1748), 19.

93. Pope, *An Essay on Criticism* (1711), in *Poems*, I (1961), line 152.

94. Thomas Middleton, *A Mad World, My Masters* (1608), B2ᵛ.

95. Richard James, ed., "The legend and defence of yᵉ Noble knight and Martyr Sir Jhon Oldcastel," Bodleian Library, MS James 34.

96. *Allusion-Book*, I, 443.

97. *Hamlet* (1676), sig. D4ᵛ (2.1.78/886).

98. *The Guardian*, No. 155 (September 8, 1713).

99. Eliza Haywood, *The Female Spectator*, 4 vols. (1744–46), III, 159.

100. *The Spectator*, No. 92 (June 15, 1711); see also No. 37 (April 12, 1711).

101. David Green, *Sarah Duchess of Marlborough* (1967), 171.

102. *The Complete Letters of Lady Mary Wortley Montagu*, ed. Robert Halsband, 3 vols. (1965–67), II, 27; Lady Louisa Stuart, "Biographical Anecdotes" (1837), in

Lady Mary Wortley Montagu, *Essays and Poems*, ed. Robert Halsband and Isobel Grundy (1977), 52.

103. *An Essay in Defence of the Female Sex . . . Written by a Lady* (1696), 48; sometimes attributed—probably wrongly—to Mary Astell.

104. *The Female Tatler*, No. 32 (September 16, 1709). This journal, which began publication on July 8, 1709, originally claimed to be published by a "Mrs. Crackenthorpe," later displaced by "a Society of Ladies"; its true authorship remains unknown.

105. *The Female Tatler*, No. 98 (February 24, 1710).

106. Margaret Cavendish, *CCXI Sociable Letters* (1664), Letter CXXIII (pp. 244–48); also Letter CLXII (p. 338).

107. Montagu, "Wrote at the Desire of Mr. Wortley, suppress'd at the desire of Mr. Adison" (1713), in *Essays and Poems*, 64.

108. Francis Lynch, *The Independent Patriot* (1737), sig. A4 (note to the Prologue, first performed on February 12, 1737).

109. Emmett L. Avery, "The Shakespeare Ladies Club," *Shakespeare Quarterly* 7 (Spring 1956), 153–58.

110. Haywood, *The Female Spectator*, I, 323.

111. Alexander Pope, *The Dunciad*, ed. James Sutherland (1943; rev. 1963), A.I.55, A.II.64.

112. Ibid., A.I.1.

113. Richard Savage, ed., *A Collection of Pieces in Verse and Prose, Which have been publish'd on Occasion of the DUNCIAD* (1732), vi.

114. Pope, *Prose Works*, II, 23.

115. Pope, *Epistle to Dr. Arbuthnot*, 164 ("pidling *Tibalds*"), in *Poems*, IV, 108.

116. "The Preface," in *The Works of Shakespeare*, ed. Lewis Theobald, 7 vols. (1733), I, xxxvi–xxxvii.

117. *The Country Journal: or, The Craftsman*, 72 (November 18, 1727), unsigned article addressed "*To* CALEB D'ADVERS, *Esq;*"

118. *Dunciad*, B.I.127–34.

119. Ibid., A.I.161–64.

120. Ibid., 61–70.

121. Ibid., 75; *Midsummer Night's Dream* 2.1.109–10/464–65; quoted from Pope's edition (I, 96), where "chin" makes the image especially ludicrous; modern editors emend to "thin."

122. Voltaire, *Letters concerning the English nation* (1733), in *Voltaire on Shakespear*, ed. Theodore Besterman (1967), 44.

123. *Dunciad*, A.I.238.

Chapter 3: 1790

1. *The Times* (London), July 20, 1789, p. 2.

2. Jane Austen, *Northanger Abbey* (composed in 1797–98; first published 1818), Book I, chap. xiv, p. 268.

3. *Speeches of the Right Honourable Richard Brinsley Sheridan*, 5 vols. (1816), III, 89.

4. Edmund Burke, *Reflections on the Revolution in France* (1790), 105–6.

5. *Lectures 1808–1819 on Literature*, ed. R. A. Foakes, 2 vols. (1987), in *The Collected Works of Samuel Taylor Coleridge*, gen. ed. Kathleen Coburn: II, 293 (manuscript note dated January 7, 1819).

6. *Specimens of the Table Talk of the late Samuel Taylor Coleridge*, ed. H. N. Coleridge, 2 vols. (1835), I, 69 (June 24, 1827).

7. Coleridge, *Lectures 1808–1819*, I, 386, 390.

8. Ibid., 540, 542.

9. *The Literary Remains of Samuel Taylor Coleridge,* ed. H. N. Coleridge, 4 vols. (1836), II, 135.

10. William Wordsworth, *The Borderers,* ed. Robert Osborn, Cornell Wordsworth (1982), III.v.60–65 (1797 manuscript).

11. *The Borderers,* 812 (1842 note).

12. *The Letters of John Keats 1814–21,* ed. Hyder Edward Rollins, 2 vols. (1958), II, 115–16 (June 9, 1819).

13. *Letters of John Keats,* II, 312 (August [?] 1820).

14. *The Letters of Charles and Mary Anne Lamb,* ed. Edwin W. Marrs, Jr., 3 vols. (1975–78), III, 243–44 (May 12, 1817).

15. "Hamlet," from *Characters of Shakespear's Plays* (1817), in *The Complete Works of William Hazlitt,* ed. P. P. Howe, 21 vols. (1930), IV, 232–37.

16. "Byron and Shelley on the Character of Hamlet," *New Monthly Magazine* 29 (1830), 328, 329, 336. The authenticity of the account is defended by Earl Wasserman, "Shelley's Last Poetics: A Reconsideration," in *From Sensibility to Romanticism,* ed. Frederick W. Hilles and Harold Bloom (1965), 505–11; evidence for Mary Shelley's authorship of the unsigned article is given by Charles E. Robinson, *Shelley and Byron: The Snake and Eagle Wreathed in Fight* (1976), 270. The 1830 article does not date the conversation, but the independent testimony of Samuel Rogers places it in Pisa in April 1822.

17. Hermann Ulrici, *Shakspeare's dramatische Kunst* (1839), trans. as *Shakspeare's Dramatic Art* (1846), 238–39.

18. Wordsworth's Muse, in the 1812 manuscript of *The Waggoner,* "scents the morning air" (MS 3, line 680; *Benjamin the Waggoner,* ed. Paul Betz, Cornell Wordsworth [1981], 305); at *Hamlet* 1.5.58/675, the Ghost "scent[s] the morning air." The parallel is discussed by Jonathan Bate, *Shakespeare and the English Romantic Imagination* (1986), 103–5.

19. George Vandenhoff, *Leaves from an actor's note-book* (1860), 22; George Henry Lewes, *On Actors and the Art of Acting* (1875), 5.

20. Siegbert Prawer, *Heine's Shakespeare: An Inaugural Lecture* (1970), 37, translating an account written by Heine in 1938; quoting *Merchant of Venice* 1.3.126–27/443–44.

21. Leigh Hunt, "Theatrical Examiner. No. 163," *The Examiner* (February 26, 1815), 138–39.

22. Coleridge, *Table Talk,* I, 24 (April 27, 1823).

23. Alluding to *Romeo and Juliet* 3.5.9/1943 and *1 Henry IV* 4.1.100/2234.

24. Jonathan Bate, "Parodies of Shakespeare," *Journal of Popular Culture* 19 (1985–86), 75–89.

25. John Poole, *Hamlet Travestie,* 2nd ed. (1811), 10.

26. A. Jonathan Bate, "Hazlitt's Shakespearean Quotations," *Prose Studies* 7 (1984), 26.

27. *Letters of John Keats,* II, 139 (August 14, 1819).

28. James Beattie, Letter XXI (January 1, 1768), in Sir William Forbes, *An Account of the Life and Writings of James Beattie, LL.D.,* 2 vols. (1806), I, 110–11.

29. *The Letters of David Garrick,* ed. David M. Little and George M. Kahrl, 3 vols. (1963), II, 542 (September 12, 1766).

30. *The Correspondence of Edmund Burke,* ed. Alfred Cobban and Robert A. Smith, 10 vols. (1958–70), VI, 10 (letter of August 9, 1789).

31. Burke, *Reflections,* 11.

32. Burke, *Correspondence,* VI, 126 (July 29, 1790), quoting *Hamlet* 1.2.158/314.

33. Ibid., 86 (February 19, 1790, from Philip Francis), 90 (February 20, 1790).

34. *Hamlet* 2.2.558–63/1488–93; quoted from Malone's edition, 9.280–81.

35. Burke, *Correspondence*, VI, 182 (ca. November 29, 1790).
36. Edmond Malone, ed., *The Plays and Poems of William Shakspeare*, 10 vols. (1790), vol. I, pt. 1, lxviii.
37. Burke, *Correspondence*, VI, 206 (note).
38. Ibid., VIII, 456.
39. Jane Austen, *Mansfield Park*, 3 vols. (1814), III, 60 (Chapter 34 in modern editions).
40. Coleridge, *Biographia Literaria* (1817), ed. James Engell and W. Jackson Bate, 2 vols. (1983), in *Collected Works*: II, 27.
41. Hazlitt, *Lectures on the English Poets* (1818), in *Works*, 5.161–64.
42. Ibid., 162.
43. Hazlitt, *Characters of Shakespear's Plays*, in *Works*, IV, 216, 214.
44. Thomas Paine, *Rights of Man* (1791), 16, 15, 9.
45. Ibid., 39, 28.
46. William Cobbett, *A Year's Residence, in the United States of America* (1818), pars. 270–71 (pp. 278–85).
47. William Hawkins, *Praelectiones poeticae in schola naturalis philosophiae Oxon. habitae* (1758); see J. W. Binns, "Some Lectures on Shakespeare in Eighteenth-Century Oxford: The *Praelectiones poeticae* of William Hawkins," in *Shakespeare: Text, Language, Criticism: Essays in Honour of Marvin Spevack*, ed. Bernhard Fabian and Kurt Tetzeli von Rosador (1987), 19–33.
48. *Thraliana: The Diary of Mrs. Hester Lynch Thrale (Later Mrs. Piozzi)*, 1776–1809, ed. Katherine C. Balderston, 2 vols. (1942; rev. 1951), I, 97 (June 1777).
49. Thomas Francklin, *A Dissertation on Antient Tragedy* (1760), 59; "An Essay on the Merits of *Shakespear* and *Corneille*," *The British Magazine* 1 (June 1760), 362–65; *The Critical Review* 10 (September 1760), 247; George Lyttleton, *Dialogues of the Dead* (1760), 118.
50. J. H. Plumb, "The Commercialization of Leisure," in Neil McKendrick, John Brewer, and J. H. Plumb, *The Birth of a Consumer Society: The Commercialization of Eighteenth-Century England* (1982), 276.
51. Stone, "The Making of the Repertoire," 201.
52. C. B. Hogan, *The London Stage, 1660–1800. Part 5: 1776–1800*, 3 vols. (1968), I, clxxi–clxxiii.
53. Burke, *Correspondence*, I, 360–61 (letter of uncertain date; apparently 1750s or 1760s).
54. *The London Chronicle*, No. 280 (October 12–14, 1758), 367.
55. Jeanne Addison Roberts, "Shakespearean Comedy and Some Eighteenth-Century Actresses," in *Shakespeare, Man of the Theater: Proceedings of the Second Congress of the International Shakespeare Association, 1981*, ed. Kenneth Muir, Jay L. Halio, and D. J. Palmer (1983), 212–30.
56. Eliza Haywood, *The Female Spectator*, II, 93.
57. Samuel Johnson, *Prologue and Epilogue, Spoken at the Opening of the Theatre in Drury-Lane* (1747), 2.
58. Henry Fielding, *The History of Tom Jones, a Foundling* (1749), ed. Martin C. Battestin and Fredson Bowers, 2 vols. (1975), I, 493 (Book IX, chap. 1).
59. Henry Fielding, *The Jacobite's Journal*, ed. W. B. Coley (1975), 153 (February 6, 1748).
60. Fielding, *Amelia*, 43; *The Covent-Garden Journal*, February 8, 1752.
61. *Thraliana*, II, 725 (January 11, 1789).
62. George Winchester Stone, Jr., and George M. Kahrl, *David Garrick: A Critical Biography* (1979), 505.
63. *The Gray's Inn Journal*, No. 17 (January 19, 1754).

64. Stone and Kahrl, 656 (combining his appearances as Benedick in *The Jubilee* and in *Much Ado*).
65. Arthur Murphy, *The Gray's Inn Journal*, No. 12 (December 15, 1753).
66. Joseph Warton, *An Essay on the Writings and Genius of Pope* (1756), 202.
67. *The Critical Review*, 10 (September 1760), 248.
68. Edward Capell, ed., *MR. WILLIAM SHAKESPEARE his Comedies, Histories, and Tragedies*, 10 vols. (1768), I, sig. a3ᵛ–a4.
69. David Garrick, *An Ode Upon Dedicating A Building, And Erecting A Statue, To Shakespeare, At Stratford Upon Avon* (1769), "Advertisement."
70. Carlo Goldoni, *Malcontenti* (1754), quoted in Lacy Collison-Morley, *Shakespeare in Italy* (1916), 35–38.
71. Pope, "The Preface of the Editor to The Works of William Shakespear," *Prose Works*, II, 16; *Shakespeare, traduit de L'Anglois*, trans. Pierre Le Tourneur, 20 vols. (1776–83), I, xciii.
72. Johann Wolfgang von Goethe, *Wilhelm Meister's Apprenticeship*, trans. Thomas Carlyle (1824), Book IV, chap. 13.
73. Jonathan Bate, "Shakespearean Allusion in English Caricature in the Age of Gillray," *Journal of the Warburg and Courtauld Institutes* 49 (1986), 196–210.
74. Joseph-Léopold Borgerhoff, *Le Théâtre Anglais à Paris sous la Restauration* (1912), 14.
75. John Boydell, "A Catalogue of the Pictures in the Shakespeare Gallery" (May 1789), in *Collection of Prints, from pictures painted for the purpose of illustrating the dramatic works of Shakspeare, by the artists of Great-Britain* (1803); reprinted as *The Boydell Shakespeare Prints* (1968).
76. Winifred H. Friedman, *Boydell's Shakespeare Gallery* (1976), 5.
77. "Historical Chronicle," *Universal Magazine* 84 (May 1789), 274.
78. William Hogarth, "Autobiographical Notes" (British Library Add. MS. 27,991), fol. 10; printed in *The Analysis of Beauty*, ed. Joseph Burke (1955), 209.
79. Laurence Sterne, *The Life and Opinions of Tristram Shandy, Gentleman* (1759–67), ed. Melvyn New and Joan New, 3 vols. (1978–84), I, 26 (chapter XI).
80. *The Tempest* 1.2.354–65/420–31.
81. *Johnson on Shakespeare*, ed. Arthur Sherbo, 2 vols. (1968), in *The Yale Edition of the Works of Samuel Johnson:* II, 737 (added in 1773).
82. Edmond Malone *et al.*, *Supplement to the edition of Shakspeare's Plays Published In 1778*, 2 vols. (1780), I, 152; Isaac Reed, ed., *The Plays of William Shakspeare*, 10 vols. (1785), IX, 607–8.
83. George Walton Williams, "The Publishing and Editing of Shakespeare's Plays," in *William Shakespeare: His World, His Work, His Influence*, ed. John F. Andrews, 3 vols. (1985), III, 595–98.
84. G. E. Lessing, *Hamburg Dramaturgy*, trans. Helen Zimmern (1962), 173 (No. 73: January 12, 1768); A. W. von Schlegel, *Vorlesungen über dramatische Kunst und Litteratur* (1809–11), II, ii, 181–82, trans. by John Black as *A Course of Lectures on Dramatic Art and Literature*, 2 vols. (1815), II, 217.
85. Joseph Addison (?), *A Discourse on Ancient and Modern Learning* (1739), 23, 2.
86. Pope, "Preface," *Prose Works*, II, 23.
87. *The Gentleman's Magazine and Historical Chronicle* 58 (1788), 778: unsigned letter dated September 11, 1788.
88. Paine, 5.
89. Dryden, letter to John Dennis, in *Letters Upon several Occasions*, ed. Dennis (1696), 55.
90. Addison, *The Spectator*, No. 592 (September 10, 1714).

91. Dryden, "Epistle to the Right Honourable, My Lord Radcliffe," *Examen Poeticum* (1693), sig. A6.

92. Rowe, I, xv–xvi, xxxiv–xxxv.

93. *Johnson on Shakespeare*, I, 68, 65–66.

94. Haywood, *The Female Spectator*, II, 74–75.

95. Edward Burnaby Greene, *Critical Essays* (1770), 226.

96. [John Palmer], *The Trial of Mr. John Palmer* (1787), 18.

97. Justice Aston, opinion in *Millar v. Taylor*, 4 Burr. 2303, 2345; 98 Eng. Rep. 201 (1769), 224.

98. Justice Yates, *Tonson v. Collins*, 1 Black. W. 321, 333; 96 Eng. Rep. 180 (1762), 185.

99. Edward Young, *Conjectures on Original Composition. In a Letter to the Author of Sir Charles Grandison* (1759), 80.

100. Capell, ed., *Comedies, Histories, and Tragedies*, I, 20.

101. Capell, *Prolusions; or, select Pieces of antient Poetry* (1760), v–vi.

102. Folger MS S.a.163.

103. Malone, "Advertizement," *Supplement*, I, iii–iv.

104. Joseph Ritson, *Remarks, Critical and Illustrative, on the Text and Notes of the last Edition of Shakspeare* (1783), 241 (unnumbered last leaf). A specimen of Ritson's proposed edition—five pages of *The Comedy of Errors*, from a planned "Volume the Second"—was printed in 1787.

105. Bertrand H. Bronson, *Joseph Ritson, Scholar-at-Arms*, 2 vols. (1938), II, 462–65. Malone's portable edition offered *The Plays of William Shakspeare. Accurately printed from the text of Mr. Malone's edition; with select explanatory notes. In seven volumes.* Malone might also have been responsible for suppressing Ritson's unpublished notes on Shakespeare, after Ritson's death (II, 541–42).

106. Bodleian Library, MS. Malone 26, fol. 2ᵛ–3 (letter dated September 30, 1783).

107. Joseph Ritson, *Cursory Criticisms on the Edition of Shakspeare Published by Edmond Malone* (1792), 29.

108. Ibid., v.

109. Bronson, I, 143.

110. Ritson, *Remarks*, 188.

111. Ritson, in *The Plays of William Shakspeare*, ed. George Steevens, 15 vols. (1793), VIII, 594–96; Ritson was responding to a note by Malone, in *Plays and Poems*, V, 119–22.

112. Ritson, *Remarks*, 114. (Malone ignores Ritson's long note on Joan, instead reinforcing the traditional hostile image of Joan: *Plays and Poems*, VI, 26–27, 66.)

113. Malone, *An Inquiry into the Authenticity of certain Miscellaneous Papers . . . attributed to Shakspeare . . .* (1796), 40.

114. Ritson, *Cursory Criticisms*, 76–77.

115. Ritson, *Remarks*, 215–24; replying to a note by Steevens in *The Plays of William Shakespeare*, ed. Samuel Johnson and George Steevens, 10 vols. (1773), X, 343–44.

116. *King John* 4.2.194–201/1815–122 (quoted from Steevens' 1793 edition, VIII, 135–37). Ritson contributed almost 300 notes to Steevens' edition (many culled from his previous publications); Steevens had turned against his former friend Malone and was willing to use Ritson as a temporary ally against him. But Steevens retained control over which of Ritson's comments to print.

117. *The Letters of Joseph Ritson, Esq.*, 2 vols. (1833), I, 204.

118. Ritson, *Cursory Criticisms*, 86–87; Malone, *Plays and Poems*, vol. I, pt. 1, lv, lxv.

119. Ritson, *Cursory Criticisms*, 58.
120. *As You Like It* 2.1.59/640.
121. Malone, *Plays and Poems*, III, 145.
122. Ritson, *Cursory Criticisms*, 50–51.
123. Leigh Hunt, *Autobiography*, 2 vols. (1850), I, 162.
124. Folger MS. M. a. 129.
125. Ian Michael, *The Teaching of English: From the Sixteenth Century to 1870* (1987), 196–98.
126. *Johnson on Shakespeare*, I, 108.
127. Charles Lamb, "THEATRALIA. No. 1.—On Garrick, and Acting; and the Plays of Shakespeare, considered with reference to their fitness for Stage Representation," *The Reflector* 2 (1811), 309, 312, 308.
128. *Johnson on Shakespeare*, II, 704.
129. George Chalmers, *An Apology for The Believers in the Shakspeare-Papers* (1797), 42–66; A. W. von Schlegel, *A Course of Lectures on Dramatic Art and Literature* (1808), trans. John Black and A. J. W. Morrison (1846), 352; Wordsworth, "Essay, Supplementary to the Preface" (1815), in *The Prose Works of William Wordsworth*, ed. W. J. B. Owen and Jane Worthington Smyser, 3 vols. (1974), III, 69; "Scorn not the Sonnet," in *The Poetical Works of William Wordsworth*, 5 vols. (1827), II, 305.
130. *Letters of John Keats*, I, 188–89 (November 22, 1817).
131. Malone, *Supplement*, I, 403, 574–75; *Plays and Poems*, X, 72.
132. Hazlitt, *Characters*, in *Works*, IV, 358, 360.
133. Rowe, I, vi.
134. Edmond Malone, "An Attempt to ascertain the Order in which the Plays attributed to Shakspeare were Written," in *The Plays of William Shakespeare*, ed. George Steevens, 10 vols. (1778), I, 269–396; Edward Capell, *Notes and Various Readings to Shakespeare*, 3 vols. (1783), II.ii.183–86; Malone, *Plays and Poems*, vol. I, pt. 1, 261–386.
135. Coleridge, *Lectures*, I, 275.
136. *Letters of John Keats*, II, 115–16 (June 9, 1819).
137. Hunt, "Theatrical Examiner. No. 412," *The Examiner* (November 12, 1820), 734.
138. Keats, *Letters*, I, 242 (March 13, 1818); I, 394 (October 14, 1818).
139. Ibid. I, 192 (December 21, 1817).
140. Hazlitt, *Characters*, in *Works*, IV, 257.
141. Percy Bysshe Shelley, *A Defence of Poetry* (composed 1821), in *Essays, Letters from Abroad, Translations and Fragments*, ed. Mary Shelley, 2 vols. (1840), I, 21.
142. Coleridge, *Table Talk*, I, 3 (December 29, 1822).
143. *The Tragedy of King Lear* 3.6.20–21/1867–8; for Wordsworth see *The Prelude: A Parallel Text*, ed. J. C. Maxwell (1971), X, 456–66 (1805), 498–510 (1850); for Burke see David Bromwich, *Hazlitt: The Mind of a Critic* (1983), 314.
144. Lamb, "On Garrick, and Acting," 308.
145. Coleridge, *Table Talk*, II, 73 (April 5, 1833); *Coleridge's Shakespearean Criticism*, ed. T. M. Raysor, 2 vols. (1930), I, 59, 65.
146. Hazlitt, *Characters*, in *Works*, IV, 271–2.
147. Heinrich Heine, *Werke und Briefe in Zehn Bänden*, ed. H. Kaufman (1961–62), IV, 354.
148. Hazlitt, *Characters*, in *Works*, IV, 214.
149. *The Tragedy of King Lear* 1.1.136/137.

Chapter 4: Victorian Values

1. Georges Cuvier, "Discours Préliminaire," in *Recherches sur les ossemens . . . les révolutions du globe . . .*, 4 vols. (1812), I, 10, 11; trans. by Robert Kerr, with notes by Robert Jameson, as *Essay on the Theory of the Earth* (1817), 15, 16. The "Discours Préliminaire" was later published separately as *Discours sur les révolutions de la surface du globe* (1825).
2. Charles Lyell, *Principles of Geology*, 3 vols. (1830–33), III, 6.
3. Ibid., I, 84.
4. Ibid., III, 3.
5. Ibid., 6.
6. Ibid., I, 2.
7. Ibid., III, 3.
8. On the date of composition of the introductory chapter of volume III (not published until 1833), in which for the first time Lyell fully articulates his position, see Leonard G. Wilson, *Charles Lyell: The Years to 1841: The Revolution in Geology* (1972), 346–52; on Lyell and the agitation for reform, 320–26.
9. Frederick James Furnivall, "The New Shakspere Society: The Founder's Prospectus Revised," in *The New Shakspere Society's Transactions 1874*, vol. I, Appendix, p. 7.
10. Furnivall, quoted in "Notices of Meetings," *Transactions 1874*, I, vi.
11. Charles Dickens, *Hard Times. For These Times* (1854), 4, 5, 3–4.
12. F. G. Fleay, "On Metrical Tests as Applied to Dramatic Poetry," *Transactions 1874*, I, 2.
13. "George Sand" (1884), in *The Complete Prose Works of Matthew Arnold*, ed. R. H. Super, 11 vols. (1960–78), X, 188.
14. Furnivall, *Transactions 1874*, I, vi.
15. "To B. W. Proctor, Esq." (May 1825), in *The Works of Thomas Lovell Beddoes*, ed. H. W. Donner (1835), 85; Thomas Carlyle, "The Hero as Poet" (May 12, 1840), *On Heroes, Hero-Worship, & the Heroic in History* (1841), 180; Arnold, "A French Critic on Milton" (1877), in *Prose Works*, VIII, 170.
16. G. W. F. Hegel, *Aesthetics: Lectures on Fine Art* (1835), trans. T. M. Knox, 2 vols. (1975), II, 1227; H. H. Hoben, *Gespräche mit Heine* (1855), second edition (1948), 995; F. M. Dostoievsky, *The Diary of a Writer*, trans. Boris Brasol, 2 vols. (1949), II, 961 (1880).
17. Stendhal, *Racine et Shakespeare* (1823–25), ed. Roger Fayolle (1970), 106. For a fuller account of French reactions in this period, see also J. J. Jusserand, *Shakespeare in France Under the Ancien Régime* (1899).
18. Arnold, "Address to the Wordsworth Society: May 2nd, 1883," in *Prose Works*, X, 133.
19. Richard Roderick, "Remarks on Shakespear," in Thomas Edwards, *The Canons of Criticism . . . The Sixth Edition, with Additions* (1758), 212–38. Roderick's remarks were published posthumously; he had died in 1756.
20. Malone, "An Attempt to Ascertain the Chronology" (1778), I, 280–81.
21. John Payne Collier, *History of English Dramatic Poetry*, 3 vols. (1831), I, 327–28; Peter Cunningham, *Revels at Court, Being Extracts from the Accounts of the Revels at Court in the Time of Queen Elizabeth and James I* (1842), 203–17; James Halliwell, ed., *The Works of William Shakespeare*, 16 vols. (1853–65), XIII, 374. Although the evidence for dating *Twelfth Night* was first published by Collier in *New Particulars Regarding the Works of Shakespeare* (1836), the manuscript was actually discovered by W. H. Black in 1832: see J. Dover Wilson and R. W. Hunt, "The Authenticity of Simon Forman's *Bocke of Plaies*," *Review of English Studies* 23 (1947), 193–200.

22. *Letters of John Keats,* II, 67 (February 19, 1819).
23. Coleridge, *Lectures 1808–1819,* I, 239.
24. Thomas Campbell, "Remarks on The Life and Writings of William Shakspeare," in *The Dramatic Works of William Shakspeare* (1838), lxiii–lxiv.
25. J[ames] S[pedding], "Who Wrote Shakspere's Henry VIII?" *The Gentleman's Magazine,* n.s. 34 (August 1850), 115–23.
26. Henry Hallam, *Introduction to the Literature of Europe, in the Fifteenth, Sixteenth, and Seventeenth Centuries,* 4 vols. (1837–39), III, 568–89.
27. *As You Like It* 2.7.139–66/1062–89 (quoted from the Globe edition, 214).
28. Edward Dowden, *Shakspere,* Literature Primers, gen. ed. John Richard Green (1877), 58. Although Dowden does italicize the labels that he gives to each period, he does not place them at the head of each paragraph; I have done so here, for clarity.
29. Dowden, *Shakspere: A Critical Study of His Mind and Art* (1875), 43.
30. Dowden, *Shakspere,* 58–59.
31. Ibid., 59; Carlyle, "Hero as Poet," 175.
32. Dowden, *Shakspere,* 60.
33. Dowden, "The Scientific Movement and Literature," in *Studies in Literature 1789–1877* (1878), 97.
34. Dowden, "The Teaching of Literature," in *New Studies in Literature* (1895), 441.
35. Dowden, "Scientific Movement," 117.
36. Ibid., 104.
37. Dowden, "Teaching of Literature," 447.
38. Dowden, "Scientific Movement," 106.
39. Dowden, *Mind and Art,* 7, 6.
40. Dowden, "Scientific Movement," 86.
41. Arnold, "The Literary Influence of Academies" (1864), in *Prose Works,* III, 238.
42. Dowden, *Mind and Art,* 32, 33, 23, 37, 9–10, 46.
43. Dowden, "Teaching of Literature," 445.
44. Dowden, *Mind and Art,* 9, 8.
45. Dowden, "Scientific Movement," 114–15.
46. I have based this count upon editions listed in William Jaggard's *Shakespeare Bibliography* (1911).
47. R. D. Altick, *The English Common Reader: A Social History of the Mass Reading Public 1800–1900* (1957), 352.
48. The price is mentioned in a letter from Furnivall to James Murray, quoted in K. M. Elisabeth Murray, *Caught in the Web of Words: James A. H. Murray and the "Oxford English Dictionary"* (1977), 174.
49. W. G. Clark and W. A. Wright, eds., *The Works of William Shakespeare,* "The Globe Edition" (1864), vi.
50. Clark and Wright, Globe edition, v.
51. John Glover, W. G. Clark, and W. A. Wright, eds., *The Works of William Shakespeare,* 9 vols. (1863–66), I, x (hereafter referred to as "Cambridge Shakespeare").
52. Cambridge Shakespeare, I, xli.
53. George Dawson, President of the local Shakespeare Club, in a letter to *Aris's Birmingham Gazette* (1861): quoted in Waveney R. N. Fredrick, "Introduction," *A Shakespeare Bibliography: The Catalogue of the Birmingham Shakespeare Library,* 7 vols. (1971), I, ix.
54. Margaret E. Atkinson, *August Wilhelm Schlegel as a Translator of Shakespeare* (1958), 54.
55. Cambridge Shakespeare, I, ix.

56. "The Number of Lines in Shakspere's Works," *Transactions 1880–85,* II (Appendix I).
57. Francis Darwin and A. C. Seward, eds., *More Letters of Charles Darwin,* 2 vols. (1903), II, 229 (March 9, 1850).
58. *A New English Dictionary on Historical Principles,* 10 vols. (1888–1928), I, vi.
59. James Murray, "Lecture on Dictionaries" (1910), quoted in *Caught in the Web,* 187.
60. Jürgen Schäfer, *Documentation in the O.E.D.: Shakespeare and Nashe as Test Cases* (1980).
61. Thomas Dale, *An Introductory Lecture Delivered in the University of London* (1828), 30.
62. Dickens, *Hard Times,* 4.
63. *The Letters of Charles Dickens,* ed. Graham Storey *et al.,* (1965–), III (1974), 512 (June 13, 1842).
64. G. W. Dasent, testimony given on February 28, 1866; quoted in *Report of the Schools Inquiry Commission,* 21 vols. (1868–70), V, 521.
65. Dowden, "Teaching," 426–27.
66. Dickens, *Hard Times,* 7, 8, 9–10.
67. Eola Willis, *The Charleston Stage in the XVIII Century* (1924), 73–74.
68. Walt Whitman, "The Bowery," reprinted in *Walt Whitman and the Civil War: A Collection of Original Articles and Manuscripts,* ed. Charles I. Glicksberg (1933), 53.
69. Alexis de Tocqueville, *Democracy in America,* trans. Henry Reeves, rev. Francis Bowen, 2 vols. (1863), II, 66 (book I, chapter xiii).
70. Horace L. Traubel, *With Walt Whitman in Camden,* 6 vols. (1906–82), II, 246; Whitman, *Specimen Days,* (1882), 14.
71. Tocqueville, *Democracy,* II, 65 (book I, chap. xiii).
72. *One Touch of Shakespeare: Letters of Joseph Crosby to Joseph Parker Norris, 1875–1878,* ed. John W. Velz and Frances N. Teague (1986), 16.
73. John Alden, "America's First Shakespeare Collection," *Papers of the Bibliographical Society of America* 58 (1964), 169–73. See also Justin Winsor, *Bibliography of the Original Quartos and Folios of Shakespeare with Particular Reference to Copies in America* (1875).
74. Robert M. Smith, "The Formation of Shakespeare Libraries in America," *Shakespeare Association Bulletin* 4 (1929), 65–74.
75. Richard Grant White, *Words and Their Uses, Past and Present* (1870), 3, 5, 6, xiv.
76. Richard Grant White, *England Without and Within* (1881), 164–65.
77. *The Diary of Philip Hone, 1828–1851,* ed. Allan Nevins, rev. ed. (1936), 752–53.
78. Charles Knight, ed., *The Pictorial Edition of Shakspere,* Part 36, *Antony and Cleopatra* (1841).
79. Herman Melville, "Hawthorne and his Mosses," *The Literary World,* No. 185 (August 17–24, 1850), 126.
80. Frances Trollope, *Domestic Manners of the Americans,* 2 vols. (1832), I, 187.
81. Nancy Webb and Jean Francis Webb, *Will Shakespeare and His America* (1964), 84 (quoting an unidentified nineteenth-century diary).
82. Tocqueville, *Democracy,* II, 88 (book I, chap. xvii).
83. "Imagination and Fact," *Graham's Magazine of Literature, Art, and Fashion* 40 (January 1852), 42.
84. "Utopia—Sir Thomas More—Jack Cade" (1834), in *A Collection of the Political Writings of William Leggett,* 2 vols. (1840), I, 131.
85. Leggett, 129.

86. Ibid., 132.
87. *The Complete Writings of Walt Whitman*, ed. R. M. Bucke, T. B. Harned, and H. L. Traubel, 10 vols. (1902), IX, 115.
88. Whitman, *Writings*, IX, 75.
89. J. O. Halliwell, "A Shakespearian Discovery," *The Athenaeum*, No. 1905 (April 30, 1864), 613.
90. Whitman, *Democratic Vistas* (1871), 32.
91. Charles H. Shattuck, *Shakespeare on the American Stage: From the Hallams to Edwin Booth* (1976), 85.
92. Karl Marx, *Economic and Philosophical Manuscripts* (1844), in *Selected Writings in Sociology and Social Philosophy*, eds. T. B. Bottomore and Maximilian Rubel, trans. T. B. Bottomore (1956), 172–73, discussing *Timon of Athens* 4.3.26–45/1454–73; Lawrence W. Levine, "William Shakespeare and the American People: A Study in Cultural Transformation," *American Historical Review* 89 (1984), 34–66.
93. James Russell Lowell, "Shakespeare Once More" (1868), in *Among My Books* (1870), 156, 157, 155, 157, 164.
94. Arthur N. Applebee, *Tradition and Reform in the Teaching of English: A History* (1974), 30, 36.
95. Richard Grant White, "On Reading Shakespeare," *Studies in Shakespeare* (1886), 2.
96. Chris Baldick, *The Social Mission of English Criticism 1848–1932* (1983), 69.
97. *Reports Issued by the Schools Inquiry Commission on the Education of Girls*, ed. D. Beale (1869), 145.
98. Charlotte Lennox, *Shakespear Illustrated*, 3 vols. (1753–54), III, 158, 99.
99. Elizabeth Montagu, *An Essay on the Writings and Genius of Shakespear* (1769), 123–24.
100. Elizabeth Griffith, *The Morality of Shakespeare's Drama Illustrated* (1775), 526, xii–xiii.
101. Ibid., 139–40, 143–44, 523.
102. Shelley, "Epipsychidion" (1821), line 130; Charles Baudelaire, "L'Invitation au Voyage," *Les Fleurs du Mal* (1857).
103. *Letters of Charles and Mary Anne Lamb*, II, 228–29 (May 30–June 2, 1806).
104. Charles and Mary Lamb, *Tales from Shakespear*, 2 vols. (1807), vi–vii.
105. [Henrietta Bowdler, ed.,] *The Family Shakespeare*, 4 vols. (1807), I, vi, vii, xi.
106. Stanley Wells, "Tales from Shakespeare," *1987 British Academy Lecture* (1988).
107. *The Letters of John Fiske*, ed. Ethel F. Fisk (1940), 278–79 (November 23, 1873).
108. *The George Eliot Letters*, ed. Gordon S. Haight, 9 vols. (1954–78), I, 22 (March 16, 1839).
109. George Eliot's manuscript journal for March 16, 1855; quoted in Gordon S. Haight, *George Eliot: A Biography* (1968), 178.
110. Michael, *Teaching of English*, 223–307.
111. Arnold, "The Study of Poetry" (1880), in *Prose Works*, IX, 168–69; "Maurice de Guérin" (1863), ibid., III, 33; "John Keats" (1880), ibid., IX, 215.
112. John Cole, *The Life and Theatrical Times of Charles Kean, F.S.A.*, 2 vols. (1859), II, 343.
113. "Imagination and Fact," 40.
114. For these and other accounts see Michael R. Booth, "Pictorial Acting and Ellen Terry," in *Shakespeare and the Victorian Stage*, ed. Richard Foulkes (1986), 78–86.
115. Edward Ravenscroft, "To the reader," *Titus Andronicus, or the Rape of Lavinia* (1687), sig. A2; Rowe, I, vii.

116. Pope, I, xx.
117. Charles Knight, ed., *The Pictorial Edition of Shakspere,* Part XVII, *Timon of Athens* (1840), "Introductory Notice," 331–43.
118. Clark and Wright, eds., *Macbeth,* Clarendon Shakespeare (1869), viii–xiii.
119. Edmund Gosse, *Father and Son* (1907), ed. James Hepburn (1974), 61, discussing his father's (Philip Gosse) book *Omphalos* (1857).
120. [Samuel Mosheim Schmucker], *The Errors of Modern Infidelity Illustrated and Refuted* (1848), reprinted as *Historic Doubts Respecting Shakspeare; Illustrating Infidel Objections against the Bible* (1853). I quote the reprint title, which more usefully defines the book's contents.
121. Dickens, *Hard Times,* 14.
122. Charles Darwin and Thomas Henry Huxley, *Autobiographies,* ed. Gavin de Beer (1974), 23, 83–84.
123. Dowden, *Mind and Art,* 18.
124. Dowden, "The Scientific Movement," 99.
125. Alfred Harbage, *A Kind of Power: The Shakespeare–Dickens Analogy* (1975), 12.
126. Dowden, "Teaching," 436; *Mind and Art,* 5.
127. Whitman, *Writings,* IX, 72.
128. Samuel Smiles, *Self-Help; with illustrations of Character And Conduct* (1859), 9, 191.
129. Halliwell, ed., *Works of William Shakespeare,* I, 151.
130. Richard Grant White, *Memoirs of the Life of William Shakespeare* (1865), 111.
131. *Hamlet,* 5.2.89–90/3356–57, 5.1.95–109/3066–80.
132. Dowden, *Mind and Art,* 34, 36–37.
133. Christian Deelman, *The Great Shakespeare Jubilee* (1964), 291.
134. Richard Foulkes, *The Shakespeare Tercentenary of 1864* (1984), 36.
135. Arnold, *Culture and Anarchy* (1869), in *Prose Works,* V, 102.
136. *"As You Like It* at Coombe House," *Dramatic Review* (June 6, 1885), in *Literary Criticism of Oscar Wilde,* ed. Stanley Weintreub (1968), 127–29.
137. Tieck's suggestion was made in the notes following Schlegel's translation (1830); see *A Midsommer Nights Dreame,* ed. H. H. Furness, New Variorum edition (1895), 259.
138. Walter Bagehot, "Shakespeare—The Individual" (1853; revised 1858), in *The Collected Works,* ed. Norman St. John-Stevas, 15 vols. (1965–86), I, 204.
139. Whitman, *Democratic Vistas,* 52.
140. F. G. Fleay, "Shakespeare and Puritanism," *Anglia* 7 (1884), 223–31.
141. Richard Simpson, "The Politics of Shakspere's Historical Plays," *Transactions 1874,* II, 396–441.
142. Dowden, "Teaching," 451.
143. Arnold, "The Study of Poetry" (1880), in *Prose Works,* X, 177.
144. Arnold, "Joubert" (1864), in *Prose Works,* III, 209.
145. A. C. Bradley, *Shakespearean Tragedy* (1904), 5.
146. Ibid., vii.
147. Ibid., 48, 71.
148. The verse was originally written by Guy Boas and published in *Lays of Learning* (1926); see Katherine Cooke, *A. C. Bradley and His Influence on Twentieth Century Shakespearean Criticism* (1972), 191–92.
149. *The Tragedy of King Lear* 4.5.109–126/2316–33 (quoted from the Globe edition, pp. 871–72).
150. Bradley, "Shakespeare the Man," in *Oxford Lectures on Poetry* (1909), 328–29.
151. Charles I (?), *Eikon Basilike* (1648), 78; *Hamlet* 1.4.54/602.

152. *Julius Caesar* 2.1.67–69/529–31 (quoted from the Globe edition).
153. *Hamlet* 3.4.72–78/2285–92. (The Globe edition adopts the revised reading, "panders.")
154. *Venus and Adonis* 792; *King John* 2.2.59/934 (quoting the Globe edition).
155. Bradley, "Note to the Second Edition," *Oxford Lectures* (1909), viii.
156. Bradley, *The Study of Poetry: A Lecture* (1884), 6.
157. John Stuart Mill, "Thoughts on Poetry and Its Varieties" (1833), in *Dissertations and Discussions*, 2 vols. (1859), I, 71.

Chapter 5: Good-bye to All That

1. Virginia Woolf, "Mr. Bennett and Mrs. Brown" (originally read to The Heretics at Cambridge on May 18, 1924), in *The Captain's Death Bed and Other Essays* (1950), 96.
2. T. S. Eliot, "The Love Song of J. Alfred Prufrock," *Poetry* 6 (June 1915), 130–35.
3. E. E. Stoll, "Criminals in Shakespeare and in Science," *Modern Philology* 10 (1912–13), 65, 62–63, 71.
4. Maurice Baring, "King Lear's Daughter," *Dead Letters* (1910), 116–17.
5. Eliot, "Four Elizabethan Dramatists. I. A Preface," *Criterion*, II, 6 (February 1924), 117; I have altered Eliot's present tenses to past.
6. *Shaw on Shakespeare: An Anthology of Bernard Shaw's Writings on the Plays and Production of Shakespeare*, ed. Edwin Wilson (1961), 25, 179, 159, 55–56 (from *The Saturday Review*, October 9, 1897; September 28, 1895; May 29, 1897; September 26, 1896).
7. Eliot, "The Perfect Critic," *The Sacred Wood: Essays on Poetry and Criticism* (1920), 1–16.
8. Woolf, *Orlando* (1928), 53–54.
9. *Shaw on Shakespeare*, 25 (from *The Saturday Review*, October 9, 1897).
10. W. H. Auden, quoted in *Shaw on Music*, ed. Eric Bentley (1955), iv.
11. *Shaw on Shakespeare*, 7 (from *The Saturday Review*, February 2, 1895).
12. *Shaw on Music*, 264–65 (March 23, 1889).
13. *Shaw on Shakespeare*, 160 (from *The Saturday Review*, May 29, 1897).
14. Eliot, "The Beating of a Drum," *Nation and Athenaeum* 34 (October 6, 1923), 12.
15. Eliot, "Poetry and Propaganda," *The Bookman* 70 (February 1930), 600.
16. Eliot, "Some Notes on the Blank Verse of Christopher Marlowe," *Art and Letters*, II, 4 (Autumn 1919), 194.
17. Eliot, "Introduction," in G. Wilson Knight, *The Wheel of Fire* (1930), xviii–xix.
18. John Dover Wilson, "The Study of Shakespeare," *University of Edinburgh Journal* 8 (Summer 1936), 12.
19. L. C. Knights, "How Many Children Had Lady Macbeth? An Essay in the Theory and Practice of Shakespeare Criticism" (1933), in *Explorations* (1947), 20, 24, 31, 41, 33, 16.
20. C. J. Sisson, "The Mythical Sorrows of Shakespeare" (1934), reprinted in *Studies in Shakespeare: British Academy Lectures*, ed. Peter Alexander (1964), 20, 31.
21. Eliot, *The Waste Land* (1922), ed. Valerie Eliot (1971), line 430.
22. Chambers, *William Shakespeare*, I, 26.
23. James Joyce, *Finnegans Wake* (1939), 295, 274.
24. Joyce, *Ulysses* (1922), in *Ulysses: A Critical and Synoptic Edition*, ed. Hans Walter Gabler, 3 vols. (1984), Episode 9 (Scylla and Charybdis), 119, 879–84. Further quotations from this episode are taken, in order, from lines 846, 308,

582–83, 410, 419, 734, 729–30, 439–40, 519–20, 660–61, 1062–63, 1065–67, 147–49, 1046–47.

25. Æ [George William Russell], "Shakespeare and the Blind Alley," *The Irish Statesman,* February 9, 1924; George Moore, *Conversations in Ebury Street* (1924), 69; *Pound/Joyce: The Letters of Ezra Pound to James Joyce, with Pound's Essays on Joyce,* ed. Forrest Read (1967), 207 (originally published in 1922).

26. I. A. Richards, *Principles of Literary Criticism* (1924), 282.

27. Sisson, "Mythical Sorrows," 24.

28. Eliot, "Hamlet and his problems," *Athenaeum,* 4665 (September 26, 1919), 940.

29. Frederick S. Boas, *Shakspere and His Predecessors* (1896), 345.

30. *Shaw on Shakespeare,* 10 (from *The Saturday Review,* February 2, 1895).

31. Eliot, "Preface to the 1928 Edition," *Sacred Wood,* rev. ed. (1928), viii.

32. Richards, *Principles,* 36.

33. Richards, *Practical Criticism: A Study of Literary Judgement* (1929), 15–16, 235–54.

34. Q. D. Leavis, *Fiction and the Reading Public* (1932), 270.

35. F. R. Leavis, *For Continuity* (1933), 189.

36. W. Trotter, *Instincts of the Herd in Peace and War* (1916; rev. 1919), 259.

37. Francis A. March, "Recollections of Language Teaching," in "Proceedings of the Tenth Annual Meeting of the Modern Language Association of America, Held at Washington, D.C., December 28, 29, 30, 1892," *PMLA* 8 (1893), xxi.

38. Robert Bridges, "On the Influence of the Audience," *The Works of William Shakespeare,* 10 vols. (1904–7), X, 322, 321, 323, 324, 325.

39. Q. D. Leavis, *Reading Public,* 85.

40. Gerald Gould, "A New Reading of *Henry V,*" *The English Review* 29 (1919), 42–55.

41. *The Letters of Ezra Pound 1907–1941,* ed. D. D. Paige (1950), 101–2 (January 10, 1917).

42. *The Letters of D. H. Lawrence,* ed. James T. Boulton *et al.,* 7 vols. (1979–), I, 546 (574: May 2[?], 1913).

43. *The Letters of Virginia Woolf,* ed. Nigel Nicholson and Joanne Trautmann, 6 vols. (1975–80), III, 416 (1805: September 2, 1927).

44. Ibid., IV, 412 (2481: December 10, 1931).

45. Ibid., III, 6 (1348: January 19, 1923).

46. Ibid., II, 520 (1237: April 13, 1922).

47. *A Victorian Diarist: Later Extracts from the Journals of Mary, Lady Monkswell 1891–1909,* ed. E. C. F. Collier (1946), 21 (February 10, 1897).

48. Chambers, "The Occasion of *A Midsummer Night's Dream,*" in *A Book of Homage to Shakespeare,* ed. Israel Gollancz (1916), 154–60.

49. Peter Alexander, "*Troilus and Cressida,* 1609," *The Library* IV, 9 (1929), 267–86.

50. John Dover Wilson, ed., *Twelfth Night,* New Shakespeare edition (1930), viii.

51. Leslie Hotson, *Shakespeare versus Shallow* (1931).

52. J. W. Draper, *The 'Twelfth Night' of Shakespeare's Audience* (1950), 258–59. Draper's suggestion was developed by Leslie Hotson in *The First Night of 'Twelfth Night'* (1954).

53. G. E. Bentley, "Shakespeare and the Blackfriars Theatre," *Shakespeare Survey* 1 (1948), 38–50.

54. Richards, *Principles,* 2nd ed. (1926), 291.

55. Knights, "Shakespeare's Sonnets," in *Scrutiny* (1934); reprinted in *Explorations,* 55–81.

56. John Middleton Murry, "The Nature of Poetry" (1922), in *Discoveries* (1924), 25. For the enthusiastic comments of Saintsbury (1910), Masefield (1911), and

Rylands (1934) see H. E. Rollins, ed., *Poems*, New Variorum Shakespeare (1938), 554–56; Richards cites it as an example of the fact that "the greatest lyrics have so often a high-level appeal only" (*Principles*, 214).

57. T. W. Baldwin, *William Shakspere's Small Latine & Lesse Greeke*, 2 vols. (1944), II, 663.

58. Wilson, *The Essential Shakespeare: A Biographical Adventure* (1932), 64–65.

59. W. W. Greg, *The Library* II, 7 (1906), 208.

60. See, for instance, Greg's review of F. S. Boas' edition of *The Works of Thomas Kyd*, in *Modern Language Quarterly* 4 (1901), 186.

61. Greg, review of J. Churton Collins' edition of *The Plays and Poems of Robert Greene*, in *Modern Language Review* 1 (1906), 246.

62. Greg, *The Editorial Problem in Shakespeare* (1942), l–li.

63. Greg, *Biographical Notes 1877–1947* (1960), 13.

64. Misquotation of Eliot, *The Waste Land*, lines 62–63.

65. Arthur M. Eastman, *A Short History of Shakespearean Criticism* (1968).

66. Wilson, *The Essential Shakespeare*, viii.

67. Woolf, "Mr. Bennett and Mrs. Brown," 118.

68. Caroline Spurgeon, "Shakespeare's Iterative Imagery" (1931), reprinted in *Studies in Shakespeare*, 200.

69. T. E. Hulme, "Searchers After Reality: Haldane" (1909), in *Further Speculations*, ed. Samuel Hynes (1955), 10.

70. Spurgeon, *Shakespeare's Imagery and What It Tells Us* (1935), 4.

71. Ibid., 203–6.

72. Eastman, *Short History*, 257.

73. Richards, *Practical Criticism*, 311.

74. Madeleine Doran, *"Henry VI, Parts II and III": Their Relation to the "Contention" and the "True Tragedy"* (1928); *The Text of "King Lear"* (1931); "Imagery in *Richard II* and *Henry IV*," *Modern Language Review* 37 (1942), 113–22 (the first of many admired studies of style and imagery).

75. Muriel St. Clare Byrne, "Bibliographical Clues in Collaborate Plays," *The Library*, IV, 13 (1932), 21–48.

76. *The Woman's Part: Feminist Criticism of Shakespeare*, ed. Carolyn Ruth Swift Lenz, Gayle Greene, and Carol Thomas Neely (1980), 314–35. (Doran is mentioned but only in relation to her later work.)

77. Woolf, *A Room of One's Own* (1929), 80–84, 142–45.

78. Joyce, *Ulysses*, Episode 9, lines 810, 259, 859, 1021, 664, 458.

79. D. H. Lawrence, "Introduction to These Paintings," in *The Paintings of D. H. Lawrence* (1929); reprinted in *Selected Literary Criticism*, ed. Anthony Beal (1966), 53, 57.

80. Eliot, "Hamlet and his problems," 941.

81. Ernest Jones, "The Oedipus-Complex as an Explanation of Hamlet's Mystery: A Study of Motive," *American Journal of Psychology* 21 (1910), 73, 102.

82. Eliot, "London Letter: May, 1921," *Dial*, 70 (June 1921), 687.

83. Wyndham Lewis, *The Lion and the Fox: The Role of the Hero in the Plays of Shakespeare* (1927), 232–33.

84. *The Letters of Virginia Woolf*, VI, 11 (February 2, 1936).

85. Eliot, "Hamlet and his problems," 941.

86. Spurgeon, "Iterative Imagery," 180.

87. *Julius Caesar*, 3.1.39–46/1126–33 (quoted from Spurgeon, "Iterative," 181).

88. Edward A. Armstrong, *Shakespeare's Imagination: A Study of the Psychology of Association and Inspiration* (1946), 31.

89. Ibid., 118, 125.

90. Spurgeon, *Leading Motives in the Imagery of Shakespeare's Tragedies* (1930), 3.
91. Woolf, *"Twelfth Night* at the Old Vic" (1933), *The Death of the Moth and Other Essays* (1942), 34.
92. Woolf, "On Being Ill," *The Criterion* 4 (January 1926), 41–42; revised in *The Moment, and Other Essays* (1947), 19–20.
93. Harley Granville-Barker, *"Twelfth Night* at the Vieux Colombier," *The Observer,* January 1, 1922; reprinted in *Twelfth Night: Critical Essays,* ed. Stanley Wells (1986), 71–78.
94. Eliot, *The Waste Land,* lines 128–30.
95. "That Shakespearian Rag," words by Gene Buck and Herman Ruby, music by David Stamper, copyright by Edward B. Marks Music Corporation (1912). See B. R. McElderry, Jr., "Eliot's 'Shakespeherian Rag,' " *American Quarterly* 9 (1957), 185–86.
96. *Macbeth,* 3.4.59/1083, 5.10.33/2104.
97. Eliot, "Tradition and the Individual Talent," *The Egoist* 6, no. 4 (September 1919), 55; no. 5 (December 1919), 72. (Eliot later changed "passive" to "neutral.")
98. Eliot, "London Letter: May, 1921," 687.
99. *Victorian Diarist,* 21.
100. "Theatricals in the Middle Temple," *The Times* (London), February 11, 1897, p. 2.
101. Sir Lewis Casson, "William Poel and the Modern Theatre," *The Listener* (January 10, 1952), 58.
102. William Poel, *Shakespeare in the Theatre* (1913), 60; correspondence to *Times Literary Supplement,* February 24, 1921, p. 127.
103. " 'Hamlet' in Modern Dress," *The Times* (London), August 26, 1925, p. 8.
104. Eliot, "Ulysses, Order, and Myth," *Dial* 75 (1923), 483.
105. David Jones, *In Parenthesis* (1937), xiv (alluding to *1 Henry IV,* 4.1.105/2229); 196 (note on the phrase "The Disciplines of the Wars," p. 24); xi (alluding to *Henry V,* Prologue, 12–14/12–14).
106. Ivor Brown, "To Breech or not to Breech?" *Saturday Review,* August 29, 1925, p. 233.
107. Hubert Griffith, in *The Observer,* August 30, 1925.
108. Muriel St. Clare Byrne, "Fifty Years of Shakespearian Production: 1898–1948," *Shakespeare Survey* 2 (1949), 12.
109. Christine Dymbowski, *Harley Granville-Barker: A Preface to Modern Shakespeare* (1986), 6–67; William Winter, *Shakespeare on the Stage,* 3 vols. (1916), III, 290, 292.
110. Eliot, " 'The Duchess of Malfi' at the Lyric: and Poetic Drama," *Art and Letters* 3 (Winter 1919–20), 38–39.
111. Eliot, "Four Elizabethan Dramatists," 119–20.
112. Jack J. Jorgens, "Shakespeare on Film and Television," in *World, Work, Influence,* III, 683.
113. Marianne Moore, "Poetry," *Selected Poems* (1935), 53.
114. *The Times* (London), October 30, 1918.
115. Shaw, *Our Theatres in the Nineties,* 3 vols. (1932), II, 184 (from *The Saturday Review:* July 11, 1896).
116. Edward Gordon Craig, *On the Art of the Theatre* (1911), 73.
117. Yeats, "At Stratford on Avon" (1901), reprinted in *Essays and Introductions* (1961), 100.
118. *The Letters of W. B. Yeats,* ed. Allan Wade (1954), 579 (March 16, 1913).
119. Yeats, "The Theatre of Beauty," *Harper's Weekly* 55 (November 11, 1911), 11.

120. Nigel Playfair, *The Story of the Lyric Theatre Hammersmith* (1925), 96.
121. Eliot, "Four Elizabethan Dramatists," 117, 120.
122. Knight, quoted in Jorgens, *Shakespeare on Film* (1977), 43.
123. *The Diary of Virginia Woolf*, III, 104 (July 31, 1926), 182 (April 24, 1928), 300–1 (April 13, 1930).
124. G. Wilson Knight, *The Wheel of Fire*, 205.
125. Ibid., 28.
126. Spurgeon, *Shakespeare's Imagery*, 214–15.
127. Ibid., 243, 259, 300, 310, 316, 323.
128. Peter Alexander, *'Henry VI'* and *'Richard III'* (1929); Knights, "Lady Macbeth," 25–44; A. M. Sampley, "Plot Structure in Peele's Plays as a Test of Authorship," *PMLA* 51 (1936), 689–701; Hereward T. Price, "The Authorship of *Titus Andronicus*," *Journal of English and Germanic Philology* 42 (1943), 55–81; Una Ellis-Fermor, "*Timon of Athens:* An Unfinished Play," *Review of English Studies* 18 (1942), 270–83.
129. Spurgeon, "Iterative Imagery," 186–90; G. Wilson Knight, "The Writing of *Pericles*," in *The Crown of Life* (1947), 32–75.
130. Samuel Johnson, *Proposals for Printing, by Subscription, the Dramatick Works of William Shakespeare* (1756), in *Johnson on Shakespeare*, I, 52.
131. Sidney Lee, "Introduction," *Shakespeares Comedies, Histories, & Tragedies, Being a Reproduction in Facsimile of The First Folio Edition 1623* (1902), xii.
132. William Shakespeare, *Comedies, Histories, & Tragedies* (1623), sig. A3; reprinted in *Complete Works* (1986), xliii.
133. Woolf, *Letters*, V, 218 (2783: August 22, 1933).
134. Alfred W. Pollard, *Shakespeare's Fight with the Pirates and the Problems of the Transmission of his Text*, 2nd ed. (1920), vii.
135. R. W. Chambers, "The Expression of Ideas—Particularly Political Ideas—in the Three Pages and in Shakespeare," in *Shakespeare's Hand in the Play of 'Sir Thomas More,'* ed. Alfred W. Pollard (1923), 165.
136. F. P. Wilson, "Ralph Crane, Scrivener to the King's Players," *The Library*, ser. IV, vol. 7 (1926), 194–215.
137. Eliot, "Hamlet and his problems," 941, 940.
138. Alexander, *"Henry VI"* and *"Richard III"* (1929); John S. Smart, *Shakespeare: Truth and Tradition*, ed. Peter Alexander (1928); E. A. J. Honigmann, "Studies in the Chronology of Shakespeare's Plays," unpublished B. Litt. thesis (University of Oxford, 1950). Honigmann's views were expanded in his Arden edition of *King John* (1954).
139. G. I. Duthie, *The 'Bad' Quarto of 'Hamlet'* (1941); Harry R. Hoppe, *The Bad Quarto of 'Romeo and Juliet': A Bibliographical and Textual Study* (1948).
140. Misquotation of *Coriolanus*, 5.3.36–37/2946–47.
141. Knight, *Wheel of Fire*, 3.
142. Eliot, "Coriolan," in *Collected Poems 1909–1935* (1936), 136.
143. Eliot, *Knowledge and Experience in the Philosophy of F. H. Bradley* (1964; printing his unrevised doctoral dissertation of 1916), 60; "Tradition and the Individual Talent" (1919), 55.
144. Eliot, "John Ford," *Times Literary Supplement* (May 5, 1932), 317.
145. Eliot, "The Function of Criticism," *Criterion*, II, 5 (October 1923), 31–32.
146. Cleanth Brooks, "Shakespeare as a Symbolist Poet," *Yale Review* 34 (1944–45), 642–65; reprinted as "The Naked Babe and the Cloak of Manliness," in *The Well Wrought Urn* (1947), 21–46. Quotations from Brooks below are taken from the 1947 printing of this essay, unless noted otherwise.
147. *Richard II*, 2.1.40/654.

148. L. C. Knights, "Shakespeare and Shakespeareans" (1934), *Explorations*, 96.
149. Knights, "Lady Macbeth," 35.
150. Brooks, "Symbolist Poet," 642.
151. *Macbeth*, 1.7.21–23/417–19, 2.3.111–16/725–30 (quoted from Brooks' essay).
152. E. A. Abbott, *A Shakespearian Grammar*, 3rd ed. (1870), para. 529.
153. *Letters of Ford Madox Ford*, ed. Richard M. Ludwig (1965), 55 (January 23, 1913); Hulme, "A Lecture on Modern Poetry" (1908?), *Further Speculations*, 69.
154. Pound, "How to Read" (1929), *Literary Essays of Ezra Pound*, ed. Eliot (1954), 38, 29; "Lionel Johnson" (1915), *Literary Essays*, 362.
155. Robert Graves, *Good-bye to All That* (1929), 14, 16, 294.
156. Robert Graves and Laura Riding, "A Study in Original Punctuation and Spelling," in *A Survey of Modernist Poetry* (1927), 63–82; revised in *The Common Asphodel* (1949), 84–95.
157. "The Golden Thoughts of Granville-Barker," *Play Pictorial*, xxi, no. 126 (1912), iv.
158. Spurgeon, *Shakespeare's Imagery*, x.
159. Pound, *Make It New* (1935); Eliot, "Tradition," 55.
160. Pound, "A Retrospect" (1918), in *Literary Essays*, 6.
161. Granville-Barker, "Introduction to *The Players' Shakespeare*" (1923), in *More Prefaces to Shakespeare*, ed. Edward M. Moore (1974), 46.
162. Granville-Barker, "A Note upon Chapters xx and xxi of *The Elizabethan Stage*," *Review of English Studies* 1 (1925), 69–70.
163. " 'Hamlet' in Modern Dress," 8.
164. Eliot, "Reflections on Contemporary Poetry" (IV), *The Egoist*, VI, no. 3 (July 1919), 39.
165. Woolf, *Letters*, IV, 4 (January 8, 1929).

Chapter 6: Present Tense

1. Robert Weimann, *Shakespeare and the Popular Tradition in the Theater*, ed. Robert Schwartz (1978), xi.
2. See J. Philip Brockbank, "Shakespeare Renaissance in China," *Shakespeare Quarterly* 39 (1988), 195–204; Zha Peide and Tian Jia, "Shakespeare in Traditional Chinese Operas," 204–11.
3. Royal Shakespeare Company, *One Hundred and Eleventh Report of the Council 1986/7* (November 1987).
4. "Shakespeare: Annotated World Bibliography for 1986," ed. Harrison T. Meserole, *Shakespeare Quarterly* 38 (1987).
5. Books by Christine Dymkowski, *Granville-Barker;* Ann Fridén, *Macbeth;* Gianfranco Bartalotta, *Amleto; Shakespeare Around the Globe: A Guide to Notable Postwar Revivals*, ed. Samuel L. Leiter; Graham Nichols, *Measure for Measure: Text and Performance*, gen. ed. Michael Scott.
6. Terence Hawkes, *That Shakespeherian Rag: Essays on a Critical Process* (1986), 117–18.
7. Adrian Noble, " 'Well, This Is the Forest of Arden': An Informal Address," *Images of Shakespeare: Proceedings of the Third Congress of the International Shakespeare Association, 1986*, ed. Werner Habicht, D. J. Palmer, and Roger Pringle (1988), 341.
8. Trevor Nunn, quoted in Ralph Berry, *On Directing Shakespeare: Interviews with Contemporary Directors* (1977), 56.
9. Jan Kott, *Szkice o Szekspirze* (1961), published in English as *Shakespeare Our Contemporary*, trans. Boleslaw Taborski (1964), 52.

10. Weimann, xi.
11. Stanley Wells, "General Introduction," *Complete Works*, xxix, xxxv.
12. Stanley Wells, "A New Oxford Shakespeare" (typescript of a lecture delivered at the Sheldonian Theatre on October 28, 1986); an abbreviated version of this essay was published in *Oxford Magazine* 26 (1987). Further quotations from Wells in this section are taken from the typescript, unless otherwise noted.
13. Alan Dessen, *Elizabethan Stage Conventions and Modern Interpreters* (1984), 12–52.
14. Ann Pasternak Slater, *Shakespeare the Director* (1982).
15. G. K. Hunter, "Flatcaps and Bluecoats: Visual Signals on the Elizabethan Stage," *Essays and Studies*, n.s. 33 (1980), 16–47.
16. John Doebler, *Shakespeare's Speaking Pictures: Studies in Iconic Imagery* (1974), 21–38; Huston Diehl, *An Index of Icons in English Emblem Books, 1500–1700* (1986).
17. David Bevington, *Action Is Eloquence: Shakespeare's Language of Gesture* (1984), 92–93.
18. "The Language of Gesture in the Renaissance: Selected Proceedings of the Conference Held in Toronto, November 1983," *Renaissance and Reformation*, n.s. 10 (1986).
19. Julius Fast, *Body Language* (1970).
20. *Shakespeare Survey 39*, ed. Stanley Wells. *Shakespeare Survey* is published annually; volume 39, scheduled for the end of 1986, did not appear until January 1987.
21. John Bayley, *The Guardian*, October 31, 1986.
22. Stanley Wells, *Re-Editing Shakespeare for the Modern Reader* (1984), 3.
23. Wells, "Modernizing Shakespeare's Spelling," in Stanley Wells and Gary Taylor, *Modernizing Shakespeare's Spelling, with Three Studies in the Text of 'Henry V'* (1979), 3.
24. G. Blakemore Evans, ed., *The Riverside Shakespeare* (1974), 39.
25. Randall McLeod, "Spellbound," in *Play-Texts in Old Spelling: Papers from the Glendon Conference*, ed. G. B. Shand with Raymond C. Shady (1984), 81–96.
26. Thomas M. Greene, "Anti-Hermeneutics: The Case of Shakespeare's Sonnet 129" (1982), in *The Vulnerable Text* (1986), 164, 162, 174.
27. *Shakespeare Translation*, vols. 1–10 (1974–84); thereafter rechristened *Shakespeare Worldwide: Translation and Adaptation*.
28. Maik Hamburger, "A Spate of *Twelfth Night*s: Illyria Rediscovered?" in *Images of Shakespeare*, 236–44.
29. Terry Eagleton, *William Shakespeare* (1986), 1–2.
30. Ibid., ix–x.
31. Ibid., 2–5.
32. Allan Bloom, *The Closing of the American Mind: How Higher Education Has Failed Democracy and Impoverished the Souls of Today's Students* (1987), 378–79, 375. Bloom's preface is datelined "Chicago, May 1986."
33. Allan Bloom with Harry V. Jaffa, *Shakespeare's Politics* (1964), 80.
34. Ibid., 4.
35. Bloom, 353, 374, 375.
36. Norman Rabkin, "Either/Or: Responding to *Henry V*," in *Shakespeare and the Problem of Meaning* (1981), 33–62.
37. Stephen Orgel, "Prospero's Wife," in *Rewriting the Renaissance: The Discourses of Sexual Difference in Early Modern Europe*, ed. Margaret W. Ferguson, Maureen Quilligan, and Nancy J. Vickers (1985), 52.
38. Mitchell Patrick, speaking at a panel on audience response at the University of Maryland Drama Conference, November 22, 1987.

39. Malcolm Bradbury, *Eating People Is Wrong* (1959), reprinted with an afterword by the author (1986), 35, 261, 267–70.
40. David Lodge, *Small World: An Academic Romance* (1984; rev. 1985), 197, 231–33.
41. Bloom, 65.
42. *Shakespeare's Politics*, 57–58.
43. Stephen Booth, "Liking *Julius Caesar*" (author's typescript of a paper publicly delivered on August 21, 1987, at the Twenty-second International Shakespeare Conference at Stratford-upon-Avon); quotations from Booth in this section are all drawn from this unpublished typescript.
44. E. A. J. Honigmann, " 'There Is a World Elsewhere': William Shakespeare, Businessman," in *Images of Shakespeare*, 40–46.
45. Edward Bond, *Bingo* (1974), vii, ix.
46. Leon Rooke, *Shakespeare's Dog* (1981; Ecco Press [paperback] edition, 1986), 8, 35, 34, 149, 52, 15.
47. S. Schoenbaum, *William Shakespeare: A Compact Documentary Life* (1977), 3.
48. *Northrop Frye on Shakespeare*, ed. Robert Sandler (1986), 43–47.
49. C. L. Barber and Richard P. Wheeler, *The Whole Journey: Shakespeare's Power of Development* (1986), 77.
50. Norman Holland, *Psychoanalysis and Shakespeare* (1966), 134–35, 285–86, 338; paraphrased in *The Whole Journey*, 77.
51. Leo Salingar, *Shakespeare and the Traditions of Comedy* (1974), 256; quoted in *The Whole Journey*, 62.
52. *The Whole Journey*, 91.
53. Random Cloud [Randall McLeod], "The Psychopathology of Everyday Art," in *The Elizabethan Theatre IX*, ed. G. R. Hibbard (1986), 150, 167, 132.
54. I owe this anecdote to Michael Warren, Barber's colleague at the University of California at Santa Cruz.
55. For full details of these authorship studies see my survey of "The Canon and Chronology of Shakespeare's Plays," in *Textual Companion*, 69–144.
56. Gary Taylor, "General Introduction," *Textual Companion*, 15, adapting a concept articulated by Jerome McGann in *A Critique of Modern Textual Criticism* (1983).
57. Charlton Hinman, *The Printing and Proof-Reading of the First Folio of Shakespeare*, 2 vols. (1963), II, 513.
58. M. C. Bradbrook, "Social Nuances in Shakespeare's Early Comedies," in *Essays in Honor of Kristian Smidt*, ed. Peter Bilton *et al.* (1986), 1–8.
59. Linda Woodbridge, *Women and the English Renaissance: Literature and the Nature of Womankind, 1540–1620* (1984; Illini Books edition, 1986), 99.
60. Germaine Greer, "The Ethos of Love and Marriage in Shakespeare's Early Comedies," Ph.D. dissertation (University of Cambridge, 1967).
61. Germaine Greer, *Shakespeare* (1986), 109.
62. Bloom, 65.
63. Juliet Dusinberre, *Shakespeare and the Nature of Women* (1975), 153.
64. Coppélia Kahn, *Man's Estate: Masculine Identity in Shakespeare* (1981), 20.
65. Madelon Sprengnether, "Annihilating Intimacy in *Coriolanus*," in *Women in the Middle Ages and the Renaissance*, ed. Mary Beth Rose (1986), 89–111.
66. Lodge, 322–23.
67. *The Whole Journey*, 330.
68. Erica Jong, *Serenissima: A Novel of Venice* (1987). The novel was completed in 1986 (the year when its jacket illustration and calligraphy were copyrighted).

69. Kathleen E. McLuskie, " 'The Emperor of Russia Was My Father': Gender and Theatrical Power," in *Images of Shakespeare*, 174–87.

70. Kathleen McLuskie, "The Patriarchal Bard: Feminist Criticism and Shakespeare: *King Lear* and *Measure for Measure*," in *Political Shakespeare: New Essays in Cultural Materialism*, ed. Jonathan Dollimore and Alan Sinfield (1985), 88–108.

71. Peter Erickson, *Patriarchal Structures in Shakespeare's Drama* (1985), 182.

72. Woodbridge, *Women and the English Renaissance*, 8.

73. Diane Elizabeth Dreher, *Domination and Defiance: Fathers and Daughters in Shakespeare* (1986).

74. Marilyn L. Williamson, *The Patriarchy of Shakespeare's Comedies* (1986), 18, 20–21.

75. Peter W. M. Blayney, *The Texts of "King Lear" and Their Origins*, Volume I: *Nicholas Okes and the First Quarto* (1982), 425–28.

76. Hinman, I, 227.

77. Paul Werstine, "Line Division in Shakespeare's Dramatic Verse: An Editorial Problem," *Analytical and Enumerative Bibliography* 8 (1984), 73–125. Although this issue is dated "1984," it was not published until early 1986.

78. D. F. McKenzie, *The Cambridge University Press 1696–1712: A Bibliographical Study*, 2 vols. (1966), and "Printers of the Mind: Some Notes on Bibliographical Theories and Printing-house Practices," *Studies in Bibliography* 22 (1969), 1–75.

79. D. F. McKenzie, *Bibliography and the Sociology of Texts*, The Panizzi Lectures 1985 (1986), 5.

80. The Folger Shakespeare Library, *Annual Report of the Director for the Fiscal Year Ending June 30, 1986*, 26.

81. Stephen Greenblatt, "Martial Law in the Land of Cockaigne," in *Shakespearean Negotiations: The Circulation of Social Energy* (1988), 129–63. All quotations from Greenblatt in this section are taken from this chapter, which in its printed form does not materially differ from the tape of his talk, preserved at the Folger.

82. Leonard Tennenhouse, *Power on Display: The Politics of Shakespeare's Genres* (1986).

83. Harold Bloom, *The Anxiety of Influence: A Theory of Poetry* (1973), 11. (In later works Bloom allows Shakespeare some anxiety, but it always remains marginal.)

84. James Gleick, *Chaos: Making a New Science* (1987); Gleick's research covers the period through December 1986 (see page 318).

85. Malcolm Evans, *Signifying Nothing: Truth's True Contents in Shakespeare's Text* (1986), 38.

86. Evans, 20, 19.

87. Erickson, "Rewriting the Renaissance, Rewriting Ourselves," *Shakespeare Quarterly* 38 (1987), 337, quoting Greenblatt.

88. Margot Heinemann, "How Brecht Read Shakespeare," in *Political Shakespeare*, 202–3, quoting an interview with Nigel Lawson in *The Guardian*, September 5, 1983.

89. Alan Sinfield, "*Macbeth*: History, Ideology, and Intellectuals," *Critical Quarterly* 28 (1986), 63–77. The Reagan parallel, spoken at Harvard but not published, was recounted to me in a letter from Sinfield (February 5, 1988).

90. *Political Shakespeare*, viii.

91. Evans, 186.

92. Steven Urkowitz, "Five Women Eleven Ways: Changing Images of Shake-

spearean Characters in the Earliest Texts," in *Images of Shakespeare,* 292–304.

93. Steven Urkowitz, "Shakespeare as a Revising Artist," unpublished typescript. A substantially revised version of this lecture appeared as "Good News about Bad Quartos," in *"Bad" Shakespeare,* ed. Maurice Charney (1988).

94. G. K. Hunter's lecture was delivered extemporaneously, from notes; my account of it has been compiled by consultation with several witnesses and from correspondence with Prof. Hunter. What follows is therefore less a transcription of Hunter's exact words on that occasion, more a generic rendering of the anticonflationist position in the mid-1980s.

95. G. K. Hunter, private correspondence (May 1, 1988).

96. Michael J. Warren, "Quarto and Folio *King Lear* and the Interpretation of Albany and Edgar," in *Shakespeare, Pattern of Excelling Nature,* ed. David Bevington and Jay L. Halio (1978), 95–107.

97. P. W. K. Stone, *The Textual History of 'King Lear'* (1980); Gary Taylor, "The War in *King Lear,*" *Shakespeare Survey 33* (1980), 27–34.

98. Randall McLeod, *"Gon.* No more, the text is foolish.," in *The Division of the Kingdoms: Shakespeare's Two Versions of 'King Lear,'* ed. Gary Taylor and Michael Warren (1983; paperback edition, 1986), 169, 167.

99. Beth Goldring, *"Cor.'s* Rescue of Kent," in *The Division of the Kingdoms,* 143–51; Urkowitz, "Five Women," 292.

100. Hawkes, *Shakespeherian Rag,* 94–95.

101. Joel Fineman, *Shakespeare's Perjured Eye: The Invention of Poetic Subjectivity in the Sonnets* (1986), 317.

102. Alan Sinfield (personal letter, February 5, 1988).

103. *Shakespeare's Politics,* 75.

104. Fineman, 1–2.

105. William Shakespeare, *The Sonnets and A Lover's Complaint,* ed. John Kerrigan (1986), 12–13, 21, 157.

106. E. A. J. Honigmann, "Re-enter the Stage Direction: Shakespeare and Some Contemporaries," *Shakespeare Survey 29* (1976), 117–25; *Representing Shakespeare,* ed. Murray Schwartz and Coppélia Kahn (1980); *Shakespeare Reproduced: The Text in History and Ideology,* ed. Jean Howard and Marion F. O'Connor (1987); *Rewriting the Renaissance,* ed. Ferguson, Quilligan, Vickers (1986).

107. Jonathan Goldberg, *Voice Terminal Echo: Postmodernism and English Renaissance Texts* (1986), 94.

108. Fineman, 15.

109. Ibid., 16, 27; Kerrigan, 23.

110. Misquotation of *Macbeth,* 3.2.51–52/995–96.

111. Ron Silliman, ed., *In the American Tree,* 485.

112. Randall McLeod, *"IMAGINATION,"* unpublished typescript (dated March 1986) circulated at the textual seminar of the 1986 World Shakespeare Congress.

113. Silliman, 486.

114. James L. Calderwood, *If It Were Done: 'Macbeth' and Tragic Action* (1986), ix.

115. Tom Stoppard, "Is It True What They Say About Shakespeare?" (delivered April 12, 1980), International Shakespeare Association, occasional paper No. 2 (1982), 11.

116. Eugene Ionesco, *Macbett* (1972), trans. Donald Watson (1973).

117. Hawkes, *Shakespeherian Rag,* ix. Hawkes does not mention that "Swisser-Swatter" had been previously published in *Shakespeare Today: Directions and Methods of Research,* ed. Keir Elam (1984).

118. As an example of a paper that could easily have been added to the book see Terence Hawkes, "Take Me to Your Leda," *Shakespeare Survey 40* (1988), 21–32 (delivered at the 1986 Stratford conference).
119. Hawkes, 94.
120. Honigmann, "Businessman," 43–44; Stephen Orgel, "What Is a Text?" *Research Opportunities in Renaissance Drama* 24 (1981), 3–6; Michael Hattaway, *Elizabethan Popular Theatre* (1982), 10.

Chapter 7: Singularity

1. Alfred Harbage, *Conceptions of Shakespeare* (1966), 54.
2. Kenneth Muir, *The Singularity of Shakespeare and Other Essays* (1977).
3. Schoenbaum, *Compact Documentary Life*, 185.
4. *The Cambridge History of Classical Literature: Latin Literature*, ed. E. J. Kenney (1982), 808–11.
5. The most skeptical survey of the biographical evidence on Sophocles and his fellow Greek dramatists is Mary Lefkowitz, *The Lives of the Greek Poets* (1981).
6. G. E. Bentley, *Shakespeare: A Biographical Handbook* (1961), 119–121.
7. Andrew Gurr, "Theatres and the Dramatic Profession," in *World, Work, Influence*, I, 116.
8. Honigmann, "William Shakespeare, Businessman"; Honigmann does not specifically suggest that Shakespeare bought his way into the company, but his analysis of Shakespeare's business interests opens up that possibility.
9. Rowe, I, ix–x.
10. Thomas Heywood, *The English Traveller* (1633), sig. A3.
11. John Lough, *Seventeenth-Century French Drama: The Background* (1979), 52.
12. Rowe, I, xxxv.
13. "Preface," in *Johnson on Shakespeare*, I, 59–60.
14. Harry Levin, "The Primacy of Shakespeare," delivered at the Folger Library in Washington on March 11, 1973; published in *Shakespeare Quarterly* 26 (1975), and in *Shakespeare and the Revolution of the Times: Perspectives and Commentaries* (1976), 235–60.
15. Northrop Frye, *Anatomy of Criticism* (1957), 20.
16. Qi-Xin He, "China's Shakespeare," *Shakespeare Quarterly* 37 (1986), 149–59.
17. A. L. Rowse, "Shakespeare's Universal Appeal," *Deutsche Shakespeare-Gesellschaft West Jahrbuch 1980*, 59.
18. Francis Meres, *Palladis Tamia* (1598), 282.
19. Dryden, *Of Dramatick Poesie*, 55.
20. Bernard Knox, "Euripidean Comedy" (originally published in 1970), collected in *Word and Action: Essays on the Ancient Theatre* (1979), 250–74.
21. Aristotle, *Poetics* 1453a25.
22. Pope, *Prose Works*, II, 16.
23. *OED* "illiterate," a. 1a; Olivia Smith, *The Politics of Language, 1791–1819* (1984), 235.
24. "Preface," *Johnson on Shakespeare*, I, 60.
25. Arthur Sherbo, *The Birth of Shakespeare Studies* (1986), 1–2.
26. "Preface," *Johnson on Shakespeare*, I, 60–61.
27. Eliot, "Marlowe," 119.
28. Walter Savage Landor, *Imaginary Conversations of Literary Men and Statesmen: Southey and Landor* (1846), in *The Complete Works of Walter Savage Landon*, ed. T. Earle Welby, 16 vols. (1927–36), V, 318.
29. Bagehot, *Works*, I, 470.

30. Gerald Langbaine, *An Account of the English Dramatick Poets* (1691), 133, 150.
31. Harry Levin, "Critical Approaches to Shakespeare from 1660 to 1904," *The Cambridge Companion to Shakespeare Studies* (1986), 216.
32. *Shaw on Shakespeare*, 217.
33. William Prynne, *Histrio-Mastrix* (1633), 148.
34. Anthony Munday, *A Second and Third Blast of Retrait from Plaies and Theaters* (1580), 3. For further evidence see Ann Jennalie Cook, " 'Bargaines of Incontinencie': Bawdy Behavior in the Playhouses," and Wallace Shugg, "Prostitution in Shakespeare's London," *Shakespeare Studies* 10 (1977), 271–90, 291–313.
35. *Hamlet* 2.2.553–61, 584–89/1483–91, 1514–19.
36. Thomas Dekker and Thomas Middleton, *The Roaring Girl* (1611), 3.1.90–96, in *The Dramatic Works of Thomas Dekker*, ed. Fredson Bowers, 4 vols. (1953–61); for Middleton's authorship of this particular passage see MacDonald P. Jackson, *Studies in Attribution: Middleton and Shakespeare* (1979), 95–101.
37. Coleridge, *Table Talk*, I, 73 (June 24, 1827).
38. *Textual Companion*, 116–17.
39. David Young, "Shakespeare as a Writer of Comedy," in *World, Work, Influence*, II, 489–90.
40. Anthony Burgess, *Shakespeare* (1970), 47–50.
41. Anne Barton, introduction to *The Comedy of Errors*, in *The Riverside Shakespeare* (1974), 80; Plautus, *Amphitruo*, ed. W. B. Sedgwick (1960), 6.
42. Eliot, "Little Gidding," lines 253–54, in *Four Quartets* (1944), ed. Helen Gardner in *The Composition of "Four Quartets"* (1978).
43. William Shakespeare, *The Comedy of Errors*, ed. Paul Jorgensen, in *The Complete Works*, "The Pelican Text Revised," gen. ed. Alfred Harbage (1969), 56.
44. William Shakespeare, *The Complete Works*, ed. David Bevington, 3rd ed. (1980), 96–97.
45. John Lahr, *Prick Up Your Ears: The Biography of Joe Orton* (1978), 88.
46. Ralph Waldo Emerson, "Shakspeare, or the Poet" (1846), in *Representative Men: Seven Lectures* (1850), ed. Willace E. Williams and Douglas Emory Wilson, in *The Collected Works of Ralph Waldo Emerson*, vol. IV (1987), 125.
47. George Santayana, "The Absence of Religion in Shakespeare," *Interpretations of Poetry and Religion* (1900), 147–65.
48. Ludwig Wittgenstein, *Culture and Value*, trans. Peter Winch (1980); see also George Steiner, "A Reading Against Shakespeare," The W. P. Ker Lecture for 1986 (University of Glasgow, 1986).
49. Leo Tolstoy, *Shakespeare and the Drama*, trans. V. Tschertkoff and I. F. M., with an introduction by G. B. Shaw (1906), 3, 4, 80, 81–82, 94, 92, 93, 97.
50. George Lyttleton, *Dialogues of the Dead. The Fourth Edition, Corrected* (1765), 127.
51. George Orwell, "Lear, Tolstoy and the Fool," in *Shooting an Elephant* (1950), 33–56.
52. Oliver Goldsmith, *An Enquiry into the Present State of Polite Learning in Europe* (1759), in *Collected Works*, ed. Arthur Friedman, 4 vols. (1966), I, 326.
53. *Boswell's Life of Johnson*, ed. George Birkbeck, rev. L. F. Powell, 6 vols. (1934), II, 96.
54. Arnold, "A Guide to English Literature" (1877), in *Prose Works*, VIII, 245.
55. J. J. Thompson, *Recollections and Reflections* (1937), 317.
56. *Diary and Letters of Madame d'Arblay*, ed. Charlotte Barrett, 7 vols. (1842–46), II, 398 (December 19, 1785).
57. *Letters of Ezra Pound: 1907–1941*, 324 (357: August 6, 1939).

58. Barton, 80.
59. Erich Segal, *Roman Laughter: The Comedy of Plautus* (1968; 2nd ed., 1987), 44, 43, 49, 50.
60. *The Tragedy of King Lear* 3.2.84/1612.
61. Muir, "Shakespeare's Open Secret," *Shakespeare Survey* 34 (1981), 9.
62. "The Theme of the Three Caskets" (1913), in *The Standard Edition of the Complete Psychological Works of Sigmund Freud,* trans. James Strachey et al., 24 vols. (1953–74), XII, 241.
63. Lewis Theobald, "Preface of the Editor," in *Double Falshood; or, The Distrest Lovers* (1728), sig. A5.
64. Brian Gibbons, *Jacobean City Comedy* (1968), 205.
65. Philip Edwards, *Shakespeare and the Confines of Art* (1968), 134.
66. Charles Knight, ed., *Pictorial Edition,* XVII, 331–43; William Wells, "*Timon of Athens,*" *Notes and Queries* 112 (1920), 226–29; Dugdale Sykes, *Sidelights on Elizabethan Drama* (1924), 1–48.
67. For all these studies see *Textual Companion,* 127–28.
68. Philip Edwards, *Shakespeare: A Writer's Progress* (1986), 130–31. Edwards was informed of Holdsworth's work, and my own, in advance of its publication.
69. Rowe, vi–vii.
70. Ludwig Wittgenstein, *Tractatus Logico-Philosophicus,* trans. D. F. Pears and B. F. McGuinness (1961; rev. 1974), 35 (Proposition 4.463).
71. Emerson, "Shakspeare," 117.
72. *Hamlet* 3.2.58–59/1785–86.

INDEX

(Italic numerals refer to illustrations and their captions; numbers in parentheses identify pages where a person is quoted or referred to, but not named in the text itself.)

447

About the Author

Gary Taylor was born in Kansas in 1953 and holds degrees from the University of Kansas and the University of Cambridge. He worked for nine years as joint general editor of the new Oxford University Press edition of Shakespeare's works. In 1985 he sparked an international—and ongoing—controversy by publishing and discussing, for the first time, an untitled poem attributed to Shakespeare in a seventeenth-century manuscript ("Shall I die?"). He now teaches at Brandeis University. Dr. Taylor has published widely in scholarly journals and the popular press; his previous books include *William Shakespeare: A Textual Companion* and *The Division of the Kingdoms: Shakespeare's Two Versions of "King Lear"* (both written in collaboration), and *To Analyze Delight: A Hedonist Criticism of Shakespeare*.